MCAT

PHYSICS and MATH

Content Review

Printed in the United States of America

Third Printing, 2017

ISBN 978-1-944935-09-2

Next Step Pre-Med, LLC
4256 N Ravenswood Ave
Suite 303
Chicago, IL 60613

www.nextstepmcat.com

ABOUT THE AUTHORS

Bryan Schnedeker is Next Step Test Prep's Vice President for MCAT Tutoring and Content. He manages all of our MCAT and LSAT instructors nationally and counsels hundreds of students when they begin our tutoring process. He has over a decade of MCAT and LSAT teaching and tutoring experience (starting at one of the big prep course companies before joining our team). He has attended medical school and law school himself and has scored a 44 on the old MCAT, a 525 on the new MCAT, and a 180 on the LSAT. Bryan has worked with thousands of MCAT students over the years and specializes in helping students looking to achieve elite scores.

Anthony Lafond is Next Step's MCAT Content Director and an Elite MCAT Tutor. He has been teaching and tutoring MCAT students for nearly 12 years. He earned his MD and PhD degrees from UMDNJ - New Jersey Medical School with a focus on rehabilitative medicine. Dr. Lafond believes that both rehabilitative medicine and MCAT education hinge on the same core principle: crafting an approach that puts the unique needs of the individual foremost.

To find out about MCAT tutoring directly with Anthony or Bryan visit our website:

http://nextsteptestprep.com/mcat

Updates may be found here: http://nextsteptestprep.com/mcat-materials-change-log/

If you have any feedback for us about this book, please contact us at mcat@nextsteptestprep.com

Version: 2017-01-01

FREE ONLINE MCAT DIAGNOSTIC and

FULL-LENGTH EXAM

Want to see how you would do on the MCAT and understand where you need to focus your prep?

TAKE OUR FREE MCAT DIAGNOSTIC EXAM

Timed simulations of all 4 sections of the MCAT

Comprehensive reporting on your performance

Continue your practice with a free Full Length Exam

These two exams are provided free of charge to students who purchased our book

To access your free exam, visit:

http://nextsteptestprep.com/mcat-diagnostic/

TABLE OF CONTENTS

PHYSICS

CHAPTER 1
INTRODUCTION

A. THE NEXT STEP APPROACH TO MCAT CONTENT

The Next Step Physics and Math Review is designed to help you understand major concepts in these areas and to use this knowledge to solve problems. Each chapter contains a large number of practice questions to help you review your content in the only format that matters: MCAT-style multiple choice questions.

The MCAT questions are written to test your understanding of basic science concepts and your problem solving abilities; they stress the memorization that is a necessary first step in mastering the MCAT. It is important to note that you cannot prepare for the MCAT the way you have successfully prepared for science exams in school. In your college classes, simple rote memorization is typically all it takes to get a good grade. On the MCAT, memorizing science material is only the first step in a very long journey.

After memorizing the content, you will then need to practice this material on full, timed practice sections and then on full practice tests. This timed work is the only way to simulate the real conditions of test day.

It is critical to note that the time pressure combined with the lengthy and often confusing presentation of facts in the MCAT's passages make for a very demanding exam. It is not enough to learn MCAT content at the level of recognition that is required by most college classes. For the MCAT, you must absolutely master the content. This means that it is not simply enough to recognize a term when you see it. You must know the content so well that you could give a small 10-minute lecture on a given topic, off the top of your head, with no notes whatsoever. This level of mastery requires repetition, practice, and more repetition. That's the main reason we've included hundreds and hundreds of questions through our content review books.

To develop the level of mastery needed, test yourself after completing each chapter. Flip to the table of contents at the front of the book. Using the table of contents as an outline, can you give a little 5-minute lecture on each bullet point? Test yourself here – make yourself speak out loud to an empty room. If you can, great! It means you've really mastered the content at the level needed. If not, go back and re-read the chapter. Take careful notes.

Finally, one of the best ways to memorize MCAT content is to make study sheets. While flashcards and notes are good and can help, a study sheet is far more effective. A study sheet is a single piece of paper summarizing the important ideas, concepts, relationships, or structures involved in a given MCAT topic. For example, you might make a study sheet of all of the hormones tested on the MCAT – where they are secreted from, where they go, what they do when they get there, what causes them to be released, etc. Then take that study sheet and make a copy, but blank out a dozen pieces of information. Then make a second blank with another dozen pieces of information missing. Then make a final study sheet with almost the whole page blanked out.

Start your practice by filling in the blank spaces on your first copy. Do this over and over, checking the original study sheet until you can get it perfect. Then fill in the spaces on the second blank over and over until you've mastered it. Finally, take the third copy (which is nearly just a blank sheet of paper) and re-create the entire study sheet from memory. That is the level of mastery demanded by the MCAT (and med school!).

B. PHYSICS AND MATH

Physics is fundamentally the study of energy and motion – the kinds of energy systems can have, how that energy converts from one form to another, how moving systems behave, and why systems don't move. With the recent revision to the MCAT, the exam has an extensive focus on how the various sciences all tie back into living systems, especially those living systems that underpin human physiology. As such, you can expect the test to assess your understanding of classic physics concepts like torque, but the passages on the MCAT are likely to deal with the elbow joint rather than a playground see-saw.

The typical first-year physics courses cover an exceptionally broad variety of topics. Physics is infamous for being the class where the professor makes you memorize an endless list of equations only to have you promptly forget them all the day after the test. When it comes to mastering these topics, you want to start with a broad-based review of all the topics that the MCAT may ask about. This book has been designed with that goal in mind. To make working with the material more intuitive, we have arranged the chapters as they are usually presented in a typical college textbook. However, the AAMC have chosen to outline the science topics around certain big concept categories. For your reference, here is an outline of the AAMC's concept categories:

Physics

Chemical and Physical Foundations of Biological Systems

4A: Kinematics

A. Translational Motion: Units, Vectors, Velocity, Acceleration
B. Force: Newton's Laws, Friction, Center of Mass
C. Equilibrium: Vector Analysis, Torque
D. Work: Mechanical Advantage, Work Energy Theorem, Conservative Forces
E. Energy: Kinetic, Potential (Gravity, Spring), Conservation, Power, Units
F. Periodic Motion
   a. Amplitude, Frequency, Phase
   b. Transverse and Longitudinal Waves: Wavelength, Speed

A. Liquids: Density, Specific Gravity, Buoyancy, Pressure, Viscosity, Continuity, Turbulence, Surface Tension, Bernoulli's Equation, Venturi Effect, Pitot Tube
B. Gas Phase
   a. Temperature in Kelvin, Pressure and Barometer
   b. Ideal Gases: Boyle's Law, Charles's Law, Avogadro's Law
   c. Kinetic Molecular Theory: Heat Capacity, Boltzmann's Constant
   d. Real Gases: Qualitative and Quantitative
   e. Partial Pressure, Dalton's Law

4B: Fluids

4C: Electrostatics and Circuits

A. Electrostatics: Charge, Conservation, Coulomb's Law
   a. Electric Field: Field Lines, Charge Distribution
   b. Electrostatic Energy, Potential
B. Circuits
   a. Current, EMF, Voltage, Ammeters, Voltmeter
   b. Resistance: Ohm's Law, Series, Parallel, Resistivity
   c. Capacitance: Parallel Plate Capacitor, Energy, Series, Parallel, Dielectric
   d. Conductivity: Metallic, Electrolytic
C. Magnetism: Field, Lorentz Force

4D: Light and Sound

A. Sound
   a. Sound Production
   b. Pitch, Speed, Intensity, Attenuation
   c. Doppler Effect
   d. Resonance
   e. Ultrasound
   f. Shock Waves
B. Light
   a. Interference, Young Double-Slit, Thin Films, Diffraction Grating, Single-Slit Diffraction, X-ray Diffraction
   b. Polarization: Linear, Circular
   c. Speed, Oscillating E and B Fields
   d. EM Spectrum, Visual Spectrum, Color, Photon Energy

C. Optics
   a. Reflection, Refraction, Snell's Law, Dispersion
   b. Total Internal Reflection
   c. Mirrors: Curvature, Focal Length, Real and Virtual Images
   d. Lenses: Converging, Diverging, Diopters, Combinations of Lenses
   e. Aberrations
   f. Optical Instruments, the Eye

4E: Nuclear and Electronic Structure

A. Nucleus: Atomic Number and Weight, Nucleons, Decay
B. Electronic Structure
   a. Ground State, Excited State, Bohr Model
   b. Absorption and Emission Spectra
   c. Paramagnetism and Diamagnetism
   d. Heisenberg Uncertainty Principle
   e. Photoelectric Effect

5E: Thermodynamics and Kinetics

A. Thermodynamic System: Zeroth Law, First Law, Second Law
   a. PV Diagram, Work
   b. Conduction, Convection, Radiation
   c. Coefficient of Expansion

General Mathematical Concepts

1. Recognize and interpret graphs and calculate slopes for: linear, semilog, log-log scales

2. Understand significant digits and use reasonable approximation when performing calculations and making measurements.

3. Use metric units and do conversions between metric units and English units (conversion factors for English units will be provided), do dimensional analysis

4. Perform arithmetic operations, including operations for probability, proportions, ratios, percents, root estimates.

5. Demonstrate general understanding (at the level of a high school Algebra 2 course) of exponents, logs, scientific notation, and systems of equations.

6. Use general trigonometry concepts to solve problems: $\sin$, $\cos$, $\tan$, $\sin^{-1}$, $\cos^{-1}$, $\tan^{-1}$, sin and cos values for 0º, 30º, 45º, 60º, 90º, 180º) special right triangles (30-60-90; 45-45-90)

7. Use vector addition and subtraction and the right-hand rule.

C. THE SCIENTIFIC METHOD

As with all sciences, physics research involves methodically searching for information. The procedure associated with this search is called the *scientific method*. It involves

1. asking questions, which are then followed by one or more *hypotheses* (educated guesses or hunches that answer or explain the question).

2. making predictions from the hypothesis, usually in the form of "if....then" statements (*if* the influenza virus causes the flu, *then* those exposed to it will become ill).

3. testing the predictions through experimentation, observation, model building, etc., including appropriate controls with which to compare the results.

4. repeating the investigations and devising new ways to further test the hypothesis (this may include modification of the hypothesis based on the results of the tests).

5. reporting the results and drawing conclusions from them.

A *theory* is similar to a hypothesis in that it is subjected to the scientific method, but a theory usually explains a broad range of related phenomena, not a single one. Theories are well supported hypotheses, shown to be valid under many different circumstances.

In science, there is no real beginning or end. All hypotheses are based on previous work, and all results and conclusions can be expanded in the future. Often experiments raise more questions than they answer.

Understanding this methodical approach to scientific evidence and conclusions is essential for success on the MCAT. Most of the passages you will see in the science sections are ones that describe an experimental procedure and it is critically important that you understand the procedure so that you can answer the questions. You should read the passage carefully, often taking "flowchart" style notes to make sure you've understood the experiment.

D. PHYSICS AND MATH PROBLEM-SOLVING

The process of solving physics or math-based questions under the time constraints of test day is a daunting task for many students. The temptation is to dive in immediately and start working, but often this rushing ends up costing more time than it saves – you start down one path only to realize you've been solving for the wrong thing.

When working your way through any calculation-based problems, always take a stepwise approach:

1. **What is the question asking me to solve for?** Write it down on the scratch paper. This could be something like "v = ?" or "# of moles of OH^- = ?" or "r = ?"

2. **Look at the answer choices!** Before doing any calculations at all, look to the choices. What are the units? How spread out are the choices? Do they have similar coefficients? Exponents? Often you can eliminate some choices immediately because they don't make any sense. For example, the question might involve a titration with adding acid, yet some answer choices will show the pH going up.

3. **Next, what is given?** Information may be presented in the question itself, in the passage, in a figure, etc. Write this down, including the units!

4. **What can I do with what's given?** It can help to jot down any relevant equations. You'll obviously need to check the passage and its figures as well. Typically you won't need to do a whole lot of very precise math – the MCAT is remarkably forgiving when it comes to rounding things off.

5. Finally, once you have your answer: "**Does this make sense?**" Often the wrong answers are written in such a way that if you used the wrong equation, you'll get one of the wrong answers. But that answer won't make any sense if you stop and put it in context. It may be a number that's lower than 7 for a solution you know is basic, for example.

E. CONSERVATION

If there's a single topic the MCAT loves more than any other, it's conservation – especially conservation of energy. Conservation of matter, conservation of charge, of angular momentum all make frequent appearances as well. In crime shows they always say "follow the money" – but on the MCAT it's, "follow the joules". Remember that joules can be neither created nor destroyed so it's your job to figure out where they're going and what they're doing.

F. UNITS

A widely held belief is that unit analysis is the least interesting activity of the physical sciences. Indeed, carefully carrying units through a difficult formula is sometimes about as interesting as painting a barn. But there are several good reasons to pay attention to units.

You can lose valuable points if you drop units, substitute into a formula, and forget to convert cm to m or the like. One way to guard against this type of error is to automatically convert any number to MKS (meters, kilograms, and seconds) as you read the passage, or at least flag the units that are nonstandard (i.e., not meters, kilograms, and seconds). Another way is to keep track of the units any time the units in the problem are nonstandard.

Another reason to pay attention to units is that they can alert you if you have written an equation the wrong way. For example, you may remember that flow rate f is the volume (m³) flowing past a point per unit time (s) and that it is related to the velocity v and cross-sectional area A of the pipe. But how do you relate

$$f \, [\mathrm{m^3/s}], \, v \, [\mathrm{m/s}], \text{ and } A \, [\mathrm{m^2}]?$$

The only way to correctly obtain the units is to write something like:

$$f = Av$$

that is:

$$\left[\frac{\mathrm{m^3}}{\mathrm{s}}\right] = \left[\mathrm{m^2}\right]\left[\frac{\mathrm{m}}{\mathrm{s}}\right]$$

where we may have left out a proportionality constant. In this case the formula is correct as written. Units may bring back to mind an equation you would have forgotten, counting for valuable points.

A third reason for keeping track of units is that they sometimes guide you to an answer without your having to use a formula or do much work, as the next example shows.

Example: How much volume does 0.4 kg of oxygen gas take up at $T = 27°$ C and $P = 12$ atm? (Use the gas constant $R = 0.0821$ L atm/K mol.)

Solution: Well, to the question, "How much oxygen?", we can answer either in kilograms or in liters. The problem gives kilograms and asks for liters, so this is a complicated units conversion problem. We will essentially construct the ideal gas equation using the units of the elements in the problem. We start with 0.4 kg.

$$(\text{amount of } O_2) = 0.4 \text{ kg } O_2$$

In order to apply the ideal gas equation we need to convert to moles. We can do this by including the factors:

$$\left(\frac{10^3 \mathrm{g O_2}}{1 \mathrm{kg O_2}}\right)\left(\frac{1 \mathrm{mole O_2}}{32 \mathrm{g O_2}}\right)$$

Both are equivalent to 1, but the units cancel, leaving us with moles.

$$\left(\text{amount of } O_2\right) = 0.4 \cancel{\mathrm{kg O_2}}\left(\frac{10^3 \cancel{\mathrm{g O_2}}}{1 \cancel{\mathrm{kg O_2}}}\right)\left(\frac{1 \mathrm{mole } O_2}{32 \cancel{\mathrm{g O_2}}}\right)$$

Now we include a factor of R because it has liters in the numerator and moles in the denominator. We obtain

$$\left(\text{amount of } O_2\right) = 0.4 \cancel{\mathrm{kg O_2}}\left(\frac{10^3 \cancel{\mathrm{g O_2}}}{1 \cancel{\mathrm{kg O_2}}}\right)\left(\frac{1 \cancel{\mathrm{mole } O_2}}{32 \cancel{\mathrm{g O_2}}}\right)\left(\frac{0.0821 \, \mathrm{L \, atm}}{\mathrm{K} \cancel{\mathrm{mol}}}\right)$$

This leaves us with units of atm and K which we want to get rid of. In order to cancel them, we can just put them in. This may seem strange, but it works. (Recall $27°$ C = 300 K.) Thus we obtain

$$\left(\text{amount of O}_2\right) = 0.4\,\cancel{\text{kg O}_2}\left(\frac{10^3\,\cancel{\text{g O}_2}}{1\,\cancel{\text{kg O}_2}}\right)\left(\frac{1\,\text{mole O}_2}{32\,\cancel{\text{g O}_2}}\right)\left(\frac{0.0821\,\text{L}\,\cancel{\text{atm}}}{\cancel{\text{K}}\,\cancel{\text{mol}}}\right)300\,\cancel{\text{K}}\frac{1}{12\,\cancel{\text{atm}}} = \frac{0.4\cdot1000\cdot0.0821\cdot300}{32\cdot12}\,\text{L}$$

For MCAT problems we generally work to one digit of accuracy, so we replace 0.0821 with 0.08, so that we have

$$\left(\text{amount of O}_2\right) = \frac{0.4\cdot1000\cdot0.0821\cdot300}{32\cdot12}$$
$$= \frac{4\cdot8\cdot300}{8\cdot5} = 24\,\text{L}$$

It is generally safe to round to one significant digit. If it happens that two choices are close, then you can always go back and gain more accuracy.

This example involved more arithmetic than most MCAT problems, but its purpose was to point out that attention to units can speed up the solution to a problem. If this is the way you normally do such a problem, good. Most readers, however, would take longer working through this type of problem, using up valuable seconds on the MCAT. Remember that seconds can add up to points.

G. EQUATIONS

Students generally have one of three attitudes toward equations:

    1 sheer hatred (enough said),

    2. cold pragmatism (plug in numbers and get an answer), and

    3. warm fondness.

Try adopting the last attitude. Many students do not realize that equations are merely a way to contain useful information in a short form. They are sentences in the concise language of mathematics. You should not have to memorize most equations in the text, because by the time you learn each chapter, the equations should feel natural to you. They should feel like natural relationships among familiar quantities.

For example, consider one of the first equations you ever encountered, distance equals rate times time, that is

$$\Delta x = v\Delta t \qquad (1)$$

It makes sense that, in a given time, we can go twice as far if we go twice as fast. Thus Δx is proportional to v. On the other hand, for a given speed, we can go twice as far if we travel twice as long a time. Thus Δx is proportional to Δt. We would never be tempted to write

$$v = \Delta x\Delta t$$

or

$$\Delta t = v\Delta x$$

because these equations give relationships among the quantities that we know to be wrong. Note also that the units work out correctly only in equation (1).

Another example is the second law of motion, which we will encounter in Section 3.B. If an object has a single force on it, then its acceleration is proportional to the magnitude of the force and inversely proportional to its mass. Instead of words, we simply write

$$a = F/m \qquad (2)$$

Now let's think about the equation. What would we do if we forgot it? If we stop to think about it, we could figure it out. First, we know that force, mass, and acceleration are connected somehow. If we have two objects of the same mass, and we apply three times as much force to the second object as to the first, then we have a picture like that in Figure 1-1. The greater force causes the greater acceleration, so we can guess that they are proportional. We write

$$a \sim F$$

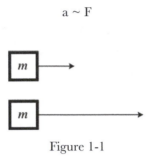

Figure 1-1

If we apply the same force to two objects of different masses, then we expect the smaller object to accelerate more (Figure 1-2). Thus we can guess that the acceleration is *inversely* proportional to the mass, so we write

$$a \sim 1/m$$

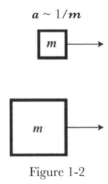

Figure 1-2

Combining these two proportions we get

$$a = F/m$$

as in equation (2).

When you take the MCAT, you really should have the equation $F = ma$ in your head, but if you train yourself to think this way, it will be easier to keep the formulas in your head. This will make it possible to recover the formula if you forget it. And you will understand physics better. Most importantly, you will be better able to apply the concept behind the equation.

Some equations are a little more complicated. An example is Newton's law of gravity, which gives the force of gravity between two objects:

$$F_{\text{grav}} = \frac{Gm_1m_2}{r^2}$$

(3)

where G is a constant, m_1 and m_2 are masses of objects, and r is the distance between them. How would you ever remember this equation?

Well, start with the idea that objects with more mass have a greater force of gravity between them, so write

$$F_{\text{grav}} \sim m_1m_2$$

Also, if objects are far apart, the force of gravity between them is less, so write

$$F_{\text{grav}} \sim \frac{m_1m_2}{r}$$

There is a constant, so write

$$F_{\text{grav}} \sim \frac{Gm_1m_2}{r}$$

The only part that needs to be memorized is the "square" in the denominator, so that we have

$$F_{\text{grav}} = \frac{Gm_1m_2}{r^2}$$

That's why we call gravity an inverse-square force.

The MCAT will not ask you to substitute into an equation like equation (3), but it may ask a question like, "What happens to the gravitational force between two objects if the distance between the objects is increased by a factor of four?"

We can tell from equation (3) that an increase in distance results in a decrease in force, because r is in the denominator. Because the r is squared, a factor of 4 in r will result in a factor of $4^2 = 16$ in F_{grav}. The answer is that the gravitational force decreases by a factor of 16.

If this last point seems opaque to you, try some numbers on a more familiar equation, such as that for the area of a circle

$$A = \pi r^2 \quad (4)$$

What happens to the area when the radius increases by a factor of 3? (Answer: It increases by a factor of 9.) Try it with $r_1 = 4$ m and $r_2 = 12$ m, or with some other numbers.

Another equation is that for the surface area of a sphere

$$A = 4\pi r^2 (5)$$

What happens to the surface area of a sphere when the radius increases by a factor of 3? (Answer: It increases by a factor of 9. Surprised? What about the factor of 4? Try it with $r_1 = 4$ m and $r_2 = 12$ m.) The surface area of a sphere is an equation that you just have to memorize. It is difficult to get an intuitive grasp why the 4π should be there. On the other hand, the r^2 is natural in this equation. Why? (Think about units.)

Another example concerns the volume of a sphere

$$V = \frac{4\pi}{3} r^3$$

(6)

What happens to the volume when the radius is doubled?

In this chapter we discussed the importance of units in solving problems. If a problem involves only simple proportionalities and there are no unitless proportionality constants, then we can obtain a quick solution simply by keeping track of units. The example in the text demonstrates all the techniques involved.

We also looked at equations as the language of physics. If you read equations as sentences containing information for you to understand, then the equations will seem less foreign than if you look at them as abstract collections of symbols. Each time you encounter a boxed equation in this book, you should spend some time thinking about what the equation means.

H. USING THIS BOOK

Remember: the MCAT stresses your problem solving skills and your knowledge of basic science concepts. Therefore, the work you do in understanding these concepts is a necessary first step, but the first step only. Next Step's Content Review books will help you in this foundational work through a thorough treatment of the major topics included in the MCAT. Study to understand these topics, not just to memorize them.

If you've purchased this book as a part of the Next Step Science Content Review package you are also entitled to a free copy of Next Step's online MCAT Diagnostic and Science Content Diagnostic exam. See the back of this book with details for how to activate your free online test. If you've purchased this book by itself, we strongly recommend that you consider purchasing the rest of the Next Step Science Content Review package. Success on the MCAT will require a good foundation in Biology, Biochemistry, Chemistry, Organic Chemistry, Psychology, Sociology, and Physics.

It's not enough to simply go through this book as you would one of your textbooks in a class. On the MCAT, you must truly master the content. You have to know it so well that you could write this book yourself. To gain that mastery, you should follow a few simple steps:

1. **Don't write in the book**. You will want to be able to come back and re-do the questions to check your mastery.
2. **Begin by taking the Final Exam** at the end of the book. This test is a pure content assessment of the relevant content on the MCAT. Taking this test first can help guide you for which chapters merit extra attention.
3. **Go through each chapter three times using a "spaced repetition"** approach. Spaced repetition has been shown to vastly increase a student's ability to recall information.
   Day 1: Start by skimming the chapter quickly. Get a general sense of the content. Then go back and read the chapter slowly and carefully. Take notes in a separate notebook, make flashcards or study sheets as needed.
   Day 2: Then wait a day.

Day 3: Come back to the chapter. Re-skim the content and only then do the questions at the end of the chapter. Be sure to analyze all of the questions to make sure you've fully understood them.

Day 4-5: Then wait two days.

Day 6: Come back a third and final time. No need to re-skim – simply re-do the questions at the end of the chapter to solidify your understanding.

5. After working your way through the whole book, **come back to the Final Exam and re-take it**. As you wrap up your content review work, you should be scoring nearly 100% on this exam.

I. STUDY PLANS

It's absolutely essential that you develop a clear and rigorous study plan and stick to it. Each student's situation is different so you'll need to develop a plan that fits your unique situation.

The best place to start is with Next Step's online Study Plan. We have posted the plan on our MCAT blog on our website. You can find this plan here:

http://nextsteptestprep.com/category/mcat-blog/

J. OTHER RESOURCES

Good MCAT Prep fundamentally requires three things: content review, practice passages, and full test simulation. The book you're holding in your hands can fulfill the first of those goals. To really prepare for the exam, you will also want to pick up materials to provide you with practice and full test simulation

For practice passages, there's no better resource than Next Step's Strategy and Practice books. We have produced one book for each of the four sections on the exam. Each of our Strategy and Practice books includes a concise, focused discussion on strategies for how to deal with the passages, followed by full timed section practice. The timed sections are in the format of the exam, but made slightly harder than the real thing in order to help build up those MCAT muscles.

To get practice simulating the real exam, you'll want to use Next Step's online Full Length exams. These tests are simply the best approximation available of what you'll see on the real test. We're the only MCAT prep company in the world to build our exams from the ground up for the new MCAT. While other big companies are simply re-purposing their old exams into the new MCAT format, we started totally fresh. Our practice tests simulate the content, format, and difficulty level of the real test perfectly.

Finally, the single best resource for MCAT practice is the testmaker: the AAMC. Every student preparing for the MCAT should purchase the official guide, the official AAMC practice test, and any other AAMC practice sets available.

Good luck!

CHAPTER 1 PROBLEMS

In any of the following problems you may want to use one of the constants

$$N_A = 6.02 \times 10^{23}$$
$$R = 0.0821 \text{ L atm/K mol}$$

1. In a certain assay, a number of microbes is measured by determining the mass of the sample. It is known that the average mass of a microbe (of this species) is 6.0×10^{-16} g. How many microbes are in a sample of mass 1.1×10^{-12} g?

   A. 1800
   B. 5500
   C. 6.6×10^4
   D. 6.6×10^{28}

2. A certain substance has a density 8.4 μg/mL. What is the mass of 422.4 mL?

   A. 0.020 mg.
   B. 3.55 mg.
   C. 350.3 mg.
   D. 3550 mg.

3. What is the mass of a water molecule?

   A. 9.2×10^{-26} g.
   B. 1.7×10^{-24} g.
   C. 3.0×10^{-23} g.
   D. 0.018 g.

4. An electrical resistor is installed in a container of water to heat it. The resistor dissipates heat at a rate of 2.0 W, and the container holds 10 kg of water. How long would it take to raise the temperature of the water 5° C? (Note: The specific heat of water is 4.2 x 10^3 J/kg °C, and 1 W is 1 J/s.)

   A. 2.4×10^{-2} seconds.
   B. 4.2×10^3 seconds.
   C. 1.05×10^5 seconds.
   D. 4.2×10^5 seconds.

5. Two liters of argon gas are at 10 atm of pressure. If the sample is 16 g, what is the temperature?

   A. 16,000 K
   B. 610 K
   C. 6 K
   D. 4 K

Use the following for questions 6–10:

For a circle we have the formula for the circumference

$$C = 2\pi r$$

and the area

$$A = \pi r^2$$

where r is the radius. For a sphere, the surface area is

$$A_{surf} = 4\pi r^2$$

and the volume is

$$V = 4/3 \ \pi r^3$$

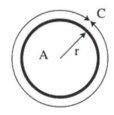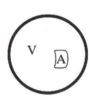

6. If the diameter of a circle is increased by a factor of 4, what happens to the circumference?

   A. It increases by a factor of 2.
   B. It increases by a factor of 4.
   C. It increases by a factor of 8.
   D. It increases by a factor of 16.

7. If the radius of a circle increases by a factor of 4, what happens to its area?

   A. It increases by a factor of 2.
   B. It increases by a factor of 4.
   C. It increases by a factor of 16.
   D. It increases by a factor of 64.

8. If the radius of a sphere increases by a factor of 4, what happens to its volume?

   A. It increases by a factor of 2.
   B. It increases by a factor of 4.
   C. It increases by a factor of 16.
   D. It increases by a factor of 64.

9. If the volume of a sphere decreases by a factor of 27, what happens to its diameter?

   A. It decreases by a factor of 9.
   B. It decreases by a factor of 3.
   C. It decreases by a factor of 4.5.
   D. It decreases by a factor of 1.5.

10. If the radius of a circle is increased by 30%, how does the area change?

    A. It increases by 30%.
    B. It increases by 60%.
    C. It increases by 69%.
    D. It increases by 75%.

Use the following for questions 11–13:

A pendulum is a mass connected to a light string or rod which is connected to the ceiling. The period is the amount of time it takes the bob (as the mass is called) to swing from one side to the other and back. It is given by

$$T = 2\pi\sqrt{\frac{l}{g}}$$

where T is in s, l is the length of the string or rod (in m), and g is the acceleration due to gravity (m/s^2). (See Figure.)

11. If the length of the string of a pendulum is increased by a factor of 4, how does the period change?

    A. It decreases by a factor of 16.
    B. It increases by a factor of 2.
    C. It increases by a factor of 4.
    D. It increases by a factor of 16.

12. The length of the rod of a certain pendulum is decreased, and the period then decreases by 20%. By how much was the rod length decreased?

    A. 20%
    B. 36%
    C. 40%
    D. 44%

13. If a pendulum is transported to the Moon, where the acceleration due to gravity is six times less than that here on Earth, how would the period of the pendulum change?

    A. It would decrease by a factor of 36.
    B. It would increase by a factor of 2.4.
    C. It would increase by a factor of 6.
    D. It would increase by a factor of 36.

Use the following for questions 14–16:

A spring is characterized by a spring constant k (in N/m) which gives the stiffness of the spring, or how hard you have to pull to stretch it. If you connect a mass m on one end, and connect the other end to a fixed wall or ceiling, then the resulting system will vibrate. This vibration has period T given by

$$T = 2\pi\sqrt{\frac{m}{k}}$$

The frequency of the vibration is defined as

$$f = 1/T$$

14. If a mass of 60 g is connected to a certain spring, the frequency is 30 Hz. If a mass of 240 g is connected to the same spring, what is the frequency?

    A. 7.5 Hz
    B. 15 Hz
    C. 60 Hz
    D. 120 Hz

15. In two trials, two masses are attached to a spring and the periods recorded. Mass P resulted in a period 36 times larger than the period of mass Q. What can be concluded?

    A. Mass P is 1296 times larger than mass Q.
    B. Mass P is 6 times larger than mass Q.
    C. Mass P is 6 times smaller than mass Q.
    D. Mass P is 1296 times smaller than mass Q.

16. If the period increases by 50%, how does the frequency change?

    A. It decreases by 50%.
    B. It decreases by 40%.
    C. It decreases by 33%.
    D. It increases by 33%.

Use the following information for questions 17–19:

The volume of a pyramid with a square base is given by

$$V = \frac{1}{3}s^2 h$$

where s is the length of a side, and h is the perpendicular height.

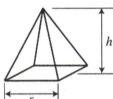

17. How does the volume of a square pyramid change if the base side length is increased by a factor of 9 and the height is unchanged?

    A. It increases by a factor of 3.
    B. It increases by a factor of 9.
    C. It increases by a factor of 27.
    D. It increases by a factor of 81.

18. How does the volume of square pyramid change if the height is increased by a factor of 12 and the base side length is unchanged?

    A. It increases by a factor of 4.
    B. It increases by a factor of 12.
    C. It increases by a factor of 36.
    D. It increases by a factor of 72.

19. If every linear dimension of a square pyramid were increased by a factor of 3, how would the volume change?

    A. It would increase by a factor of 3.
    B. It would increase by a factor of 9.
    C. It would increase by a factor of 27.
    D. It would increase by a factor of 81.

Passage 1

[You do not need to have any prior knowledge of electricity to deal with this passage.]

In a parallel-plate capacitor, two parallel metal plates are connected to a voltage source which maintains a potential V across the plates. Positive charges collect on one side of the capacitor and negative charges on the other side, thus creating an electric field E between the plates. The magnitude of the electric field is related to the potential and the separation between the plates according to

$$V = Ed$$

where V is measured in volts, E in J/m, and d in m. A charged particle placed between the plates will experience a force given in magnitude by

$$F = qE$$

where q is the charge of the particle in coulombs, and F is the force in N.

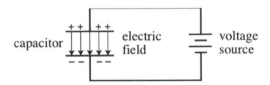

20. If a new battery is installed, so that the voltage between the plates is increased by a factor of 9, how is the electric field affected?

    A. It decreases by a factor of 9.
    B. It increases by a factor of 3.
    C. It increases by a factor of 9.
    D. It increases by a factor of 81.

21. If the voltage in a given experiment is held constant, but the distance between the plates is increased by a factor of 3, how is the electric field affected?

    A. It decreases by a factor of 9.
    B. It decreases by a factor of 3.
    C. It stays the same.
    D. It increases by a factor of 3.

22. In a given experiment, both a proton and a bare helium nucleus are between the plates. How does the force on the helium nucleus compare to the force on the proton?

    A. It is the same.
    B. It is twice as great.
    C. It is four times as great.
    D. There is no force on the helium.

23. In a given experiment, all other things being held constant, what happens to the force on a proton between the plates if the separation of the plates is increased by a factor of 2?
    A. It decreases by a factor of 4.
    B. It decreases by a factor of 2.
    C. It stays the same.
    D. It increases by a factor of 2.

24. Which graph best show the relationship between the potential V and the electric field E?

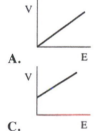

A.

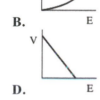

B.

C.

D.

Passage 2

Two charged balls which are near each other will exert a force on each other: attractive if they are oppositely charged, and repulsive if they are similarly charged. The magnitude of the force is given by

$$F = \frac{kq_1q_2}{r^2}$$

where F is in N, k is a constant 9×10^9 N m^2/C^2, q_1 and q_2 are the charges on the balls measured in C, and r is the distance between the balls in m.

25. In a certain experiment, the separation between the balls is halved, while the charges on the balls are undisturbed. How would this affect the force between them?

    A. The force would decrease by a factor of 4.
    B. The force would decrease by a factor of 2.
    C. The force would increase by a factor of 2.
    D. The force would increase by a factor of 4.

26. In an experiment, the distance separating the balls is increased by 25%. How does this affect the force between the balls?

    A. It decreases by 50%.
    B. It decreases by 36%.
    C. It decreases by 25%.
    D. It increases by 25%.

27. If the force between the balls stays the same, but the charge q_2 is multiplied by 4, which is a possibility?

    A. The charge q_1 is also multiplied by 4, and all else is unchanged.
    B. The separation is decreased by a factor of 2, and all else is unchanged.
    C. The separation is increased by a factor of 2, and all else is unchanged.
    D. The separation is increased by a factor of 4, and all else is unchanged.

28. In a hypothetical situation, two balls of positive charge exert a force 12 N on each other. The charge on ball A is 2 C. If the charge on ball A is increased to 8 C, and all else unchanged, what would the force be?

    A. 8 N
    B. 16 N
    C. 18 N
    D. 48 N

29. Which graph best shows the relationship between the force between two balls F and their separation r?

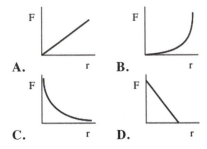

30. In a certain experiment two balls are both given a charge q, they are set a distance r away from each other, and the force between them is recorded. Which graph best represents the relationship between F and q?

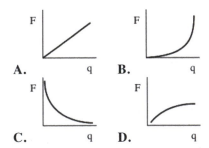

PHYSICS

SECTION 1
MOTION AND FORCE

As we mentioned earlier, physics is fundamentally the student of energy and motion. Appropriately enough, this first section that covers the foundations of motion is the longest in the book.

As you work your way through the chapters in this section, put an extra emphasis on trying to really *understand* the equations you encounter rather than simply rote memorizing them. One of the best ways to develop this understanding is to create study sheets for the equations. A study sheet consists of a series of questions down the left-hand side of the page and the answers on the right-hand side. The study sheet should focus on the relationships and units involved, rather than just the equation itself and doing calculations. Here's a small example:

Force due to gravity	$F = \frac{GMm}{r^2}$
Variables	F=force G=gravitational constant=$6.67 \times 10^{-11} \frac{m^3}{Kg \times s^2}$ m_1, m_2=mass of object r=distance between the center of the two objects
Units	newtons=kg x (m/s^2)
If the mass of both planets were doubled, the gravitational force:	Would quadruple
If the mass of one planet were doubled and the mass of the other planet was reduced by half, the gravitational force:	Would remain the same
If the gravitation force was reduced to ¼ and the mass of the balls remained the same, the distance between the objects:	Doubled
The radius of both balls was ½d, and the distance between the surfaces of the two balls was d. If the distance between the surfaces of the balls and their masses remained the same but the radius of both balls was tripled, the gravitational force:	Is cut by ¼
If mass and the distance between the center of the planets remained the same but the density of the planets increased, the gravitational force:	Would remain the same

CHAPTER 2
MOTION BASICS

A. INTRODUCTION

Mechanics is about the motion of things. Before we can talk about motion in depth, we need to be able to describe motion and the things which affect it. Objects move, and we talk of how fast they go, that is, velocity. Their velocity changes, so we talk of acceleration. We can think of changes in acceleration, but it turns out (happily) that we rarely need to. Mechanics is concerned mainly with changes in velocity.

In this chapter we look at the fundamental elements of mechanics: force, mass, distance, velocity, and acceleration. Comparatively this chapter has a lot of equations (six that you should memorize) and the least interesting physics. It is an unpleasant way to begin, but it must be done.

B. FORCE, MASS, AND VECTORS

A *force* is a push or pull, and the units for force are [newtons = N]. (Some countries continue to use an archaic unit called the "pound".) A newton is approximately the amount of force that you would exert on an apple near the Earth's surface to keep it from falling.

Examples of forces include the force of a horse pulling a cart, the force of a spring pushing the chassis of a car, the force of gravity pulling you down, and the force on your head due to pressure when you are at the bottom of a pool.

MASS

We can think about mass in several ways. First, the *mass* of an object is a measure of the total amount of material (or stuff) in the object. The amount of stuff in an object is a fundamental property of the object. It doesn't change if you move the object to a new place, like a mountaintop or to Mars.

There is another way to think of mass. The mass of an object is a measure of how difficult it is to get it moving at a certain velocity if it starts from rest. For example, if John wants to set a car, initially at rest, to moving at 1 m/s, he has to push hard for a little while. We are assuming the car's motion has no friction. If John and the car were on the Moon, his task would be equally difficult. The fundamental concept here is the mass of the car, not the astronomical body the car is on. (See Figure 2-1.)

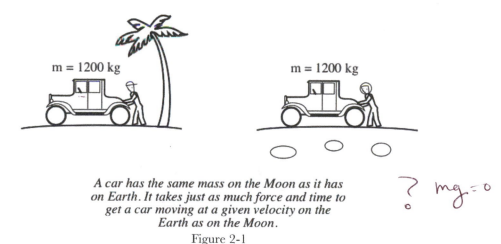

m = 1200 kg   m = 1200 kg

A car has the same mass on the Moon as it has on Earth. It takes just as much force and time to get a car moving at a given velocity on the Earth as on the Moon.

Figure 2-1

Saying this another way, the mass of an object is a measure of how much it hurts if you stub your toe on it. Stubbing your toe on a bowling ball is a painful proposition, even on the Moon.

There is a *wrong* way to think about mass. Many people think the mass of an object is a measure of how difficult it is to pick it up. But that definition depends on where you are. It is easy to pick up a bowling ball on the Moon, but nearly impossible on the surface of Jupiter. The difficulty in picking up an object is a matter of weight, which is a force. And weight **does** depend on the astronomical body nearby.

VECTORS

In physics we often need to describe direction as well as size. For example, two forces F_1 and F_2 may both be 100 N and acting on a crocodile, but the crocodile's experience will be very different depending on whether the forces are both pointing north or one north and one south (Figure 2-2). In the former case he gets stretched, and in the latter case he goes flying. To describe forces we need to specify size and direction. That is, we need to use vectors. Force is a vector.

We denote vectors in diagrams by arrows, the length of the arrow showing the size of the vector and the direction of the arrow showing its direction.

We can add vectors by the tip-to-tail method. We leave the first vector fixed, and move the second vector so its tail is at the first vector's tip. If there are other vectors, then each vector gets added to the previous tip. The sum is the vector pointing from the first tail to the last tip.

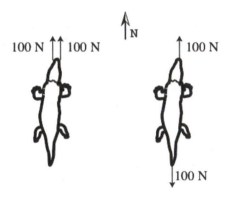

Two forces on an object may add in different ways, depending on the relative directions of the forces.
Figure 2-2

Example 1: For the crocodiles mentioned before, if the vectors (both 100 N) both point north, then the sum is a force of 200 N pointing north (Figure 2-3, where the sum is shown dashed).

If one vector points north and the other south, then the first tail coincides with the last tip and the sum is zero (Figure 2-3).

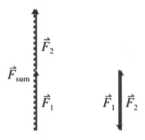

Forces are vectors and they add according to the tip-to-tail method.

Figure 2-3

Example 2: A crocodile has three forces acting on him: a 100-N force north, a 100-N force east, and a 100-N force southwest. What is the direction of the net force (that is, total force)?

Solution: We DRAW A DIAGRAM (Figure 2-4). The sum is a vector pointing northeast, about 40 N.

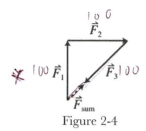

Figure 2-4

Note that, when you add vectors, the magnitude of the sum is equal to, at most, the sum of the individual magnitudes (and that only if they are pointing in the same direction). For instance, if three vectors of 100 N are acting on a crocodile, the sum can be anything from 0 N to 300 N, but no greater.

For MCAT problems, vector addition need not get more sophisticated than this. It is useful to keep in mind the Pythagorean theorem and elementary trigonometry.

Example 3: A force of 4 N is acting to the north on a rock and a force of 3 N is acting to the east.

a. What is the magnitude of the total force?
b. What is $\cos\phi$, if ϕ is the deviation from north of the direction of the total force?

Solution: We DRAW A DIAGRAM (Figure 2-5). There is a right triangle, so we can write

Figure 2-5

$$F^2_{sum} = (3N)^2 + (4N)^2 = 25N^2$$

$$F_{sum} = 5\ N$$

Also we write

$$\cos\phi = 4N/5N = 0.8$$

If your trigonometry is rusty, now is a good time to relearn the definitions of sine, cosine, and tangent.

A vector is denoted by a half-arrow on top of a letter, $\overrightarrow{F}$, for example.

C. POSITION, DISPLACEMENT, AND TIME

To specify position, we must give three coordinates x, y, and z, generally measured in [meters = m]. The symbol s stands for the coordinates (x, y, z). If an object moves from one position to another, the vector giving the change in position is the **displacement vector**, $\Delta s = s_2 - s_1$. The magnitude of the displacement vector is called the **displacement**.

Time is a fundamental quantity in classical physics, denoted t, measured in [seconds = s]. Often we will speak of a **time interval** $\Delta t = t_2 - t_1$, that is, the time between a beginning time t_1 and ending time t_2. An **instant** is a single moment of time.

D. VELOCITY, SPEED, AND ACCELERATION

We can think of the **velocity vector** in terms of a speedometer reading with units [meters/second = m/s] and a direction. The magnitude of the velocity vector (that is, just the speedometer reading) is called **speed**. The word "velocity" is sometimes used to refer to the vector and sometimes to the magnitude. When in doubt, you should assume it refers to the vector.

If an object is traveling such that its velocity vector is constant, we say it is in ***uniform motion***. An example is a car going a constant 30 m/s (freeway speed) west. We can write the following equations for uniform motion in one dimension:

$$v = \frac{\Delta x}{\Delta t} \tag{1a}$$

$$v = \frac{x_2 - x_1}{\Delta t} \tag{1b}$$

When you see a formula in this text, instead of speeding by it, slow down and look at it. Ask yourself, "What is this equation telling me?" Equation (1a) is just another form of "distance equals rate times time" for an object in uniform motion. Since v is constant, this tells you, for instance, that a car will travel twice as far if it travels for twice the time. This makes sense.

Equation (1b) is like the first, only Δx is replaced by its definition $x_2 - x_1$. Do you see why it is this and not $x_1 - x_2$ or $x_2 + x_1$?

But in some problems the velocity does change, and we must pay attention to several velocities, that is,

$$v_1 \quad \text{initial velocity,}$$

$$v_2 \quad \text{final velocity,}$$

and

$$v_{avg} \quad \text{average velocity.}$$

The average velocity is defined as

$$v_{avg} = \frac{\Delta s}{\Delta t} \tag{2}$$

This is different from equation (1). Equation (2) is the definition of an average velocity over a time interval when velocity is changing, whereas equation (1) defines a constant velocity and only holds for time intervals when the motion is uniform.

Example: A car goes west at 10 m/s for 6 s, then it goes north at 10 m/s for 5 s, and then it goes west again at 4 m/s for 15 s. What are v_1, v_2, and v_{avg}?

Solution: Well, we have $v_1 = 10$ m/s and $v_2 = 4$ m/s. For the average velocity we need to DRAW A DIAGRAM (Figure 2-6). The Pythagorean theorem gives us $\Delta s = 130$ m. Thus

$$v_{avg} = 130\text{m}/26\text{s} = 5 \text{ m/s}$$

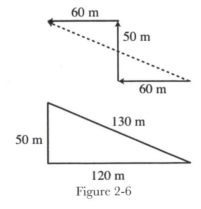

Figure 2-6

ACCELERATION

When an object's velocity vector is changing, the object is **accelerating**. Examples include a car speeding up ("accelerating" in common parlance), slowing down or braking ("decelerating", but physicists prefer to say "negatively accelerating"), and turning. In three dimensions, we define acceleration by

$$\vec{a} = \frac{\vec{\Delta v}}{\Delta t} \qquad (3a)$$

$$= \frac{\vec{v}_2 - \vec{v}_1}{\Delta t} \,. \qquad (3b)$$

The numerator for equation (3a) gives the change in the velocity vector, so there is an acceleration if either the magnitude or the direction of the velocity vector change. We will talk more about this in Chapter 6. In one dimension the definition of acceleration is

$$a = \frac{\Delta v}{\Delta t} \qquad (4a)$$

$$= \frac{v_2 - v_1}{\Delta t} \qquad (4b)$$

The units for acceleration are $[(m/s)/s = m/s \cdot 1/s = m/s^2]$.

Example 1a: Take north to be positive. A car is traveling south and speeding up. What is the sign of the acceleration?

Solution: Since the velocity vector points south and the car is speeding up, the acceleration vector must point south. With this sign convention, acceleration is negative.

Example 1b: Take north to be positive. A car traveling south speeds up from 10 m/s to 15 m/s in 10 s. What is its acceleration?

Solution: We write

$$a = \frac{-15\frac{m}{s} - (-10)\frac{m}{s}}{10s} = 0.5\frac{m}{s^2}$$

This confirms our thinking in Example 1a.

Example 2a: Take north to be positive. A car is traveling north and slowing for a red light. What is the sign of the acceleration?

Solution: The velocity vector points north. Since this vector is shrinking, the acceleration vector must point south. Thus the acceleration is negative.

Example 2b: What is the acceleration for the car in Example 2a slowing from 10 m/s to 8 m/s in 1 s?
Solution: We write

$$a = \frac{8\frac{m}{s} - 10\frac{m}{s}}{1s} = -2\frac{m}{s^2}$$

Example 3: An Oldsmobile takes a certain amount of time to accelerate from 0 to 60 mph. A Porsche takes less time by a factor of 3 to accelerate from 0 to 60 mph. How does the Porsche acceleration compare with that of the Oldsmobile?

Solution: We look at equation (4)

$$a = \frac{\Delta v}{\Delta t}$$

Since Δv is constant, if Δt is smaller by a factor of 3, then a is larger by a factor of 3.

E. GRAPHS

Now we have three quantities, position, velocity, and acceleration, all related to each other algebraically. Often it is helpful to visualize these quantities graphically. The following principles apply

1. Given a graph of x versus t, the instantaneous slope at time t is the velocity v at time t.
2. Given a graph of v versus t, the instantaneous slope at time t is the acceleration a at time t.
3. Given a graph of a versus t, the area under the curve during interval Δt gives the change in velocity v during that interval.
4. Given a graph of v versus t, the area under the curve during interval Δt gives the change in position x during that interval.

Example 1: The graph of a versus t for a car which undergoes constant acceleration is shown in Figure 2-7. Sketch the graph of v versus t. Assume $v = 0$ m/s at $t = 0$ s.

Solution: The area under the curve between 0 and Δt is shown in a "forward-slash" hatch. This area is Δv, that is, the change in velocity during Δt. The reason for principle 3 above becomes clear if we recall the formula for the area of the rectangle representing the hatched region:

$$\text{area} = \text{height x length}$$
$$\Delta v = a\Delta t$$

This is how we defined acceleration in equation (4). During the second interval Δt, the area is a Δt again. Thus the change in velocity is the same, as shown in Figure 2-8. For the next intervals of time, the quantity Δv is constant.

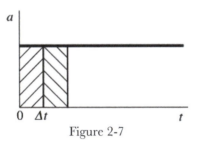

Figure 2-7

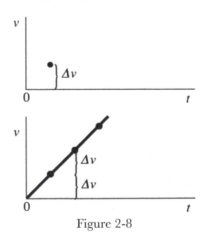

Figure 2-8

Note that Figures 2-7 and 2-8 give (almost) the same information in different forms. Figure 2-7 has the information that the acceleration is positive and constant, so the car is speeding up (if it is going forward). Figure 2-8 has the information that the velocity is increasing at a constant rate. This is the same thing.

Before you read the next example, consider an object thrown straight up. When it reaches the top of its path, what is the direction of its velocity? What is the direction of its acceleration?

Example 2: An apple is tossed straight up in the air. The graph of y versus t is shown in Figure 2-9. Sketch the graphs of v versus t and a versus t.

Solution: To obtain an instantaneous slope, we can use an imaginary electron microscope to look at a small portion of the graph. A small section of Figure 2-9 has been enlarged using such a microscope. This portion looks almost straight, so we could calculate its slope if we had some numbers. We can at least read that the slope is positive and very large, hence the first point in Figure 2-10.

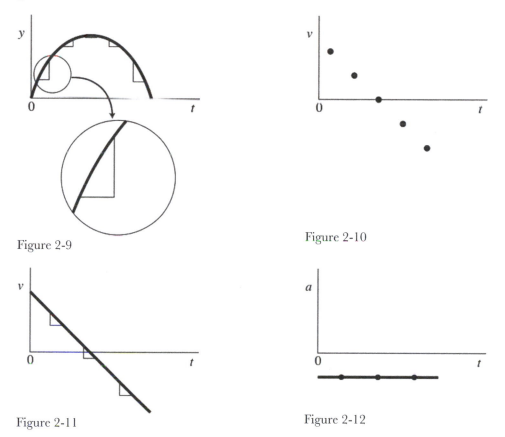

Figure 2-9

Figure 2-10

Figure 2-11

Figure 2-12

The second point on Figure 2-10 still has a positive slope, but smaller. The third point has a zero slope (see uppermost point in Figure 2-9). The fourth point has negative slope, and the fifth point has a slope more negative still.

It will not come as a surprise if we draw a straight line through these points, as in Figure 2-11. We take the slope at three points, but it is easy to see that the slope is constant and negative. We graph the acceleration in Figure 2-12.

Does this match your expectation? Particularly at the top of flight, did you know that the direction of the acceleration would be down?

Example 3: Figure 2-13 shows v versus t for a car. Sketch the graphs for x versus t and for a versus t. (Say $x = 0$ at $t = 0$.)

Solution: Let's graph x versus t first. From $t = 0$ to 1 s, there is no area under the curve, so x stays constant. From $t = 1$ to 2 s, the area under the curve is 0.5 m. (Recall the area of a triangle is $A = 1/2$ base x height.)

From $t = 2$ to 3 s the area under the curve is 1.5 m, so that the x value jumps to 2 m (see the first graph of Figure 2-14). Between $t = 3$ and 4 s, the area is 2 m and x jumps to 4 m, and so on. Figure 2-14 shows the result.

For the graph of a versus t, the slope of v versus t for any point between $t = 0$ and 1 s is zero. The slope jumps to 1 m/s² for the interval from 1 to 3 s and drops back down to zero for times after 3 s. (See Figure 2-15.)

Think about all three graphs for a while and note how they give the same information in different forms.

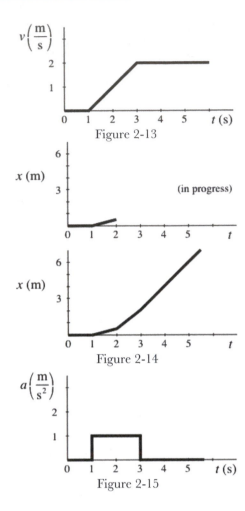

Figure 2-13

Figure 2-14

Figure 2-15

F. UNIFORM ACCELERATION

If an object has a constant acceleration vector, we say it undergoes *uniform acceleration*. Most MCAT problems involving acceleration will involve uniform acceleration. For uniform acceleration, we have the following:

$$v_{avg} = \frac{1}{2}(v_1 + v_2)$$

(5)

that is, the average velocity over a period of time is the average of the beginning and ending velocities. This may seem like a natural definition of average velocity, but the definition of v_{avg} is given by equation (2), and equation (5) holds only for uniform acceleration.

See Figures 2-7 and 2-8 for an example. The velocity v_1 is small, v_2 is large, and v_{avg} is exactly between them.

If we start with the definition of average velocity, we can write

$$\Delta x = v_{avg}\Delta t$$

$$\Delta x = \frac{1}{2}(v_1 + v_2)\, t$$

This is a useful equation if you do not have and do not need the acceleration (see equation [7] below). Furthermore, if we substitute $v_2 = v_1 + a\Delta t$ (from equation [4]), then we obtain

$$\Delta x = \frac{1}{2}\left(v_1 + (v_1 + a\Delta t)\right)\Delta t$$

$$\boxed{\Delta x = v_1\Delta t + \frac{1}{2}a\Delta t^2 \qquad (6)}$$

This is the first equation which may seem a bit arcane. You should memorize it anyway. Working through the algebra will help you memorize it.

Example: A car is accelerating uniformly from rest. If it goes a distance **d** in the first second, how far will it go in the first four seconds?

Solution: We want an equation involving the quantities mentioned in the problem, **a**, $v_1 = 0$, Δx, and Δt, so equation (6) is it. With $v_1 = 0$, we obtain

$$\Delta x = \frac{1}{2}\Delta a \; t^2$$

If Δt increases by a factor of 4, the Δx increases, and it increases by a factor of $4^2 = 16$.

G. KINEMATIC EQUATIONS FOR CONSTANT ACCELERATION

For uniform acceleration there are four equations you should know:

$$\boxed{\begin{aligned}
\Delta x &= \frac{1}{2}\left(v_1 + v_2\right)\Delta t & (7)\\
v_2 - v_1 &= a\Delta t & (8)\\
\Delta x &= v_1\Delta t + \frac{1}{2}a\Delta t^2 & (9)\\
v_2^2 &= v_1^2 + 2a\Delta x & (10)
\end{aligned}}$$

The first equation we have seen before, the modified "distance equals rate times time" when velocity is changing. It should be easy to remember. The second equation is just the definition of acceleration. The third equation was in the last section. The last equation is the only one which is new, obtained by eliminating Δt from equations (7) and (8). It is useful for problems in which the time interval is neither specified nor desired.

Example 1: A cat drops from a ledge 2 m above the ground. If he accelerates 10 m/s² downward due to gravity, how much time does it take him to drop?

Solution: Let's choose "up" to be positive and DRAW A DIAGRAM (Figure 2-16). We write the quantities we know:

$$\Delta y = -2 \text{ m}$$
$$v_0 = 0 \text{ m/s}$$
$$a = -10 \text{ m/s2}$$
$$\Delta t = ?$$

(handwritten annotations:)

2m |

$$\Delta x = \frac{1}{2}at^2$$

$$\sqrt{\frac{2\Delta x}{a}} = \sqrt{t}$$

$$\frac{2(-2)}{-10} = \sqrt{0.4}$$

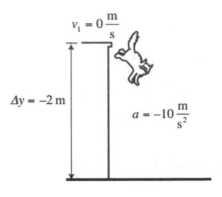

Figure 2-16

We look for an equation which involves these quantities and no others. Equation (9) fits, so that

$$-2\text{m} = 0\text{m} + \frac{1}{2}\left(-10\frac{m}{s^2}\right)\Delta t^2$$

$$\Delta t^2 = 0.4\ \frac{s^2}{m}$$

$$\Delta t = 0.63\text{s}$$

Example 2: A man drops from the sixth floor of a building (20 m). As he is falling, his acceleration is a constant 10 m/s² downward. What is his velocity just before reaching the ground?

Solution: First we DRAW A DIAGRAM (Figure 2-17). The impact velocity is the man's velocity just before he hits the ground v_2. Thus our information summary is

$$v_1 = 0 \text{ m/s}$$

$$\Delta y = -20 \text{ m}$$

$$a = -10 \text{ m/s2}$$

$$v_2 = ?$$

The formula which contains this information and nothing else is (10), so that

$$v_2^2 = v_1^2 + 2a\,\Delta y$$

$$v_2^2 = \left(0\frac{m}{s}\right)^2 + 2\left(10\frac{m}{s^2}\right)(20\ \cancel{m})$$

$$v_2^2 = 400\frac{m^2}{s^2}$$

$$v_2 = -20\frac{m}{s}$$

His final velocity is 20 m/s.

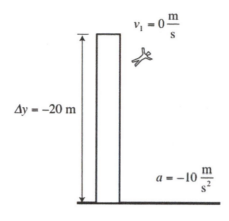

$$v_1 = 0 \frac{m}{s}$$

$$\Delta y = -20 \text{ m}$$

$$a = -10 \frac{m}{s^2}$$

Figure 2-17

In this chapter we looked at the quantities which describe motion, that is, displacement, velocity, and acceleration, and the quantities which affect motion, that is, force and mass. Displacement is a change in location. Velocity is a measure of the change in location per unit time, while acceleration is a measure of the change in velocity per unit time. Displacement, velocity, acceleration, and force are all vectors, that is, they have direction as well as magnitude. We will be dealing with the vector nature of these quantities in future chapters. Most of the mechanics problems on the MCAT involve one dimension and uniform acceleration. In this case we can derive four equations.

In addition, you should know the equations for the definition of velocity for uniform motion and of average velocity.

CHAPTER 2 PROBLEMS

1. The gravitational field of a planet or spherical astronomical body depends on its mass and on its radius. When the Moon is compared to Earth, its smaller mass makes for a smaller gravitational field, while its smaller radius favors a larger one. The net effect is that the gravitational field of the Moon at its surface is one sixth that of the Earth. A 10,000-kg mobile unit is transported to the Moon. What is its mass on the Moon?

   A. 1/36 (10,000) kg
   B. 1/6 (10,000) kg
   C. 10,000 kg
   D. 60,000 kg

Use the following for questions 2 and 3:

A car is driving north at 2 m/s, and a fly in the car is flying west at 0.3 m/s (relative to the car).

2. Which of the following best shows the appropriate diagram for the fly's velocity relative to the ground (thick arrow)?

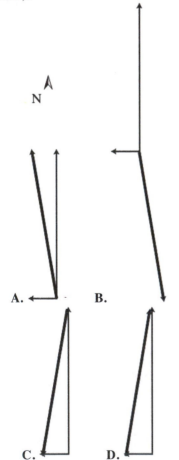

3. What is the speed of the fly?

   A. 1.7 m/s
   B. 2.02 m/s
   C. 2.3 m/s
   D. 4.09 m/s

4. The following diagram represents three vectors in a plane:

   What arrow best represents the direction of the sum?

   A. →
   B. ←
   C. ↑
   D. ↓

5. The following diagram represents three vectors in a plane:

   What arrow best represents the direction of the sum?

   A. ↓
   B. ↑
   C. The sum is zero.
   D. The diagram is invalid.

6. Two men pull on ropes connected to a large refrigerator with forces 3000 N and 4000 N. If there are no other (unbalanced) forces, which of the following is NOT a possibility for the magnitude of the net (total) force?

   A. 500 N
   B. 1000 N
   C. 3500 N
   D. 7000 N

7. If, in question 6, the two men are pulling at right angles to each other, what is the magnitude of the net force?

   A. 1000 N
   B. 5000 N
   C. 7000 N
   D. 8000 N

Use the following for questions 8–11:

A woman is going to a friend's house to discuss opening a business. At 11:00 (exactly) she starts from rest and accelerates at a constant 2.5 m/s^2 for 9 s to get to her cruising speed. She then drives for 15 minutes at constant speed before she hits city traffic. She comes to a stop at her friend's house, which is 27 km away (straight-line distance), at 12:15 (exactly). Consider the interval from 11:00 to 12:15.

8. What is her initial velocity?

   A. 0 m/s
   B. 2.1 m/s
   C. 5.6 m/s
   D. 22.5 m/s

9. What is her final velocity?

   A. 0 m/s
   B. 2.1 m/s
   C. 5.6 m/s
   D. 22.5 m/s

10. What is her average velocity?

    A. 0 m/s
    B. 6 m/s
    C. 12 m/s
    D. 22.5 m/s

11. What is her velocity 9 s after 11:00?

    A. 0.28 m/s
    B. 6 m/s
    C. 11.25 m/s
    D. 22.5 m/s

Use the following for questions 12–14:

A car accelerates uniformly in one dimension from 5 m/s to 30 m/s in 10 s.

12. What is the car's acceleration?

    A. 1.75 m/s^2
    B. 2.5 m/s^2
    C. 3.5 m/s^2
    D. 15 m/s^2

13. What is the car's average velocity for this time interval?

    A. 2.5 m/s
    B. 3.5 m/s
    C. 17.5 m/s
    D. This cannot be determined from the information given.

14. How far does the car travel during this time?

    A. 1.75 m
    B. 17.5 m
    C. 175 m
    D. This cannot be determined from the information given.

15. A car travels a certain distance at a constant velocity *v* for a time *t*. If the car were to travel three times as fast, covering the same distance, then the time of travel would be

    A. decreased by a factor of 9.
    B. decreased by a factor of 3.
    C. increased by a factor of 3.
    D. increased by a factor of 9.

16. A sparrow cruising at 1.5 m/s begins to accelerate at a constant 0.3 m/s^2 for 3 s. What is its change in velocity?

    A. 0.9 m/s
    B. 1.5 m/s
    C. 1.95 m/s
    D. 2.4 m/s

Use the following for questions 17 and 18:

A dropped ball falls from a height of 10 m to the ground. Its acceleration is a constant 9.8 m/s^2 downward.

17. How long does it take to fall?

    A. 1.02 s
    B. 1.43 s
    C. 2.04 s
    D. This cannot be determined from the information given.

18. What is its velocity just before hitting the ground?

    A. 0.98 m/s
    B. 14 m/s
    C. 98 m/s
    D. This cannot be determined from the information given.

19. A car is going 20 m/s in traffic. When the traffic breaks, the driver steps on the accelerator pedal, accelerating at a constant 1.2 m/s^2 for 5 s. How far does he travel during these 5 s?

    A. 30 m
    B. 115 m
    C. 130 m
    D. 160 m

20. A car is going up a slight slope decelerating at 0.1 m/s^2. It comes to a stop after going for 5 s. What was its initial velocity?

    A. 0.02 m/s
    B. 0.25 m/s
    C. 0.5 m/s
    D. 1.0 s

Use the following for questions 21 and 22:

A ball is initially rolling up a slight incline at 0.2 m/s. It decelerates uniformly at 0.05 m/s^2.

21. At what time does the ball come to a stop?

    A. 2 s
    B. 4 s
    C. 8 s
    D. 16 s

22. What is the ball's net displacement after 6 s?

    A. 0.3 m
    B. 0.4 m
    C. 0.5 m
    D. 1.7 m

Use the following for questions 23 and 24:

A car is going backwards at 5 m/s. After 10 s of uniform acceleration, the car is going forward at 10 m/s.

23. What is the acceleration?

    A. 0.5 m/s^2
    B. 0.75 m/s^2
    C. 1.5 m/s^2
    D. 5 m/s^2

24. What is the net distance traveled?

    A. 25 m
    B. 41.7 m
    C. 45 m
    D. 50 m

25. A bicycle traveling at speed v covers a distance Δx during a time interval Δt. If a car travels at speed $3v$, how much time does it take the car to go the same distance?

    A. $\Delta t + 3$
    B. $3\Delta t$
    C. $\Delta t/3$
    D. $\Delta t - 3$

26. A car is traveling 25 m/s when it passes kilometer-marker 3000. The car accelerates at 0.02 m/s^2 for the next 500 s. What kilometer marker will the car pass at that time?

    A. 3015 km
    B. 3030 km
    C. 12000 km
    D. 18000 km

27. A squirrel is running along a wire with constant acceleration. If it has an initial velocity 0.4 m/s and final velocity 1.8 m/s after 4 s, how far does it run in that time?

    A. 1.6 m
    B. 4.4 m
    C. 5.6 m
    D. 8.8 m

28. If a bicycle starts accelerating uniformly from rest (at $t = 0$), it attains a certain velocity v after a time t. How fast would it be going after a time $3t$ (that is, a time $3t$ after the start $t = 0$)?

    A. $v + 9$
    B. $3v$
    C. $6v$
    D. $9v$

For questions 29 and 30, consider the following figure representing the velocity of a car along a street.

Consider also the following graphs:

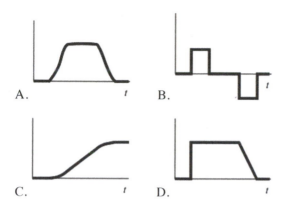

A.   t   B.   t

C.   t   D.   t

29. Which best represents the graph of displacement versus time?

A. A
B. B
C. C
D. D

30. Which best represents the graph of acceleration versus time?

A. A
B. B
C. C
D. D

Passage 1

A man is driving out of his driveway by backing up. He realizes he has forgotten his lunch, so he pulls back into the driveway. Car experts agree that the best way to do this is to press on the brake until the car comes to a complete stop, shift from reverse into first gear, then accelerate forward.

The driver, however, shifts into first gear while the car is rolling backward and pushes on the accelerator until he is going forward. This causes some wear on the transmission. The following chart shows some data about his progress. (Negative velocity = backwards.)

t (s)	x (m)	v (m/s)
0.0	1.35	-1.8
0.5	0.60	-1.2
1.0	0.15	-0.6
1.5	0.00	0.0
2.0	0.15	0.6
2.5	0.60	1.2
3.0	1.35	1.8

31. What is the value of his initial velocity?

A. –1.8 m/s
B. 0.0 m/s
C. 1.2 m/s
D. 1.8 m/s

32. What is the value of his average velocity?

A. –1.8 m/s
B. 0.0 m/s
C. 1.2 m/s
D. 1.8 m/s

33. Which of the following is evidence that the acceleration is uniform?

A. The displacement x is always nonnegative.
B. The velocity is always increasing.
C. The velocity becomes zero at $t = 1.5$ s.
D. Equal intervals of time correspond to equal intervals of velocity.

34. What is the magnitude of the acceleration from $t = 1.0$ s to 2.0 s?

A. 0.0 m/s^2
B. 0.6 m/s^2
C. 1.0 m/s^2
D. 1.2 m/s^2

35. What is the direction of the acceleration vector?

    A. forward
    B. backward
    C. up
    D. down

36. Which best represents acceleration versus time?

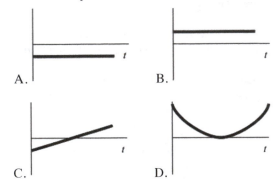

CHAPTER 3
LAWS OF MOTION

A. FIRST LAW OF MOTION

The following is *not* a law of physics:

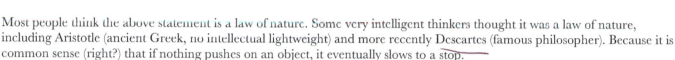

If an object is moving, there must be a force on it.

Most people think the above statement is a law of nature. Some very intelligent thinkers thought it was a law of nature, including Aristotle (ancient Greek, no intellectual lightweight) and more recently Descartes (famous philosopher). Because it is common sense (right?) that if nothing pushes on an object, it eventually slows to a stop.

But sometimes closer scrutiny conflicts with common sense, and when that happens we have to change our thinking, to retune our intuition, so that what once seemed wrong now seems right. That can be difficult, but that's physics.

First Law of Motion
If the forces on an object are balanced, then the object moves with constant velocity (constant speed in a straight line). Conversely, if an object has constant velocity, then the forces on it are balanced. Some people use the term *inertia* to describe this property of matter.

Galileo discovered this law, although it's generally called Newton's first law of motion.

What does it mean for the forces to be balanced? Before we answer that question, let's look at a few cases. In the following

figures (Figures 3-1a–f) we denote the motion of an object by "motion marks", so that 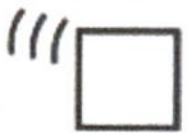 means the object is moving to the right.

Case a. There are no forces. In this case think of a rock in deep space moving along. The velocity vector is constant, meaning the rock continues traveling at constant speed to the right indefinitely.

Figure 3-1a

Case b. There are two opposed forces, equal in magnitude, perpendicular to the motion. In this case think of a marble rolling along a smooth level floor (no friction). Gravity pulls down, but the floor pushes up. The velocity vector is constant.

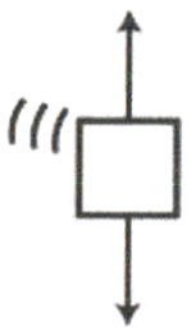

Figure 3-1b

Case c. This scenario is a nonexample, in which the right force is larger than the left force (hence unbalanced). The object will speed up.

37

Figure 3-1c

Case d. This scenario is also a nonexample with the left force larger than the right force. The object will slow down.

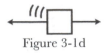

Figure 3-1d

Case e. Two opposed forces, left and right, are equal in magnitude. The case is between cases c and d. The object has constant velocity, that is, it will keep its speed indefinitely. Think about this one for a while. This stumps many people.

Figure 3-1e

Case f. The forces in all three directions are balanced. The object's velocity vector is constant.

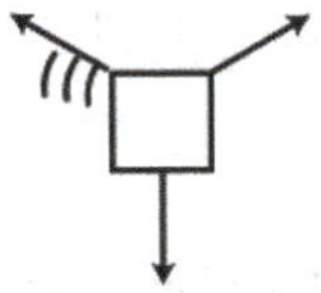

Figure 3-1f

The forces are balanced if the vector sum of all the forces on the object is zero. We define F_{net} by

$$F_{net} = F_1 + F_2 + \dots$$

where F_1, F_2, …, are all the forces acting on an object. The vector F_{net} is the total force on the object.

Example: A woman kicks a soccer ball, and it rolls for a while at constant speed, then another woman stops it. Draw a diagram showing all the forces on the ball at the three times: kicking, rolling, and stopping.

Solution: Part a: The ball is kicked (see Figure 3-2). The vector F_{grav} is the force of gravity, and F_{kick} is the force of the foot on the ball. The symbol N stands for "normal", a physics word meaning perpendicular to the ground. It is force the ground exerts on the ball.

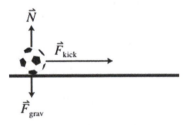

The woman kicks the ball.
Figure 3-2

Part b: The ball rolls along. It has only two forces acting on it (Figure 3-3). The ball does not remember (or care) what started it rolling. According to the first law, the balanced forces guarantee it will keep rolling indefinitely at constant speed.

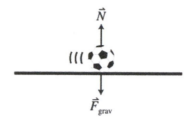

The ball rolls without friction.
Figure 3-3

Part c: The ball is stopped. Now there is a force of a foot on the ball as well (Figure 3-4).

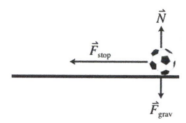

The woman stops the ball.
Figure 3-4

Over the next several chapters there will be many problems to test your intuition on the first law.

B. SECOND LAW OF MOTION

So what happens if the forces on an object are not balanced? If the net force on an object is nonzero, then the velocity vector changes. There must be acceleration. In fact the larger the force, the larger the acceleration. (See Figure 3-5.) On the other hand, if we apply the same push to both a small car and a large car (Figure 3-6), the small car will have the larger acceleration.

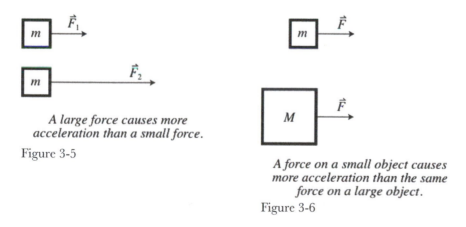

*A large force causes more
acceleration than a small force.*

Figure 3-5

*A force on a small object causes
more acceleration than the same
force on a large object.*

Figure 3-6

We can write (in one dimension)

$$a = \frac{F_{net}}{m} \qquad (1)$$

We have not proven this equation, but the discussion in the previous paragraph should make it seem reasonable to you.

In three dimensions, we write what is often called Newton's second law:

> **Second Law of Motion**
> If an object has forces $\vec{F}_1, \vec{F}_2, \cdots$, acting on it, then the total force on the object is the vector sum
>
> $$\vec{F}_{net} = \vec{F}_1 + \vec{F}_2 + \cdots,$$
>
> and the acceleration $\vec{a}$ of the object is given by
>
> $$\vec{F}_{net} = m\vec{a}. \tag{2}$$

Most often, however, we will break up equation (2) into components:

$$\left(F_{net}\right)_x = ma_x \tag{3a}$$
$$\left(F_{net}\right)_y = ma_y \tag{3b}$$

Equation (3a), for example, states that the sum of all the horizontal forces is mass times the horizontal acceleration.

Finally, we are able to make the connection between the units for force [N] and for mass [kg], introduced in Chapter 1. The newton is defined by

$$N = \frac{kgm}{s^2}$$

Example 1: Bruce pushes a car (500 kg) on level ground starting from rest with a force 100 N. How long does it take to get the car rolling 1 m/s? (Assume no friction.)

Solution: We have the information m = 500 kg, v_1 = 0 m/s, F = 100 N, and v_2 = 1 m/s, and we want Δt. We can find acceleration from equation (1), so we obtain

$$a = 100N/500kg$$

$$= 0.2 \ N/kg$$

Then we can find Δt from

$$a = \frac{\left(v_2 - v_1\right)}{\Delta t}$$

$$\Delta t = 5 \ s.$$

Example 2: A rocket provides a constant force to wagon A that rolls without friction. It starts from rest and after time t attains velocity v. A similar rocket providing the same force is attached to wagon B, which has five times the mass of A (Figure 3-7). How much time does it take wagon B to go from rest to velocity v? (Assume no friction.)

Figure 3-7

Solution: This one looks difficult, but if we write down the relevant equations, it is not so hard. We need to connect force and velocity, so we write,

$$F = ma$$

$$a = \frac{v_2 - v_1}{\Delta t} = \frac{v_2}{\Delta t}$$

We set v_1 to zero because the wagons start from rest. Substitution gives

$$F = m\frac{v_2}{\Delta t}$$

Since the problem asks about the change in time, we can solve for Δt to obtain

$$\Delta t = m\frac{v_2}{F}$$

Now, F and v_2 stay the same, but m is five times larger for wagon B, so Δt is five times larger. The answer is 5t.

C. THIRD LAW OF MOTION

The third law of motion is not so much a law about motion as it is a rule of thumb about pairs of forces. It is usually stated thus:

To every action there is an equal and opposite reaction.

This is certainly poetic, but what does it mean? More clear (and less poetic) is the following:

The Third Law of Motion
If object 1 exerts a force $\vec{F}_{12}$ on object 2,

then object 2 exerts a force $\vec{F}_{21}$ on object 1

which is equal in magnitude, opposite in direction, and of the same type (gravity, friction, etc.):

$\vec{F}_{12} = -\vec{F}_{21}$.

Example 1: The Sun and the Earth exert a force of gravity on each other. Draw a force diagram.

Solution: See Figure 3-8.

Figure 3-8

F_{ES} = gravitational force of the Earth on the Sun,

F_{SE} = gravitational force of the Sun on the Earth.

Example 2: Two spacecraft push off from each other. Draw a force diagram.

Solution: See Figure 3-9.

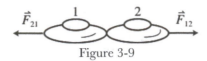

Figure 3-9

F_{12} = contact force of craft 1 on craft 2,

F_{21} = contact force of craft 2 on craft 1.

Example 3: A basketball player jumps up. While he is in the air, he pushes the basketball horizontally. Draw all the forces *while* he is pushing the ball. Ignore the tiny gravitational force between the player and the ball.

Solution: See Figure 3-10.

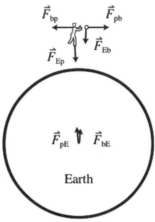

Figure 3-10

F_{pb} = contact force of player on ball,
F_{bp} = contact force of ball on player,
F_{Ep} = gravitational force of Earth on player,
F_{pE} = gravitational force of player on Earth,
F_{Eb} = gravitational force of Earth on ball,
F_{bE} = gravitational force of ball on Earth.

Notice that the magnitude of the force of the player on the ball is the same as that of the ball on the player. But the player moves hardly at all, while the ball springs toward another player. Why is the basketball affected more than the player? (Hint: Look at equation 1.)

D. FORCE DIAGRAMS

Already in this chapter we have seen a number of force diagrams. In this section we discuss some rules for drawing force diagrams. There are two types of force diagrams:

1. a diagram in which all the objects appear and the forces come in third-law pairs, and
2. a diagram featuring one object and all its forces (or maybe several objects, but not all the objects in the situation).

In most problems we will want the second type, but it is important to know how to draw both, and knowing diagrams of the first type will help with the second type.

To draw the first type of diagram, we ask four questions:

1. What gravitational forces are important?
2. What things are touching? (These give contact forces.)
3. Does the problem mention any specific forces?
4. Do the net forces in the diagram conform to expectation?

For each force we draw an arrow whose tail lies on the object **on which the force acts**. This may seem unnatural at first, but it makes things easier in the end. For some examples, look at the diagrams we drew in Section C.

Example 1: A girl jumps horizontally from a boat in the water. Draw all the forces on the boat, the girl, and the Earth. Ignore the tiny gravitational force between the girl and the boat, and ignore the drag force of the water on the boat.

Solution: First we add the gravitational forces in pairs (Figure 3-11).

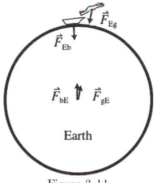

Figure 3-11

Then we add the forces due to the boat and girl touching (F_{bg} and F_{gb}) and the contact force between the Earth and the bat (N_{eb} and N_{bE}). See Figure 3-12.

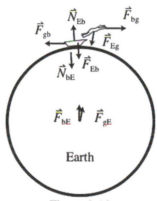

Figure 3-12

The net forces on the boat indicate that it accelerates backwards, which seems right. The net force on the girl indicates she would accelerate forward and down, which seems right. It is difficult to tell what is going on with the Earth.

Example 2: A vase sits on a table, which sits on the Earth. List all pairs of forces. Do this example on your own before you look at the solution.

Solution: See Figure 3-13.

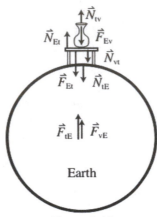

Figure 3-13

$\boldsymbol{F_{Ev}}$ = gravitational force of Earth on the vase,
$\boldsymbol{F_{vE}}$ = gravitational force of vase on the Earth,
$\boldsymbol{F_{Et}}$ = gravitational force of Earth on the table,
$\boldsymbol{F_{tE}}$ = gravitational force of table on the Earth,
$\boldsymbol{N_{tv}}$ = contact force of table on vase,
$\boldsymbol{N_{vt}}$ = contact force of vase on table,
$\boldsymbol{N_{Et}}$ = contact force of Earth on table,
$\boldsymbol{N_{tE}}$ = contact force of table on Earth.

Drawing a diagram of the second type is easier, but you have to be careful not to leave out any forces nor to add any ghost forces.

Example 3: A roller skate is rolling frictionlessly on level ground to the left. Draw all the forces on the roller skate. STOP! Try doing this problem before looking at the solution.

Solution: Gravity is pulling down (question 1). And the ground is touching the skate, pushing up (question 2). There is no friction, nor any other forces, so the force diagram is Figure 3-14.

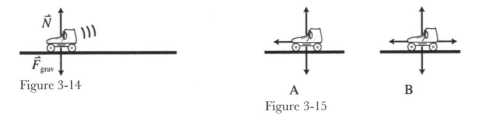

Figure 3-14

A   B

Figure 3-15

Did your diagram look like Figure 3-15 A or B? If so, you have not yet tuned your intuition about the first law of motion. Just because the skate is going to the left does not mean there is a force to the left. Only if the skate were speeding up to the left would we be forced to conclude that there was a force to the left.

In this chapter we studied Newton's laws of motion. In a sense, the first law of motion is the most subtle. If an object is moving at a constant velocity, then the forces on the object add to zero, and if the vector sum of the force vectors for an object is zero, then the object moves at constant velocity. Constant velocity means constant speed in a straight path. No force is required to keep an object moving.

The second law of motion concerns objects whose force vectors' sum is not zero: The acceleration of such an object is in the same direction as the total force, proportional to its magnitude and inversely proportional to the object's mass. That is $\boldsymbol{a} = \boldsymbol{F}_{net}/\boldsymbol{m}$. Do you see why we use equations?

The third law states that forces come in pairs: If object 1 pushes object 2, then object 2 pushes object 1 in the opposite direction.

Pay special attention to Section D on force diagrams. In solving problems, we are always interested in the forces on an object at a given instant in time. These include gravity, usually, and forces due to things touching the object at that moment. No other forces need to be included. In particular, do not include a force in a direction just because the object in moving in that direction.

CHAPTER 3 PROBLEMS

1. Consider a paratrooper who has jumped from an airplane. After an initial accelerating plunge, he begins to fall at a constant speed in a straight vertical plunge (at *terminal velocity*). During the latter portion of his fall, are the forces on the paratrooper balanced?

   A. No, since a force balance exists only if an object is not moving.
   B. No, since gravity is not balanced by anything.
   C. No, since gravity is greater than the drag force.
   D. Yes, since he is moving at a constant velocity.

2. There is one force acting on an object. What can we definitely conclude from this?

   A. The object is speeding up or slowing down.
   B. The object is going at a constant speed, not necessarily in a straight line.
   C. The object is going at a constant speed in a straight line.
   D. None of the above may be definitely concluded.

3. A car's engine has died, and the car is slowing down as it coasts. What may we conclude about the forces acting on the car?

   A. There are no forces acting on the car.
   B. There are forces acting on the car, but the net force is zero.
   C. The net force acting on the car is not zero.
   D. None of the above may be definitely concluded.

4. An object is moving with uniform motion, that is, at constant speed in a straight line. There are two forces acting on the object. What can we definitely conclude from this?

   A. The net force is in the same direction that the object is moving.
   B. Both forces are in a direction perpendicular to the object's motion.
   C. The two forces have equal magnitudes but point in opposite directions.
   D. None of the above may be definitely concluded.

5. In the following diagram, the magnitude of force F_A is 400 N, and that of F_B is 300 N. What is the magnitude of the net force in the three cases?

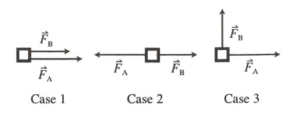

Case 1   Case 2   Case 3

   A. In case 1, the net force is 100 N; case 2, 700 N; and case 3, 500 N.
   B. In case 1, the net force is 700 N; case 2, 100 N; and case 3, 500 N.
   C. In case 1, the net force is 350 N; case 2, 50 N; and case 3, 450 N.
   D. In case 1, the net force is 350 N; case 2, 50 N; and case 3, 550 N.

Use the following for questions 6 and 7:

A man is pulling his son in a toy wagon. The son and the wagon are 60 kg. For 3 s the man exerts a force which has the effect of uniformly accelerating the wagon from 1.5 m/s to 3.5 m/s.

6. What is the acceleration of the wagon with the son?

   A. 0.67 m/s²
   B. 0.84 m/s²
   C. 1.66 m/s²
   D. 20 m/s²

7. What is the net force on the wagon and son?

   A. 40 N
   B. 50 N
   C. 120 N
   D. 1200 N

Use the following for questions 8–11:

A tiger (100 kg) sees a wildebeest and accelerates uniformly from rest to 20 m/s in 12 s.

8. What is the acceleration of the tiger?
   A. 0.60 m/s²
   B. 0.83 m/s²
   C. 1.67 m/s²
   D. 240 m/s²

9. How much distance does the tiger cover in those 12 s?

   A. 120 m
   B. 240 m
   C. 480 m
   D. 960 m

10. What is the magnitude of the net force on the tiger?

    A. 60 N
    B. 83 N
    C. 167 N
    D. 24000 N

11. What are all the forces acting on the tiger?

    A. Gravity, down.
    B. Gravity, down; and the normal force, up.
    C. Gravity, down; the normal force, up, and a horizontal force of the ground pushing the tiger.
    D. None of the above is correct.

12. Three men push on a station wagon with a net force F, producing an acceleration. (Assume there is no friction.) If they push with the same net force on a compact car (with half the mass), the acceleration of the compact car is

    A. four times the acceleration of the station wagon.
    B. twice the acceleration of the station wagon.
    C. half the acceleration of the station wagon.
    D. one quarter the acceleration of the station wagon.

13. Object A is acted upon by a net force F_A to produce an acceleration. If object B has three times the mass of A and is acted on by three times the force as A, the acceleration of B is

    A. 9 times that of A.
    B. 3 times that of A.
    C. the same as that of A.
    D. one third that of A.

14. At time $t = 0$ s, two dung beetles are pushing a small ball (0.5 g). One pushes east with a force 0.0015 N; the other pushes west with a force 0.0010 N. At $t = 0$ s, what is the acceleration of the ball?

    A. 1 m/s^2
    B. 2.5 m/s^2
    C. 3 m/s^2
    D. 5 m/s^2

15. A rocket ship (500 kg) is firing two jets at once. The two jets are at right angles, with one firing to yield a force of 5000 N and the other to yield a force of 12000 N. What is the magnitude of the acceleration of the rocket ship?

    A. 24 m/s^2
    B. 26 m/s^2
    C. 34 m/s^2
    D. 36 m/s^2

16. A girl shoves a 4-kg toy cart across the level floor with a speed of 15 m/s (so it is going 15 m/s when it leaves her hand). It slides to a rest in 5 s. Assuming a constant force slowing the cart, what is the magnitude of the force?

    A. 0.75 N
    B. 1.33 N
    C. 12 N
    D. 18.75 N

17. A piece of steel of mass 0.8 kg hangs from a string over the edge of a table. The string passes over a pulley and is connected in such a way as to maintain a tension force of 6 N (see figure).

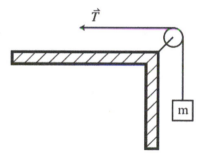

The force due to gravity on the steel is given by $F_{grav} = mg$, where $g = 10$ m/s^2 is the acceleration due to gravity. We allow the piece of steel to fall from rest for 5 s. What is the final acceleration of the piece of steel?

    A. 2 m/s^2
    B. 2.5 m/s^2
    C. 10 m/s^2
    D. 12.5 m/s^2

18. A woman is riding in an elevator which is going up at constant speed. The force of the floor against her feet

    A. is less than the force of gravity on her.
    B. is the same as the force of gravity on her.
    C. is greater than the force of gravity on her.
    D. has no relationship with the force of gravity on her that can be determined by the given information.

19. On September 12, 1966, astronauts conducted an experiment using the second law of motion. A Gemini spacecraft (measured to be 3400 kg) connected with an orbiting rocket case. The thrusters were fired to provide a force of 890 N for 7.0 s. The change in velocity of the spacecraft and rocket case was found to be 0.93 m/s. What was the mass of the rocket case?

    A. 120 kg
    B. 3300 kg
    C. 10,100 kg
    D. 15,400 kg

20. Car A starts from rest and accelerates uniformly for a period of time *t* to travel a distance *d*. Car B, which has four times the mass of car A, starts from rest and accelerates uniformly as well. If the magnitudes of the forces accelerating A and B are the same, how long does is take B to travel the same distance *d*?

    A. 16*t*
    B. 4*t*
    C. 2*t*
    D. *t*/4

21. A car trailer is connected to a car, and both are traveling forward at velocity 3 m/s at time *t* = 5 s. The force the car exerts on the trailer is 105 N, the force of friction on the trailer is 30 N, and the force of air resistance on the trailer is 70 N. The force of gravity on the trailer is 8000 N, and the road exerts an upward force of 8000 N. What conclusion may be drawn about the trailer?

    A. It is speeding up.
    B. It is staying the same speed.
    C. It is slowing down.
    D. It is speeding up or staying the same speed.

22. A car is accelerating from rest at an intersection after the light has turned green. What is the force which accelerates the car?

    A. The horizontal force of the wheels on the road.
    B. The vertical force of the wheels on the road.
    C. The horizontal force of the road on the wheels.
    D. The normal force of the road on the car.

Passage 1

We perform an experiment which involves two masses *m* and *M* connected by a string which we will consider to be massless. Mass *m* hangs over the edge of a table. The string passes over a pulley at the edge of the table and mass *M* sits on the table, such that it moves along the table without friction. (See figure.) The tension in the string is the force that the string exerts where it is connected to another object or to more string. It is generally true that the tension anywhere along the string is the same as the tension anywhere else in the string.

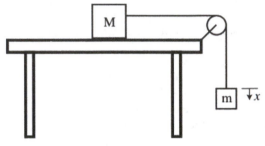

In this experiment the mass *m* is initially at rest and allowed to drop. Its position *x* is measured downward from its initial position. At various times, the position *x* and velocity *v* of mass *m* are measured and the results are recorded in the table which follows:

t (s)	*x* (m)	*v* (m/s)
0.0	0.00	0.0
0.2	0.01	0.1
0.4	0.04	0.2
0.6	0.09	0.3

23. Which of the following is evidence that the acceleration is uniform?

    A. The entries for *x* are nonnegative and increasing.
    B. The entries for *v* are nonnegative and increasing.
    C. The entries for *v* are always greater than *x*.
    D. Any interval Δv is proportional to the interval Δt.

24. Assuming that acceleration remains uniform, what is a likely entry *x* for *t* = 0.9 s?

    A. 0.18 m
    B. 0.20 m
    C. 0.22 m
    D. 0.24 m

25. What are the forces on the mass *m*?

    A. The force of gravity.
    B. The force of gravity and the tension of the string.
    C. The force of gravity and the force due to mass *M*.
    D. The force of gravity, the tension of the string, and the force due to *M*.

26. What are the forces on the mass *M*?

A. The force of gravity and the upward force of the table.
B. The force of gravity, the upward force of the table, and the tension in the string.
C. The force of gravity, the upward force of the table, and the force due to *m*.
D. The force of gravity, the upward force of the table, the force due to *m*, and the tension in the string.

27. What is the average velocity v_{avg} for the interval of time shown in the table?

A. 0.0 m/s
B. 0.1 m/s
C. 0.15 m/s
D. 0.3 m/s

28. After the experiment has run a while, the mass *m* hits the floor and the string goes slack. But mass *M* continues going forward until it hits the pulley. After the string goes slack but before *M* hits the pulley, what are the forces on mass *M*?

A. There are no forces on *M*.
B. The force of gravity.
C. The force of gravity, and the upward force of the table.
D. The force of gravity, the upward force of the table, and a forward force.

This page intentionally left blank.

CHAPTER 4
GRAVITY

A. THE LAW OF GRAVITATION

When a person does a great deal of work in a scientific field, it often happens that that person eventually receives credit for almost everything done by anybody. For instance, Newton is given credit, at least in popular accounts, for almost every interesting thing that happened in science during the Renaissance. In fact, then as now, science is the activity of a community, with many people contributing to the revolution in thinking. For example, the essentials of Newton's first law of motion were discovered by Galileo, and Robert Hooke surmised the essential parts of the law of gravitation.

Newton's genius lay in his ability to see a simple underlying law for very different phenomena and to synthesize diverse branches of science. An example of this is his realization that both the motion of the Moon and the motion of a falling apple could be explained by the same force, the force of gravity. In this chapter we will study the physics of the gravitational force.

Newton's law of gravity states that any two objects exert an attractive force on each other given by

$$F_{grav} = \frac{Gm_1m_2}{d^2} \qquad (1)$$

Here F_{grav} is the magnitude of the gravitational force between two objects, m_1 and m_2 are the masses of the objects, d is the distance between the centers of the objects, and G is a universal constant 6.67×10^{-11} m³/kg s². Do not memorize G, but do remember the equation. We discussed it in Chapter 1.

Example 1: What is the force on a cow (200 kg) standing on the surface of the Earth? (Assume $M_{Earth} = 6.0 \times 10^{24}$ kg, $R_{Earth} = 6.4 \times 10^6$ m.)

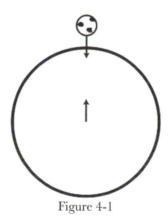

Figure 4-1

Solution: Let's assume we have a spherical cow (Figure 4-1). We calculate

$$F_{grav} = \frac{GM_{Earth}m_{cow}}{R_{Earth}^2}$$

$$= \frac{\left(6.67 \times 10^{-11} \frac{m^3}{kgs^2}\right)\left(6.0 \times 10^{24} kg\right)}{\left(6.4 \times 10^6 m\right)^2} \, m_{cow}$$

$$= m_{cow}\left(9.8 \frac{m}{s^2}\right)$$

$$= 1960 \text{ N}$$

Example 2: What is the motion of an apple (0.1 kg) which has let go of its tree?

Solution: First, we DRAW A DIAGRAM (Figure 4-2) showing all the forces on the apple while it is falling. There is only the force of gravity (nothing else is touching it), so we write

$$F_{grav} = \frac{GM_{Earth}m_{apple}}{R_{Earth}^2}$$

$$= \frac{\left(6.67 \times 10^{-11} \frac{m^3}{kgs^2}\right)\left(6.0 \times 10^{24}\,kg\right)(0.1kg)}{\left(6.4 \times 10^6\,m\right)^2}$$

$$= 0.98\ N$$

Figure 4-2

Since the total force is simply the gravitational force, we write

$$m_{apple}a = F_{net}$$

$$a = \frac{0.98 \frac{kgm}{s^2}}{0.1kg} = 9.8 \frac{m}{s^2}$$

So the apple accelerates downward at 9.8 m/s².

Equation (1) is easy to use in two types of problems:

1. obtaining the force between two planets (*d* is much larger than the radii of the planets), and
2. obtaining the force between a planet and a small object on its surface (*d* is essentially the radius of the planet).

The previous examples illustrated this second use.

B. SURFACE OF THE EARTH

Most of us will spend most of our lives on or near the surface of the Earth. What is the force of gravity of the Earth on an object of mass *m*? The force is

$$F_{grav} = \frac{GM_{Earth}m}{R_{Earth}^2} = \left(9.8 \frac{m}{s^2}\right)m$$

where we use a calculation from the previous section. This number 9.8 m/s² comes up so often in introductory physics that we have given it a name: The ***acceleration due to gravity*** is

$$\boxed{g = 9.8 \frac{m}{s^2}} \qquad (2)$$

In working problems, however, we ***always*** approximate this as ***g*** = 10 m/s² (even if the problem says to use 9.8 m/s²).

Please note: ***Whenever*** there is gravity and we are at the surface of the Earth, which is in most problems, we will use

$$\boxed{F_{grav} = mg \qquad\qquad (3)}$$

C. FREE FALL

An object is said to be in *free fall* when nothing is touching it, so that the only force on it is gravity. Such an object is called a *projectile*. The simplest problem in free fall involves dropping objects near the surface of the Earth. We want to know which falls faster, a heavy object or a light one? Things become complicated if the object is too light, like a leaf fluttering to the ground, so at first we will consider two objects for which air resistance is only a small consideration. (We discuss air resistance in Chapter 6.) Let us start by doing a pair of examples.

Example 1: How long does it take a small rock (0.02 kg) to fall from rest 2 meters to the ground?

Solution: First, we DRAW A DIAGRAM (Figure 4-3). There is only one force since nothing touches the rock and we are neglecting air resistance. Second, we find the net force

$$F_{net} = F_{grav} = -mg$$
$$= -(0.02 \text{ kg})(10 \text{ m/s}^2)$$
$$= -0.2 \text{ N}$$

where the negative sign reminds us that gravity points down.

Figure 4-3

Third, we obtain acceleration by writing

$$F_{net} = ma$$
$$a = F_{net}/m = -0.2 \text{ N}/0.02 \text{ kg} = -10 \text{ m/s}^2$$

(This result should look familiar.)

We also have

$$v_1 = 0$$
$$\Delta y = -2 \text{ m}$$

so that

$$\Delta y = v_1\Delta t + 1/2\ a_y\Delta t^2$$
$$-2 \text{ m} = 1/2\ (-10\text{m/s}^2)\Delta t^2$$
$$\Delta t = 0.63 \text{ s}$$

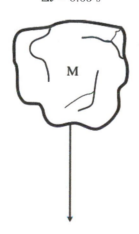

Figure 4-4

Example 2: How long does it take a medium-sized rock (0.2 kg) to fall 2 meters from rest?

Solution: The rock is larger, and so is the force of gravity (and the force arrow, see Figure 4-4). We write

$$\boldsymbol{F}_{net} = \boldsymbol{F}_{grav} = -\boldsymbol{Mg} = -(0.2 \text{ kg})(10 \text{ m/s}^2) = -2 \text{ N}$$

The acceleration is

$$\boldsymbol{a} = \boldsymbol{F}_{net}/\boldsymbol{M} = -2 \text{ N}/0.2 \text{ kg} = -10 \text{ m/s}^2$$

The rest of the problem is the same, so $\Delta\boldsymbol{t} = 0.63$ s.

WHAT HAPPENED? The force of gravity was larger in Example 2, BUT the acceleration is inversely proportional to mass in the second law of motion. The net effect is that the acceleration is the same 9.8 m/s² for both rocks. Try this at home with a pen and a stapler or some such thing. It is difficult to gain an intuitive grasp of this situation, but think about it until you also understand **why** the two rocks have the same acceleration.

Let us revisit Example 2 in Section 2.H. There we saw an apple tossed straight up. It rose, came to a stop, and fell. We claimed that the acceleration was always negative (that is, down), even at the top point. We are now at a better position to understand why. Once the apple leaves the hand, there is only one force on the apple, the downward force of gravity. (See Figure 4-5.) The acceleration must be down as well. In fact, we now know the acceleration is a constant 9.8 m/s², down.

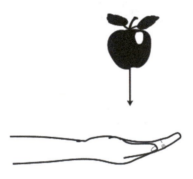

A tossed apple at the top of its flight
is accelerating down at $9.8 \frac{\text{m}}{\text{s}^2}$.

Figure 4-5

D. HORIZONTAL AND VERTICAL MOTION

This section has no new equations but it does present one new idea, so prepare your imagination. A pencil and paper may prove handy.

Imagine you are sitting at the shore of a bay, and you see a boat traveling along at constant speed in a straight line. A sailor at the top of a vertical mast drops a grapefruit. (See Figure 4-6.) We will pretend air resistance plays no role (mostly true). Where will the grapefruit land?

A. In front of the mast.
B. At the foot of the mast.
C. Behind the mast.

Choose your answer before you read any further.

A boat moves with uniform motion.
A grapefruit falls from the mast.
Where does it land?
Figure 4-6

Few people choose A. Not many people choose B. If you are like most people, you chose C, thinking that somehow the boat moves out from under the grapefruit. If that was your answer, then you need to do some rethinking. Here is what really happens. Figure 4-7 shows two ships at four successive times, one ship at rest and the other in uniform motion. Sailors at the tops of the masts drop grapefruits at the same time. Both grapefruits drop to the foot of the corresponding mast.

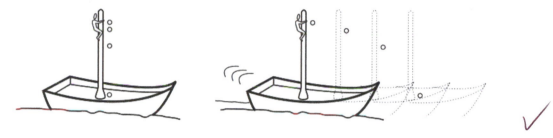

The grapefruit on the moving ship retains its
horizontal motion regardless of vertical motion, and
it drops vertically regardless of its horizontal motion.
Figure 4-7

What is going on in the previous example? Just after the grapefruit is released from the hand on the second ship, it still has its horizontal motion. If air resistance does not affect it, then it maintains its same horizontal motion from start to finish. The vertical motion, on the other hand, proceeds on schedule regardless of the horizontal motion. At $t = 0.2$ s, both grapefruits have moved **vertically** 0.05 m (the second has moved horizontally as well). As time goes on, the second grapefruit keeps up with the ship, and both grapefruits hit the deck at the same time.

If you do not believe the figure, try the experiment yourself. While walking at a constant speed, release an apple above your head (and a little forward). It will fall in front of your face and land at your feet. (See Figure 4-8.)

Figure 4-8

The picture of a boat in the bay and the resulting principle are due to Galileo:

Horizontal and vertical motion are independent. That is, motion in the x- and y-directions can be considered independently.

Now let's leave the bay and travel to the edge of a cliff with a large plain at the bottom. We have two cannonballs, and at the same time, we shoot one horizontally off the cliff and drop the other. Which will hit the plain first?

Again, most people will say the dropped ball hits first. As long as air resistance plays at most a small role, they will hit at the same time. (See Figure 4-9.) For the second ball, the vertical motion of falling is not affected at all by its horizontal motion. It may help your intuition to realize that the shot cannonball does have a larger total velocity all the way down. Notice that Figure 4-9 looks just like Figure 4-7 with the boats removed. It is the same physical principle.

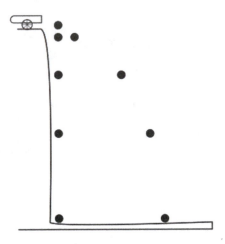

A dropped cannonball falls at the same rate as one shot horizontally.

Figure 4-9

Up until now we have been using v_1, v_2, and a to denote velocities and acceleration in one dimension. For these problems we will need to keep track of the vertical and horizontal pieces separately, so we need the symbols v_{1x}, v_{2x}, a_x, v_{1y}, v_{2y}, and a_y.

The following box shows how this principle gets translated into equations:

If the net vertical force is $(F_{net})_y$, then we can determine the vertical motion using

$$\left(F_{net}\right)_y = ma_y,$$

$$\Delta y = \frac{1}{2}\left(v_{1y} + v_{2y}\right)\Delta t,$$

$$v_{2y} = v_{1y} + a_y\Delta t,$$

$$\Delta y = v_{1y}\Delta t + \frac{1}{2}a_y\Delta t^2,$$

$$v_{2y}^2 = v_{1y}^2 + 2a_y\Delta y.$$

Similarly, we can determine the horizontal motion using similar equations with y replaced by x.

Objects in free fall experience only the force of gravity, so we can say more:

For an object in free fall at the surface of the Earth, we have

$$a_y = -9.8 \, \frac{m}{s^2},$$ (4a)

$$a_x = 0 \, \frac{m}{s^2},$$ (4b)

where "up" is positive and we use *the estimate* $10 \, \frac{m}{s^2}$.

Example 1: A cliff stands 80 m above a flat plane. One cannonball is dropped, and another is fired horizontally at 120 m/s at the same time. How far from the first ball will the second ball land?

Solution: The first ball falls straight down, of course. Let's DRAW A DIAGRAM for the second ball while it is in flight (Figure 4-10). Note that the cannon exerts a force on the cannonball while it is in the cannon, but after the ball leaves the cannon, *the only force is gravity*.

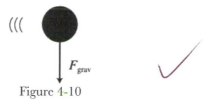

Figure 4-10

We record the information we have. We do not know the mass of the ball, but from Section B we know we do not need it. The acceleration vector is 10 m/s², down.

Vertical
$v_{1y} = 0$
$\Delta y = -80$ m
$a_y = -10$ m/s²
$\Delta y = v_{1y}\Delta t + 1/2 \, a_y\Delta t^2$
-80 m $= 1/2 \, (-10$ m/s²$)\Delta t^2$
$\Delta t = 4$ s

Horizontal
$v_{1x} = 120$ m/s
$\Delta x = ?$
$a_x = 0$ m/s²

$\Delta t = 4$ s
$\Delta x = v_{1x}\Delta t + 1/2 \, a_x\Delta t^2$
$\Delta x = (120$ m/s$)(4$ s$)$
$\Delta x = 480$ m

We solved the vertical problem first because we had more vertical information than horizontal information. The time $\Delta t = 4$ s was the connection between the horizontal and vertical parts. You should work through this example yourself without looking at the book.

The following example involves a *projectile*.

Example 2: A cannon is fired on level ground, so that the ball's initial velocity is 300 m/s and directed 30° up from the horizontal. How far from the cannon will the ball fall? (See figure 4-11.)

Figure 4-11

Interruption: We need to know the horizontal and vertical components of the initial velocity v_1. We need to find a horizontal vector v_{1x} and a vertical vector v_{1y} so that their sum is the original vector v_1 (see Figure 4-12). We can find the magnitudes of v_{1x} and v_{1y} using simple trigonometry. (You may need to review trigonometry at this point.)

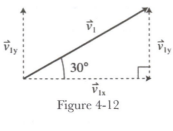

Figure 4-12

$$\frac{v_{1y}}{v_1} = \sin 30°$$

$$v_{1y} = v_1 \sin 30°$$

$$v_{1y} = 300\left(\frac{1}{2}\right)\frac{m}{s}$$

$$v_{1y} = 150\frac{m}{s}$$

$$\frac{v_{1x}}{v_1} = \cos 30°$$

$$v_{1x} = v_1 \cos 30°$$

$$v_{1x} = 300\left(\frac{\sqrt{3}}{2}\right)\frac{m}{s}$$

$$v_{1x} = 150\sqrt{3}\frac{m}{s}$$

Solution: The force diagram is the same as in Figure 4-10. The cannonball rises and then falls to the same height from which it started, so we have $\Delta y = 0$ m.

Vertical

$\Delta y = 0$ m

$v_{1y} = 150$ m/s
$a_y = -10$ m/s^2
$\Delta y = v_{1y}\Delta t + 1/2\ a_y\Delta t^2$
$0 = v_{1y}\Delta t + 1/2\ a_y\Delta t^2$
$0 = v_{1y} + 1/2\ a_y\Delta t$

Horizontal

$\Delta x = ?$

$$v_{1x} = 150\sqrt{3}\frac{m}{s}$$

$a_x = 0$ m/s^2

In the last line, we have divided by a factor of Δt.

$0 = (150$ m/s$) + 1/2\ (-10$ m/s$^2)\ \Delta t$
$\Delta t = 30$ s

$\Delta t = 30$ s
$\Delta x = v_{1x}\Delta t + 1/2\ a_x\Delta t^2$

$$\Delta x = \left(150\sqrt{3}\frac{m}{s}\right)(30s)$$

$\Delta x = 4500\sqrt{3}$ m
$\Delta x = 7800$ m

We have been talking about grapefruits and cannonballs so far. Objects with a more complicated shape obey the same rules, as long as we use the center of mass to talk about the position of the object. Figure 4-13 shows a baseball bat fired from a cannon. The center of mass moves in a parabola, just like the cannonball in the previous example, even though the bat is rotating. In fact this is a definition of the center of mass. If an object is set to freely rotating, the center of mass is the point which refuses to rotate. The gravitational force acts as if it were exerted only at the center of mass.

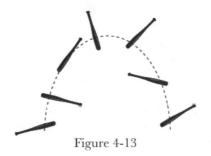

Figure 4-13

In this chapter we looked at the law of gravitation, whose grand form is

$$F_{grav} = Gm_1m_2/d^2$$

For most problems near the surface of the Earth we can use simply

$$F_{grav} = mg$$

where $g = GM_{Earth}/R_{Earth}^2 = 10\text{m/s}^2$

When any object near the Earth's surface has only gravity acting on it (freefall), it has a downward acceleration vector of magnitude 10 m/s². This curious result comes from the fact that the force of gravity is proportional to the mass, while the second law of motion states that the acceleration in inversely proportional to the mass.

We also explored the principle that horizontal and vertical motion are independent. This allows us to solve problems involving projectiles, that is, objects with only gravity acting on them. We will see more of this principle in the following chapter.

CHAPTER 4 PROBLEMS

Use the following for questions 1–3:

In a binary star system, two stars revolve about their combined center of mass. They are held together by the force of gravity. For a certain system, the force of gravity between the stars (masses M_1 and M_2) is F_0.

1. If the mass of one of the stars could somehow be decreased by a factor of 2 at a given moment, how would this affect the force between them?

    A. It would decrease by a factor of 4.
    B. It would decrease by a factor of 2.
    C. It would stay the same.
    D. It would increase by a factor of 2.

2. If the distance between the stars were doubled, how would this affect the force between them?

    A. It would decrease by a factor of 4.
    B. It would decrease by a factor of 2.
    C. It would increase by a factor of 2.
    D. It would increase by a factor of 4.

3. In some binary systems, one star transfers material onto the other. If star 1 dumps half of its material onto star 2, which thus increases its mass by a factor of 5, how is the force affected if the distance between the stars' centers remains the same?

    A. The force increases by a factor of 5.
    B. The force increases by a factor of 2.5.
    C. The force remains the same.
    D. The force decreases by a factor of 2.5.

Use the following for questions 4–6:

For a spherical planetary body, the gravitational field depends on its mass and radius. The strength of the gravitational field determines the acceleration due to gravity of freely falling objects at the planet's surface. At the surface of the Earth, for example, the acceleration due to gravity is $g_{Earth} = 9.8$ m/s². The Moon has a smaller mass and a smaller radius. The net result is that the acceleration due to gravity is $g_{Moon} = 1.6$ m/s². A metal block (12 kg on Earth) is taken to the Moon.

4. What is the mass of the block on the Moon?

    A. 2 kg
    B. 12 kg
    C. 24 kg
    D. 72 kg

5. The block is dropped from a height of 2 m to the surface of the Moon. How long does it take to drop to the surface?

    A. 1.6 s
    B. 2.4 s
    C. 6.3 s
    D. There is not enough information to answer this question.

6. What is the weight of the block on the Moon?

    A. 2 kg
    B. 12 kg
    C. 19 N
    D. 118 N

Use the following for questions 7 and 8:

Mars is a smaller planet than Earth and further from the Sun. Its radius is 0.5 times that of Earth, and its mass is 0.1 times that of Earth. It is 1.5 times further from the Sun than Earth. (Note: On Earth, the acceleration due to gravity is 10 m/s². Also, we have $G = 6.67 \times 10^{-11}$ N m²/kg².)

7. If a person were standing on the surface of Mars and dropped a Martian rock, what is the approximate acceleration of the rock's fall?

    A. 0.3 m/s²
    B. 1 m/s²
    C. 2 m/s²
    D. 4 m/s²

8. How does the force of attraction between the Sun and Mars compare with that between the Sun and Earth?

    A. 0.04 times weaker.
    B. 0.07 times weaker.
    C. 0.10 times weaker.
    D. There is not enough information to answer this question.

Use the following for questions 9 and 10:

The Earth's radius is 3.67 times that of the Moon, and the Earth's mass is 81 times that of the Moon. The acceleration due to gravity on the surface of the Moon is one sixth the acceleration due to gravity on the Earth's surface.

9. How would the force of gravity between the Earth and the Moon be affected if the distance between the Earth and the Moon were decreased by a factor of 3?

    A. It would decrease by a factor of 9.
    B. It would decrease by a factor of 3.
    C. It would stay the same.
    D. It would increase by a factor of 9.

10. How does the Earth's gravitational pull on the Moon differ from the Moon's pull on the Earth?

    A. It is the same.
    B. It is 3.67 times larger.
    C. It is 6 times larger.
    D. It is 81 times larger.

Use the following for questions 11 and 12:

A new planet is discovered whose mass is the same as that of Earth, although the acceleration of freely falling objects at the surface of this planet is three times larger than that corresponding to Earth. (That is, we have g_{Earth} = 9.8 m/s^2 and n_{ew} = 29.4 m/s^2.)

11. What is the radius of this new planet?

    A. 9 times smaller than the radius of Earth.
    B. 3 times smaller than the radius of Earth.
    C. 1.7 times smaller than the radius of Earth.
    D. 3 times larger than the radius of Earth.

12. If an object were dropped from a height h on this planet, how much time would it take to reach the ground compared to the time it would take on Earth to drop the same distance h? (Assume no atmospheric resistance.)

    A. It would take the same amount of time.
    B. The time would be less by a factor of 1.7.
    C. The time would be less by a factor of 3.
    D. The time would be less by a factor of 9.

Use the following for questions 13–15:

An astronaut is in a spaceship traveling at constant velocity toward the star Rigel and is far away from any other objects (planets and stars, etc.). There is racquet ball moving at 0.5 m/s on the spaceship. An astronaut blows air on the racquet ball, producing a small force of 0.08 N in the direction opposite the ball's velocity. The ball slows to a stop in 4 s.

13. What is the weight of the racquet ball?

    A. 0 N
    B. 0.016 N
    C. 0.4 N
    D. 6.4 N

14. What is the magnitude of the acceleration of the racquet ball?

    A. 0 m/s^2
    B. 0.125 m/s^2
    C. 0.2 m/s^2
    D. 0.4 m/s^2

15. What is the mass of the racquet ball?

    A. 0 kg
    B. 0.64 kg
    C. 1.6 kg
    D. 2.5 kg

Use the following for questions 16–20:

In a certain sports event, called the appliance toss, men and women test their strength by hurling an electric can opener horizontally over a cliff. (See figure.) The cliff is very high, standing over a plain, and judges at the bottom determine where the openers land. When Barbara heaves her opener at $t = 0$ s, the opener has horizontal velocity 1.5 m/s when it leaves her hand. After 2 s, it is still in the air (point B in the diagram). (Use $g = 10$ m/s^2.)

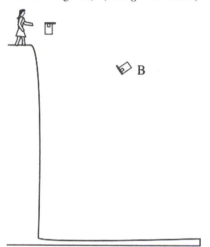

16. Which of the following best shows a force diagram for the can opener at point B?

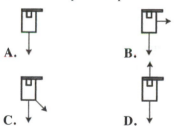

17. What vertical distance has the can opener fallen in the two seconds?

    A. 3 m
    B. 20 m
    C. 20.2 m
    D. 23 m

18. What horizontal distance has the can opener traversed in the two seconds?

    A. 3 m
    B. 20 m
    C. 20.2 m
    D. 23 m

19. At $t = 2$ s, what is the opener's vertical velocity?

    A. 0 m/s
    B. 1.5 m/s
    C. 20 m/s
    D. 21.5 m/s

20. At $t = 2$ s, what is the opener's horizontal velocity?

    A. 0 m/s
    B. 1.5 m/s
    C. 20 m/s
    D. 21.5 m/s

Use the following for questions 21–27:

A ball (0.2 kg) rolls along a level table at 1.5 m/s and then rolls off the edge. The table is 1.25 m off the floor. Consider the time from the moment just after the ball leaves the table till the moment just before the ball touches the floor. See figure. (Use $g = 9.8$ m/s^2, and ignore any air resistance.)

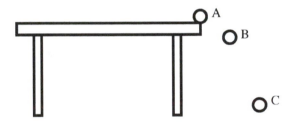

21. What is the ball's initial horizontal velocity?

    A. 0 m/s
    B. 1.5 m/s
    C. 5.0 m/s
    D. 5.2 m/s

22. What is the ball's initial vertical velocity?

    A. 0 m/s
    B. 1.5 m/s
    C. 5.0 m/s
    D. 5.2 m/s

23. When the ball is in midair (point B), what is the net force on the ball?

    A. 1.96 N
    B. 3.92 N
    C. 9.8 N
    D. 19.6 N

24. What is the vertical displacement of the ball during the fall?

    A. 0.76 m
    B. 1.47 m
    C. 1.25 m
    D. 2.25 m

25. How much time does the drop take?

    A. 0.26 s
    B. 0.51 s
    C. 0.83 s
    D. 1.01 s

26. What is the horizontal acceleration of the ball at point B?

    A. 0 m/s^2
    B. 0.2 m/s^2
    C. 1.96 m/s^2
    D. 9.8 m/s^2

27. What is the horizontal displacement of the ball during the fall?

    A. 0.76 m
    B. 1.47 m
    C. 1.25 m
    D. 2.25 m

Passage 1

A sport at a nearby educational institute involves running along the roof of an apartment building, jumping off the edge, and falling into the pool below. This dangerous sport involves a combination of strength of spirit, braggadocio, and inebriation.

Let's say a student (50 kg) accelerates uniformly from rest at one side of the building to the jumping edge, a distance of 5 m. Just after his feet leave the building, he is traveling horizontally at a speed 5 m/s. The building is 7.2 m high, and the pool is 4.5 m from the edge of the building. Use $g = 10$ m/s^2.

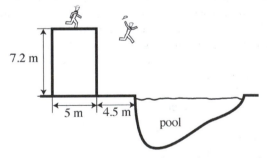

28. How much time does it take the student to accelerate as he is running along the roof?

    A. 1.00 s
    B. 1.20 s
    C. 1.44 s
    D. 2.00 s

29. How much time does it take him to fall?

    A. 1.00 s
    B. 1.20 s
    C. 1.44 s
    D. 2.00 s

30. Which diagram best represents the force diagram for the student while he is on the roof?

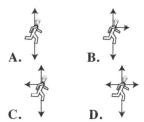

31. Which diagram best represents the force diagram for the student while he is in the air?

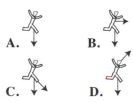

32. Where does he land?

    A. 2.5 meters from the edge of the building, that is, on the pavement.
    B. 4.5 meters from the edge of the building, that is, on the edge of the pool.
    C. 5.0 meters from the edge of the building, that is, in the pool.
    D. 6.0 meters from the edge of the building, that is, in the pool.

33. What is his horizontal velocity just before he lands?

    A. 0 m/s
    B. 5 m/s
    C. 12 m/s
    D. 13 m/s

This page intentionally left blank.

CHAPTER 5
INCLINED PLANES AND CIRCULAR MOTION

A. HORIZONTAL AND VERTICAL MOTION, AGAIN

In the last chapter we solved problems with gravity as the only force. Well, gravity is a fine force indeed, but we need to understand problems in which other forces are present. That is the goal of this chapter.

In the last chapter we discussed the independence of vertical and horizontal motion for objects in freefall, but it turns out the principle works when other forces are acting as well:

> **Independence of Vertical and Horizontal Motion**
> An object has forces $\vec{F}_1, \vec{F}_2, \ldots$, acting on it. If $F_{1y}, F_{2y}, \ldots$, are the vertical components of the forces, then we have
> $$F_{net.y} = F_{1y} + F_{2y} + \cdots, \tag{1}$$
> $$a_y = \frac{F_y}{m}. \tag{2}$$
> Similarly, if $F_{1x}, F_{2x}, \ldots$, are the horizontal components of the forces, then we have
> $$F_{net.x} = F_{1x} + F_{2x} + \cdots, \tag{3}$$
> $$a_x = \frac{F_x}{m}. \tag{4}$$

This is a more useful form of $\boldsymbol{F_{net} = ma}$, the equation that we discussed in Section 3.B. An example will help illustrate how the principle in the above box is used to solve problems.

In the following example, we find a toy wagon rolling on the ground. In general, when an object is on the ground or some other surface, that surface exerts one or two forces on it: always a normal force $\boldsymbol{N}$ pointing perpendicular to the surface and sometimes a frictional force $\boldsymbol{F}_{fric}$ pointing parallel to the surface. We will postpone discussing friction until Chapter 6.

Example: A boy pulls a red wagon (10 kg) with a constant force 20 N. The handle makes an angle 30° with the horizontal. Assume there is no friction.

a. If the wagon starts from rest, how fast is it going after 3 seconds?
b. What is the normal force acting on the wagon?

Solution: First we DRAW A DIAGRAM (Figure 5-1) showing all the forces on the wagon body. The handle and the ground are the only two things which touch it. So in addition to gravity, there are the tension due to the handle and the normal force. The tension $\boldsymbol{T}$ points along the handle, that is, 30° from the horizontal.

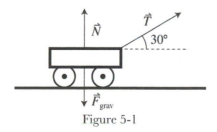
Figure 5-1

In Figure 5-2 we resolve the tension into components (recall trigonometry), so we have

$$\frac{T_y}{T} = \sin 30°$$

$$T_y = (20\text{N})\sin 30°$$

$$T_y = 10\text{N}$$

$$\frac{T_x}{T} = \cos 30°$$

$$T_x = (20\text{N})\cos 30°$$

$$T_x = 17\text{N}$$

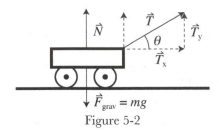

Figure 5-2

The normal force and gravity do not have horizontal components, so the only horizontal force is T_x. Thus we write

$$(F_{net})_x = ma_x,$$
$$T_x = ma_x,$$
$$a_x, = T_x/m = 17\text{N}/10\text{kg} = 1.7 \text{ m/s}^2$$

Using this and $v_{1x} = 0$ m/s and $\Delta t = 3$ s, we derive a horizontal velocity

$$v_{2x} = v_{1x} + a_x\Delta t$$
$$= 0 \text{ m/s} + 1.7 \text{ m/s}^2(3\text{s}) = 4.1 \text{ m/s}$$

which is the answer to part a.

If we consider the vertical components of force, then we can find $(F_{net})_y$ just by looking at the diagram, so we write

$$(F_{net})_y = N + T_y - F_{grav}$$

where we use the positive sign for forces which point up; negative for down. Now the second law of motion connects this with vertical acceleration, so that

$$(F_{net})_y = ma_y$$

But the cart is not moving vertically, so we know that v_y is constant (and zero) and thus a_y is zero. This means $(F_{net})_y$ is zero, so we have

$$0 = N + T_y - F_{grav},$$
$$N = F_{grav} - T_y$$
$$= mg - T_y$$
$$= (10\text{kg})(10\text{m/s}^2) - 10\text{N}$$
$$= 90 \text{ N}.$$

Notice that the normal force is not the same as the gravitational force, a mistake often made by students. Why is the normal force not the same as gravity?

Note that in solving part a, we used information about forces to obtain the horizontal acceleration a_x and then the answer. In part b we reasoned the other way, using information about the vertical acceleration $a_y = 0$ to obtain information about the normal force. This strategy of reasoning in both directions will be useful in many problems.

B. INCLINED PLANES

The following method generally works for force problems in two dimensions:

1. DRAW A DIAGRAM.
2. Draw all the forces on the object(s) in question (see Section 3.D).

3. Decide the orientation of the axes ("horizontal" and "vertical").
4. Divide the forces into components if necessary.
5. Solve $(F_{net})_y = ma_y$ and $(F_{net})_x = ma_x$.

For the last step, note that we often have $a_y = 0$, leading to $(F_{net})_y = 0$. Also, be on the lookout for the words "constant velocity" or the equivalent, since that implies $a_x = 0$ and $a_y = 0$, a force balance.

The principle of the independence of the components of the $F = ma$ equation is valid even when the axes are tilted, as the next example will show.

Example: A toy car of mass 40 grams is released at the top of an incline of plastic track, inclined 30° from the horizontal. The car starts from rest and travels 4 m to the floor. Assuming there is no friction, how much time does it take the car to reach the floor?

Solution: First we DRAW A DIAGRAM (Figure 5-3). In addition to gravity, the track touches the car and exerts a normal force. Since the track is inclined, the normal force points not up but perpendicular to the surface. There is no frictional force.

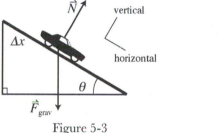

Figure 5-3

We will call "horizontal" the direction along the track and "vertical" the direction perpendicular to the track (Figure 5-3).

Next, we divide the gravitational force into components (Figure 5-4). Note that F_x and F_y are not new forces but pieces of F_{grav}. If we add F_x and F_y together like vectors (tip-to-tail), then we get F_{grav}. It may not be obvious that the two angles shown in Figure 5-4 should both be $\theta = 30°$. Note that both angles labeled θ are complementary to the angle between F_x and F_{grav}. On the other hand, in physics it is generally true that two small angles which look congruent are congruent(!).

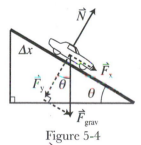

Figure 5-4

Now if we look at the triangle in Figure 5-4, we can write

$$\frac{F_x}{F_{grav}} = \sin\theta \qquad\qquad \frac{F_y}{F_{grav}} = \cos\theta$$

$$F_x = F_{grav}\sin\theta \qquad\qquad F_y = F_{grav}\cos\theta$$

$$F_x = mg\sin\theta \qquad\qquad F_y = mg\cos\theta$$

We care about the horizontal motion, so we write

$$(F_{net})_x = ma_x$$

The only horizontal force is F_x, so we write

$$F_x = ma_x$$

$$mg \sin \theta = ma_x$$

$$g \sin \theta = a_x$$

$$a_x = (10 \text{ m/s}^2)\sin 30° = 5 \text{ m/s}^2$$

We have $v_{1x} = 0$ m/s and $\Delta x = 4$ m, so we can find Δt by writing

$$\Delta x = v_1 t + \frac{1}{2}a_x t^2$$

$$\Delta t = \sqrt{\frac{2\Delta x}{a_x}}$$

$$= \sqrt{\frac{2(4\text{m})}{5\dfrac{\text{m}}{\text{s}^2}}}$$

$$= 1.3 \text{ s}$$

C. CIRCULAR MOTION

Let's think a minute about a toy car moving along the floor and pretend the movement is frictionless. Figure 5-5 shows a top view, with the car moving to the right (see the motion marks behind the car). If we were to apply a rightward force F_A, by blowing the car with a portable hair dryer, for instance, this would clearly speed up the car. If we were to apply a leftward force F_B, this would slow it down. A force F_C applied (for just a moment) perpendicular to the motion would neither speed it up nor slow it down, but it would cause the car to veer from its straight path.

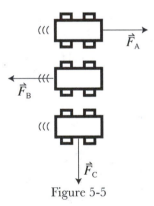

Figure 5-5

If we are using a hair dryer to exert F_C, then we can keep adjusting the direction of the force to keep it perpendicular to the motion of the car. The car will end up traveling in a circle (Figure 5-6). Given this discussion, the following box should seem reasonable.

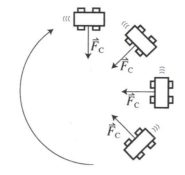

An object moving in a circle with constant speed has an acceleration vector pointed towards the center of the circle.

Figure 5-6

If an object is moving at constant speed in a circle, then the net force on the object points toward the center of the circle, and the acceleration vector points towards the center as well.

In normal English, we do not say that the car is accelerating when it is turning. But in physics language, an object that is moving at constant speed in a circle is "accelerating toward the center of the circle", because the **velocity vector** is changing. We call this **centripetal acceleration**, which is Latin for "toward the center". (Parenthetically, "centrifugal" means "away from the center".) The force which provides the centripetal acceleration is the **centripetal force**.

Example 1: The Earth moves around the Sun. What force provides the centripetal force?

Solution: The gravitational force provides the centripetal force (Figure 5-7).

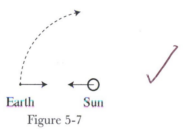

Earth   Sun

Figure 5-7

Example 2: A car goes around a curve to the left. What force provides the centripetal force?

Solution: This example is a bit more complicated. The driver turns her wheels to the left, so the wheels exert a force on the road to the right. By Newton's Third Law of Motion, the road exerts a force to the left on the wheels, turning the car left. In this case friction provides the centripetal force (Figure 5-8). (Think what would happen if there were no friction, for instance, if there were oil on the road.)

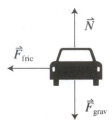

*The car, seen from the rear, is
turning left, and the frictional force
provides the centripetal
acceleration.*

Figure 5-8

Example 3: A father is driving a car and turns to the left. There is a sack of groceries in the front passenger seat which crashes into the passenger door. The little brother Samson in the back seat asks the father why the groceries crashed into the door. The father says that was due to centrifugal force. The older sister Cadenza rolls her eyes at this, thinking about how much physics her brother will have to unlearn as he grows up. What is the correct explanation for the groceries' crashing into the door?

Solution: Figure 5-9 gives the real story. The groceries are going along a straight path, as we would expect according to the first law of motion. The car door is pulled into the path of the groceries. The father invents the word "centrifugal force" in order to hide his ignorance. Whenever you are tempted to explain something by centrifugal force, it is likely that you can explain it better with the ideas of first law of motion and a turning frame of reference (like the car).

*The groceries in the passanger's seat
crash into the car door because the
door turns into their path (not
because of "centrifugal force").*

Figure 5-9

An object moving in a circle has an acceleration which has, in general, two components: the centripetal acceleration and the tangential acceleration. The former is directed toward the center and is responsible for changing the direction of the object. The latter is responsible for changing the speed. The acceleration is given by

Tangential acceleration	$a_{\text{tang}} = \dfrac{\Delta \text{speed}}{\Delta t}$,	(5)
Centripetal acceleration	$a_{\text{cent}} = \dfrac{v^2}{r}$.	(6)

Example 1: A bombardier beetle sits on a blade of a windmill which is going counterclockwise and slowing down. The blade is at the top of its cycle. Sketch the acceleration vector.

Solution: In Figure 5-10, if the beetle is going left and slowing down, then the tangential acceleration must be to the right. The centripetal acceleration vector is down, and the total acceleration a is shown.

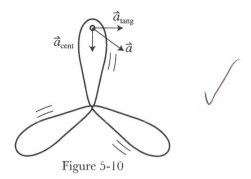

Figure 5-10

Example 2: Use the following information to find the mass of the sun:

$$G = 6.67 \times 10^{-11} \text{ m}^3/\text{kg s}^2$$
$$R = 1.5 \times 10^{11} \text{ m (distance from the Sun to the Earth)}$$

Solution: First, we DRAW A DIAGRAM showing all the forces (Figure 5-11). Some students are tempted to draw two forces on the Earth: a gravitational and a centripetal force. But the only force is gravity, and this provides the centripetal force in this problem. This last sentence provides the clue for solving the problem. We know expressions for gravitation and for centripetal acceleration, so that we have

$$F_{grav} = F_{cent}$$

$$\frac{GM_{sun}M_{Earth}}{R^2} = M_{Earth}\frac{v^2}{R} \quad (7)$$

We use M_{Earth} on the right-hand side of the equation, because it is the Earth's acceleration we are concerned about. The Sun's acceleration is much smaller because its mass is larger. (Recall that the force the Earth exerts on the Sun is the same as that which the Sun exerts on the Earth.) Note that M_{Earth} cancels.

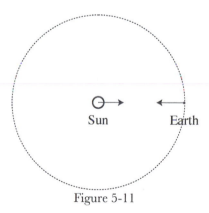

Sun   Earth

Figure 5-11

What expression shall we use for v? What is the velocity of the Earth? If the Earth travels a full circuit in a year, then velocity is simply distance per time, where the distance is the circumference of the circle. Thus we write

$$v = \frac{2\pi R}{T} \quad (8)$$

where T is 1 year. Do not simply memorize this, but take a minute to think about why this equation is true, so it will come immediately to mind in any similar situations. Substituting this into equation (7) and doing some algebra gives

$$M_{sun} = \frac{4\pi^2 R^3}{GT^2}$$

into which we can substitute the values given in the problem, along with

$$T = 365 \text{days} \left(\frac{24 \text{ hours}}{1 \text{ day}} \right) \left(\frac{3600 \text{ s}}{1 \text{ hour}} \right) = 3 \quad 10^7 \text{ s}$$

to yield

$$M_{sun} = 2 \times 10^{30} \text{ kg}$$

The importance of this example does not lie in the arithmetic. The important parts are the method of setting two expressions for the same force equal to each other and the use of equation (8).

Example 3: A fan spins at a frequency of 50 cycles per second, and its plastic blades are 0.4 meters long. What is the centripetal acceleration of a piece of plastic at the tip of one of the blades?

Solution: You should try to work this out before you read the solution.

If the fan spins at 50 cycles per second, it must undergo one cycle in one fiftieth of a second, so $T = 1/50 \text{ s} = 0.02 \text{ s}$. The velocity is given by

$$v = \frac{2\pi r}{T} = \frac{2\pi(0.4\text{m})}{0.02\text{s}} = 126 \frac{\text{m}}{\text{s}}$$

so the acceleration is given by

$$a = \frac{v^2}{r} = \frac{\left(126 \frac{\text{m}}{\text{s}}\right)^2}{0.4\text{m}} = 4 \quad 10^4 \frac{\text{m}}{\text{s}^2}$$

Example 4: A space warrior must fly his spacecraft at constant speed around a spherical space station "Bad Star". Bad Star is large but not large enough to have an atmosphere or gravity worth considering. It is important for the warrior to stay close to the surface and maintain constant speed. A conventional rocket provides the thrust to maintain course, so the plume appears in the opposite direction of the desired thrust. In which direction (Figure 5-12) would we see the plume?

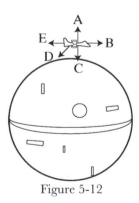

Figure 5-12

Stop! Think about his question and answer it before you look at the solution on the next page.

Solution: No one chooses B. Few people choose A. In fact, almost everyone chooses E, because they are thinking about a car driving on the surface of the Earth. But a car on the Earth's surface encounters the force of drag, both by friction and by air resistance, whereas the space warrior encounters neither. No force is required to maintain constant speed. If you chose E, it means you need to study the first law of motion again.

Okay, what is the correct way to think of this problem? The net force of the spacecraft is down, toward the center of Bad Star, because the craft is moving at constant speed in a circle. there is no gravity, no friction, no air drag, so the only force on the craft is due to the rockets. Therefore the rocket plume points in the direction of A.

Some students object that a rocket firing in the direction of A would push the craft into the Bad Star. This is the same as objecting that if the Earth pulls on the Moon, it ought to fall down. What holds up the Moon? The answer in both cases is that the centripetal force is large enough to keep the object (spacecraft or Moon) from moving away but not so large as to pull them into the ground. That is, in Figure 5-13, path 1 is the path the spacecraft takes if the warrior does not fire his rockets at all (no force). Path 2 is the path if he does not fire the rockets enough; and path 4, if he fires them too much. Path 3 is just right.

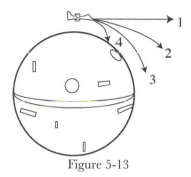
Figure 5-13

The most important concept in this chapter is the independence of horizontal and vertical motion. We saw this concept for the first time in Chapter 4. In this chapter we have used the concept to solve problems involving inclined planes and oblique forces, that is, forces which are neither horizontal nor vertical.

We also looked at circular motion. If an object is moving in a circle, its velocity vector is not constant, and the object must be accelerating. If the object is moving at constant speed, then the direction of the acceleration vector is toward the center, called centripetal acceleration, and its magnitude is $a_{cent} = v^2/r$.

D. TORQUE

Now let's consider a 10-kg bicycle wheel of diameter 1 meter and a 10-kg pipe of diameter 5 cm, both at rest (Figure 5-14). Now we want to set them spinning by giving them a twist. Which is more difficult to set spinning?

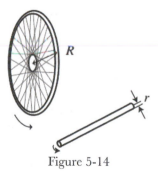
Figure 5-14

Even though they have the same mass, the bicycle wheel has a greater *moment of inertia* than the pipe, and applying a twist to it will not have as great an effect as applying the same twist to the pipe. For the simple shape of a ring (or pipe) turning about a central axis, the moment of inertia is

$$I = MR^2 \quad (9)$$

where M is the mass of the object and R is the radius. Do not memorize the equation, but do remember the general rule: If two objects have the same mass, then the object with greater radius will have a greater moment of inertia and thus will be more difficult to set spinning from rest.

If an object, like a bicycle wheel, is spinning, then the *period T* is the time it takes for one revolution. The *frequency f* is the number of revolutions per unit time, so

$$f = 1/T \ (10)$$

which is measured in [1/s = Hertz = Hz].

A *torque* is a twist, which can change the frequency at which an object is spinning. A large torque on an object with a small moment of inertia will produce a large change in its frequency of rotation. Note the similarity with the second law of motion.

Notice that the moment of inertia depends also on the axis about which an object is turning. We can twist a barbell about its central axis, or about a perpendicular axis (see Figure 7-2). The moment of inertia with respect to the perpendicular axis is greater than that with respect to the central axis, because of the greater radius.

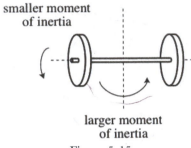

smaller moment
of inertia

larger moment
of inertia

Figure 5-15

TORQUE EQUATION AND SIGN CONVENTIONS

In order to calculate a torque, we always have a pivot P_0 (where the axis is) and a force acting at another point P_1. For example, in Figure 5-16, the pivot is at the crocodile's belly, and the force F acts at his snout at P_1.

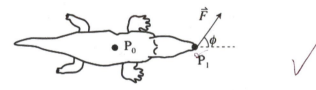

*The force produces a
torque about point P_0'.*
Figure 5-16

The torque is defined by

$$\tau = rF \sin \phi \ (11)$$

where τ is the torque, r is the distance from P_0 to P_1, F is the size of the force, and ϕ is the angle between the direction of the force and the line P_0 and P_1. But is ϕ the big angle or the little angle? Well, it turns out it doesn't matter, since we are taking the sine, and the sines of supplementary angles are the same. Recall that

$$\sin 0° = 0,$$
$$\sin 90° = 1,$$
$$\sin 180° = 0.$$

Also the convention is that

counterclockwise = positive torque
clockwise = negative torque.

Up until this chapter, we have drawn force vector arrows anywhere as long as the tail of the arrow sat on the object the force acted on. In doing torque problems, we must be more careful to put the arrows in the right place.

Example 1: A large tarot card (the Fool) measuring 0.3 m by 0.4 m lies at the lower left in the first quadrant of the *xy*-plane, so that one corner is at (0.4 m, 0.3 m). See Figure 5-17. There is a force of 1.5 N in the *y*-direction located at point (0.4 m, 0.3 m). The pivot is at the origin. What is the torque?

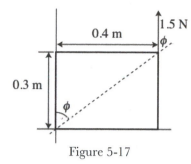

Figure 5-17

Solution: We can see that the force tends to turn the card counterclockwise, so the torque is positive. We can find the radius by the Pythagorean theorem:

$$r = \sqrt{(0.3 \text{ m})^2 + (0.4 \text{ m})^2} = 0.5 \text{ m}$$

The angle ϕ is shown in the two places in the diagram (corresponding angles with the parallel lines). The sine of ϕ can be obtained by looking at the portion of the diagram shown in Figure 5-17:

$$\sin\phi = \frac{opposite}{hypotenuse} = \frac{0.4 \text{ m}}{0.5 \text{ m}} = 0.8$$

Putting all this together gives us

$$\tau = rF\sin\phi$$
$$= (0.5 \text{ m})(1.5 \text{ N})(0.8)$$
$$= 0.6 \text{ Nm.}$$

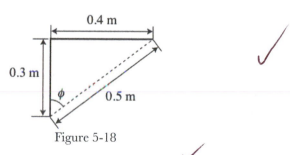

Figure 5-18

Example 2: A massless meter stick is supported by a fulcrum at the mark 0.3 m (point B). A mass A of 10 kg is sitting at the 0.1-m mark (point A). A mass C of 4 kg is sitting at the 0.8-m mark (point C). Consider the forces on the ruler (Figure 5-19).

a. What is the torque due to the weight of A about point B?
b. What is the torque due to the weight of C about point B?
c. What is the torque due to the force of the fulcrum about point B?

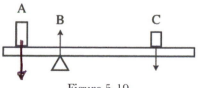

Figure 5-19

Solution:
a. In this case, we have $r = 0.2$ m, $F = mg = 100$ N, $\sin\phi = 1$, and the torque is counterclockwise, so

$$\tau = (0.2 \text{ m})(100 \text{ N})(1) = 20 \text{ Nm}.$$

b. In this case, the torque is clockwise, so we have

$$\tau = -(0.5 \text{ m})(40 \text{ N})(1) = -20 \text{ Nm}.$$

c. In this case, $r = 0$ m, so $\tau = 0$ Nm.

Example 3: A massless meter stick is hanging from the ceiling at the mark 0.3 m, point B. Mass A (10 kg) is hanging by string A (0.2 m long) connected to point A at the 0.1-m mark on the meter stick. Mass C (4 kg) is hanging by string C (0.3 m long) connected to point C at the 0.8-m mark on the meter stick. (See Figure 5-20.)

a. What is the torque due to the weight of A about point B?
b. What is the torque due to the weight of C about point B?
c. What is the torque due to the force of the fulcrum about point B?

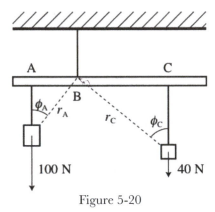

Figure 5-20

Solution: This example looks exactly like the previous example; the strings are only a slight modification. If we apply the strict definition for torque (equation [3]), however, we will end up making an enormous effort, calculating r_A and $\sin\phi_A$, and so on. Thankfully, there is an easier way.

> **Trick:** The torque due to a force is not changed by moving the force vector to a new point, as long as that point lies on the line of the vector. That is, the new point must be on a line containing the old point and running in the same direction as the vector. We can think of this as sliding the vector along the direction it is already pointing until we have $\phi = 90°$.

In this example, this trick is the equivalent of sliding the force up the string to the meter stick. In fact, the example is exactly equivalent to Example 2.

a. $\tau = 20$ Nm.
b. $\tau = -20$ Nm.
c. $\tau = 0$ Nm.

Example 1, revisited solution: We can slide the 1.5-N force down the edge of the card to the *x*-axis. In this case we have $r = 0.4$ m and $\sin\phi = 1$, so we have

$$\tau = (0.4 \text{ m})(1.5 \text{ N})(1) = 0.6 \text{ Nm}$$

Once we move the force to a new point, so that $\phi = 90°$ (and $\sin\phi = 1$), the torque is especially easy to calculate. The line segment from the pivot to the new position of the force is called the **lever arm**. In Figure 5-21, the lever arm is the line segment $\overline{P_0 P_1}$.

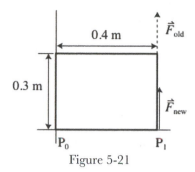

Figure 5-21

In drawing torque diagrams, it is helpful to keep the following principles in mind:

1. Gravity acts at the center of mass. ✓
2. A string or rope exerts only a pulling force at the point of connection. ✓
3. When a stick or pole meets a wall or floor, the force acts at the point of contact. ✓
a. If the surface is frictionless, then there is only a normal force. ✓
b. If the stick is connected by a hinge, then the force is along the stick (either pushing or pulling). ✓
c. If the stick is connected to the wall or floor, then there are two forces, one normal and one parallel to the surface. ✓

E. EQUILIBRIUM

Torques are useful in problems involving rolling and spinning, although most such problems lie outside the scope of the MCAT. Torques are also useful in solving for forces in structural problems, even if there is no motion. For these problems we use the following principle:

If a system is in static equilibrium, then

$$(F_{net})x = 0 \quad (12a) \quad ✓$$
$$(F_{net})y = 0 \quad (12b) \quad ✓$$

and

$$\tau_{net} = 0 \quad (12c) \quad ✓$$

no matter which point you choose as the pivot.

Equations (12a) and (12b) assure **translational equilibrium**, and equation (12c) assures **rotational equilibrium**. The following examples illustrate methods for calculating forces in static equilibrium. ✓

Example 1: Consider the pulley system shown in Figure 5-22. Mass m_1 is 2 kg, the radius of pulley A is 0.15 m, the radii of pulley B are 0.3 m and 0.1 m, and the radius of pulley C is 0.05 m. What mass m_2 is required for equilibrium?

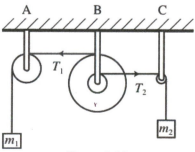

Figure 5-22

Solution: A string has one tension throughout its length, no matter what pulleys it goes around. Thus the tension $T_1 = m_1g$, and $T_2 = m_2g$. The radii of pulleys A and C are irrelevant.

For equilibrium, we can take torques about the pivot of pulley B, keeping in mind that counterclockwise is positive and clockwise is negative, so that

$$\tau_{net} = 0$$
$$\tau_1 - \tau_2 = 0$$
$$(0.3 \text{ m})(2 \text{ kg} \cdot 10 \text{ m/s}^2)(1) - (0.1 \text{ m})(m_2 \cdot 10 \text{ m/s}^2)(1) = 0$$
$$m_2 = 6 \text{ kg}$$

For problems involving torque balance, the following methods often work:

1. DRAW A DIAGRAM.
2. Label all forces acting on the system.
3. Choose a pivot.
4. Calculate torques and set $\tau_{net} = 0$.
5. Use $(F_{net})_x = 0$ and $(F_{net})_y = 0$, or choose another pivot.

Example 2: A pole of mass m_1 and length L sticks out perpendicularly from a wall at point A. A wire connects the end of the pole to a point B above point A, making an angle θ with the pole. A lamp of mass m_2 hangs from a wire at the end of the pole. (See Figure 5-23.)

a. What is the tension in the wire from B to C in terms of m_1, m_2, g, L, and θ?
b. What is the vertical force exerted by the wall on the pole?

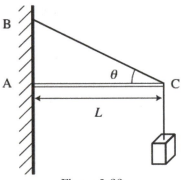

Figure 5-23

Solution: First, we DRAW A DIAGRAM with all the forces on the pole (Figure 5-24).

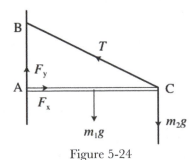

Figure 5-24

We know m_1g and m_2g but not T, F_x, and F_y. Let us make a chart showing the torques about A and C.

Force	Torque about A	Torque about C
m_1g	$-Lm_1g/2$	
m_2g		
T	$LT\sin\theta$	
F_x		
F_y		

Make sure you understand why these two entries are correct. Then fill in the rest of the chart on your own. The completed chart is shown below.

Force	Torque about A	Torque about C
m_1g	$-Lm_1g/2$	$Lm_1g/2$
m_2g	$-Lm_2g$	0
T	$LT\sin\theta$	0
F_x	0	0
F_y	0	$-LF_y$

In the second column the entries for the torque due to F_x and F_y about A are zero, since $r = 0$ for these entries. In the third column, the entry for the torque due to F_x about C is zero because $\sin\phi = 0$. The torque due to T about C is zero because $r = 0$.

a. In order to find T, we can take torques about point A, since that eliminates F_x and F_y. The net torque must be zero because the system is in equilibrium, so we have (taking the sum of the first column)

$$-\frac{L}{2}m_1g - Lm_2g + LT\sin\theta = 0$$

We solve for T and divide through by L to obtain

$$T = \frac{m_1g + 2m_2g}{2\sin\theta}$$

b. In order to find F_y, we can use one of two methods. Using torques and choosing point C as a pivot yields

$$Lm_1g/2 - LF_y = 0$$

$$F_y = m_1g/2$$

On the other hand, we could add up all the vertical forces and use $(F_{net})_y = 0$, so that

$$F_y + T\sin\theta - m_1g - m_2g = 0$$

$$F_y = m_1g + m_2g - T\sin\theta$$

$$= m_1g + m_2g - \frac{m_1g + 2m_2g}{2\sin\theta}\sin\theta$$

$$= \frac{1}{2}m_1g$$

This was a longer solution, so using torques is clearly the way to go.

Example 3: A pole of length L is connected to a hinge at point A on a vertical wall, making an angle α with the wall. A horizontal string connects to the wall at point B and the end of the pole at point C. A box of candy of mass m hangs from a string at the end of the pole. (See Figure 5-25)

a What is the tension in the horizontal string?
b. What is the magnitude of the force of the wall on the pole at point A?

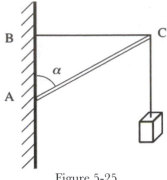

Figure 5-25

Solution: First we DRAW A DIAGRAM with all the forces on the pole (Figure 5-26). We have the tension T in the horizontal string and tension mg in the vertical string. We are left with a choice for the force of the wall on the pole F_s: pushing or pulling? No matter, we can draw it either way, and physics will tell us later on if we have it right. Let's make the force tensile, that is, pulling.

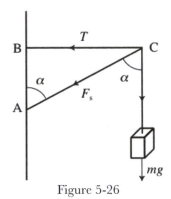

Figure 5-26

a. We choose A for the pivot, since that choice kills the force F_s but keeps T and mg. Setting the sum of the torques equal to zero gives

$$LT \sin(90° - \alpha) - Lmg \sin\alpha \quad 0$$
$$LT \cos\alpha - Lmg \sin\alpha = 0$$
$$T = mg \frac{\sin\alpha}{\cos\alpha}$$

b. In order to find F_s, we set the sum of vertical forces to zero, so that

$$(F_{net})_y = 0$$
$$-F_s \cos\alpha - mg = 0$$
$$F_s = -mg/\cos\alpha$$

The negative sign tells us that we drew the F_s vector the wrong way. (Perhaps you knew this already.) The force is compressional.

CHAPTER 5 PROBLEMS

Use the following for questions 1–5:

A cannon shoots an orange (3 kg) straight up in the air with initial velocity 5 m/s (see figure). A horizontal wind exerts a force of 6 N on the orange while it is in the air. Use 10 m/s² for the acceleration due to gravity.

1. Which is the best force diagram while the orange is in the air?

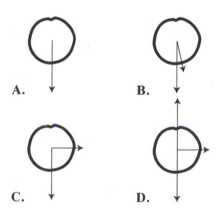

A.

B.

C.

D.

2. What is the vertical component of the net force on the orange while it is in the air?

    A. 0 N
    B. 2 N
    C. 30 N
    D. 32 N

3. How much time does it take the orange to reach the top of its path?

    A. 0.25 s
    B. 0.4 s
    C. 0.5 s
    D. 2.5 s

4. What is the horizontal component of the acceleration of the orange while it is in the air?

    A. 0 m/s²
    B. 2 m/s²
    C. 10 m/s²
    D. 18 m/s²

5. What is the horizontal velocity of the orange at the top of its path?

    A. 0 m/s
    B. 1 m/s
    C. 5 m/s
    D. 1.25 m/s

6. A shoe is being dragged to the right at constant velocity along a level floor by its string. The string is horizontal and bears a tension T in magnitude. The magnitude of the frictional force is F, the magnitude of the gravitational force is G, and the magnitude of the normal force is N. What can definitely be concluded?

    A. $T < F$
    B. $T = F$
    C. $T > F$
    D. $T + F = G + N$

Use the following for questions 7–11:

A winch pulls a crate of oranges (300 kg) up an incline (30° with the horizontal) by maintaining a tension on a rope over a pulley. The crate is moving at a constant speed 0.2 m/s. There is no friction. (Using $g = 10$ m/s².)

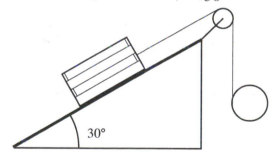

7. What is the component of the gravitational force perpendicular to the surface on which the crate sits?

    A. 0 N
    B. (3000 N) sin30°
    C. (3000 N) cos30°
    D. 3000 N

8. What is the component of the gravitational force parallel to the surface on which the crate sits?

    A. 0 N
    B. (3000 N) sin30°
    C. (3000 N) cos30°
    D. 3000 N

9. What is the normal force on the crate?

    A. 0 N
    B. (3000 N) sin30°
    C. (3000 N) cos30°
    D. 3000 N

10. What is the net force on the crate?

    A. 0 N
    B. (3000 N) sin30°
    C. (3000 N) cos30°
    D. 3000 N

11. What is the tension on the rope?

    A. 0 N
    B. (3000 N) sin30°
    C. (3000 N) cos30°
    D. 3000 N

Use the following for questions 12–17:

A boy (60 kg) is pushing a sled (5 kg) with a stick, so that the stick makes a 30° angle with the vertical. He applies a force of 20 N, so that the force acts along the stick (i.e., there is no shear or friction force). There is negligible friction between the sled and the ground. At time $t = 0$ s, the sled is at rest.

12. Which of the following is the best force diagram for the sled after $t = 0$ s?

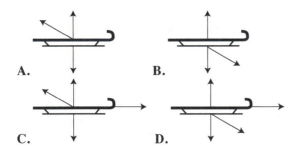

    A.   **B.**

    C.   **D.**

13. What is the horizontal component of the force due to the stick?

    A. 10 N
    B. 17 N
    C. 20 N
    D. 50 N

14. What is the vertical component of the force due to the stick?

    A. 10 N
    B. 17 N
    C. 20 N
    D. 50 N

15. What is the normal force of the ground on the sled?

    A. 17 N
    B. 33 N
    C. 50 N
    D. 67 N

16. What is the net force on the sled?

    A. 0 N
    B. 10 N
    C. 50 N
    D. 67 N

17. What is the acceleration of the sled?

    A. 0 m/s^2
    B. 0.5 m/s^2
    C. 2.0 m/s^2
    D. 9.8 m/s^2

18. A woman is driving a car along a road when she realizes, almost too late, that she needs to make a left hand turn. She quickly turns the wheel, and the books which were in the passenger seat go crashing against the passenger door. Consider the following statements:

I. The books were pushed against the door by a centrifugal force.
II. The books were pushed against the door by a centripetal force.
III. The forces acting on the books while they are crashing against the door are gravity, the normal force, and a force toward the right.

Which is (are) true?

    A. I and III are true.
    B. II and III are true.
    C. III only is true.
    D. None is true.

Use the following for questions 19–23:

A stopper is swung on a string, one end of which is fixed at a point P. The diagram shows the stopper and string from the top, and the stopper is swinging counterclockwise at constant speed.

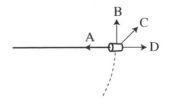

19. Which arrow best shows the direction of the velocity vector?

    A. A
    B. B
    C. C
    D. D

20. Which arrow best shows the direction of the acceleration vector?

    A. A
    B. B
    C. C
    D. D

21. Which arrow best shows the direction of the net force?
    A. A
    B. B
    C. C
    D. D

22. What provides the centripetal force?

    A. Gravity.
    B. Tension.
    C. Friction.
    D. Normal.

23. Which arrow best shows the direction the stopper would go if the string were to break at the moment shown in the diagram?

    A. A
    B. B
    C. C
    D. D

Use the following for questions 24–27:

A '79 Buick Regal (1200 kg) is being driven at a constant speed 3 m/s and turning to the right on a curve of road which has effective radius 4 m.

24. Consider the car as viewed from the top. Ignore the gravitational and normal forces (which are vertical and add to zero anyway). Which is the best force diagram?

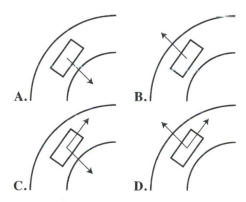

25. What is the acceleration of the Buick?

    A. 0 m/s^2
    B. 0.75 m/s^2
    C. 2.25 m/s^2
    D. 9.8 m/s^2

26. What is the net force on the Buick?

    A. 0 N
    B. 900 N
    C. 2700 N
    D. 11760 N

27. What force provides the centripetal force on the Buick?

    A. Gravity.
    B. Tension.
    C. Friction.
    D. Normal.

Use the following for questions 28–29:

A bicycle wheel (mass 3 kg, radius 0.5 m) is spinning at a constant angular speed. It is situated horizontally, and a beetle (5 g) is sitting on the rim. The beetle is traveling at a speed 2 m/s. Use $g = 10$ m/s^2.

28. In the following diagrams, the wheel is viewed almost from the side, so that "down" is toward the bottom of the page. Which is the best force diagram?

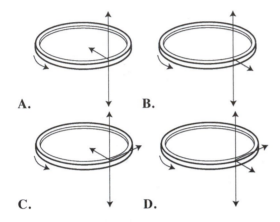

A.   **B.**

C.   **D.**

29. What is the acceleration of the beetle?

    A. 0 m/s^2
    B. 2 m/s^2
    C. 8 m/s^2
    D. 10 m/s^2

30. The figure shows a ball (from the top view) rolling on a table with a partial hoop. Which arrow best describes the path of the ball after it leaves the hoop?

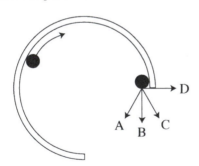

    A. A
    B. B
    C. C
    D. D

Use the following for questions 31–33:

A student nails a meter stick to a board at the meter stick's 0.0-m mark. A force *A* of 10 N acts at the 0.5-m mark perpendicular to the meter stick as shown in the figure. Force *B* of 5 N acts at the end of the meter stick, making a 30° angle, as shown. Force *C* of 20 N acts at the same point providing tension but no shear. (Use counterclockwise to be positive.)

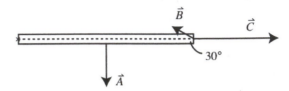

31. What is the torque of force *A* about the fixed point?

    A. −5 Nm
    B. 0 Nm
    C. 5 Nm
    D. 10 Nm

32. What is the torque of force *B* about the fixed point?

    A. −4.33 Nm
    B. 2.5 Nm
    C. 4.33 Nm
    D. 5 Nm

33. What is the torque of force *C* about the fixed point?

    A. −20 Nm
    B. 0 Nm
    C. 10 Nm
    D. 20 Nm

34. A massless meter stick sits on a fulcrum at its 0.4-m mark. A 6-kg mass sits on the meter stick at the 0.2-m mark. What mass is required to sit at the 0.9-m mark in order to have torque balance?

    A. 2.4 kg
    B. 4.5 kg
    C. 10 kg
    D. 15 kg

Use the following for questions 35–38:

A book (4 kg) is hanging by a string connected to a rope at point B. One end of the rope is connected to the wall at point A, and the other end is pulled by a person at point C with a tension T. The rope from A to B is 1.5 m long and horizontal, while the rope from B to C makes an angle 30° with the horizontal. (See figure, in which we take counterclockwise to be positive.) (Use $g = 10$ m/s²)

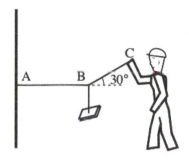

35. What is the torque due to the weight of the book about point B?

    A. −60 Nm
    B. −30 Nm
    C. 0 Nm
    D. 60 Nm

36. What is the torque due to the weight of the book about point A?

    A. −60 Nm
    B. −30 Nm
    C. 0 Nm
    D. 60 Nm

37. What is the torque due to tension T about point B?

    A. −60 Nm
    B. −30 Nm
    C. 0 Nm
    D. 60 Nm

38. What is the torque due to tension T about point A?

    A. −60 Nm
    B. −30 Nm
    C. 0 Nm
    D. 60 Nm

39. Scott and Tina are playing on a seesaw which is 4 meters long with a fulcrum in the middle. Tina is 30 kg and sits at one end, while Scott, 40 kg, sits so that they balance. Assume the seesaw itself is uniform and balanced. How far from the end should Scott sit in order to achieve balance?

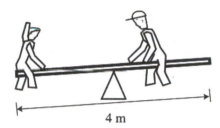

    A. 0.5 m
    B. 1 m
    C. 1.5 m
    D. 3 m

40. A meter stick of mass 0.6 kg sits on a fulcrum located at the 0.3-m mark at equilibrium. At the 0.0-m mark hangs a mass m. What is m?

    A. 0.4 kg
    B. 0.9 kg
    C. 1.4 kg
    D. 1.8 kg

Use the following for questions 41 and 42:

Pulley B hangs from the ceiling and has a diameter d. A string twined about the pulley leads around pulley A, hanging from the ceiling, and to a mass M. A beam of length L is attached to the pulley B itself and stretches out horizontally. A mass m is connected to the end. The system is in static equilibrium. (See figure.)

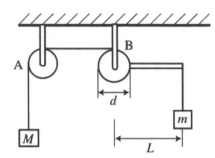

41. What is the magnitude of the torque due to the weight of mass m about the axis of pulley B?

   A. $mgd/2$
   B. mgd
   C. $mgL/2$
   D. mgL

42. Which gives an expression for M?

   A. $mL/2d$
   B. mL/d
   C. $2mL/d$
   D. $md/2L$

Use the following for questions 43–45:

The bones of the forearm (radius and ulna) are hinged to the humerus at the elbow. The biceps muscle connects to the bones of the forearm about 2 cm beyond the joint, forming a second-class lever. Assume the forearm is 2 kg in mass and 0.4 m long. The humerus and biceps are (nearly) vertical and the forearm is horizontal. The hand holds a mass A of 1.5 kg. The arm and mass are in static equilibrium. (Use $g = 10$ m/s^2.)

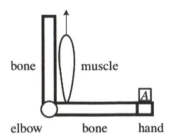

43. What is the magnitude of the torque of the weight of mass A about the elbow?

   A. 3 Nm
   B. 4 Nm
   C. 6 Nm
   D. 8 Nm

44. What is the magnitude of the torque of the weight of the forearm about the elbow?

   A. 3 Nm
   B. 4 Nm
   C. 6 Nm
   D. 8 Nm

45. What is the force exerted by the muscle?

   A. 300 N
   B. 350 N
   C. 500 N
   D. 700 N

CHAPTER 6
FRICTION AND AIR RESISTANCE

A. INTRODUCTION

So far in this book, we have ignored friction in order to make problems easier and to understand the basic principles behind motion. On the other hand, there cannot be too many practical applications of such a theory without friction, since few of the surfaces in this world are frictionless, and it is difficult to go anywhere without air resistance (especially if you go by car).

Friction is a force that opposes the slipping of two surfaces, so it acts parallel to the boundary between the surfaces. We generally think of friction as the force that slows things down, but that is not the best way to consider it. When you step on the accelerator of a car, what force makes the car go faster? None other than the friction between the tires and the road. What happens when you try to accelerate on ice?

There are two types of friction: *static friction*, which is relevant when the surfaces are not slipping, and *kinetic friction*, which is relevant when the surfaces are slipping.

B. STATIC FRICTION

Let us consider an example. Muffin the cat is trying to budge a waste-paper basket in order to see what is under it. Before she starts, the forces on the basket are those shown in Figure 6-1. She begins to push, but the basket does not budge. The force of friction has shown up and exactly balances her pushing force (Figure 6-2). When she pushes harder, the frictional force becomes larger, frustrating her effort (Figure 6-3).

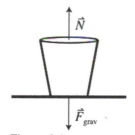

Figure 6-1

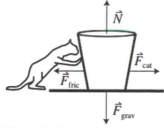

Figure 6-2

There is a maximum for friction, and that is shown in Figure 6-4 as a dashed vector, labeled F_{max}. If she can manage to push harder than the theoretical maximum, then the basket will move. At that time we no longer have a problem in static friction.

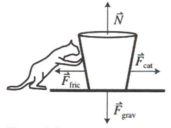

Figure 6-3

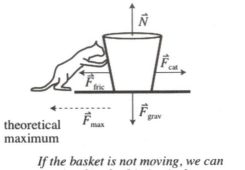

If the basket is not moving, we can surmise that the friction is the same magnitude as the push force.

Figure 6-4

There are two principles here:

> If there are no slipping surfaces, then the static friction, which acts parallel to the surface, has whatever magnitude it needs in order to maintain nonslipping surfaces. This generally involves solving the whole force equation with $a_x = 0$ and $a_y = 0$.

Also

> If the calculated force of friction is greater than the theoretical maximum, then static friction is not relevant, and the problem needs to be reconsidered with kinetic friction. The maximum is given by
>
> $$F_{s,max} = \mu_s N,$$
>
> where μ_s, the coefficient of static friction, depends only on the materials involved. It has no units and is generally less than 1.

Example: Beth (45 kg) has tied a rope around her brother's waist. Vincent (20 kg) is on the slippery slope of a river bank making an angle 30° with the horizontal. The coefficient of static friction between him and the bank is 0.2.

a. If she does not pull on the rope, will he slide down into the river, which is infested with crocodiles?
b. If so, what is the smallest force she must exert parallel to the bank in order to keep him from slipping?

Solution: First, we need to DRAW A DIAGRAM (Figure 6-5). First, there is the force of gravity. The bank is touching him, so there is a normal force. There is also friction and possibly the rope. At any rate, these act along the bank, so we label them F_{need}, that is, the force needed to keep him from sliding.

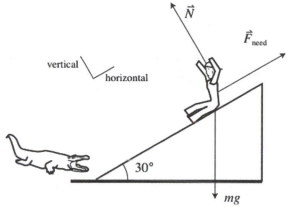

Figure 6-5

In Figure 6-6 we divide gravity into components.

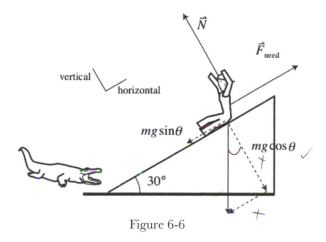

Figure 6-6

The "vertical" equation becomes

$$N - mg \cos 30° = (F_{net})_y = 0$$

because if Vincent does not move, then $a_y = 0$. Thus we have

$$N = mg \cos 30° = (20 \text{ kg})(10 \text{ m/s}^2)(0.87)$$

$$= 170 \text{ N}$$

The "horizontal" equation becomes

$$F_{need} - mg \sin 30° = (F_{net})_x = 0$$

If Vincent is being held still by friction, or by friction and his sister's rope, then we must have $a_x = 0$. Then we have

$$F_{need} = mg \sin 30° = (20 \text{ kg})(10 \text{ m/s}^2)(1/2)$$

$$= 100 \text{ N}$$

Equation (1) becomes

$$F_{s, max} = \mu N = 0.2(170 \text{ N}) = 34 \text{ N}$$

which is clearly insufficient. Beth must pull with a force

$$\boldsymbol{F}_{\text{Beth}} = (100 - 34)\text{N} = 66 \text{ N}$$

If Beth pulls with a force 66 N, then static friction provides 34 N, enough to keep Vincent from slipping down. If she wants to pull Vincent up the slope, then she must pull hard enough to exceed the static friction maximum in the other direction. That is, friction would pull **down** the slope, and she would have to pull up the slope with a force (100 + 34)N = 134 N.

C. KINETIC FRICTION

Once the static friction maximum is exceeded, the surface involved in a problem begins to slip, and we have a problem involving kinetic friction.

If there is slipping between surfaces, then the kinetic frictional force is given by

$$F_k = \mu_k N,$$

where μ_k is the coefficient of kinetic friction, N is the normal force, and the direction of the force is parallel to the surface in opposition to the slipping. In general μ_k is less than μ_s, so once an object is moving, the force of friction is less than the maximum friction when the object is still.

You might have thought that, the faster an object slides, the more friction it experiences. This is **not** true. (It is true for air resistance, but not friction.)

Also, you might have thought that there would be more friction for an object with more surface touching (see the second picture in Figure 6-7), but again, this is not true. The friction depends only on the coefficient of friction and the normal force.

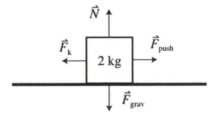

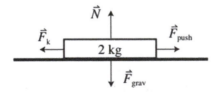

The kinetic friction depends only on the normal force and the slipping surfaces.

Figure 6-7

Example 1: Brad pushes a stove (100 kg) in a straight path across the level floor at constant speed 0.2 m/s. The coefficient of kinetic friction is 0.3 for the stove and the floor. What is the force that Brad must apply?

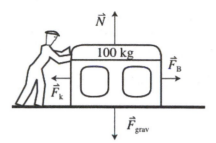

Figure 6-8a

Solution: First, we DRAW A DIAGRAM (Figure 6-8a). The words "constant speed" and "straight path" should send bells off in our head. There is no acceleration, so the vertical equation becomes,

$$N - mg = (F_{net})_y = 0$$

$$N = mg = (100 \text{ kg})(10 \text{ m/s}^2) = 1000 \text{ N}$$

Equation (2) gives the friction

$$F_k = \mu_k N = 0.3(1000 \text{ N}) = 300 \text{ N}$$

The horizontal equation becomes

$$F_B - F_k = (F_{net})_x = 0$$

$$F_B = F_k = 300 \text{ N}$$

Think about this. Brad's pushing force is equal in magnitude to the frictional force.

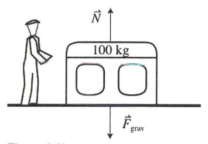

Figure 6-8b

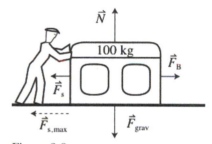

Figure 6-8c

"But wait a minute!" some readers will cry. "Doesn't Brad have to **overcome** the force of friction for the stove to be moving? Brad's force must be **greater** than the frictional force!" But that is exactly not the case. If the stove is moving at **constant speed**, then the forces must balance. If Brad exceeded the force of friction, the stove would be accelerating.

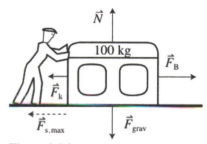

Figure 6-8d

Perhaps it would help if we looked at the whole Brad/stove story. When Brad approaches the stove, the force diagram on the stove looks like Figure 6-8b. As Brad begins to push on the stove, the friction vector gets larger, as in Figure 6-8c. The moment Brad exceeds $F_{s,max}$, the stove budges, and the force of friction shrinks from $F_{s,max}$ to F_k. Now there is a net force on the stove, and it accelerates from rest (Figure 6-8d). Once the stove is moving, it gets away (a little) from his hands, and Brad's force decreases to become F_k. At this point the stove has attained some constant speed, which it keeps. See Figure 6-8a, where the two horizontal vectors are equal in magnitude.

Example 2: A student is pushing a chalk eraser (0.1 kg) across a level desk by applying a force 0.3 newtons at an angle directed downward, but 30° from the horizontal. The eraser is moving at constant speed 0.1 m/s across the desk (in a straight line). What is the coefficient of friction between the eraser and the desk?

Solution: First, we DRAW A DIAGRAM (Figure 6-9). Constant velocity tells us that $(F_{net})_x$ and $(F_{net})_y$ are zero. The vertical equation becomes

$$N - T_y - mg = (F_{net})_y$$

$$N = T_y + mg = T\sin 30° + mg$$

$$N = (0.3 \text{ N})\sin 30° + (0.1 \text{ kg})(10 \text{ m/s}^2)$$

$$N = 1.15 \text{ N}.$$

The horizontal equation becomes

$$T_x - F_k = (F_{net})_x = 0$$

$$F_k = T_x = T\cos 30° = 0.26 \text{ N}$$

Thus we can calculate μ_k

$$\mu_k = F_k/N = 0.26\text{N}/1.15\text{N} = 0.23$$

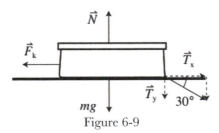

Figure 6-9

Example 3: A car (1000 kg) is traveling downhill at 20 m/s in the rain. The grade of the road is 20%, which means that for every 100 meters of road, the vertical drop is 20 meters. The driver sees Bambi in the road and slams on the brakes. The coefficient of kinetic friction between the tires and the road is 0.5. How much time does it take the car to skid to a halt? (Hint: If θ is the angle between the horizontal and the road, then $\cos\theta = 0.98$ and $\sin\theta = 0.2$. Also $g = 10 \text{ m/s}^2$.)

Solution: Here we will merely sketch a solution. You should try to work out the details. Figure 6-10 shows the force diagram. Working out the vertical equation with $(F_{net})_y = 0$ gives

$$N = 9800 \text{ N}.$$

Kinetic friction is then

$$F_k = 4900 \text{ N}.$$

Working out the horizontal equation (there is a net force) gives

$$(F_{net})_x = 2900 \text{ N}$$

$$a_x = 2.9 \text{ m/s}^2$$

Using the acceleration, the initial velocity, and the final velocity $v_{2x} = 0$, we obtain

$$\Delta t = 7 \text{ s}.$$

(Bambi was unscathed, but only because he jumped off the road in time.)

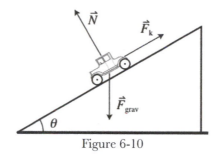

Figure 6-10

D. STICK/SLIP

The fact that μ_k is generally less than μ_s means that, in many situations, the friction will switch back and forth from kinetic to static. Picture pulling a potato with a rubber band, so static friction initially prevails. After the rubber band stretches enough, the potato moves and kinetic friction takes over. But then the rubber band has contracted again, so the potato stops, and static friction prevails. By this time you are pulling again. This is called *stick/slip*, for obvious reasons.

The stick/slip phenomenon is responsible for the squeal of bus brakes. It is also responsible for the eh-eh-eh-eh-eh sound when you rub your hair after a shower or your dishes after washing. These are some very practical applications of physics.

E. AIR RESISTANCE

We have neglected air resistance thus far mainly for one reason, and that is that air resistance makes problems more difficult. Air resistance, or drag, depends on the velocity that an object is going, and not always in a simple way. Thus it is difficult to work problems without a computer.

There are a few things we can say about drag. Consider an object moving through a substance, such as air or water. It is reasonable that a larger object would experience more drag than a smaller one. We might also expect that the drag would be larger for a faster moving object. Finally it is reasonable to expect that a dense fluid would exert more drag than a "thin" fluid. It will not be a surprise, then, that the formula for drag is

$$F_{drag} = C\rho A v^2$$

where C is a constant equal to about 0.2, ρ is the density of the fluid, A is the cross-sectional area of the moving object, and v is its velocity. This equation is reasonably accurate if the fluid is "roughed up" a bit by the object's passing through. For cars driving and people walking through air and for fish swimming through water, this is a reasonable assumption.

You do not have to memorize this equation, but do know how to use it. The force is placed in the force diagram like all the other forces, except it points necessarily opposite the direction of motion.

Example 1: A dog Nikki (7 kg) falls five stories (3.3 meters each) down from a roof with his stomach pointing down. He is 0.2 meters tall, and 0.15 meters wide and 0.4 meters from nose to tail. The density of air is 1.29 kg/m3.

a. If we ignore air resistance, what is the terminal velocity of the dog?
b. What is the air resistance by the time the dog gets to the bottom?
c. Is air resistance a small or large effect in this problem?

Solution: a. First, we DRAW A DIAGRAM (Figure 6-11). We are hoping that the force of air resistance is small. We have

$$F_{net} = F_{grav} = -mg$$
$$a = -g = -10 \text{ m/s}^2$$
$$v_1 = 0$$
$$\Delta y = -16.5 \text{ m}$$

We use the kinematic equation that does not involve Δt, so we have

$$v_2^2 = v_1^2 + 2a\,\Delta y$$

$$v_2^2 = 2\left(-10\frac{m}{s^2}\right)(-16.5m) \quad 330\frac{m^2}{s^2}$$

$$v_2 = -18\frac{m}{s}$$

b. The cross-sectional area presented by the dog is (0.4 m)(0.15 m) = 0.06 m². It does not matter how tall Nikki is. Thus

$$F_{air} = (0.2)\left(1.29\frac{kg}{m^3}\right)(0.06m^2)\left(330\frac{m^2}{s^2}\right)$$

$$= 5N$$

c. Air resistance is about 10% of the dog's weight (70 N). This implies that the dog's weight is the dominant force all the way down, and we are justified in ignoring air resistance. Our answer is good with no more than about 10% error.

Nikki is a stunt dog. He was unharmed.

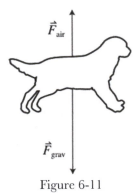

Figure 6-11

Example 2: A rubber ball (radius 2 cm, mass 5 grams) is dropped from a height of 50 meters. What is its velocity when it reaches the ground?

Solution: If we work out the problem as in Example 1a above, we run into trouble. Ignoring air resistance yields v² = 32 m/s. (You should work this out.) The cross-sectional area is the area of a circle πr^2, not the total surface area of a sphere. If we calculate the force due to air resistance at the bottom of flight, we obtain

$$F_{air} = (0.2)\left(1.29\frac{kg}{m^3}\right)\left[\pi(0.02m)^2\right]\left(32\frac{m}{s}\right)^2$$

$$= 0.33 \text{ N}$$

whereas the weight of the ball is $F_{grav} = mg = 0.05$ N. The calculated force F_{air} is not small at all in comparison. In fact, it is much larger than the force of gravity. Any assumption that air resistance is negligible is not valid. We need a new idea in order to solve this.

The new idea follows. If the ball has fallen so far that it has stopped accelerating then the gravity force down and the air resistance force up are balanced. Then the force diagram would look like the one in Figure 6-12. The force equation becomes

$$F_{air} - mg = (F_{net})_y = 0$$

$$C\rho Av^2 - mg = 0$$

$$v^2 = \frac{mg}{C\rho A} = \frac{(0.005\text{kg})\left(10\,\frac{\text{m}}{\text{s}^2}\right)}{0.2\left(1.29\,\frac{\text{kg}}{\text{m}^3}\right)\left(1.3 \times 10^{-3}\,\text{m}^2\right)}$$

$$= 149\,\frac{\text{m}^2}{\text{s}^2}$$

$$v = 12\,\frac{\text{m}}{\text{s}}$$

As the ball falls, its velocity increases until it begins to get close to 12 m/s. The air resistance increases until it balances the force of gravity. Force balance occurs when $v = 12$ m/s. This velocity is called **terminal velocity**.

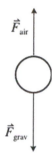

Figure 6-12

Example 3: A man (60 kg) falls from a very tall building (200 m). The cross-sectional area for his fall is 0.3 m².

a. What equation governs the fall?
b. What is his velocity when he reaches the bottom?

Figure 6-13

Solution: a. First, we DRAW A DIAGRAM (Figure 6-13). The force equation becomes

$$F_{\text{air}} - mg = ma$$
$$C\rho Av^2 - mg = ma$$

b. An analysis similar to the one in Example 1 shows that ignoring air resistance yields $v_2 = 63$ m/s. If we calculate F_{air}, as in Example 1, we obtain 310 N, about half of the man's weight. This shows that ignoring air resistance is wrong since 310 N is not small compared to $F_{\text{grav}} = 600$ N. But F_{air} is not large compared to F_{grav} either. Our calculations show that air resistance is too large to be ignored, but not so large as to assure force balance. This problem is just too hard.

In this chapter we looked at friction and air resistance. Friction is a force which opposes the slipping of surfaces, and it always acts parallel to the surface. Situations involving friction fall into two categories: static and kinetic. If the surfaces are not slipping, then static friction is the force which maintains the status. We solve for the frictional force using force balance. The static friction cannot be larger than the maximum, given by $F_{\text{s,max}} = \mu_s N$.

If the surfaces are slipping, then kinetic friction opposes the slipping. Its magnitude is given by $F_k = \mu_k N$.

The MCAT does not have many problems involving air resistance. Generally you just need to know that air resistance is a retarding force that depends on the surface area, density of the medium, and velocity of the object.

CHAPTER 6 PROBLEMS

Use the following for questions 1–3:

Sam is pulling a block of ice (mass m) along a smooth level floor with a rope on which he maintains a tension of magnitude T. The rope makes an angle α with the horizontal. The block is moving at velocity v for a time Δt. The coefficient of friction between the ice and the floor is μ_k.

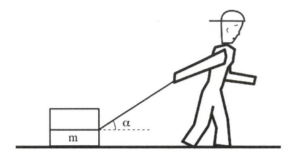

1. What is the horizontal component of the tension?

    A. 0
    B. $T\cos\alpha$
    C. $T\sin\alpha$
    D. T

2. What is the magnitude of the normal force?

    A. mg
    B. $mg - T\cos\alpha$
    C. $mg + T\cos\alpha$
    D. $mg - T\sin\alpha$

3. What is the magnitude of the force of friction F_{fr}?

    A. 0
    B. $\mu_k mg$
    C. $T\cos\alpha$
    D. $T\sin\alpha$

Use the following for questions 4–8:

In a laboratory experiment, a student places a block of copper (2 kg) on a surface of a flat piece of steel and tilts the steel. The student determines that for any angle up to 30° (with respect to the horizontal), friction will prevent the block from sliding, but larger angles necessarily allow the block to slide. Consider the situation in which the block is not moving, and the angle of the tilt is its maximum 30°. (Use 9.8 m/s² for the acceleration due to gravity.)

4. What frictional force prevents the block from sliding?

    A. Air resistance.
    B. Static friction.
    C. Kinetic friction.
    D. Rolling friction.

5. What is the magnitude of the normal force on the copper block?

    A. 0 N
    B. 9.8 N
    C. 17.0 N
    D. 19.6 N

6. What is the net force on the block?

    A. 0 N
    B. 9.8 N
    C. 17.0 N
    D. 19.6 N

7. What is the magnitude of the force of friction on the block?

    A. 0 N
    B. 9.8 N
    C. 17.0 N
    D. 19.6 N

8. What is the value of μ, the coefficient of friction?

    A. 0.58
    B. 0.97
    C. 1.00
    D. 1.73

Passage 1

The Drum of Discomfort is an amusement park ride which consists of a large vertical hollow cylinder which turns on its axis. A person of mass M enters the drum (inside-radius R) while the drum is still and stands against the wall. The drum begins to turn, until it achieves uniform rotation with period T and the rider feels as if some force is pushing him against the wall (see figure). Then the floor drops down, so there is nothing touching the bottoms of the rider's shoes.

Assume the coefficient of friction between the rider's clothes and the surface of the drum is μ.

9. During uniform rotation, after the floor drops, what are the forces acting on a rider, besides gravity acting down and a force acting up?

    A. There is a force pointing inward.
    B. There is a force pointing inward and a force pointing in the same direction the rider is moving.
    C. There is a force pointing outward.
    D. There is a force pointing outward and a force pointing in the same direction the rider is moving.

10. After the floor drops, what force provides the centripetal force?

    A. The normal force.
    B. Friction.
    C. Gravitation.
    D. Tension.

11. After the floor drops, which direction does the acceleration vector point?

    A. Toward the center of rotation.
    B. Away from the center of rotation.
    C. In the direction of the rider is moving.
    D. The acceleration is zero.

12. Which gives an expression for the speed v the rider is going?

    A. $R/2\pi T$
    B. R/T
    C. $2\pi R/T$
    D. $2\pi T/R$

13. What is the magnitude of the upward force on the rider?

    A. Mg
    B. μMg
    C. Mv^2/r
    D. $\mu Mv^2/r$

14. What values of μ assure that the rider will not slide down when the floor drops?

    A. μ must be less than v^2/Rg.
    B. μ must be greater than v^2/Rg.
    C. μ must be less than Rg/v^2.
    D. μ must be greater than Rg/v^2.

Passage 2

When an object moves through a fluid, there is a drag force which retards its motion. Its magnitude is given by

$$F_{drag} \approx C\rho Av^2 \qquad (1)$$

where C ($= 0.2$) is a constant, ρ is the density of the fluid, A is the cross-sectional area of the object normal to the flow direction, and v is its velocity relative to the fluid.

Equation (1) is valid only if the fluid flow develops whirls and eddies, that is, approaching the onset of turbulence. (If the fluid is essentially undisturbed, then the drag force is actually greater than the value given in equation [1].) The extent to which a fluid is disturbed is determined by a dimensionless constant called the Reynolds number, defined by

$$Re = \rho vl/\eta \qquad (2)$$

where l is the linear size of the object and η is the viscosity of the fluid, a measure of its stickiness. A table of densities and viscosities is shown below.

substance	ρ (kg/m^3)	η (kg/m s)
air	1.29	1.8×10^{-5}
water	1.0×10^3	1.0×10^{-3}
mercury	1.36×10^4	1.6×10^{-3}

If Re is greater than about 100, then equation (1) for F_{drag} is fairly accurate. The Reynolds number also determines when turbulence begins. If Re is greater than about 2×10^5, then the fluid develops whirls and eddies that break off from the flow in an essentially unpredictable manner, i.e., turbulence.

(Note: $g = 9.8$ m/s^2.)

15. For a cube 2 m by 2 m by 2 m moving through the air, what velocities would make equation (1) valid?

    A. Any velocity less than about 10^{-3} m/s.
    B. Any velocity greater than about 10^{-3} m/s.
    C. Any velocity less than about 1 m/s.
    D. Any velocity greater than about 1 m/s.

16. For a car 1.5 m high, 2 m wide, and 3 m long, what is the cross-sectional area A appropriate for equation (1)?

    A. 3.5 m^2
    B. 3 m^2
    C. 6 m^2
    D. 9 m^2

17. Consider a car (1000 kg) of dimensions in the above question. What is the drag force on such a car if it is going 30 m/s?

    A. 700 N
    B. 9800 N
    C. 20,000 N
    D. 40,000 N

18. How fast would a car have to be going for turbulence to develop behind it?

    A. Any velocity less than about 10^{-3} m/s.
    B. Any velocity greater than about 10^{-3} m/s.
    C. Any velocity less than about 1 m/s.
    D. Any velocity greater than about 1 m/s.

19. For a fish (0.1 m by 0.1 m by 0.1 m) swimming at constant velocity in the ocean at 2 m/s, what thrust would it exert?

    A. 0.01 N
    B. 8 N
    C. 80 N
    D. 2×10^5 N

20. On Venus, rain presumably consists of sulfuric acid droplets in a carbon dioxide atmosphere. Consider a water raindrop on Earth, and a drop of equal size and mass of sulfuric acid on Venus. The acceleration due to gravity on Earth's surface is approximately the same as the acceleration due to gravity on the surface of Venus. Consider the following possibilities:

    I. The chemical composition of the drop.
    II. The temperature of the atmosphere.
    III. The pressure of the atmosphere.

    Which of the above affect(s) the terminal velocity with which rain falls?

    A. I only.
    B. II and III.
    C. I and III.
    D. I, II, and III.

SECTION 1

CONTENT REVIEW PROBLEMS

Passage 1

In a certain experiment, we are investigating the retarding force that a fluid exerts on an object moving through it. We guess that the size of the object is a factor, so we include A, the cross-sectional area, in an equation. The relative velocity between the object and the fluid is a factor v, as well as the density of the fluid ρ. So we guess

$$F = k\rho^m A^n v^p$$

where k is a proportionality constant with some appropriate units. Before we run the experiment, we do not know the values of the exponents m, n, and p.

The chart gives the data for a certain fluid.

Experiment	object	A (cm^2)	v (m/s)	F (N)
1	cork ball	1.5	7.0	0.020
2	cork ball	1.5	3.5	0.005
3	steel ball	1.5	3.5	0.005
4	steel ball	3.0	3.5	0.010
5	steel ball	4.5	3.5	0.015
6	steel ball	3.0	14.0	0.160

1. Which pair of experiments could be used to determine n?

    A. 2 and 3
    B. 3 and 4
    C. 4 and 6
    D. 5 and 6

2. What is the approximate value of p?

    A. −1
    B. 0
    C. 1
    D. 2

3. Which pair of experiments indicates that retarding force does not depend on the density of the object?

    A. 1 and 2
    B. 2 and 3
    C. 1 and 6
    D. 4 and 6

4. Let us say m and n are known. What combination of experiments would be considered a minimum set for determining p and k?

    A. 1 and 2
    B. 1, 2, and 3
    C. 3, 4, and 5
    D. 3 only

Passage 2

The amount of energy a car expends against air resistance is approximately given by

$$E = 0.2\rho_{air} A D v^2$$

where E is measure in joules, ρ_{air} is the density of air (1.2 kg/m^3), A is the cross-sectional area of the car viewed from the front (in m^2), D is the distance traveled (in m), and v is the speed of the car (in m/s). Julie wants to drive from Tucson to Phoenix and get good gas mileage. For the following questions, assume that the energy loss is due solely to air resistance, and there is no wind.

5. If Julie increases her speed from 30 mph to 60 mph, how does the energy required to travel from Tucson to Phoenix change?

    A. It increases by a factor of 2.
    B. It increases by a factor of 4.
    C. It increases by a factor of 8.
    D. It increases by a factor of 16.

6. Julie usually drives at a certain speed. How much more energy will she use if she drives 20% faster?

    A. 20% more energy.
    B. 40% more energy.
    C. 44% more energy.
    D. 80% more energy.

7. Scott drives a very large 50s style car, and Laura drives a small 90s style car, so that every linear dimension of Scott's car is double that of Laura's car. *On the basis of energy loss due to air resistance alone,* how much more energy would you expect Scott's car to expend getting from Tucson to Phoenix than Laura's car?

   A. Twice as much energy.
   B. Four times as much energy.
   C. Eight times as much energy.
   D. Sixteen times as much energy.

8. How does Julie's energy usage change if she changes from driving 50 mph to 55 mph?

   A. It increases by 10%.
   B. It increases by 20%.
   C. It increases by 21%.
   D. It increases by 40%.

9. Julie modifies her car, so that the effective cross-sectional area is reduced by 20%. How much further can she drive and still use the same amount of energy?

   A. 10% further.
   B. 20% further.
   C. 25% further.
   D. 44% further.

For questions 10 and 11, consider the following figure representing the displacement of an object in one dimension.

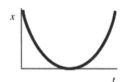

10. Which best represents the graph of acceleration versus time?

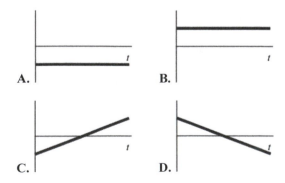

11. What can be concluded about the net displacement?

   A. It is zero.
   B. It is positive except for one point, where it is zero.
   C. It is negative, then zero, then positive.
   D. It is always positive?

For questions 12–14, consider the following figure representing the velocity of an object in one dimension.

Consider also the following graphs:

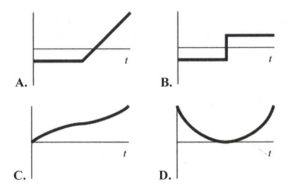

12. Which best represents the graph of displacement versus time?

   A. A
   B. B
   C. C
   D. D

13. Which best represents the graph of acceleration versus time?

   A. A
   B. B
   C. C
   D. D

14. What can be said about the net velocity change Δ*v*?

    A. It is positive.
    B. It is zero.
    C. It is negative.
    D. It is positive, except for one point.

Use the following for questions 15 and 16:

A car backs up at constant velocity, then slows to a stop. After it is stopped for a while, it accelerates and then goes forward at constant velocity. Consider also the following graphs:

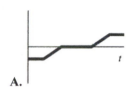

    A.   **B.**

    C.   **D.**

15. Which best represents the graph of velocity versus time?

    A. A
    B. B
    C. C
    D. D

16. Which best represents the graph of acceleration versus time?

    A. A
    B. B
    C. C
    D. D

Passage 3

A physics student leans out of the fortieth story of the physics building and drops two balls of the same size at the same time. One is 0.8 kg and made of iron, and the other is 1.2 kg and made of lead. Not only do the two balls hit the ground at the same time, the heights of the two balls match all the way down.

This somewhat counterintuitive result is an example of a general principle: If air resistance is negligible, then an object in free fall at the surface of the Earth has a downward acceleration of $g = 9.8$ m/s^2. Free fall means that only the force of gravity is acting on an object.
In the following questions, consider a ball dropped from the fortieth story of a building, and consider "down" to be in the positive direction. Consider air resistance negligible

unless noted otherwise.

17. How far does the object fall in the time interval from $t = 0$ to 4 s?

    A. 39.2 m
    B. 78.4 m
    C. 156.8 m
    D. 313.6 m

18. Which expression gives the change in velocity between $t_1 = 3$ s and $t_2 = 4$ s?

    A. $g(t_2 - t_1)/2$
    B. $g(t_2 - t_1)$
    C. $g(t_2 + t_1)/2$
    D. $g(t_2 + t_1)$

19. Which graph best represents velocity versus time?

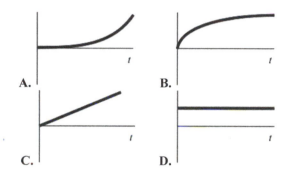

    A.   **B.**

    C.   **D.**

20. How does the change in velocity from $t = 1$ to 2 s compare with the change in velocity from $t = 3$ to 4 s?

    A. It is less.
    B. It is the same.
    C. It is greater.
    D. It depends on the object.

21. How does the change in height from $t = 1$ to 2 s compare with the change in height from $t = 3$ to 4 s?

    A. It is less.
    B. It is the same.
    C. It is greater.
    D. It depends on the object.

22. If an object falls a distance Δ*x* during the first *t* seconds, how far does it fall during the first 3*t* seconds?

    A. $\Delta x + 3$
    B. $3\Delta x$
    C. $\Delta x + 9$
    D. $9\Delta x$

23. A styrofoam ball of the same size as the lead ball takes a longer time to reach the ground. Which is a good explanation for this?

    A. The force of gravity does not act on the styrofoam ball.
    B. The force of gravity on the styrofoam ball is less than that on the lead ball.
    C. Air resistance is a significant force in this problem.
    D. There is a gravitational force between the ball and the building.

Use the following for questions 24–27:

An antique stove is sitting on the ground. (See figure) Assume for this problem that the Earth is not rotating.

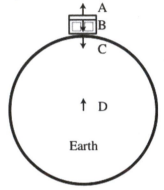

24. Which arrow represents the gravitational force of the Earth on the stove?

    A. A
    B. B
    C. C
    D. D

25. Which arrow represents the force paired with the gravitational force of the Earth on the stove, according to the third law of motion?

    A. A
    B. B
    C. C
    D. D

26. Why is the force vector A equal in magnitude to the force vector B?

    A. The first law of motion states that an object which is motionless has balanced forces.
    B. The first law of motion states that an object in motion will remain in motion only if acted upon by an *unbalanced* force.
    C. The second law of motion states that force and acceleration are proportional.
    D. The third law of motion states that forces come in equal and opposite pairs.

27. Why is the force vector A equal in magnitude to the force vector C?

    A. The first law of motion states that objects which are motionless have balanced forces.
    B. The first law of motion states that an object in motion will remain in motion unless acted upon by an unbalanced force.
    C. The second law of motion states that a force on an object and acceleration of the object are proportional.
    D. The third law of motion states that forces come in equal and opposite pairs.

28. A car's engine has died, and the car is slowing down as it coasts. What forces are acting on the car?

    A. Gravity, down.
    B. Gravity, down; and the road's force, up.
    C. Gravity, down; the road's force, up; and friction, backwards.
    D. Gravity, down; the road's force, up; friction, backwards; and a forward force.

29. An arrow is shot into the air. When the arrow is in the air, what forces are acting on the arrow?
    A. There are no forces.
    B. There is the force of gravity.
    C. There is the force of gravity and an upward normal force.
    D. There is the force of gravity and a forward force.

30. The planet Mars is traveling around the Sun. What forces are acting on Mars?

    A. There are no forces.
    B. There is the force of gravity.
    C. There is the force of gravity and a forward force.
    D. There is the force of gravity, a forward force, and an outward force.

Passage 4

The space shuttle is a spaceship which was designed for transporting a payload to near-earth orbits and to be used many times. When it stands on the launching pad, it consists of the orbiter itself, the external tank, and two booster rockets. The orbiter is 7.32×10^4 kg, while the whole assembly is 2.0×10^6 kg. The thrust at liftoff is 2.86×10^7 N, which is achieved by burning 3400 kg of fuel each second. The force provided by the engines is given by the product of the velocity of the exhaust gases relative to the ship and the rate (mass per time) at which fuel is burned.

As the space shuttle ascends, the rate of fuel burning is approximately constant, and so the mass of the shuttle decreases.

The following chart shows hypothetical data for the liftoff of a shuttle. We are assuming the shuttle moves in one dimension upward. Use 10 m/s^2 for the acceleration due to gravity. The force due to gravity is $F_{grav} = Mg$, where M is the mass of the object, and g is the acceleration due to gravity.

t (s)	x (m)	v (m/s)
0	0.0×10^4	0
90	2.0×10^4	490
180	9.6×10^4	1240
270	25.5×10^4	2400

31. What is the initial acceleration of the shuttle just as it begins leaving the launch pad?

    A. 4.3 m/s^2
    B. 5.4 m/s^2
    C. 8.9 m/s^2
    D. 14.3 m/s^2

32. What is the approximate mass of the shuttle after 300 s?

    A. 1.0×10^6 kg
    B. 1.2×10^6 kg
    C. 1.5×10^6 kg
    D. 2.0×10^6 kg

33. Referring to the chart, what evidence is there that the acceleration is increasing?

    A. The velocity v is linear with time.
    B. The velocity v increases with time.
    C. The ratio of Δv to Δt increases with time.
    D. The ratio of Δx to Δv increases with time.

34. Which gives the best reason for the increase in acceleration?

    A. The first law of motion states that an unbalanced force implies a change in velocity.
    B. The second law of motion states that acceleration is proportional to force.
    C. The second law of motion states that acceleration is inversely proportional to mass.
    D. The third law of motion states that there must be a second force, equal in magnitude but of opposite direction to the force accelerating the shuttle.

35. Consider a situation when the shuttle is in space and fires its engines, creating a force accelerating the shuttle. Which of the following BEST describes the force accelerating the shuttle?

    A. The force of the shuttle on the air.
    B. The force of the exhaust gases on the shuttle.
    C. The force of the shuttle on the exhaust gases.
    D. If there is no air, then the shuttle cannot accelerate.

Use the following for questions 36–39:

Two girls are sitting on the edge of a building tossing coins over the edge. Alice is actually dropping her coins, each of which is 10 g. Barbara is tossing her coins horizontally at 0.3 m/s, and her coins are 40 g each. (See figure.) (Ignore air resistance.)

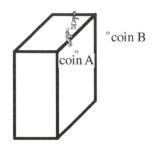

36. When the coins are in midair, how does the gravitational force on one of Alice's coins compare with the force on one of Barbara's?

    A. It is one fourth as large.
    B. It is the same.
    C. It is four times as large.
    D. It depends on the height at which the force is recorded.

37. When the coins are in midair, how does the acceleration of one of Alice's coins compare with the acceleration of one of Barbara's?

    A. It is one fourth as large.
    B. It is the same.
    C. It is four times as large.
    D. It depends on the height at which the acceleration is recorded.

38. How does the time to reach the ground for one of Alice's coins compare with the time of fall for Barbara's?

    A. The time for Alice's coins is less.
    B. The times are the same.
    C. The time for Alice's coins is greater.
    D. It depends on the height of the building.

39. Just before Alice's coin reaches the ground, it has speed s_A. Just before Barbara's coin reaches the ground, it has speed s_B. How does s_A compare with s_B?

    A. The speed s_A is less than s_B.
    B. The speed s_A is the same as s_B.
    C. The speed s_A is greater than s_B.
    D. It depends on the height of the building.

Use the following for questions 40–44:

A woman (50 kg) is pulling a wagon behind her. In the wagon is her daughter by her first marriage; the daughter and the wagon are 60 kg. (See figure.) The woman pulls the handle with a tension 200 N, and the handle makes a 30° angle with the horizontal. There is a horizontal force of friction, and the wagon moves at a constant 2 m/s. (Use $g = 10$ m/s^2.)

40. What is the horizontal component of the force of the wagon handle on the wagon body?

    A. 0 N
    B. (200 N) (sin 30°)
    C. (200 N) (cos 30°)
    D. 200 N

41. What is the vertical component of the force of the wagon handle on the wagon body?

    A. 0 N
    B. (200 N) (sin 30°)
    C. (200 N) (cos 30°)
    D. 200 N

42. What is the horizontal component of the gravitational force on the wagon and daughter?

    A. 0 N
    B. (600 N) (sin 30°)
    C. (600 N) (cos 30°)
    D. 600 N

43. What is the vertical component of the gravitational force on the wagon and daughter?

    A. 0 N
    B. (600 N) (sin 30°)
    C. (600 N) (cos 30°)
    D. 600 N

44. What is the magnitude of the net force?

    A. 0 N
    B. 173 N
    C. 600 N
    D. 800 N

Use the following for questions 45–47:

A bale of hay (500 kg) is dropped from the second story of a barn (9 m) with no initial velocity. A rope is tied to the hay to control its fall. The rope extends up from the bale and maintains a tension of 4000 N. (Use $g = 10$ m/s^2.)

45. What are the forces acting on the bale of hay?

    A. The tension in the rope only.
    B. Gravity only.
    C. The tension in the rope and gravity.
    D. The tension in the rope, gravity, and an additional downward force once the bale is moving.

46. What is the magnitude of the net force on the bale of hay?

    A. 0 N
    B. 1000 N
    C. 5000 N
    D. 9000 N

47. What is the acceleration of the bale of hay?

    A. 0 m/s^2
    B. 2 m/s^2
    C. 10 m/s^2
    D. 18 m/s^2

48. On the Moon there is very little atmosphere (several centimeters of thin gas). An astronaut drops a hammer and a feather at the same time from about shoulder height. What happens?

    A. The hammer lands first.
    B. The feather lands first.
    C. The hammer and the feather land at the same time.
    D. Neither lands but instead fly off the Moon's surface.

Use the following for questions 49 and 50:

A large ball (2 kg) is rolling (at the surface of the Earth) on a large, flat plain, so large that we will idealize it as an infinite plain. It is rolling 0.3 m/s to the right at time $t = 0$ s. Take the acceleration of gravity to be 10 m/s^2. Assume there is no friction.

49. Which of the following represents the best force diagram at times after $t = 0$ s?

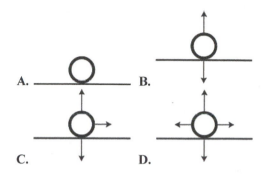

50. How long would it take the ball to come to a stop?

    A. 0.3 s.
    B. 3.33 s.
    C. 30 s.
    D. There is no answer.

Passage 5

When a massive star uses up its nuclear fuel, there is no longer enough heat to hold up its core against gravitational forces, and the core collapses. The result is an explosion, called a supernova, which leaves behind a very dense core, called a neutron star.

A neutron star is composed mainly of neutrons. It has approximately the mass of the Sun, but the radius is about 14 km, that is, 50,000 times smaller than the Sun's. The structure inside a neutron star is different from anything known on Earth, and the gravity on the surface is strong enough to crush any ordinary material. The only thing which creates a stronger gravitational field is a black hole.

Away from the surface, the tidal forces near a neutron star are nevertheless prodigious. A man falling toward a neutron star would be stretched out as he fell. He would be killed when he was about 2000 km away, and as he got closer he would be drawn as thin as a wire. Finally he would land on the surface, creating a shower of X-rays.

For these problems you may want to use the following:

    $G = 6.67 \times 10^{-11}$ N m^2/kg^2
    $M_{Sun} = 2.0 \times 10^{30}$ kg
    $V_{sphere} = 4/3\ \pi r^3$ (volume of a sphere)
    $A_{sphere} = 4\pi r^2$ (surface area of a sphere)

$A_{circle} = \pi r^2$ (area of a circle)

51. What is the approximate density of a neutron star?

    A. 2×10^{17} kg/m^3
    B. 8×10^{20} kg/m^3
    C. 1×10^{24} kg/m^3
    D. 1×10^{27} kg/m^3

52. How does the acceleration due to gravity at the surface of a neutron star compare with that near the surface of the Sun?

    A. $\sqrt{50,000}$ times stronger.
    B. 50,000 times stronger.
    C. $(50,000)^2$ times stronger.
    D. $(50,000)^3$ times stronger.

53. The Earth is 1.5×10^{11} meters away from the Sun. If there were a planet of the same mass which was 1.5×10^{11} meters away from a neutron star, how would the neutron star's gravitational pull on that planet compare with the Sun's pull on the Earth?

    A. It would be the same.
    B. It would be 50,000 times stronger.
    C. It would be $(50,000)^2$ times stronger.
    D. It would be $1.5 \times 10^{11}/14$ times stronger.

54. What is the best explanation for the stretching of an object in free fall as it approaches a neutron star?

    A. The density of the neutron star is huge.
    B. The parts of an object which are nearer the neutron star are pulled more strongly than the parts which farther away from the star.
    C. The strong surface gravity is due to the fact that surface gravity varies inversely as the radius.
    D. The strong surface gravity is due to the fact that surface gravity varies inversely as the square of the radius.

Use the following for questions 55 and 56:

A winch pulls a crate of apples (mass M) up an incline (making an angle α with the horizontal). (See figure.) The tension exerted by the winch is T. At the bottom of the incline the crate begins at rest at $t = 0$. Assume there is no friction.

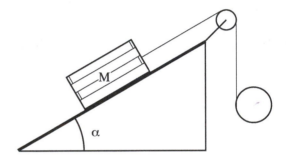

55. What is the normal force of the incline on the crate?

    A. Mg
    B. $Mg\cos\alpha$
    C. $Mg\sin\alpha$
    D. $Mg\sin\alpha - T$

56. What is the acceleration of the crate?

    A. 0
    B. g
    C. $N/M - g\cos\alpha$
    D. $T/M - g\sin\alpha$

SECTION 1 CONTENT REVIEW PROBLEMS

Use the following for questions 57 and 58:

A runner (50 kg) is running around a track (see figure). The curved portions of the track are arcs of a circle, and the dimensions of the track are shown. The runner is running a constant speed 8 m/s. Use 10 m/s² for the acceleration due to gravity.

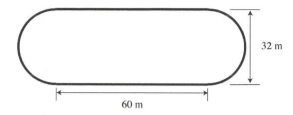

57. When the runner is on the curved portions of the track, what are the forces acting on her?

   A. Gravity, up; the normal force, down; and a force, inward.
   B. Gravity, up; the normal force, down; a force, inward; and a force, forward.
   C. Gravity, up; the normal force, down; and a force, outward.
   D. Gravity, up; the normal force, down; a force, outward; and a force, forward.

58. What is the net force on the runner on the curved portion of the track?

   A. 0 N
   B. 100 N
   C. 200 N
   D. 5000 N

Use the following for questions 59–61:

A Ferris wheel (radius R) is turning in a counterclockwise direction at a given frequency (f).

59. How would the velocity of a chair on the Ferris wheel change if the frequency were doubled?

   A. It would stay the same.
   B. It would increase by a factor of 2.
   C. It would increase by a factor of 4.
   D. It would increase by a factor of 8.

60. How would the centripetal acceleration of a chair on the Ferris wheel change if the frequency were doubled?

   A. It would stay the same.
   B. It would increase by a factor of 2.
   C. It would increase by a factor of 4.
   D. It would increase by a factor of 8.

61. A person is sitting on a seat at the bottom of a Ferris wheel which is going counterclockwise and speeding up. Which arrow best shows the acceleration vector?

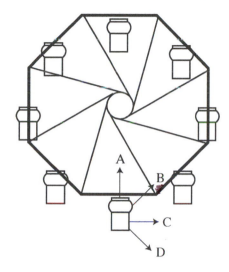

   A. A
   B. B
   C. C
   D. D

62. In a centrifuge, the bottoms of the centrifuge tubes are 10 cm away from the axis of rotation. The centrifuge spins with a frequency of 50 rps (revolutions per second). Which expression gives the velocity of a sample at the bottom of a spinning tube?

   A. 10π m/s
   B. 20π m/s
   C. 100π m/s
   D. 200π m/s

63. In the following diagram Jupiter is revolving about the Sun. If the gravity of the Sun were somehow cut off when Jupiter was at point P, what path would Jupiter take?

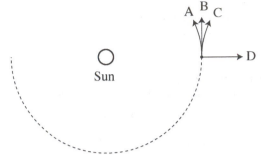

A. A
B. B
C. C
D. D

Passage 6

Consider an object sitting on a scale at the surface of the Earth. The scale reading is the magnitude of the normal force which the scale exerts on the object. To a first approximation, there is force balance, and the magnitude of the scale's force is the magnitude of the gravitational force:

$$F_{grav} = \frac{GM_{Earth}m}{R_{Earth}^2} \qquad (1)$$

where G is Newton's constant, M_{Earth} is the mass of the Earth, and R_{Earth} is the radius of the Earth. The simple result is that the force of gravity, and the reading of the scale, is proportional to the mass:

$$F_{grav} = mg \qquad (2)$$

where g has the value $GM_{Earth}/R_{Earth}^2 = 9.8$ m/s^2. We have made several idealizations, however, and if we want to calculate the scale reading, we need to be more careful.

For example, we have ignored the rotation of the Earth. Consider a man standing on a scale at the equator. Because he is moving in a circle, there is a centripetal acceleration. The result is that the scale will not give a reading equal to the force of gravity (equation [1]).

We have also assumed that the Earth is a perfect sphere. Because it is rotating, the distance from the center of the Earth to the equator is greater than the distance from center to pole by about 0.1%.

A third effect we have ignored is that the Earth has local irregularities which make it necessary to measure g in the local laboratory, if we need an exact value of the effective acceleration due to gravity.

64. For a man standing at the equator of a rotating Earth, which expression gives the best expression of his velocity? (Let T_{day} be the time of one rotation, 1 day.)

A. R_{Earth}/T_{day}
B. $2\pi R_{Earth}/T_{day}$
C. gT_{day}
D. $2\pi gT_{day}$

65. If we know the period of the man's motion, and we want to calculate the centripetal force on him, what is the minimum number of other data that we need?

A. 1: the radius of the Earth.
B. 2: the radius of the Earth and the velocity of the man.
C. 2: the radius of the Earth and the mass of the man.
D. 3: the radius of the Earth, the velocity of the man, and the mass of the man.

66. Which is the best force diagram for a man standing at the equator of a rotating Earth?

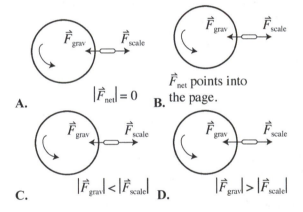

67. If the man at the equator stood on a scale, how would the scale read compared to the scale reading for an identical man standing at the equator of a nonrotating Earth?

    A. It would read less than on a nonrotating Earth.
    B. It would read the same as on a nonrotating Earth.
    C. It would read greater than on a nonrotating Earth.
    D. It would depend on where the man is.

68. If two identical men stood on scales at the south pole and at the equator of an Earth identical to this one but nonrotating, how would the reading of the polar scale compare to the equatorial one?

    A. It would be less.
    B. It would be the same.
    C. It would be greater.
    D. There is not enough information to answer this question.

Use the following for questions 69–71:

A rectangular piece of metal (0.3 m by 0.4 m) is hinged (⊗) as shown in the upper left corner, hanging so that the long edge is vertical. Force *A* (20 N) acts to the left at the lower left corner. Force *B* (10 N) acts down at the lower right corner. Force *C* (30 N) acts to the right at the upper right corner. (Take counterclockwise to be positive.)

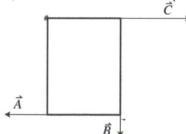

69. What is the torque of force *A* about the pivot?

    A. –8 Nm
    B. –4 Nm
    C. 0 Nm
    D. 4 Nm

70. What is the torque of force *B* about the pivot?

    A. –5 Nm
    B. –4 Nm
    C. –3 Nm
    D. 0 Nm

71. What is the torque of force *C* about the pivot?

    A. –9 Nm
    B. 0 Nm
    C. 4.5 Nm
    D. 9 Nm

Use the following for questions 72–74:

One end of a massless rod connects to a vertical wall at point B, and the other end (point C) is connected to the wall at point A by a second massless rod, this one horizontal (see figure). Point A is a distance *d* above B, and the horizontal rod has a length *l*. In addition, a brick of mass *m* hangs from a wire connected to the rod at point C.

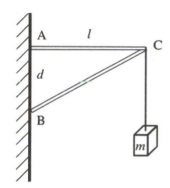

72. What is the horizontal force of the wall exerted on the oblique rod at point B?

    A. lmg/d, to the left
    B. dmg/l, to the left
    C. lmg/d, to the right
    D. dmg/l, to the right

73. What is the horizontal force of the wall exerted on the horizontal rod at point A?

    A. lmg/d, to the left
    B. dmg/l, to the left
    C. lmg/d, to the right
    D. dmg/l, to the right

74. What is the sum of the vertical forces of the wall exerted on the rods?

    A. lmg/d
    B. dmg/l
    C. $2dmg/l$
    D. mg

Use the following for questions 75–78

A rod (mass $m_1 = 1$ kg, length 2 m) of uniform cross section sticks out perpendicularly from a vertical wall at point A. A mass ($m_2 = 2$ kg) hangs from a string connected to the middle of the rod. A wire connects the opposite end of the rod B to a point C, which is 1 m directly above A. (See figure.) (Use $g = 10$ m/s^2.)

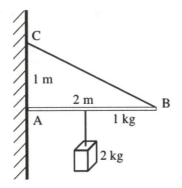

75. If the torque due to the tension T in the wire BC about point A is τ, what is the ratio $\tau{:}T$?

    A. $m/2$
    B. 2 m
    C. $\dfrac{1}{\sqrt{5}}$ m
    D. $\dfrac{2}{\sqrt{5}}$ m

76. What is the tension in the wire?

    A. $3\sqrt{5}$ N
    B. $6\sqrt{5}$ N
    C. $15\sqrt{5}$ N
    D. $30\sqrt{5}$ N

77. What is the vertical force exerted by the wall on the rod?

    A. $3\sqrt{5}$ N
    B. $6\sqrt{5}$ N
    C. 15 N
    D. 30 N

78. What is the horizontal force exerted by the wall on the rod?

    A. $3\sqrt{5}$ N
    B. $6\sqrt{5}$ N
    C. 15 N
    D. 30 N

Use the following for questions 79–81:

The femur of a human leg (mass 10 kg, length 0.9 m) is in traction (see figure). The center of gravity for the leg is one third of the way from the pelvis to the bottom of the foot. Two masses are hung via pulleys to provide an upward support: the mass m_1 at the pelvis and the mass m_2 at the foot. A third mass of 8 kg is hung to provide tension along the leg. The body itself provides tension but no shear.

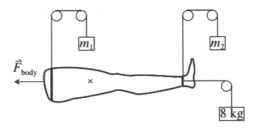

79. What is the mass m_1?

    A. 3.33 kg
    B. 6.67 kg
    C. 10 kg
    D. 30 kg

80. What is the ratio of m_2 to m_1?

    A. 0.3333
    B. 0.5
    C. 2
    D. 3

81. What is the tension provided by the body?

    A. 33 N
    B. 67 N
    C. 80 N
    D. 100 N

Use the following for questions 82–85:

A playing card (4 grams) is held against a vertical wall by a pencil (20 grams). The pencil is perpendicular to the wall and exerts a horizontal force 0.4 N. The coefficient of static friction between the wall and the card is 0.2. Assume the card is still. (We will investigate this assumption in question 12.) (Use $g = 10$ m/s^2.)

82. What is the gravitational force on the card?

    A. 0 N
    B. 0.04 N
    C. 0.08 N
    D. 0.4 N

83. What is the magnitude of the normal force on the card?

    A. 0 N
    B. 0.04 N
    C. 0.08 N
    D. 0.4 N

84. What is the magnitude of the force of static friction on the card?

    A. 0 N
    B. 0.04 N
    C. 0.08 N
    D. 0.4 N

85. Is the force of friction sufficient to maintain the card from sliding?

    A. Yes, the frictional force is less than $\mu_s N$.
    B. Yes, the frictional force is greater than $\mu_s N$.
    C. Yes, the frictional force is greater than mg.
    D. No, the frictional force is insufficient to hold up the card.

Use the following for questions 86–88:

A man is trying to push a washer (100 kg) along a level floor, but the washer is not moving. He is pushing with a horizontal force 700 N. The coefficients of friction are $\mu_{static} = 0.8$ and $\mu_{kinetic} = 0.6$. (Use $g = 10$ m/s^2.)

86. What is the normal force on the washer?

    A. 600 N
    B. 700 N
    C. 800 N
    D. 1000 N

87. What is the force of friction on the washer?

    A. 600 N
    B. 700 N
    C. 800 N
    D. 1000 N

88. How hard would the man have to push to get the washer moving?

    A. 600 N
    B. 700 N
    C. 800 N
    D. 1000 N

Use the following for questions 89–93:

A car (mass m) is going up a shallow slope (angle θ with the horizontal) when the driver sees a red light and suddenly applies the brakes. The car goes into a skid as it comes to a stop. The static coefficient of friction between the tires and the road is μ_s, and the kinetic coefficient of friction is μ_k.

89. Which of the following best represent the force diagram for the car during the skid?

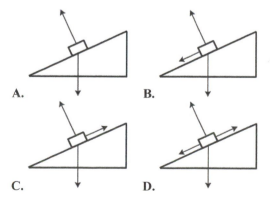

A.   B.

C.   D.

90. What is the magnitude of the component of the force of gravity parallel to the surface of the road?

    A. mg
    B. $mg\cos\theta$
    C. $mg\sin\theta$
    D. $mg\tan\theta$

91. Which expression gives the normal force on the car?

    A. mg
    B. $mg\cos\theta$
    C. $mg\sin\theta$
    D. $mg\tan\theta$

92. Which expression gives the force of friction on the car?

    A. mg
    B. $mg\sin\theta$
    C. $\mu_k N$
    D. $\mu_s N$

93. What is the net force on the car during the skid?

    A. 0
    B. $\mu_k N$
    C. $\mu_k N + mg\sin\theta$
    D. $\mu_k N - mg\sin\theta$

Use the following for questions 94–99:

A car (1000 kg) is driving on level road at a constant speed 8 m/s when it attempts to execute a turn about a curve of effective radius 10 m. For the following questions, we will assume the turn is successful, that is, the car performs in the turn as the driver intends. The static coefficient of friction between the tires and the road is 0.9, the kinetic coefficient of friction is 0.7, and the acceleration due to gravity is 10 m/s^2.

94. What forces are acting on the car besides the gravitational force (down) and the normal force (up)?

    A. A force toward the turn axis.
    B. A force away from the turn axis.
    C. A force in the direction the car is traveling and a force toward the turn axis.
    D. A force in the direction the car is traveling and a force away from the turn axis.

95. What force provides the centripetal force?

    A. Gravity.
    B. The normal force.
    C. Static friction.
    D. Kinetic friction.

96. What is the acceleration of the car?

    A. 0 m/s^2
    B. 0.08 m/s^2
    C. 6.4 m/s^2
    D. 10 m/s^2

97. What is the normal force on the car?

    A. 6400 N
    B. 7000 N
    C. 9000 N
    D. 10,000 N

98. What is the net force on the car if the turn is successful?

    A. 6400 N
    B. 7000 N
    C. 9000 N
    D. 10,000 N

99. Is the turn successful?

A. Yes, the net force F_{net} is less than $\mu_s N$.
B. Yes, the net force F_{net} is greater than $\mu_s N$.
C. No, the net force F_{net} is less than $\mu_s N$.
D. No, the net force F_{net} is greater than $\mu_s N$.

Passage 7

Most physical situations are quite complicated, involving a number of forces or interactions even in the simplest of cases. Much of the praxis of physics is breaking a problem into parts, treating some parts exactly and ignoring other parts. Once we have solved the idealized problem, we can use the solution to evaluate the appropriateness of the idealizing assumptions.

A simple example of this is the analysis of a tennis ball falling from a height at the surface of the Earth. The ball consists of many atoms, connected by chemical forces. In addition to the chemical forces, each atom is pulled by all the pieces of the Earth. The first idealization we make is that we can treat the ball as a point mass located at its center and the Earth as a point mass located at its center. Second, we ignore the gradient of the gravitational field, so that allows us to approximate the force of gravitation on the ball as $F_{grav} = mg$, where $g \approx 9.8$ m/s^2 is a constant.

The third effect we generally ignore is air resistance. If we ignore air resistance, we can calculate the idealized maximum velocity of the falling ball and then calculate the force of air drag. This is given by

$$F_{drag} \approx C\rho A v^2 \qquad (1)$$

where C (= 0.2) is a constant, ρ (= 1.3 kg/m^3) is the density of air, A is the cross-sectional area of the ball, and v is its velocity relative to the air. If the air resistance is small, then we were justified in ignoring it.

If air resistance is important, it is possible that we can still do the problem. If the ball falls far enough for there to be a force balance $F_{net} = 0$, then we can use equation (1) to solve the problem. (Actually we can only require that F_{net} be small compared to the other forces in the problem.)

For the following problems, consider a ball of radius 0.03 m and mass 0.05 kg which is tossed upward at initial velocity 3 m/s.

100. If there were no air, to what idealized height would the ball travel?

A. 0.46 m
B. 0.92 m
C. 1.84 m
D. 176.4 m

101. What is the initial drag force on the ball?

A. 3×10^{-4} N
B. 7×10^{-3} N
C. 0.7 N
D. 50 N

102. If we are going to ignore air resistance, the drag force must be small compared to

A. the normal force.
B. the centripetal force.
C. the gravitational force.
D. the frictional force.

103. We have idealized the gravitational field as being uniform. If we remove that idealization, what happens to the force of gravity as the ball travels toward the top of its flight?

A. The force of gravity decreases.
B. The force of gravity increases.
C. The force of gravity decreases, then disappears at the top.
D. The force of gravity decreases, then increases.

104. In the idealized problem, the ball attains a certain maximum height and afterward attains a final velocity just before it reaches the ground. If air resistance is included,

A. the height is less, and the terminal velocity is less.
B. the height is less, but the terminal velocity is greater.
C. the height is greater, but the terminal velocity is less.
D. the height is greater, and the terminal velocity is greater.

105. Cats falling from large heights often survive the fall. In fact, it has been found that a cat falling from a building at very great height (e.g., ten stories) has a better chance of surviving than a cat falling from a lesser height (five stories). Which, if true, could best explain this?

A. The air is more dense near the ground.
B. The force of gravity on the cat is greater near the ground.
C. Cats falling for a while tend to stretch out their legs.
D. Greater velocity leads to a greater force of drag.

SECTION 2
ENERGY

The next section includes only a single chapter, because it addresses one of the most fundamental and important concepts in MCAT physics – energy.

As we said at the start of the book, physics is fundamentally the study of motion and energy. Before moving on to study the various ways that energy can be moved (waves) and the forms it can take (electrical, nuclear, etc.), we must start with the basics – kinetic and potential energies and how we can use energy in different contexts.

This page intentionally left blank.

CHAPTER 7
ENERGY

A. INTRODUCTION

To understand politics, it is said you need to follow the money. To understand physics, it is said you need to follow the energy. If we understand where energy is coming from, how it flows, and where it ends up in any physical situation, then we understand a lot about the physics of the situation.

"What is energy?" you may ask. Actually energy is harder to explain than you may think. In the history of physics, the concept of energy did not suddenly arrive as a mature concept out of Newtonian theory, like Athena emerging from Zeus's head. Rather, it began as a hazy idea which grew in richness and clarity during the 1800s. In this chapter we can do no better, so we will introduce the concept slowly.

In standard English, **energy** is defined as the capacity for performing something useful. We can obtain energy from various places and then we can use it usefully or squander it, and once it is gone, it is gone.

In physics also, energy is the capacity for doing useful things. On the other hand, energy is a thing that cannot be created from nothing or destroyed, only transformed from one form to another. Following energy through its forms is what much of physics is all about.

As you can see, the physics understanding is distinct from the popular understanding, and we will want to pay attention to the differences between the two.

B. WORK

Work is a measure of the energy flowing into an object or system due to a force on it. When a force F (which can be due to a pair of hands, a rope, gravity, or anything) acts on an object, that moves a distance Δx, the **work** done by the force on the object is

$$W = F\Delta x \cos\phi , \qquad (1)$$

where ϕ is the angle between the direction of the force F and the direction of the displacement Δx. The units for work are [kg m^2/s^2 = Nm = joule = J].

The **total work** done on an object is

$$W_{tot} = F_{net}\Delta x \cos\phi , \qquad (2)$$

where F_{net} is the magnitude of the net force and ϕ is the angle between F_{net} and Δx.

Keep in mind that if the force is in the same direction as the motion, then $\cos\phi = 1$. If the force exactly opposes the motion, then $\cos\phi = -1$. If the force acts perpendicular to the motion, then $\cos\phi = 0$. You should know these angles without pausing to think about them.

Hint: *Whenever* a problem on the MCAT mentions a force and a distance, you should think "WORK!" and write down the equation for work. Even if work and energy are not mentioned, it is probably a key idea for understanding at least one of the problems.

Example 1: A woman is pushing a cart of mass m slowly at constant speed up an incline that makes an angle θ with the horizontal. The cart goes from the floor level to a height h.

a. How much work does the woman do on the cart in terms of m, g, h, and θ?
b. What is the total work done on the cart?

Solution: a. First, we DRAW A DIAGRAM (Figure 7-1).

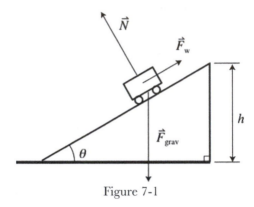

Figure 7-1

We need to find F_W and Δx. We choose a "horizontal" and "vertical" and resolve the gravity vector into components (Figure 7-2).

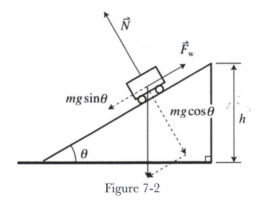

Figure 7-2

First we look at the "horizontal" components. The words "constant speed" and "straight path" imply that the cart's acceleration is zero, and the net force on it is zero, so we write

$$(F_{net})_x = 0$$

From Figure 7-2 we obtain

$$(F_{net})_x = F_W - mg\,\sin\theta$$

Combining these equations gives us

$$F_w - mg\sin\theta = 0$$
$$F_w = mg\sin\theta$$

We can find Δx by trigonometry. If we look at the large triangle in Figure 9-2, then we have

$$\sin\theta = h/\Delta x$$

$$\Delta x \sin\theta = h$$

$$\Delta x = h/\sin\theta$$

The vectors F_W and Δx point in the same direction, so $\cos\phi = 1$. Thus the work done by the woman on the cart is

$$W_w = (mg\sin\theta)\frac{h}{\sin\theta}$$

$$W_w = mgh$$

This is the answer to question a.

But what is this? The quantity θ dropped out of the equation (!). It takes the same energy to go a long way up a shallow incline as it does to go a short way up a steep incline. In fact:

> The work done depends only on the height climb h from the begnning to end and not at all on the path between the two.

The energy a woman requires to push a cart from one point to a point that is height h higher is mgh, even if the path is complicated. See Figure 7-3.

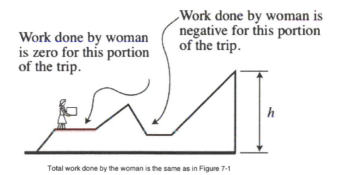

Figure 7-3

b. What is the total work done? Well, since the speed and direction are constant, the acceleration is zero, and $F_{net} = 0$, so that

$$W_{tot} = 0$$

What? The poor woman works from dawn till dusk, and the total work done is zero? Where did the energy go? Well, if we were to figure out the work done by gravity, we would find that it comes to $-mgh$, so the work done by gravity cancels the work done by the woman. It seems like a sad story, perhaps, but this will not be the final word on gravity (see Section D).

Example 2: How much work is done by the gravity of the Sun on the Earth in one day?

$G = 6.67 \times 10^{-11}$ m³/kg s²,
$M_{Sun} = 2 \times 10^{30}$ kg,
$M_{Earth} = 6 \times 10^{24}$ kg,

distance from Earth to Sun = 1.5 x 10^{11} m.

Solution: First, we DRAW A DIAGRAM (Figure 7-4). Once we draw the diagram, the answer is clear. The vector F_{grav} is perpendicular to the displacement Δx, so we have $\cos\phi = 0$ and $W_{tot} = 0$.

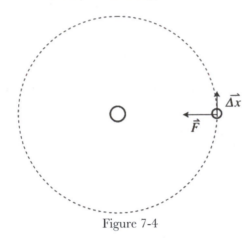

Figure 7-4

C. ENERGY OF MOTION

So how much energy do we put into an object if we push it for a while? Let's try another simple example, this time in one dimension.

Example: Consider an orange, which we have smeared with grease so there is essentially no friction. It is initially at rest, so $v_1 = 0$. We push it in one direction with a force F over a distance Δx. What is the work done by the force, in terms of the mass m and final velocity v_2 of the orange?

Solution: We have an expression for the force given by the second law of motion:

$$F = ma$$

$$= m\frac{\Delta v}{\Delta t} \qquad \text{(definition of acceleration)}$$

$$= m\frac{v_2 - v_1}{\Delta t}$$

$$= m\frac{v_2}{\Delta t} \qquad \text{(since the orange starts from rest } v_1 = 0\text{)}$$

Also we have

$$\Delta x = \frac{1}{2}\left(v_1 + v_2\right)\Delta t \qquad \text{(from Chapter 2)}$$

$$= \frac{1}{2}v_2\Delta t$$

Since $\cos\phi = 1$, we have

$$W = F\Delta x$$

$$= \left(m\frac{v_2}{\Delta t}\right)\left(\frac{1}{2}v_2\Delta t\right)$$

$$= \frac{1}{2}mv_2^{2}$$

Notice that the factor Δt drops out.

120

If we push on an orange initially at rest until it is going at velocity v_2, then the amount of work we have done on it is $1/2$ mv_2^2. This indicates that we can define the ***kinetic energy***, the energy of an object due solely to its motion, as

$$E_K = \frac{1}{2}mv^2. \tag{3}$$

Work and change in kinetic energy are related by the following expression.

Work-energy theorem, simple version
If the total work done on an object is W_{tot}, then its change in kinetic energy is given by

$$W_{tot} = \Delta E_K$$
$$= \frac{1}{2}mv_2^2 - \frac{1}{2}mv_1^2. \tag{4}$$

Some examples should clarify this.

Example 1: What is the change in kinetic energy for the woman's cart in the previous section?

Solution: We calculated $W_{tot} = 0$, which tells us that the change in kinetic energy is zero. The cart is going the same speed at the end of the problem as at the beginning. Thus we have $\Delta E_K = 0$. So this result is consistent with the above equation.

Example 2: What is the change in kinetic energy of the Earth in one day?

Solution: According to the previous section, $W_{tot} = 0$, and indeed the Earth's speed is constant from one day to the next. The kinetic energy change is zero. Here we are assuming a circular orbit, which is almost correct.

Example 3: A bullet of mass 20 grams is fired from a gun, so that its speed is 700 m/s in air. The bullet enters a tree stump and embeds 2 meters inside. What is the average force exerted by the stump on the bullet? (Ignore gravity.)

Solution: First, we DRAW A DIAGRAM (Figure 7-5). At first this problem looks like a conservation of momentum problem, because of the collision and crunching of wood. If we try to apply conservation of momentum, however, we just do not get anywhere.

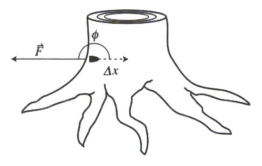

When a bullet embeds in a stump,
kinetic energy is converted to heat.

Figure 7-5

The key is to notice that force and distance are both mentioned in the problem. ***Immediately*** we think of energy. We know the change in kinetic energy of the bullet

$$\Delta E_K = E_{K2} - E_{K1}$$

$$= 0\,J - 1/2\,(.020\ \text{kg})(700\ \text{m/s})^2$$
$$= -4.9 \times 10^3\,J.$$

This is also W_{tot}, and we can set W_{tot} to $F\Delta x \cos\phi$, where $\cos\phi$ is -1. Thus $-4.9 \times 10^3\,J = F(2\ \text{m})(-1)$, $F = 2.45 \times 10^3\,N$.

Sometimes, as an object moves along a path, the net force acting on it changes, or else the displacement changes direction. We can still consider calculating the total work on the object.

Work-energy theorem, complicated version
If an object moves along a path, we can calculate the total work done on the object by dividing the path into tiny pieces and calculating the work done for each piece. The total work W_{tot} is the sum of the work for these pieces. The change in kinetic energy is given by

$$W_{tot} = \Delta E_K$$

(the same formula as before).

We will see examples of this in future chapters.

D. POTENTIAL ENERGY AND CONSERVATIVE FORCES

Potential energy is the energy of an object due to position alone. *Gravitational potential energy* is the energy associated with the position of an object in a gravitational field. How does this work?

Remember the woman in Section B? She pushed a cart to a new height h, doing work $W = mgh$. It would make sense to define gravitational potential energy as

$$E_P = mgh\,, \qquad\qquad\qquad (5)$$

where m is the mass of the object in question, g is the acceleration due to gravity, and h is the height. The height is measured relative to some standard, such as sea level or street level. It does not matter what the standard is, because we are always interested in changes in height or changes in potential energy. This formula works for all situations near the surface of the Earth.

Any force with an associated potential energy is called a *potential force* or a *conservative force*. Examples include the forces due to springs and the electrostatic force. The force the woman exerts on the cart and magnetic forces are not conservative forces.

Example: We are now in a position to FOLLOW THE ENERGY for the woman and the cart. It is clear that the energy ends up as potential energy. How does the energy start? Kinetic? No, because the cart is hardly moving both before and after its trip. The energy starts in her muscles, where it was stored as chemical energy. Thus the flow of energy is chemical to gravitational potential energy.

E. CONSERVATION OF ENERGY

Sometimes physicists use strange words to mean normal things (They say "scalar" when they mean "number", for example.) Sometimes they use normal words to mean normal things, but they mean it a little differently; for example, force and energy. Sometimes they use normal words to mean something completely different from the standard meaning, and this leads to much confusion.

In common parlance, "conservation of energy" means frugal use of energy, a responsibility of good citizens.

In physics, "conservation of energy" means that energy, by decree of Nature, cannot be created from nothing nor destroyed, but it can flow from one form to another or from one place to another. If we calculate the total energy in a closed system at one time, the total energy some time later will be the same. Energy is conserved.

> **Energy Conservation**
> The energy in a closed system is conserved, that is, constant in time.

In the table are listed some of the energy forms which may appear on the MCAT.

Type of Energy	Description
kinetic	bulk motion
potential	object's position
gravitational potential	object's position in gravity
mechanical	MCAT word for kinetic + potential
chemical	batteries, muscles, etc.
electrical	moving electrons
nuclear	energy in the nucleus, radioactivity, fission reactor
sound	pressure waves
light	electric, magnetic field waves
heat	random motion of particles

The principle of energy conservation in the previous box is the Grand Statement, almost too grand to be useful in most problems. For doing problems it is better if the kinds of energy considered are few, like two: kinetic and potential.

> **Energy Conservation, Simple Statement**
> If there is no friction, or crunching, or nonpotential forces (except forces perpendicular to the motion), then
> $$E_{K1} + E_{P1} = E_{K2} + E_{P2}.$$ (6)

Use this principle in problems where gravity does all the work.

Example 1: The woman of Section B lets go of the cart at the top of the incline. The cart rolls to the bottom.

a. What is the final velocity?
b. Describe the energy flow from start to finish.

Solution: a. First, we DRAW A DIAGRAM (Figure 7-6). We need to check all the forces. Although the normal force is nonpotential, it is perpendicular to the motion, so it does no work. The gravitational force is a potential force. We conclude that the simple version of energy conservation applies. Thus we write

$$E_{K1} + E_{P1} = E_{K2} + E_{P2}$$

$$0 + mgh = 1/2\, mv_2^2 + 0$$

Solving for v_2 yields

$$v_2 = \sqrt{2gh}$$

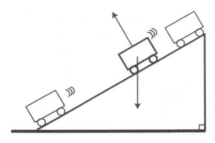

When the cart rolls down,
gravitational potential energy is
converted to kinetic energy.
Figure 7-6

Note that the mass has dropped out. This should remind you of the situation in which a massive object and a light object are dropped at the same time. They fall at the same rate with the same acceleration and same velocity as each other, all the way down.

b. The energy flow is chemical (woman's muscles) to potential to kinetic.

Example 2: A pendulum of length 0.7 meters is pulled so that its bob (0.2 kg) is 0.1 meters higher than its resting position. From that position it is let go.

a. What is its kinetic energy at the bottom of the swing?
b. What is its velocity at the bottom of the swing?
c. What is the work done by the string tension during the swing from start to the bottom?

Solution: a. First, we DRAW A DIAGRAM (Figure 7-7).

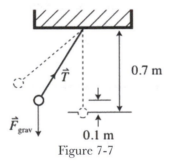

Figure 7-7

We check the forces. The tension is perpendicular to the direction the bob is moving at every moment. This is true even though the bob is moving in an arc and the tension is changing direction during the swing. Thus tension does no work. Gravity is a potential force, so equation (6) applies and we can write

$$E_{K1} + E_{P1} = E_{K2} + E_{P2},$$
$$0 + mgh_1 = E_{K2} + 0,$$
$$E_{K2} = mgh_1$$
$$= (0.2 \text{ kg})(10 \text{ m/s}^2)(0.1) = 0.2 \text{ J}$$

b. Now, we obtain the final velocity from

$$\frac{1}{2}mv_2{}^2 = mgh_1$$
$$v_2 = \sqrt{2gh_1} = 1.4 \text{ m/s}$$

c. We have already decided that the tension does no work.

F. EFFICIENCY OF ENERGY CONVERSION

Often we have energy in one form and we want to convert it into another form, for example, from chemical energy in gasoline to kinetic energy of a car. It may be the case that energy cannot be destroyed, but it can end up in an inconvenient form such as heat. In this case we define the *efficiency* of energy conversion as follows:

$$\text{Efficiency} = \frac{\text{energy in desired form}}{\text{energy in original form}} \times 100\% \qquad (7)$$

Example 1: A car (800 kg) goes slowly up a hill from the base to a height of 300 meters. It uses 245 grams of fuel in the form of 2,2,4-trimethylpentane. The following overall reaction occurs in the car:

$$C_8H_{18(g)} + \frac{25}{2}O_{2(g)} \rightarrow 8CO_{2(g)} + 9H_2O_{(g)} \qquad \Delta H_{\text{reaction}} = 1310 \frac{\text{kcal}}{\text{mol}}$$

What is the efficiency of the engine? Assume no energy loss due to air resistance. Use 1 kcal = 4184 J.

Solution: First we calculate the energy in desired form, which is the potential energy:

$$E_{\text{des}} = \textbf{\textit{mgh}}$$
$$= (800 \text{ kg})(10 \text{ m/s}^2)(300 \text{ m})$$
$$= 2.4 \times 10^6 \text{ J}$$

Next we calculate the energy used:

$$E_{\text{orig}} = 245\text{g}\left(\frac{1 \text{ mol } C_8H_{18}}{114 \text{ g } C_8H_{18}}\right)\left(\frac{1310 \text{ kcal}}{1 \text{ mol } C_8H_{18}}\right)\left(\frac{4184 \text{ J}}{1 \text{ kcal}}\right)$$
$$= 1.2 \times 10^7 \text{ J}$$

The efficiency is

$$\frac{2.4 \times 10^6 \text{ J}}{1.2 \times 10^7 \text{ J}} \times 100\% = 20\%$$

(See Figure 7-8.)

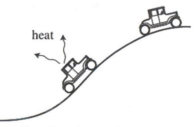

Gasoline chemical energy is converted to gravitational potential energy and heat.
Figure 7-8

We can speak of efficiency in a collision as well. In a collision, kinetic energy is often converted to heat and chemical energy. If this is not the case, that is, if kinetic energy before the collision is the same as after, then the collision is called *elastic*. Otherwise it is called *inelastic*. If everything is stuck together in the end, the collision is called *completely inelastic*.

Example 2: Two cars collide in one dimension in a completely inelastic collision. One car is 1000 kg, initially going east at 10 m/s. The other car is 1500 kg, initially going west at 15 m/s.

a. What is the velocity of the twisted metal afterward?
b. What is the efficiency of the collision?

Solution: a. Did you remember that crunching or smashing generally means we must use the conservation of momentum? Let us take east to be positive (see Figure 7-9) and we write

$$p_1 = p_2,$$

$$(1000 \text{ kg})(10 \text{ m/s}) + (1500 \text{ kg})(-15 \text{ m/s}) = (2500 \text{ kg})v_f$$

$$v_f = -5 \text{ m/s}$$

b. Now we need to know the kinetic energy both before and after the collision.

$$E_{K1} = 1/2 \ (1000 \text{ kg})(10 \text{ m/s})^2 + 1/2 \ (1500 \text{ kg})(-15 \text{ m/s})^2$$

$$= 2.19 \times 10^5 \text{ J},$$

$$E_{K2} = 1/2 \ (2500 \text{ kg})(-5 \text{ m/s})^2$$

$$= 3.1 \times 10^4 \text{ J}$$

Thus the efficiency is

$$\frac{3.1 \times 10^4 \text{ J}}{2.2 \times 10^5 \text{ J}} \times 100\% = 14\%$$

before:

after:

During the collision, some kinetic energy is converted to heat.

Figure 7-9

G. POWER

Power is the rate at which energy is produced, consumed, or transformed, that is,

$$P = \frac{\Delta E}{\Delta t}.$$ (8)

Example 1: A car (1000 kg) traveling 55 mph has a forward cross-sectional area of about 4 m². What is the power dissipated by air resistance? (Use 1 mph ≈ 0.45 m/s. Recall that the formula for air resistance is $F_{air} = C\rho A v^2$, where ρ, the density of air, is 1.29 kg/m³ and $C \approx 0.2$.)

Solution: First, we DRAW A DIAGRAM (Figure 7-10).

126

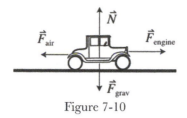

Figure 7-10

We have only one formula to work with ($P = \Delta E / \Delta t$), but we have neither energy nor a time. But we have several formulas for energy, so let's try to connect it with the force given in the problem. We have

$$P = \frac{\Delta E}{\Delta t} = \frac{F_{air} \Delta x \cos\phi}{\Delta t} = \frac{F_{air} \Delta x}{\Delta t}$$

since $\cos\phi = -1$. We can substitute for F_{air}. And the expression $\Delta x / \Delta t$ reminds us of velocity, so we have

$$P = -F_{air}v = -(C\rho Av^2)v$$

$$-(0.2)\left(1.29\,\frac{kg}{m^3}\right)(4\ m^2)\left(55\ mph\,\frac{0.45\,\frac{m}{s}}{mph}\right)^3$$

$$= -1.6 \times 10^4\ W.$$

The minus sign indicates that energy is removed from the system.

Example 2: The same car is traveling 65 mph. What is the power dissipated by air resistance?

Solution: $P = -2.6 \times 10^4$ W.

Why is there such a large difference?

H. PULLEYS

Pulleys are somewhat tricky, but with some practice, problems including pulleys become simpler. There are two underlying principles:

---

1. The tension in a single rope is the same all along the rope, even if it goes over and under pulleys.
2. If a rope is pulled at a constant rate by a hand, the work done by the hand on the rope is the same as the work done by the rope on some load.

Let's look at some examples.

Example 1: A person is hanging in air by grabbing the two ends of a rope that is draped around a pulley. If the person is 60 kg, what is the tension in the rope?

Solution: First, we DRAW A DIAGRAM (Figure 7-11) showing the forces on the man. The tension on the two sides of the rope is the same, so we can call it T. The person is not accelerating, so the forces add to zero, giving

$$T + T - mg = 0$$

$$T = mg/2$$

$$= (60 \text{ kg})(10 \text{ m/s}^2)/2$$

$$= 300 \text{ N}$$

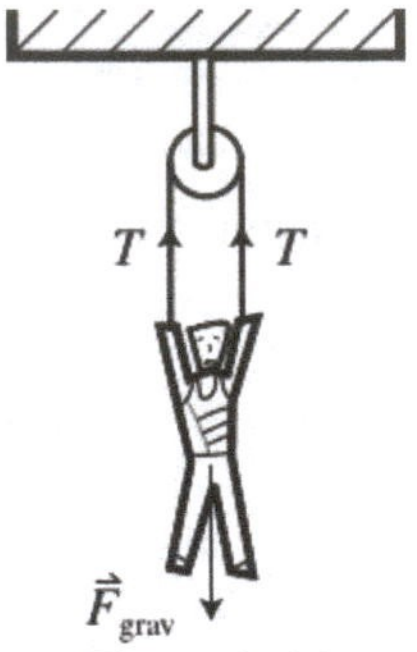

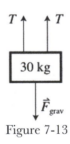

Figure 7-11

Example 2: A rope, one end of which is connected to the ceiling, passes through a pulley and then goes up, so that an upward tension is maintained. A mass 30 kg is hung on the pulley. What is the tension in the rope? (See Figure 7-12.)

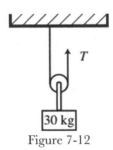

Figure 7-12

Solution: There are two ways to do this problem. One is to realize that this is essentially the same as Example 1, so that $T = 1/2 \, mg = 150$ N. (See Figure 7-13.)

$T \uparrow \qquad \uparrow T$

30 kg

$\downarrow \vec{F}_{grav}$

Figure 7-13

The other way is to imagine pulling up on the rope 1 meter. A bit of study of the diagram will show that the mass will rise 0.5 meters, since 0.5 meters of rope will be pulled from each side of the pulley. The work done by T must be the same as the work done on the mass. The work done by the rope is $W_1 = F\Delta x \cos\phi = T(1 \text{ m})$. The work done on the mass is the change in potential energy $W_2 = mg\Delta h = mg(0.5 \text{ m})$. Thus

$W_1 = W_2$,

$T(1 \text{ m}) = mg(0.5 \text{ m})$,

$T = 1/2 \, mg = 150 \text{ N}$.

Example 3: A rope has one end connected to the ceiling. It loops through a pulley with a downward weight of 500 N, goes up to the ceiling where it loops over a second pulley and connects to a mass m. If everything is in equilibrium, what is m? (See Figure 7-14.)

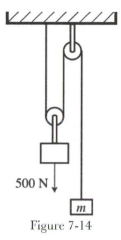

500 N

m

Figure 7-14

Solution: This looks different from the previous problem, but in fact it is essentially the same. The tension T which pulls up on mass m is numerically the same as the tension T pulling up on both sides of the first pulley. So we have

$$T = 1/2 \, (500 \text{ N}) = 250 \text{ N}$$

$$T = mg$$

So $m = 25$ kg

Another way to obtain the above equation is to DRAW A DIAGRAM showing the forces on both masses (Figure 7-15).

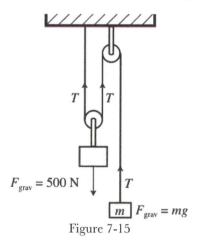

T T

$F_{grav} = 500$ N T

m $F_{grav} = mg$

Figure 7-15

I. MECHANICAL ADVANTAGE

The concept of mechanical advantage is pretty simple. In ideal simple machines employing things like ramps, levers, gears or pulleys, the total amount of power put into the system P_i and put out by the system P_o must be equal, according to the law of conservation of energy. We can obtain the following relationships by remembering that power is the amount of work W per unit time t and that work is force F times displacement Δx.

$$P_i = P_o \quad (9)$$
$$W_i/t = W_o/t \quad (10)$$
$$F_i \Delta x_i/t = F_o \Delta x_o/t \quad (11)$$

For most simple machines the time that work is done is the same for the input and output, so this equation can simply be stated in terms of work, or torque for rotational systems, as in levers or gears.

$$F_i \Delta x_i = F_o \Delta x_o \quad (12)$$

Furthermore, since the displacement per unit time, is velocity v, we can get yet another equation that applies to simple machines.

$$F_i v_i = F_o v_o \quad (13)$$

All a simple machine does is reduce the amount of force that is applied to the system, at the expense of increasing the distance over which the force is applied. The mechanical advantage MA is defined as the ratio of the output force to the input force, which leads to two other simple ratios in terms of displacement and velocity.

$$MA = F_o/F_i = \Delta x_i/\Delta x_o = v_i/v_o \quad (14)$$

Perhaps the simplest of the simple machines is the inclined plane. The work required to push an object at a constant velocity up a frictionless incline must equal the work done against gravity, in the vertical direction, to create gravitational potential energy. Less force f is required to push an object up an incline, than to lift it straight up (opposite of mg), because the displacement of the incline (Δx_i) is greater than the vertical component of displacement (Δx_o), as seen in Figure 7-2.

Example 1: A college student needs to move into her dorm room and she is using a nearly frictionless cart to help carry her books into the main entrance of the dorm. She uses the ramp which has a 30° angle with respect to the ground and she pushes the cart at an angle such that the applied force is parallel with the incline. What is the mechanical advantage provided by the ramp?

Solution: The ramp is a 30°, 60°, 90° special right triangle, with the length of its sides being in the ratio of x:x√3:2x opposite to the respective angles. The MA is the ratio of the length of the hypotenuse to the vertical side, so the MA = 2x/x = 2.

Another example of a simple machine that involves rotational motion and torque is the fulcrum and lever. If the fulcrum is placed in the center of the lever there is no mechanical advantage since the input distance and output distance are the same, requiring that the input and output force are the same. But, if the fulcrum is shifted towards the object that must be lifted against gravity, Figure 7-16, the input displacement will be greater than the output displacement, and a MA greater than one results.

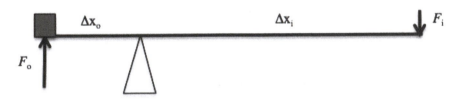

Figure 7-16

Example 2: A student wants to make a simple balance using an essentially massless meter stick and a wooden triangle. The student has a standard 100 g brass mass that he hangs at one end of the meter stick and he hangs an object of unknown mass at the other end of the meter stick. He then carefully sets the meter stick on the triangular wooden block and adjusts the position of the fulcrum until the meter stick is horizontal. If the tip of the fulcrum is located at the 0.25 m mark (from the unknown), what is the mechanical advantage of the system and what is the mass of the unknown object?

Solution: The MA in this case is the ratio of the distance between the fulcrum and the standard mass (Δx_i = 0.75 m) to the distance between the fulcrum and the unknown mass (Δx_o = 0.25 m). Hence the MA = 0.75/0.25 = 3. This means that the weight of the unknown object must be three times greater than the weight of the brass standard. Since the acceleration due to gravity for both objects is the same, the unknown has a mass of 300 g.

Finally, pulley systems can provide considerable mechanical advantage. For a frictionless pulley system in which a person pulls down on a essentially massless rope strung over a single pulley with a constant speed to lift an object as seen in Figure 7-17.1, there is no mechanical advantage, **MA** = 1, since the tension in the rope is the same as the force required to lift the mass against gravity. Also note that the distance the end of the rope moves (10 cm) is the same distance that the weight is lifted. In this case there is only one supporting rope, since ropes that are pulled down do not exert tension in a direction opposite to the force of gravity acting on the weight being lifted.

However when there are two pulleys and two supporting ropes, Figure 7-17.2, the input force pulling down on the rope and tension in the rope is halved and the **MA** = 2. It would be easier for a person to lift the weight, but the end of the rope would have to travel twice as far (20 cm) as the weight is lifted (10 cm). Likewise, in these simple cases, the **MA** is increased in proportion to the number of pulleys and supporting ropes, Figure 7-17.3 and 7-17.4. In real systems with friction and where the rope has significant mass, the added **MA** obtained by adding pulleys is offset by an increase in friction and at some point, adding pulleys would not result in further mechanical advantage due to a loss in efficiency.

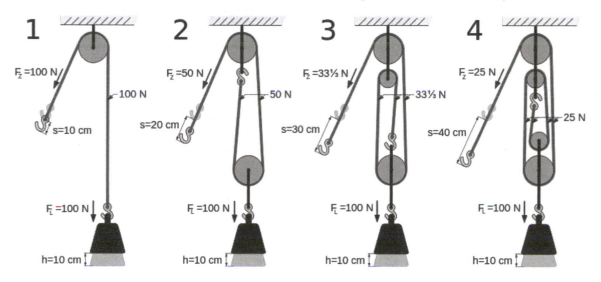

Figure 7-17 (https://commons.wikimedia.org/wiki/File:Four_pulleys.svg)

J. CHAPTER SUMMARY

In this chapter we explored the concept of energy. Whenever you read about a force and a distance through which the force acts, you should think immediately of work $W = F\Delta x \cos\phi$. This will be the key to answering some of the questions, even if no numbers are involved.

If a net force acts on an object, the kinetic energy $E_K = 1/2\ mv^2$ of the object is changed according to $W_{net} = \Delta E_k$. The total work gives the size of the energy flow into an object. Another form of energy is gravitational potential energy given by $E_P = mgh$. It is important to keep track of the energy flow because energy is conserved. That is, energy cannot be created from nothing or destroyed, but it can be transferred from one form to another. The rate at which energy is transformed is called power $P = \Delta E/\Delta t$. Mechanical advantage is the ratio of the output force to the input force for simple machines.

CHAPTER 7 PROBLEMS

Use the following information for questions 1–5:

A woman pulls her daughter on a sled by a rope on level, packed snow. The woman is 70 kg with red hair, earnest looking. The daughter is 20 kg with brown hair and wild curls. The sled is a Firestone-200 of mass 10 kg which slides along the snow with a coefficient of friction 0.09. The tension in the rope is 30 N, making an angle of 30° with the ground. They are going a constant 2.5 m/s for 4 s. (Use $g = 10$ m/s².)

1. What is the work done by the rope on the sled?

    A. 0 Joules
    B. 150 Joules
    C. 260 Joules
    D. 3000 Joules

2. What is the work done by the normal force on the sled?

    A. 0 Joules
    B. 150 Joules
    C. 1500 Joules
    D. 3000 Joules

3. What is the work done by the force of gravity on the sled?

    A. −3000 Joules
    B. 0 Joules
    C. 1500 Joules
    D. 3000 Joules

4. What is the total work done on the sled?

    A. 0 Joules
    B. 150 Joules
    C. 260 Joules
    D. 3000 Joules

5. What is the work done by friction on the sled?

    A. −3000 Joules
    B. −260 Joules
    C. 0 Joules
    D. 3000 Joules

Use the following for questions 6 and 7.

A man is carrying a heavy box (mass 30 kg) at constant velocity 1.5 m/s across a room. It takes 10 seconds. (Use $g = 10$ m/s².)

6. What are the forces acting on the box?

    A. The force of gravity, down.
    B. The force of gravity, down; and the man's force, up.
    C. The force of gravity, down; normal force, up; and man's force, forward.
    D. The force of gravity, down; man's force, up; and man's force, forward.

7. What is the work done by the man on the box during this time?

    A. 0 Joules
    B. 2250 Joules
    C. 3000 Joules
    D. 4500 Joules

Use the following for questions 8 and 9:

A toy cart (4 kg) is rolling along level ground. At a given time it is traveling 3 m/s and accelerating at 4 m/s².

8. What is the magnitude of the cart's momentum at this time?

    A. 12 kg m/s
    B. 8 kg m/s
    C. 32 Joules
    D. 64 Joules

9. What is the cart's kinetic energy at this time?

    A. 12 kg m/s
    B. 8 kg m/s
    C. 18 Joules
    D. 32 Joules

Use the following for questions 10 and 11:

A horse pulls with a horizontal force *F* on a wagon full of belongings (mass *M*). The horse and wagon are traveling at a constant speed *v* on level ground. (Use $g = 10$ m/s^2.)

10. How much work is done by the horse on the wagon in time Δt?

    A. $-Fv\Delta t$
    B. 0 Joules
    C. $Fv\Delta t$
    D. There is not enough information to answer this question.

11. How much work is done by gravity on the wagon in time Δt?

    A. $-Mgv\Delta t$
    B. 0 Joules
    C. $Mgv\Delta t$
    D. There is not enough information to answer this question.

12. A toy cart is initially at rest. A constant force of 10 N is applied horizontally for 20 seconds, so the cart begins to move along the level frictionless floor. What is the kinetic energy of the cart just after the 20 seconds?

    A. 100 Joules
    B. 200 Joules
    C. 2×10^4 Joules
    D. There is not enough information to answer this question.

Use the following for questions 13–16:

A car (1000 kg) is going 20 m/s on a level road and slams on the brakes. The skid marks are 25 meters long.

13. What forces are acting on the car while it is coming to a stop?

    A. Gravity, down; and normal force, up.
    B. Gravity, down; normal force, up; and a force backwards.
    C. Gravity, down; normal force, up; and a force forwards.
    D. Gravity, down; normal force, up; the engine force forwards; and a brake force, backwards.

14. What is the change in kinetic energy during the braking?

    A. -2×10^5 Joules
    B. 0 Joules
    C. 2×10^5 Joules
    D. 4×10^5 Joules

15. What is the work done by the road on the car?

    A. -2×10^5 Joules
    B. 0 Joules
    C. 2×10^5 Joules
    D. 4×10^5 Joules

16. If the force of the road on the car during the stop is constant, what is that force?

    A. 500 Newtons
    B. 3000 Newtons
    C. 5000 Newtons
    D. 8000 Newtons

Use the following for questions 17–18:

A cat (4 kg) drops from the roof to the ground, a distance of 3 meters. (Use $g = 10$ m/s^2.)

17. What is its kinetic energy just before it reaches the ground?

    A. 0 Joules
    B. 18 Joules
    C. 120 Joules
    D. There is not enough information to answer this question.

18. What is its velocity just before it reaches the ground?

    A. 3.9 m/s
    B. 5.5 m/s
    C. 7.7 m/s
    D. There is not enough information to answer this question.

Use the following for questions 19–20:

A hammer of mass *m* is dropped from the roof, so that it falls a distance *h* to the ground.

19. If the height *h* were doubled, how would the terminal kinetic energy of the hammer be changed? (The terminal kinetic energy is the kinetic energy just before it hits the ground.)

    A. The kinetic energy would be the same.
    B. The kinetic energy would increase by 41%.
    C. The kinetic energy would double.
    D. There is not enough information to answer this question.

20. If the height h were doubled, how would the terminal velocity of the hammer be changed? (The terminal velocity is the velocity just before it hits the ground.)

    A. The terminal velocity would increase by 41%.
    B. The terminal velocity would increase by 59%.
    C. The terminal velocity would double.
    D. There is not enough information to answer this question.

Use the following for questions 21–23:

Cart A (1 kg) and Cart B (2 kg) run along a frictionless level one-dimensional track. Cart B is initially at rest, and Cart A is traveling 0.5 m/s toward the right when it encounters Cart B. After the collision, Cart A is at rest.

21. Which of the following is true concerning the collision?

    A. Momentum is conserved.
    B. The collision is an elastic collision.
    C. The collision is a completely inelastic collision.
    D. Kinetic energy is conserved.

22. What is the final velocity of Cart B?
    A. 0.25 m/s
    B. 0.35 m/s
    C. 0.5 m/s
    D. 1.0 m/s

23. What is the efficiency of the collision (for kinetic energy)?

    A. 0.2
    B. 0.25
    C. 0.5
    D. 0.75

Use the following for questions 24–26:

A cart runs along a straight level road by burning propane. For the cart, we can define efficiency as the ratio of energy expended to overcome air resistance to the energy available in the propane. The enthalpy for the combustion of propane

$$C_3H_{8(g)} + 5O_{2(g)} \rightarrow 3CO_{2(g)} + 4H_2O_{(g)}$$

is given by

$$\Delta H_{rea} = -2.22 \times 10^6 \text{ J/mol}$$

In a given experiment, the cart (of mass m) travels a distance D at constant velocity v on a level road. It consumes n moles of propane during that time. The force due to the air resistance is F_{air}, which is proportional to the square of the velocity.

24. Which expression gives the efficiency of the cart?

    A. $\dfrac{n\Delta H_{rea}}{F_{air}D}$

    B. $\dfrac{F_{air}D}{n\Delta H_{rea}}$

    C. $\dfrac{F_{air}v}{n\Delta H_{rea}}$

    D. $\dfrac{n\Delta H_{rea}}{F_{air}v}$

25. If the cart travels the same distance D at a larger velocity, what is a necessary consequence?

    A. The efficiency must decrease.
    B. The efficiency must stay the same.
    C. The efficiency must increase.
    D. The energy expended to overcome air resistance is increased.

26. Where does the energy go which is not used to overcome air resistance?

    A. kinetic energy
    B. potential energy
    C. heat and sound
    D. chemical energy

Use the following for questions 27–28:

A winch pulls a box on wheels (1000 kg) at a very slow speed up an incline which makes an angle $\theta = 30°$ with the horizontal. The mass starts at ground level, and the winch exerts a power 2000 Watts, working for 200 seconds. (Use $g = 10$ m/s^2.)

27. Assuming no friction and 100% efficiency, to what height above the ground does the winch pull the box?

    A. 10 meters
    B. 20 meters
    C. 35 meters
    D. 40 meters

28. Which is the best description of the energy flow?

    A. Electric to potential.
    B. Electric to kinetic.
    C. Kinetic to potential.
    D. Electric to potential to kinetic.

Use the following for questions 29–30:

A motor is connected to a power supply which supplies 6 amperes of current with a 20-volt potential difference. The motor is used to lift a mass which is 40 kg. The motor has a 10% efficiency rating.

The power provided by a power supply is given by

$$P = I\Delta V$$

where P is power in Watts, I is current in amperes, and ΔV is the potential difference in volts. (Use $g = 10$ m/s^2.)

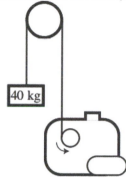

29. If the motor is run for 60 seconds, how high does the mass rise?

 A. 1.8 meters
 B. 5.4 meters
 C. 18 meters
 D. 180 meters

30. How long would it take to bring the mass to the same height if the current and the potential difference were both doubled? (Assume constant efficiency.)

 A. 15 seconds
 B. 30 seconds
 C. 60 seconds
 D. 120 seconds

31. In the pulley system shown, the angle α is the angle the rope makes with the horizontal.

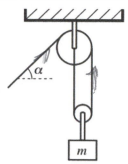

The hanging mass has mass m. If the rope is slowly pulled at a constant rate with tension T, what is that tension?

 A. $mg\cos\alpha$
 B. $mg\sin\alpha$
 C. mg
 D. $mg/2$

32. A painter hangs by connecting two ends of a rope to a harness, so that the rope wraps over a pulley. There is a tension T_1 in the rope.

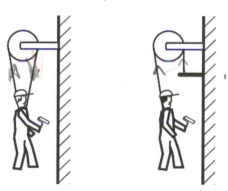

A second painter of the same mass connects one end of the rope to his harness, and the other end wraps over a pulley and connects to a flagpole. The tension in his rope is T_2.

Which is true?

 A. $T_2 = 2T_1$
 B. $T_2 = T_1$
 C. $T_2 = T_1/2$
 D. There is not enough information to determine a relationship between T_1 and T_2.

33. In the figure shown, what is the force reading on the force meter?

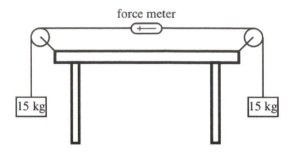

(Take 10 m/s² for the acceleration due to gravity.)

A. 0 Newtons
B. 30 Newtons
C. 150 Newtons
D. 300 Newtons

34. In the figure shown, a tension T is exerted in order to lift the mass m.

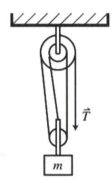

Which expression gives the tension?

A. $mg/4$
B. $mg/3$
C. $mg/2$
D. mg

SECTION 2

CONTENT REVIEW PROBLEMS

Use the following to answer questions 1 and 2:

Bob the runner (50 kg, runner's build) takes about 3 strides, which is 12 meters all together, to accelerate from rest at the starting block to the speed at which he plans to run. At that speed, his kinetic energy is 1600 Joules.

1. What is his final running velocity?

A. 4.0 m/s
B. 8.0 m/s
C. 16.0 m/s
D. 32.0 m/s

2. What is the average force accelerating him during the first 3 strides?

A. 2.7 Newtons
B. 32 Newtons
C. 130 Newtons
D. There is not enough information to answer this question.

Use the following to answer questions 37–40:

A cannon fires a cannonball (20 kg) at an angle, so that its initial speed upon leaving the cannon is 100 m/s. The cannonball reaches a height of 180 meters. Use 10 m/s^2 for the acceleration due to gravity, and assume there is no air resistance.

3. What forces are acting on the cannonball after it leaves the cannon?

A. Gravity.
B. Gravity, and a forward force.
C. Gravity, and the normal force.
D. Gravity, the normal force, and a forward force.

4. What is the initial kinetic energy?

A. 3.6 x 10^4 Joules
B. 6.4 x 10^4 Joules
C. 1.0 x 10^5 Joules
D. There is not enough information to answer this question.

5. What is the gravitational potential energy at the top of flight?

A. 3.6 x 10^4 Joules
B. 6.4 x 10^4 Joules
C. 1.0 x 10^5 Joules
D. There is not enough information to answer this question.

6. What is the velocity at the top of flight?

A. 10 m/s
B. 20 m/s
C. 80 m/s
D. There is not enough information to answer this question.

Use the following to answer questions 7–8:

Consider a ball tossed into the air. Point A shows the ball just after the release, and point D show it at the top of its flight.

7. Consider the following statements:

I. From points A to D, the kinetic energy is conserved.
II. From points A to D, the potential energy is conserved.
III. From points A to D, the sum of the kinetic energy and potential energy is conserved.

Which is true?

A. Only I is true.
B. Only II is true.
C. Only III is true.
D. I, II, and III are true.

8. From A to D, is the momentum of the ball conserved?

A. Yes, the ball is isolated from other objects.
B. Yes, gravity and the force due to the hand are balanced.
C. No, gravity is an unbalanced external force.
D. No, there are no internal forces.

9. Which is true?

A. The total work done on the ball from A to D is zero.
B. As the ball travels from A to D, the kinetic energy is converted to potential energy.
C. As the ball travels from A to D, the potential energy is converted to kinetic energy.
D. The work done on the ball from A to D is due to the force by the hand.

Use the following to answer questions 10–14:

A bullet (5 grams) is fired horizontally into a block of wood (2 kg) suspended from the ceiling by strings of length 1.5 meters.

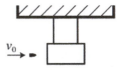

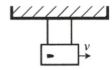

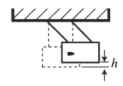

The bullet embeds itself in the block of wood. Immediately after the bullet embeds in the wood, the wood and bullet are moving 1.5 m/s.

The event can be divided into two parts:

1) In a very little time the bullet embeds itself into the wood. Gravity can be ignored in this part.
2) The wood block with the bullet, which is suspended by the strings, swings upward by height *h*.

10. Immediately after the bullet embeds itself in the wood, which is the best approximation of the kinetic energy of the block and bullet?

A. 2.25 Joules
B. 4.5 Joules
C. 9 Joules
D. 18 Joules

11. What is the velocity of the bullet just before it enters the block?

A. 30 m/s
B. 300 m/s
C. 600 m/s
D. 3000 m/s

12. How high does the block (and bullet) swing on the strings before it comes to rest?

A. 6 cm
B. 11 cm
C. 22.5 cm
D. 225 cm

13. Which best describes the energy flow during part 1?

A. kinetic to potential
B. potential to kinetic
C. kinetic to heat and kinetic
D. potential and kinetic to heat

14. Which best describes the energy flow during part 2?

A. kinetic to potential
B. potential to kinetic
C. kinetic to heat
D. potential and kinetic to heat

Use the following to answer questions 15–17:

Consider a winch which is operating to pull a cart slowly at constant speed up an incline, as shown in the figure. Point A is at the bottom of the incline and point B is at the top.

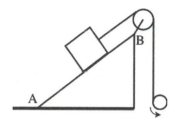

15. Consider the following statements:

I. From points A to B, the kinetic energy of the cart is conserved.
II. From points A to B, the potential energy of the cart is conserved.
III. From points A to B, the sum of the kinetic energy and potential energy of the cart is conserved.

Which is true?

A. Only I is true.
B. Only II is true.
C. Only III is true.
D. I, II, and III are true.

16. Is the momentum of the cart conserved?

A. Yes, the cart is isolated from other objects.
B. Yes, gravity, the normal force, and the force due to the winch are balanced.
C. No, gravity is an unbalanced external force.
D. No, there are internal forces.

17. Which is true?

A. The total work done on the cart from A to B is zero.
B. Kinetic energy is converted to potential energy.
C. Potential energy is converted to kinetic energy.
D. The total work done on the cart from A to B is due to the force of the winch alone.

Use the following to answer questions 18–21:

A rock of mass M slides without friction from a height h above some ground level along a slope making angle α with the horizontal. It takes time t_1 to reach the bottom, at which time it is traveling a velocity v_1.

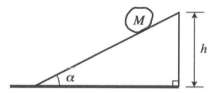

A rock of mass m, less than M, slides without friction from the same height h along a slope of the same angle α. It takes time t_2 to reach the bottom, at which time it is traveling a velocity v_2.

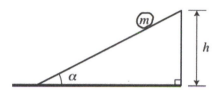

A rock of mass m slides without friction from the same height h along a slope making angle β (greater than α) with the horizontal. It takes time t_3 to reach the bottom, at which time it is traveling a velocity v_3.

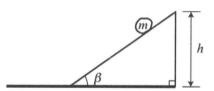

18. What is the relationship between v_1 and v_2?

A. The velocity v_1 is less than v_2.
B. The velocity v_1 is the same as v_2.
C. The velocity v_1 is greater than v_2.
D. There is not enough information to answer this problem.

19. What is the relationship between v_2 and v_3?

A. The velocity v_2 is less than v_3.
B. The velocity v_2 is the same as v_3.
C. The velocity v_2 is greater than v_3.
D. There is not enough information to answer this problem.

20. What is the relationship between t_1 and t_2?

A. The time t_1 is less than t_2.
B. The time t_1 is the same as t_2.
C. The time t_1 is greater than t_2.
D. There is not enough information to answer this problem.

21. What is the relationship between t_2 and t_3?

A. The time t_2 is less than t_3.
B. The time t_2 is the same as t_3.
C. The time t_2 is greater than t_3.
D. There is not enough information to answer this problem.

Use the following to answer questions 22–24:

A car (mass M) has a cross-sectional area A in the direction of motion. If it is moving at constant speed v, then the force due to air resistance is

$$F_{air} = C\rho A v^2$$

where $C \approx 0.2$ and ρ is the density of air, 1.3 kg/m^3. The power dissipated by a car moving at constant velocity is $P = Fv$, where F is the force required to overcome drag. Consider only the drag due to air resistance, and consider a car driving at speed v from city A to city B. For these problems consider C to be constant.

22. How does the energy required to get from A to B change if the velocity were doubled?

A. The energy required would stay the same.
B. The energy required would increase by a factor of 2.
C. The energy required would increase by a factor of 4.
D. The energy required would increase by a factor of 8.

23. How does the energy required to get from A to B change if the velocity were increased from 50 mph to 55 mph?

A. The energy required would stay the same.
B. The energy required would increase by 10%.
C. The energy required would increase by 21%.
D. The energy required would increase by 33%.

24. How would power dissipated change if the velocity increased from 35 to 70 mph?

A. The power would stay the same.
B. The power would double.
C. The power would increase by a factor of 4.
D. The power would increase by a factor of 8.

Passage 1

In a certain experiment, a piston chamber is used as part of a primitive engine. The apparatus consists of a pipe closed at one end with a piston at the other end. A valve in the cylinder allows fuel gases to be introduced or waste gases to be expelled.

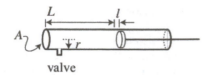

valve

In the operation of this engine, hydrogen and oxygen are introduced in a 2:1 ratio (in order to ensure complete combustion) at ambient temperature T_{amb} and atmospheric pressure P_{atm}. The following reaction is ignited

$$2H_{2(g)} + O_{2(g)} \rightarrow 2H_2O_{(g)}$$

with a heat of reaction

$$\Delta H_{rea} = -4.8 \times 10^5 \text{ J/mol}$$

The pressure rises to P_{burn}.

Next the piston slowly moves back a distance l, from which the engine derives useful work. The distance l is short enough that the pressure and temperature inside the chamber remain roughly constant.

The waste gases are then expelled, and the piston is restored to its original position.

The radius of the cylinder is r, and the cross-sectional area is A. The length of the cylinder before the piston moves back is L, which is much larger than l. The number of moles of oxygen introduced is n.

25. After the combustion occurs, why does the pressure go up?

A. There are more gas particles on the left side of the reaction.
B. The temperature rises considerably.
C. The reaction is spontaneous.
D. The heat of reaction is negative.

26. Which expression expresses the efficiency of the engine?

A. $\dfrac{2}{3}\dfrac{P_{burn} A l}{n\Delta H_{rea}}$

B. $\dfrac{2}{3}\dfrac{P_{burn} A L}{n\Delta H_{rea}}$

C. $\dfrac{P_{burn} A l}{n\Delta H_{rea}}$

D. $\dfrac{P_{burn} A L}{n\Delta H_{rea}}$

27. The second paragraph refers to what kind of ratio?

A. mass
B. volume
C. neutron
D. temperature

28. What would happen if the ratio in the second paragraph were not 2:1?

A. The heat of reaction would be less than 4.8 x 10^5 J/mol.
B. The combustion would not ignite.
C. Some of the waste gas would be intermediate products of incomplete combustion.
D. Some of the waste gas would be oxygen or hydrogen.

29. If the reaction shown were performed in a closed chamber isothermally at 500°C , what would happen to the pressure?

A. The pressure would decrease.
B. The pressure would stay the same.
C. The pressure would increase.
D. There is not enough information to solve this problem.

30. Which is an expression giving the number of moles of oxygen introduced in the chamber?

A. $\dfrac{1}{3}\dfrac{P_{atm}AL}{RT_{amb}}$

B. $\dfrac{1}{2}\dfrac{P_{atm}AL}{RT_{amb}}$

C. $\dfrac{2}{3}\dfrac{P_{atm}AL}{RT_{amb}}$

D. $\dfrac{P_{atm}AL}{RT_{amb}}$

31. What would be the consequence of making *l* larger? During the piston movement,

A. pressure in the chamber would decrease, and temperature would decrease.
B. pressure in the chamber would decrease, and temperature would increase.
C. pressure in the chamber would increase, and temperature would decrease.
D. pressure in the chamber would increase, and temperature would increase.

Passage 2

A swiftly moving charged particle, called an incident particle, moving through a material composed of neutral atoms and molecules, such as gas or biological tissue, loses kinetic energy to the material. For instance, a massive positive particle, such as a bare nucleus, moving at a speed near that of light will ionize the atoms or molecules of the medium it is moving through. In the process, there is a drag force on the incident particle and hence a loss of energy.

The energy loss depends not on the mass of the incident particle, interestingly enough, but it does depend on its charge z, as well as on the average number of electrons Z per atom or molecule in the material. The following equation gives energy loss per distance traveled:

$$\frac{\Delta E}{\Delta x} = 4\pi NZ \frac{z^2 e^4}{m_e c^2}\ln B \qquad (1)$$

where N is the number of atoms per unit volume of material,

Z is the average number of electrons per atom or molecule in the material,

z is the charge (number of elementary charges) of the incident particle,

e is the electron charge (in Coulombs),

m_e is the electron mass,

c is the speed of light,

$\ln B \approx 10$ (approximately constant).

Use this equation to answer the questions. If you have forgotten notation like ^{4}He, then look forward to Chapter 16 and review it.

32. Consider the following statements:

I. Momentum is conserved.
II. Kinetic energy is conserved.
III. Total energy is conserved.

In an isolated collision between a fast charged particle and an electron, if the collision is elastic, then what can be definitely concluded?

A. I only
B. III only
C. I and III only
D. I, II and III

33. What sort of quantity is on the left hand side of equation (1)?

A. mass
B. acceleration
C. force
D. energy

34. A hydrogen nucleus (^{1}H) and a helium nucleus (^{4}He) have the same initial kinetic energy, with near light speed. They travel through the air. Which tends to lose more energy in a given distance?

A. ^{1}H, by a factor of 4
B. They lose approximately the same amount of energy per distance.
C. ^{4}He, by a factor of 2
D. ^{4}He, by a factor of 4

35. A hydrogen nucleus (^{1}H) and a tritium nucleus (^{3}H) have the same initial kinetic energy, with near light speed. They are traveling through water. Which tends to lose more energy in a given distance?

A. ^{1}H, by a factor of 3
B. They lose approximately the same amount of energy per distance.
C. ^{3}H, by a factor of 3
D. ^{3}H, by a factor of 9

36. A relativistic proton beam is incident upon helium gas at STP. A second relativistic proton beam is incident upon neon gas at STP. Which beam loses more energy in a given distance?

A. The beam in helium, by a factor of 5.
B. They lose approximately the same in a given distance.
C. The beam in neon, by a factor of 5.
D. The beam in neon, by a factor of 25.

Passage 3

A large amount of energy is lost each time a car is brought to a stop by applying the brakes. The kinetic energy is converted into heat energy, which is useless in getting the car going again. For this reason, some engineers have experimented with the idea of storing energy in a flywheel when a car comes to a stop.

A flywheel is a massive ring which is free to spin about its center, like a bicycle wheel. The kinetic energy of a flywheel is given by

$$E_K = I\omega^2/2$$

where I is the moment of inertia and ω is the angular frequency in radians per unit time. Thus the frequency f (in cycles per unit time) is $f = \omega/2\pi$. The moment of inertia is given by

$$I = MR^2$$

where M is the mass of the flywheel and R is the radius.

Ideally the kinetic energy of the car would be transferred to the flywheel as the car comes to a stop. When the driver wants to go again, the energy would be transferred back to forward kinetic motion. Unfortunately, the efficiency of the two transfers will be less than 100%, so energy will be lost to heat. This energy can, of course, be made up by conventional means, such as burning gasoline.

For the following questions, use the notation:

M_{car} is mass of the car
M is mass of the flywheel
R is radius of the flywheel
$\omega = 2\pi f =$ angular frequency of the flywheel

37. Consider the whole car as a physical system in the situation in which it is braking on level ground using conventional brakes. If we consider the system as closed with respect to energy, then we would say the energy of the system is conserved. Which of the following statements tends to contradict the idea of the car as a closed system?

A. Since the car is slowing, there is an unbalanced external force.
B. Since the brake pads are growing hotter, entropy is increasing.
C. Since the brake pads are growing hotter, some heat is transferred to the air.
D. Since the situation is not spontaneous, the free energy change is greater than zero.

38. If the mass of the brake pads is m_{brake}, and the heat capacity is C_V (in J/kg K), which expression gives an approximate temperature change in the brake pads if a car going velocity v slows to a stop?

A. $\dfrac{M_{car}v}{2C_V m_{brake}}$

B. $\dfrac{M_{car}v}{C_V m_{brake}}$

C. $\dfrac{M_{car}v^2}{C_V m_{brake}}$

D. $\dfrac{M_{car}v^2}{2C_V m_{brake}}$

39. The efficiency of conversion of forward kinetic energy to rotational energy is a. Assume the flywheel is initially nonrotating and the car is moving at velocity v. Then what is an expression giving the angular velocity ω after the car comes to a stop?

A. $a\sqrt{\dfrac{M_{car}}{2M}}\,\dfrac{v}{R}$

B. $\sqrt{\dfrac{aM_{car}}{2M}}\,\dfrac{v}{R}$

C. $\sqrt{\dfrac{aM_{car}}{M}}\,\dfrac{v}{R}$

D. $a\sqrt{\dfrac{M_{car}}{M}}\,\dfrac{v}{R}$

40. Consider a small portion of the flywheel Δm. Which expression gives the centripetal force experienced by that piece?
A. $\Delta m\omega^2 R/2$
B. $\Delta m\omega^2 R$
C. $\omega^2 R/2$
D. $\omega^2 R$

41. The efficiency for converting forward kinetic energy to rotational energy is a, and the efficiency for converting rotational energy to kinetic energy is b. The car is initially going velocity v and the flywheel is still. The car slows to a stop by converting energy to the flywheel, and then it gains velocity again until the flywheel is still. What is the resulting speed of the car?

A. $\sqrt{ab}\,v$

B. abv

C. $(ab)^2 v$

D. av/b

42. A conventional car (500 kg) rolls down a hill, such that the efficiency of conversion of potential energy to kinetic energy is 40%. If the car starts from rest at a point 600 meters above sea level and coasts to a point 550 meters above sea level, what is the resulting speed of the car? (Use $g = 10$ m/s^2.)

A. 12.6 m/s
B. 20 m/s
C. 31.6 m/s
D. 40 m/s

Passage 4

People began to make roller coasters around the early 1900s. These early roller coasters were made of wood, and people learned how to construct them using the principles of physics and by a certain amount of experimentation.

Beginning in the 1980s, constructers of roller coasters began to use computers to design them. In this way they were able to create a great many designs and simulate them, thus finding a roller coaster's weakest points and determining the cost of making them fail-safe. This, and the practice of making them of steel, made the new roller coasters larger, safer, and more fun.

Nevertheless, a fair amount of knowledge about a roller coaster can be learned by applying simple physics without the aid of a computer. For the most part, the two forces acting on the car are gravity and the normal force, for we will ignore the force of friction during the ride. A force due to a motor carries the car to the top of the first hill. Finally there is a frictional force due to rubber bumpers pressing against the car which serve to stop it at the end of the ride so that other riders can get on.

The feeling a rider experiences in the car is related to the force exerted by the car's seat on his body perpendicular (normal) to the car's motion. This is expressed as a number of g's, where g is the acceleration due to gravity. For instance, if the rider (mass m) experiences a force $2mg$, then he is said to experience 2g's.

Consider the figure below, a very simple roller coaster, in answering the following questions. A motor brings the car from point A to B, where it is has very little velocity at a height H_1 above the ground. The slope of the first hill is an angle θ from the horizontal. The loop is a circle of whose highest point is H_2 above the ground. The mass of the car is M. The velocity of the car at point F is v_F.

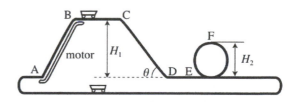

43. What is the kinetic energy of the car at point E?

A. $MgH_1\cos\theta$
B. $MgH_1\sin\theta$
C. MgH_1
D. $2MgH_1$

44. What is the velocity of the car at point E?

A. $\sqrt{\dfrac{gH_1}{2}}$

B. $\sqrt{gH_1}$

C. $\sqrt{2gH_1}$

D. $\sqrt{2gH_1 \cos\theta}$

45. What is the velocity of the car at point F, v_F?

A. $\sqrt{\dfrac{1}{2}g(H_1 - H_2)}$

B. $\sqrt{g(H_1 - H_2)}$

C. $\sqrt{2g(H_1 - H_2)}$

D. $\sqrt{g(H_1 + H_2)}$

46. What is the work done by the normal force from point C to point D?

A. 0

B. $-MgH_1\sin\theta$

C. $MgH_1\cos\theta$

D. $MgH_1\sin\theta$

47. How many forces are acting on the car at point F?

A. One, the force of gravity down.

B. Three, the force of gravity down, the normal force down, and a centripetal force toward the center of the circle.

C. Three, the force of gravity down, the normal force down, and a force forward.

D. None of the above.

48. What force pulls the blood to the rider's feet when the car is at point F?

A. The centripetal force.

B. The force of gravity.

C. The normal force.

D. None of the above.

49. What expression best gives the normal force on the car at point F?

A. $\dfrac{Mv_F^2}{H_2} - Mg$

B. $\dfrac{Mv_F^2}{H_2} + Mg$

C. $\dfrac{2Mv_F^2}{H_2} - Mg$

D. $\dfrac{2Mv_F^2}{H_2} + Mg$

50. When it rains, the park operators run the ride with fewer people in the cars. Which of the following is a good explanation of why this is?

A. The rain reduces the friction on the tracks and makes the cars go faster.

B. The rain reduces the coefficient of static friction between the bumpers and the car.

C. The rain reduces the coefficient of kinetic friction between the bumpers and the car.

D. The rain decreases the efficiency of the motor.

51. Which of the following best describes the energy flow in this ride?

A. electrical to potential and kinetic to heat

B. electrical to kinetic to electrical, in a circuit

C. electrical to kinetic to potential

D. electrical to heat to potential

Passage 5

A cannon is a device for imparting a large velocity to a mass of iron, generally for the purpose of warfare. Over the centuries, the manufacture of cannons has taken many forms, but the basic construction has remained the same.

A cylinder (or *barrel*) is closed at one end (the *breech*) and open at the other (the *muzzle*). An explosive (or *charge*) is placed in the cylinder at the breech, and a ball is placed in the cylinder on top of the charge. The explosive is ignited and the reaction produces hot gases which increase the pressure. Thus the gases push the ball along the cylinder and out the muzzle at great velocity.

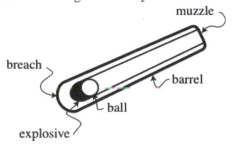

Beginning in the 1500s, gunners began using large-grained explosive in order to decrease the rate of burning. Faster burning charge creates a large pressure very quickly, thus creating stress on the cannon and creating a risk of failure. The slower burning charge ensures that the pressure behind the ball stays more nearly constant as the ball travels the length of the barrel.

For the following questions, consider a cannon which is 2.3 meters long with a bore (hole) of radius 5 centimeters. Assume the pressure inside the cannon after the explosive has been set off is constant. While the ball is in the cannon, the forces due to the gases are so much greater than the force of gravity that the force of gravity can be ignored.

52. What additional piece of information would be sufficient to allow the calculation of the kinetic energy of the ball upon leaving the cannon?

A. The mass of the cannonball.
B. The final velocity of the cannonball.
C. The force the cannonball experiences in the barrel.
D. None of the above.

53. What additional piece of information would be sufficient to allow the calculation of the pressure in the barrel while the cannonball is still inside?

A. The temperature of the gas in the barrel.
B. The final velocity of the cannonball.
C. The force the cannonball experiences in the barrel.
D. None of the above.

54. Which of the following would best explain why a large-grained charge would burn more slowly than a small-grained charge?
A. The rate of reaction depends on the surface area.
B. The rate of reaction depends on the concentration of reactants.
C. The rate of reaction depends on the temperature of reactants.
D. The activation energy is reduced for smaller-grained charge.

55. Which of the following is necessarily true?

A. The entropy change during burning is zero.
B. The free energy change during burning is negative.
C. The free energy change during burning is zero.
D. The free energy change during burning is positive.

56. Which of the following best describes the energy flow in the passage?

A. chemical to kinetic to heat
B. chemical to heat to kinetic
C. chemical to potential to heat
D. chemical to potential to kinetic

57. For this question, assume the cannon points straight up, and assume we know the velocity of the cannonball when it leaves the muzzle of the cannon. What additional piece of information would be sufficient to allow the calculation of the height to which the cannonball would travel?

A. The mass of the cannonball.
B. The kinetic energy of the ball upon just leaving the barrel.
C. The force the cannonball experiences in the barrel.
D. No more information is needed.

This page intentionally left blank.

SECTION 3
FLUIDS AND WAVES

One of the major ways the MCAT focuses on physics is in discussions of how physical phenomena interact with living systems. In this next section dealing with fluids and waves, a wide variety of different phenomena are covered. They're also essential since so much of modern medicine involves manipulating waves in order to, in some way, assess the human body.

We will begin with a discussion of fluids. Needless to say, these concepts are critical when it comes to thinking about the body's circulatory system. For the purposes of this book we'll focus on the more simple, abstract situations that let us understand these phenomena more clearly. To get more in-depth practice applying concepts about fluids to biological systems, check out Next Step's Strategy and Practice books or our Full Length tests.

After talking about fluids, we'll move on to a discussion about waves. It's important to remember that sound and light are also waves, so this will be a fairly lengthy discussion covering three chapters. This material comes easily to some students, but is often very counter-intuitive for a lot of students. To that end, you may need to review these chapters several times to get a real mastery of the material.

This page intentionally left blank.

CHAPTER 8
FLUIDS

A. INTRODUCTION

In studying mechanics, we have generally looked at one object and the forces on it. For most people, the difficult part of mechanics is unlearning the misconception that a moving object needs a force to maintain its motion. (Recall Example 4 in Section 5.D.)

In this chapter we study fluids. A fluid is a large number of interacting particles, so it is somewhat more complicated. The key concept here is pressure. In any given problem you should be thinking, "Do I know the pressure everywhere? Can I figure out the pressure where the crocodile is?" and that sort of thing. Even if pressure is not mentioned in the problem, often it is the concept that leads you to the answer. For instance, when a teenager sips a soft drink through a straw, does he pull the refreshing liquid into his mouth? As you will soon discover, the answer is no.

For the MCAT, you need to know only a few basic principles of elementary fluid mechanics. The tricky part is learning how to apply them in diverse situations. One way to do this is to look at so many examples that any new situation reminds you of something you have seen or worked before. Hence you should pay close attention to the problems and solutions at the end of the chapter.

B. SOME DEFINITIONS

Density is a measure of how packed a substance is. Its symbol is the Greek letter rho, ρ, and it is defined by

$$\rho = m/V \ (1)$$

where m is the mass of a piece of fluid and V is its volume. *Specific gravity* is the ratio of the density of something to the density of water:

$$\text{specific gravity} = \frac{\rho}{\rho_{H_2O}} \ (2)$$

(This is a misnomer, by the way, since "specific gravity" has nothing to do with gravity.) The density of almost all biological tissue is approximately the same as the density of water (remember this):

$$\rho_{H_2O} = 1\frac{g}{cm^3} = 10^3 \frac{kg}{m^3} \ (3)$$

Pressure is like a push (that is, force), except we also consider the area over which the push is extended. If you are barefoot and step on the sidewalk, the sidewalk pushes up on you with about 1000 N. If you step on an upright tack, it pushes up on you with the same 1000 N. Why then does your face look so different when it's a tack that you stepped on? In this case, pressure is the important concept. Pressure is defined as

$$P = F/A \ (4)$$

where F is a force, and A is the area over which it acts. Consider this definition carefully, so that you do not confuse force and pressure. The point of a tack has a much smaller area than the bottom of your foot, so the pressure on that point is quite large.

The units for pressure are N/m², and these have a name:

$$1\frac{N}{m^2} = 1 \text{ Pascal} = 1 \text{ Pa} \ (5)$$

Pressure can also be measured in pounds per square inch, or psi. The pressure of the atmosphere at sea level varies, but its average is given by

$$1 \text{ atm} = 1.01 \times 10^5 \text{ Pa} = 14.7 \text{ psi} \quad (6)$$

C. BUOYANT FORCE

When an object is floating on or immersed in a fluid, such as an iceberg in water or a whale in the ocean, the fluid pushes on the object from many directions. This situation might seem too complicated to analyze mathematically, but it turns out that it is not. We can summarize the effect of the fluid in one force, the buoyant force. The following principle is called *Archimedes' principle*, after its discoverer:

If an object is floating on or immersed in a fluid, then the fluid exerts an upward buoyant force given by

$$F_B = \rho V g, \quad (7)$$

where F_B is the buoyant force, ρ is the density of the fluid, and V is volume of the displaced fluid.

The method for solving problems involving Archimedes' principle follows:

1. DRAW A DIAGRAM, including the buoyant force.
2. Write a force equation.
3. Get rid of m and F. (Use $m = \rho V$, $F = PA$, and of course $F_B = \rho V g$.)
4. Solve.

Example 1: A bathtub duck floats in water with one third of its volume above the water line. What is its specific gravity?

Solution: First, we DRAW A DIAGRAM. (See Figure 8-1.)

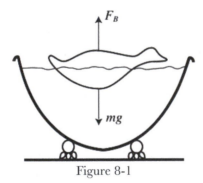

Figure 8-1

Second, we write a force equation, which is a force balance equation, since the duck is not accelerating:

$$0 = F_B - mg$$

Next we replace F_B with $\rho_{H_2O} V_{disp} g$, and we replace m with ρV, where ρ is the density of the duck, and V is its volume:

$$0 = \rho_{H_2O} V_{disp} g - \rho V g$$

Since one third of the duck is shown above the water, the displaced volume is $2V/3$, and we write

$$0 = \rho_{H_2O} \frac{2}{3} Vg - \rho Vg$$

$$0 = \rho_{H_2O} \frac{2}{3} - \rho$$

$$\frac{\rho}{\rho_{H_2O}} = \frac{2}{3}$$

Here we canceled the factors V and g. The answer is 2/3

Example 2: A crown, apparently made of gold, is weighed in air, and the weight is 50 N. The crown is weighed again by hanging it from a string and submerging it in water. (See Figure 8-2.) What reading will the force meter give if the crown is true gold? (Use for the density of gold 19.3 g/cm³; and for water, 1.0 g/cm³. Also, use g = 10 m/s².)

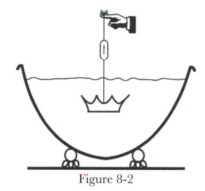

Figure 8-2

Solution: First, we DRAW A DIAGRAM with all the forces on the crown. (See Figure 8-3.)

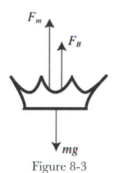

Figure 8-3

We draw the force of gravity first. Next, what is touching the crown? The fluid and the string are, so we know to draw the buoyant force and the force of tension. It is the force of tension that the meter reads. (That is what a force meter does: it provides a force and then tells you what that force is.)

We have force balance because there is no acceleration:

$$0 = F_m + F_B - mg$$

In this equation m is the mass of the crown, and mg is 50 N. Let's first solve for F_m (which we want), then replace F_B and m. We obtain

$$F_m = mg - F_B$$
$$= \rho_{Au} V g - \rho_{H_2O} V g$$
$$= (\rho_{Au} - \rho_{H_2O}) V g$$
$$= (\rho_{Au} - \rho_{H_2O}) \frac{m}{\rho_{Au}} g$$
$$= \frac{\rho_{Au} - \rho_{H_2O}}{\rho_{Au}} mg$$
$$= \frac{19.3 - 1.0}{19.3} (50 \text{ N})$$
$$= 47 \text{ N}$$

D. PRESSURE

We want to answer the question: Given the pressure at one point in a fluid, what is the pressure at any other point? In fact, the key intuition on many problems is to understand what the pressure is, everywhere.

Let us start with the simple situation shown in Figure 8-4. Point 1 is directly above point 2 in a fluid. The pressure at point 1 is P_1. What is the pressure at point 2?

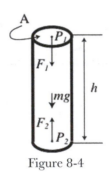

Figure 8-4

Consider a vertical pipe filled with fluid and consider the body of fluid between points 1 and 2 as an object. The pipe's height is h and its cross-sectional area is A.

There are three vertical forces: the force of gravity, the force of the pressure pushing up from below, and the force of the pressure pushing down from above. The fluid is not accelerating, so the net force is zero, and we have

$$0 = F_2 - F_1 - mg$$
$$= P_2A - P_1A - \rho V g$$
$$= P_2A - P_1A - \rho A h g$$

We can cancel the factor A:

$$0 = P_2 - P_1 - \rho h g$$
$$P_2 = P_1 + \rho h g$$

This equation applies not only to this situation but also to any situation involving two vertically separated points in a fluid. The pressure is greater at point 2 because more fluid is pressing down on top of point 2 than on top of point 1.

We can obtain pressures at other points in the fluid using a principle, discovered by Blaise Pascal: "Pressure applied to an enclosed fluid is transmitted to every portion of the fluid and the walls of the containing vessel in all directions." The language is a bit obscure, but it translates into principles 2 and 3 below.

> **Law of Hydrostatic Equilibrium**
> In a body of fluid,
> 1. the pressures at two points separated vertically by height h are related by
>
> $$P_2 = P_1 + \rho g h, \qquad (8)$$
>
> 2. the pressures at two points separated only horizontally are the same,
> 3. and the pressure at a given point is the same in all directions.

Example 1: We are standing on the fifty-first story of a hotel, where each story is 4 meters high. How much less is the pressure on the fifty-first story than the pressure at the ground floor? (Use 1.2×10^{-3} g/cm³ for the density of air.)

Solution: This is a straightforward application of the formula:

$$P_2 = P_1 + \rho g h,$$

$$P_2 - P_1 = \left[1.2 \times 10^{-3} \frac{g}{cm^3} \; 50 \cdot 4\,m \; \frac{1\;kg}{10^3 g} \left(\frac{100\;cm}{1\;m} \right)^3 \right] \; \frac{m}{s^2} \; .$$

$$= 2400 \; kg/ms^2$$
$$= 2400 \; Pa$$

This pressure is fairly small compared to P_{atm}, but it is enough to make your ears pop. Notice what is going on here. The people on the ground floor have to deal with not only the air column on top of us at the fifty-first floor, but also they have the air column between us and the ground floor sitting on their head.

Example 2: An underground cave is almost filled with water as shown in Figure 8-5. The air pressure above point S is 1 atm. The point Q is 20 m directly below point S, and T is at the same height as Q. R is 5 m vertically below S.

a. What is the pressure at point Q?
b. What is the pressure at point T against the floor?
c. What is the pressure at point T against the walls?
d. What is the pressure in the air chamber above R?

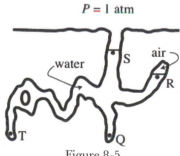

Figure 8-5

Solution: a. The pressure at Q is given by the formula:

$$P_Q = P_S + (10^3 \; kg/m^3)(10 \; m/s^2)(20 \; m)$$
$$= 1.01 \times 10^5 \; Pa + 2.0 \times 10^5 \; Pa$$
$$= 3.01 \times 10^5 \; Pa$$

b and c.

$$P_T = 3.01 \times 10^5 \; Pa$$

d.

$$P_R = P_S + (10^3 \text{ kg/m}^3)(10 \text{ m/s}^2)(5 \text{ m})$$
$$= 1.5 \times 10^5 \text{ Pa}$$

The pressure inside the air chamber varies slightly with height but it is approximately equal to the pressure at R.

Example 3: A pan contains a pool of mercury, with an inverted tube, as shown in Figure 8-6.

Point A is 38 cm above the surface of the mercury in the pan. Point B is 75 cm above the surface of the mercury in the pan. Point C is 76 cm above the surface of the mercury in the pan. The pressure of the air on the mercury in the pan is 1.01325×10^5 Pa, the density of mercury is 1.36×10^4 kg/m^3, and the acceleration due to gravity is 9.8 m/s^2.

a. What is the pressure at point A?
b. What is the pressure at point B?
c. What is the pressure at point C?

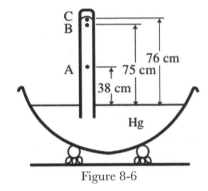

Figure 8-6

Solution: a. When we apply the equation to point A, we obtain

$$P_{atm} = P_A + \rho g h,$$
$$P_A = P_{atm} - \rho g h$$
$$= 1.01325 \times 10^5 \text{ Pa} - (1.36 \times 10^4)(9.8)(0.38) \text{ Pa}$$
$$= 5.1 \times 10^4 \text{ Pa}$$

b. At point B, we obtain

$$P_B = P_{atm} - \rho g h$$
$$= 1.01325 \times 10^5 \text{ Pa} - (1.36 \times 10^4)(9.8)(0.75) \text{ Pa}$$
$$\approx 10^3 \text{ Pa}$$

c. At point C, we obtain

$$P_C = P_{atm} - \rho g h$$
$$= 1.01325 \times 10^5 \text{ Pa} - (1.36 \times 10^4)(9.8)(0.76) \text{ Pa}$$
$$\approx 0 \text{ Pa}$$

Thus the pressure vanishes at the top of the column.

This is a simple barometer. Above the mercury column is a vacuum, or, more accurately, mercury vapor. The last calculation shows that the height of the mercury column is proportional to the outside pressure. For this reason, the height of a hypothetical mercury column is often given as units of pressure:

1 torr = 1 mm of mercury = pressure sufficient to lift Hg 1 mm   (9)

760 torr = 1 atm

These are the units used in a sphygmomanometer. But the numbers reported in blood pressure measurements are the pressures in excess of atmospheric pressure, called the **gauge pressure**. For instance, the systolic pressure of a woman with blood pressure 110/60 is actually (760 + 110) torr = 870 torr (assuming 760 torr atmospheric pressure). Thus:

$$P_{gauge} = P - P_{atm}. \qquad\qquad (10)$$

E. SURFACE TENSION

The molecules in the middle of a fluid exert an attractive force on each other, called cohesion. This is what holds the fluid together. The molecules at the surface of the fluid, however, experience a cohesive force directed into the fluid. If the surface becomes bent for some reason, there is a restoring force making the surface smooth or flat. The larger the distortion, the larger the force, up to a maximum:

$$F_{max} = \gamma L \qquad (11)$$

where γ is the surface tension (a function of the fluid) and L is the length of the edge of the object in contact with the fluid. This will become clearer with some examples.

Example 1: Water has a surface tension of 7.2 x 10^{-2} N/m at 25° C. A six-legged water bug stands on the surface of the water. The radius of each foot is 2 x 10^{-4} m. What is the maximum force on the bug due to the water? That is, what is the maximum weight the water surface tension can support?

Solution: In this case, L is the circumference of a foot. (See Figure 8-7.) Applying the formula yields $F_{max} = 6\gamma (2\pi r) = 5$ x 10^{-4} N, where 6 is the number of legs on the bug.

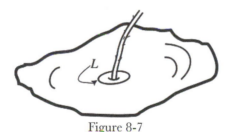

Figure 8-7

Example 2: A needle floats on the surface of the water as shown in Figure 8-8. Its length is l = 3 cm, and its width is very small. What is the maximum force exerted on the needle by the surface tension of the water?

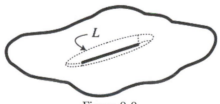

Figure 8-8

Solution: In this case, L is the circumference of the dimple, that is, the length of distorted surface **around** the needle or the length of the dashed line in Figure 9-8. Notice the similarity between Figures 10-7 and 10-8. We use the formula for the perimeter of a rectangle:

$$L = 2l + 2w \approx 2l$$

since the width w is very small. Thus we have

$$F_{max} = \gamma(2l) = 4.3 \text{ x } 10^{-3} \text{ N}$$

Example 3: A straight piece of wire has loops at both ends, and the two hoops fit on the arms of a U-shaped frame. A water film fills the interior of the U-shape. (See Figure 8-9.) In this case the surface tension exerts its maximum force.

If the length of the wire is l and the width of the film is w, what is the force of surface tension?

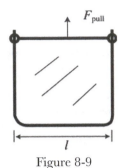

Figure 8-9

Solution: The circumference is the distance around the wire, as in the previous example. In Figure 8-9 we measure the length of the wire along the front of the page and then along the back of the page:

$$F_{max} = \gamma(2l)$$

F. CONTINUITY

The dynamics of flowing fluids are more difficult to understand than the statics, but this is good news. It means the MCAT will test only some of the basic principles.

The first principle is **continuity**. Figure 8-10 shows a river, in which point 1 is in a slow, lazy flow, while point 2 is in the rapids. Why does the water flow faster at point 2? During one second the number of gallons flowing past point 1 is the same as the number flowing past point 2. (Think about it. If the water level between 1 and 2 is constant, then the inflow must equal the outflow.) The difference is that point 2 has a smaller cross-sectional area.

The rate at which a fluid passes by a point, measured in volume per time, is called the **flow rate f**. In a steady state, the flow rate is the same at each point along the flow:

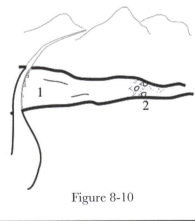

Figure 8-10

$$f_1 = f_2 \qquad (12)$$

Now we can relate the flow rate to the actual speed of the fluid. Think of water going through a garden hose. If we turn up the faucet, then the flow rate and the flow velocity both increase. We can also obtain a greater flow rate by increasing the cross-sectional area. We would guess (correctly) that we could write

$$f = Av. \tag{13}$$

The discussion in this section refers to any incompressible fluid, that is, liquids. It also applies to compressible fluids, like air, if the fluids are not, in fact, compressed.

G. VISCOSITY AND TURBULENCE

Viscosity is a measure of the stickiness of a fluid. Molasses is stickier, for instance, than water, and water is stickier than air. A precise definition of viscosity looks like this: Say we have a floor covered with a fluid to a depth *d*. A hockey puck of area *A* is traveling along at velocity *v*. The drag force on the hockey puck due to the stickiness of the fluid is given by

$$F_{viscous} = \eta \frac{Av}{d} \tag{14}$$

where η is the viscosity in kg/ms (that is, kilograms per meter per second, not kilograms per millisecond). You should understand this equation but need not memorize it. Just remember that viscosity is stickiness.

Viscosity often calms down a flow. Consider a stream of water flowing past a rock or the flow of air past a weather vane. The flow can break off into wild swirls and chaotic patterns, called **turbulence**. Smooth flow is called **streamline** or **laminar**. If we pull a spoon through a bowl of molasses, the molasses is mostly undisturbed (laminar flow around the spoon), whereas if we pull the spoon through a cup of tea with cream at the bottom, the tea and cream undergo turbulent motion. What's the difference? The more viscous the fluid, the less turbulent the flow.

An important parameter for determining the type of flow is the Reynolds number:

$$Re = \frac{l\rho v}{\eta} \tag{15}$$

where *l* is the size (in m) of the obstacle in the flow (spoon or whatever), ρ is the density of the fluid (in kg/m³), *v* is the velocity of the flow (in m/s), and η is viscosity (in kg/m s).

The flow starts getting rough when *Re* is around 40, and it is starts to become turbulent (in a pipe) if *Re* is greater than 2,000. Do not memorize this equation, but do realize that the presence of η in the denominator means that higher viscosity reduces turbulence. It should also make sense to you that *v* is in the numerator.

Example: What is the Reynolds number for a spoon moving through tea with cream in it? (Use $\eta = 1.0 \times 10^{-3}$ kg/ms and estimate other values.)

Solution: We can use information corresponding to water, so the density is 10^3 kg/m³, and the viscosity is 1.0×10^{-3} kg/m s. A good rate to stir tea is 0.1 m/s, and a typical spoon has size 0.03 m. Thus

$$Re \approx \frac{(0.03)(10^3)(0.1)}{10^{-3}} = 3 \times 10^3$$

H. BERNOULLI'S PRINCIPLE

For laminar flow there is an equation that relates conditions at one point in the flow with points downstream. Consider two points, 1 and 2, along a streamline. Point 1 is at some height h_1 above a standard height, and point 2 is at height h_2. (See Figure 8-11.)

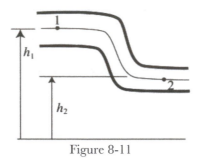

Figure 8-11

For incompressible, laminar, inviscid (no viscosity) flow, if points 1 and 2 are on the same streamline, we have

$$P_1 + \rho g h_1 + \frac{1}{2}\rho v_1{}^2 = P_2 + \rho g h_2 + \frac{1}{2}\rho v_2{}^2 \qquad (16)$$

Let's see if we can make sense of this equation, which can also be written

$$P + \rho gh + 1/2\ \rho v^2 = \text{const} \qquad (17)$$

The expression ρgh reminds us of mgh, the difference being only a factor of ΔV, that is, volume. If we multiply the above expression by ΔV, then we obtain

$$P\Delta V + mgh + 1/2\ mv^2 = \text{const}$$

Wait! This looks like an energy conservation equation, the second and third terms being potential and kinetic energy. But what is the first term? This is a bit more difficult, but we can make this look like an expression for work. For a moving fluid, ΔV can be replaced with $A\Delta x$ so that $P\Delta V = PA\Delta x = F\Delta x$. Thus, $P\Delta V$ is the work that one portion of the fluid does on another portion of the fluid as it moves along.

Bernoulli's principle is an expression of energy conservation, and that is why there are so many caveats in the statement of the principle: we are trying to make sure energy does not leak out into heat and ruin the equation.

Example: A large barrel of water has a hole near the bottom. The barrel is filled to a height of 4.5 meters above the bottom of the barrel, and the hole is a circle of radius 1 centimeter in the side of the barrel at a height 0.5 meters above the bottom.

a. What is the flow velocity v just outside the hole?
b. What is the flow rate f out of the hole?

Solution: a. First, we DRAW A DIAGRAM with a streamline. (See Figure 8-12).

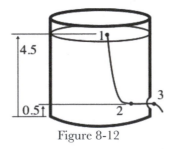

Figure 8-12

Bernoulli's principle applies, so we have

$$P_1 + \rho g h_1 + 1/2\ \rho v_1{}^2 = P_3 + \rho g h_3 + 1/2\ \rho v_3{}^2$$

We are looking for v_3. At point 1, the pressure is atmospheric pressure P_{atm}, and at point 3, we have $P_3 = P_{atm}$ as well. Also, $h_1 = 4.5$ m and $h_3 = 0.5$ m.

The tricky part is realizing that v_1 is very, very small. This is because continuity guarantees that $A_1v_1 = A_3v_3$, where A_1 is the cross-sectional area of the barrel and A_3 is the area of the hole. Thus we can set v_1 to zero in the above equation:

$$P_{atm} + \rho gh_1 = P_{atm} + \rho gh_3 + 1/2\, \rho v_3^2$$

$$\rho gh_1 = \rho gh_3 + 1/2\, \rho v_3^2$$

$$gh_1 = gh_3 + 1/2\, v_3^2$$

$$(10 \text{ m/s}^2)(4.5 \text{ m}) = (10 \text{ m/s}^2)(0.5 \text{ m}) + 1/2\, v_3^2$$

$$v_3^2 = 80 \text{ m}^2/\text{s}^2$$

$$v_3 = 9 \text{ m/s}$$

Another way to get the same result is to realize that the pressure at point 2 must be (from Section D)

$$P_2 = P_1 + \rho gh = P_{atm} + (10^3 \text{ kg/m}^3)(10 \text{ m/s}^2)(4 \text{ m})$$

$$= P_{atm} + 4 \times 10^4 \text{ Pa}$$

Then we can use Bernoulli's principle between points 2 and 3 and use $h_2 = h_3$ to obtain

$$P_2 + \rho gh_2 + 1/2\, \rho v_2^2 = P_3 + \rho gh_3 + 1/2\, \rho v_3^2$$

$$(P_{atm} + 4 \times 10^4 \text{ Pa}) + 1/2\, \rho v_2^2 = P_{atm} + 1/2\, \rho v_3^2$$

Again, we set the very small velocity v_2 to zero to obtain

$$4 \times 10^4 \text{ Pa} = 1/2\, (10^3 \text{ kg/m}^3)\, v_3^2$$

$$v_3 = 9 \text{ m/s}$$

b. The answer to part b we get through the definition of flow rate, so we have

$$f_3 = A_3v_3$$

$$\pi (0.01 \text{ m})^2(9 \text{ m/s})$$

$$3 \times 10^{-3} \text{ m}^3/\text{s}$$

I. THE VENTURI EFFECT AND PITOT TUBES

We now need to consider what happens to the pressure and flow rate of a fluid in a tube when we change the radius of the tube, or the so-called Venturi effect. Simply stated, when a tube's radius is constricted, in order to maintain continuity, the flow rate must increase, which also results in a reduction in the pressure that the fluid exerts on the surface of the tube. Figure 8-13 shows a tube in which a fluid is flowing horizontally from left to right with laminar flow. The cross-sectional area A_1 at point P_1 is larger than the cross-sectional area A_2 at point P_2. The velocities $v_1 < v_2$ are shown for the volume flow rate at points P_1 and P_2, respectively. Note that the vertically oriented tubes above P_1 and P_2 are open to the atmosphere and that fluid is pushed up against gravity into these tubes due to the relative pressure exerted by the fluid. Remember that pressure is the force per unit area, so the diameter of the vertically oriented tubes are the same, but the heights of the fluid are different, indicating that the force that the fluid exerts in the portion of the tube above P_1 is greater than the force that the fluid exerts above P_2. Also remember that the force that the fluid exerts comes from the random collisions of molecules that have a certain average kinetic energy at a given temperature. If the velocity of the fluid molecules moving in the horizontal direction is increased in going from P_1 to P_2, then to maintain the same average kinetic energy, the number of molecules moving in the vertical direction must decrease. Hence a decrease pressure on the surface of the tube.

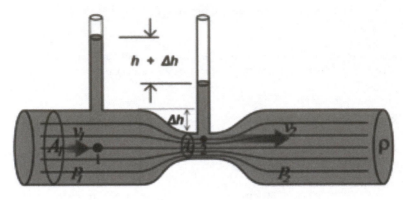

Figure 8-13

An equation for the relationship between the pressure and flow rate of a fluid, in such a tube, can be derived from combining the continuity equation (13) and Bernoulli's equation (16). It is highly unlikely that you would need to derive this equation for the MCAT. The important things to know here are the qualitative relationships between tube radii, flow rates and pressures.

Example 1: As a practical example, let us consider using a hose to water your garden, but the hose is not quite long enough for you to reach all of the plants in your garden. When you open the spigot, water begins to flow out the end of the hose and travels through the air in a parabolic path, just like a projectile. You angle the end of the hose at 45° (maximum range) and hold it as high as possible, but you still can't get water to your prized rose bush. What do you do to water your roses? Note that you are a good physics student (you understand projectile motion and fluids), but you are not wealthy due to all your student loans and can't afford to buy a longer hose.

Solution: Well it's quite simple and I'm sure you have done this, put your finger over the opening of the hose and restrict the diameter of the tube. The smaller you make the opening, the harder you will have to push against the water, meaning the pressure of the water inside the hose is increased compared to the pressure of the water as it hits the air (ca. 1 atm). What happens to the velocity of the water coming out the end of the hose with you finger partially blocking the opening? It is much faster, the Venturi effect, and now you can water those roses.

A Pitot tube is a pretty simple device used to measure the pressure of a flowing fluid and is often used to measure airspeed for aircraft. The tube is open at one end and the other end is attached to a sensor, such as a piezoelectric material. The tube is oriented horizontally and parallel with the flow of the fluid, such that the fluid is forced into the opening and molecules strike the pressure sensor. This device can also be used to indirectly measure the flow rate of the fluid, i.e. air speed of an aircraft or measure blood flow rates.

J. CHAPTER SUMMARY

In this chapter we studied fluids in static equilibrium and fluids in motion. Pressure is a unifying concept for fluids in equilibrium. Pressure is related to force by the equation $P = F/A$ (where the units of pressure are often Pa = N/m²). Pressure at one point in a body of fluid can be related to pressure at another point using $P_2 = P_1 + \rho gh$ (for vertical separation) and Pascal's law (for horizontal separation). If we know the pressure everywhere in a situation, we can often understand the physics and answer questions about it.

The important concepts for fluids in motion are continuity and Bernoulli's principle. Continuity expresses the conservation of mass as the fluid flows, so we have the product Av being a constant along a streamline. Bernoulli's principle expresses the conservation of energy along the fluid flow, so we have the sum $P + 1/2\rho v^2 + \rho gh$ being a constant along a streamline, as long as energy is not lost to heat or other energy sinks. These two principles allow you to solve most simple problems involving flowing fluids. The Venturi effect is a necessary consequence of Bernoulli's relationship in which the ρgh term is held constant. By changing the radius of the tube, thereby changing the cross-sectional area of the tube, and maintaining a constant volume flow rate (continuity), the pressure of the fluid in a particular portion of the tube is directly related to the radius and the linear flow rate is inversely related to the radius.

CHAPTER 8 PROBLEMS

1. A typical human head has the approximate shape of a cylinder of diameter of 0.2 meters and height 0.3 meters. If the pressure of the atmosphere is 1.01×10^5 N/m², let F_{atm} be the force acting down on a human head due to the atmosphere. How many kilograms taken together would weigh F_{atm}?

    A. 12
    B. 94
    C. 320
    D. 1300

2. A cork floats with three quarters of its volume in and one quarter of its volume out of the water. What is the specific gravity of the cork?

    A. 0.25
    B. 0.5
    C. 0.75
    D. 2.0

3. An object floats with one tenth of its volume out of the water. What is its specific gravity?

    A. 0.1
    B. 0.9
    C. 1.0
    D. 1.11

4. Iron has a density of $\rho_{Fe} = 7.9$ g/cm³, and mercury has a density of $\rho_{Hg} = 13.6$ g/cm³. A piece of iron is placed in a pool of mercury. Which expression gives the ratio of volume of iron above the surface to volume below the surface of the liquid?

    A. ρ_{Fe}/ρ_{Hg}
    B. ρ_{Hg}/ρ_{Fe}
    C. $1 - \rho_{Fe}/\rho_{Hg}$
    D. $\rho_{Hg}/\rho_{Fe} - 1$

5. A 70-kg man would weigh $mg = (70 \text{ kg})(9.8 \text{ m/s}^2) = 686$ N if there were no air. How much weight does the buoyancy due to air take off the man's weight? (The density of the man is about 1 g/cm³, and the density of air is about 1.2×10^{-3} g/cm³.)

    A. 0.08 N
    B. 0.12 N
    C. 0.8 N
    D. 8 N

Use the following for questions 6 and 7:

Sarah is in a basket hanging from a balloon filled with helium.

M = mass of basket, Sarah, and empty balloon
ρ_{He} = density of helium gas at 27° C and 1 atm
ρ_{air} = density of air at 27° C and 1 atm

6. Which expression is an approximation for the density of helium in g/cm³?

    A. $\dfrac{1}{(0.0821)(27)(1000)}$

    B. $\dfrac{4}{(0.0821)(27)(1000)}$

    C. $\dfrac{1}{(0.0821)(300)(1000)}$

    D. $\dfrac{4}{(0.0821)(300)(1000)}$

7. To what volume should the balloon be filled to achieve neutral buoyancy? (Ignore the volume of Sarah, but include the weight of the helium.)

    A. $\dfrac{M}{\rho_{He}} - \dfrac{M}{\rho_{air}}$

    B. $\dfrac{M}{\rho_{He}}\left(1 - \dfrac{\rho_{He}}{\rho_{air}}\right)$

    C. $\dfrac{M}{2\rho_{He}}\left(1 - \dfrac{\rho_{He}}{\rho_{air}}\right)$

    D. $\dfrac{M}{\rho_{air} - \rho_{He}}$

8. What is the pressure 5 meters below the surface of the ocean? ($\rho_{water} = 10^3$ kg/m³, $P_{atm} = 1.01 \times 10^5$ Pa)

    A. 5×10^4 Pa
    B. 7.5×10^4 Pa
    C. 1.0×10^5 Pa
    D. 1.5×10^5 Pa

9. What is the gauge pressure 5 meters below the surface of the ocean? ($\rho_{water} = 10^3$ kg/m³, $P_{atm} = 1.01 \times 10^5$ Pa)

   A. 5×10^4 Pa
   B. 7.5×10^4 Pa
   C. 1.0×10^5 Pa
   D. 1.5×10^5 Pa

Use the following for questions 10 and 11:

A man is swimming in the ocean and breathing through a snorkel.

When his chest is about 1 meter under water, he has a difficult time breathing.

Use the following information:

$P_{atm} = 1.01 \times 10^5$ Pa
$\rho_{water} = 10^3$ kg/m³
$\rho_{air} = 1.2$ kg/m³
$g = 10$ m/s²

10. Why is it difficult for the man to breathe?

   A. His lungs are expanding against a net 10^4 Pa of pressure.
   B. His lungs are expanding against a net 1.01×10^5 Pa of pressure.
   C. His lungs are expanding against a net 1.1×10^5 Pa of pressure.
   D. His lungs are expanding against a net 2.02×10^5 Pa of pressure.

11. Which expression most nearly gives the force his muscles must exert to push out his chest?

   A. (gauge pressure of the water)x(area of his chest)
   B. (gauge pressure of the water)x(area of snorkel hole)
   C. (pressure of the atmosphere)x(area of his chest)
   D. (pressure of the atmosphere)x(area of snorkel hole)

12. The figure shows a simple barometer which consists of a U-tube with one end closed (1) and the other end open to the atmosphere (2).

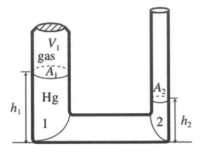

The liquid in the barometer is mercury, with a density of $\rho_{Hg} = 13.6$ g/cm³. The height of mercury in column 1 is h_1, and the cross-sectional area is A_1. The height of mercury in column 2 is h_2, and the cross-sectional area is A_2. Volume 1 is filled with an unknown gas.

What is the best expression for the pressure in volume 1?

   A. $\frac{h_2 - h_1}{h_1} P_{atm}$
   B. $\frac{A_1 h_1}{A_2 h_2} P_{atm}$
   C. $\frac{h_2}{h_1} P_{atm}$
   D. $P_{atm} - \rho_{Hg} g (h_1 - h_2)$

Use the following for questions 13–15:

A hydraulic press is used to lift heavy objects, such as cars. It consists of a U-tube, one end having large cross-sectional area A_1; and the other, small cross-sectional area A_2. The tube is filled with an incompressible fluid, and the load is placed on a platform fitted to area A_1. (See figure.)

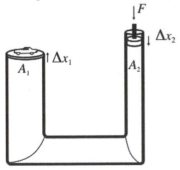

The object is lifted by applying a force to a piston fitted to area A_2. If the piston moves down a distance Δx_2, then the load moves up a distance Δx_1. These distances are small compared to the other dimensions of the device. We assume losses due to friction are negligible.

13. If the piston and the load are at the same height, and the pressure of the fluid near the piston is P_2, what is the pressure of the fluid near the load?

    A. P_2

    B. $\dfrac{A_1}{A_2} P_2$

    C. $\dfrac{A_2}{A_1} P_2$

    D. $\dfrac{A_1 + A_2}{A_1} P_2$

14. If the force exerted by the piston is F_2, what load can be lifted?

    A. $\dfrac{A_1}{A_2} F_2$

    B. $\dfrac{A_2}{A_1} F_2$

    C. $\dfrac{A_1 + A_2}{A_1 A_2} F_2$

    D. $\dfrac{A_1 A_2}{A_1 + A_2} F_2$

15. If the work done by the piston on the fluid is W_2, and the work done by the fluid on the load is W_1, which is correct?

    A. W_1 is less than W_2.
    B. W_1 is equal to W_2.
    C. W_1 is greater than W_2.
    D. There is not enough information to determine a relationship between W_1 and W_2.

16. The two flasks shown in the figure have no ambient atmosphere, that is, they exist in a chamber in which the atmosphere has been removed.

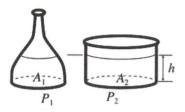

    Both flasks contain mercury to a height h. The volume of mercury in the second flask is three times the volume of mercury in the first flask. The area at the bottom of the second flask is twice that of the first flask. Pressure P_1 is the pressure at the bottom of the first flask, and P_2 is the pressure at the bottom of the second flask. Which equation holds?

    A. $P_2 = P_1/2$
    B. $P_2 = P_1$
    C. $P_2 = 3P_1/2$
    D. $P_2 = 3P_1$

17. The figure shows a simple barometer, which is essentially a U-tube with one end leading to a reservoir whose pressure is desired and the other end open to the atmosphere.

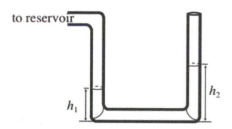

    The liquid in the tube is water, with a density of $\rho = 1.0$ g/cm^3. The height of water in the reservoir column is h_1. The height of water in the open column is h_2. What would happen to the height difference $h_2 - h_1$ if the water were replaced by salt water with a density 1.2 g/cm^3?

    A. It would decrease.
    B. It would stay the same.
    C. It would increase.
    D. There is not enough information to answer this question.

18. A thread (diameter d) in the shape of a rectangle (length l, width w) is lying on the surface of the water. If γ is the surface tension of water ($\gamma = 7.2 \times 10^{-2}$ N/m), then what is the maximum weight that the thread can have without sinking?

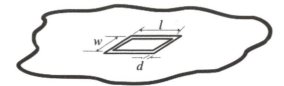

A. $2\gamma(l + w)$
B. $4\gamma(l + w)$
C. $\gamma d(l + w)$
D. $\gamma \pi d(l + w)$

19. A wire circle is sitting on the surface of the water, and a solid circle of the same diameter is also sitting on the water. Which one can have the larger maximum mass without sinking?

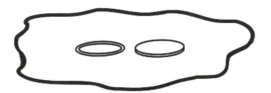

A. The wire circle, by a factor of 2.
B. They have the same maximum mass.
C. The solid circle, by a factor of 2.
D. The solid circle, by a factor of 4.

Use the following for questions 20–21:

A pipe with a circular cross section has water flowing in it from A to B. The radius of the pipe at A is 6 cm, while the radius at B is 3 cm. At end A the flow rate is 0.06 m³/s.

20. What is the flow rate at end B?

A. 0.03 m³/s
B. 0.06 m³/s
C. 0.12 m³/s
D. 0.24 m³/s

21. A tiny propeller is inserted at point A in order to measure the velocity of the water. What does it read?

A. 21 m/s
B. 67 m/s
C. 85 m/s
D. 96 m/s

22. A pipe has a circular cross section, such that the radius of the pipe at point A is r_A, while the radius at B is r_B. An incompressible fluid is flowing through the pipe at flow rate f. The velocity of the fluid particles at point A is v_A. Which expression gives the velocity of the fluid particles at point B?

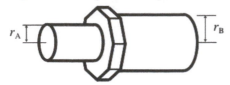

A. fr_B^2
B. $f\pi r_B^2$
C. f/r_B^2
D. $v_A \dfrac{r_A^2}{r_B^2}$

Use the following for questions 23–24:

A piston fits into a sleeve, so that the pressure from combustion in the reaction chamber is used to push the piston back at a constant rate and do useful work. The movement of the piston is lubricated by oil which has a viscosity η. Recall: The force due to viscosity is given by $F_{vis} = \eta A v/d$, where A, v, and d are the relevant surface area, relative velocity, and separation.

The piston has a radius r and a length l, and it moves with velocity v. The sleeve has a radius slightly larger than the piston $r + \Delta r$, such that Δr is very small compared to r. The pressure in the chamber is P_{cham}, and the pressure outside the chamber is P_{amb}.

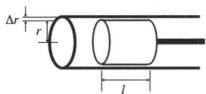

23. Which expression gives the force due to viscosity?

A. $2\pi r l \eta v/\Delta r$
B. $\pi r^2 \eta v/\Delta r$
C. $2\pi r^2 \eta v/\Delta r$
D. $\pi r^2 \eta v/l$

24. Which expression gives the magnitude of the work done by the pressure outside the chamber on the piston during the time Δt?

A. $P_{amb} r^2 v \Delta t$
B. $P_{amb} \pi r^2 v \Delta t$
C. $P_{amb} 2\pi r^2 v \Delta t$
D. $P_{amb} \pi r l v \Delta t$

Use the following for questions 25–26:

A hockey puck of area A and mass m rides on an air hockey table, so that the puck sits on a cushion of air (which has a thickness d and viscosity η). The puck is connected to a thread whose other end is attached to a vertical small rod, so the puck travels a large circle of radius R (R is much larger than the radius of the puck, as shown in the figure). The rod exerts a small torque to maintain the circular motion over time, since otherwise the puck would gradually slow down and stop. The puck turns with frequency f (revolutions per unit time). The force due to viscosity is $F_{vis} = \eta A v / d$.

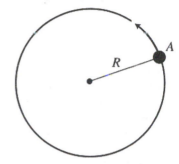

25. If v is the velocity of the puck, which gives the best expression for v?

    A. Rf
    B. πRf
    C. $2\pi Rf$
    D. $\pi R^2 f$

26. Which expression gives the torque which the rod must exert?

    A. $\dfrac{R\eta A v}{d}$

    B. $\dfrac{2\pi R\eta A v}{d}$

    C. $m\dfrac{v^2}{R}$

    D. $R\left(m\dfrac{v^2}{R}\right)$

27. Reynold's number is given by $Re = l\rho v/\eta$, where l is the length scale of the pipe or of obstacles, ρ is the density of the fluid, v is the velocity of the fluid, and η is the viscosity. The greater Reynold's number for a given flow, the more likely it is that turbulence will develop. Consider water flowing in a pipe. Which of the following would tend to reduce the likelihood of turbulent flow?

    A. Increase the flow rate.
    B. Make the joints in the pipe smooth.
    C. Raise the temperature.
    D. Increase the radius of the pipe.

Use the following for questions 28–30:

Water in a certain sprinkler system flows through a level hose connected to a nozzle which is directed upward. The water leaves the nozzle and shoots to a height h before falling back down again into a pool. (See figure.)

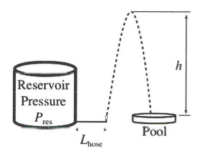

The hose is connected to a reservoir which maintains the water there at a pressure P_{res}. Assume the flow has no viscosity from the reservoir until it gets out of the nozzle. Use the following notation:

A_{noz} = cross-sectional area of the nozzle
L_{hose} = length of the hose
P_{atm} = pressure of the outside atmosphere
ρ = density of water.

28. Which gives the best expression for the velocity of the water just after it leaves the nozzle?

    A. $\sqrt{\dfrac{P_{res} - P_{atm}}{\rho}}$

    B. $\sqrt{\dfrac{2\left(P_{res} - P_{atm}\right)}{\rho}}$

    C. $\dfrac{P_{res} - P_{atm}}{\rho}\sqrt{\dfrac{L_{hose}}{gA_{noz}}}$

    D. $\dfrac{P_{res}}{\rho}\sqrt{\dfrac{L_{hose}}{gA_{noz}}}$

29. Which gives the best expression for the height h?

    A. $\dfrac{P_{res} - P_{atm}}{\rho g}$

    B. $\dfrac{2(P_{res} - P_{atm})}{\rho g}$

    C. $\dfrac{P_{res} - P_{atm}}{\rho g}\dfrac{L_{hose}^{2}}{A_{noz}}$

    D. $\dfrac{P_{res} - P_{atm}}{\rho g}\dfrac{A_{noz}}{L_{hose}^{2}}$

30. Does Bernoulli's principle apply for the water which falls into the pool?

    A. No, because the water develops viscosity.
    B. No, because the water develops turbulence.
    C. No, because the water returns to the level of the nozzle.
    D. No, because the pool is not part of the flow.

Use the following for questions 31–32:

A tank of water has a hose coming out of the top. The hose is filled with water and the other end is below the tank, so that the system acts as a syphon. The end of the hose outside the tank is at height $h = 0$ meters. The bottom of the tank is at height h_1, the end of the hose inside the tank is at height h_2, and the top of the water is at height h_3. Assume the flow is without viscosity.

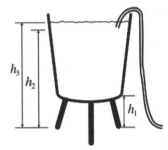

31. Which is the best expression for the velocity of the flow coming out of the hose?

    A. $\sqrt{2gh_1}$
    B. $\sqrt{2gh_2}$
    C. $\sqrt{2gh_3}$
    D. $\sqrt{2g(h_3 - h_1)}$

32. Which is the best expression for the pressure at the bottom of the tank?

    A. $P_{atm} - \rho g(h_3 - h_1)$
    B. $P_{atm} + \rho g(h_3 - h_1)$
    C. $P_{atm} - \rho g(h_3 + h_1)$
    D. $P_{atm} + \rho g(h_3 + h_1)$

Use the following for questions 33–35:

In a chemistry laboratory it is often useful to create a partial vacuum. A simple way to do this involves connecting a wide pipe to a narrow pipe which is connected to a reservoir of water (just the water line). The reservoir has pressure greater than the ambient atmospheric pressure, but once flow is established, the pressure in the narrow tube is less than atmospheric pressure. A valve can be placed in the narrow tube to take advantage of the partial vacuum. Assume that there is no viscosity and that gravity plays no role. Use the following notation:

    ρ = density of water
    ρ_{air} = density of air
    P_{res} = pressure of the reservoir
    P_{atm} = atmospheric pressure
    A_1 = cross-sectional area of the narrow tube
    A_2 = cross-sectional area of the wide tube
    v_1 = velocity of water in the narrow tube
    v_2 = velocity of water in the wide tube

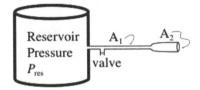

33. Which gives the best expression for v_2?

    A. $\sqrt{\dfrac{P_{res} - P_{atm}}{\rho}}$
    B. $\sqrt{\dfrac{2(P_{res} - P_{atm})}{\rho}}$
    C. $\sqrt{\dfrac{P_{res} - P_{atm}}{\rho}}\left(\dfrac{A_2}{A_1}\right)$
    D. $\sqrt{\dfrac{P_{res} - P_{atm}}{\rho}}\left(\dfrac{A_1}{A_2}\right)$

34. Which gives the best expression for v_1?

    A. $\left(\dfrac{A_1}{A_2}\right)v_2$
    B. $\left(\dfrac{A_2}{A_1}\right)v_2$
    C. $\left(\dfrac{P_{res}}{P_{atm}}\right)v_2$
    D. $\left(\dfrac{P_{atm}}{P_{res}}\right)v_2$

35. Which gives the best expression for P_1, the pressure in the narrow tube?

A. $\left(\dfrac{\rho_{air}}{\rho}\right) P_{atm}$

B. $\left(\dfrac{A_1}{A_2}\right) P_{atm}$

C. $P_{res} - \dfrac{1}{2}\rho v_1{}^2$

D. $P_{atm} - \dfrac{1}{2}\rho v_1{}^2$

This page intentionally left blank.

CHAPTER 9
PERIODIC MOTION AND WAVES

A. INTRODUCTION

This chapter begins the study of waves. Waves govern many of the phenomena we experience every day, such as sound and light. In this chapter we look at what these various wave phenomena have in common, their so-called "wavelike" nature. In the following two chapters we will look at sound and light separately.

For these chapters it will be important to have pen and paper ready to recopy diagrams and rework problems. But it is especially important to have ready a mental pad of paper. You need to visualize the to-and-fro motion of the medium, the shape of waves, and the bending and reflecting of waves. Only in this way will the few formulas and ideas become intuitive.

B. SPRINGS

If you stretch a spring, the spring exerts a pull on you. The more you stretch it, the more it pulls. If you compress a spring capable of being compressed, then it exerts a push. Hooke's law states that the force is proportional to the extension or compression.

Hooke's Law
If a spring has resting length l_0 and it is stretched (or compressed) to a length l_0+x, then it exerts a force

$$F_{spring} = kx \quad , \quad (1)$$

where k is the spring constant in [N/m], and the force of the spring is opposite the direction of the push or pull. (See Figure 9-1)

Let's be clear about the forces involved here. Figure 9-2 shows a spring attached to a wall stretched by a hand. Figure 9-3 shows all the forces involved. The force F_1 is the force the spring exerts on the wall, and F_2 is the force the wall exerts on the spring. These forces are equal in magnitude because of the third law of motion. The force F_3 is the force the hand exerts on the spring, and F_4 is the force the spring exerts on the hand. The forces F_3 and F_4 are equal in magnitude because of the third law of motion as well. The forces F_2 and F_3 add to zero because of the **second** law of motion, because the spring is not accelerating, giving force balance. All these forces are equal in magnitude (for various reasons), but there are four forces.

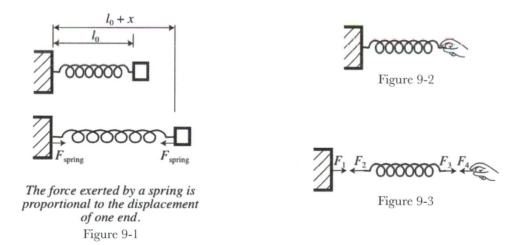

The force exerted by a spring is
proportional to the displacement
of one end.
Figure 9-1

Figure 9-2

Figure 9-3

In spring problems, as in many types of physics problems, it is important to follow the energy. The potential energy of a stretched or compressed spring is as follows:

$$E_p = \frac{1}{2}kx^2. \qquad (2)$$

This energy is the second type of potential energy we have encountered. In many problems, we can treat this potential energy like gravitational potential energy.

Conservation of Energy, Again

If there is no friction, no crashing, no heat generation, and if each force is a potential force or does no work, then the sum of kinetic and potential energies is constant, so we have

$$E_K + E_P = \text{constant.} \qquad (3)$$

The expression E_P includes both gravitational and spring energies, although in most problems it represents just one or the other.

Example: One end of a horizontal spring ($k = 20$ N/m) is connected to a wall, and the other end is connected to a mass m (0.2 kg). The spring is compressed 0.1 m from equilibrium. After it is released, how much work does the spring do in order to push the mass to the equilibrium position?

Solution: Our first idea is to write the work equation: $W = F_{spring}\Delta x \cos\phi = F_{spring}\Delta x = (20$ N/m 3 0.1 m$)$ (0.1 m) = 0.2 J. But this would be WRONG. The force of the spring begins at $(20$ N/m$)$ (0.1 m) = 2 N, but then it decreases as the spring moves the mass. (See Figure 9-4, showing the system at three different times.) In the work equation we assume the force is constant. What shall we do?

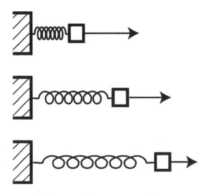

The spring's force changes as the mass moves, so the equation $W = F\Delta x$ does not apply.

Figure 9-4

Let's think about the flow of energy after the release. The work done by the spring on the mass is the same as the change in kinetic energy of the mass (by energy conservation), that is,

$$W_{tot} = \Delta E_K$$

But the kinetic energy of the mass comes from the potential energy of the spring, so we have

$$W_{tot} = \Delta E_K = -\Delta E_P$$

$$= E_{P1} - E_{P2}$$

$$= 1/2\ kx^2 - 0$$

$$= 1/2\ (20\text{ N/m})(0.1\text{ m})^2 = 0.1\text{ J}$$

This is one of those problems in which blind plugging into the formulas is to no avail, but thinking about the energy flow is the key to success.

C. PERIODIC MOTION: ONE OSCILLATOR

Let's think about a mass m connected to a horizontal spring (resting length l_0, spring constant k) which is connected to a wall. The mass is sitting on a frictionless floor (so we can ignore vertical forces). We stretch the spring to length $l_0 + A$ and let go. What happens?

At first the spring pulls the mass back towards equilibrium. As the mass goes faster, the displacement x and force F_{spring} decrease. When the spring is length l_0, the mass is moving velocity $-v_{max}$. Because the length is l_0 (and thus $x = 0$), the restoring force and acceleration are zero. The maximum displacement occurs when $v = 0$ and the magnitude of the spring force is very large. Figure 9-5 shows the movement at five times. Spend some time making sure you understand every entry on the table. In the first line the negative sign of the acceleration indicates the acceleration vector points left, the same as the force of the spring. This motion is called ***simple harmonic motion***.

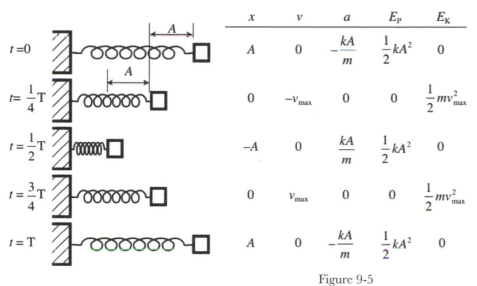

	x	v	a	E_P	E_K
$t = 0$	A	0	$-\dfrac{kA}{m}$	$\dfrac{1}{2}kA^2$	0
$t = \dfrac{1}{4}T$	0	$-v_{max}$	0	0	$\dfrac{1}{2}mv_{max}^2$
$t = \dfrac{1}{2}T$	$-A$	0	$\dfrac{kA}{m}$	$\dfrac{1}{2}kA^2$	0
$t = \dfrac{3}{4}T$	0	v_{max}	0	0	$\dfrac{1}{2}mv_{max}^2$
$t = T$	A	0	$-\dfrac{kA}{m}$	$\dfrac{1}{2}kA^2$	0

Figure 9-5

Energy changes from potential to kinetic and back again, but the total energy is conserved. We have

$$
\begin{aligned}
E_T &= E_P + E_K \quad (= \text{constant}) \\
&= \frac{1}{2}kx^2 + \frac{1}{2}mv^2 .
\end{aligned}
\tag{4}
$$

The maximum displacement of the mass from equilibrium is the ***amplitude A***. The ***period T*** is the time it takes for the system to go through one cycle, and it has units [s]. The ***frequency f*** is the number of cycles a system goes through in a unit of time, and it has units [1/s = Hertz = Hz]. We have

$$
T = \frac{1}{f} .
\tag{5}
$$

The frequency is related to the spring constant and the mass as follows:

$$
f = \frac{1}{2\pi}\sqrt{\frac{k}{m}}
\tag{6}
$$

Let's see if this equation makes sense. We would guess that a system with a stiff spring would have a high frequency (think about it), so it makes sense that k should be in the numerator. As k increases, f increases. Also a larger mass will decrease the frequency, so it makes sense that m is in the denominator. The square root is needed to make the units agree.

Let's consider a similar set up. In a pendulum we have a bob connected to a string or a light rod, which is connected to a ceiling of some sort. In this case, the restoring force is provided not by a spring but by a component of gravity. In Figure 9-6, the solid arrows are the two forces on the bob, and the dashed arrows show the gravitational force divided into components, along the supporting rod and perpendicular to it. The restoring force is the latter

$$F_\perp = mg \sin\theta \approx mg\theta \qquad (7)$$

where $\sin\theta$ is approximately equal to θ (measured in radians) for small angles. Note the similarity of this equation to equation (1). In both, the force is proportional to the displacement, so the motion is similar.
The frequency of a pendulum is given by

$$f = \frac{1}{2\pi}\sqrt{\frac{g}{l}} \qquad (8)$$

Note that the mass of the bob m does not appear in this equation, so a 10-kg mass swings on a 3-m string with the same period as a 0.1-kg mass swinging on a 3-m string. You need not memorize this equation, but you should be familiar with the fact that m does not appear in it.

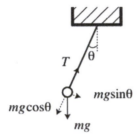

A pendulum operates by a principal similar to that of a spring with a mass.
Figure 9-6

D. PERIODIC MOTION: TWO CONNECTED OSCILLATORS

In the last section we looked at a single oscillator moving in one dimension. Figure 9-7 shows a slightly more complicated system with two similar pendulums connected by a weak spring. Let's look at some general characteristics of this system.

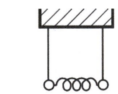

Two pendulums connected by a weak coupling (spring).
Figure 9-7

If one of the pendulums is set to swinging, the other pendulum hardly moves at first because the coupling is weak. Gradually, the second pendulum swings higher and higher, while the first pendulum swings less and less. Then the first pendulum comes almost to a stop while the second one swings with the original amplitude of the first. The energy of swinging has transferred from the first pendulum to the second. (See Figure 9-8.)

Now the situation is reversed from the original set up. The second pendulum now transfers energy to the first pendulum. This continues until the second one is at rest and the first is swinging.
This is an example of a general principle.

> If two weakly connected oscillators have similar frequencies, and if the energy starts in one oscillator, then the energy tends to be slowly transfer back and forth between the oscillators. This is called *resonance*.

Figure 9-8 shows two pendulums with a very weak spring connecting them.

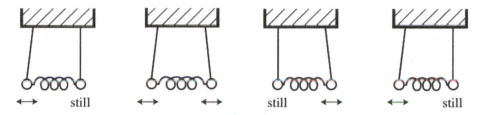

These are two pendula weakly connected by a spring. The energy in the first pendulum is slowly transferred to the second then slowly back again.

Figure 9-8

Another example of resonance involves a soprano, a wine glass, and the air between them. The soprano can tap the glass to hear its natural frequency. If she sings that note very loudly, then the energy starts in one oscillator, her vocal cords, and transfers to the other oscillator, the wine glass, by the weak coupling, the air. In this case, enough energy enters the wine glass to cause it to go into a nonlinear regime, and it bursts.

E. WAVES, AN INTRODUCTION

When you throw a rock into an otherwise calm lake, the circular ripples carry energy and momentum away from the original disturbance. These ripples are waves (Figure 9-9). When you see a ripple across a field of grain, that is not a wave, because it is the wind pushing the grain, and the grain itself does not carry any energy or momentum.

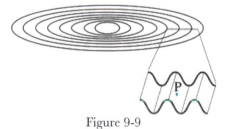

Figure 9-9

> A *wave* is a disturbance (small movement or change) in a medium such that, although the medium moves hardly at all, the disturbance travels a long distance, transporting energy.

Figure 9-10 shows water waves frozen at several moments in time. The waves are moving to the right. A water skater sitting at point P goes up and down and up with period T, measured in [s]. Of course, his frequency is $f = 1/T$. The **wavelength** λ is the length from peak to peak (or trough to trough or ascending zero point to ascending zero point). The wavelength is measured in [m]. The **amplitude A** is a measure of the size of the disturbance, measured from the equilibrium point to the high point. The units depend on the kind of wave it is and on how we measure it.

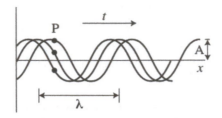

*A water wave moves to the
right but keeps its shape.*

Figure 9-10

The velocity of a wave is given by

$$v = \lambda f. \tag{9}$$

In many cases the velocity is constant, and this formula simply relates frequency and wavelength. Watch for this on the MCAT.

In a wave, if the disturbance of the medium is in the same direction as the direction of wave travel, then the wave is called **longitudinal**. Figure 9-11 shows a longitudinal wave on a spring. The small arrows show the direction of the displacement, and the large arrow shows the direction of travel.

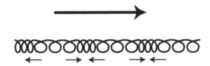

*The arrows show the
displacement in this longitudinal
wave. The large arrow shows the
direction of wave travel.*

Figure 9-11

If the disturbance of the medium is perpendicular to the direction of wave travel, then the wave is called **transverse**. Figure 9-12 shows two examples of transverse waves. Transverse waves are capable of being **polarized**, that is, they can be confined to moving in one of two dimensions. Unpolarized transverse waves are a random mixture of the two polarizations. Longitudinal waves cannot be polarized.

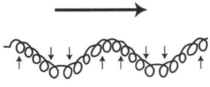

up and down

in and out of page

*The arrows show the displacement
in these polarized transverse
waves. The large arrow shows the
direction of wave travel.*

Figure 9-12

The table below shows most of the examples of waves that you need to know for the MCAT.

Wave	Longitudinal/Transverse	Medium
water wave	both	water
wave on plucked string	T	string
sound	L	air
earthquake	both	earth
light	T	electric, magnetic fields

F. INTERFERENCE

When two particles come together, like two balls or two cars, they generally collide in some manner. When two waves come together, they do not collide but jumble together in a process called *interference*. It is not as complicated as it sounds. For example, consider a wave on a lake (amplitude 7 cm, wavelength 4 m) arriving from the north, such that at point A at time 12:30 (exactly) its height would be +5 cm if it were the only wave around (Figure 9-13). Now another wave (amplitude 10 cm, wavelength 6 m) arrives from the east, such that at time 12:30 its height would be −2 cm if it were the only wave around. The resulting height of the water at 12:30 at point A is (+5 + −2) cm = +3 cm. (These heights are measured relative to the equilibrium height of the water.) Three seconds later, let's say, wave 1 would have height +7 cm and wave 2, −1 cm. Then the new height, with both waves, would be (+2 + −1) cm = +1 cm.

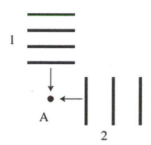

When two waves come together, they interfere.

Figure 9-13

Principle of Superposition
When two waves come together, the resulting displacement of the medium is the sum of the individual displacements.

Figure 9-14 shows another example of this, in which two wave pulses come together, one from the right and one from the left.

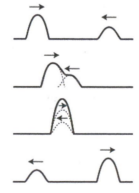

Transverse pulses interfere.

Figure 9-14

Figure 9-15 shows a third example of interference on water. In this example a wave train from the left encounters a wave train from the right with the same wavelength. Water skaters are sitting on the water at points A, B, and C.

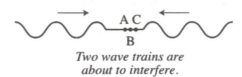

*Two wave trains are
about to interfere.*
Figure 9-15

The skater at point A experiences the up–down–up–down–up from the wave on the left and the up–down–up–down–up from the wave on the right. Superposition tells us that the resulting motion is added, so A experiences increased amplitude UP–DOWN–UP–DOWN–UP. This is called ***constructive interference***, when two wave forms add in such a way as to create maximal displacement of the medium. The two waves are said to be ***in phase***, and point A is called an ***antinode***. Their relative phase is said to be 0. The resulting amplitude is the sum of the individual amplitudes.

For the water skater at C, the left wave is up–down–up–down–up, and the right wave is down–up–down–up–down. By superposition we see that the resulting motion is no displacement at all. This is called ***destructive interference***, when the wave forms tend to cancel and give minimal displacement. The two waves are said to be ***out of phase***, and point C is called a ***node***. Their relative phase is said to be 180°. The resulting amplitude is the difference of the individual amplitudes.

For the water skater at B, the relative phase is between 0° and 180°, and the interference is neither in phase nor out of phase but somewhere in between. The resulting amplitude is somewhere in between as well.

Figure 9-16 shows a fourth example of interference, this time with sound waves. Stereo speakers are at points 1 and 2, both producing a pure tone (sine wave) of wavelength λ in phase. Alice and Bob are listening to the speakers.

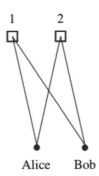

*Sound waves arriving from
speakers 1 and 2 interfere where
Alice sits (and where Bob sits).*
Figure 9-16

Alice is an equal distance from both speakers. Figure 9-17 shows the waves traveling from speakers to Alice. Since the waves begin in phase and travel equal distances, they arrive in phase. If only speaker 1 were making sound, the wave arriving at her ear would look like that shown in Figure 9-18. If only speaker 2 were making a sound, the wave arriving at her ear would look like that shown in the same figure. Note that these figures show displacement of air particles versus time. Figure 9-19 shows what Alice hears with both speakers. She experiences constructive interference, so she hears a sound of greater intensity than that from one speaker.

Figure 9-17

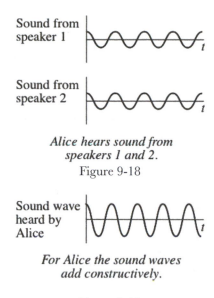

Sound from speaker 1

Sound from speaker 2

Alice hears sound from speakers 1 and 2.

Figure 9-18

Sound wave heard by Alice

For Alice the sound waves add constructively.

Figure 9-19

Bob, however, is further away from speaker 1 than from speaker 2 by half a wavelength. What difference does half a wavelength make? The wave arriving from speaker 1 has further to go, so when a peak is coming from speaker 2, a trough is just arriving from speaker 1. (See Figure 9-20.) Figure 9-21 shows the sound waves from the two speakers. Figure 9-22 shows what Bob hears, nothing.

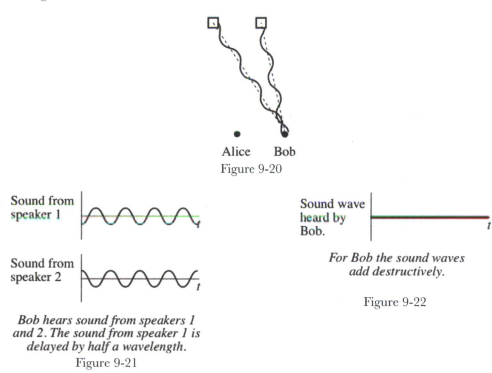

Alice   Bob

Figure 9-20

Sound from speaker 1

Sound from speaker 2

Bob hears sound from speakers 1 and 2. The sound from speaker 1 is delayed by half a wavelength.

Figure 9-21

Sound wave heard by Bob.

For Bob the sound waves add destructively.

Figure 9-22

Note: In real life it is difficult to hear this phenomenon fully, since the amplitudes of the two speakers are rarely exactly the same. However, architects of orchestra halls often must guard against the possibility of "dead spots", where certain notes made by the concert master's violin, for example, cannot be heard well.

Calculations of this type get complicated fairly quickly, beyond the scope of the MCAT. But you should recognize constructive and destructive interference when you see it (or hear it). In any wave phenomenon, when there are bands of strong and weak amplitude, you should suspect that constructive and destructive interference is the cause. And you should recognize this:

> Constructive interference occurs when two waves differ by no wavelengths, or one, or two, or cetera. Destructive interference occurs when two waves differ by half a wavelength, or 3/2, or 5/2, or cetera.

G. STANDING WAVES

So far we have been talking of waves that are unconstrained by boundaries, or *traveling waves*. *Standing waves* are waves constrained inside a cavity. The main difference is that traveling waves may have any frequency at all, whereas standing waves have only certain allowed frequencies, and there is a lowest frequency.

Think about a wave on an infinite string. There is nothing to constrain your imagination to think of waves of any wavelength. Now think about a wave on a guitar string. The fixed ends now constrain your imagination, so that the longest wavelength you can imagine would look something like that shown in Figure 9-23. How could it be any longer, with the ends forced to be at equilibrium points?

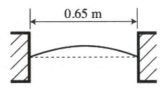

*Lowest frequency mode for
a string held at both ends.*

Figure 9-23

> Waves trapped in a cavity may have only certain allowed frequencies. Generally there are an infinite number of allowed frequencies, but there is a lowest possible frequency, a next lowest, and so on. These are standing waves.

A mode of motion in which every part of the medium moves back and forth at the same frequency is called a normal mode. The example of the guitar string will help make this clear.

Example 1: A guitar string has a wave velocity 285 m/s, and it is 0.65 m long. What is the lowest frequency that can be played on it? (The lowest frequency corresponds to the normal mode with no nodes except at the ends.)

Solution: Figure 9-23 shows the normal mode for the lowest frequency.

A full wavelength looks like

So, Figure 9-23 is half a wavelength. We write

$$\lambda = 1.3m,$$

$$f = v / \lambda$$

$$= \frac{285 \frac{m}{s}}{1.3m}$$

$$= 220\frac{1}{s} = 220Hz$$

This frequency is called the *fundamental*.

Example 2: What is the second lowest frequency that can be excited on the same guitar string?

Solution: Figure 9-24 shows the normal mode with one node between the ends. That is, the midpoint of this string experiences destructive interference and thus no motion at all. For this mode the wavelength is $\lambda - 0.65$ m. We write

$$f = v/\lambda$$

$$= 440 \text{ Hz}$$

This frequency is called the **second harmonic** (the first harmonic being the fundamental, but that is always called the *fundamental*).

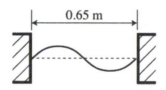

0.65 m

*Next lowest frequency mode
for a string held at both ends.*

Figure 9-24

Example 3: What is the third lowest frequency that can be excited on the guitar string?

Solution: Figure 9-25 shows the normal mode with two nodes between the ends. The wavelength is given by

$$\lambda = \frac{2}{3}(0.65m) = 0.433m,$$

$$f = \frac{285\frac{m}{s}}{0.433}$$

$$= 660Hz$$

This is the **third harmonic**.

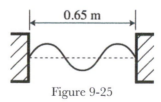

0.65 m

Figure 9-25

When you pluck a guitar string, you hear all these frequencies with varying amplitudes, so the guitar string is not in a normal mode but in a mixed state.

These normal modes are all sine waves on a string. Here are some general rules for drawing normal modes:

1. It is important to get the ends correct (for example, the ends of a guitar string are nodes).
2. For the fundamental there are as few nodes as possible, usually none, excluding the end points.
3. Each following harmonic adds one node (only rarely more).

In this chapter we explored springs and waves. To solve problems involving stationary springs, it is important to draw accurate force diagrams and remember the spring equation $F_{spring} = kx$. To solve problems involving moving springs, it is often more important to follow the energy flow. The potential energy of a spring stretched (or compressed) by a distance x is $E_p = kx^2/2$. You should practice doing this sort of problem.

Waves involve a small movement of a medium which propagates to great distances, transporting energy. Often waves have a characteristic frequency f and a wavelength λ, and these are connected by the wave velocity $v = f\lambda$. When waves come together they exhibit interference. If they interfere constructively, they create a wave with large amplitude. If they interfere destructively, they create a wave with small amplitude. Whenever you encounter bands of light and dark (light waves) or loud and soft (sound waves), it is likely that interference is part of the explanation as to why the bands formed.

Standing waves are waves trapped in a cavity. They have the distinguishing characteristic that only certain frequencies are allowed: a lowest, and a next lowest, and so on.

CHAPTER 9 PROBLEMS

Use the following for questions 1 and 2:

An ideal, massless spring (spring constant 2.5 N/m and resting length 0.15 m) is hanging from the ceiling. (Use acceleration due to gravity $g = 10$ m/s^2.)

1. A mass of 0.8 kg is added to the bottom end of the spring, and the system is allowed to reach a static equilibrium. What is the length of the spring?

    A. 0.47 m
    B. 3.05 m
    C. 3.20 m
    D. 3.35 m

2. If the 0.8 kg mass in the previous question were pulled down an additional 10 cm (that is, below its equilibrium length) and released, what is the magnitude of the net force on the mass just after the release?

    A. 0.25 N
    B. 7.75 N
    C. 8.00 N
    D. 8.25 N

Use the following for questions 3–5:

One end of a spring (spring constant 50 N/m) is fixed at point P, while the other end is connected to a mass m (which is 5 kg). The fixed end and the mass sit on a horizontal frictionless surface, so that the mass and the spring are able to rotate about P. The mass moves in a circle of radius $R = 2$ m, and the force on the mass is 10 N.

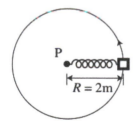

3. How long does it take for the mass to go around P once?

    A. 1.00 s
    B. 3.14 s
    C. 4.00 s
    D. 6.28 s

4. What is the resting length of the spring?

    A. 0.2 m
    B. 1.8 m
    C. 2.0 m
    D. 2.2 m

5. What is the amount of potential energy stored in the spring?

    A. 1 J
    B. 2 J
    C. 100 J
    D. 200 J

The figure shows a pendulum at the bottom of its swing. Use this figure for questions 6 and 7.

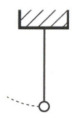

6. What is the direction of the acceleration vector for the bob?

    A. ↑
    B. ↓
    C. ↗
    D. There is no acceleration at this point.

7. What is the direction of the net force on the pendulum bob?

    A. ↑
    B. ↓
    C. ↘
    D. The net force is zero.

Refer to the figure below for questions 8 and 9.

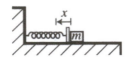

8. A massless spring with spring constant k is connected on one end to a wall and on the other end to a massless plate. A mass m is sitting on a frictionless floor. The mass m is slid against the plate and pushed back a distance x. After its release, it reaches a maximum speed v_1. In a second experiment, the same mass is pushed back a distance $4x$. After its release, it reaches a maximum speed v_2. How does v_2 compare with v_1?

   A. $v_2 = v_1$
   B. $v_2 = 2v_1$
   C. $v_2 = 4v_1$
   D. $v_2 = 16v_1$

9. A massless spring with spring constant k is connected on one end to a wall and on the other end to a massless plate. A mass m is sitting on a frictionless floor. The mass m is slid against the plate and pushed back a distance x. After its release, it reaches a maximum speed v_1. In a second experiment, a larger mass $9m$ is pushed back the same distance x. After its release, it reaches a maximum speed v_2. How does the final kinetic energy E_1 of the first mass compare with the final kinetic energy E_2 of the second mass?

   A. $E_1 = E_2/3$
   B. $E_1 = E_2$
   C. $E_1 = 3E_2$
   D. $E_1 = 9E_2$

Use the following for questions 10 and 11:

A ball of mass m falls from rest from a height and encounters a spring, thus compressing it (see figure). When the ball comes to a momentary stop, it has moved a distance L, compressing the spring a distance x.

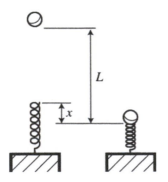

10. Which describes the flow of energy referred to in the problem?

    A. potential to kinetic
    B. kinetic to potential
    C. potential to kinetic to potential
    D. kinetic to potential to kinetic

11. Which expression is an expression for x?

    A. $x = \sqrt{\dfrac{mgL}{2k}}$

    B. $x = \sqrt{\dfrac{mgL}{k}}$

    C. $x = \sqrt{\dfrac{2mgL}{k}}$

    D. $x = \dfrac{g}{mk}$

Use the following information for questions 12–18:

A massless ideal spring projects horizontally from a wall and connects to a mass (0.1 kg). The mass is oscillating in one dimension, such that it moves 0.3 m from one end of its oscillation to the other. It undergoes 20 complete oscillations in 60.0 s. (The frequency is related to the spring constant by $f = \dfrac{1}{2\pi}\sqrt{\dfrac{k}{m}}$.)

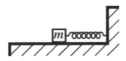

12. What is the period of the oscillation?

    A. 0.333 s
    B. 2.09 s
    C. 3.00 s
    D. 18.8 s

13. What is the frequency of the oscillation?

    A. 0.333 Hz
    B. 2.09 Hz
    C. 3.00 Hz
    D. 18.8 Hz

14. What is the spring constant k?

A. $(0.1)\left(2\pi\dfrac{20}{60}\right)^2$

B. $(0.1)\left(2\pi\dfrac{60}{20}\right)^2$

C. $(0.1)\left(2\pi\dfrac{20}{60}\right)^{1/2}$

D. $(0.1)\left(2\pi\dfrac{60}{20}\right)^{1/2}$

15. What is the amplitude of the oscillation?

A. 0.15 m
B. 0.3 m
C. 0.6 m
D. 3 m

16. How would the frequency change if the spring constant were increased by a factor of 2?

A. It would decrease by a factor of 2.
B. It would increase by 41%.
C. It would increase by a factor of 2.
D. It would increase by a factor of 4.

17. How would the amplitude change if the spring constant were increased by a factor of 2?

A. It would decrease by a factor of 2.
B. It would increase by a factor of 2.
C. It would increase by a factor of 4.
D. None of the above is true.

18. What is the energy flow in such a system?

A. potential to kinetic to heat
B. back and forth from spring potential to kinetic
C. back and forth from gravitational potential to spring potential
D. back and forth from potential to kinetic to heat

Use the following for questions 19–24:

Blocks A (0.1 kg) and B (0.4 kg) ride on a frictionless level surface in one dimension and have Velcro on their sides, so that they stick when they touch. Block B is also connected to a massless, ideal spring (k = 50 N/m) which extends horizontally and is connected to a wall. Initially block B is at rest, and block A approaches from the left (see figure).

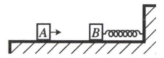

Immediately after the hit, the two blocks are going 0.2 m/s. They then oscillate. Consider the following three statements in questions 19 and 20.

I. Momentum is conserved.
II. Kinetic energy is conserved.
III. The sum of kinetic and spring potential energy is conserved.

19. Which of the statements is true during the collision?

A. I only
B. II only
C. II and III
D. I, II, and III

20. Which of the statements is true during the oscillation?

A. I only
B. III only
C. II and III
D. I, II, and III

21. What is the velocity of block A before the collision?

A. 0.45 m/s
B. 1.0 m/s
C. 2.0 m/s
D. 5.0 m/s

22. How far does the spring get compressed from its resting position?

A. 0.02 m
B. 0.04 m
C. 0.08 m
D. 0.16 m

23. During the oscillation, when is the magnitude of the acceleration the greatest and the direction of the acceleration directed to the right?

    A. When the spring is extended.
    B. When the spring is at its resting length.
    C. When the spring is compressed.
    D. None of the above.

24. Which best describes the flow of energy during the collision?

    A. kinetic to potential
    B. kinetic to chemical
    C. kinetic to potential and chemical
    D. kinetic to kinetic and heat

25. A research and development lab has just built a prototype for a potato peeler. It has many moving parts, but one particular part, the blade patroller, is not supposed to move. When the researchers turn on the machine, they notice that this piece vibrates a little at first, then more, until it is flopping around uselessly. If resonance is responsible for this phenomenon, what can you conclude? Consider the following statements.

    I. There is a weak connection between this vibration and another vibration.
    II. There is a strong connection between this vibration and another vibration.
    III. The two vibrations have similar or equal frequencies.

    A. II only.
    B. I and III.
    C. II and III.
    D. I or II is true, and III is true.

Use the following for questions 26–29:

A water wave is traveling down a narrow channel in a rundown district in Manhattan. A Styrofoam cup is floating on the surface of the water, tossed there by some careless passerby rushing to work. The city, in its rush, ignores this assault to civility, but you are waiting for a taxi, and you notice that it bobs from up to down to up in every two seconds. You decide to take a photograph in order to use up a roll of film. The data for the figure is taken from the photo.

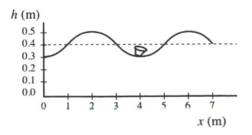

26. What is the wavelength for this wave?

    A. 1 m
    B. 2 m
    C. 4 m
    D. 8 m

27. What is the frequency of this wave?

    A. 0.5 Hz
    B. 1 Hz
    C. 2 Hz
    D. 4 Hz

28. What is the velocity of the wave?

    A. 2 m/s
    B. 3.14 m/s
    C. 4 m/s
    D. 6.28 m/s

29. What is the amplitude of the wave?

    A. 0.1 m
    B. 0.2 m
    C. 2 m
    D. 4 m

Passage 1

When a guitar string is plucked, there are many frequencies of sound which are emitted. The lowest frequency is the note we associate with the string, while the mix of other frequencies gives the sound its *timbre*, or sound quality. The lowest frequency is the *fundamental*, while the higher frequencies make up the *harmonic series*. The next lowest frequency is the second harmonic; the next to lowest, the third harmonic, and so on. The timbre depends on the material of the string (steel or plastic or catgut), on the way it is plucked (middle or at the end), and on the sounding board.

Sometimes some of the frequencies may be suppressed, for example, by lightly holding a finger at a point along the string to force a node there. This is not the same as fretting the string, which involves holding the string all the way down to the neck in order to effectively change the length of the string.

The wave velocity is given by

$$v = \sqrt{T/\mu}$$

where T is the tension in the string, and μ is the linear mass density, which is the product of material density and cross-sectional area.

For the following questions, consider an E string (frequency 660 Hz) which is made of steel. It has a mass of 0.66 grams for each meter of wire and has a circular cross section of diameter 0.33 mm. The string length when strung on a guitar is 0.65 m.

Also note that the D string has a wave velocity of 382 m/s.

30. What is the velocity of a wave on the E string mentioned in paragraph 4?

    A. 214.5 m/s
    B. 429 m/s
    C. 858 m/s
    D. 1716 m/s

31. What is the frequency of the fundamental of the D string?

    A. 294 Hz
    B. 588 Hz
    C. 882 Hz
    D. 1175 Hz

32. What is the frequency of the fourth harmonic of the D string?

    A. 588 Hz
    B. 882 Hz
    C. 1175 Hz
    D. 2350 Hz

33. If the guitarist places her left finger lightly on the D string one fourth way from the neck end to the base, what is the lowest frequency that will be heard?

    A. 588 Hz
    B. 882 Hz
    C. 1175 Hz
    D. 2350 Hz

34. What is the wavelength of the sixth harmonic of the E string?

    A. 0.22 m
    B. 0.325 m
    C. 3.25 m
    D. 20.8 m

35. If we want to increase the frequency of the fundamental of a string by 3%, by how much do we want to change the tension in the string?

    A. increase it by 1.5%
    B. increase it by 3%
    C. increase it by 4.5%
    D. increase it by 6%

This page intentionally left blank.

CHAPTER 10
SOUND

A. INTRODUCTION

Sound is a longitudinal wave in some material medium, usually in air. Alternatively, we can say that sound is a wave of pressure variation, as Figure 10-1 shows.

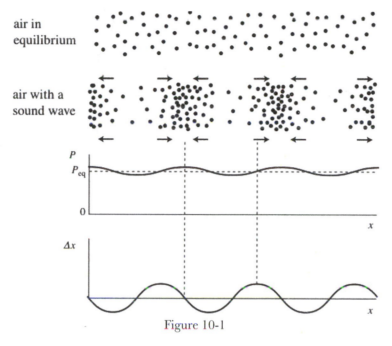

Figure 10-1

Notice several things about the above graphs. The variations of pressure are much smaller than the barometric pressure itself, that is, the equilibrium pressure P_{eq}. In fact, the pressure variations are much exaggerated in the figure. The quantity Δx gives the displacement of an air particle from its equilibrium position to its position with the sound wave, so that a positive Δx corresponds to displacement to the right. Where $\Delta x = 0$, the pressure is a maximum or minimum, and where $P = P_{eq}$, we have Δx a maximum or minimum. We denote the variation of the pressure from the equilibrium pressure as $\Delta P = P - P_{eq}$.

There are many ways in which energy can be converted into the energy of sound; for example, an underground nuclear explosion creates pressure waves in the solid Earth. The vibrating column of air in the plaintive oboe creates pressure waves in air.

In general, sound waves travel faster in a stiff material than in a material which is not as stiff. Thus waves travel a little faster in solids than in liquids, and a lot faster in solids and liquids than in a gas. (See table.)

Material	Speed of Sound
air	340 m/s
water	1600 m/s
steel	16000 m/s

B. INTENSITY AND PITCH

The *intensity* of a wave is a measure of the amount of energy a wave transports. If there is a stereo speaker producing music on one side of the room, then sound waves transport energy across the room. On the other side of the room we hear the sound with a certain intensity, so that a certain amount of energy per time falls on an ear. A person with bigger ears would have a proportionally greater energy per time falling on them, so a sensible definition of intensity is energy per time *per area*:

$$I = \frac{\Delta E}{A \Delta t}$$ (1)

The units are [W/m²]. (See Figure 10-2.)

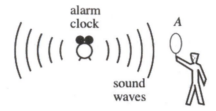

alarm
clock

A

sound
waves

*The intensity is the power (energy
per unit time) going through the hoop
divided by the area of the hoop.*

Figure 10-2

The human ear can hear sounds from the barely perceptible rush of air at intensity 10^{-12} W/m² to the painful roar at intensity 1 W/m². In order to make these numbers correspond more closely to our perception of sound, we often convert intensity into decibels:

$$\beta = 10 \log_{10} \frac{I}{I_0}$$ (2)

where I_0 is the intensity 10^{-12} W/m².

> Note that an increase by a factor of 10 in intensity I corresponds to adding 10 to β, which is in decibels.

The chart shows the results of some sample decibel calculations.

Description	$I (W/m^2)$	I/I_0	Log I/I_0	β (decibels)
rush of air	10^{-12}	1	0	0
wind	10^{-9}	10^3	3	30
conversation	10^{-6}	10^6	6	60
water fall	10^{-3}	10^9	9	90
pain	1	10^{12}	12	120

Example 1: A loud argument takes place in the next room, and you hear 70 dB. How much energy lands on one ear in one second? (An ear is about 0.05 m by 0.03 m.)

Solution: The intensity is given by

$$70 = 10 \log_{10} \frac{I}{I_0}$$

$$\log_{10} \frac{I}{I_0} = 7$$

$$\frac{I}{I_0} = 10^7$$

$$I = 10^{-5} \frac{W}{m^2}$$

Thus,

$$\Delta E = IA\Delta t$$
$$= 10^{-5} \text{ W/m}^2 \cdot (0.05 \cdot 0.03 \text{ m})(1 \text{ s})$$
$$1.5 \times 10^{-8} \text{ J.}$$

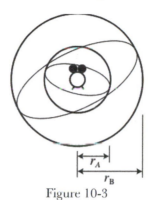

Figure 10-3

As you go further from a source of sound, the intensity of the sound decreases. In order to figure out how much it decreases, think of an alarm clock in the center of two concentric spheres (Figure 10-3). The alarm clock produces a certain amount of energy each second. That same amount of energy flows out of sphere A each second, and the same amount flows out of sphere B each second. Thus we have

[power going through surface A] = [power going through surface B],

$$P_A = P_B$$

If there is a woman listening at radius A, the intensity she experiences is

$$I_A = \frac{P_A}{4\pi r_A^2}$$

because the surface area of the sphere is $4\pi r_A^2$. Similarly, a man at radius r_B experiences intensity

$$I_B = \frac{P_B}{4\pi r_B^2}$$

Putting this all together yields

$$4\pi r_A^2 I_A = 4\pi r_B^2 I_B$$

$$I_A = \left(\frac{r_B}{r_A}\right)^2 I_B$$

or, in general,

$$I = I_0 \left(\frac{r_0}{r}\right)^2 . \tag{3}$$

In words, the intensity decreases as the square of the radius (inverse square law).

Memorize the formula, but also understand the reasoning that led to the formula.

Example 2: Jack and Jill are in a field, and Jill is playing a violin. If the intensity of the sound Jack hears is β_0 (in decibels) when he is 63.2 m away, how much louder is the sound when he is 2 m away?

Solution: If Jack moves from 63.2 m to 2 m, then the radius decreases by a factor of $63.2/2 = 31.6$. Then equation (3) indicates that I increases by a factor of $(31.6)^2 = 1000$. Three factors of 10 is equivalent to adding 10 to β three times, so $\beta = \beta_0 + 30$. The violin sounds 30 decibels louder.

The pitch you hear depends on the frequency of the sound wave; the lower the frequency, the lower the note. For instance, the wave in Figure 10-4, with period $T = 0.8$ ms, corresponds to D#$_6$. The wave in Figure 10-5, with period double the first one, corresponds to D#$_7$, the same note one octave higher.

Figure 10-4   Figure 10-5

C. RESONATING CAVITIES

In the last chapter we looked at the sound produced by a plucked guitar string or a struck piano string. Now we will look at resonating pipes, like organ pipes. While the resonating cavity of a soft drink bottle or of an oboe are more complicated than the pipes in this section, the principle behind all these pipes is the same. Standing waves are set up in the cavities, and these produce sound of a particular pitch and timbre.

A **closed pipe** is a pipe closed at one end and open at the other. If we excite the air column, the air in the pipe vibrates longitudinally. The variable x gives the location along the length of the pipe, and Δx gives the tiny displacement an air particle can have. (See Figure 10-6.) The double arrow shows the air particle moving back and forth. Since its equilibrium point is in the middle, the distance from one side to the other side of the displacement is $2\Delta x$.

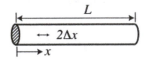

A closed pipe has a
displacement node on one end
and an antinode on the other.

Figure 10-6

At the closed end, the air cannot move back and forth, while it is completely free to do so at the open end. Thus the closed end is a displacement node, and the open end is an antinode. Any graph we draw for a closed pipe must have a node on one end and an antinode on the other. The fundamental has no nodes in the middle of the pipe away from the ends (Figure 10-7).

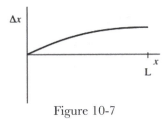

Figure 10-7

What is shown ends up being one fourth of a wave. A full wave looks like this:

The graph shows the first fourth: from zero point to maximum. Thus the full wave is four times the length of the pipe.

Example 1: A boy blows across the top of a bullet casing (a cylinder closed at one end, open at the other) which is 0.03 m long. What is the frequency of the note he hears (the fundamental)? (The speed of sound is 343 m/s.)

Solution: The fundamental mode is shown in Figure 10-7, and the wavelength is $\lambda = 4$ (0.03 m) = 0.12 m. Thus $f = v/\lambda = 2860$ Hz. (At a different temperature the sound speed will be different.)

For closed pipes, each successive harmonic has one additional node.

Now try drawing the second harmonic without looking at Figure 10-8.

For the second harmonic we have drawn three fourths of a wave, so $L = 3/4\ \lambda$, and $\lambda = 4/3\ L$. The next harmonic is shown in Figure 10-9, but try to draw it also without looking. What is λ? (Did you get 4/5 L?)

Let's go back and look at the fundamental. Note this peculiar fact: If we are thinking in terms of displacement of air particles, then the node is at the closed end and the antinode is at the open end. If we are thinking in terms of pressure variation (see the beginning of the chapter), then the closed end is the antinode and the open end is the node. Figure 10-10 shows the fundamental in both cases. The frequency we calculate comes to the same, of course. You should check this point.

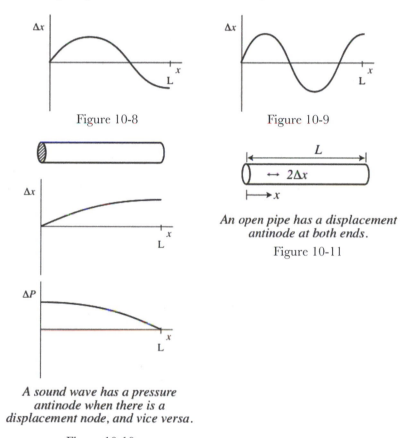

Figure 10-8

Figure 10-9

An open pipe has a displacement
antinode at both ends.

Figure 10-11

A sound wave has a pressure
antinode when there is a
displacement node, and vice versa.

Figure 10-10

An **open pipe** is open at both ends, like an organ pipe (Figure 10-11). If we consider displacement of air particles, then both ends are antinodes. We find that we cannot draw a mode with no nodes in the middle of the pipe, since such a mode would make no sound. Thus the fundamental has one node (Figure 10-12).

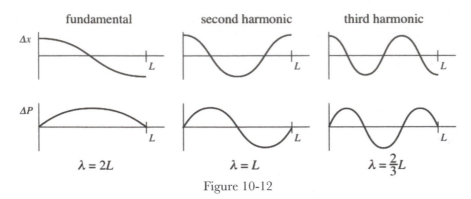

Figure 10-12

If we consider pressure variation, then both ends are nodes, and we can draw a mode with no nodes in the middle. Try drawing these graphs yourself without looking. They represent the fundamental and the second and third harmonics. Draw also the graphs for the fourth harmonic.

D. BEATS

If you play the lowest two notes of a piano you may hear the notes separately, but you may also hear a beating pattern, like aaaaaaaah–ooooooo–aaaaaaaah–ooooooo–aaaaaaaah about twice a second. Try this if a piano is available.

If you have a guitar, you can hear this effect by playing an A on the fifth fret of the sixth string and an A on the fifth string open. If the two strings are slightly out of tune, you will hear a single note that gets louder and quieter, louder and quieter. This is called **beats**.

What is happening? The first two graphs of Figure 10-13 show the two notes that have similar frequency. At $t = 0$, they are in phase, and the amplitude of the combination is large. This is shown in third graph, where their sum is shown. A little while later, however, the two waves are out of phase, and the amplitude of the sum is a minimum. So this is the origin of the loud-soft-loud sound of the two notes. The **beat period** is shown in the third graph, and **beat frequency** is given by

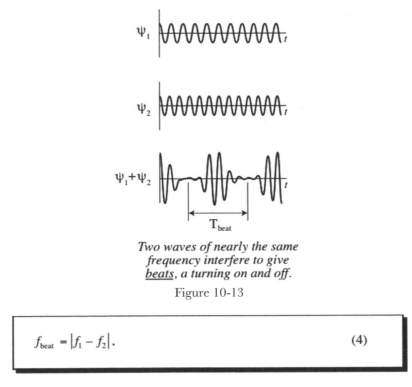

Two waves of nearly the same frequency interfere to give beats, a turning on and off.

Figure 10-13

$$f_{\text{beat}} = |f_1 - f_2|. \qquad (4)$$

Example: Jessica is tuning a guitar by comparing notes to a piano that she knows is in tune. She plays an A on the piano (220 Hz) and loudly plucks the A-string. She hears a loud-soft ringing whose maxima are separated by 3 seconds.

a.   What is the guitar string's current fundamental frequency?

b.   Jessica tightens the string (increases the tension) of the guitar slightly, and the beat gets faster. Should she continue to tighten the string?

Solution: a. The beat period is 3 s, so the beat frequency is 0.33 Hz. The string may be producing 220.33 Hz or 119.67 Hz, that is, too sharp or too flat.

b. By tightening the string, Jessica increases its frequency. If the resulting frequency were closer to 220 Hz, the beat period would get longer. She should reduce the tension in the string.

E. DOPPLER SHIFT

If you have ever been standing around where a train or car goes by, you are familiar with the eeeeeeeeee–aaaaaaaaaah sound it makes as it passes. Why does this happen?

Figure 10-14–Figure 10-16 show this phenomenon. Figure 10-14 shows a train whistle making sound waves when it is still. The man hears these pressure waves, so that his ear records a certain frequency of pressure-maxima arrival times. In Figure 10-15, the train whistle is approaching, so the man perceives the pressure maxima coming more frequently. He perceives a higher frequency note. In Figure 10-16 the train is receding, each successive pressure maximum has a longer way to travel, and the man perceives pressure maxima less frequently.

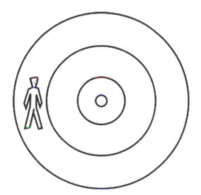

A person hears a note from a whistle.
Figure 10-14

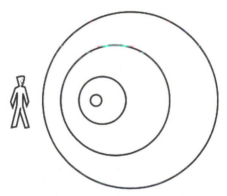

*A person hears a higher note from
an approaching whistle.*
Figure 10-15

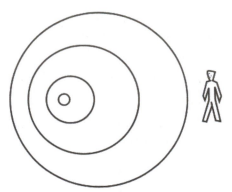

A person hears a lower note from a receding whistle.

Figure 10-16

When the emitter of a wave and the detector are moving relative to each other, the detector detects a different frequency from the one emitted—a **Doppler shift**. The frequency is higher if they are coming together and lower if they are going apart.

There is one special case that deserves note. If a wave strikes a moving object and bounces back, then there are two Doppler shifts. For example, when a police officer uses a radar device to detect the speed of an oncoming vehicle, there is one shift when the radar is intercepted by the car and another shift when the reflected signal is intercepted by the police device.

Example: A police officer uses sonar to determine the speed of an approaching car. (Actually police use electromagnetic waves, but that is in the next chapter.) It emits a frequency of 60 kHz. The car is approaching at 38 m/s. The Doppler shift is

$$f_{det} = f_{em} \frac{v_s \pm v_{det}}{v_s \pm v_{em}}$$

where f_{det} is the detected frequency, v_s is the speed of the wave in the medium, v_{det} is the speed of the detector, v_{em} is the speed of the emitter, and f_{em} is the emitted frequency. The speed of sound is 343 m/s.

a. What frequency would the car detect if it could detect the sonar?
b. What frequency would the officer detect from the reflection?

Solution: a. The frequency that the car would pick up if it could intercept the police sonar is

$$f_{car} = f_0 \frac{v_s + v_{car}}{v_s}$$

where $f_0 = 60$ kHz and $v_{car} = 38$ m/s. We know to choose the positive sign because we know the result must be a higher frequency. Thus,

$$f_{car} = (60 \text{kHz}) \frac{(343 + 38) \frac{m}{s}}{343 \frac{m}{s}}$$

$$= 66.7 \text{Hz}$$

b. The frequency that the police intercepts is given by

$$f_{det} = f_{car} \frac{v_s}{v_s - v_{car}}$$

We choose the negative sign because, again, we know the result must be a higher frequency. Thus,

$$f_{det} = (66.7\text{kHz})\dfrac{343\,\frac{m}{s}}{(343-38)\,\frac{m}{s}}$$

$$= 75\text{Hz}$$

F. SHOCK WAVES

If an object, such as a jet aircraft, or a bullet, travels faster than the speed of sound, a shock wave will be produced that can be perceived as a large sharp crack or sonic boom. As we have seen in the previous section, a moving source of a sound with a particular frequency will cause an increase in the frequency of the pressure waves as it moves towards a receiver. An object moving through the air can be thought of as a point source for pressure waves producing a phenomenon similar to the Doppler effect. If an object such as a fighter jet, Figure 10-17, approaches the speed of sound, Mach one (Ma = 1), the pressure waves begin to merge and overlap, producing constructive interference at the leading edge of the moving point source. Once the jet exceeds the speed of sound (Ma > 1), the constructive interference edge, or shock cone angle, is reduced to less than 180°. As the shock wave travels through the air its energy is dissipated, like any other wave. Since the shock wave is the result of constructive interference the amplitude and hence energy carried by the shock wave can produce very loud sounds.

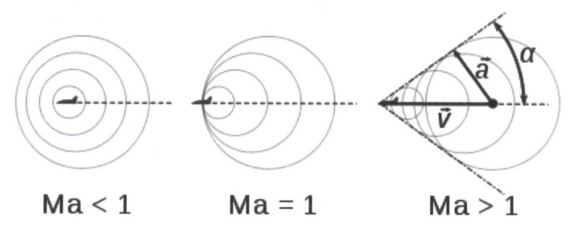

Figure 10-17

As can be seen in the figure, the plane's velocity v and the velocity of the sound a can be represented as vectors. If the velocity of the sound is taken to be perpendicular to the shock wave, these two vectors represent two sides of a right triangle, where the angle α, is half of the cone angle for the shock wave. This provides the basis for the trigonometric relationship seen in equation (5), where the inverse of the a/v ratio is the Ma value. Under certain atmospheric conditions, the shock wave can reveal itself due to condensation of water vapor.

$$\sin \alpha = a/v \qquad (5)$$

Example 1: Estimate the Ma value of a jet aircraft whose shock cone angle is 120°. Note that sin 120° = sin 60° ≈ 0.86.

Solution: Using the information provided for the cone angle, sin α is 0.86. While it is unlikely that the MCAT will make you know that the sine of 60° (or 120°) is 0.86, they may give it to you (and you probably should know that the sine of 30° is 0.5). Inserting this value into equation 5 gives

$\sin \alpha = a/v$
$0.86 = a/v$

Since Ma is the inverse of a/v, the inverse of 0.86 is Ma = 1/0.86 ~ 1.1. The plane is going approximately 10% faster (390 m/s) than the speed of sound, which is about 340 m/s (760 mph).

G. ULTRASOUND

Ultrasound imaging is based on the same principles that the Navy uses for active sonar and by certain animals, like bats and dolphins for echolocation. Similar to the electromagnetic spectrum, the acoustic spectrum can be divided up into various regions, with respect to the audio range for human hearing, Figure 10-19. The ultrasound region that is used for imaging purposes has frequencies in the low megahertz range.

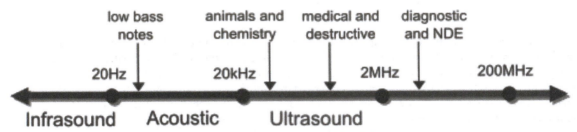

Figure 10-19 https://commons.wikimedia.org/wiki/File:Ultrasound_range_diagram.svg

Like all waves, when sound waves pass from one material to a different material, a portion of the wave is transmitted into the new material and a portion of the wave is reflected. If the speed of the sound wave is known, it is possible to calculate the distance between the source of the sound and the reflecting material, by measuring the time required to detect the echo. This non-invasive technology has improved dramatically since its initial applications for imaging back in the early 20th century, with improvements in computers and digital detector arrays driving this leap forward. Furthermore, changes in the frequencies of the sound can be used to provide information about the motion of materials, like blood in the heart, forming the basis for Doppler Ultrasound imaging.

Example 1: Assuming that the ultrasound source and detector are at the same distance from a highly reflective tissue, like a bone, what is the distance between the bone and the ultrasound device if the time required to detect the sound pulse is 65 μs. Assume that the speed of sound in body tissue is the same as the speed of sound in water, which is 1540 m/s.

Solution: First we need to convert the time from microseconds to seconds. Then multiplying by the speed of the sound, gives the distance that the sound pulse traveled.

$$65 \text{ μs} \times (10^{-6} \text{ m}/1 \text{ μs}) \times (1540 \text{ m/s}) = 0.10 \text{ m}$$

We are not yet finished, and have to remember that the sound was reflected and that the distance between the ultrasound device and the bone is half the distance that the sound pulse traveled, or 5 cm.

Example 2: Doppler ultrasound having a frequency of 1.000 MHz was used to image blood flow in the heart of a patient. If the detected frequency was 1.003 MHz, what was the speed of the blood that was imaged if the speed of the sound is 1540 m/s?

Solution: Using the Doppler equation

$$f_{\text{det}} = f_{\text{em}} \frac{v_s \pm v_{\text{det}}}{v_s \pm v_{\text{em}}}$$

where f_{em} = 1.0000 MHz, f_{det} = 1.0003 MHz and the v_s = 1540 m/s. We can assume that the emitting source v_{em} is not moving. Inserting these values into the equation gives

$$1.0003 = 1.0000 \, [1450 + v_{\text{det}}]/1450$$

Rearranging and solving for v_{det}, gives

$$v_{\text{det}} = [(1.0003/1.0000) \times (1450)] - 1450$$
$$v_{\text{det}} = 0.44 \text{ m/s}$$

The blood was flowing towards the ultrasound device because the frequency increased.

H. CHAPTER SUMMARY

In this chapter we looked at sound as an example of waves. We especially noted resonating cavities of air that exhibit standing waves just like the waves on the guitar string in the previous chapter. The key to doing problems involving these cavities is drawing the pictures correctly.

The most important thing to remember about the Doppler shift is that the detected frequency is greater than the emitted frequency if the emitter and the detector are approaching each other, and less if they are receding.

CHAPTER 10 PROBLEMS

In the following use

$$\beta = 10 \log_{10} \frac{I}{I_0}$$

where I_0 is a barely perceptible noise 10^{-12} W/m^2.

Use the following for questions 1 and 2:

A copier machine is making a rattling sound whose intensity is 10^{-6} W/m^2 where you are sitting 2 m away from it.

1. What is the sound level in decibels for this noise?
    A. 10 decibels
    B. 30 decibels
    C. 60 decibels
    D. 120 decibels

2. If you move to a point 6 m away, what would be the intensity?

    A. 1.11×10^{-7} W/m^2
    B. 3.33×10^{-7} W/m^2
    C. 3×10^{-6} W/m^2
    D. 9×10^{-6} W/m^2

3. A speaker is producing 40 W of sound and you are standing 6 m away. (Assume the sound goes out equally in all directions.) What would be the intensity of sound energy at your ear?

    A. 0.088 W/m^2
    B. 1.11 W/m^2
    C. 6.67 W/m^2
    D. 240 W/m^2

4. A speaker is producing a total of 5 W of sound, and you hear 10 dB. Someone turns up the power to 50 W. What level of sound do you hear?

    A. 15 dB
    B. 20 dB
    C. 40 dB
    D. 100 dB

Use the following for questions 5–7:

In a quiet room just before she drops off to sleep, Betsy hears the barely perceptible buzz of a mosquito one meter away from her ear. (Hint: A barely perceptible noise is 10^{-12} W/m^2.)

5. How much energy does a mosquito produce in 100 s?

    A. 10^{-10} J
    B. 3.1×10^{-10} J
    C. 1.3×10^{-9} J
    D. 1.6×10^{-8} J

6. If you could harness the sound energy of mosquitoes, how many would it take to power a 10-W bulb?

    A. 10^9
    B. 8×10^9
    C. 10^{11}
    D. 8×10^{11}

7. If a swarm of mosquitoes were 10 m away, how many mosquitoes would there have to be in order for you to just be able to hear it?

    A. 10
    B. 100
    C. 1000
    D. 10,000

8. You hear a 20-decibel noise which comes from a cricket 30 m away. How loud would it sound if you were 3 m away?

    A. 30 decibels
    B. 40 decibels
    C. 120 decibels
    D. 2000 decibels

Use the following for questions 9–13:

Richard is preparing a mailing tube. Before he inserts his papers, he accidentally lets the mailing tube drop to the floor, and it produces a note. The mailing tube is 1.5 m long with a cylindrical cross section of 4-cm diameter. It is sealed at one end and open at the other. The speed of sound in air is 343 m/s at 20° C.

9. What is the wavelength of the fundamental?

    A. 0.04 m
    B. 0.08 m
    C. 3 m
    D. 6 m

10. What is the frequency of the note that Richard heard?

    A. 60 Hz
    B. 100 Hz
    C. 4000 Hz
    D. 9000 Hz

11. What is the wavelength of the second harmonic?

    A. 1.5 m
    B. 2 m
    C. 3 m
    D. 6 m

12. What is the wavelength of the fifth harmonic?

    A. 0.7 m
    B. 3.8 m
    C. 6 m
    D. 7.5 m

13. If the tube were filled with helium, which has a sound speed of 965 m/s, what would be the frequency of the fundamental?

    A. 160 Hz
    B. 320 Hz
    C. 430 Hz
    D. 970 Hz

Use the following for questions 14–17:

An organ pipe is a cylindrical tube which is open at both ends. The air column is set to vibrating by air flowing through the lower portion of the pipe. The shape of the hole where the air exits affects the timbre of the pipe.

In the diagram the length of the pipe is 0.1 m and the diameter is 0.02 m. The velocity of sound at 20° C is 343 m/s.

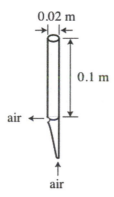

14. What is the wavelength of the fundamental?

    A. 0.05 m
    B. 0.1 m
    C. 0.13 m
    D. 0.2 m

15. What is the frequency of the fundamental?

    A. 200 Hz
    B. 400 Hz
    C. 1700 Hz
    D. 3400 Hz

16. What is the wavelength of the fourth harmonic?

    A. 0.025 m
    B. 0.05 m
    C. 0.067 m
    D. 0.1 m

17. On a cold day (10° C) the speed of sound is 2% slower than on a warm day (20° C). How would that affect the frequency?

    A. It would be 4% lower.
    B. It would be 2% lower.
    C. It would be the same.
    D. It would be 2% higher.

18. The two lowest notes on the piano are A_0 (27.5 Hz) and $A\#_0$ (29.1 Hz). If you play the notes simultaneously, the resulting sound seems to turn off and on and off and on. How much time exists between the successive "on"s?

    A. 0.6 s
    B. 1.6 s
    C. 28.3 s
    D. 56.6 s

Use the following for questions 19 and 20:

Sarah has correctly tuned the B string of a guitar. She frets the string to play an E (660 Hz). The E string is not yet in tune. When she plucks the true E (on the B string) and the E string together, she hears a note that changes from loud to soft to loud twice a second.

19. What is the fundamental frequency on the untuned E string?

    A. 0.5 Hz.
    B. 2 Hz.
    C. 660 Hz.
    D. Either 658 Hz or 662 Hz.

20. What best describes the energy flow in this problem?

    A. Sound to mechanical.
    B. Sound to heat.
    C. Sound to mechanical to heat.
    D. Kinetic and potential in one medium to kinetic and potential in another medium.

Use the following for questions 21–23:

On a piano tuned to the American equal-tempered scale, the frequency of the third harmonic of C_4 string is 784.87 Hz. The fundamental frequency of G_5 string is 783.99 Hz. Beats between these frequencies can be heard in the following way:

Hold the key for C_4 down, so that the string can vibrate. Strike the G_5 key loudly, so that the third harmonic of the C_4 string will be excited. Before that note dies down, let the G_5 key go (this quiets the G string). Then strike the G string again more softly, so that the volume of the two strings are matched.

21. What phenomenon is demonstrated when the G_5 string is used to excite the vibration of the C_4 string?

   A. beats
   B. interference
   C. resonance
   D. dispersion

22. What is the frequency of the beat between the notes?

   A. 0.88 Hz
   B. 1.1 Hz
   C. 784.43 Hz
   D. 1569 Hz

23. What is the frequency of the C_4 fundamental?

   A. 0.88 Hz
   B. 262 Hz
   C. 392 Hz
   D. 785 Hz

Use the following for questions 24–27:

When the source of waves and a detector are moving with respect to each other, the frequency of the detected wave is shifted from the frequency of the emitted wave (Doppler shift). The effect of this is to increase the detected frequency when the source and detector are approaching each other and to decrease the detected frequency when they are receding from each other.

In two or three dimensions this is complicated, but in one dimension the formula is relatively simple:

$$f_{det} = \frac{v_s \pm v_{det}}{v_s \pm v_{em}} f_{em}$$

where f_{det} is the detected frequency, v_s is the speed of the wave in the medium, v_{det} is the speed of the detector, v_{em} is the speed of the emitter, and f_{em} is the emitted frequency. Choose the sign in the numerator to reflect the direction the detector is going (negative if approaching), and choose the sign in the denominator to reflect the direction the emitter is going (positive if approaching).

A fast train (50 m/s) is moving directly toward Samuel, who is standing near the tracks. The train is emitting a whistling sound at 420 Hz. The speed of sound is 350 m/s at the outdoor temperature of 31° C.

24. What frequency does Samuel hear?

   A. 360 Hz
   B. 367.5 Hz
   C. 480 Hz
   D. 490 Hz

25. In the above question, Samuel whistles at 420 Hz. If a passenger on the train could hear him, what frequency would she hear?
   A. 360 Hz
   B. 367.5 Hz
   C. 480 Hz
   D. 490 Hz

26. After the train passes Samuel, what frequency does he hear from the whistle?

   A. 360 Hz
   B. 367.5 Hz
   C. 480 Hz
   D. 490 Hz

27. A police sonar detector operates by emitting a sound at 42 kHz. This sound bounces off an approaching vehicle going 50 m/s. What is the frequency of the signal received back at the detector? ($v_s = 350$ m/s)

   A. 36 kHz
   B. 48 kHz
   C. 49 kHz
   D. 56 kHz

Passage 1

Bats are mammals which have acquired the ability of flight and of echolocation. Echolocation involves using vibrating membranes to direct a high frequency sound, with frequencies ranging from 12 kHz to 150 kHz. If the sound encounters a flying insect or obstacle which is larger than the wavelength of the sound, then a portion of the sound wave is reflected, and the bat detects it.

Beyond this basic framework, different species of bats use different strategies in echolocation. Some species emit a series of pulses, determining the distance to an object by the delay in return of the signal. Some emit a constant frequency, using the frequency of the returned sound to determine information about the velocity of the insect. Others use a sweep of frequencies, presumably to determine size information or directional information. Some emit a sound with a high harmonic content. Many use some combination of these strategies.

Several adaptations provide for better processing of the returned signal, including isolation of the detection apparatus from the emitting apparatus and specializations in the middle ear.

For the questions, use the following: The speed of sound is 343 m/s, and the Doppler-shifted frequency for a detector and emitter moving relative to each other is

$$f_{det} = \frac{v_s \pm v_{det}}{v_s \pm v_{em}} f_{em}$$

28. What frequency would a bat use to locate an insect 1 cm wide which is 10 m away?

　A. Any frequency less than 34 kHz.
　B. Any frequency greater than 34 kHz.
　C. Any frequency less than 34 Hz.
　D. Any frequency greater than 34 Hz.

29. If an insect is 3 m away, and a bat emits a pulse signal, how long is the delay in the return signal?

　A. 0.009 s
　B. 0.017 s
　C. 0.09 s
　D. 0.17 s

30. A bat is in pursuit of an insect. The bat is flying 10 m/s to the east, and the insect is flying 10 m/s to the east. If the bat emits a constant frequency sound of 30 kHz, what frequency will he detect?

　A. 29 kHz
　B. 30 kHz
　C. 31 kHz
　D. 32 KHz

31. What is a possible reason for using a sound with high harmonic content?

　A. The harmonic frequency can determine the distance to an insect.
　B. The harmonic frequency can stun the insect.
　C. The harmonic frequency might be reflected even if the fundamental is not.
　D. The harmonic frequency might be Doppler shifted even if the fundamental is not.

32. A bat is traveling west at 15 m/s, emitting a constant–frequency sound of 50 kHz. If it encounters an obstacle, such as a tree, what frequency sound does it detect?

　A. 2.2 kHz
　B. 48 kHz
　C. 50 kHz
　D. 55 kHz

33. Which is an adaptation which might aid an insect?

　A. An ability to emit a sound with frequency much lower than that of a bat.
　B. An ability to emit a sound with frequency about the same as that of a bat.
　C. An ability to emit a sound with frequency much higher than that of a bat.
　D. A secretion of an obnoxious tasting chemical.

This page intentionally left blank.

CHAPTER 11
LIGHT

A. INTRODUCTION

Light is pretty mysterious: sometimes it acts just like a wave, interfering with itself and undergoing Doppler shifts and so on, and sometimes it acts like a particle, such as when it interacts with an electron. In this chapter we will explore the wavelike properties of light.

So light is a wave, like sound and water ripples. But sound involves the motion of air, and water ripples involve the motion of water, but what motion happens in a light wave? Well, it turns out to be a hard question. The answer is not "this molecule" or "that substance" but rather a combination of electric and magnetic fields. When all the material is removed from a piece of space, we call that piece of space a *vacuum*, but electric and magnetic fields are still there, and light disturbs these fields. That is why light can travel in a vacuum.

Here is another strange property of light, or perhaps it is a property of the space and time in which light travels. Its speed is the same $c = 3.00 \times 10^8$ m/s to every observer. Think of how strange this is. If you are driving 60 mph down the freeway, a car may pass you going 75 mph, and a car on the other side of the yellow stripe may be going 60 mph in the other direction. From the point of view *of your car*, the first car is going 15 mph and the second is going −120 mph. This makes sense.

In the super fast space freeway, your spacecraft may be going 1.00×10^8 m/s and another spacecraft passes you going in the same direction going 2.00×10^8 m/s. A light beam passes both of you in the same direction going 3.00×10^8 m/s. From the point of view *of your spacecraft*, it is going (not 2.00×10^8 m/s but) 3.00×10^8 m/s, and from the point of view of the other spacecraft it is going 3.00×10^8 m/s. Go figure.

The speed of light is this mysterious $c = 3.00 \times 10^8$ m/s only in a vacuum. In other materials the speed is a little slower.

B. GENERAL PROPERTIES OF LIGHT

Since light acts like a wave, it has a wavelength. Light of different wavelengths goes by different names. (See Figure 11-1).

Light waves of a very long wavelength (greater than one centimeter) are used for broadcast, so the information about television images is encoded on the light waves and broadcast to your television set, if you have one. These are called *radio waves* or *microwaves*.

Much of the heat from an electric heater is transported by *infrared radiation*, with wavelengths on the order of 10^{-5} m to 10^{-4} m.

If light of a wavelength between 400 nm and 700 nm enters the pupil of your eye, it is likely to interact with the electrons of certain cells in the retina, producing a chemical change in the photoreceptor cells, leading to an action potential in neurons. For this reason, light in this range is called *visible light*.

Light with shorter wavelengths is *ultraviolet light*, responsible for sun tans and melanoma.

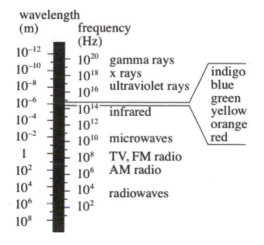

Figure 11-1

X-rays have shorter wavelengths still (less than 10^{-9} m) and can pass through soft biological tissue, but not so easily through bones. They are used in imaging. Nuclear decay produces gamma rays (see Chapter 16), which have even shorter wavelengths, and this is the most penetrating electromagnetic radiation. **Gamma rays** are able to pass through the Earth like visible light passes through glass.

Light waves can be polarized. In fact, the light from the sky is polarized in most places, as well as light which is reflected from the hot layer of air on a desert road. You can detect the polarization using special glasses. Look through the glasses at the shimmering surface of a hot road and rotate the glasses. You can see the light become dimmer and brighter.

To see what is happening, look at Figure 11-2. Beth is holding a rope and waving her hands up and down sending waves to Sam. The waves easily pass through the picket fence as it stands, but if the slats were horizontal, the waves would not be transmitted to Sam. Polaroid glasses allow the vertically polarized portion of light to go through but absorb the horizontally polarized portion.

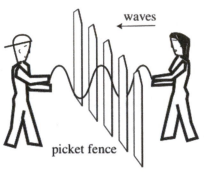

Transverse waves can be polarized, so that the displacements lie along one direction (defined here by the picket fence).

Figure 11-2

When electromagnetic waves are polarized, the electric and magnetic components are orthogonal (mutually perpendicular) to the direction of wave propagation, as seen in Figure 11-3.

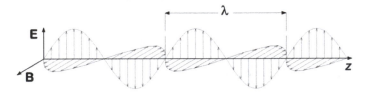

Figure 11-3

If two equal amplitude light waves are orthogonal to one another, propagate in the same direction and have a 90° phase-difference, the resulting interference produces a spiral, or circularly, polarized light wave.

C. REFLECTION AND REFRACTION

We mentioned in Section A that light traveling in a medium other than a vacuum has a speed slower than c. In fact it is given by

$$v_{\text{light}} = \frac{c}{n}, \tag{1}$$

where **n** is the **index of refraction**. The chart at right gives some values of indices of refraction (do not memorize this chart, but note that **n** is always greater than 1).

substance	n
vacuum	1
air	≈ 1
water	≈ 1.3
glass	≈ 1.5

When light traveling in one medium encounters a boundary to another medium, some of the light is **reflected** and some is **transmitted** into the second medium. If the incident light comes in at an angle, then the transmitted light is **refracted**, or bent, from its original direction. Figure 11-4 shows the wave fronts of light waves incident on glass from air.

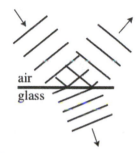

Light waves in air encounter glass.
Figure 11-4

When working with diagrams of light waves, it is customary (and convenient) to use light rays rather than wave fronts. Rays point perpendicular to the front, and in the direction the light is going. Figure 11-5 is equivalent to Figure 11-4, using rays instead. Also, the normal to the surface (remember that "normal" means perpendicular) is shown as a dashed line.

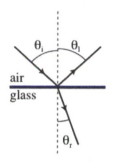

Incident light beam is both reflected and refracted.
Figure 11-5

This is the most important figure of the chapter, so take a moment to study it. Notice the following:

    1. The angles are measured from the normal; the reflected angle θ_l is the same as the incident angle θ_i.
    2. The refracted angle θ_r (in glass) is smaller than the incident angle (in air). That is, the slower medium has the ray closer to the normal.

Example 1: A light beam encounters a piece of glass as shown (Figure 11-6). Sketch the refracted path of the beam.

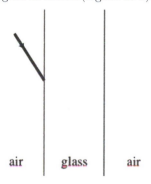

air   glass   air

Figure 11-6

Solution: In Figure 11-7 the normal is shown as a dashed line. The dotted line shows the path the beam would take if there were no glass. The ray bends, however, toward the normal. Now when it hits the other side of the glass, the beam bends away from the normal. The answer, then, is the solid line.

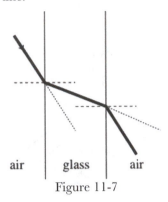

air   glass   air

Figure 11-7

Snell's law gives the value of the refracted angle:

> **Snell's Law**
> If a beam of light encounters a boundary, and if the beam is transmitted, the transmitted beam is refracted, or bent, according to
>
> $$n_i \sin \theta_i = n_r \sin \theta_r, \qquad\qquad (2)$$
>
> where n_i and n_r are the indices of refraction of the media housing the incident and refracted beams, and θ_i and θ_r are the angles of the beams, measured from the normal.

You will want to memorize this equation since it is in the MCAT study guide, but knowing how to use this equation is more important.

Example 2: A beam of light in air strikes the surface of pure liquid hydrogen peroxide ($n = 1.414$) making an angle 30° with the normal to the surface.

    a. What angle does the reflected beam make with the normal?
    b. What angle does the transmitted beam make with the normal?

Solution: a. The diagram for this problem is similar to Figure 11-5, with glass replaced by hydrogen peroxide. The reflected angle is the same as the incident angle, 30°.

b. The refracted angle is given by

$$n_{air}\sin \theta_r = n_{dia}\sin \theta_i$$
$$1.414 \sin \theta_r = 1.0 \sin 30°$$
$$\sin \theta_r = 0.354$$
$$\theta_r = \sin^{-1} 0.354$$
$$= 20.7°$$

where that last equation must be solved on a calculator. Since calculators are not allowed on the MCAT, additional information concerning the $\sin^{-1}$ would probably be provided.

Example 3: A beam of light in a piece of diamond encounters an interface with air. The beam makes a 30° angle with the normal. What is the angle of refraction? (The index of refraction for diamond is 2.42.)

Solution: Figure 11-8 shows the diagram for this problem. Snell's law becomes

$$n_{air}\sin \theta_r = n_{dia}\sin \theta_i$$
$$1.0 \sin \theta_r = 2.42 \sin 30°$$
$$\sin \theta_r = 1.21$$

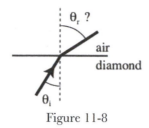

Figure 11-8

Now we need to find an angle whose sine is 1.21. But wait a minute! There is no such thing as a sine that is greater than one. This equation has no solution. What is going on? Figure 11-9 shows a beam of light in diamond with an angle of incidence of 20°. The refracted ray bends away from the normal. Figure 12-10 shows a beam of light in diamond making a 24.4° angle with the normal. Once the beam gets into the air, it has bent so far from the normal that it is parallel with the surface. This angle, 24.4°, is called the **critical angle** for a diamond-air interface. It is the incident angle for which the refracted angle is 90°.

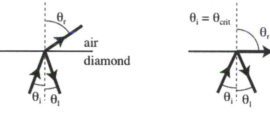

The refracted ray bends away from the normal.

Figure 11-9

With a large angle of incidence, the refracted ray bends all the way to 90°

Figure 11-10

Figure 11-11 shows our situation with 30°, but the refracted beam cannot bend any further away from the normal than it did for 24°. In fact, there is no refracted ray in this case. This phenomenon is called **total internal reflection**, because all of the light stays in the diamond and none goes into the air.

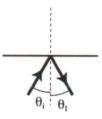

With a larger angle of incidence, there is only reflection (total internal reflection).

Figure 11-11

Example 4: In a fiber optic cable, light travels down a light pipe with very little energy loss. You may have seen these cables in toys that were popular in the 1970s, where the tips of clear thin fibers light up with different colors. The cables have a high index of refraction, so that light gets totally internally reflected off the surface and thus does not leak out the sides. When it arrives at the tip, the light is transmitted into the air (Figure 11-12).

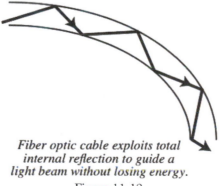

Fiber optic cable exploits total internal reflection to guide a light beam without losing energy.

Figure 11-12

Although we have discussed reflection and refraction only in the context of light waves, all waves in fact get reflected and refracted at boundaries. Figure 11-13 shows ocean waves coming toward the shore, as seen from above. As they approach, they encounter more and more shallow water, with smaller wave speed. Thus we would guess that they would bend toward the normal, so that the wave fronts would arrive roughly parallel to the shore. Compare Figure 11-13 to Figure 11-4. The difference here is that the air–glass boundary is sharp, whereas the boundary from deep to shallow water is gradual. Notice how the waves come in to the shore the next time you are at the beach.

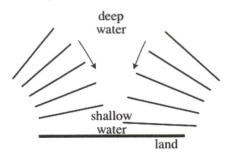

Ocean waves are refracted toward the normal as they approach the shore.

Figure 11-13

Also note (Figure 11-4 and Figure 11-13) that when a wave travels from one medium to another, the frequency stays the same, whereas the wavelength changes if the wave speed changes. This is easier to see with ocean waves than with waves of light. Imagine ocean waves in the deep portion of the ocean going up-down-up-down once every five seconds. If this goes on for a long time, it must be that the ocean waves arriving at shallow water go up-down-up-down once every five seconds as well.

D. LENSES

Figure 11-14 shows a *converging lens*. A light ray incident on the lens bends twice, once when entering the lens (usually glass) and once when leaving it, both times bending toward the axis. You should work this out by tracing the rays in an exaggerated diagram. The lens is designed so that parallel light rays on the left converge to a point on the right. The distance from the lens to the point of convergence is the *focal length f*. Light rays from the right will also focus to a point after a distance *f*.

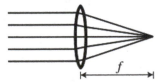

A converging lens focuses parallel beams to a point.

Figure 11-14

A *diverging lens* has the property that parallel light rays incident from the left spread apart after going through the lens, as if they were coming from a point source a distance –*f* from the lens. Figure 11-15 shows such a lens. For diverging lenses, the focal length is negative.

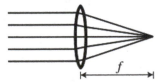

A diverging lens causes parallel beams to diverge, as if from a point.

Figure 11-15

For lens problems, there are two formulas and a ray-tracing method. It is probably worth your while to learn both. The formulas are better for calculating numbers, but ray tracing is better at answering qualitative questions. The method of ray tracing will sound confusing at first, but it will become clearer as you work through the examples.

If the distance from the lens to the object is d_o, the distance from the lens to the image is d_i, and the focal length of the lens is f, then we have

$$\frac{1}{f} = \frac{1}{d_i} + \frac{1}{d_o},\qquad(3)$$

and

$$m = -\frac{d_i}{d_o}\qquad(4)$$

is the magnification of the image. If d_i is greater than zero, this indicates that the image is on the other side of the lens from the object.

Ray-tracing method for a converging lens
1. Draw the lens, the object being observed, and both focuses.
2. Draw a ray parallel to the principal axis and passing through the lens. Bend the ray to go through the opposite focus.
3. Draw a ray passing through the object and the focus on the same side of the lens. This ray becomes parallel to the principal axis when it passes through the lens.
4. The intersecting point is the location of the image. If the rays do not intersect on the side opposite the object, extend them backwards until they do.

Ray-tracing method for a diverging lens
1. Draw the lens, object, and focus on the same side as the object.
2. Draw a ray parallel to the principal axis. After it passes through the lens it bends up, as if it came from the focus. Extend the ray backwards.
3. Draw a ray going through the vertex (center) of the lens and passing straight through.
4. The intersection of the extended ray in step 2 and the ray in step 3 gives the location of the image.

Example 1: A boy uses a magnifying glass (converging lens with focal length 0.03 m) to observe a bug that is 0.02 m from the lens.

   a. Draw a ray diagram.
   b. What is the magnification of the image?

Solution: Figure 11-16 shows the ray diagram.

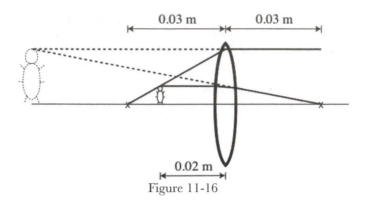

Figure 11-16

In this example, we had to extend the rays backwards in step 4 in order to find the image. For this reason the image is *virtual*, meaning light rays are not actually coming from the position from which they seem to come.

If the light rays pass through the point from which they seem to come, then the image is said to be *real*. We can get the magnification by first calculating the exact position of the image:

$$\frac{1}{f} = \frac{1}{d_i} + \frac{1}{d_o}$$

$$\frac{1}{0.03 \text{ m}} = \frac{1}{d_i} + \frac{1}{0.02 \text{ m}}$$

$$\frac{1}{d_i} = \left(\frac{1}{0.03} - \frac{1}{0.02}\right) \text{m}^{-1}$$

$$\frac{1}{d_i} = \left(\frac{100}{3} - \frac{100}{2}\right) \text{m}^{-1}$$

$$\frac{1}{d_i} = -\frac{100}{6} \text{m}^{-1}$$

$$d_i = -0.06 \text{ m}$$

Then

$$m = -\frac{-0.06 \text{ m}}{0.02 \text{ m}} \quad 3$$

The negative sign for d_i means the image is on the same side as the object. The positive sign for m means the image is upright (not inverted).

It is a general rule that if only one lens or mirror is involved in a problem, then the image is either both real and inverted or both virtual and upright. It will never be real and upright, for example.

E. MIRRORS

The methods and formulas for mirrors are almost identical to those for lenses, except that a mirror has only one focus. There are three kinds of mirrors: convex, plane, and concave (Figure 11-17). For a convex mirror, incoming parallel rays diverge after reflection, so the focal length is negative. For a plane mirror, the focal length is infinity. And for a concave mirror, incoming parallel rays converge after reflection, so the focal length is positive.

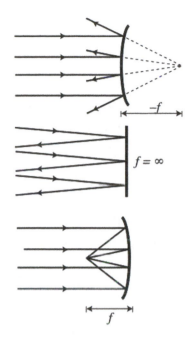

There are three types of mirrors:
convex, plane, and concave.

Figure 11-17

For mirrors, you use the same equations, but you have to be careful, because the meaning of the sign for d_i is different from that for lens. A positive sign for d_i means that the image is on the same side of the mirror as the object, that is, in front. You use the same kinds of ray diagrams, but since there is only one focus, you use that same focus in steps 2 and 3.

Ray-tracing method for a converging mirror
1. Draw the mirror, object, and focus.
2. Draw a ray parallel to the principal axis which reflects from the mirror and passes through the focus.
3. Draw a ray from the object passing through the focus and reflecting off the mirror to become parallel to the axis.
4. The intersecting point is the location of the image. If the rays do not intersect, extend the rays behind the mirror.

Ray-tracing method for a diverging mirror
1. Draw the mirror, object, and focus (behind mirror).
2. Draw a ray parallel to the principal axis which reflects and goes up, as if it came from the focus. Extend the ray behind the mirror.
3. Draw a ray going toward the focus of the mirror and reflecting as a horizontal ray. Extend the horizontal ray behind the mirror.
4. The intersection of rays behind the mirror is the location of the image.

Example 1: The passenger mirror in Larry's car is a diverging mirror with focal length 0.8 meters. A car is 10.0 meters away from the mirror.

    a. Where is the image of the car?
    b. What is the magnification of the image?
    c. Is the image real or virtual?
    d. Is the image upright or inverted?

Solution: Figure 11-18 shows the ray diagram.

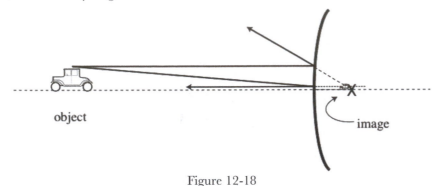

Figure 12-18

Note that the second ray uses the same focus as the first ray. The image of the car is behind the mirror and is virtual and tiny. The location is given by

$$\frac{1}{f} = \frac{1}{d_i} + \frac{1}{d_o}$$

$$\frac{1}{-0.8m} = \frac{1}{d_i} + \frac{1}{10m}$$

$$\frac{1}{d_i} = (-1.25 - 0.1)m^{-1} \quad 1.35m^{-1}$$

$$d_i = -0.74 \text{ m}$$

where the negative sign indicates the image is behind the mirror. The magnification is given by

$$m = -\frac{d_i}{d_o}$$

$$= -\frac{-0.74m}{10m}$$

$$= 0.074$$

where the positive sign indicates the image is upright. You do not need to pay attention to the sign conventions if you get the diagram right.

So why is there a warning "Objects in mirror are closer than they appear"? There are two things going on. The first is that the image is much closer to Larry than the object itself, and the second is that the image is smaller than the image Larry would see if he turned around and looked. Larry's brain does not care about where the image is and does not notice from which point the light rays appear to be diverging. Larry's brain compares the size of the image to what it knows is the size of a car in order to obtain a distance to the car. The distance thus calculated is about a factor of two too far away.

Example 2: Alice looks at herself in a plane mirror, standing 4 meters away.

    a. Where is her image?
    b. What is the magnification?
    c. Is the image real or virtual?
    d. Is the image upright or inverted?

Solution: Figure 11-19 shows a ray diagram, with which we can be a bit creative, since the focuses are an infinite distance away.

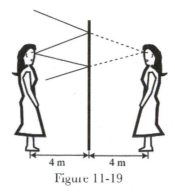

Figure 11-19

The image is 4 meters on the other side of the mirror, the magnification is 1, and the image is virtual and upright. To see this in the equations, we calculate

$$\frac{1}{f} = \frac{1}{d_i} + \frac{1}{d_o}$$

$$\frac{1}{\infty} = \frac{1}{d_i} + \frac{1}{4m}$$

$$0 = \frac{1}{d_i} + \frac{1}{4m}$$

$$d_i = -4m$$

Also

$$m = -\frac{d_i}{d_o}$$

$$= -\frac{-4m}{4m} \quad 1$$

Example 3: The image of a candle lies 10.0 meters behind a converging mirror (focal length 5.0 m). Where is the object?

Solution: Figure 11-20 shows the ray diagram. Treat the image as the object and thus the origin of light rays. The hard part of this problem (if you have to do the calculation) is remembering the sign $d_i = -10$ m. Then

$$\frac{1}{f} = \frac{1}{d_i} + \frac{1}{d_o}$$

$$\frac{1}{5.0m} = \frac{1}{-10m} + \frac{1}{d_o}$$

$$\frac{1}{d_o} = (\frac{1}{5.0} + \frac{1}{10})m^{-1}$$

$$= \frac{3}{10}m^{-1}$$

$$d_o = 3.33 \text{ m}$$

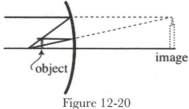

Figure 12-20

F. DISPERSION

In Section C we discussed the idea that the speed of light in each substance is related to its index of refraction n, and the index of refraction governs the bending of light as it crosses a boundary. While this is true, it is not the whole truth.

A more complete version of the truth is that the index of refraction depends slightly on the frequency of the light. (Sometimes not so slightly, but that is another story.) The chart shows the index of refraction for glass. You can see that n is *approximately* 1.5, but not exactly. So blue light bends a little more when going from air to glass than red light. This is the principle behind the prism (Figure 12-21). The phenomenon is called *dispersion*. There are not many simple calculations we can do at this point, but you should study the diagram of the prism until it makes sense to you. It should be noted that the red light travels through the glass faster than the blue light. Since red light has a lower frequency than blue light, it has a lower probability of interacting with the electric and magnetic fields generated by the moving electrons of the atoms in the glass.

f	color	n
4.6×10^{14} Hz	red	1.4566
4.9×10^{14} Hz	orange	1.4578
5.1×10^{14} Hz	yellow	1.4584
5.8×10^{14} Hz	green	1.4614
6.5×10^{14} Hz	blue	1.4649
7.5×10^{14} Hz	indigo	1.4702

Different colors (different frequencies) refract slightly differently, causing a separation of colors in a prism.
Figure 11-21

G. COMBINATION OF LENSES

When we view an object through several lenses that are near each other, then it is possible to treat the combination of lenses as one lens.

Combination of Lenses
When several lenses with focal lengths $f_1, f_2, \ldots$, are near each other, then the combination has a focal length f_{total} given by

$$\frac{1}{f_{total}} = \frac{1}{f_1} + \frac{1}{f_2} + \cdots .$$
(5)

The quantity $1/f$ for a lens is called the *power* of the lens, measure in [m^{-1} = diopters = D]. This word power has nothing to do with the other definition of power, that is, energy per time. The point here is that the power of a combination of lenses is the sum of the power of the lenses.

Example: Dieter has an eye which, when the eye is at rest, focuses light to a point 0.024 m behind the lens, which is 0.001 m in front of the retina. What is the power of the corrective lens he must wear?

Solution: The power of Dieter's eye is $P_{eye} = 1/0.024$ m = 41.67 D. The combination of lenses should have a focal length 0.024 m + 0.001 m = 0.025 m, so the power of the combination of the two lenses needs to be $P_{combo} = 1/0.025$ m = 40 D. Since $P_{combo} = P_{eye} + P_{correct}$, we have $P_{correct} = -1.67$ D.

H. IDEAL LENSES AND NONIDEAL LENSES

In our discussion of lenses, we assumed that the lens was able to focus all parallel rays to a single focus. Such an assumption is called an *ideal-lens* or *thin-lens* approximation. Real lenses are not so good. The deviation from ideality is called an *aberration*. For one thing, lenses that are very thick cannot focus light to a single point, so the image ends up distorted. If you look through a glass sphere, like a bead or a paperweight, you will notice that the image looks bent out of shape. This is called a *spherical aberration*.

I. THE EYE AND OPTICAL INSTRUMENTS

From a physics point of view, the most important aspect concerning the function of the eye is the focusing of light by the lens and aqueous humor on the retina. The eye acts as a converging lens that generally produces a real image focused on the retina, which is located in the back of the eye. The retina contains photoreceptors (rods and cones) that detect both the intensity and color of electromagnetic radiation in the visible portion of the spectrum. The brain converts the inverted real image into the perceived erect psychological image of appropriate dimensions to stimulate responses by the nervous system.

The shape of the lens can be adjusted by contraction of muscles within the eye. Figure 11-22 illustrates the range of positions for which a person can clearly focus on an object. The far point is the furthest point that an object can be placed in front of the eye and still be seen clearly. This corresponds to the maximum relaxation of the eye muscles connected to the lens, allowing the lens to flatten out due to pressure from the vitreous humor. This reduced curvature maximizes the focal length of the lens. The near point is the closest point that an object can be located in front of the eye and still be seen clearly. This corresponds to the maximum contraction of the eye mussels causing the lens to thicken, producing a shorter focal length so that the image can remain focused on the retina.

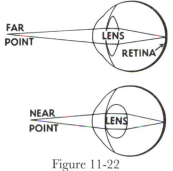

Figure 11-22

There are two general types of corrective lenses that compensate for farsightedness (hyperopia) and nearsightedness (myopia). As seen in Figure 11-23A, hyperopia results when the image is focused behind the retina, and can be corrected by using a converging lens of appropriate optical power to focus the image on the retina, Figure 11-23B. As seen in Figure 11-23C, myopia results from the image being focused in front of the retina, and can be corrected by using a diverging lens of appropriate optical power to likewise refocus the image on the retina.

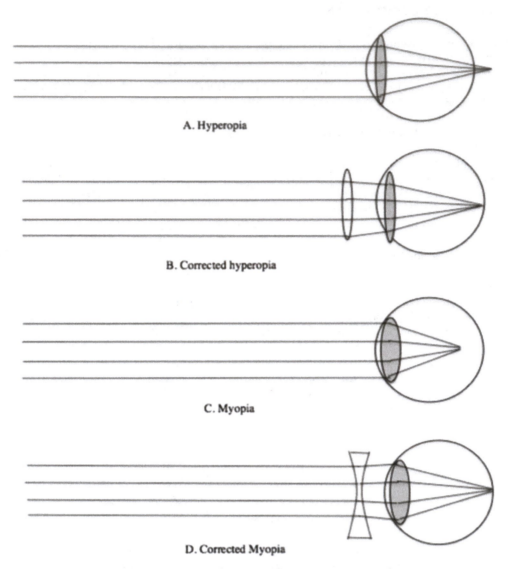

A. Hyperopia

B. Corrected hyperopia

C. Myopia

D. Corrected Myopia

Figure 11-23

Example 1: The eye contains a lens whose focal length can be adjusted. A candle (2 cm long) sits 0.1 m from the lens of the eye, and the image is focused on the retina. Assume the length of the eye from front to back is 2.5 cm.

a. What is the focal length of the lens?
b. Is the image upright or inverted?

Solution: We calculate the focus as follows:

$$\frac{1}{f} = \frac{1}{d_i} + \frac{1}{d_o}$$

$$\frac{1}{f} = \frac{1}{0.025\text{m}} + \frac{1}{0.1\text{m}}$$

$$\frac{1}{f} = 40\text{m}^{-1} + 10\text{m}^{-1} = 50\text{m}^{-1}$$

$$f = 0.02 \text{ m}$$

Figure 11-24 shows the appropriate diagram.

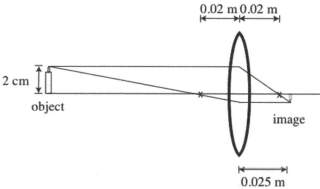

0.02 m 0.02 m

2 cm

object

image

0.025 m

Figure 11-24

We draw the horizontal line on the left of the lens in step 2. The other line, you will notice, takes the **near** focus into account. The image is where the lines meet, inverted and very small.

Because the image is located where light rays actually converge, the image is real. Figure 11-24 is a physics diagram. In an actual eye, there are many rays that converge to a point, and none of them need to be the two that we have drawn here. See Figure 11-25 for a more realistic diagram.

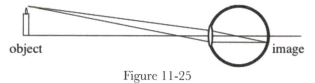

object   image

Figure 11-25

Example 2: The diverging lens on a pair of glasses has a focal length of 3.0 m. A candle is 9.0 cm tall and 6.0 m away.

    a. Where is the image of the candle when viewed through the lens?
    b. What is the size of the image?
    c. Is the image inverted or upright?
    d. Is the image real or virtual?

Solution: You should try this solution yourself before you read about it. Then work it out with the book. Figure 11-26 shows the ray diagram.

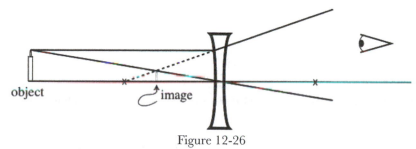

object   image

Figure 12-26

We had to extend a ray backwards in step 2. That means the image is virtual. Also the image is upright. The location of the image can be gotten from the equation:

$$\frac{1}{f} = \frac{1}{d_i} + \frac{1}{d_o}$$

$$\frac{1}{-3m} = \frac{1}{d_i} + \frac{1}{6m}$$

$$\frac{1}{d_i} = \left(-\frac{1}{3} - \frac{1}{6}\right)m^{-1}$$

$$= -\frac{1}{2}m^{-1}$$

$$d_i = -2\ m$$

where the negative result indicates the image is behind the lens, which we knew from the diagram. The magnification is given by

$$m = -\frac{d_i}{d_o}$$

$$= -\frac{-2 \text{ m}}{6 \text{ m}} = \frac{1}{3}$$

where the positive result indicates the image is upright. That gives the magnification. The size is then $(0.333)(9.0 \text{ cm}) = 3.0$ cm.

Optical instruments, such as microscopes and telescopes, are used to magnify the images of very small objects or objects located very far away, using multiple lenses arranged in a specific configuration within a tube, allowing for the adjustment of the distance between the lenses to adjust the magnification. Shown in Figure 11-27A, is a schematic diagram of a simple visible light microscope, with multiple objective lenses. Coarse and fine focusing adjustments allow for the modification of the distance between the objective lenses. Figure 11-27B provides a ray diagram for the images produced from a small object, by both the objective lens (Image 1) and the eyepiece lens (image 2). Both lenses are converging convex lenses of a specified optical power. The image produced by the objective lens is real and inverted with respect to the object. The location of Image 1 is between the focal point and the surface of the eyepiece lens. As a result, when a person looks through the eyepiece, they observe a Image 2, which is virtual (see Figure 11-16) and appears to be much larger than the original object.

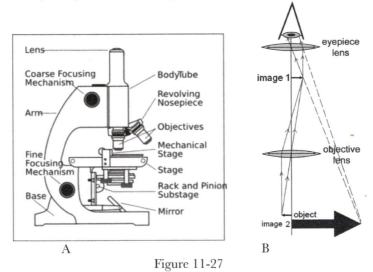

Figure 11-27

Example 3: What is the magnification of a compound microscope whose objective lens has a magnification of -1.5 and whose eyepiece lens has a magnification of +4.0?

Solution: The key to solving problems involving multiple lenses is to remember that the image created by the first lens will be the object for the second lens. The magnification equation is $M = h_i/h_o = -d_i/d_o$. If we assume that the height of the object is 1, the height of the image created by the first lens will be -1.5. This image is a real, since it is inverted with respect to the object. If we now use -1.5 as the h_o for the second lens, $h_i = -1.5 \times 4 = -6$. This means that the image will be six times larger than the original object, and inverted with respect to the orientation of the original object. Essentially the total magnification is the product of the magnifications of the component lenses.

J. INTERFERENCE

All waves, mechanical waves like sound or water waves, electromagnetic radiation and even particle waves of electrons, protons or neutrons are capable of creating interference patterns when more than one oscillation interacts. If two oscillations moving in different directions, or two waves with different frequencies moving in the same direction interact within the same space and time, an interference pattern due to the additive properties of amplitude will result. For two in-phase waves having the same wavelengths, traveling in the same direction, the amplitudes of the crests and troughs will coincide and result in a new wave that has twice the amplitude (Figure 11-28A). Out of phase combinations result in destructive interference (Figure 11-28B), or a wave with reduced amplitude (or no amplitude?).

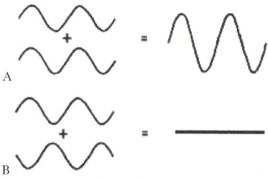

A

B

Figure 11-28

If two (or more) waves with slightly different wavelengths interact, as in Figure 11-29, complicated repeating interference patterns can result (see also Figure 11-13).

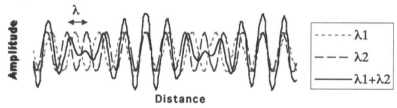

Figure 11-29

K. GRATINGS AND FILMS

Diffraction is a phenomenon that results when a wave moving through a medium, interacts with the surface of a material such that the wave fronts are bent by the surface. This phenomenon is distinct from refraction, because the wave direction is changed without passing from one material into the other. As an example, if a water wave is observed from some altitude above the surface of the water, a series of moving parallel lines would be observed, corresponding to the crests and troughs of the wave. If the wave encounters a levee with an opening that is the same as the wavelength of the water wave, a portion of the wave will pass through the opening and come out the other side, but the wave crests are no longer parallel, but have been bent due to diffraction. The new wave behaves as if it was generated by a point source, with crests and troughs forming concentric circles radiating from the opening. If the opening is slightly larger than the wavelength, the diffracted waves emerging from the other side, will appear to be generated by multiple point sources in the opening *d*, Figure 11-30A. This diffraction phenomenon is common to all types of waves, including electromagnetic radiation passing through a single slit, and results in an interference pattern, which manifests itself in a plot of light intensity versus *n* for the ***destructive*** interference, Figure 11-30B, where q is the angle that the destructive interference occurs relative to the perpendicular.

$$d \sin q = nl$$

In this plot a strong central peak is observed with additional fringe peaks of decreasing intensity. The mathematical model describing this behavior is based on right triangles and simple trigonometric relationships that we will describe in detail for diffraction gratings.

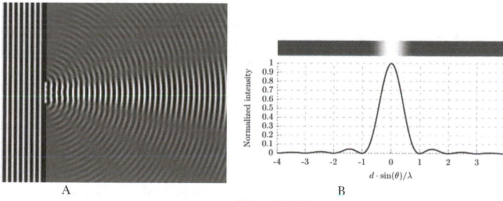

A   B

Figure 11-30

We next should consider the interactions of a wave with two openings comparable to the wavelength, but the distance $d*$ between the openings is slightly greater than the wavelength. Again an interference pattern is observed, as seen in Figure 11-31. To compare and contrast to the single slit experiment, the mathematical model for **constructive** interference in the double slit experiment is

$$d* \sin q = nl$$

It is now well accepted that light has both wave and particle properties. The significance of the double slit experiment for electromagnetic radiation, is that it clearly demonstrates the wave nature of light, since a purely particle description for this experiment would result in only two bright spots on a screen, rather than the bright central peak, with associated decreasing intensity fringe peaks that are experimentally observed.

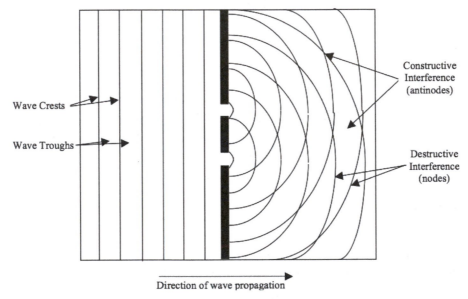

Figure 11-31

A diffraction grating can best be described as a series of parallel lines imprinted on a transparent material, such as a plastic. Let us first consider the interaction of highly coherent monochromatic light from a red laser (l = 650 nm), where the openings are of comparable size to the wavelength of light. If the laser is focused such that the light rays are perpendicular to the surface (Figure 11-32), Fraunhofer diffraction is observed, in which bright spots are seen on a screen, with a specific pattern of intensity, corresponding to the order (n = 1, 2, 3 ...) of diffraction on either side of the central peak. The angle of diffraction f' can be easily determined by measuring the distance between the parallel surfaces of the diffraction grating and the screen D and the distance between the bright spots d', representing the adjacent and opposite sides of a right triangle, respectively. Remember that these diffraction spots result from constructive interference of the light waves.

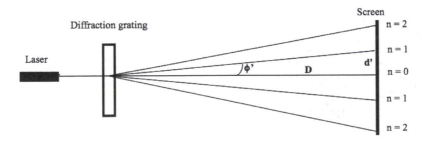

Figure 11-32

Now let us consider a ray diagram for the diffraction grating that results in constructive interference. As seen in Figure 11-33, as the wave passes through the openings, the angle q, is equal to f' in Figure 11-32. Note that constructive interference will result when each wave travels distances that are multiples of $n\Delta l$, where in this case n is an integer corresponding to the order of the diffraction fringe shown in Figure 11-32 and Δl is equal to the wavelength (l) of the light. Subsequently, as seen by the trigonometric relationship for the resulting right triangle, it is possible to calculate the spacing d between the openings in the diffraction grating.

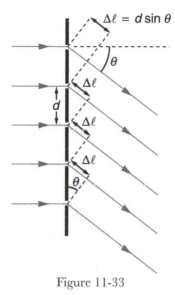

Figure 11-33

Example 1: What is the number of diffraction lines per centimeter, for a diffraction grating that produces a first order (m = 1) diffraction angle q = 30° for constructive interference using a red laser whose wavelength is 650 nm?

Solution: The appropriate mathematical relationship is nΔl = d sin q, as seen in Figure 11-33, where m represents integers for the order of the diffraction fringe. If the angle of diffraction that corresponds to constructive interference is 30°, then sin 30° = 0.5. Since Δl is equal to the wavelength of the laser light, then l = 650 nm, which is 650 x 10⁻⁹ m = 6.5 x 10⁻⁷ m, or 6.5 x 10⁻⁵ cm. The distance between the openings d, which is d = (6.5 x 10⁻⁵ cm) ÷ 0.5 = 13 x 10⁻⁵ = 1.3 x 10⁻⁴ cm per line. However, the question asks for the number of lines per centimeter, therefore we need the inverse, or 7.7 x 10³ lines per centimeter. Common sense should remind us that diffraction gratings have a large number of very small lines that are nearly impossible to see with the naked eye.

If white light, or light consisting of multiple wavelengths, is focused on a diffraction grating, dispersion will occur, however, there is a significant difference in the mechanism and the observed order in which the colors are bent as compared with a prism. When the spectra obtained from a diffraction grating and from a prism are compared, longer wavelengths (red) are diffracted more, but refracted less, than shorter wavelengths (violet), resulting in an inversion of the order in which the colors are observed.

When monochromatic light strikes the surface of a thin film of a material, such as a soap bubble, oil, or a sheet of plastic, at an incident angle as seen in Figure 11-34, a portion of the light is reflected, and the remaining portion is transmitted and refracted by the upper surface. When the ray reaches the bottom surface, again a portion of the wave will be reflected back to the upper surface, where a portion can be transmitted and refracted. The path of this ray exiting the upper surface will be parallel to the originally reflected ray. If the difference in the distances that the two rays travel (AD) after exiting the upper surface are multiples of the wavelength of the light, then constructive interference will occur. The interference is dependent upon the thickness of the film, the angle of incidence and the wavelength of the light. When white light is focused on the film, dispersion will occur, resulting is a series of rainbow like repeating patterns of color.

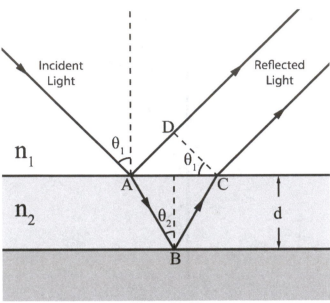

Figure 11-34

Example 2: What is the thickness of the an oil film, if the smallest angle of incidence of red light (l = 650 nm) that produces constructive interference is 30°, where n_1 is the index of refraction of air and $n_2 = 1.5$ is the index of refraction of the oil?

Solution: Notice that the angle of incidence q_1 is the same angle as in the right triangle ACD. For constructive interference, the distance AD must equal the wavelength of the light, 650 nm = 6.5×10^{-7} m and is opposite of the angle q_1, where AC is the hypotenuse of this right triangle. Therefore AC = $1 \div \sin q_1$ = (6.5×10^{-7} m) $\div 0.5 = 1.3 \times 10^{-6}$ m. We can determine the value of $\sin q_2$ by using Snell's law, $n_1 \sin q_1 = n_2 \sin q_2$.

$$\sin q_2 = (1.0 \times 0.5)/(1.5) = 0.333$$

Now we can turn our attention to the right triangle within the film with an angle of q_2 and hypotenuse of AB, which requires that $\sin q_2 = (AC/2)/AB$, which now allows us to calculate the distance AB

$$AB = (6.5 \times 10^{-7} \text{ m})/0.333 = 1.95 \times 10^{-6} \text{ m}$$

Since we have a right triangle, applying the Pythagorean theorem gives

$$(1.95 \times 10^{-6})^2 = (6.5 \times 10^{-7})^2 + d^2$$
$$d^2 = (3.8 \times 10^{-12}) - (4.22 \times 10^{-13})$$
$$d^2 = 3.38 \times 10^{-12}$$
$$d = 1.84 \times 10^{-6} \text{ m}$$

L. STRUCTURAL ANALYSIS BY X-RAY DIFFRACTION

Crystalline solids have three-dimensional structures in which the repeating patterns of atoms form unit cells that act like three-dimensional diffraction gratings. By using electromagnetic radiation (X-rays) with short wavelengths similar to the spacing between the atoms, diffraction patterns can be mathematically analyzed to discern the planes of atoms, symmetry and three-dimensional structures of the molecular orientations within the unit cell. The Bragg equation describes the diffraction by the planes of atoms, with spacing d, angle q between the X-ray and the plane and the usual integer n representing the order of diffraction. This equation should seem similar to the equations previously presented for the single slit experiment and diffraction gratings, because it is based on similar trigonometric relationships for right triangles, but the details of its derivation are probably beyond the scope of our current discussion. It is unlikely that you will have to memorize the Bragg equation for the MCAT, but you might have to interpret information in a passage about X-ray diffraction.

$$2d \sin q = nl$$

X-ray diffraction has become a very powerful tool for understanding the structures of all sorts of materials, ranging from high-temperature superconductors to important biomolecules, such as enzymes.

In 1952 Gosling and Franklin, used X-ray diffraction to help determine the structure of a crystalline form of deoxyribonucleic acid (DNA). After performing numerous experiments, they were able to orient the crystal such that the long axis of the unit cell was perpendicular to the path of the X-ray beam. In her notes she (Franklin) wrote, "The results suggest a helical structure (which must be very closely packed) containing 2 (Figure 11-35A), 3 or 4 co-axial nucleic acid chains per helical unit, and having the phosphate groups near the outside." This was well before Watson and Crick published their Nobel award winning description of DNA, which was based in part on Franklin's experiments. This insight into the helical structure of crystalline DNA can be easily understood by analogy to the shape of a coiled spring. If one were to look closely at a spring held with the principle axis oriented vertically, you would see two sets of parallel straight lines (Figure 11-35B) (ignoring the curved shapes that would be seen on the ends) forming an angle of 2α, where α represents the pitch angle of the helix. If one were to imagine a large number of springs (DNA molecules), all oriented vertically, the straight portions would appear to form a series of intersecting diffraction grating lines, that would produce two series of intersecting bright diffraction spots (Figure 11-35C), similar to what Gosling and Franklin observed in "Photo 51". Additionally, less pronounced diffraction spots and patterns resulted from the layers formed by the nucleic bases and other repeating atomic patterns in the crystalline structure.

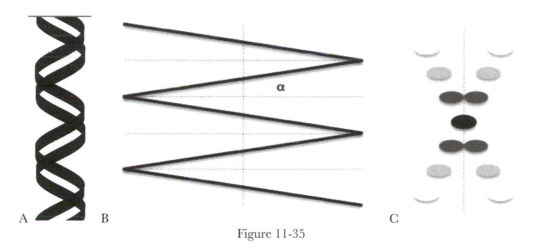

Figure 11-35

Example 1: In the famous "Photo 51", the vertically oriented angle between the two sets of diffraction spots was 76°. What is the pitch angle a for the DNA?

Solution: The series of spots are always oriented perpendicular to the orientation of the diffracting planes in the crystal, the value of 2α would also be 76°. In this case the pitch angle is with respect to the horizontal plane, and $\alpha = 76/2 = 38°$.

In Section F we noted that different frequencies of light have slightly different indices of refraction, which can cause different colors to have different focal lengths. This is called a ***chromatic aberration***.

M. CHAPTER SUMMARY

In this chapter we looked at light as an example of waves, looking specifically at reflection, refraction, diffraction and lens effects. The properties of waves we have studied in the past three chapters include:

1. interference (by superposition),
2. frequencies in standing waves,
3. beats,
4. Doppler shift,
5. reflection,
6. refraction,
7. diffraction, and
8. dispersion.

All waves exhibit these properties, so the way we have divided them up among chapters titled "Waves", "Sound", and "Light" is somewhat artificial. Refraction is most often observed in light waves, so it is generally studied in the context of light. Likewise, beats are usually observed in sound waves and only extremely rarely in light. You should be aware that sound waves reflect and refract just like light, bending toward the normal of the interface when they pass from a fast medium to a slow one.

If you visualize this principle in diagrams such as Figures 11-4 and 11-12 and practice the ray-tracing diagram, then you should do well on problems that this chapter covers.

CHAPTER 11 PROBLEMS

Use the following indices of refraction for problems 1–12:

substance	n
air	1
water	$1.3 \approx 4/3$
hydrogen peroxide	1.414
glass	$1.5 \approx 3/2$
ammonium bromide	1.7

1. Which of the following best shows the refracted ray at a glass-air-glass interface?

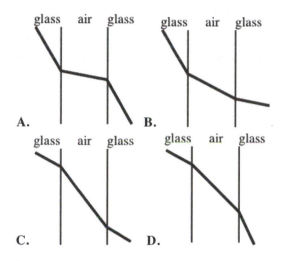

2. In the following figures, there is a triangle of glass in air. Which best shows the refracted ray of light?

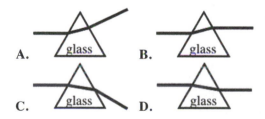

3. In the figure, a ray of light approaches normal to the surface on the left. Which best represents the refracted ray which leaves the right surface?

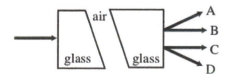

4. A ray of light in air is incident on an interface with glass, followed by an interface with water, such that the air-glass interface is parallel to the glass-water interface. Which best represents the refracted ray?

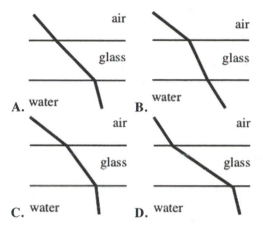

5. A spherical air bubble is embedded in glass, and a ray of light (incident ray I) approaches the bubble as shown in the figure. Which best represents the refracted ray which passes through the bubble?

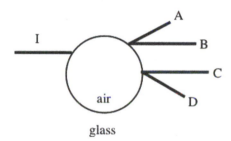

Use the following information in questions 6–8:

A beam of light in water encounters a boundary with air, so that the angle between the beam and the normal to the surface is 30°. (See figure.)

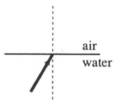

6. Which expression best expresses the angle the refracted ray makes with the normal?

   A. 30°
   B. $\sin^{-1} 1/3$
   C. $\sin^{-1} 2/3$
   D. $\sin^{-1} 3/4$

7. Which expression best expresses the angle the reflected ray makes with the normal?

   A. 30°
   B. 60°
   C. sin⁻¹ 2/3
   D. sin⁻¹ 3/4

8. Which expression best expresses the critical angle for the interface of water with air?

   A. sin⁻¹ 1/3
   B. sin⁻¹ 2/3
   C. sin⁻¹ 3/4
   D. None of the above.

Use the following information in questions 9 and 10:

A light beam of frequency 1.4 x 10¹⁴ Hz in air encounters a surface with hydrogen peroxide (index of refraction = $\sqrt{2}$). (See figure.)

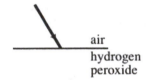

air
hydrogen
peroxide

9. What is the critical angle for this encounter?

   A. 30°
   B. 45°
   C. 60°
   D. None of the above.

10. If the angle of encounter is less than the critical angle, which of the following is the frequency of the light beam in the hydrogen peroxide?

    A. 9.9 x 10¹³ Hz
    B. 1.4 x 10¹⁴ Hz
    C. 2.0 x 10¹⁴ Hz
    D. 2.8 x 10¹⁴ Hz

Use the following information in questions 11 and 12:

A light beam of wavelength 510 nm in air encounters a flat surface of ammonium bromide (index of refraction = $\sqrt{3} \approx 1.7$), such that the smallest angle the beam makes with the surface is 30°. (See figure.)

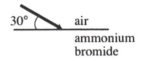

30°   air
        ammonium
        bromide

11. What is the smallest angle the refracted ray makes with the surface?

    A. 17°
    B. 30°
    C. 45°
    D. 60°

12. What is the wavelength of the refracted ray?

    A. 300 nm
    B. 510 nm
    C. 867 nm
    D. 1020 nm

Use the following information in questions 13–15:

We observe a candle through a converging lens with focal length 4 m. The candle is 0.1 m tall and 2 m away from the lens. (See figure.)

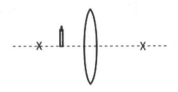

13. Where is the resulting image?

    A. 1.333 m from the lens on the same side as the object.
    B. 4 m from the lens on the same side as the object.
    C. 1.333 m from the lens on the opposite side from the object.
    D. 4 m from the lens on the opposite side from the object.

14. Which of the following characterizes the image?

    A. upright and real
    B. upright and virtual
    C. inverted and real
    D. inverted and virtual

15. What is the magnification of the image?

    A. 0.5
    B. 0.6667
    C. 1.5
    D. 2

Use the following information in questions 16 and 17:

A sodium emission tube produces light of frequency 5.1 x 10^{14} Hz. It sits 6 m from a converging lens of focal length 2 m.

16. Which of the following characterizes the image?

    A. upright and real
    B. upright and virtual
    C. inverted and real
    D. inverted and virtual

17. For a different frequency of the light, the focal length of the lens is different from 2 m. This phenomenon is called

    A. interference.
    B. refraction.
    C. dispersion.
    D. incidence.

Use the following information in questions 18 and 19:

A candle 21 cm tall sits 4 m away from a diverging lens with focal length 3 m. (See figure.)

18. Where is the resulting image?

    A. 12 m from the lens on the same side as the object.
    B. 12/7 m from the lens on the same side as the object.
    C. 12 m from the lens on the opposite side from the object.
    D. 12/7 m from the lens on the opposite side from the object.

19. What is the size of the image?

    A. 7 cm
    B. 9 cm
    C. 49 cm
    D. 63 cm

Use the following information in questions 20 and 21:

A candle is viewed through a lens. The candle is 4 m from the lens, while the image is 2 m from the lens on the other side.

20. What is the focal length of the lens?

    A. –4 m
    B. –4/3 m
    C. 4/3 m
    D. 4 m

21. What is the magnification of the image?

    A. Half as large and erect.
    B. Half as large and inverted.
    C. Twice as large and erect.
    D. Twice as large and inverted.

Use the following information in questions 22–27:

We view an object at various distances using a mirror with focal length 12 m. (See figure.)

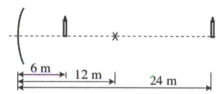

22. If the object is 6 m in front of the mirror, where is the image?

    A. 6 m in front of the mirror.
    B. 6 m behind the mirror.
    C. 12 m in front of the mirror.
    D. 12 m behind the mirror.

23. If the object is 6 m in front of the mirror, what is its magnification?

    A. It is half as large, and the image is upright.
    B. It is half as large, and the image is inverted.
    C. It is twice as large, and the image is upright.
    D. It is twice as large, and the image is inverted.

24. If the object is 24 m away from the mirror, where is the image?

    A. 12 m in front of the mirror.
    B. 12 m behind the mirror.
    C. 24 m in front of the mirror.
    D. 24 m behind the mirror.

25. If the object is 24 m away from the mirror, what best characterizes the image?

    A. upright and real
    B. upright and virtual
    C. inverted and real
    D. inverted and virtual

26. If the object is an infinite distance away, where is the image?

    A. 6 m in front of the mirror.
    B. 6 m behind the mirror.
    C. 12 m in front of the mirror.
    D. 12 m behind the mirror.

27. What happens when a candle is placed at the focus?

    A. An image is formed 6 m in front of the mirror.
    B. An image is formed 6 m behind the mirror.
    C. Light rays end up parallel going to infinity.
    D. Light rays reconverge at the focus.

Use the following information in questions 28–31:

A light bulb is placed 12 m in front of a diverging mirror with focus 6 m. (See figure.)

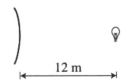

28. Where is the resulting image?

    A. 4 m behind the mirror.
    B. 4 m in front of the mirror.
    C. 12 m behind the mirror.
    D. 12 m in front of the mirror.

29. What is the absolute magnification of the image?

    A. 0.333
    B. 1.5
    C. 2
    D. 3

30. The image is

    A. upright and real.
    B. upright and virtual.
    C. inverted and real.
    D. inverted and virtual.

31. What happens if a light bulb is placed 6 m in front of the mirror?

    A. An image is formed 6 m behind the mirror.
    B. An image is formed 3 m behind the mirror.
    C. An image is formed 6 m in front of the mirror.
    D. No image is formed and the rays end up traveling parallel to infinity.

Use the following information in questions 32 and 33:

A light bulb is 2 m in front of a mirror, and the image is 4 m behind the mirror.

32. What can be said about the mirror?
    A. It is a converging mirror with focal length 1.33 m.
    B. It is a converging mirror with focal length 4 m.
    C. It is a diverging mirror with focal length 1.33 m.
    D. It is a diverging mirror with focal length 4 m.

33. What is the magnification of the image?

    A. The magnification is 0.5, and the image is upright.
    B. The magnification is 0.5, and the image is inverted.
    C. The magnification is 2, and the image is upright.
    D. The magnification is 2, and the image is inverted.

Passage 1

Electromagnetic radiation from an incandescent source, such as a light bulb, is unpolarized, which means that the electric field of the wave points in random directions perpendicular to wave travel. One way to produce polarized radiation involves applying an alternating voltage to a straight piece of wire to form an antenna (See figure below). Radiation is emitted from the antenna perpendicular to the wire with a polarization which is parallel to the wire.

In this diagram the small arrows show the direction of the electric field, and the large arrows show the direction of the wave.

Another way to obtain polarized radiation involves allowing unpolarized radiation to be incident on a film or material which transmits radiation of one polarization but absorbs radiation of the perpendicular polarization. Such a film is called a *polarizer*. If unpolarized light of intensity I_0 is incident on a vertical polarizer, the radiation that passes through is vertically polarized with intensity $1/2\ I_0$. The figure below shows this schematically.

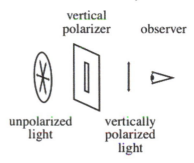

vertical polarizer   observer

unpolarized   vertically
light   polarized
                 light

If polarized radiation is incident on a polarizer, the amount of energy that is transmitted depends on the relative angle of the radiation polarization and the polarizer axis. If they are aligned, then all the radiation is transmitted. If the angles differ by θ, then the intensity of the transmitted radiation is $\cos^2\theta$ of the original intensity.

All of the foregoing refers to ideal polarizers. All manufactured polarizers have less than ideal efficiency which comes from reflection off the two surfaces and absorption of the parallel component.

In questions 1–4, an unpolarized radiation source is incident on a series of polarizers. Without the polarizers the intensity of the source is I_0. Assume the polarizers are ideal.

34. In the figure below, unpolarized light is incident on polarizers A and B in series. Polarizers A and B are both oriented vertically. What is the intensity of the resultant beam?

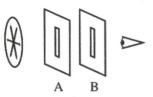

A   B

A. I_0
B. $I_0/2$
C. less than $I_0/2$ but greater than zero intensity
D. 0

35. In the figure below, unpolarized light is incident on polarizers A and B in series. Polarizer A is oriented vertically, while polarizer B is oriented horizontally. What is the intensity of the resultant beam?

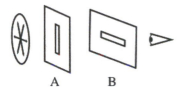

A   B

A. I_0
B. $I_0/2$
C. less than $I_0/2$ but greater than zero intensity
D. 0

36. An optically active substance is a substance which rotates the plane of polarization of a beam. The figure shows a modification of the figure in Problem 2, with an optically active substance between the polarizers. What is the intensity of the resultant beam?

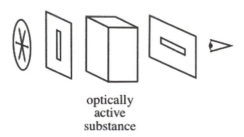

optically
active
substance

A. I_0
B. $I_0/2$
C. It could have any intensity less than (or equal to) $I_0/2$
D. 0

37. Where does the energy of the original beam go which is not in the resultant beam?

   A. chemical energy
   B. potential energy
   C. heat
   D. nuclear energy

38. A horizontal antenna is aligned along a north-south axis. This antenna has an alternating voltage applied to it, so it is emitting electromagnetic radiation. An observer is due north of the antenna. (See the figure.) What polarization does he detect from the antenna?

 observer

N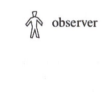

   A. He observes horizontal polarization.
   B. He observes vertical polarization.
   C. He observes an unpolarized beam.
   D. He observes no radiation.

SECTION 3
CONTENT REVIEW PROBLEMS

1. A silver necklace has a mass of 50 grams and a volume 4.82 cm^3. It is tied to a string and lowered into a glass of water. The other end of the string is connected to a force meter. What is the reading on the force meter? (Take the density of water to be 1 g/cm^3, and use 9.8 m/s^2 for the acceleration due to gravity.)

   A. 0.44 N
   B. 0.49 N
   C. 0.54 N
   D. There is not enough information to answer the question.

2. A coffee cup sits fully submerged at the bottom of the sink filled with water. The coffee cup is 120 grams and is able to hold 0.1 liters of coffee. If the density of water is 10^3 kg/m^3, what is the force that the sink exerts on the coffee cup? (Use 9.8 m/s^2 for the acceleration due to gravity.)

   A. 0.20 N
   B. 1.18 N
   C. 2.16 N
   D. There is not enough information to answer the question.

Use the following to answer questions 3 and 4:

The restaurant Bistro-an-Maine-Street is located on the fourth floor of a certain building. Part of the restaurant's "character" is that the beverages are served on the first floor with a straw leading up to the fourth-floor customers 12 meters up. The joke is that customers cannot manage to drink their beverages. One night a chemist brings along a vacuum pump from her laboratory. Assume the pump can draw a perfect vacuum.

Assume also that surface tension of the beverage plays no role, and we have

$P_{atm} = 10^5$ Pa,
$\rho_{beverage} = 10^3$ kg/m^3,
$g = 10$ m/s^2,
$\rho_{air} = 1.2$ kg/m^3,
$R = 0.0821$ L atm/K mol,
and the radius of the straw $r_{straw} = 3 \times 10^{-3}$ m.

3. What happens when the chemist connects her pump to the straw?

   A. The pump is able to draw the liquid to the fourth floor and quench her thirst.
   B. The pump is theoretically able to draw the liquid to the fourth floor, but it requires an infinite amount of time.
   C. The beverage will not rise past a certain point, no matter how good the pump is.
   D. There is not enough information to answer this question.

4. Consider the following possibilities:

   I. Use a straw of smaller radius.
   II. Drink a beverage which has a smaller density. Which option will help a customer to draw the beverage up the straw?

   A. I only.
   B. II only.
   C. Either I or II would work.
   D. Neither I nor II would work.

5. A metal box in the shape of a cube which is 0.1 m on a side floats in space, where there is a vacuum. The box has 8 grams of oxygen gas in it at 2 atm. Use $R = 0.0821$ L atm / K mol, and 1 atm = 1.01 x 10^5 Pa. What is the best estimate of the force the gas exerts on one face of the cube?

   A. 210 N
   B. 420 N
   C. 2100 N
   D. 2.1 x 10^6 N

Use the following to answer questions 6–8:

When the dike sprang a leak, the little Dutch boy placed his finger in the hole to stop the flow. We can model the dike as a dam 20 m high and 100 km long on top of an ocean which is another 980 m deep, 100 km wide, and 100 km long. Let's say the hole is a square 0.01 m by 0.01 m located 1 m below the surface of the water.

Assume that viscosity is negligible. We have

$P_{atm} = 10^5$ Pa, $\rho_{water} = 10^3$ kg/m^3, and $g = 10$ m/s^2.

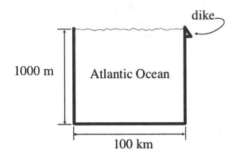

Use the following to answer questions 9 and 10:

A steel hammer ($m_h = 790$ grams) is tied to a string which is hung from a force meter. A container of water ($m_w = 5$ kg) sits on a scale. The hammer is lowered completely into the water but it does not touch the bottom.

Assume the density of steel is 7.9 g/cm^3 and the density of water is 1.0 g/cm^3. The acceleration due to gravity is 10 m/s^2.

6. What would be the velocity of the stream if the little Dutch boy removed his finger from the hole?

    A. 4.5 m/s
    B. 45 m/s
    C. 140 m/s
    D. There is not enough information to answer this question.

7. What would be the flow through the hole if the little Dutch boy removed his finger?

    A. 4.5×10^{-4} m^3/s
    B. 4.5×10^2 m^3/s
    C. 4.5×10^4 m^3/s
    D. There is not enough information to answer this question.

8. What force does the little Dutch boy have to exert in order to keep his finger in the dike?

    A. 1 N
    B. 10^2 N
    C. 10^4 N
    D. There is not enough information to answer this question.

9. What does the force meter read?
    A. 6.9 N
    B. 7.9 N
    C. 8.9 N
    D. There is not enough information to answer this question.

10. What does the scale holding the water read?

    A. 49 N
    B. 50 N
    C. 51 N
    D. There is not enough information to answer this question.

Passage 1

When we place a straw (a hollow cylindrical tube) in water, the water inside the straw rises above the surface level outside and a meniscus (curvature of the surface) forms. Consider the column of water in the straw from the height of the water outside the straw to the top of the column. (See figure, where the column is shown shaded.) Let P_1 be a point in the straw at the bottom of the column and let P_2 be a point inside the water column at the top.

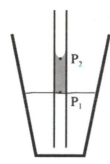

The force due to surface tension for a maximally stretched surface is given by $F_{surf} = \gamma L$, where γ is the coefficient of surface tension (which depends only on the substance) and L is the length of the line of contact between an object and the fluid. For this problem use the following:

ρ = density of water
γ = surface tension of water
r = radius of the straw
h = height of the column
P_{atm} = atmospheric pressure
g = acceleration due to gravity

11. Which pressure is greater, the pressure at P_1 or at P_2?

    A. Pressure at P_1 is greater than at P_2 by the term ρgh.
    B. Pressure at P_1 and at P_2 are both P_{atm}.
    C. Pressure at P_1 and at P_2 are the same but not P_{atm}.
    D. Pressure at P_2 is greater than at P_1 by the term ρgh.

12. What are the forces acting on the column?

    A. Gravity, down.
    B. Gravity, down; force due to pressure on top surface; force due to pressure on bottom surface.
    C. Gravity, down; force due to pressure on top surface; force due to pressure on bottom surface; and surface tension, up.
    D. Gravity, down; force due to pressure on top surface; force due to pressure on bottom surface; and surface tension, down.

13. What expression gives the magnitude of the force due to pressure on the top of the column?

    A. $F = \pi r^2(P_{atm} - \rho gh)$
    B. $F = 2\pi r^2(P_{atm} - \rho gh)$
    C. $F = \pi r^2 P_{atm}$
    D. $F = 2\pi r^2 P_{atm}$

14. What expression gives the force due to gravity on the column?

    A. $F_{grav} = r^2 hg$
    B. $F_{grav} = 2r^2 hg$
    C. $F_{grav} = \pi r^2 h\rho g$
    D. $F_{grav} = 2\pi r^2 h\rho g$

15. What expression approximates the force due to surface tension?

    A. $2r\gamma$
    B. $\pi r\gamma$
    C. $2\pi r\gamma$
    D. $2\pi r^2 \gamma/h$

16. What happens if r decreases by a factor of 2?

    A. The height h would stay the same.
    B. The height h would increase by a factor of 2.
    C. The height h would increase by a factor of 4.
    D. There is not enough information to answer this question.

You should understand the last passage before going on to the next one.

Passage 2

Vascular plants transport water by a passive transport system using xylem, a cell tissue which forms thin, long cylinders along branches of plants. In particular, trees use this tissue to transport water against the force of gravity to great heights.

In one model (Model 1, shown in first figure below), xylem is a tube or pipe, and water is "pulled" up by reducing the pressure at the top of the column of water in the xylem. The figure shows a tube whose bottom end is in a reservoir of water. The top end is closed and has a cavity whose pressure is less than atmospheric pressure. It turns out not to be a good model for Nature.

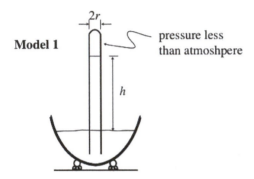

Model 1 — pressure less than atmoshpere — h

In another model (Model 2, shown in figure below), xylem is a narrow tube which exerts a force on water by surface tension, the same force that causes water to rise in a thin straw when it is sitting in water. In this case the forces on the column of water have to be balanced, so the downward force of gravity is equal to the upward force of surface tension. The force of surface tension is the product of the coefficient of surface tension γ (0.072 N/m for water) and the circumference of the cylinder.

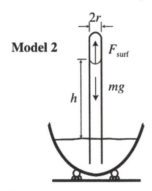

Model 2 — F_{surf} — mg — h

In both models the height of the column is h and the radius of the tube is r, which is about 2×10^{-7} m. Use the estimate $P_{atm} = 10^5$ N/m^2 for atmospheric pressure. Use 10^3 kg/m^3 for the density of water and 10 m/s^2 for the acceleration of gravity.

17. What is maximum height of a column of water in xylem in Model 1?
    A. 1 meter
    B. 10 meters
    C. 20 meters
    D. 200 meters

18. How could the maximum height be increased in Model 1?

    A. Decrease the radius of the cylinder.
    B. Increase the radius of the cylinder.
    C. Increase the density of xylem.
    D. None of the above will increase the maximum height.

19. What is maximum height of a column of water in xylem in Model 2?

    A. 3.6 meters
    B. 36 meters
    C. 72 meters
    D. 144 meters

20. How could the maximum height be increased in Model 2?

    A. Decrease the radius of the cylinder.
    B. Increase the radius of the cylinder.
    C. Increase the density of xylem.
    D. None of the above will increase the maximum height.

Note: The tallest trees are the redwoods, which can be as high as 100 meters.

Passage 3

When the bombardier beetle is attacked or provoked, it sprays a jet of hot liquid toward its attacker. The jet comes out of an opening at the tip of its abdomen, which it can move in order to direct the stream.

The physical mechanism for creating the hot spray consists of two chambers in the abdomen: an inner chamber which stores hydrogen peroxide and hydroquinone in water solution, connected by a valve to an outer chamber which contains oxidative enzymes (peroxidase and catalase) adhered to the walls. The beetle squeezes the hydrogen peroxide and hydroquinone into the outer chamber where the following reaction takes place to form quinone (also called 1,4 benzoquinone):

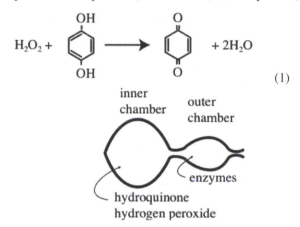

(1)

The heats of formation of the various compounds are shown in the table.

species	$\Delta H° \left(\dfrac{kcal}{mole} \right)$
hydrogen peroxide	−45.68
hydroquinone	−44.65
quinone	−44.84
water	−68.32

This reaction in the outer chamber creates a solution of the products of reaction (1) in water. This solution has enough heat and pressure to create a hot stream to shoot out of an opening (radius 0.1 mm) in the tip of the abdomen at a speed $v = 12$ m/s.

We can model this outer chamber as a volume (reaction flask) with a nozzle. The pressure in the chamber P_{cham} is greater than the outside pressure P_{atm}, and this provides the force on the fluid in the nozzle. The nozzle has radius r and cross-sectional area A, and the entire chamber has volume V_{cham}. The temperature of the fluid in the chamber is T_{cham}.

chamber

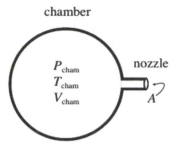

21. What is the primary reason that the reaction rate of the reaction (1) increases when the reactants go from the inner chamber to the outer chamber?

   A. The temperature is increased.
   B. The concentration of the reactants is increased.
   C. The surface area of reaction is increased.
   D. The activation energy is decreased.

22. What is the flow rate out of the beetle's abdomen?

   A. 4×10^{-8} cm³/s
   B. 4×10^{-6} cm³/s
   C. 4×10^{-4} cm³/s
   D. 0.4 cm³/s

23. What is the approximate height to which the spray would travel if it were directed straight up? (Ignore air resistance.)

   A. 0.6 meters
   B. 1.2 meters
   C. 7.2 meters
   D. 14.4 meters

24. How does the catalyst affect the heat of reaction for reaction (1)?

   A. The catalyst decreases the heat of reaction.
   B. The catalyst does not affect the heat of reaction.
   C. The catalyst increases the heat of reaction.
   D. The catalyst may decrease or increase the heat of reaction depending on the temperature.

25. Which of the following expressions gives the *best* approximation of the pressure inside the chamber?

   A. $P_{atm} + 1/2\ \rho v^2$, where ρ is the density of the fluid.
   B. $n_q RT/V_{cham}$, where n_q is the number of moles of quinone in the chamber.
   C. nRT/V_{cham}, where n is the number of moles of molecules in the chamber.
   D. $P_{atm} + nRT/V_{cham}$, where n is the number of moles of molecules in the chamber.

26. In reference to the model in the last paragraph, which gives the best expression for the total force on the part of the fluid in the nozzle?

A. $(P_{cham} - P_{atm})A$

B. $(P_{cham} + P_{atm})A$

C. $\dfrac{(P_{cham} - P_{atm})V_{cham}}{r}$

D. $\dfrac{(P_{cham} + P_{atm})V_{cham}}{r}$

27. Once reaction (1) takes place in the outer chamber, a scientist wants to determine whether there is enough heat to raise the temperature to the boiling point of the solution. In addition to the information given in the passage and the boiling point of the product solution, what information does she need to do the calculation?

A. Heat capacity of the solution.

B. Heat capacity of the solution and the concentration of quinone.

C. Heat capacity of the solution, the concentration of quinone, and the heat of reaction (1).

D. Heat capacity of the solution, the concentration of quinone, and volume of the outer chamber.

Passage 4

A recent innovation in automobile safety is the airbag. In the event of a collision, an airbag in front of the driver inflates in about 0.02 seconds. As the driver's body comes to a rapid stop, the airbag provides a soft cushion, softer than the steering wheel in any case.

The essential mechanism of the airbag consists of a sealed combustion chamber containing iron(III) oxide and sodium azide, which react to form the nitrogen gas which fills the airbag:

$$Fe_2O_{3(s)} + 6NaN_{3(s)} \rightarrow$$
$$9N_{2(g)} + 3Na_2O_{(s)} + 2Fe_{(s)} \qquad (1)$$

In the same chamber is an igniter, consisting of an electric coil, zirconium and potassium hyperchlorate, which react somewhat as follows:

$$4Zr_{(s)} + KClO_{4(s)} \rightarrow 4ZrO_{(s)} \quad KCl_{(s)} \qquad (2)$$

The main active ingredient in the airbag is the sodium azide. This ingredient is prepared using the reaction of sodium amide and nitrous oxide:

$$NaNH_{2(s)} + N_2O_{(g)} \xrightarrow[180°C]{} NaN_{3(s)} + H_2O_{(g)} \qquad (3)$$

During a collision, an electric coil starts reaction (2). This provides the heat which ignites reaction (1). After 1–5 ms, the seal of the combustion chamber bursts and releases the products (see figure). A filter screen removes the solid products of reaction (1) and other trace reaction products (some possibly noxious) while passing the nitrogen gas.

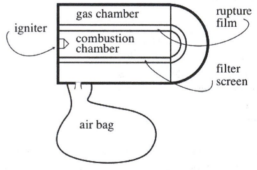

The nitrogen gas fills the bag in about 20 ms, and the whole reaction (1) continues for about 50 ms. The bag is porous, so as the driver presses against it, the bag deflates. Thus, it is almost completely deflated by the time the accident is over. After that, it is hoped that the driver can walk away from the collision with no injuries worse than abrasions from the inflating bag.

28. What is a possible purpose for keeping the combustion chamber sealed during the first 1–5 ms of reaction?

    A. This ensures that poisonous byproducts are prevented from entering the bag.
    B. The concentration of reactants is kept high to speed the reaction.
    C. The reactants are protected from water vapor, which could contaminate the reaction.
    D. This keeps the reactants near the catalyst.

29. Of reactions (1), (2), and (3), which has the greatest entropy increase?

    A. (1)
    B. (2)
    C. (3)
    D. All three have zero entropy increase.

30. Assume that the final gas has temperature 27° C at 1 atmosphere of pressure. If 1000 liters of gas are desired, which expression gives the grams of sodium azide required?

    A. $\dfrac{1000}{(0.0821)(300)} 65$

    B. $\dfrac{1000}{(0.0821)(300)} \dfrac{2}{3} 65$

    C. $\dfrac{1000}{(0.0821)(300)} \dfrac{3}{2} 65$

    D. $\dfrac{1000}{(0.0821)(300)} \dfrac{2}{3} 65(1000)$

31. What is the best possible purpose for having the bag deflate as the driver presses into it?

    A. As the bag deflates, the temperature of the gas decreases to safe levels.
    B. Allowing the gas to flow out of the bag ensures that the bag does not burst.
    C. The bag's deflation decreases the energy of the collision.
    D. Increasing the distance over which the deceleration occurs decreases the required force.

32. What is the advantage of having an airbag with larger area (as one views it from the driver seat)?

    A. Increasing the area increases the gas flow rate.
    B. Increasing the area decreases the gas flow rate.
    C. Increasing the area decreases the pressure on any given body part.
    D. Increasing the area decreases the density of the gas inside the bag.

33. Which of the following is the best description of the energy flow for the airbag inflation?

    A. chemical to heat
    B. chemical to gravitational potential.
    C. chemical to kinetic to heat.
    D. chemical to heat to work against the atmosphere.

34. Which of the following is the *least* likely byproduct for reaction (1) referred to in Paragraph 3?

    A. NaO_2
    B. Na
    C. FeO
    D. Na_3N

Passage 5

A barometer, that is, a device that measures pressure, can be constructed from a tube which is open at both ends and shaped like a U. A fluid, like mercury, is placed inside, filling the bottom portion of the U. If the height of the mercury column at one end is greater than at the other end, then the pressure above the liquid on that end is less.

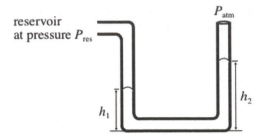

A modification of a barometer can be used to measure flow speed. Consider a pipe which carries an inviscid, incompressible fluid moving a speed v and pressure P_1 far upstream. Barometer 1 does not interrupt the flow, so it measures P_1. If Barometer 2 is placed in the flow as shown in the figure below, then the tip of the barometer forms an obstruction in the flow.

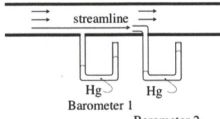

The flow just in front of the tip comes to stop at what is called a *stagnation point*. Nevertheless, we can consider the line shown in the figure, which comes to an end at the stagnation point, to be a streamline.

The figure below shows a flow with a constriction. The flow far upstream has a speed v_3, pressure P_3, and a cross-sectional area A_3. In the constriction the flow has a velocity v_4, pressure P_4, and a cross-sectional area A_4.

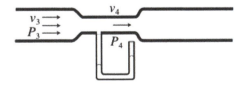

For the following problems, let ρ be the density of mercury.

35. In the first figure, the heights of the left and right columns of mercury are h_1 and h_2, respectively. Which expression gives the reservoir pressure P_{res}?

  A. $P_{atm} - \rho g(h_2 - h_1)$
  B. $P_{atm} + \rho g(h_2 - h_1)$
  C. $P_{atm} - \rho g(h_2 + h_1)$
  D. $P_{atm} + \rho g(h_2 + h_1)$

36. If the pressure measured by Barometer 1 in the second figure is P_1 and that measured by Barometer 2 is P_2, then what is the upstream velocity of the flow?

  A. $\sqrt{\dfrac{(P_2 - P_{atm})}{2\rho}}$

  B. $\sqrt{\dfrac{(P_2 - P_1)}{2\rho}}$

  C. $\sqrt{\dfrac{(P_2 - P_1)}{\rho}}$

  D. $\sqrt{\dfrac{2(P_2 - P_1)}{\rho}}$

37. How does the speed v_4 compare with the speed v_3?

  A. The speed v_4 is less than v_3.
  B. The speed v_4 is the same as v_3.
  C. The speed v_4 is greater than v_3.
  D. This cannot be determined from the information given.

38. How does the pressure P_4 compare with the pressure P_3?

  A. The pressure P_4 is less than P_3.
  B. The pressure P_4 is the same as P_3.
  C. The pressure P_4 is greater than P_3.
  D. This cannot be determined from the information given.

39. Suppose the fluid were replaced with an incompressible fluid that had viscosity, but v_3, P_3, A_3, and A_4 remained the same. How would the velocity, v_{4new}, in the constriction be changed from v_4?

  A. The speed would be less than v_4.
  B. The speed would be the same as v_4.
  C. The speed would be greater than v_4.
  D. This cannot be determined from the information given.

40. Again, suppose the fluid were replaced with a fluid that had viscosity, but v_3, P_3, A_3, and A_4 remained the same. How would the new pressure in the constriction be changed from P_4?

  A. The new pressure would be less than P_4.
  B. The new pressure would be the same as P_4.
  C. The new pressure would be greater than P_4.
  D. This cannot be determined from the information given.

Use the following for questions 41–44:

The velocity of a wave on a wire or string is not dependent (to a close approximation) on frequency or amplitude and is given by $v^2 = T/\mu$, where T is the tension in the wire and μ is the linear mass density. The linear mass density is the mass per unit length of wire, so that the linear mass density μ is the product of the mass density and the cross-sectional area.

A certain wire A (see figure) has tension 2000 N and a circular cross section of diameter 0.4 mm. A sine wave is traveling to the right with frequency 200 Hz.

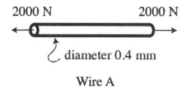

Wire A

Wire B is made of the same material as wire A with half the diameter.

41. How would the cross-sectional area change if the diameter were increased by a factor of 4?

  A. It would decrease by a factor of 4.
  B. It would increase by a factor of 2.
  C. It would increase by a factor of 4.
  D. It would increase by a factor of 16.

42. What is the linear density of wire B?

  A. One quarter that of wire A.
  B. One half that of wire A.
  C. The same as that of wire A.
  D. Double that of wire A.

43. If we want to increase the wave velocity on a wire by 30%, by how much should we increase the tension?

  A. 30%
  B. 60%
  C. 69%
  D. 81%

44. One long, straight wire has a diameter of 0.4 mm made of steel (density 8.0 g/cm³). Another wire has the same tension, made of a synthetic material (density 2.0 g/cm³). What must the diameter of the second wire be in order to have the same wave velocity?

  A. 0.1 mm
  B. 0.8 mm
  C. 1.6 mm
  D. 6.4 mm

45. The wave shown is traveling to the right. Which of the waves below, traveling to the left, will momentarily cancel this wave?

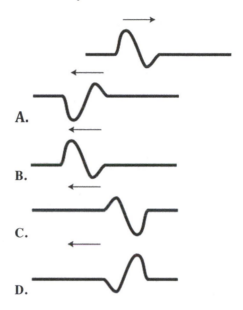

46. There are two water waves (velocity 16 m/s) which arrive at point P, where a duck is sitting. The first wave comes from the north with amplitude 3 m and wavelength 60 m. The second wave comes from the west with amplitude 4 m and wavelength 60 m. What is the amplitude of the duck's oscillation?

  A. 1 m
  B. 3.5 m
  C. 7 m
  D. There is not enough information to answer this question.

Use the following for questions 47–49:

Two speakers are located $L = 2$ m from each other, and both are producing a sound wave (in phase) with wavelength 0.8 m (see figure). A microphone is placed between the speakers to determine the intensity of the sound at various points. Use $v = 343$ m/s for the speed of sound.

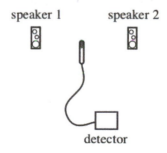

47. What kind of point exists exactly midway between the two speakers?

    A. An antinode.
    B. A node.
    C. Neither an antinode nor a node.
    D. Both an antinode and a node.

48. What kind of point exists exactly 1.3 m to the right of the left-hand speaker?

    A. An antinode.
    B. A node.
    C. Neither an antinode nor a node.
    D. Both an antinode and a node.

49. What kind of point exists exactly 0.4 m to the left of the right-hand speaker?

    A. An antinode.
    B. A node.
    C. Neither an antinode nor a node.
    D. Both an antinode and a node.

50. Two sounds waves of the same frequency arrive at point P, one with amplitude 0.3 Pa, and the other with amplitude 0.5 Pa. Which of the following gives the range of possible amplitudes for sound at point P?

    A. 0 – 0.5 Pa
    B. 0.2 – 0.5 Pa
    C. 0.2 – 0.8 Pa
    D. 0.3 – 0.8 Pa

Use the following information for questions 51–56:

A taut string (2 m) is fixed at both ends and plucked. The speed of waves on this string is 3×10^4 m/s. (See figure.)

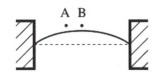

51. If the fundamental has wavelength λ_1, and the second harmonic has wavelength λ_2, what is the ratio λ_1/λ_2 ?

    A. 0.5
    B. 1
    C. 2
    D. 4

52. If the fundamental has a frequency of f_1, and the first harmonic has frequency of f_2, what is the ratio f_1/f_2?

    A. 0.5
    B. 1
    C. 2
    D. 4

53. What is the wavelength corresponding to the third harmonic?

    A. 2/3 m
    B. 1 m
    C. 4/3 m
    D. 2 m

54. What is the wavelength corresponding to the fourth harmonic?

    A. 2/3 m
    B. 1 m
    C. 4/3 m
    D. 2 m

55. A finger is placed at point B (see figure; B is midway between the ends), and the string is lightly plucked, so that a waveform exists on the whole string. (Thus a node exists at B.) What is the lowest frequency that may be heard in this case?

    A. 7.5×10^3 Hz
    B. 1.5×10^4 Hz
    C. 2.25×10^4 Hz
    D. 3×10^4 Hz

56. A finger is placed at point A (point A is one third way from one end to the other), and the string is lightly plucked, so that a waveform exists on the whole string. What is the lowest frequency that may be heard in this case?
    A. 7.5×10^3 Hz
    B. 1.5×10^4 Hz
    C. 2.25×10^4 Hz
    D. 3×10^4 Hz

Passage 6

Sometimes we are concerned with what happens when a wave in one medium encounters a sharp boundary with a second medium. If the properties of the second medium are similar to those of the first medium, the wave passes from the first medium to the second, or is *transmitted* (see figure).

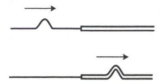

If the properties of the second medium are markedly different from the first, there is said to be an *impedance mismatch*, and much of the wave energy is reflected (see figure), while some is transmitted.

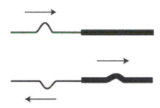

The situation is slightly more complicated if the boundary between the two media is gradual. In this case most of the energy of a wave may be transmitted to the second medium even if there is an impedance mismatch. This occurs if the length of the transition region is large compared with the wavelength of the wave (see figure). If not, then the wave "sees" the boundary as being sharp.

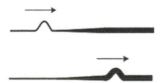

In addition to being reflected and transmitted, sometimes wave energy is *absorbed*. Certain media convert wave energy into heat energy. This can happen, for instance, for a wave traveling along a rope. The rope fibers rub against each other and the energy dissipates as heat (see figure).

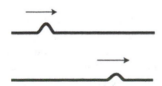

For the following questions, refer to the following chart, which shows the typical wavelengths of various waves.

wave	typical wavelength
ocean wave	10–100 m
swimming pool wave	0.1 m
sound wave	1 m
visible light	10^{-7} m

57. Water waves which strike the edge of a swimming pool are reflected, while ocean waves approaching the shore are generally not reflected back to sea. Which is a good explanation for this?

 A. Ocean waves have a longer wavelength than waves in pools.
 B. There is a gradual slope to shallower water at a shore.
 C. Ocean waves are generally parallel to the shore.
 D. Ocean waves are waves in a denser medium (salt water) than pool waves (fresh water).

58. What happens to the energy of ocean waves as they approach and break on the shore?

 A. The energy is converted from kinetic to potential.
 B. The energy is converted from potential to kinetic.
 C. The energy is converted from mechanical to chemical.
 D. The energy is converted from mechanical to heat.

59. Waves are approaching the ocean shore from the left in the following figure. According to the passage, which is true?

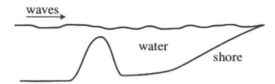

 A. Waves with a long wavelength have the best chance of arriving at the shore.
 B. Waves with a short wavelength have the best chance of arriving at the shore.
 C. Waves of a large amplitude have the best chance of arriving at the shore.
 D. Waves of a small amplitude have the best chance of arriving at the shore.

60. A photographer's lens often has a thin plastic coating on the surface of a glass lens. What is a likely purpose for that coating?

 A. The coating increases the efficiency of converting light to heat.
 B. The coating prevents absorption of light.
 C. The coating increases the reflectivity of the lens.
 D. The coating decreases the reflectivity of the lens.

61. One morning you go outside and find a blanket of newly fallen snow several centimeters thick. The outdoors seems very quiet. What is the best explanation for this?

  A. The snow tends to reflect sound.
  B. The snow tends to transmit sound energy to the ground.
  C. The snow tends to absorb sound energy.
  D. The cold temperature makes the air unable to carry sound.

62. When sound waves encounter a closed door, what is most likely to happen?

  A. The sound energy is likely to be transmitted into the wood.
  B. The sound energy is likely to be reflected.
  C. The sound energy is likely to be absorbed.
  D. The frequency of the sound is likely to be changed as it enters the door.

Passage 7

The human ear can hear sounds with frequencies from 20 Hz to 20,000 Hz. Frequencies of sound higher than this are called ultrasound. Although they cannot be heard, they are used in the technique of ultrasound imaging, for example, to take the image of a fetus in the womb. The sound waves are reflected off the interface between the fetus and the surrounding fluid. In order for this to provide information, the wavelength of the sound has to be smaller than the object being observed. Otherwise the wave passes right around the object.

At the other end of the sound spectrum there are very low frequency sounds. These can be highly injurious to humans if they have sufficient intensity. The sounds can cause internal organs to vibrate and eventually rupture, tearing the connective tissue holding the organ in place. For this reason, there are limits in the workplace as to how intense low frequency sounds can be.
For the following, use 1500 m/s for the speed of sound in biological tissue. Use 343 m/s for the speed of sound in air. A mass m on a spring (constant k) has a frequency given by

$$f = \frac{1}{2\pi}\sqrt{\frac{k}{m}}$$

63. For a sound wave of frequency 10^2 Hz in air, what is its wavelength?

  A. 0.29 m
  B. 0.56 m
  C. 1.7 m
  D. 3.4 m

64. If a doctor wanted to take the image of a fetus and wanted to resolve features of size on the order of one millimeter, what frequency sound could she use?

  A. Any frequency less than about 3×10^5 Hz.
  B. Any frequency greater than about 3×10^5 Hz.
  C. Any frequency less than about 1.5×10^6 Hz.
  D. Any frequency greater than about 1.5×10^6 Hz.

65. What period corresponds to the lowest frequency a human ear can hear?

  A. 0.05 seconds
  B. 0.05 meters
  C. 17 seconds
  D. 17 meters

66. Which best describes the flow of energy in paragraph 2?

  A. sound to potential
  B. sound to heat
  C. sound to gravitational
  D. sound to chemical and heat

67. In paragraph 2, which of the following would result in an increase in intensity?

  A. An increase in frequency.
  B. A decrease in frequency.
  C. An increase in the mass of the internal organ.
  D. None of the above.

68. Which of the following would be part of an explanation of why low frequency sounds are injurious?

  A. The wavelength of the sound is smaller than the size of the organ.
  B. The wavelength of the sound is larger than the size of the organ.
  C. The sound is reflected by the organ.
  D. The frequency of the natural oscillation of the organ is similar to that of the sound.

69. A scientist wants to model an internal organ with connective tissue as a mass on a spring. The mass of the organ is 0.5 kg, and its natural period of oscillation is 0.2 s. What would be the spring constant for the spring in the scientist's model?

  A. 0.1 N/m
  B. 0.8 N/m
  C. 2.5 N/m
  D. 490 N/m

Passage 8

It is possible to construct a device for determining the speed of moving objects using sonar. The device consists of a sound emitter and a detector. The emitter creates a sound of a single frequency. The outgoing sound reflects from a moving target and is Doppler shifted. When the incoming signal arrives at the detector, the incoming signal and outgoing signal are combined, so that the detector actually detects the beat between them. The detector is a square-amplitude detector, which is thus able to pick up the beat (see figures below).

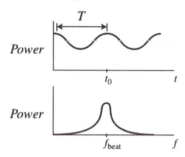

In one experiment with the device, the emitter created an outgoing signal of 80 kHz, which was reflected from a vehicle. The received signal was 70 kHz. The two graphs above were obtained. The top figure shows the output of the detector in terms of power versus time. The bottom figure shows power as a function of frequency (Fourier analyzed function of the top figure above).

For these questions, use 343 m/s for the speed of sound.

70. What is the wavelength corresponding to a 80 kHz wave?

    A. 4.3 mm
    B. 8.6 mm
    C. 27 mm
    D. 54 mm

71. What is the beat frequency referred to in this passage?

    A. 5 kHz
    B. 10 kHz
    C. 75 kHz
    D. 150 kHz

72. In the top figure above, what is T?

    A. 1.25×10^{-5} s
    B. 1.33×10^{-5} s
    C. 1.43×10^{-5} s
    D. 10^{-4} s

73. At time $t = t_0$ (in the top figure above), the incoming and outgoing waves are

    A. in phase.
    B. out of phase.
    C. coherent.
    D. resonant.

74. Which can be concluded from the passage?

    A. The vehicle is approaching the detector directly.
    B. The vehicle is approaching the detector, but not necessarily directly.
    C. The vehicle is receding from the detector directly.
    D. The vehicle is receding from the detector, but not necessarily directly.

Passage 9

A certain wind chime is a hollow pipe 0.8 m long and 0.025 m in diameter, and it is suspended by a string about 0.2 m from the top, about one-fourth way down (see figure). A hammer hits the chime about one-half way down. The note that the chime plays is a D at 262 Hz.

The ends are free to vibrate, so they are antinodes. The place where the hammer strikes also vibrates, but the place where the string connects is not free to vibrate.

For the following use 343 m/s for the speed of sound in air.

75. What is the wavelength of the wave in the pipe which produces the 262 Hz tone?

    A. 0.27 m
    B. 0.4 m
    C. 0.8 m
    D. 1.31 m

76. How would the frequency change if the length of the pipe were doubled, and the velocity of sound in the pipe stayed the same?

    A. It would be halved.
    B. It would stay the same.
    C. It would be doubled.
    D. It would increase by a factor of 4.

77. Which is true?

    A. The waves in the pipe and the sound waves in air are longitudinal.
    B. The waves in the pipe are longitudinal, whereas the waves in air are transverse.
    C. The waves in the pipe are transverse, whereas the waves in air are longitudinal.
    D. The waves in the pipe and the sound waves in air are transverse.

78. What is the wavelength in the pipe corresponding to the second harmonic?

    A. 0.2 m
    B. 0.27 m
    C. 0.4 m
    D. 0.8 m

Passage 10

The ear converts a series of pressure variations, that is, a sound wave, into a Fourier-analyzed signal traveling on nerves to the hearing center of the brain. In a highly idealized model of the ear, each frequency of sound wave corresponds to one neuron leading from the ear to the brain. For example, if a sound wave were to enter the ear consisting of two frequencies f_1 and f_2, then two neurons would be excited, one corresponding to f_1 and the other to f_2.

A physical ear is more complicated than this model, however, and these differences from ideal can be observed by simple experiment. For instance, if a sound wave of two very similar frequencies enters the ear, the brain hears not two frequencies but one average frequency which slowly turns on and off. The turning on and off is called *beats*, and the beat frequency is the difference between the two frequencies:

$$f_{beat} = f_1 - f_2$$

Another similar example involves a sound wave of two frequencies, which are not similar but have some harmonic relationship. In this case the brain sometimes hears a third tone, a *difference tone*, corresponding to the difference of the frequencies of the input:

$$f_3 = f_1 - f_2$$

This seemingly unfortunate phenomenon was a boon to the listeners of early phonographs. The phonographs were not really able to reproduce the lowest frequencies in the music, corresponding to the fundamental of the notes being played, although they would reproduce the harmonics. Often the ear would reconstruct the difference tone which would be the missing fundamental, making it seem as if the phonograph reproduced sound better than it in fact did.

79. When waves of two frequencies combine to make one wave, this phenomenon is called

    A. diffraction.
    B. interference.
    C. beats.
    D. difference tones.

80. On a piano, someone plays the notes B_0 (30.87 Hz) and C_1 (32.70 Hz) simultaneously. A single note is heard beating. What is the frequency of the note which is heard to beat?

    A. 0.55 Hz
    B. 1.83 Hz
    C. 31.79 Hz
    D. 63.57 Hz

81. In the question above, how many times per second does the beat turn on and off?

    A. 0.55
    B. 1.83
    C. 31.79
    D. 63.57

82. If a phonograph fails to reproduce the fundamental tone 110 Hz, which of the following sets of harmonics might cause the ear to reproduce it?

    A. 27.5 Hz and 137.5 Hz
    B. 55 Hz and 165 Hz
    C. 220 and 330 Hz
    D. 220 and 440 Hz

83. If the equilibrium pressure in the room is 10^5 Pa, which best represents pressure as a function of time for a sound wave of one frequency?

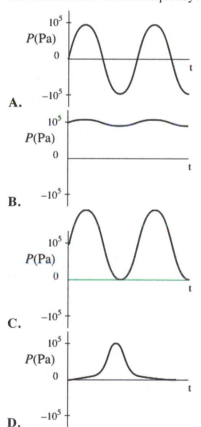

84. Which best represents a power spectrum of the sound entering the ear in paragraph 3 of the passage?

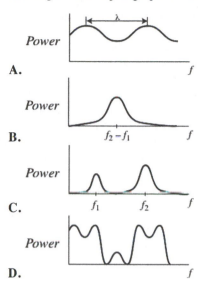

Passage 11

Alice places two stereo speakers a distance d apart. She sends a signal which is a sine wave of frequency f, so that the speakers are producing the same pure tone in phase. The sound wave in air has a wavelength λ.

She enlists her friend Bob to do an experiment. Alice sits directly in front of the speakers on the line which bisects the line segment connecting the speakers (see figure) but relatively far away from the speakers. Bob starts at the same place, but he slowly moves to the right. For him the sound gets quieter as he moves right, until he can barely hear it. Then it begins to get louder again. The figure shows Bob's position: where he first can barely hear the sound. This is the set up.

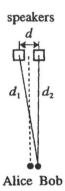

speakers

Alice Bob

In Experiment 1, Alice and Bob keep their positions, and Alice changes the frequency of the signal sent to both speakers, so that both speakers are still producing a sound in phase at the same frequency (a different frequency from the set up).

In Experiment 2, Alice changes the frequency of the second speaker slightly, but the first speaker remains at the original frequency.

The distance d is large compared to the wavelength, and it is small compared to the distance Alice and Bob sit from the speakers. The distance from Bob to the left speaker is d_1, and his distance to the right speaker is d_2.

85. Which is true concerning the set up?

   A. Alice and Bob are both at antinodes.
   B. Alice is at an antinode, and Bob is at a node.
   C. Alice is at a node, and Bob is at an antinode.
   D. Alice and Bob are both at nodes.

86. Which is the best explanation that Bob hears little sound where he sits in the set up?

   A. The sound is blocked by the speakers.
   B. Alice's body is absorbing the sound.
   C. Waves from the two speakers are out of phase and add to zero.
   D. Waves from the two speakers are in phase and add to zero.

87. Which of the following is the best expression for $d_1 + d_2$?

   A. λ^2/d
   B. d^2/λ
   C. $\dfrac{d^2 + \lambda^2}{\lambda}$
   D. There is not enough information in the passage to answer this question.

88. Which of the following is the best expression for $d_1 - d_2$?
   A. $d/2$
   B. d
   C. $2d$
   D. $\lambda/2$

89. In Experiment 1, what is the best prediction for what Alice and Bob will observe?

   A. Alice will hear very little sound, and Bob will hear sound clearly.
   B. Alice will continue to hear sound, and Bob will continue to hear little.
   C. Alice will continue to hear sound, and Bob's hearing of sound depends on the chosen frequency.
   D. Nothing can be predicted, in that Alice and Bob's hearing of sound depends on the chosen frequency.

90. In Experiment 2, what is the best prediction for what Alice and Bob will observe?

   A. Alice will continue to hear sound, and Bob will continue to hear little.
   B. Alice will continue to hear sound, and Bob's hearing of sound depends on the chosen frequency.
   C. Alice and Bob will hear a sound which grows and fades and grows.
   D. Neither Alice nor Bob will hear very much sound.

91. Two thin converging lenses are near each other, so that the lens on the left has focal length 2 m and the one on the right has focal length 4 m. What is the focal length of the combination?

   A. 1/6 m
   B. 3/4 m
   C. 4/3 m
   D. 6 m

92. A certain lens has focal length 2 m. What lens could you combine with it to give a combination with focal length 3 m?

A. A lens of power –6 diopters.
B. A lens of power – 1/6 diopters.
C. A lens of power 1/6 diopters.
D. A lens of power 6 diopters.

93. If parallel light rays were incident on a lens of power 3 D, what would the rays do on the other side of the lens?

A. They would converge with a focal length of 3 m.
B. They would converge with a focal length of 1/3 m.
C. They would diverge as if from a point 1/3 m behind the lens.
D. They would diverge as if from a point 3 m behind the lens.

94. Two thin lenses (6 D and 4 D) are positioned near each other. What is the power of the combination?

A. 1/10 D
B. 5/12 D
C. 12/5 D
D. 10 D

Passage 12

The mammalian eye is designed to collect light and focus it onto the retina. The retina consists of an array of cells, each having the ability to detect light falling on its surface. Most of the refraction (and thus focusing) of incoming light rays takes place at the interface between air and the cornea. The lens does the fine tuning, changing the focal length so the image lands exactly on the retina. The tuning is necessary since the eye must be able to bring into focus light from objects as close as 0.1 m as well as light from an infinitely distant source.

Spatial resolution is the ability of the eye to distinguish waves coming from different directions. For example, if a distant car is facing you at night with its headlights on, you can see two distinct headlights, since the light from the two headlights approaches your eye from two directions (see figure). If the car is far enough away, however, your eye lacks the resolution to distinguish the headlights, and you see only one light source.

Resolution is measured in degrees or radians. For instance, if your eye can just resolve two headlights which are 1.5 m apart on a car which is 1 km away, then the angular separation of the lights is approximately 1.5 m/1000 m = 1.5 x 10^{-3} radians. The resolution of your eye is 1.5 x 10^{-3} rad or 0.09 degrees (since 1 rad ≈ 57°) or 5 seconds of an arc. To a good approximation, the angular separation of two light sources (or features on any sort) is the ratio of spatial separation Δx to distance from the point of reference L. (See figure.) Thus the better the resolution, the smaller the resolution angle.

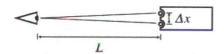

Ultimately the spatial resolution of any detector, including the eye, is limited by *diffraction*, which is the spreading of waves. When waves pass through an aperture, they spread on the other side subtending an angle given by

$$\theta_{diff} = \lambda/d \qquad\qquad (1)$$

where θ_{diff} is measured in radians, λ is the wavelength of the wave involved, and d is the diameter of the hole through which the waves must pass. Of course, diffraction is the physical limit of the resolution. The actual resolution of a detector may be much poorer than equation (1) would indicate if it is poorly designed. The human eye, when functioning properly, is essentially diffraction limited.

For the following problems use c = 3.0 x 10^8 m/s. Green light has a wavelength of 520 nm in a vacuum. (1 nm = 10^{-9} m)

95. What is the frequency of green light?

    A. 64×10^{-3} Hz
    B. 160 Hz
    C. 5.8×10^{14} Hz
    D. 1.2×10^{15} Hz

96. A human eye is focused on a moth of size 0.01 m located 0.25 m away. The front to back length of the eye is 0.025 m. What is the size of the image on the retina?

    A. 10^{-4} m
    B. 2.3×10^{-4} m
    C. 10^{-3} m
    D. 0.023 m

97. In question 2, what angle is subtended by the moth in the view of the eye?

    A. $2.3°$
    B. $4.6°$
    C. $15°$
    D. $30°$

98. A certain eye does not focus correctly, being either near- or far-sighted. The front to back length of the eye is 0.025 m, but the focusing power of the resting eye is 35 diopters. What should be the approximate power of the appropriate corrective lens?

    A. –5 diopters
    B. –3 diopters
    C. 3 diopters
    D. 5 diopters

99. The cornea is made of a material which has a larger index of refraction for blue light than for red light. If the eye is focusing a beam of red light onto the retina, where would the focus for a beam of blue light fall?

    A. In front of the retina.
    B. On the retina.
    C. Behind the retina.
    D. Both in front of and behind the retina.

100. An engineer is working on a camera to photograph the distant landscape in foreign countries. He has designed a camera with a lens which focuses incoming light on a detector. The camera is essentially diffraction limited, but the resolution is not good enough. Which of the following could improve the resolution?

    A. Increase the distance from the lens to the detector.
    B. Improve the lens shape.
    C. Change the material of the lens to be more transparent.
    D. Increase the size of the whole camera.

101. A Seurat painting consists of many dots of paint about 0.002 m in diameter. If you view it from a great enough distance, the dots of color appear to blend together, and you see a coherent picture. The resolution of your diffraction-limited eye is 2×10^{-4} radians. If you wanted to know how far away need you be for the dots to blur together, which paragraph in the passage gives the information to calculate this?

    A. Paragraph 3, and you must stand 2 m away.
    B. Paragraph 3, and you must stand 10 m away.
    C. Paragraph 4, and you must stand 2 m away.
    D. Paragraph 4, and you must stand 10 m away.

102. The figure shows a cross section of the Hubble Space Telescope (HST) (length 13.1 m and diameter 4.3 m). Light comes in from the right and is focused by the primary mirror (focal length 13 m). The focus is directed by a secondary mirror into detection apparatus (not shown). The perimeter of the mirror is a circle whose diameter is 2.4 m. If the HST is used for viewing galaxies in visible light, which of the following gives an estimate for the best resolution we could hope for?

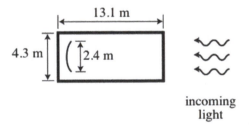

    A. 2×10^{-7} radians
    B. 0.045 radians
    C. 0.09 radians
    D. 0.18 radians

103. The Hubble Space Telescope in question 8 above also has detectors for ultraviolet light. Assuming diffraction limitation, we would expect that the resolution in the ultraviolet would be

A. not as good as that for visible light.
B. about the same as that for visible light.
C. better than that for visible light.
D. sometimes not as good as, sometimes better than that for visible light.

104. A cat's eye, adapted for seeing at night, has a larger pupil than a human eye and a much larger lens. The resolution for a cat's eye, however, is not better than that of a human eye, which is almost diffraction limited. Which of the following is a possible explanation for the lack of resolution in a cat's eye?

A. The larger pupil allows more light to enter the eye.
B. The larger pupil restricts the amount of directional information entering the eye.
C. The large lens introduces chromatic aberration.
D. The large lens introduces spherical aberration.

This page intentionally left blank.

SECTION 4
ELECTROMAGNETISM, NUCLEAR PHYSICS, AND THERMODYNAMICS

In this final section of our physics review we come to topics that have a very direct application to biological systems. The function of neurons is directly related to the ideas of electrostatics and circuits that will be discussed here.

We'll then wrap up our discussion of physics with chapters on atomic nuclear phenomena and thermodynamics. Many of these ideas are also discussed in the Chemistry content review book, but they merit discussion here. Many biological and medical assay techniques are based on radiolabeling molecules, and it is valuable to review the basics of radiation to understand the basis of such radiolabeling.

This page intentionally left blank.

CHAPTER 12
ELECTROSTATICS AND MAGNETISM

A. INTRODUCTION

Many students find electrodynamics difficult because it is the physics of things you cannot see, things no one talks about outside of physics circles. In mechanics we used words like "car" and "force" and "wave". In electrodynamics we use phrases like "electric field". What *is* an electric field?

It's a reasonable question, but if you ask your physics teacher, it's unlikely you'll get a satisfactory answer. Well, then, is the electric field real? Well, yes, it is as real as anything, but everyday life does not bring us in direct experience with the electric field, and so it is less familiar.

The key to building an intuition about electrodynamics is visualizing these unfamiliar concepts: concepts such as charge, electric and magnetic fields, and electric potential. We can not see them directly, but we can become familiar with their properties. In this chapter there are only a few equations and concepts, but the implications are profound. There is no doubt that this is a difficult chapter, but if you spend some effort actively creating mental pictures, electrodynamics will become far less arcane.

B. ELECTRIC CHARGE

A long time ago, someone noticed that when amber is rubbed with a cloth it attracts small seeds or pieces of straw. No one knew why. (Amber is a soft ochre "stone" of hardened tree sap.) Many years and many experiments later, the following story has emerged as the best explanation:

Most material on Earth is composed of three particles, called *protons*, *neutrons*, and *electrons*. The protons and neutrons hold together in tight lumps, called *nuclei*. The much less massive electrons exist in a cloud around the nuclei, forming *atoms*. Sometimes the electrons hold the atoms together, forming *molecules* and so on. The electrons are sometimes quite mobile, and this mobility results in most of the changes we observe.

But that's chemistry. That is not our story.

This is our story: Electrons have a *negative charge*, and protons have a *positive charge*. Two charges of like sign exert a repulsive force on each other, while two charges of unlike sign exert an attractive force on each other (Figure 12-1). Most objects are neutral, that is, they have nearly the same number of protons as electrons. When our unknown predecessor rubbed the neutral amber it acquired a few extra electrons, giving it a net negative charge.

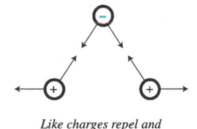

Like charges repel and unlike charges attract.
Figure 12-1

Under normal circumstances, as in physical and chemical reactions, electrons, protons, and neutrons are permanent objects. They may move around, but they do not spontaneously disappear or appear. Thus we have the following:

Conservation of Charge
If a system is closed (no matter goes in or out), then the total charge of that system is conserved (stays constant as time passes).

Clearly this is true in chemical reactions, which are just rearrangements of electrons and nuclei, but it turns out to be true even in unusual circumstances, such as the radioactive decay of nuclei or reactions of exotic particles.

CHARGES AND MATERIALS

There are some materials, most of them metals, in which electrons are able to move freely from atom to atom. Such materials are called **conductors**. A material which does not conduct electrons is called either a **nonconductor**, or an **insulator**, or a **dielectric**, depending on the mood of the speaker.

If we place a bunch of electrons (a negative charge) on an isolated conducting sphere (like a metal ball), the electrons repel and move away from one another. So all the charge ends up evenly distributed on the surface. (See Figure 12-2.)

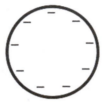

Negative charges migrate to the
surface of a conducting sphere.

Figure 12-2

If we examine the interior of a piece of the sphere, the total charge on that piece will be zero. (This has to be. If there were any excess electrons, they would repel each other and move out of the piece, until they cannot go any further.) All the excess charge is on the surface.

The same holds for positive charge. If a positive charge is placed on a conducting sphere, then the excess positive charge will spread out on the surface, with no positive excess charge in the interior. In other words, any interior piece has a total charge of zero (Figure 12-3). (Although the positive charge is caused by a **deficit** of electrons, you will never go wrong by thinking in terms of positive charges repelling each other.)

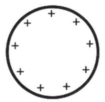

Positive charges migrate to the
surface of a conducting sphere.

Figure 12-3

This is a general rule: The total charge of a piece of the interior of a conductor is zero. Any excess charge lies on the surface of the conductor.

If a charged object is brought near a neutral conductor, electrons will move away or toward the charged object, depending on the object's charge. This is called **induced charge**, since the charged object induces a charge on the neutral conductor (Figure 12-4).

A charged object (left) can induce
a charge in a conductor (right).

Figure 12-4

We can induce a charge on a nonconductor, too. Even though charges do not move freely in it, each molecule in a nonconductor can have its electron density move to one side (Figure 12-5a).

Generally the induced charge on nonconductors is smaller than that on conductors. Instead of drawing all the polarized molecules, we generally summarize these with a picture like Figure 12-5b.

A charged object (left) can induce a charge in a nonconductor (right) as well.

Figure 12-5a

The induced charge in a nonconductor is not as large as in a conductor.

Figure 12-5b

A **ground** is any hug reservoir and depository of electrons. If you touch a charged object to a wire connected to ground, the charge will be neutralized where you touch it (Figure 12-6).

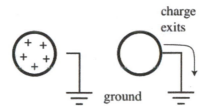

A ground is able to supply a charge to or drain a charge from any object it touches.

Figure 12-6

The following example illustrates these concepts. In the illustrations, a slight excess in the number of electrons over the number of protons is indicated by a − sign, and a deficit of electrons is indicated by a + sign.

Example: In a physics lab text, the following procedure is given for charging by induction a metal sphere connected to an insulating rod:

1. Rub a piece of amber with cotton cloth.
2. Bring the amber near but not touching the metal sphere.
3. Touch the other side of the sphere with your finger (which acts as a ground).
4. Remove your finger.
5. Remove the amber.

Sketch what happens to charges. (Hint: Amber tends to pick up electrons.)

Solution: 1. We rub amber with a cloth.

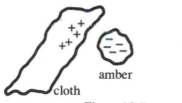

Figure 12-7a

2. We bring the amber near the sphere.

Figure 12-7b

3. We touch the other side with a finger.

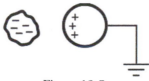

Figure 12-7c

4. We remove the finger

Figure 12-7d

5. We remove the amber.

Figure 12-7e

C. COULOMB'S LAW

Knowing that like charges repel (and unlike attract) is only a part of the story. We can calculate numbers as well. For this we must introduce the unit for charge

[Coulombs = C]. A Coulomb is a large amount of charge, and most laboratory situations involve the accumulation of at most 10^{-6} C.

Coulomb's Law

If two simple charges q_1 and q_2 are a distance d apart, then they exert a force on each other, of magnitude

$$F_{Coul} = \frac{kq_1q_2}{d^2} , \qquad\qquad (1)$$

where $k = 9 \times 10^9 \dfrac{Nm^2}{C^2}$ is Coulomb's constant. This force is attractive if the charges have unlike sign and repulsive if they have like sign.

Note that the distance appears in the denominator as a square, so it is called an inverse-square law, just like the law of gravitation.

Example: A piece of amber rubbed with a cloth acquires a negative charge on a cold day. If the amber is brought near neutral seeds, the seeds are attracted to it.

    a. Show the charge distribution for the amber and the seeds.
    b. Explain why the seeds are attracted to the amber.

Solution: Figure 12-8 shows the charge distribution, taking into account the induced charge in the seed. At first it looks as if the attractive and repulsive forces balance, giving no net force. But the distance from the amber to the left side of the seed is less than the distance to the right side. The inverse-square relationship in Coulomb's law makes the arrow on the left slightly longer than the arrow on the right, and the net force is to the left.

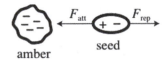

A charged object may attract a neutral object because of induced charge and the inverse-square relationship of electric force.

Figure 12-8

We have explained our predecessor's observation (Section B), that is, we have explained why a rubbed piece of amber attracts seeds and small objects.

D. ELECTRIC FIELD

Coulomb's law is simple, but it is not the only way we can explain the forces which charges experience. Often in physics, there are two viewpoints which explain the same phenomena. Usually, only one eventually prevails. Sometimes it prevails because it is easier to use, and sometimes it prevails because it provides a deeper insight into the working of the universe. The electric field is an example of a deeper insight.

Again, we consider two charges, now call them **Q** and **q,** and assume they are positive. Fix **Q** at some point. If we place charge **q** nearby, it experiences a force away from **Q**. Now, using Coulomb's law, we **can** explain this phenomenon as a repulsive force that **Q** exerts on **q**.

Or we **can** explain this as follows: The charge **Q** creates a "field of arrows" around itself, directed outward and getting shorter with distance from the charge **Q**. When we place **q** at a point, charge **q**, being nearsighted, does not see **Q** over there. But it does see the arrow, which tells it what force to feel (Figure 12-9).

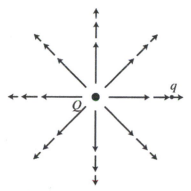

*In another viewpoint, q does not feel the
force from Q directly, but Q creates an
electric field, and q feels this field.*
Figure 12-9

Stop for a minute and think about this. Both viewpoints explain the observations, but they are very different perspectives. The second viewpoint introduces a new animal: a field of arrows (or **vector field**). Charge **Q** creates an electric field, and the electric field tells charge **q** what force to feel.

So why do we introduce a new viewpoint? Isn't Coulomb's law adequate for our needs? Actually, there are good reasons to talk about an independent existence of an electric field. One is that Coulomb's law is not really designed to deal with moving charges. What happens if we abruptly move charge **Q**. If **Q** is moved to a different place, then **q** must experience a different force. But does it feel it immediately, or is there a delay, and if so, how much of a delay?

If **d** (in Coulomb's Law) is the actual distance between the charges, then Coulomb's Law indicates **q** feels the change immediately.

It turns out, however, that there is a delay. The information about the change in position spreads out quickly, but not immediately (Figure 12-10 a,b,c). The easiest way to explain this is to say that a disturbance in the **electric field** propagates outward at a finite speed—the speed of light. In fact, that's what light is: a disturbance in the electric field which propagates away from the source, which is an accelerating charge. This is worth remembering. (**Fiat lux**.)

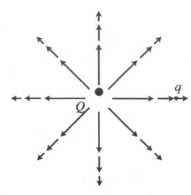

In this figure charge Q has been moved up suddenly. If the charge Q moves quickly, then the electric field does not respond immediately. The electric field is the same as it was before the move and charge q feels a force as if Q were in its old place.

Figure 12-10a

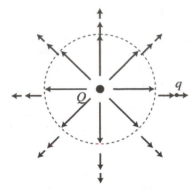

The information has moved outward to the dotted line. The electric field outside the dotted line is the same as before the charge Q moved up. Charge q still feels a force as if Q were in its old place.

Figure 12-10b

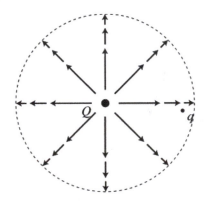

Now q experiences force to the right, but also down. This demonstration indicates that the electric field has an existence independent of the charges and that the second viewpoint is better than Coulomb's law. (See text.)

Figure 12-10c

The important concept is this: The universe is filled with arrows, that is, an electric field. Charges (some stationary and some moving) create the electric field. The electric field tells charges what force to feel.

There are three rules for the electric field which you need to know for the MCAT.

Rule 1

A stationary charge Q creates at every point an electric field $\vec{E}$ of magnitude

$$E = \frac{kQ}{d^2} \ ,$$

where d is the distance from the charge to the point in question. The direction of this field is away from Q if Q is positive and toward Q if it is negative.

> **Rule 2**
> Assume there are several stationary charges Q_1, Q_2, and so on. Charge Q_1 creates electric field $\vec{E}_1$ at point P, charge Q_2 creates electric field $\vec{E}_2$ at point P, and so on. The electric field at P is the vector sum
> $$\vec{E} = \vec{E}_1 + \vec{E}_2 + \dots.$$

> **Rule 3**
> A charge q placed at point P will experience a force given by
> $$\vec{F} = q\vec{E}.$$

Figure 12-9 shows the electric field due to a single positive charge. A sketch of the electric field due to a single negative charge would look the same except the arrows would point toward the charge.

Example 1: A *dipole* is a positive charge and an equal-magnitude negative charge separated by a distance. Sketch the electric field around a dipole.

Solution: Figure 12-11a shows such a sketch. Each electric field vector shown is actually the sum of two vectors. Figure 12-11b shows this explicitly for point P.

A positive charge q placed at point P would experience a force to the right, while a negative charge would experience a force to the left.

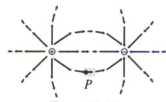

Figure 12-11a

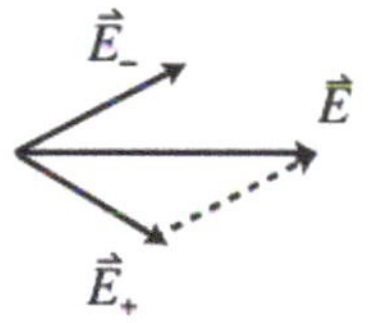

The electric field at any point is the vector sum of the individual electric fields.

Figure 12-11b

Example 2: Square ABCD has sides of length 10^{-6} meters. Charges of $Q = 1.1 \times 10^{-17}$ C are placed at corners B and D. (The charge of a proton is 1.6×10^{-19} C.)

    a. What is the electric field at point A?
    b. What force would an electron placed at point A experience?
    c. If a proton were placed at point A, what would be the ratio of the magnitude of the force it would experience to that which the electron in b experiences?

Solution: a. First, we DRAW A DIAGRAM showing the electric fields caused by the two charges (Figure 12-12).

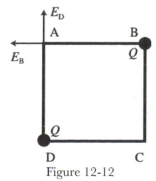

Figure 12-12

The magnitude of the electric field at A due to the charge at B is

$$E_B = \frac{kQ}{d^2}$$

$$= \frac{\left(9 \times 10^9 \, \frac{Nm^2}{C^2}\right)\left(1.1 \times 10^{-17} \, C\right)}{\left(10^{-6} \, m\right)^2}$$

$$= 10^5 \, \frac{N}{C}$$

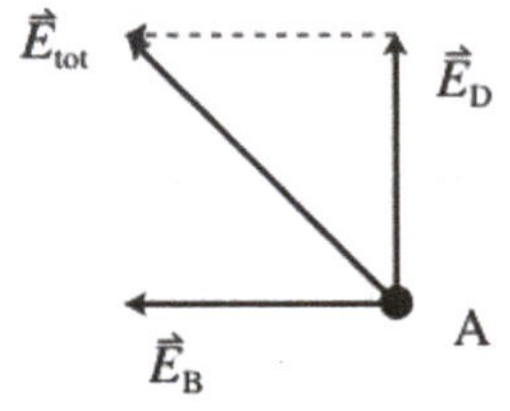

Figure 12-13

This is the magnitude of the electric field due to the charge at D as well. The two electric fields add like vectors. Figure 12-13 shows this sum, in which we may use the Pythagorean theorem, so we write

$$E_{tot}^2 = E_B^2 + E_D^2$$

$$E_{tot} = \sqrt{\left(10^5\right)^2 + \left(10^5\right)^2} \, \frac{N}{C}$$

$$= 1.4 \times 10^5 \, \frac{N}{C}$$

This is the answer to part a.

b. We simply calculate

$$F = qE$$

$$= (1.6 \times 10^{-19} \, C)(1.4 \times 10^5 \, N/C)$$

$$= 2.2 \times 10^{-14} \, N$$

The force the electron at point A experiences is directed toward C, since the charge of the electron is negative.

c. The force on the proton at point A is obtained in the same way, except the direction of the force is away from C, since the sign of the proton is positive. The ratio of the magnitudes of the forces on the proton and the electron is 1.

The following example shows how important it is to have a mental picture of the charges, electric field, and forces, much more important than memorizing several equations.

Note: A water molecule is a complicated object, with three nuclei and ten electrons interacting quantum mechanically. But for many purposes (as in the following example), we can model the water molecule as a simple dipole: a molecule with a positive end and a negative end. (See Figure 12-14.)

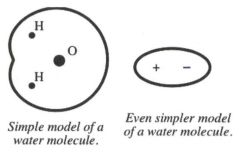

Simple model of a
water molecule.

Even simpler model
of a water molecule.

Figure 12-14

Note also: In problems of this sort, you should ignore gravity unless the problem tells you to include it.

Example 3: An electric field exists in the xy-plane directed in the positive y-direction with constant magnitude E_0. (Use q_e for the elementary charge, or the charge of the proton.)

    a.   If a chloride ion (Cl⁻) is placed in the xy-plane, what is the force on the ion?
    b.   If a water molecule is placed in the xy-plane with its oxygen end pointing in the $+x$-direction and hydrogen end pointing in the $-x$-direction, which direction is the torque?
    c.   What is the direction of the net force on the water molecule?

Solution: a. Figure 12-15a shows the electric field.

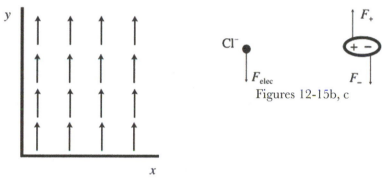

Figures 12-15b, c

Figure 12-15a

Chloride has one more electron than it has protons, so its charge is $-q_e$. The magnitude of the force on the ion is

$$F = q_e E_0$$

The force is directed in the $-y$-direction (Figure 12-15b).

b. For the torque on a water molecule, think of a water molecule as having a positive end and a negative end. Figure 12-15c shows the forces on the two ends, so the torque is clockwise. Adding the two forces in Figure 12-15c yields zero net force.

Example 4: A positive charge due to a sodium ion (Na⁺) is at the origin. A hydrogen fluoride molecule (HF) is on the positive x-axis with its hydrogen end further from the ion than its fluoride end. What direction is the net force due to the sodium ion on the hydrogen fluoride molecule?

Solution: First we DRAW A DIAGRAM showing the electric field (Figure 12-16).

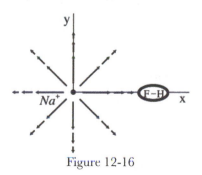

Figure 12-16

Figure 12-17 shows the force diagram for the molecule. Notice that the force on the fluoride part of the molecule is larger than the force on the hydrogen part, because the hydrogen part is located where the electric field is smaller. The net force is in the $-x$-direction.

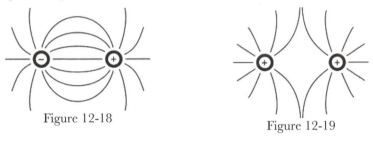

$$\xleftarrow{\quad F_{att}\quad} \left(\; F-H \;\right) \xrightarrow{\quad F_{rep}\quad}$$

Figure 12-17

Notice the difference between Example 4 and Example 3. In Example 3 the electric field is uniform, so the net force on the dipole is zero. In Example 4 the electric field is not uniform. (This is like the seeds beings attracted to the amber in Section D.)

One last note here: To draw electric field lines, simply connect the arrows of the electric field, each arrow directing your pen to the next arrow. Figure 12-18 shows an example for a dipole, and Figure 12-19 exemplifies two positive charges. This is just another way of graphically representing the same information.

Figure 12-18

Figure 12-19

E. ELECTRIC POTENTIAL

We begin this section with an analogy.

Analogy: Sisyphus, of Greek legend, was condemned to move a large stone of mass M to the top of a mountain (with no friction). His sister moved a similar stone up a different path to the top of the mountain. His son moved a smaller rock (mass m) to the top of the same mountain. (Figure 12-20 shows them in action.) Each carefully calculated the work required. (They calculated $W = F\Delta x \cos\phi$ for each piece of the journey and then added the pieces.)

  a. Who did the most work?
  b. Who had the greatest work per mass ratio?

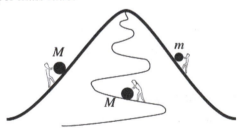

*The ratio of work required to roll a rock
from the bottom to the top to the mass of
the rock is independent of the path.*

Figure 12-20

Solution: This is a problem we have done before. For Sisyphus' task, there is a flow of energy from his muscles into another form, the gravitational potential energy of the stone. The latter is given by MgH, where H is the height of the mountain. But by the conservation of energy, that must be the same as the work that Sisyphus performs. By the same argument, Sisyphus' sister performs the same work MgH, and his son performs work mgH.

If they calculate the work to mass ratio, all obtain gH. At the top of the mountain they could drive a stake in the ground with the title "Work/mass is 1200 J/kg," or whatever it happened to be. Each point on the mountain would have its own work/mass ratio. The work/mass ratio is independent of path because gravity is a conservative force, and it has a potential energy associated with it.

The electric force is also a conservative force.

How would we create and analogy with electric forces? Let's say a positive charge Q is fixed in space. (See Figure 12-21.)

a. A honeybee carries a positive charge q_1 along Path 1 from A to B.
b. Another bee carries the same amount of charge along Path 2 from A to B.
c. A third bee carries a negative charge q_2 along Path 2.

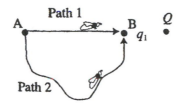

Path 1

A   B Q
                  q_1

Path 2

*For bees carrying charges from A to B
the work-to-charge ratio is independent
of path and sign of charge.*

Figure 12-21

Honeybees <u>a</u> and <u>b</u> perform the same amount of work. Although honeybee <u>c</u> performs a different amount of work, it is different only because of the different charge. The work per charge is the same in all cases. This work per charge is called ***electric potential***. We could drive a stake into space at point B with the title "7 J/C to get to this point from A" or something to that effect. This is analogous to gravitational potential energy per mass or roughly analogous to height.

Thus, to every point in space we assign a number, the electric potential. In physics, point A is often set at infinity as a standard. In that case, we refer to the absolute electric potential.

> Each point P in space has an absolute electric potential V_P.
> The work required to bring a charge from infinity to P is
> independent of the path taken and is given by
>
> $W = qV_P$.
>
> The units are [J/C = volts = V].

Now the analogy to gravitational potential energy works only so far. For one thing, mass is always positive, while charge may be positive or negative. So Sisyphus performs a large amount of work with his large rock, and his son performs a smaller amount of work. Honeybee <u>a</u> performs a large amount of work, but honeybee <u>c</u> performs a negative amount of work, so she is able to derive work from the system.

Another difference is that the Earth's surface is two dimensional, and the third dimension, height, is equivalent to the work/mass ratio to get to that point. Each point on the Earth's surface may be labeled by a height or the work/mass ratio. On the other hand, the honeybees can fly in three dimensions, and the electric potential is in a fourth dimension that we can only imagine. Figure 12-22 is an attempt to illustrate this. The bee carries a charge of 10^{-8} C, and the flower has an electric potential of 600 volts. Figure 12-22a shows how it looks to us. But since it takes a lot of energy to get to the flower, the situation appears like Figure 12-22b to the bee.

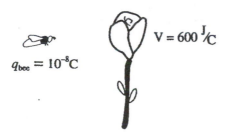

$q_{bee} = 10^{-8}C$

$V = 600 \; {}^J\!/C$

Figure 14-22a

Figure 12-22b

If we want to know how much energy is required to move a rock from A to B, we don't need the exact heights of A and B above sea level. We need only the difference in height, the mass of the rock, and the acceleration due to gravity. Similarly, in most electrostatic problems, we do not care about the absolute potential; we need only the *potential difference*.

The work required to move a charge q from point A to B is given by

$$W = q\Delta V_{AB}$$
$$= q(V_B - V_A),$$

where V_A and V_B are the electric potentials at A and B, respectively.

Example 1: A **DC battery** is rated at 6 volts. How much energy would be required to remove an electron from the positive terminal and move it to the negative terminal? (The charge of an electron is -1.6×10^{-19} C.)

Solution: Note that going from a positive terminal to a negative terminal is "downhill", so ΔV is negative. We apply the formula

$$W = q\Delta V$$
$$= (-1.6 \times 10^{-19} \text{ C})(-6 \text{ J/C})$$
$$= 1.0 \times 10^{-18} \text{ J}$$

We need to check the sign. Does such an action require work? Or can we derive work from it? Removing an electron from a *positive* terminal requires work, and placing it on a *negative* terminal requires work as well, so the positive sign in our answer is correct.

It is a good thing to know the amount of work to move a charge from one place to another, and we know how to do that now, if we know the electric potentials at the various points. But how do we calculate the potentials? In many situations, this is easier than it sounds.

Consider a lone charge Q. The potential at point P due to that charge is given by

$$V = k\frac{Q}{d},$$

where d is the distance from P to the center of the charge.

Note that there is no d^2 in the denominator, only d.

For a positive charge q, such a positive potential (if Q is positive) looks like a high steep mountain. (Figure 12-23). For a negative charge, it looks like a deep pit (since the energy change is negative for getting close to Q).

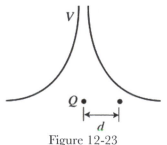

Figure 12-23

> If there are several charges $Q_1, Q_2, \ldots$, then the potential at P is given by the simple sum (no vectors):
>
> $$V = k\frac{Q_1}{d_1} + k\frac{Q_2}{d_2} + \cdots .$$

When we move charge q from A to B, we increase its electric potential energy by the same amount as the work we have performed. The *electric potential energy* of a group of charges is the work required to assemble the charges by moving them from an infinite distance away. So now we have an electric potential energy in addition to the gravitational potential energy.

Example 2: Two charges $Q_1 = Q_2 = 1.1 \times 10^{-8}$ C are 2×10^{-2} meters apart. Point A is exactly between them, and point B is 10^{-1} meters from both of them. How much work is required to move a charge $q = 10^{-9}$ C from A to B?

Solution: First we DRAW A DIAGRAM (Figure 12-24).

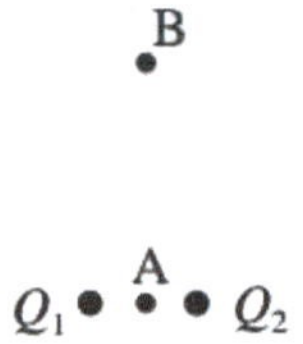

B

Q_1 • A • Q_2

Figure 12-24

Let's apply the formula:

$$V_A = \frac{kQ_1}{d_{1A}} + \frac{kQ_2}{d_{2A}}$$

$$= \frac{\left(9\times10^9\,\frac{\text{Nm}^2}{\text{C}^2}\right)\left(1.1\times10^{-8}\,\text{C}\right)}{10^{-2}\,\text{m}} + \frac{\left(9\times10^9\,\frac{\text{Nm}^2}{\text{C}^2}\right)\left(1.1\times10^{-8}\,\text{C}\right)}{10^{-2}\,\text{m}}$$

$$= 2\times10^4\,\frac{\text{Nm}}{\text{C}}$$

$$= 2\times10^4\,\text{V}$$

$$V_B = \frac{kQ_1}{d_{1B}} + \frac{kQ_2}{d_{2B}}$$

$$= 2\times10^3\,\text{V}$$

$$W = q(V_B - V_A)$$

$$= \left(10^{-9}\,\text{C}\right)\left(2\times10^3\,\frac{\text{J}}{\text{C}} - 2\times10^4\,\frac{\text{J}}{\text{C}}\right)$$

$$= -1.8\times10^{-5}\,\text{J}$$

Now let's check the sign. Since the test charge is positive, we imagine the two charges Q are mountains next to each other, and A is a mountain pass. Point B is further down, so the energy change is negative. No energy is required, but instead energy can be derived. Therefore the negative answer is justified.

Example 3: Two charges Q_1 and Q_2 (both 1.1×10^{-7} C and both 10^{-6} grams) are initially 0.01 m apart. They are released, and they go flying apart.

    a. How much potential energy is in the system initially?
    b. How much kinetic energy is in the system finally?

Solution: a. The potential energy is the work needed to assemble the system. Let's regard Q_1 as fixed and move Q_2 toward it from infinity (Figure 12-25).

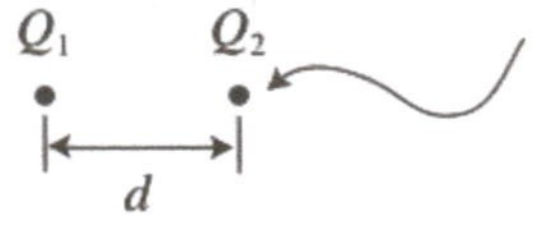

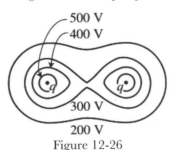

For part a, we assemble the system by regarding Q_1 as fixed and moving Q_2 from infinity.

Figure 12-25

With this viewpoint, the initial electric potential (at infinity) is zero and the final electric potential is kQ_1/d, where $d = 0.01$ m. The work done to bring Q_2 to this point is

$$W = Q_2\left(\frac{kQ_1}{d} - 0\right)$$

$$= \left(1.1\times10^{-7}\ \text{C}\right)\frac{\left(9\times10^9\ \frac{\text{Nm}^2}{\text{C}^2}\right)\left(1.1\times10^{-7}\ \text{C}\right)}{0.01\ \text{m}}$$

$$= 1.1\times10^{-2}\ \text{J}$$

The other way to do this problem is to regard Q_2 as fixed and move Q_1 toward it, but of course we would get the same answer. Or we could move them both from infinity. This would be harder to calculate, but since the energy is independent of path, the answer must be the same.

b. After the particles are released, the potential energy is converted to kinetic energy. Since there are no external forces and no heat generation, energy is conserved, and the final kinetic energy is 1.1×10^{-2} J.

> **Major hint:** *Whenever* there is a question about energy in a problem involving charges or electricity, chances are near certain you will use potential differences to solve the problem (rather than $W = F\Delta x \cos \phi$).

One last note: In topographic maps of the Earth's surface, points at the same height are connected by lines and labeled according to height. We can do the analogous thing with charges by connecting points of equal potential, forming *equipotential lines*. Figure 12-26 shows such a diagram for two equal positive charges.

500 V
400 V
q
q
300 V
200 V
Figure 12-26

F. MAGNETIC FIELDS

Electric fields are not enough to explain everything in electrodynamics. It turns out that we need to consider a second field as well, called the *magnetic field*. Both stationary and moving charges generate an electric field, but only moving charges generate a magnetic field.

Magnetic fields appear outside the wires in which there is current flowing. A *current* is a flow of charge, that is, the quantity of charge moving past a point per unit of time. The units of current are [C/s = amperes = amps = A]. For most problems it does not matter whether we think of (negative) electrons moving left or of some positive charge moving right. In physics we generally think in terms of a positive charge moving, even though we know that it is the electrons which are moving. For this reason, if electrons are moving to the left along a wire, then we say the current is toward the right, since electrons have negative charge.

If a current is flowing in a wire, this generates a magnetic field outside the wire. This magnetic field points not toward, not away from, not along the wire, but tends to point **around** the wire. It is strongest near the wire, of course. We can remember its direction by applying the first hand rule: Use your right hand and point the thumb in the direction of the (positive) current. Bend your fingers around so the tips are as close to your wrist as possible. The fingers tend to point in the direction of the magnetic field. Figure 12-27 shows a current flowing to the right. The small arrows show the direction of the magnetic field. Figure 12-28 shows a current coming out of the page. Again, the arrows show the magnetic field. A circle with a dot in it often denotes a vector coming out of the page, like an incoming arrow. A circle with a cross in it denotes a vector going into the page, like the feathers of a receding arrow.

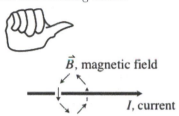

The first hand rule reminds us of the direction of the magnetic field due to current.
Figure 12-27

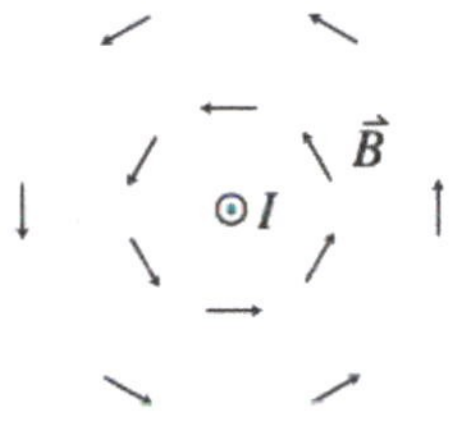

The current is coming out of the page. The arrows point in the direction of the magnetic field.
Figure 12-28

Certain materials, such as iron, generate magnetic fields as well, and at first glance there do not seem to be any currents here. The reason for magnetic fields in these cases is subtle and involves the current of electrons about the nucleus. This is almost certainly beyond the scope of the MCAT.

A charge sitting still in a magnetic field experiences no force. Furthermore, a moving charge experiences a magnetic force only if its motion has a component perpendicular to the magnetic field. In that case the particle experiences a force which is perpendicular to the magnetic field and to the charge's path. Figure 12-29 shows a situation in which the magnetic field is coming out of the page and a proton is moving to the right.

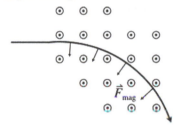

The magnetic field is coming out of the page, and the proton is traveling right. It experiences a magnetic force down the page.
Figure 12-29

The second hand rule helps you to recall the direction of the force: For a positive particle, use your right hand. Your fingers point in the direction of the magnetic field, which you can remember because the four fingers look like the field lines of a magnet. Your thumb points in the direction that the particle is going, like a hitchhiker. Your palm (which you use for pushing) points in the direction in which the particle experiences a force. For a negative particle, use your left hand.

In brief, every point in the universe has two vectors sitting on it, one being the electric field and the other being the magnetic field. Just to help you visualize it, imagine going to a field in the Northern Hemisphere on a clear day and picking a point in the air. To a close approximation, the electric field points down with a magnitude 100 N/C and the magnetic field points south (0.5 gauss, if you must know, but we have not discussed units for the magnetic field).

Now the force on a particle due to a magnetic field is always perpendicular to the displacement of the particle. For this reason magnetic forces do no work (always we have $\cos\phi = 0$). If you ever encounter a question such as "How much work does the magnetic force … ?" you need read no further. The answer is zero.

G. ELECTROMAGNETIC RADIATION

In Section D we discussed the fact that an accelerating charge will shake up the electric field around it. The shaking portion of the electric field breaks off and moves away through space. The phenomenon is called ***electromagnetic radiation*** or ***light***. The electric field is perpendicular to the wave direction, so the wave is transverse, and the orientation of the electric field gives the polarization. That is to say, if the electric field points up and down, then we say the light is vertically polarized. In Figure 12-30 a charge Q on a vertical spring moves up and down and generates the wave shown. So the polarization is in the same direction that the charge shakes.

Figure 12-30   Figure 12-31

A magnetic field also goes along with the electric field. Although Figure 12-30 does not show the magnetic field, Figure 12-31 shows both fields. The magnetic field is perpendicular to the electric field and to the direction of propagation.

Of course, this is not the full story. These waves of electric and magnetic fields come out as packets, called ***photons***, generally associated with energy transitions within a crystal, molecule, or atom.

This chapter is the most difficult of the book. In addition to visualizing the movement of electrons in various materials, you must also learn to visualize electric and magnetic fields, and an electric potential as well.

The electric field relates force to charge. Whenever you read a question involving force and charge, you will probably need to think of the electric field. You should picture arrows (vectors) filling all of space pointing away from positive charges and toward negative ones. Since the electric field is a vector field, the electric field at a point due to several charges is the vector sum of the individual electric fields at that point.

The electric potential is related to energy and charge. When a question mentions energy and charge, you should immediately think of using electric potentials. The work to move a charge from point A to point B is $W = q(V_B - V_A)$. We can find the potential at point A by simply adding the potentials ($V = kQ/r$) from the charges in the problem.

An electric field is generated by both stationary and moving charges, although we have calculated only the former. A magnetic field is generated only by moving charges and affects only moving charges. Qualitative information can be obtained by the hand rules. The MCAT will not ask for any more detailed information.

CHAPTER 12 PROBLEMS

In all of the following problems, use the following constants:

$$k = 9 \times 10^9 \frac{Nm^2}{C^2}$$

$$q_{electron} = -1.6 \times 10^{-19} \ C$$

In all problems ignore gravity unless it is explicitly mentioned.

Consider the following possibilities in answering questions 1 and 2:

I. Both balls have a positive charge.
II. Both balls have a negative charge.
III. One ball has a positive charge, and the other, a negative charge.
IV. One ball is charged and the other is neutral.

1. In a certain experiment, two balls made of cork are hung from insulating strings. There is a force to the effect of pushing the balls apart, due to charges on the balls. What can be concluded?

    A. I or II.
    B. I or II or III.
    C. III.
    D. III or IV.

2. In a certain experiment, two balls made of cork are hung from insulating strings. There is a force to the effect of pulling the balls together, due to charges on the balls. What can be concluded?

    A. I or II.
    B. I or II or III.
    C. III.
    D. III or IV.

Use the following in questions 3–5:

Two charges $Q_1 = 2 \times 10^{-10}$ C and $Q_2 = 8 \times 10^{-10}$ C are near each other, and charge Q_1 exerts a force F_{12} on Q_2.

3. How would F_{12} change if the distance between Q_1 and Q_2 were increased by a factor of 4?

    A. It would decrease by a factor of 16.
    B. It would decrease by a factor of 4.
    C. It would decrease by a factor of 2.
    D. It would increase by a factor of 4.

4. How would F_{12} change if the charges were both doubled, but the distance between them remained the same?

    A. F_{12} would decrease by a factor of 4.
    B. F_{12} would decrease by a factor of 2.
    C. F_{12} would increase by a factor of 2.
    D. F_{12} would increase by a factor of 4.

5. What is F_{21}, the force that charge Q_2 exerts on charge Q_1?

    A. $F_{12}/4$
    B. F_{12}
    C. $4F_{12}$
    D. $16F_{12}$

Use the following in questions 6 and 7:

A small metal ball having a positive charge is brought near a large solid metal disk on the right side. The ball then touches it and is removed.

6. Which of the following best shows the distribution of the charges before the ball touches the disk?

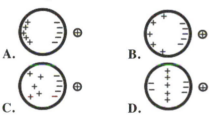

7. Which of the following best shows the distribution of the charges after the ball is removed?

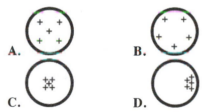

8. A small metal ball having a positive charge is brought near a large solid plastic disk. The ball then touches it on the right side and is removed. Which of the following best shows the distribution of the charges after the ball is removed?

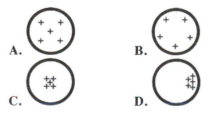

9. Two charges, a positive charge $Q = 1.1 \times 10^{-10}$ C and a negative charge of the same magnitude, are located 2×10^{-6} m apart. A third charge $q = 10^{-17}$ C is located exactly between them. What is the magnitude of the force on charge q?

    A. 0 N
    B. 2.5×10^{-12} N
    C. 2.5×10^{-6} N
    D. 2×10^{-5} N

10. One charge ($Q_1 = 3.3 \times 10^{-5}$ C) is located on the x-axis at (10^{-3} m, 0 m), and another charge ($Q_2 = 4.4 \times 10^{-5}$ C) is located on the y-axis at (0 m, 10^{-3} m). A charge $q = 10^{-16}$ C is located at the origin. What is the magnitude of the force on the charge at the origin?

    A. 10^{-5} N
    B. 2×10^{-5} N
    C. 5×10^{-5} N
    D. 7×10^{-5} N

11. Two positive charges, $Q = 1.1 \times 10^{-10}$ C, are located 10^{-6} m apart. A third charge $q = 10^{-17}$ C is located exactly between them. What is the magnitude of the force on charge q?

    A. 0 N
    B. 10^{-11} N
    C. 10^{-5} N
    D. 8×10^{-5} N

Use the following in questions 12 and 13:

In a water solution of sodium chloride, the sodium chloride dissociates into ions surrounded by water molecules. Consider a water molecule near a sodium ion.

12. What tends to be the orientation of the water molecule?
    A. The oxygen atom is nearer the ion because of the oxygen's negative charge.

    B. The oxygen atom is nearer the ion because of the oxygen's positive charge.
    C. The hydrogen atoms are nearer the ion because of their negative charge.
    D. The hydrogen atoms are nearer the ion because of their positive charge.

13. What net electrostatic force exists between a sodium ion and a water molecule oriented as shown in the figure? (Assume the overlap of electron clouds is negligible.)

    Na^+ H—O—H (figure)

    A. There is no net force.
    B. The net force is attractive.
    C. The net force is repulsive.
    D. The net force is into the page.

14. A positive charge $Q = 1.1 \times 10^{-9}$ C is located on the x-axis at $x = -10^{-3}$ m, and a negative charge of the same magnitude is located at the origin. What is the magnitude and direction of the electric field at the point on the x-axis at $x = 10^{-3}$ m? (Right means the positive x-direction.)

    A. 7.5×10^6 N/C, to the left.
    B. 10^7 N/C, to the right.
    C. 1.25×10^7 N/C, to the right.
    D. 2×10^7 N/C, to the right.

15. A positive charge $Q = 1.1 \times 10^{-11}$ C is located 10^{-2} meters away from a negative charge of equal magnitude. Point P is exactly between them. What is the magnitude of the electric field at point P?

    A. 10^3 N/C
    B. 2×10^3 N/C
    C. 4×10^3 N/C
    D. 8×10^3 N/C

16. Two positive charges $Q = 1.1 \times 10^{-10}$ C are located 10^{-3} meters away from each other, and point P is exactly between them. What is the magnitude of the electric field at point P?

    A. 0 N/C
    B. 10^6 N/C
    C. 2×10^6 N/C
    D. 8×10^6 N/C

17. In the figure, points A, B, and C are the vertices of an equilateral triangle with sides of length 10^{-4} meters. Positive charges of magnitude $Q = 1.1 \times 10^{-10}$ C are located at points B and C. What is the direction of the electric field at point A?

A

B   •C

A. ↑
B. ↓
C. →
D. ←

Use the following in questions 18 and 19:

In the figure, points A, B, and C are the vertices of an equilateral triangle with sides of length 10^{-5} meters. Point D is exactly between B and C, while point E is in the same plane as A, B, and C and equidistant from them. Positive charges of magnitude $Q = 1.1 \times 10^{-15}$ C are located at points A, B, and C.

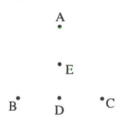

18. What is the direction of the electric field at point D?

A. It points up (↑).
B. It points down (↓).
C. It points into the page.
D. It has zero magnitude.

19. What is the magnitude of the electric field at point E?

A. 0 N/C
B. 10^5 N/C
C. 3×10^5 N/C
D. 9×10^5 N/C

Use the following in questions 20 and 21:

A positive charge of 3.3×10^{-8} C is at the point (0 m, 1 m). A negative charge -5.5×10^{-8} C is at the point (0.5 m, 0 m).

20. Which arrow best shows the direction of the electric field at the point (0.5 m, 1 m)?

A. ↗
B. ↘
C. ↙
D. ↖

21. Which arrow best shows the direction an electron would experience a force if it were placed at (0.5 m, 1 m)?

A. ↗
B. ↘
C. ↙
D. ↖

Use the information in questions 22–26:

Two parallel metal plates separated by a distance 0.01 meters are charged in order to create a uniform electric field (4×10^4 N/C) between them, which points down (see figure). A small plastic ball ($m = 0.009$ kg) has a small charge Q on it and is located between the plates. The only forces on it are the forces due to gravity and to the electric field. The ball is not moving.

Note: An alpha particle is a bare helium-4 nucleus and has a mass about four times that of a proton. The mass of a proton is 2000 times the mass of an electron. The acceleration due to gravity $g = 10$ m/s^2. The charge on a proton is 1.6×10^{-19} C.

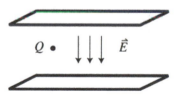

22. Which is a distribution of charge which would create the desired electric field between the plates?

A. The top plate is charged positively and the bottom plate is charged negatively.
B. The top plate is charged negatively and the bottom plate is charged positively.
C. Both plates have the same positive charge.
D. Both plates have the same negative charge.

23. What is the charge on the ball?

    A. −100 C
    B. −2.25 x 10^{-6} C
    C. 2.25 x 10^{-6} C
    D. 100 C

24. What is the magnitude of the force which would be exerted on a proton between the two plates?

    A. 6.4 x 10^{-15} N
    B. 1.28 x 10^{-14} N
    C. 2.56 x 10^{-14} N
    D. 6.4 x 10^{-5} N

25. How would the force exerted on an alpha particle between the plates compare with the force exerted on a proton between the plates?

    A. Four times as large, and in the opposite direction.
    B. The same magnitude, and in the same direction.
    C. Twice as large, and in the same direction.
    D. Four times as large, and in the same direction.

26. How would the acceleration of an electron between the plates compare with the acceleration of a proton between the plates?

    A. The same magnitude, but in the opposite direction.
    B. Twice as large, and in the opposite direction.
    C. One thousand times as large, and in the opposite direction.
    D. Two thousand times as large, and in the opposite direction.

Use the following in questions 27–29:

Two parallel metal plates are charged in order to create a uniform electric field between them which points up (see figure). A water molecule can be modeled as a simple dipole, that is, having a negative end (the oxygen atom) and a positive end (the hydrogen atoms).

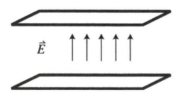

27. If a water molecule is placed between the two plates, which orientation would it take to minimize its energy?

A.   B.

C.   D.

28. If the water molecule were oriented as shown below, what would be the direction of the net force on it?

    A. No force.
    B. ↑
    C. ↓
    D. →

29. If the water molecule were oriented as in the previous problem, what effect would the electric field have on the molecule (other than net force)?

    A. The molecule would be rotated clockwise.
    B. The molecule would be rotated counterclockwise.
    C. The molecule would be compressed.
    D. The molecule would be stretched.

Passage 1

The radio waves which carry information in a standard broadcast are an example of electromagnetic radiation. These waves are a disturbance, not of a material medium, but of electric and magnetic fields. When the wave is linearly polarized, the electric field points in a direction perpendicular to the propagation of the wave, although its magnitude varies, of course, in space and time. The magnetic field points in a direction perpendicular to the wave propagation and to the electric field, and the two fields propagate in phase.

The electromagnetic radiation is generated by an antenna, which is a wire or metal rod which points perpendicular to the direction of the intended wave propagation. An alternating current is generated in the antenna, whose frequency is the same as that of the radiation to be produced. The electric field of the resulting electromagnetic radiation points along the same axis as the current.

The electric field of the electromagnetic radiation encounters electrons on the receiving antenna, which is another wire or metal rod. The electric field creates a current along the receiving antenna. One way to have good transmission and reception is to have the length of the antenna be one quarter of the wavelength of the electromagnetic wave.

For the following questions, consider a situation in which a transmitting antenna points vertically, and the receiving antenna is directly to the north. The speed of light is 3 x 10^8 m/s.

30. If the alternating current in the transmitting antenna has a frequency of 10^7 Hz, what would be a reasonable length for an efficient antenna, according to the passage?

A. 7.5 m
B. 30 m
C. 60 m
D. 120 m

31. For a point between the two antennas, what is the direction of the electric field vector for the radiation?

A. North/south.
B. East/west.
C. North/south or east/west.
D. Up/down.

32. For a point between the two antennas, what is the direction of the magnetic field vector for the radiation?

A. North/south.
B. East/west.
C. North/south or east/west.
D. Up/down.

33. What would be the best orientation of the receiving antenna?

A. North/south, that is, pointing toward the transmitting antenna.
B. Vertical.
C. East/west.
D. Any orientation would suffice.

34. In the third paragraph, how does the electric field create a current on the receiving antenna?

A. The electric field changes the resistance of the antenna.
B. The electric field exerts a force on the electrons.
C. The electric field boosts the electrons to higher energy orbitals in the atoms.
D. The electric field polarizes the electrons.

35. Which of the following best describes the energy flow?

A. Electrical to electromagnetic to electrical.
B. Electromagnetic to electrical to electromagnetic.
C. Mechanical to electromagnetic to mechanical.
D. Kinetic to electromagnetic to kinetic.

This page intentionally left blank.

CHAPTER 13
ELECTRIC CIRCUITS

A. INTRODUCTION

In the last chapter, we developed some intuition about electric fields and electric potentials, so in this chapter we will apply this intuition to electric circuits. A simple *electric circuit* consists of a voltage source, wires, and resistors, so that charge flows in a closed path or circuit. This flow of charge is called a *current*. In this chapter the concepts to watch are current and electric potential, two related but distinct concepts. Whenever you see a circuit diagram, you should imagine seeing currents and potentials. By doing this as you read this chapter, you will find that this subject becomes fairly straightforward.

A voltage source (often a *DC cell or battery*) is a potential difference enforcer, its one job being to ensure that the potential difference between the two terminals remains constant. It does this by chemically transporting electrons from the positive terminal to the negative terminal. When the potential between the terminals becomes the rated voltage (6 volts, or whatever), the chemical reaction in the cell reaches equilibrium and the electron transport stops. The symbols for a cell are shown in Figure 13-1, where the long bar is the positive end, the end with higher potential.

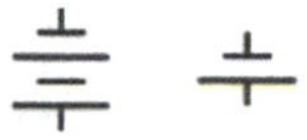

DC cells or batteries
Figure 13-1

A *wire* is simply a long, long cylinder of metal. Because it is a piece of metal, however, the potential difference between any two points in it is zero. That is to say, all along its length, a wire has one potential. In our analogy with Sisyphus and the mountain in the earlier chapter, a wire is like a plateau, all of it at one height. The reason for this is simple: If it were not so, that is, if one end of the wire were at a higher potential, then electrons, being free to move, would rush toward the higher potential and lower it. Perhaps a better analogy is a mountain lake which is, of course, flat. If one end were higher than the other, the water, free to move, would flow away from that end into the lower one.

For this reason also the electric field inside a piece of metal is always zero. If it were not so, then the electric field would push electrons to one side, and the shifting electrons would cancel the electric field.

At any rate, you should remember that inside a metal, the electric field is zero, and if the potential at one point in the wire is V_0, then the potential all along the wire is V_0.

Electric current may flow through a *resistor* as well, but the charge does not flow freely as it does in a wire. For current to flow through a resistor, there must be a potential difference across it. A simple example of a resistor is a piece of graphite (pencil lead). Other examples include a light bulb and a toaster. The symbols for these are shown in Figure 13-2.

resistor   light bulb
Figure 13-2

In order to think about circuits, it is helpful to think of an analogy. The electric current is like a current of water, and the electric potential is like the height of the water. Wires are like level streambeds (level because they have one potential). Resistors are like rocky waterfalls, and a voltage source is like a pump which pumps water from one height to another.

Let's look at the example of a 6-V battery connected to a light bulb. This is shown in Figure 13-3, and the circuit diagram is shown in Figure 13-4. The battery pumps the charge from one electric potential to another. The charge flows through a wire to the light bulb, through the light bulb, and back to the battery. The analogy is shown in Figure 13-5, in which the water flows in a circuit. Note the following very important idea: The current in the upper trough is the same as the current in the lower trough. If the current in the upper trough were larger, then more water would be going into the waterfall than coming out of it, and the waterfall would overflow. That is not what happens. Think about this scenario until it is intuitive.

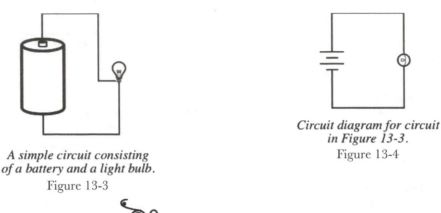

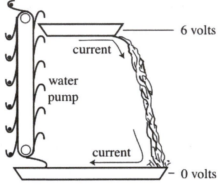

A simple circuit consisting of a battery and a light bulb.
Figure 13-3

Circuit diagram for circuit in Figure 13-3.
Figure 13-4

Water-course analogy for circuits in Figures 13-3 and 13-4.
Figure 13-5

Also, energy flow is not the same as water flow. The energy starts in the pump and becomes the energy of flowing water. As the water falls, however, the energy becomes heat. Similarly, the chemical energy of the battery is transformed into electrical energy and then into heat and light.

Whereas in the last chapter we were often interested in the absolute potential, in circuits we are interested only in changes in potential from one position to another. Therefore, we are free to choose a standard 0 volts, relative to which other potentials are measured. In this circuit, we can label the low end of the battery 0 volts. The other end of the battery is then 6 volts (Figure 13-6).

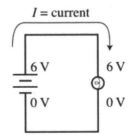

We can analyze a circuit by noting the currents and potentials.
Figure 13-6

B. OHM'S LAW AND THE COMBINATION OF RESISTORS

It turns out that the current through most resistors is approximately proportional to the electric potential across them.

> **Ohm's Law**
> If I is the current through a given resistor and ΔV is the potential across the resistor, then
>
> $$\Delta V = IR, \qquad\qquad\qquad (1)$$
>
> where R is the *resistance* of the resistor, a measure of how difficult it is for charge to flow through it. The unit for R is [volt/amp = Ohm = Ω].

In the next example we encounter a combination of resistors. Several resistors in a circuit are often either *in series* or *in parallel*. Several resistors are in series if a charge coming from the source must go through each of them before going back to the source. Several resistors are in parallel if a charge may go through any of them before going back to the source.

Example 1: Two resistors ($R_1 = 10\ \Omega$ and $R_2 = 20\ \Omega$) are connected in series with a potential source (9 volts). What is the current through resistor 1?

Solution: First, let's DRAW A DIAGRAM of the circuit (Figure 13-7).

We label the lower wire 0 volts. There is 9-volt jump across the voltage source, so the upper wire is labeled 9 volts. We label the wire between the two resistors with the potential V_m. The current is the same through both resistors and the source.

The equivalent water course is shown in Figure 15-8 in which the current in the top trough is the same as the current through both waterfalls and through the bottom trough.

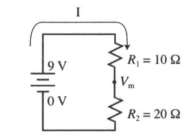

A slightly more complicated circuit
involves two resistors in series.
Figure 13-7

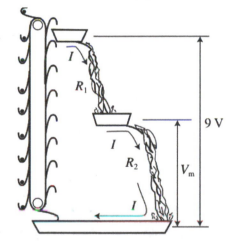

Water-course analogy for
Figure 13-7.
Figure 13-8

> If several resistors are in series, then the same current flows through all of them.

Do you see why?

Applying Ohm's law to the first resistor gives

$$9V - V_m = IR_1$$

and applying Ohm's law to the second resistor gives

$$V_m - 0 = IR_2$$

Substituting the expression for V_m gives

$$9V - IR_2 = IR_1$$

$$9V = I(R_1 + R_2)$$

$$I = 9V/(R_1 + R_2)$$

$$= 9V/(10\ \Omega + 20\ \Omega)$$

$$= 0.3\text{A}$$

Example 2: In the circuit above, what is the potential drop across resistor 1?

Solution: If we apply Ohm's law to resistor 1, then we have

$$\Delta V_1 = I_1 R_1$$
$$= (0.3\text{A})(10\ \Omega)$$
$$= 3\text{V}$$

Generally, we do not have to go through as much trouble as we did in Example 1 because there are two rules for combining resistors:

If several resistors (R_1, R_2, and so on) are in series, then we can replace them with one resistor whose resistance is the sum

$$R_T = R_1 + R_2 + \cdots. \qquad (2)$$

 becomes 〰
$R_1 \quad R_2 \quad R_3$ $\qquad R_T$

If several resistors (R_1, R_2, and so on) are in parallel then we can replace them with one resistor with resistance R_T, where

$$\frac{1}{R_T} = \frac{1}{R_1} + \frac{1}{R_2} + \cdots. \qquad (3)$$

becomes R_T 〰

Example 3: In the circuit shown (Figure 13-9), we have $R_1 = 20\ \Omega$, $R_2 = 30\ \Omega$, and $R_3 = 60\ \Omega$, and the potential source is 12 volts.

    a. What is the current through resistor R_2?
    b. What is the current through the potential source?

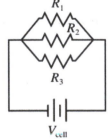

Another simple circuit involves resistors in parallel.
Figure 13-9

Solution: a. First, let's label the negative terminal of the source 0 V and the positive terminal 12 V. The potential all along the left wire is 0 volts, and along the right wire is 12 volts (Figure 13-10).

This gives us the potential drop across R_2:

$$\Delta V_2 = 12V$$
$$I_2 = \Delta V_2 / R_2$$
$$= 12V/30\Omega$$
$$= 0.4A$$

b. Note that the current splits into three parts through the resistors. To obtain the total current, we need to combine resistors to obtain an equivalent circuit (Figure 13-11):

$$\frac{1}{R_T} = \frac{1}{20\Omega} + \frac{1}{30\Omega} + \frac{1}{60\Omega}$$

$$= \frac{6}{60\Omega}$$

$$R_T = 10\Omega$$

$$I = \frac{\Delta V}{R_T} = \frac{12V}{10\Omega} = 1.2A$$

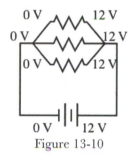

Figure 13-10

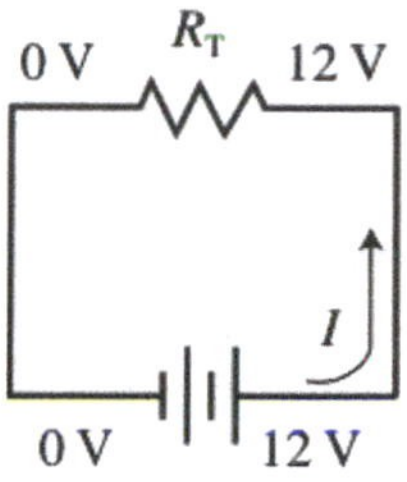

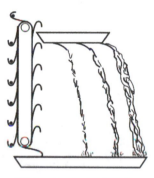

Figure 13-11

Figure 13-12 shows the analogous water-course.

Water-course analogy for the circuit in Figure 13-10.
Figure 13-12

> If several resistors are in parallel then the same potential exists across all of them.

When faced with a question concerning a circuit, there is no general procedure, which always leads to an answer, but here are some things to try:

1. Label the lower end of the battery 0 V.
2. Label other wires with voltages.
3. Label the currents going through the wires.
4. Combine resistors.
5. Apply Ohm's law.

Example 4: Consider the circuit shown in Figure 13-13, where $R_1 = 1\ \Omega$, $R_2 = R_3 = 4\ \Omega$, and $V_{cell} = 6$ V.

    a. What is the current going through resistor 1?
    b. How does I_1 change if points A and B are connected with a wire?

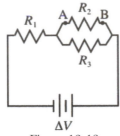

Figure 13-13

Solution: a. First we draw in the current and voltages (Figure 13-14), but this does not seem to get anywhere, because we do not know a potential difference across resistor 1 to apply Ohm's law. (Many students make the mistake here of using 6 volts and 1 Ω in Ohm's law, but the potential difference across resistor 1 is not 6 volts.)

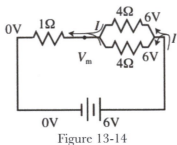

Figure 13-14

Figure 13-15 shows the result of combining the two parallel resistors. Figure 13-16 shows the final equivalent circuit, by combining the two resistors in Figure 13-15. The total current is (by Ohm's law, finally) 2 A. The total current is the same as the current through resistor 1 (see Figure 13-14), so the answer to part a is 2 A.

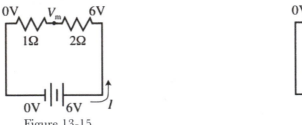

Figure 13-15   Figure 13-16

b. If we connect points A and B by a wire, then they have the same potential, and this is shown in Figure 13-17. No current flows through resistors 2 and 3, and resistor 1 has the full 6 V across it. The current through it (by Ohm's law) is 6 A.

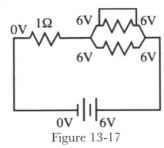

Figure 13-17

C. REAL DC CELLS AND REAL WIRES

An ideal voltage source would maintain a given potential across its terminals regardless of the circuit. Real DC cells are not so good, and we find that any current through the cell reduces the potential across the terminals. We can model a real cell as an ideal potential source in series with a resistor, as if there were a resistor inside the cell. The potential across the ideal source is the *electromotive force* or *emf*, the resistance of the internal resistor is the *internal resistance* R_{cell}, while the actual potential difference across the whole cell is the *terminal potential*.

In the simplified circuit of Figure 13-18, the circuit outside of the cell is a represented by a single resistor and dashed lines enclose the cell. The potential jump across the ideal source is V_{emf}. The current flowing through the circuit is I, so the potential drop across the internal resistor is IR_{cell}. Thus from the illustration we can give an expression for the terminal potential:

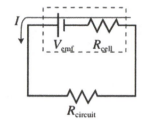

A real cell is like an ideal
potential source (V_{emf}) in series
with a resistor (R_{cell}).
Figure 13-18

$$\Delta V = V_{emf} - IR_{cell} \qquad\qquad (4)$$

In addition to knowing this equation, you should understand the discussion that leads to it.

Example 1: A battery has a measured potential difference of 6.0 volts if no circuit is connected to it. When it is connected to a 10-Ω resistor, the current is 0.57 amps. What is the internal resistance of the battery?

Solution: First let's DRAW A DIAGRAM (Figure 13-19). We label the negative terminal of the potential source 0 volts; the other side, 6 volts. The potential drop across the external resistor (10 Ω) is given by Ohm's law:

$$\Delta V_{ext} = IR_{ext}$$

$$= (0.57A)(10\ \Omega)$$

$$= 5.7V$$

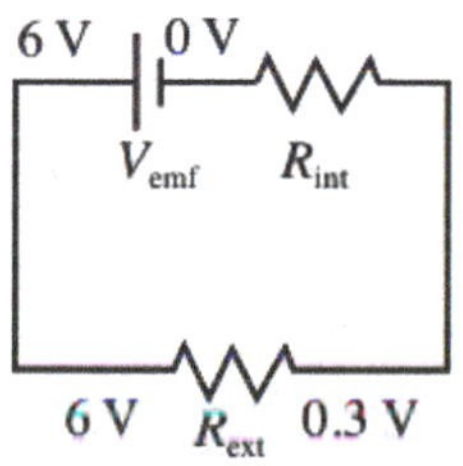

Figure 13-19

The potential on the other side of the external resistor is 0.3 volts. The potential difference across the internal resistor is 0.3 volts, and Ohm's law gives us the resistance

$$R_{int} = \Delta V_{int}/I$$

$$= 0.3V/0.57A$$

$$= 0.53\Omega$$

Another way to do this problem is to combine resistances. Notice that equation (4) does not automatically give the answer in this example, but if we draw a diagram and apply the methods of Section B, then we obtain the answer in two steps.

In addition to idealizing DC cells, we have been assuming that wires have no resistance at all. In fact, they have a small resistance that is proportional to their length and inversely proportional to their cross-sectional area. A given material has a ***resistivity*** ρ, so the resistance of the wire is given by

$$R = \rho \frac{l}{A}, \tag{5}$$

where ρ has the units [Ohm meters], l is the length of the wire (in [m]) and A is its cross-sectional area (in [m^2]).

Some resistivities are given in the table below.

substance	resistivity (Ωm)
silver	1.5×10^{-8}
copper	1.7×10^{-8}
gold	2.4×10^{-8}

You can assume wires have zero resistance unless the passage tells you otherwise.

D. POWER

Recall that power is a measure of how quickly energy is transformed, measured in [J/s = Watts = W]. The power dissipate by a resistor is

$$P_{res} = I\Delta V, \tag{6}$$

where I is the current through the resistor and ΔV is the potential difference across it.

Because of Ohm's law, we may also write

$$P_{res} = I^2R = (\Delta V)^2/R$$

(It is better to remember how to derive this equation than to memorize it.) The power provided by a DC cell to a circuit is

$$P_{cell} = I\Delta V, \tag{7}$$

where I is the current through the cell and ΔV is the potential difference across it.

Example: Light bulbs that you use around the house are designed to have 120 V across their terminals. For instance, a 120-W bulb uses 120 Watts of power when placed in a socket with a 120-V potential difference. (Actually it is a little more complicated. See Section F.) With that in mind,

    a.   what is the resistance of a "120-Watt" bulb?

    b.   What is the resistance of a "30-Watt" bulb?

    c.   If these two bulbs are connected in series, and plugged into a wall outlet, which bulb would be brighter (Figure 13-20)?

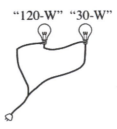

Which burns brighter when a 30-W bulb and a 120-W bulb are connected in series?

Figure 13-20

Solution: a. Figure 13-21 shows the circuit diagram for a single 120-W bulb plugged into a potential source. The equation for power is

$$P = I\Delta V$$
$$120\text{W} = I(120\text{V})$$
$$I = 1\text{A}$$

By Ohm's law, we have

$$\Delta V = IR$$
$$120\text{V} = (1\text{A})R$$
$$R = 120\ \Omega.$$

b. A similar calculation gives a resistance 480 Ω for the "30-W" bulb.

c. If we place the bulbs in series (Figure 13-22), then the current through the bulbs is the same. Since

$$P = I^2R$$

the power is proportional to the resistance. So the 480-Ω bulb (that is, the "30-W" bulb) is brighter because the bulbs are in series. (Usually the "120-W" bulb is brighter because the bulbs are connected in parallel.)

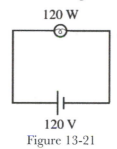

120 W

120 V

Figure 13-21

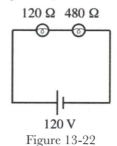

120 Ω 480 Ω

120 V

Figure 13-22

E. CAPACITANCE

A DC cell creates a potential difference between its terminals by transferring electrons from the positive to the negative terminal. As it transfers more and more electrons, the negative terminal gains a greater charge, and the terminal exerts a greater force on every additional electron the cell transfers. Thus it takes more energy to transfer each additional electron onto it. Finally, the energy cost of adding an electron is too much and the cell stops, but by that time the terminal potential has been reached (Figure 13-23).

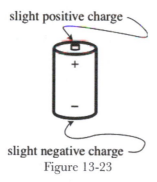

slight positive charge

+

−

slight negative charge

Figure 13-23

If, however, we connect each terminal to a plate of metal (Figure 13-24), then the cell is able to transport more electrons at a low energy cost, because the additional electrons are able to spread out across the plate. Eventually the cell tries to push one more electron onto the plate but cannot, because the energy cost is too great. In this case the potential between the plates is same as before, but the difference is that more charge is able to be contained on the plates than on the terminals of the cell.

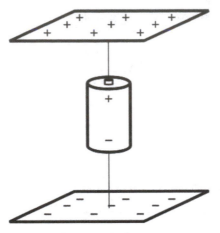

When metal plates are
connected to battery terminals,
the plates become charged.
Figure 13-24

If we bring the plates near each other but not touching (Figure 13-25), even more charge is able to be transferred through the cell. An electron arriving at the negative plate feels the opposing force from the electrons, but it also feels the attractive force of the nearby positive plate, so it does not mind so much getting onto the negative plate. (That is, it can be energetically favorable.)

Such a device, which holds a charge when a potential difference is applied to it, is called a ***capacitor***. In Figure 13-25, if a larger potential is applied to the plates, a proportionally larger charge will sit on them. The ***capacitance***, the capacity to hold charge, is defined by

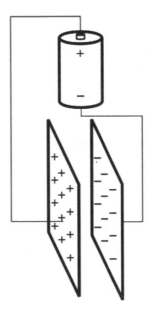

Bringing the plates near each
other increases their capacity
to hold charge.
Figure 13-25

$$C = \frac{Q}{\Delta V}, \qquad\qquad (8)$$

where Q is the charge on one plate, and ΔV is the potential difference across the plates. The units of capacitance are [Coulombs/volt = Farads = F].

To reiterate, the capacitance of a device depends on how it is built. The charge on it is proportional to the voltage applied to it: $Q = C\Delta V$.

Example: We place two metal plates parallel to each other and 0.01 meters apart. One sheet we connect by a wire to the positive end of a 6-V DC cell; and the other, to the negative end. The two plates now have a 6-V potential difference between them. The electric field between the plates is uniform (though we will not prove it), that is, the same direction and magnitude everywhere. A dust mite has a 2×10^{-14} C charge tied around his ankle.

  a. How much work is required for him to cross from the negative plate to the positive plate?
  b. What force does he experience as he crosses?
  c. What is the magnitude of the electric field between the plates?

Solution: a. First let's DRAW A DIAGRAM showing the electric field (Figure 13-26); second, a diagram showing the forces on the mite (Figure 13-27).

Figure 13-27

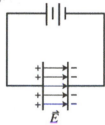

An electric field exists between the plates of a capacitor.

Figure 13-26

Moving from a negative to a positive plate is an uphill battle for the mite, so we expect the work to be positive. We write

$$W = q\Delta V$$
$$= (2 \times 10^{-14}\,\text{C})(6\,\text{J/C})$$
$$= 1.2 \times 10^{-13}\,\text{J}$$

b. If the electric field is uniform, then the force ($F_{elec} = qE$) that the mite experiences must be constant. If he goes straight across, then we have the old work equation

$$W = F_{mite}\Delta x \cos\phi$$

Now the mite moves at a constant velocity, so the forces are balanced and we can replace F_{mite} with F_{elec}. Also, we know $\cos\phi$ is 1. Thus we write

$$W = F_{elec}\Delta x$$

and

$$F_{elec} = W/\Delta x$$
$$= (1.2 \times 10^{-13}\,\text{J})/0.01\,\text{m} = 1.2 \times 10^{-11}\,\text{N}$$

c. We obtain the electric field from $F_{elec} = qE$, so that $E = 600$ N/C.

It is more important to understand the pictures and the ideas than to apply the formulas in this example.

The equation we derived is worth remembering in its own right:

$$\Delta V = E\Delta x \,, \tag{9}$$

where ΔV is the potential across a capacitor, E is the magnitude of the electric field inside of the capacitor, and Δx is the separation of the plates.

Remember what this equation is about. This is just our old $W = F\Delta x$ equation in new clothing, that is, work (per charge) is force (per charge) times displacement. In fact, the assumption made in the problem is fairly accurate: The electric field between two charged parallel plates is uniform.

Now let's complicate the situation even more. A **dielectric** is a nonconducting substance, such as plastic. Its electrons are not free to move from one atom to the next, but the electrons can slosh a little onto one side of the molecules (they are slightly polarizable). If a dielectric is placed between the plates, then the molecules in the dielectric become polarized, with electrons being pulled toward the positive plate (Figure 13-28). The result is that the DC cell can transfer still more charge from one plate to the other, since an electron arriving at the negative plate feels also the slight positive charge of the one side of the dielectric. Thus, placing the dielectric between the plates increases the capacitance.

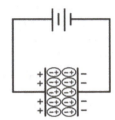

A dieletric between the metal plates increases the capacitance.

Figure 13-28

Each material which is a nonconductor has a dielectric constant κ. The capacitance of the capacitor with the dielectric in the middle is given by

$$C_{\text{dielectric}} = \kappa C_{\text{vacuum}}. \tag{10}$$

The constant κ is always greater than 1.

F. ALTERNATING CURRENT

When a DC cell is connected in a circuit, the potential difference between the terminals stays constant. This is called **direct current** (hence DC). In a wall outlet, things are more complicated.

In the United States, the long slit is the **ground**, connected to the Earth itself, which is a large supply of charge. This ensures that this terminal stays at a constant potential which we call 0 volts. The short slit is "hot". Its potential, relative to ground, varies like a sine wave between +170 volts and −170 volts. The voltage goes from high to low to high about 60 times a second, that is, with frequency 60 Hz. This is called **alternating current**, since the current in the wire is changing back and forth (Figure 13-29).

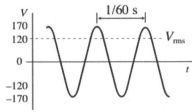

Figure 13-29

Example: Consider your toaster plugged into the wall. The power company pulls electrons out of the Earth and pushes them onto a wire. The resulting electric field pushes electrons on down the wire, until electrons are pushed into your toaster. Electrons are pushed out of the toaster into the wire, out of the wire into the Earth. Any one electron does not go very far, but the signal goes from the power company to your toaster. (See

Figure 13-30

Figure 13-30.)

Then the power company pulls electrons out of the wire and pushes them into the Earth. The resulting electric field pulls electrons along the wire, out of your toaster. Electrons in the other wire go into the toaster and are replaced with electrons pulled from the Earth. Sixty times a second. Until your bread is toasted. Note that only one wire needs to go from the power company to your house, since the Earth itself completes the circuit.

Generally, we do not talk of the line current as being 170 volts (the maximum). Instead we talk of a kind of average (root mean square) which is V_{rms} = 120 volts for the line current. The following equations hold for alternating current:

$$V_{rms} = I_{rms}R$$
$$P_{rms} = V_{rms}I_{rms}$$
(11)

So there are no new equations to memorize.

Things begin to get complicated when we connect alternating current to capacitors (and to other things), but that is beyond the scope of the MCAT.

In this chapter we built on the concepts of the previous chapter to study simple circuits. When you solve problems involving circuits, it is helpful to visualize the flow of charge as the flow of a fluid and the potential in the wires as a height above a standard. Each piece of wire is at one potential. Each individual resistor has a current I through it and a potential ΔV across it such that $\Delta V = IR$ (Ohm's law). It is important to be careful when using Ohm's law. Think about the circuit first. The power dissipated by a resistor is $P_i = I_i \Delta V_i$.

A capacitor is two parallel conducting plates which store charge when a potential is applied to them. The capacitance of a capacitor is its ability to hold charge $C = Q/\Delta V$. The capacitance is determined by the dimension and material of the capacitor and the stored charge depends on the applied potential. The electric field between the plates is given by $\Delta V = E\Delta x$, where Δx is the separation of the plates.

CHAPTER 13 PROBLEMS

Use the following in questions 1–4:

In a certain water fountain, a pump takes water from a large pool and pumps it up to a trough. The water flows along the trough and falls through a hole in the bottom. As the water falls, it turns a water wheel and returns to the pool. Assume this water fountain is analogous to an electric circuit.

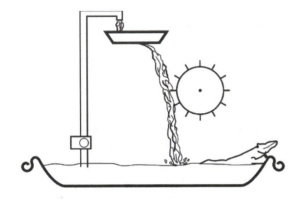

1. What would be analogous to electric current?

   A. water
   B. flow velocity
   C. volume flow rate
   D. height of water

2. What would be analogous to electric potential?

   A. water
   B. flow velocity
   C. volume flow rate
   D. height of water

3. What would be analogous to the water pump?

   A. a motor
   B. a resistor
   C. a battery
   D. a light bulb

4. What would be analogous to the pool?

   A. a resistor
   B. an inductor
   C. a ground
   D. a wire

Use the following in questions 5 and 6:

In the circuit shown, use the following:

$R_1 = 20 \ \Omega,$
$R_2 = 30 \ \Omega,$
$R_3 = 40 \ \Omega,$
$\Delta V = 18 \text{ V}.$

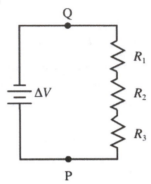

5. What is the current flowing through resistor 2?

   A. 0.2 A
   B. 0.4 A
   C. 0.6 A
   D. 1.2 A

6. How does the current flowing through the wire at point P compare with the current flowing at Q?

   A. The current at P is less.
   B. The current at P is the same.
   C. The current at P is greater.
   D. The answer depends on whether one considers positive current or negative current.

Use the following in questions 7 and 8:

In the circuit shown, $R_1 = 1 \ \Omega$, $R_2 = 2 \ \Omega$, and the emf of the cell is 6 volts.

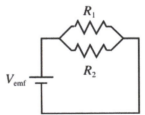

7. How does the current flowing through resistor 1 compare with the current flowing through resistor 2?

   A. The current through resistor 1 is less.
   B. The current through resistor 1 is the same.
   C. The current through resistor 1 is greater.
   D. None of the above can be concluded.

8. How does the voltage drop across resistor 1 compare with the voltage drop across resistor 2?

   A. The voltage across resistor 1 is less.
   B. The voltage across resistor 1 is the same.
   C. The voltage across resistor 1 is greater.
   D. None of the above can be concluded.

9. Two batteries are connected to a single resistor, as shown in the diagram.

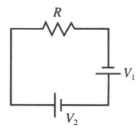

   V_1 = 6 volts
   V_2 = 9 volts
   R = 60 Ω

   What is the current through the resistor?

   A. 0.083 A
   B. 0.125 A
   C. 0.020 A
   D. 0.250 A

Use the following in questions 10–13:

Four 6-V batteries are connected in series in order to power lights A and B. The resistance of light A is 40 Ω and the resistance of light B is 20 Ω.

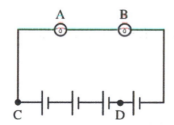

10. How does the current through light bulb A compare with the current through light bulb B?

   A. The current through light bulb A is less.
   B. The current through light bulb A is the same.
   C. The current through light bulb A is greater.
   D. None of the above is true.

11. What is the potential difference between points C and D?

   A. 6 volts
   B. 12 volts
   C. 18 volts
   D. 24 volts

12. How does the voltage drop across light A compare to the drop across light B?

   A. The voltage drop for A is less than that for B by a factor of 4.
   B. The voltage drop for A is less than that for B by a factor of 2.
   C. The voltage drop for A is the same as that for B.
   D. The voltage drop for A is greater than that for B by a factor of 2.

13. What is the current through the wire at point C?

   A. 0.1 A
   B. 0.2 A
   C. 0.4 A
   D. 1.8 A

Use the following in questions 14–16:

In the circuit diagram shown, note that

   $R_1 = 4$ Ω,
   $R_2 = 2$ Ω,
   $R_3 = 2$ Ω.

In addition, the current through resistor 1 is 2 amps.

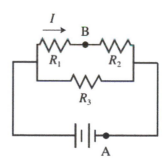

14. What is the voltage drop across resistor 1?

   A. 2 volts
   B. 4 volts
   C. 8 volts
   D. 12 volts

15. What is the current through resistor 2?

    A. 1 ampere
    B. 2 amperes
    C. 4 amperes
    D. 8 amperes

16. What is the voltage difference between points A and B?

    A. 2 volts
    B. 4 volts
    C. 8 volts
    D. 12 volts

Use the following in questions 17–20:

In the diagram, resistors 2 and 3 are in parallel, and their combination is in series with resistor 1. Point A is in the wire between the voltage source and resistor 1. Point B is in the wire between resistor 1 and the combination 2 and 3. Point C is on the other side of resistor 2.

In the circuit shown, use the following:

$R_1 = 4\ \Omega$,
$R_2 = 6\ \Omega$,
$R_3 = 3\ \Omega$,
$\Delta V = 36$ V.

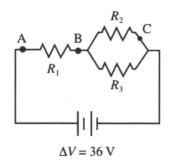

$\Delta V = 36$ V

17. What is the current through resistor 1?

    A. 2.77 amps
    B. 6 amps
    C. 8 amps
    D. 9 amps

18. How does the voltage drop across resistor 2 (that is, V_2) compare with that across resistor 3 (that is, V_3)?

    A. $V_2 = 2\ V_3$
    B. $V_2 = V_3$
    C. $V_3 = 2\ V_2$
    D. $V_2 + V_3 = 36$ V

19. How would the potential difference across resistor 2 change if points A and B were connected by a wire?

    A. It would increase.
    B. It would stay the same.
    C. It would decrease, but it would not be zero.
    D. It would be zero.

20. How would the current through the source change if points A and C were connected by a wire?

    A. It would be the same.
    B. It would increase by a factor of 4.
    C. It would increase by a factor of 24.
    D. None of the above, the circuit would be shorted.

Use the following in questions 21–24:

In the circuit shown, the light bulbs are each 20 Ω, and the potential source is 6 volts.

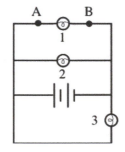

21. How much energy is dissipated by light bulb 2 in 10 seconds?

    A. 18 Joules
    B. 120 Joules
    C. 200 Joules
    D. 1200 Joules

22. What would happen to light bulb 2 if light bulb 1 were to blow (interrupting the connection)?

    A. It would go out.
    B. It would be dimmer, but it would not go out.
    C. It would burn the same.
    D. It would be brighter.

23. What would happen to light bulb 3 if light bulb 1 were to blow (interrupting the connection)?

    A. It would go out.
    B. It would be dimmer, but it would not go out.
    C. It would burn the same.
    D. It would be brighter.

24. What would happen if the points A and B were connected with a wire?

A. Light 1 would extinguish, otherwise nothing.
B. Lights 1 and 2 would extinguish, light 3 would remain the same.
C. Lights 1 and 2 would extinguish, and light 3 would be brighter.
D. All lights would extinguish, and the battery would be shorted.

Use the following in questions 25 and 26:

In the circuit shown, resistor 1 has resistance 2 Ω, and resistor 2 has resistance 4 Ω. The potential source has a potential of 12 volts.

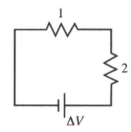

25. How much power is dissipated by resistor 1?

A. 8 Watts
B. 24 Watts
C. 48 Watts
D. 72 Watts

26. Which correctly gives a relationship between the potential drop across resistor 1, ΔV_1, and that across resistor 2, ΔV_2?

A. $\Delta V_1 = \Delta V_2$
B. $\Delta V_1 = 2\,\Delta V_2$
C. $\Delta V_1 = 4\,\Delta V_2$
D. $\Delta V_1 + \Delta V_2 = 12$ V

Use the following in questions 27–30:

In the circuit shown, each of the light bulbs has a resistance 2 Ω, and the potential source has an emf of 6 volts.

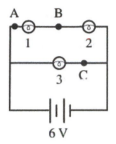

27. Which of the following would increase the power dissipated by light bulb 3?

A. Decrease the resistance of light bulb 3.
B. Increase the resistance of light bulb 3.
C. Decrease the emf of the battery.
D. Introduce another resistor at C.

28. Which graph best shows the power dissipated by light bulb 3 as a function of time?

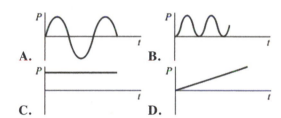

29. What would happen if light bulb 1 goes out (thus breaking the circuit)?

A. Nothing else happens.
B. Light bulb 2 goes out.
C. Light bulb 3 burns brighter.
D. Light bulb 2 goes out, and light bulb 3 burns brighter.

30. What happens to light bulb 2 if light bulb 1 is shorted, that is, if points A and B are connected by a wire?

A. It extinguishes.
B. It becomes dimmer, but it does not extinguish.
C. It burns the same.
D. It burns brighter.

Passage 1

In a certain experiment, we place two metal plates of area A parallel to each other and separated by a distance d to form a capacitor. The copper disks are mounted on nonconducting stands in a dry room which does not allow the conduction of charge through the air. The two plates are connected with wires to the opposite ends of a DC cell. The capacitance of such a device is given by

$$C = \varepsilon_0 \frac{A}{d}$$

where

$$\varepsilon_0 = 8.85 \times 10^{-12} \frac{C^2}{Nm^2}$$

In Experiment 1 we place two copper circular disks of radius R_1 a distance d_1 apart and connect them to a battery which produces a potential ΔV_{bat}. This produces a positive charge Q_1 on one of the plates and an electric field E_1 between the plates.

In Experiment 2 we use two copper circular disks of the same radius (R_1) and place them three times as far apart ($3d_1$) as in Experiment 1. Again, the two disks are connected to the opposite ends of the same battery.

In Experiment 3 we reproduce the setup in Experiment 1. Then the wires are removed from the copper plates. The copper plates are carefully separated to a new distance $2d_1$.

31. An alpha particle is a bare helium-4 nucleus. If an alpha particle is placed between the plates in Experiment 1, how would the electric force on it compare to the electric force on a proton?

A. Both experience zero force.
B. The force on the alpha particle would be the same as that on the proton.
C. The force on the alpha particle would be double that on the proton.
D. The force on the alpha particle would be four times that on the proton.

32. What charge is on the positive plate in Experiment 2?

A. $Q_1/3$
B. Q_1
C. $3Q_1$
D. $9Q_1$

33. What is the magnitude of the electric field between the plates in Experiment 2?

A. $E_1/3$
B. E_1
C. $3E_1$
D. $9 E_1$

34. What charge is on the positive plate at the end of Experiment 3?

A. $Q_1/2$
B. Q_1
C. $2 Q_1$
D. $4 Q_1$

35. What is the magnitude of the potential difference between the plates at the end of Experiment 3?

A. $\Delta V_{bat}/2$
B. ΔV_{bat}
C. $2\Delta V_{bat}$
D. $4\Delta V_{bat}$

CHAPTER 14
ATOMIC AND NUCLEAR PHYSICS

A. INTRODUCTION

In this chapter we break out of the tradition and viewpoint of classical physics and discuss results from quantum theory. In the 1890s, physicists began to realize that the very language of particles and positions, forces and fields was insufficient to discuss the world of the very small, of atoms and molecules. They needed a new language and a new way of thinking, and quantum physics was born.

In classical physics, which we have been studying thus far, if we wanted to talk about a particular electron in an atom, we would specify its position and velocity. Physics would tell us how that position changed in time.

In quantum physics, we do not even talk about position and velocity in this way, because it turns out these terms are impossible to define. Particles simply do not have a definite position nor velocity. Instead we talk about a particular electron in an atom by specifying the orbital it is in. Orbital it is in? An **orbital** is a state of being for an electron. Knowing an electron's orbital means knowing its energy (generally) and knowing something about its location (often), but not its exact position.

One way to think about it is to think that electrons are tiny particles that move so fast that we do not know where they are, and the area of space they move in is an orbital. That is one way to think about it, but it's the wrong way.

It is **not** the case that electrons have position and velocity of which we are simply ignorant. An electron truly has no exact position, existing all around the nucleus at once, although it does exist more strongly in some places than in others.

For instance, an electron in the lowest-energy orbital of a hydrogen atom exists throughout the area near the nucleus, but it exists 90% within a radius of 1.4×10^{-10} m and 10% outside of that radius. (That does not mean that it spends 10% of its time outside of 1.4×10^{-10} m. That is thinking classically again.)

B. BASIC STRUCTURE OF AN ATOM

As was mentioned earlier, an **atom** consists of a tiny positive charge center (10^{-15} m) called the **nucleus** and a surrounding cloud of electrons (10^{-10} m). Atoms connect together by interactions of their electrons to form **molecules** and **ionic solids**, which comprise almost all of the matter around us. The nucleus of the atom contains **protons** and **neutrons**. Each proton has a charge $+1.6 \times 10^{-19}$ C (chemists call this +1), each neutron has zero net charge, and each electron has charge -1.6×10^{-19} C (chemists call this −1).

The mass of the proton and the mass of the neutron are about the same (1.7×10^{-27} kg), and electrons are about 2000 times lighter. As you can see, kilograms are really too large a unit to use to talk of these masses, so we often use another mass unit, called the **atomic mass unit**, or [amu] (or sometimes just u), so that

$$1 \text{ amu} = 1.6606 \times 10^{-27} \text{ kg}$$

It is very nearly the mass of a proton or neutron, so we have

$m_{proton} = 1.0073$ amu
$m_{neutron} = 1.0087$ amu
$m_{electron} = 0.00055$ amu

The **atomic mass** (sometimes erroneously called the atomic weight) is the mass of an atom in amu. The **mass number** is the total number of protons and neutrons in the nucleus. The mass number is approximately the atomic mass of an atom in amu, since most of the mass comes from the protons and neutrons.

Thus we can describe a nucleus by specifying the number of protons in it, or **atomic number**, and the total number of protons and neutrons, or mass number. The atomic number also determines which element the atom makes up. The notation we use for a single atom contains all this information. For instance, we denote common helium by one of the two symbols:

$$^4_2\text{He} \qquad ^4\text{He}$$

(pronounced "helium four"), where the mass number is 4 and the atomic number is 2. We really do not need to specify the atomic number, since we can obtain that from the periodic table. The mass of such a nucleus is about 4 amu (actually 4.00260 amu).

Several atoms which differ in the number of neutrons but have the same number of protons are called *isotopes* of that element, for example, ^{35}Cl and ^{37}Cl. The chemical properties of ^{35}Cl and ^{37}Cl are nearly identical, since the neutrons of the nucleus have hardly any effect on the surrounding electron cloud.

The symbol ^4_2He may refer either to a nucleus having two protons and two neutrons or to an atom having such a nucleus. We write nuclear reactions using similar notation as that for chemical reactions, except now we are concerned with changes in the protons and neutrons in the nuclei.

Example 1: When a slow neutron collides with a ^{17}O nucleus, the products include a ^4He nucleus and what other nucleus?

Solution: The information given in the problem can be written

$$^1_0n + {}^{17}_8O \rightarrow {}^4_2He + \,?$$

where we have used the symbol ^1_0n for the neutron (do you see why?). The number of protons mentioned among the reactants is $0 + 8 = 8$, of which 2 went into the ^4_2He. The number of protons and neutrons all together among the reactants is $1 + 17 = 18$, of which 4 are in ^4_2He. Thus the final nucleus has a 6 in the lower left position and a 14 in the upper left, corresponding in the periodic table to ^{14}C or carbon-14, so we write

$$^1_0n + {}^{17}_8O \rightarrow {}^4_2He + {}^{14}_6C$$

When writing reactions, the sum of left superscripts for the reactants must equal the sum of left superscripts for the products. This assures that the number of heavy particles stays constant. Also, the sum of left subscripts for the reactants must equal the sum of left subscripts for the products. This assures that charge is conserved in the reaction.

There are always at least two product particles in any nuclear reaction. (Exceptions are vanishingly rare.) One of these particles is often a particle of light, called a *photon* and symbolized by *g*.

Example 2: When a proton collides with a nucleus of carbon-12, generally the result is one new nucleus (if there is a reaction at all). How do we write the reaction?

Solution: We write the reaction as follows:

$$^1_1H + {}^{12}_6C \rightarrow {}^{13}_7N + \gamma$$

or

$$^1H + {}^{12}C \rightarrow {}^{13}N + \gamma$$

where we have used ^1_1H for the proton (again, do you see why?).

C. ENERGY LEVELS AND TRANSITIONS

For an isolated atom, the electrons are in various orbitals. The atom as a whole has a certain energy, depending on what orbitals are occupied by electrons. Quantum theory predicts that only certain energies are allowed for a given atom.

For instance, a hydrogen atom can have only energies corresponding to the equation

$$E_n = -(2.18 \times 10^{-18} \text{ J}) \frac{1}{n^2}$$

where *n* is a positive integer. There is no such thing as an isolated hydrogen atom with energy -1.5×10^{-18} J or with energy -1.1×10^{-18} J, since they do not fit into the formula. This can be shown graphically on an energy level diagram (Figure 14-1), in which the vertical axis represents energy and the horizontal axis does not represent anything. Zero energy corresponds to the state in which the proton and electron are infinitely separated. Bringing the proton and electron together releases energy, so the energies for all the other states are negative.

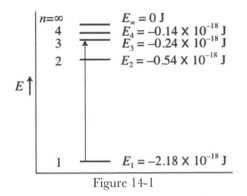

Figure 14-1

Even though the atom cannot have energies between the allowed energy states shown on the diagram, the atom can jump, or make a *transition*, from one state to another. It does this either by colliding with another atom or by absorbing or releasing a photon. The state corresponding to the lowest energy is called the ***ground state***. Other states are ***excited states***.

In previous chapters we discussed light in terms of a wave of disturbance of electric and magnetic fields. Quantum theory maintains that these disturbances come in little packets called photons. If there are a large number of photons, then they act like the classical field discussed earlier. At any rate, there is a connection between the frequency of the light and the energy of a photon of that light, so that

$$E_{photon} = hf, \qquad\qquad (1)$$

where $h = 6.63 \times 10^{-34}$ J/Hz is a constant of nature, Planck's constant.

If a photon is emitted or absorbed by an atom, then the photon must have energy, given by the energy difference between the atomic states. Several examples will make this clearer.

Example 1: A beam of laser light is incident on a sample of hydrogen gas. Most of the gas in the sample is in the ***ground state*** (lowest energy state). To what frequency should the laser be tuned so that the hydrogen atoms absorb the light and end up in the second excited state?

Solution: The ground state corresponds to $n = 1$, so its energy is

$$E_1 = -2.18 \times 10^{-18} \, J$$

The second excited state must have $n = 3$, so its energy is

$$E_3 = -0.24 \times 10^{-18} \, J$$

The energy of the photons in the laser are $(-0.24 \times 10^{-18} \, J) - (-2.18 \times 10^{-18} \, J) = 1.94 \times 10^{-18}$ J. Thus the frequency of the photons is

$$f = \frac{E_{photon}}{h}$$

$$= \frac{1.94 \times 10^{-18} \, J}{6.63 \times 10^{-34} \, \dfrac{J}{Hz}}$$

$$= 2.9 \times 10^{15} \, Hz$$

Transitions are shown in an energy level diagram by arrows from one line to another. Figure 14-1 shows the transition for Example 1.

Several things can happen after an atom has absorbed a photon. It can decay back to its previous state, emitting a photon of (almost) the same energy. This process, called *scattering*, is shown in Figure 14-2, in which the up arrow represents absorption and the down arrow, subsequent emission. Figure 14-3 shows the process differently, where absorption occurs between steps 1 and 2 and emission between steps 2 and 3.

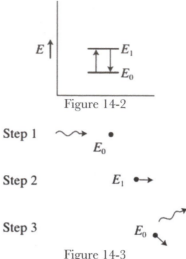

Figure 14-2

Step 1

E_0

Step 2 E_1

Step 3

E_0

Figure 14-3

An atom that has absorbed a photon may emit a photon of a different energy by making a transition to a new state. This is shown in Figure 14-4. The upward arrow represents the absorption of the original photon. The downward arrows represent emitted photons, so the atom emits two photons for each one it absorbs. This phenomenon, in which a substance absorbs one frequency of light and emits light of different frequencies, is called *fluorescence*.

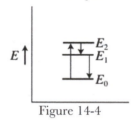

Figure 14-4

Do not get thrown off by notation. Sometimes the ground state energy is labeled E_0 and sometimes E_1. Also, sometimes we say the ground state has zero energy, but sometimes zero energy corresponds to complete ionization and the ground state energy is negative. It is a matter of convention which the problem will specify. The ground state is always the lowest-energy state.

D. RADIOACTIVITY

The nucleus is often content to spend many years undergoing no major changes. The protons and neutrons hold together, while the electrons in the electron orbitals are doing all sorts of things. Sometimes, however, the nucleus undergoes a change. If this happens spontaneously, it is called **radioactive decay**.

There are three main types of radioactive decay. Nuclei which have an especially large number of protons and neutrons will sometimes throw off a packet of two protons and two neutrons, called an **alpha particle** (**a**). Note that an alpha particle is the same as the nucleus of the common helium nucleus. This is called **alpha decay**.

Example 1: What is the reaction representing the alpha decay of the thorium-232?

Solution: The answer is

$$^{232}_{90}\text{Th} \rightarrow {}^{228}_{88}\text{Ra} + {}^{4}_{2}\text{He}$$

We know the atomic number of thorium (90) from the periodic table. The alpha particle is always represented by the symbol $^{4}_{2}\text{He}$. Figure 14-5 shows this decay. (Figure 14-5 shows this decay.)

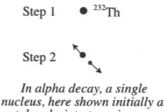

In alpha decay, a single nucleus, here shown initially at rest, breaks into two pieces, one a small ^{4}He nucleus.
Figure 14-5

Generally alpha emitters are not dangerous to biological tissue (provided you do not eat them), since the alpha particles lose energy very quickly and do not penetrate very far even in air (several centimeters). That means they generally do not get inside of you.

The second type of radioactive decay is **beta decay**. Nuclei with many neutrons, compared with protons, undergo normal beta decay (β^-). In this process, a neutron decays into a proton, an electron, and an antineutrino. The proton stays in the nucleus, and the electron shoots away from the nucleus. The speeding electron, often called a **beta particle**, can be highly injurious to biological tissue, since it is able to speed through the air and penetrate into the body. Once in the body, it slows down by ionizing molecules that it passes by, which can be very dangerous if one such molecule is DNA. The antineutrino is so penetrating that it generally passes through the body and the planet without depositing any energy, so it is mostly harmless.

Example 2: What is the reaction for the (normal) beta decay of lithium-9?

Solution: On the left side of the reaction we have ^9_3Li. On the right side we place an electron. For accounting purposes, the symbol of the electron is $^0_{-1}e$. Thus we have the incomplete equation

$$^9_3Li \rightarrow ?+ {}^0_{-1}e$$

In order to complete it, we need to make sure the upper and lower left numbers add up correctly. Also we add an antineutrino, so we write

$$^9_3Li \rightarrow {}^9_4Be + {}^0_{-1}e + \bar{\nu}$$

or we can write

$$^9Li \rightarrow {}^9Be + e^- + \bar{\nu}$$

Figure 14-6 shows this decay schematically.

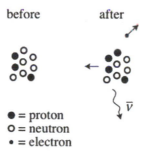

before   after

● = proton
○ = neutron
• = electron

Figure 14-6

Nuclei with many protons undergo **positron decay** (β^+). In this process, a proton decays into a neutron, a positron, and a neutrino. The neutron stays in the nucleus. The positron, which is a particle just like an electron (in mass and so on) with a positive charge, shoots away from the nucleus. The positron is dangerous to biological tissue as well, and the neutrino is innocuous.

(A word about words: Radioactivity is generally divided into alpha, beta, and gamma decays (although there are some other sorts of decays as well). Beta decays are divided into beta decays and positron decays, so the wording can be a bit tricky. Sometimes writers will be careful to say "normal beta decay" and sometimes they will not. If it matters which sort of beta decay is required, assume the normal kind unless otherwise specified.)

Example 3: What is the reaction for the positron decay of carbon-11?

Solution: On the left side of the reaction we have $^{11}_{6}\text{C}$. On the right side we place a positron, whose symbol is $^{0}_{+1}\text{e}$. Thus we have

$$^{11}_{6}\text{C} \rightarrow \,^{11}_{5}\text{B} + \,^{0}_{+1}\text{e} + \bar{\nu}$$

A third type of radioactive decay is ***gamma decay***. Just as the electrons of an atom may be in an excited state, the nucleus can also be in an excited quantum state. When the nucleus decays into the lower energy state, it releases a photon, called a ***gamma particle***, just as a photon is released in the electronic case. When the nucleus decays, however, the energies involved are much greater, about a million times greater, than for the electronic decays. This reaction is the most penetrating, able to penetrate many meters of lead. It can be harmless if it passes simply through the human body, or it can be quite harmful.

Example 4: The radioactive decay of an excited state of cobalt-60 is given by

$$^{60}_{27}\text{Co}^{*} \rightarrow \,^{60}_{28}\text{Ni}^{*} + \,^{0}_{-1}\text{e} + \bar{\nu}$$
$$\searrow$$
$$^{60}_{28}\text{Ni}^{*} + \gamma$$
$$\searrow$$
$$^{60}_{28}\text{Ni} + \gamma$$

where the asterisk indicates an excited state. In this case $^{60}\text{Co}^{*}$ decays into one excited state of ^{60}Ni, which decays into a second excited state of ^{60}Ni, which decays to the ground state.

We can measure the time it takes a nucleus to decay in terms of a ***half-life***. This is the time it takes half the atoms in a sample to decay. The lifetime of an atom is not the same as the lifetime of, say, humans.

If we imagine a population sample of 1000 humans all born in the same year, then after 75 years we would expect about half of them (or 500) to still be alive. After another eight years, only half of those would be surviving. After another five years, it would be half again. We would expect, 150 years after the birth date, that there would probably be no survivors.

Consider now a sample of 1000 gadolinium-148 atoms, all generated at the same moment. This isotope decays by alpha emission to samarium-144 with a half-life of 75 years. After 75 years we expect about half of the original Gd-148 to remain. After another 75 years, about half of those have decayed, leaving about 250 Gd-148 atoms. After yet another 75 years, there are around 125 left. Radioactive atoms do not age and die, but at any moment they have some constant risk of decaying.

Example 5: The nucleus Ru-103 decays to the stable isotope Rh-103. We obtain a pure sample and measure that its radioactivity to be 1616 millicuries. After 156 days the radioactivity is down to 101 millicuries. What is the half-life of this isotope?

Solution: The activity of the sample is down by a factor of $1616/101 = 16$, that is, down by four factors of 2. That means that four half-lives must have transpired. One half-life is (156 days)/4 = 39 days.

In Example 1, the mass of a Th-232 is 232.0381 amu. The mass of Ra-228 is 228.0311 amu, and that of He-4 is 4.0026 amu. Notice that the sum of the Ra-228 and He-4 masses is less than that of Th-232. Where did the missing mass go? This mass has been converted into energy.

There is a deep connection between mass and energy which we will mention only briefly here. In this reaction, mass is converted into energy, and the amount of energy can be determined if we know the masses sufficiently well. The ***mass deficit*** m_{def} is the difference of the mass of products and the mass of reactants, and the energy of reaction is given by

$$E = m_{\text{def}}c^2, \qquad\qquad\qquad (2)$$

where $c = 3.0 \times 10^8$ m/s is the speed of light. This is the famous $E = mc^2$ equation. In order to apply this equation we must be careful that the units agree.

Example 6: In the decay of Th-232, most of the energy of the reaction ends up in the kinetic energy of the alpha particle. After a decay,

a. how much energy (in J) does the alpha particle have?
b. How fast (approximately) is the alpha particle going?

Solution: a. The mass deficit in this reaction is $m_{def} = (232.0381 - 228.0311 - 4.0026)$ amu $= 0.0044$ amu. We convert this to kg and multiply by c^2 to obtain energy

$$E = \left(0.0044 \text{ amu} \frac{1.66 \times 10^{-27} \text{ kg}}{1 \text{ amu}}\right)\left(3 \times 10^8 \frac{\text{m}}{\text{s}}\right)^2$$

$$= 6.6 \times 10^{-13} \frac{\text{kgm}^2}{\text{s}^2}$$

$$= 6.6 \times 10^{-13} \text{ J}$$

This energy is mainly in the form of kinetic energy of the alpha particle.

b. We want to use the equation $E_K = 1/2\, mv^2$ to solve for v. We know E_K in Joules, so we want m to be in kilograms:

$$m_\alpha = 4.0026 \text{ amu} \frac{1.66 \times 10^{-27} \text{ kg}}{1 \text{ amu}} = 6.6 \ 10^{-27} \text{ kg}$$

Then we have

$$E_K = \frac{1}{2}mv^2$$

$$6.6 \times 10^{-13} \text{ J} = \frac{1}{2}\left(6.6 \ \times 0^{-27} \text{ kg}\right)v^2$$

$$v = 1.4 \times 10^7 \frac{\text{m}}{\text{s}}$$

This is quite fast, about 5% of the speed of light, but not so fast that we have to resort to the full mechanics of special relativity.

In summary for this section, here is a chart of special particles and their symbols for nuclear reactions:

Particle	Other names	Symbol
proton	p	^1_1He
neutron	n	^1_0n
helium-4	α, alpha	^4_2He
electron	β^-, e$^-$, beta minus	$^0_{-1}\text{e}$
positron	β^+, e$^+$, beta plus	$^0_{+1}\text{e}$
photon	γ, gamma	γ
neutrino	(do not need to know)	v
antineutrino	(do not need to know)	$\bar{v}$

E. ISOTOPES AND THE MASS SPECTROMETER

Mass spectroscopy has become one of the most important and versatile methods that scientist can use to identify molecular species. The basic principles associated with mass spectroscopy were discussed earlier. Specifically when a positively charged particle moves perpendicularly through a magnetic field, the charged particle experiences a force, as predicted by the right hand rule. The path that the charged particle takes is dependent upon the mass to charge ratio (m/q or m/z) of the particle. Since particles with more mass (inertia) will follow a curved path with a larger radius than lighter particles, with the m/q ratio being the critical parameter for predicting the path through the magnetic field. When a molecule is ionized, producing a molecular M^+ ion , which is often unstable, fragmentation occurs, producing unique combinations of daughter ions that facilitate the identification of the molecular species. Furthermore, the naturally occurring isotopes for the atoms that make up a molecule result in specific isotope patterns, providing further information about the composition and structure of a molecular species.

As an example, let's consider the mass spectrum of a relatively simple molecule like carbon dioxide. The naturally occurring isotopes of carbon and oxygen as well as the corresponding percent abundances are provided in the following table. Shown in Figure 14-7 is a schematic diagram showing what happens when carbon dioxide is analyzed in a mass spectrometer. When the sample is injected into the ionization chamber, the resulting ions are accelerated by an electric field and focused such that they pass through a magnetic field. For the molecular ion of carbon dioxide, three separate ions are observed, M^+, $M+1^+$ and $M+2^+$. The ion detected with the greatest relative intensity has an m/q of 44 amus, resulting from one ^{12}C and two ^{16}O atoms, which are by far the most abundant isotopes of these elements. The other two ions with much lower relative intensities have m/q ratios of 45 and 46, resulting from the presence of ^{13}C, ^{17}O or ^{18}O atoms.

Isotope	% abundance	Atomic Weight (amu)
Carbon-12	98.93	12 (exactly)
Carbon-13	1.07	13.0033548378
Oxygen-16	99.757	15.994914619
Oxygen-17	0.034	16.999132
Oxygen-18	0.205	17.999161

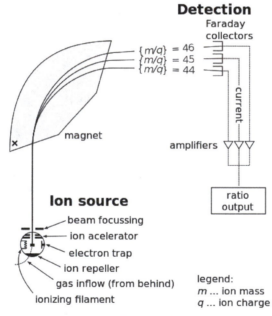

Figure 14-7

Shown in Figure 14-8 is the mass spectrum for carbon dioxide. Besides the molecular ion (m/z = 44) and its corresponding isotopic species (m/z = 45 and 46), the daughter ions corresponding to CO^+, O^+ and C^+ are also observed.

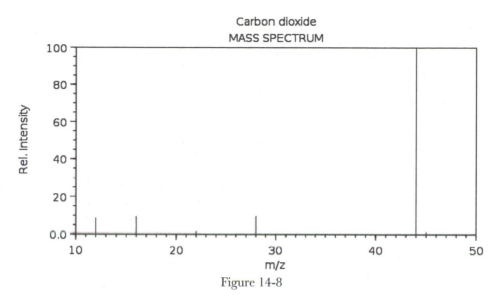

Figure 14-8

Example 7: What is the relative intensity of the M+1⁺ peak to the M⁺ peak for carbon dioxide.

Solution: The M+1⁺ peak can result from the presence of either a ^{13}C or an ^{17}O atom in the molecule. The naturally occurring percentages for these isotopes can be used to predict the M+1⁺/M⁺ ratio, by multiplying the percentage natural abundance of the isotope times the number of atoms in the molecule, followed by summing the result.

$$1 \ ^{13}C \times 1.07\% = 1.07\%$$
$$2 \ ^{17}O \times 0.034\% = 0.068$$
$$1.07 + 0.068 = 1.14\%$$

Therefore, the relative intensity of the M+1⁺ peak at 45 m/q is 1.14% of the M⁺ peak at 44 m/q.

F. CHAPTER SUMMARY

In this chapter we discussed the physics of the atom and nucleus: atomic structure, electronic energy levels, radioactivity, and nuclear reactions. The key to understanding many physical situations lies in understanding the energy level diagram. An atom or nucleus can exist only in certain discrete states of precise energy. When the atom or nucleus makes a transition from one state to another, a photon is absorbed or released with energy equal to the difference of the energies of the two states.

The key to understanding problems involving nuclear reactions, including radioactive decay, lies in visualizing the decay and in writing the nuclear reaction correctly. There are three types of radioactive decay, called alpha, beta, and gamma decay. These decays vary in the type of particle expelled from the nucleus and the effect that this expulsion has on the nucleus.

Mass spectroscopy has become an essential tool for the identification of molecular species based on isotope patterns and fragmentation patterns.

CHAPTER 14 PROBLEMS

1. A charged parallel-plate capacitor has an electric field of 160 N/C between its plates. If a proton (mass 1.7 x 10^{-27} kg, charge 1.6 x 10^{-19} C) is between the plates and starts from rest, what is its speed after 0.1 milliseconds?

    A. 1.7 x 10^{-52} m/s
    B. 1.7 x 10^{-10} m/s
    C. 5.9 x 10^1 m/s
    D. 1.5 x 10^6 m/s

Use the following in questions 2–6:

A charged parallel-plate capacitor has an electric field E_0 between its plates. Ignore the force of gravity. Note the approximations:

$$m_{proton} \approx 2000\, m_{electron},$$
$$m_{electron} \approx 9 \times 10^{-31}\ kg,$$
$$q_{proton} = 1.6 \times 10^{-19}\ C.$$

2. An electron and a deuteron (bare nucleus of ^{2}H) are placed between the plates. How does the magnitude of the force on the electron F_{elec} compare with the magnitude of the force on the deuteron F_d?

    A. $F_{elec} = 4000\ F_d$
    B. $F_{elec} = 2000\ F_d$
    C. $F_{elec} = F_d$
    D. $F_{elec} = 1/2\ F_d$

3. Two ions are placed between the plates: the fluoride ion ^{20}F$^-$ and the bromide ion ^{80}Br$^-$. The former experiences a force of magnitude F_F, and the latter a force of magnitude F_{Br}. How do these compare?

    A. $F_{Br} = F_F$
    B. $F_{Br} = 35F_F/36$
    C. $F_{Br} = 35F_F/9$
    D. $F_{Br} = 4\ F_F$

4. A proton and an electron are both between the plates, and both are at rest at $t = 0$ seconds. How does the magnitude of the acceleration of the proton a_p compare with the magnitude of the acceleration of the electron a_e?

    A. $a_p = a_e/2000$
    B. $a_p = a_e$
    C. $a_p = 2000\ a_e$
    D. $a_p = (2000)^2\ a_e$

5. The bare nuclei of ^{1}H and of ^{4}He are between the plates, and both are at rest. How does the magnitude of the acceleration of the hydrogen nucleus a_H compare with the magnitude of the acceleration of the helium nucleus a_{He}?

    A. $a_H = 1/4\ a_{He}$
    B. $a_H = a_{He}$
    C. $a_H = 2\ a_{He}$
    D. $a_H = 4\ a_{He}$

6. The bare nuclei of ^{1}H and of ^{3}H are between the plates, and both are at rest. How does the magnitude of the force of the light hydrogen nucleus F_p compare with the magnitude of the force of the heavy hydrogen nucleus F_t?

    A. $F_t = 1/3\ F_p$
    B. $F_t = F_p$
    C. $F_t = 2F_p$
    D. $F_t = 3F_p$

7. Some isolated ^{235}U atoms will spontaneously fission into two approximately equal-sized fragments. The following represents a possible reaction:

    $$^{235}U \rightarrow {}^{141}Ba + {}^{92}Kr + ?$$

    What is missing from the right side of the reaction?

    A. A proton.
    B. A neutron.
    C. A proton and a neutron.
    D. Two neutrons.

8. A common reaction in the Sun involves the encounter of two nuclei of light helium (^{3}He). If one ^{3}He nucleus encounters another, which is a possible list of products?

    A. ^{4}He + ^{2}H
    B. ^{4}He + ^{1}H + ^{1}H
    C. ^{7}Li + ^{1}H
    D. ^{2}H + ^{2}H + ^{2}H

9. If the nucleus ^{15}N is bombarded with a proton, one or more products may result. Which of the following represents a possible set of products?

    A. ^{15}O + γ
    B. ^{16}N + γ
    C. ^{12}C + ^{4}He
    D. ^{14}B + ^{2}Li

10. In the spectrum of a hypothetical atom, we discover a line with wavelength 1.5×10^{-7} m, and we discover that the transition is from the ground state. The ground state corresponds to zero energy. What other energy level must exist in the atom? (Use $c = 3.0 \times 10^8$ m/s and $h = 6.63 \times 10^{-34}$ J s.)

   A. -3.0×10^{-32} J
   B. -1.3×10^{-18} J
   C. 1.3×10^{-18} J
   D. 3.0×10^{-32} J

11. If an atom has only the three energy levels shown in the figure below, what possible frequencies might be in the spectrum of this atom? (Use $h = 4.14 \times 10^{-15}$ eV s and $c = 3.0 \times 10^8$ m/s.)

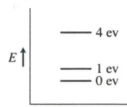

   A. 7.2×10^{14} Hz
   B. 2.4×10^{14} Hz and 7.2×10^{14} Hz
   C. 2.4×10^{14} Hz and 9.7×10^{14} Hz
   D. 2.4×10^{14} Hz, 7.2×10^{14} Hz, and 9.7×10^{14} Hz

Use the following in questions 12 and 13:

The figure below shows the energy level diagram of a hypothetical atom. Light in the visible portion of the spectrum has frequency between 4.0×10^{14} Hz and 7.5×10^{14} Hz. (Use $h = 4.14 \times 10^{-15}$ ev s and $c = 3.0 \times 10^8$ m/s.)

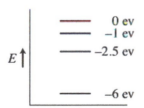

12. What is the maximum number of spectral lines for this atom?

   A. 1
   B. 3
   C. 4
   D. 6

13. How many lines are possible in the visible spectrum?

   A. 0
   B. 1
   C. 2
   D. 3

14. The figure below shows the known energy level diagram for a hypothetical atom. A brilliant young scientist discovers a new spectral line with frequency 4.8×10^{14} Hz, which she determines is a transition from the ground state to an excited state. What is the energy of the (excited) quantum state she has discovered? (Use $h = 4.14 \times 10^{-15}$ eV s and $c = 3.0 \times 10^8$ m/s.)

   $E \uparrow$ —— 0 ev
         —— -1.5 ev
         —— -5 ev

   A. -7 eV
   B. -4 eV
   C. -3 eV
   D. -2 eV

Use the following for questions 15–17:

Atoms of lithium are able to absorb photons of frequency 2.01×10^{14} Hz. This corresponds to a transition from the ground state (at -5.37 eV) to an excited state. Zero energy corresponds to the state in which one electron is completely removed from the atom. (Use $h = 4.14 \times 10^{-15}$ eV s and $c = 3.0 \times 10^8$ m/s.)

15. What is the energy of the excited state referred to in the passage?

   A. -6.20 eV
   B. -4.54 eV
   C. -0.83 eV
   D. 6.20 eV

16. What is the wavelength of light corresponding to this transition?

   A. 2.3×10^{-7} m
   B. 1.5×10^{-6} m
   C. 4.3×10^{6} m
   D. 6.7×10^{5} m

17. If a photon ionizes a lithium atom, what conclusion can be drawn about the photon?

   A. It had frequency less than 1.3×10^{15} Hz.
   B. It had frequency 1.3×10^{15} Hz.
   C. It had frequency greater than 1.3×10^{15} Hz.
   D. None of the above may be concluded.

18. What nucleus results when ^{55}Ni decays by positron emission?

    A. ^{55}Fe
    B. ^{55}Co
    C. ^{55}Ni
    D. ^{55}Ca

19. The daughter nucleus from an alpha decay was identified to be ^{222}Ra. What was the parent nucleus?

    A. ^{218}Rn
    B. ^{222}Fr
    C. ^{222}Ac
    D. ^{226}Th

20. What is the result when a ^{238}U decays by alpha emission, followed by two beta decays, and another alpha decay?

    A. ^{228}Th
    B. ^{228}Rn
    C. ^{230}Th
    D. ^{230}Rn

21. In the Sun much of the energy results from a set of reactions called the pp chain. The first step involves two protons colliding to make heavy hydrogen. Which of the following expresses this reaction?

    A. $^{1}\text{H} + {}^{1}\text{H} \rightarrow {}^{2}\text{H} + \gamma$
    B. $^{1}\text{H} + {}^{1}\text{H} \rightarrow {}^{2}\text{He} + \gamma$
    C. $^{1}\text{H} + {}^{1}\text{H} \rightarrow {}^{2}\text{H} + e^{+} + \upsilon$
    D. $^{1}\text{H} + {}^{1}\text{H} \rightarrow {}^{2}\text{H} + e^{-} + \bar{\upsilon}$

22. Another step in the pp chain is a reaction in which heavy hydrogen combines with a proton to make a third nucleus. Which of the following shows this reaction? (The third step in the pp chain is given in problem 8.)

    A. $^{1}\text{H} + {}^{2}\text{H} \rightarrow {}^{3}\text{He} + \gamma$
    B. $^{1}\text{H} + {}^{2}\text{H} \rightarrow n + {}^{2}\text{He}$
    C. $^{1}\text{H} + {}^{2}\text{H} \rightarrow {}^{4}\text{He} + \gamma$
    D. $^{1}\text{H} + {}^{2}\text{H} \rightarrow {}^{3}\text{Li} + \gamma$

23. The Curies prepared about 1 gram of Ra-226 (with half-life 1600 years). How much will be left after 8000 years (about the length of time of recorded history)?

    A. None.
    B. 3.1×10^{-10} grams
    C. 3.1×10^{-2} grams
    D. 0.5 grams

24. We measure the radioactivity of a certain sample of ^{32}P to be 300 mCi. How long before the radioactivity decreases to 20 mCi? (The half-life of ^{32}P is 14.3 days.)

    A. 26.7 days
    B. 28.6 days
    C. 55.9 days
    D. 112 days

25. A nuclear power plant provides 10^{12} J of electrical power each day to run a small community by using heat from the fission of uranium-235 to turn turbines. The mass deficit due to the fission of one uranium-235 atom is 3×10^{-25} grams. How much mass is converted to energy per day to power the community? (Hint: $c = 3.0 \times 10^{8}$ m/s, $h = 6.63 \times 10^{-34}$ J s.)

    A. 10^{-23} g
    B. 10^{-5} g
    C. 10^{-2} g
    D. 13 g

Passage 1

A hydrogen atom has energy levels given by

$$E_n = -(13.6 \text{ ev})\frac{1}{n^2}$$

where n is a positive integer. A state in which the electron is infinitely far from the nucleus corresponds to 0 eV. (Note: 1 eV = 1.602 x 10^{-19} J) The energy level diagram is shown in the figure below. An atom generally has an electron in a given energy level; however, a transition may occur if the atom absorbs or emits a photon, or particle of light.

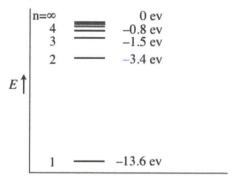

For the following questions, consider a hydrogen atom in an excited state initially at rest. It emits a photon of energy E_{ph} which travels to the right. The hydrogen atom is now in its ground state.

The energy of a photon is given by $E_{photon} = hf$, where f is the frequency and $h = 4.14$ x 10^{-15} eV s. The momentum of a photon is given by $p_{photon} = E/c$, where $c = 3.0$ x 10^8 m/s, the speed of light. The mass of a hydrogen atom is $m_H = 1.7$ x 10^{-27} kg.

26. What is the smallest energy a photon must have to boost a hydrogen atom in its ground state to an excited state?

A. 3.4 eV
B. 10.2 eV
C. 13.6 eV
D. There is no smallest energy.

27. What is the ionization energy for a hydrogen atom?

A. 1.5 eV
B. 3.4 eV
C. 10.2 eV
D. 13.6 eV

28. A hydrogen atom in its ground state absorbs a photon and ends up in the excited state corresponding to $n = 3$. What is the most restrictive statement that can be concluded about the photon?

A. The photon had an energy of 12.1 eV.
B. The photon had an energy greater than or equal to 12.1 eV.
C. The photon had an energy greater than 12.1 eV but less than 12.8 eV.
D. The photon had an energy greater than 10.2 eV.

29. In the scenario mentioned in the second paragraph, what can be concluded?

A. Momentum is conserved, but not energy.
B. Energy is conserved, but not momentum.
C. Both momentum and energy are conserved.
D. Neither momentum nor energy is conserved.

30. What is the longest wavelength corresponding to a photon which could cause a transition in a hydrogen atom?

A. 9.1 x 10^{-8} m
B. 1.2 x 10^{-7} m
C. 3.6 x 10^{-7} m
D. There is no longest wavelength.

This page intentionally left blank.

A. INTRODUCTION

Thermodynamics is the driving force behind all physical and chemical processes, in which the various parts of the universe are overall trying to become as stable as possible by distributing energy in its various forms. Without a clear understanding of how energy interacts with and affects matter, our ability to make reasonable predictions concerning future events would be reduced to what appears to be magic. For instance, if you had a black powder that spontaneously burst into flames when touched by a spark, you might conclude that all black powders would behave similarly. However, after a short period of time and after some experimentation, you discover that not all black powders behave this way. Gradually with further experimentation, it becomes clear that only certain black powders, when mixed with yellow and white powders, have these magical properties. Eventually you might see patterns and develop theories to explain your observations. These patterns and observations have now grown into what we call science.

B. THERMODYNAMIC SYSTEMS, STATE FUNCTIONS AND TEMPERATURE

A thermodynamic **system** is a defined volume of space that has a boundary separating it from everything else, the so-called **surroundings**. A system must have measurable properties such as temperature, internal energy, pressure and entropy. An **open system** permits certain quantities, such as matter and/or heat, to be transferred in and out, through the boundary. A hypothetical **isolated system** does not allow quantities such as heat or matter to pass through the boundary. A **closed system** is one in which heat (and entropy) can pass through the boundary, but matter does not pass through the boundary. If two closed systems are in contact with one another, then heat will be transferred between the systems until thermodynamic equilibrium is reached. The path that the heat takes can be through other systems with multiple boundaries, which must all eventually come to equilibrium as well. This is the so-called Zeroth Law of Thermodynamics.

A **state function** is a property of a system that depends only on its current status and not on how it achieved that situation. For example, a 25 g piece of lead at room temperature would have a volume of 2.56 cm^3 and a certain average kinetic energy associated with the motion of atoms, such that its temperature would be 25°C. This would be the same average kinetic energy, for a sample that was obtained by first starting with 25 g of molten lead at 328°C and allowing heat to transfer from the system into the surroundings at room temperature; or if you started with the same sample of lead at 0° and allowed heat to flow into the system from the surroundings at room temperature. This sample of lead may have other properties that are not state functions, such as shape, that may be different depending upon how the sample was obtained. A property is a state function only if once it has come to equilibrium with its surroundings, you can't tell how it got there without knowing its previous state properties at some moment during its transformation to the current state.

It is important to remember that heat and temperature are two very different concepts. Temperature is a measure of the average kinetic energy of a system. Galileo is widely credited with inventing the first temperature measuring device, sometimes called a thermoscope, which measures temperature based on the buoyancy of sealed glass spheres, suspended in a glass tube filled with water. Various spheres having different densities float or sink depending upon the temperature and density of the surrounding liquid. The German physicist Fahrenheit is credited with inventing thermometers, which are glass tubes filled with alcohol or mercury and having a scale divided into one hundred equally spaced divisions. As the story goes, Fahrenheit used cold salty (ocean?) water in the winter, just at its freezing point, to set the 0° mark and then placed the thermometer in his mouth to set the 100° mark. Worlnwide, perhaps the most commonly used temperature scale was established by the Swedish scientist Celsius, in which the zero and 100° marks on the centigrade scale were based on the melting point and normal boiling point of water. Of course, the related Kelvin scale eliminates the possibility of negative temperatures by setting the zero mark at the lowest possible temperature at which there is theoretically no molecular motion. The Kelvin scale is used in thermodynamic experiments, and when using the ideal gas law. The magnitude of a degree Kelvin K is identical to that of a degree Celsius °C, but we must add 273 to the Celsius temperature to obtain the K temperature. Hence, absolute zero corresponds to -273°C. Today we can also use thermal couples, rather than conventional thermometers to measure temperature. A thermal couple is a device, in which two dissimilar metal conductors are welded together, producing a temperature dependent voltage.

Example 1: What is the Kelvin temperature for the normal boiling point of water?

Solution: The normal boiling point of water is when the pressure on the surface of the water is the same as the atmospheric pressure on an average day at sea level, 101 kilopascals, or 1 atm, which is equivalent to a height of 760 mm of mercury in a barometer. By definition, boiling occurs when cavities form within the liquid because the vapor pressure within the bubble equals the external pressure. The normal boiling point of water is 100°C and by adding 273, we get the normal boiling point of water to be 373 K.

Example 2: What can we conclude about the state of Fahrenheit's health on the day he determined his temperature scale?

Solution: Since normal body temperature is 98.6°F, Fahrenheit must have been sick and he was running a slight fever at the time.

C. WORK AND ENERGY

Energy is defined as any process that is capable of doing work W with respect to the four fundamental forces: gravity, electromagnetic, strong nuclear and weak nuclear. The most difficult aspect of describing energy is the fact that it apparently can take so many different forms: (1) kinetic energy, or the energy of motion, can be associated with the movement of objects with mass on the macroscopic scale; (2) thermal energy which can be associated with the microscopic movement of atoms and molecules; (3) potential energy can be associated with an object's position with respect to other objects with mass, i.e. gravity; (4) the deformation of elastic objects, i.e. spring potential energy; (5) the stability of atoms being bonded to other atoms, i.e. chemical potential energy; and (6) the stability of associated nucleons, i.e. nuclear energy.

Previously, we have described work as a force that causes a displacement, according to the equation
$$W = F_{net} D_x \cos \theta \qquad (1)$$

The work-energy theorem, states that work can be used to interconvert energy into its various forms. At this stage it might be instructive to consider the SI units associated with work and various forms of energy. Since work, is a force, in newtons, times a displacement in meters, the unit of work is given as units of N•m, which is equivalent to the joule J. But we should also remember that a newton is mass times acceleration, or kg•m/s². Therefore, a joule is also equivalent to a kg•m²/s². The following table summarizes the equations and units for the various forms of work and energy.

Form	Equation	Units
Work	$W = F D_x$	N•m = kg (m/s²) m =kg m²/s² = J
Kinetic Energy	$KE = 1/2 \, mV^2$	kg (m/s)² = kg m²/s² = J
Gravitational Potential Energy	$PE = mgh$	kg (m/s²) m = kg m²/s² = J
Nuclear	$E = mc^2$	kg (m/s)² = kg m²/s² = J

Example 1: Nuclear reactions transform mass into energy. If a deuterium (^{2}H) atom and a tritium (^{3}H) atom undergo a fusion nuclear reaction that produces helium (^{4}He) and a neutron, having 14.1 MeV and 3.5 MeV of additional kinetic energy, respectively, how much mass was converted into the work required to accelerate the products of the nuclear reaction? Note that 1 eV = 1.6 x 10^{-19} J and c = 3.0 x 10^8 m/s.

Solution: The total additional kinetic energy of 17.6 MeV, resulted from the work done by changing mass into energy in the nuclear reaction. Converting this value into joules, provides

$$17.6 \text{ MeV} \times (10^6 \text{ eV/MeV}) \times (1.6 \times 10^{-19} \text{ J/eV}) = 2.82 \times 10^{-12} \text{ J}$$

which is E in Einstein's famous equation for when mass is converted into energy. Therefore

$$2.82 \times 10^{-12} \text{ J} = m (3.0 \times 10^8 \text{ m/s})^2$$
$$m = (2.82 \times 10^{-12} \text{ kg m}^2/\text{s}^2)/(9.0 \times 10^{16} \text{ m}^2/\text{s}^2)$$
$$m = 3.1 \times 10^{-29} \text{ kg}$$

Not much, eh? Well how about if we fused one mole of deuterium with one mole of tritium. Well the mass change would be about 18 mg, releasing 1.7 x 10^{12} J of energy, which could provide the electrical power of a small US city for a year.

D. THE FIRST LAW OF THERMODYNAMICS

Simply stated, the First Law of Thermodynamics is equivalent to the Law of Conservation of Energy. It states that the total energy ΔE_{tot} of an isolated system is equivalent to the amount of heat Q entering or leaving the system, plus the amount of work done on, or by the system. The total energy can be comprised of other more familiar forms of energy, such as the internal energy of molecular vibrations, the macroscopic kinetic energy of the system, the chemical potential energy stored in bonds, and the gravitational potential energy.

$$\Delta E_{tot} = Q + W \qquad (2)$$

The sign of the variable indicates the direction of energy flow, with the typical convention being, positive corresponds to energy flowing from the surroundings into the system, and negative corresponds to the flow of energy from the system to the surroundings. In the absence of changes in heat for a system, any change in the total energy of a system must involve work. In the context of the MCAT, in the proverbial frictionless systems, energy changes are often used to create a change in macroscopic kinetic energy and/or a change in gravitational potential energy. In reality, friction, heat flow and changes in temperature should also be considered.

Example 1: A 1.0 kg block of wood is placed on a 10 m ramp that forms a 30° angle with the horizontal. The block of wood begins to accelerate and reaches a velocity of 9.0 m/s at the bottom of the ramp. Approximately how many Joules of heat are generated due to friction between the system and its surroundings?

Solution: We first must assume that the ΔE_{tot} is the result of a change in the gravitational potential energy of the block of wood, as it slides down the ramp. The height of the ramp is

$$h = (10 \text{ m}) \sin 30° = 5 \text{ m}$$

Therefore the gravitational potential energy of the block of wood prior to sliding down the ramp is

$$PE = mgh = (1.0 \text{ kg})(10 \text{ m/s}^2)(5 \text{ m}) = 50 \text{ kg m}^2/\text{s}^2 = 50 \text{ J}$$

The kinetic energy of the block of wood, results from the work done by gravity on the block of wood.

$$W = KE = 1/2 \text{ mV}^2 = (0.5)(1.0 \text{ kg})(9 \text{ m/s})^2 = (81/2) = 40.5 \text{ J}$$

According to the First Law of Thermodynamics, the total energy change will be equivalent to the work and heat changes in the system. In this case, the heat will be the difference between the change in the gravitational potential energy and the change in the kinetic energy.

$$\Delta PE - \Delta KE = (50 - 40.5) = 9.5 \text{ J}$$

E. THE SECOND LAW OF THERMODYNAMICS

Our description of the second law must first start with the direction for heat flow. On average, heat will always flow in one direction, from a system having a higher temperature to a system with a lower temperature, unless external work is done on the system. By convention we never discuss the flow of cold, which presumably flows in the opposite direction of heat. Assuming that there is a finite amount of energy in the universe, but an infinite volume into which the matter of the universe appears to be expanding, the concentration of energy will always be dissipating in the universe. In order to explain this flow of heat, scientists developed the concept of **entropy S**, which is often described as the randomness or disorder of a system, but really is a measure of the dispersion of energy Q at a specific temperature T in degrees Kelvin for a given physical or chemical process with the equation for calculating entropy being

$$\Delta S = dQ/T \qquad (3)$$

Crystalline solids are generally more ordered and have fewer degrees of freedom of motion and hence less absolute entropy than the corresponding liquid, which has less absolute entropy than the gas phase. During the melting process, the temperature of the system will remain constant, assuming ideal thermal diffusion conditions. Energy that is added to the system from the surroundings during the phase change does not cause a temperature change, because chemical bonds are being broken. The reverse process, freezing, can be achieved when the surroundings are at a lower temperature than the freezing point of the substance. Chemical bonds will be formed to create the solid, which is the source of the energy released to the surroundings. In the case of ice, some of the intermolecular hydrogen bonds are broken during melting, resulting in a disruption in the crystal lattice. The temperature of the system will not change until the solid is completely converted to liquid. For water the ΔS of fusion is 22.0 J/mol K, whereas the ΔS of vaporization is 119 J/mol K.

Example 1: If the heat of fusion of ice is 333 J/g, what is the entropy change when 100 g of ice at 0°C is converted into liquid water at 0°C?

Solution: This is a relatively simple example, since the phase change of solid ice to liquid water occurs at a constant temperature, 273 K. The amount of heat that must flow into the ice from its surroundings for this reversible process can be calculated from the heat of fusion (freezing).

$$\Delta Q = 333 \text{ J/g x } 100 \text{ g} = 3.33 \times 10^4 \text{ J}$$

We can calculate the entropy change by dividing the heat by the temperature.

$$\Delta S = \Delta Q/T = (3.33 \times 10^4 \text{ J})/(273 \text{ K}) = 122 \text{ J/K}$$

The flow of heat against a temperature gradient is not impossible, just highly improbable unless a system is coupled with another system that involves work. For example, we would not naturally expect that heat would leave an insulated box called a refrigerator. But it is possible by doing work to compress a gas to form a liquid. If this process is done on the outside of the refrigerator compartment, the heat generated by the phase change can be dissipated into the surrounding air by passing it through a series of heat exchanging tubes. Subsequently forcing the liquid into the refrigerator compartment, and allowing it to expand causes it to be converted back into a gas that is below the temperature of the inside the refrigerator. This causes heat in the refrigerator to be transferred to the colder gas. After the gas leaves the refrigerator compartment, the gas is again compressed and the process is repeated. Energy is required to do the work necessary to compress the gas. In this real system, the key is that the rate that heat is removed from the refrigerator is initially faster than the rate at which heat can pass through the insulated walls of the refrigerator. For a constant power input to the compressor, the refrigerator temperature will eventually reach equilibrium and can be maintained below the temperature of the surrounding air, which acts as a heat sink.

F. PRESSURE-VOLUME DIAGRAMS

In order to better understand the work aspect of thermodynamics we should consider the information contained in plots of pressure versus volume for a particular system. In our first case, let us consider an ideal gas in a cylinder with a movable piston, as shown in Figure 15-1. If a force is applied to the piston, work will be done on the gas by the piston, causing the volume of the cylinder to decrease and the pressure of the gas inside the cylinder to increase, according to Boyle's law. The area under the pressure-volume curve represents the work done on the gas. This is perhaps most easily understood by considering the units of pressure and volume. If the pressure is measured in Pascals (Pa), which is equivalent to a Newton per meter squared (N/m^2), multiplying by the volume in cubic meters (m^3), gives the unit for work ($N \cdot m$), which as we have previously pointed out, is equivalent to the more commonly used energy unit of Joules (J).

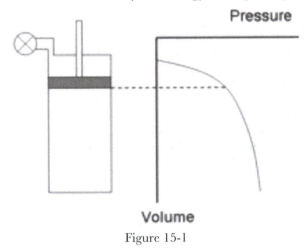

Figure 15-1

Example 1: If a gas expands from a volume of 0.50 m^3 to a volume of 1.00 m^3 and the pressure increases linearly from 100 kPa to 200 kPa during the expansion, what is the work done by the gas?

Solution: We can imagine that the graph of pressure versus volume for this process looks like a right triangle sitting on top of a rectangle, as seen below.

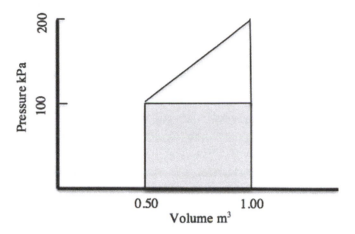

The work is the sum of the area of the rectangle and triangle. The area of a triangle is one half base times height. Therefore

$$W = [(0.50 \text{ m}^3)(100 \text{ kPa})] + [1/2 \ (1.00 \text{ m}^3 - 0.50 \text{ m}^3)(200 \text{ kPa} - 100 \text{ kPa})]$$
$$W = 50 \text{ kJ} + 25 \text{ kJ} = 75 \text{ kJ}$$

There are four basic thermodynamic processes. In each case one particular physical property remains constant. These processes are: (1) *Isovolumetric*, (*isochoric*) in which the volume of the gas does not change and therefore no work is involved; (2) *Isobaric*, in which the pressure does not change; (3) *Isothermal*, in which heat is added or removed from the system so that the temperature does not change; and (4) *Adiabatic*, in which heat is not exchanged between the system and its surroundings, such that there is a temperature change. For an adiabatic process, less work is done than the high temperature isothermal process, but more work is done than the low temperature isothermal process, as seen in Figure 15-2.

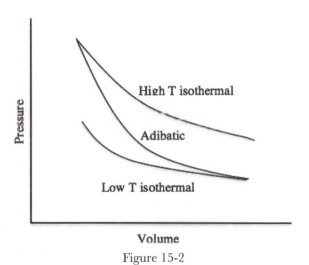

Figure 15-2

Now let us consider the work done by a reversible cyclic pumping system relevant to the MCAT. Figure 15-3 represents an idealized pressure-volume curve for the left ventricle of the heart. Point A represents the beginning of the systolic phase of contraction. At this point the aortic valve is closed and pressure inside the chamber rapidly increases and becomes higher than the pressure inside the left atrium. This causes the mitral valve to also close, causing a further rise in pressure. At point B the pressure inside the left ventricle is greater than the pressure inside the aorta, and the aortic valve opens, allowing the volume of blood in the left ventricle to decrease as blood is pumped into the aorta. At point C the pressure of blood in the left ventricle has decreased to the point where the aortic valve closes, ending the systolic phase and beginning the diastolic phase. During line segment CD the myocardium relaxes, while both the mitral and aortic valves are closed such that the pressure rapidly decreases. At point D the pressure is below the pressure in the left atrium, causing the mitral valve to open, and blood flows into the left ventricle from the left atrium. After the left ventricle has been filled with blood (point A), the cycle repeats itself. The area within the polygon ABCD, represents the total work done by the heart on the blood during one cycle. To calculate the area for this polygon we can resort to fairly simple geometric shapes, such as triangles and rectangles, however, in reality cardiologists must consider the fact that the segments corresponding to the various processes during the systolic and diastolic phases are not straight lines, requiring the use of calculus to obtain a precise value.

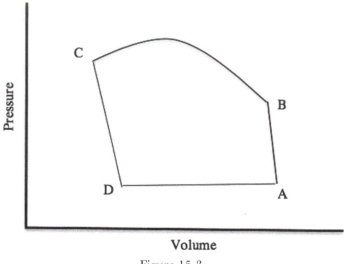

Figure 15-3

Example 2: In the idealized pressure-volume plot for the left ventricle of the heart shown in Figure 15-3, which thermodynamic process (line segment) does not involve work? Which process involves the most work?

Solution: For this example, the first part is a trick question. Sorry, stay on your toes. For a thermodynamic process to not do work, it must be isovolumetric. As seen in Figure 15-3, each of the line segments AB, BC, CD and DA involve some change in volume and hence none of the processes are truly isovolumetric. Perhaps segment AB is the closest to being isovolumetric, since liquids are relatively incompressible. Each of the processes has some area in the P-V plot and involves some amount of work. The process that involves the most work, is line segment BC, i.e. pushing blood out of the ventricle and into the aorta, since it has the greatest area for the PV plot.

G. HEAT TRANSFER

Heat is energy that is transferred from one system to another, and does not do work. Heat entering or leaving a system can cause the temperature of that system to change by altering the average kinetic energy of molecular vibrations, or in other words the **internal energy** of a system. It is worthwhile to remember that for an ideal gas, the molecules are in constant motion and collisions are almost completely elastic. Most importantly, the molecules are not all moving with the same velocity, but there is a range of velocities and kinetic energies, representing a Boltzmann distribution. As the temperature increases, the velocity with the highest probability increases and a broadening of the distribution results, as seen in Figure 15-4.

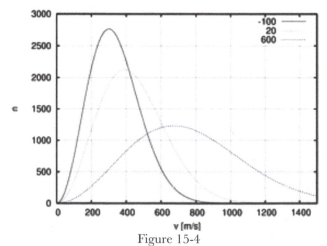

Figure 15-4

Heat can be transferred from one system to another due to the molecular collisions at the boundary of the systems involved and is referred to as thermal **conduction**. Thermal **convection** involves the transfer of heat within a fluid (liquids or gases) and involves translational motion of molecules. The last method for heat transfer is by **radiation**, in which electromagnetic energy (photons) is generated by one substance and absorbed by another. Hence radiation can transfer energy through a vacuum.

As an example, a real gas at some temperature can be in contact with a solid at a higher temperature, when a gas molecule with the average kinetic energy of the system collides with the solid, some of the vibrational kinetic energy of the solid is imparted on the gas molecule during the collision. Considering things on the microscopic scale, if this collision occurs during the proper moment in time during a vibration of the atoms in the solid, a small push will occur and the gas molecule will be accelerated, increasing its kinetic energy. This results in some of the heat content of the solid being transferred to the gas and a rise in temperature. But, this process is not just in one direction, since some of the gas molecules may have more kinetic energy that the solid. The key is that on the macroscopic scale involving huge numbers of collisions, on average heat will be transferred from the higher temperature system to the lower temperature system, until a dynamic equilibrium is established.

Example 1: One mole samples of hydrogen gas and carbon dioxide gas are both at 25°C, how many times faster is the average hydrogen molecule traveling than the average carbon dioxide molecule?

Solution: Since both gases are at the same temperature and there are the same number of molecules in both samples, we can set the kinetic energies of the two gases equal to one another. The mass of a hydrogen molecule is 2 amus, whereas the mass of a carbon dioxide molecule is 44 amus.

$$KE_{H2} = KE_{CO2}$$
$$1/2\ (2)\ V_{H2}^2 = 1/2\ (44)\ V_{CO2}^2$$
$$V_{H2}^2/\ V_{CO2}^2 = 44/2$$
$$V_{H2}/\ V_{CO2} = \sqrt{22}$$
$$V_{H2}/\ V_{CO2} = 4.7$$

For a pure substance the amount of heat required to cause a temperature change for a particular phase of matter (solid, liquid or gas) is determined by the nature of the intermolecular forces and/or bonding for that substance. The equation that relates the amount of heat Q required to cause a temperature change Δt, is

$$Q = m\ C\ \Delta t \qquad (4)$$

where C is a proportionality constant called the **heat capacity** or **specific heat** of that substance. In addition, the amount of heat required to cause phase changes is given by

$$Q = m\ H \qquad (5)$$

where H is either the heat of fusion (H_f) or heat of vaporization (H_v) for a substance. Note that as discussed above, the phase change does not involve a temperature change, since the heat involved does not change the average kinetic energy of the system, just the entropy, or stored potential energy of the system. The following table provides these constants for water.

Constant	Value
Specific Heat of ice	2.06 J/g K
Specific Heat of liquid water	4.18 J/g K
Specific Heat of steam	2.02 J/g K
Heat of fusion at 0°C	334 J/g
Heat of Vaporization at 100°C	2260 J/g

Example 1: Calculate the amount of heat energy, in kilojoules, required to change 50.0 g of ice at -25°C to steam at 125°C.

Solution: There are several parts to this calculation, the sum of which represents the total amount of heat needed. Initially we need to calculate the amount of heat needed to change the temperature of the ice from -25°C to 0°C, which is a temperature change of 25 K. Using Equation 4 and the specific heat of ice, gives

$$Q = m\ C\ \Delta t = (50.0\ g)(2.06\ J/g\ K)(25\ K) = 2575\ J$$

Using Equation 5 and the heat of fusion of ice, we can calculate the amount of heat needed to melt the ice.

$$Q = m\,H = (50\text{ g})(334\text{ J/g}) = 16700\text{ J}$$

Using Equation 4 and the specific heat of liquid water, we can calculate the heat required to warm the water from 0°C to 100°C, which is a temperature change of 100 K.

$$Q = m\,C\,\Delta t = (50.0\text{ g})(4.18\text{ J/g K})(100\text{ K}) = 20900\text{ J}$$

Next we need to calculate the heat needed to convert the liquid water into steam, using the heat of vaporization and Equation 5.

$$Q = m\,H = (50\text{ g})(2260\text{ J/g}) = 113000\text{ J}$$

Finally, we need to calculate the heat needed to raise the temperature of the steam from 100°C to 125°C which is a temperature change of 25 K, using Equation 4 and the specific heat of steam.

$$Q = m\,C\,\Delta t = (50.0\text{ g})(2.02\text{ J/g K})(25\text{ K}) = 2525\text{ J}$$

The total heat being

$$(2575\text{ J}) + (16700\text{ J}) + (20900\text{ J}) + (113000\text{ J}) + (2525\text{ J}) = 155700\text{ J or }156\text{ kJ}$$

H. COEFFICIENTS OF EXPANSION

For most materials there is a direct relationship between volume and temperature. This is primarily due to the fact that as temperature increases, molecular motion increases, causing the rebounding due to molecular collisions to increase the space between molecules and/or atoms. It is rare for a substance to have an inverse relationship between volume and temperature and typically this occurs only in limited temperature ranges. Perhaps the most important example of this is water. Liquid water reaches its maximum density at 4.0 °C, below which its volume expands due to the formation of an extensive hydrogen bonding network, which creates hexagonal pores in the structure of crystalline ice, which is significantly less dense than liquid water. Hence ice forms on the top surface of liquid water, unlike most substances where the solid has a greater density than the liquid.

The general equation for the temperature ΔT dependent volume change ΔV, is

$$\Delta V / \Delta T = a\,V \qquad (6)$$

where V is the volume of a given mass of a substance and a is the coefficient of thermal expansion. A variation of this equation can be used to predict the linear expansion of a material, where V is replaced with the variable L for length. This can be useful for mechanical engineering purposes. The following table provides the coefficients of thermal expansion for a few select materials. The volume coefficients are typically three times the linear coefficients. The expansion coefficients are temperature dependent and for some materials, highly so.

Material	Volume coefficient a_V (10^{-6} K^{-1} at 20°C)
Brass	57
Glass	25.5
Borosilicate glass	9.9
Mercury	182
Water	207

Example 1: A thermometer is constructed by sealing 1.00 cm³ of mercury in a borosilicate glass tube with an inner diameter of 0.200 mm. Assuming that the coefficient of thermal expansion is not significantly temperature dependent, and that the expansion of the borosilicate glass does not significantly affect the diameter of the tube, how much higher in the tube is the convex meniscus at 38 °C as compared with 20 °C?

Solution: We can first calculate the volume change that would occur when the mercury warms from 20 °C to body temperature, 38°C, $\Delta T = 18$ °K and $a = 182 \times 10^{-6}$

$$\Delta V = a\, V\, \Delta T = (182 \times 10^{-6}\ K^{-1})(1.0\ cm^3)(18\ K) = 0.0033\ cm^3$$

The equation for the volume of a cylinder is $V = pr^2h$ and the radius is $(0.0200\ cm)/2 = 0.0100\ cm$. Only the height of the mercury can change, not the radius.

$$\Delta h = \Delta V/pr^2 = (0.0033\ cm^3)/(3.14)(0.0100\ cm)^2 = (0.0033)/(0.000314) = 10.5\ cm$$

I. CHAPTER SUMMARY

In this chapter we discussed the concepts of temperature, heat and work as related to various thermodynamic processes. The key to understanding these concepts lies in a good foundation in the concepts of energy and the mechanics of motion, both on the macroscopic and microscopic levels. The distribution of energy in the form of entropy, is a critical driving force that influences the behavior of chemical and physical assemblies of complex systems. It is possible to design devices that couple various individual systems and do work to produce results that otherwise would not normally be expected to occur. This has resulted in in the design of complex physical and biological machines that do amazing things. Perhaps the most amazing machine of all is the human body. Comprised of various complex materials and electronic systems, the physics and chemistry of the body involves energy generation and distribution to do work. These systems are driven by the same rules of thermodynamics that govern the operation of other devices, like cars, that have internal combustion engines, electrical systems, fluid systems for heat transfer, and complex combinations of materials having a variety of other functions.

CHAPTER 15 PROBLEMS

Passage 1

It has been proposed that pressure-volume (PV) plots could be used to evaluate the effects of various lung diseases such as acute respiratory distress syndrome (ARDS), congestive heart failure, emphysema, asthma and interstitial lung disease (ILD).

Frog lungs have proven to be a useful model system for the hysteresis observed in the PV plots for humans. Hysteresis is the difference between the shapes of the PV curve for the inflation versus deflation process. In one study, a cannulated frog lung was attached to an apparatus consisting of rigid plastic tubes, three valves, two syringes (S1 and S2) and two water manometers (M1 and M2). The lung was at its natural volume when all valves were open and the barometric pressure was measured to be 745 mmHg and the temperature of the air was 20°C. When one of the valves was closed, the system could no longer exchange air with the atmosphere. Air was injected into the lung using S2. The pressure between the two water manometers was adjusted using S1 so that there was no difference in the water levels in M2. The pressure necessary to maintain a constant volume of the tubes connecting M2 to the lung was read as using M1. Incremental changes of 0.10 mL were used during the inflation/deflation cycles and pressure readings were made after waiting at least 15 seconds after the injection or withdrawal of air from the lung. A typical PV plot for a frog lung in shown below. As a control, a balloon was used to repeat the experiment and no hysteresis was observed. The upper curve represents inflation and the lower curve represents deflation.

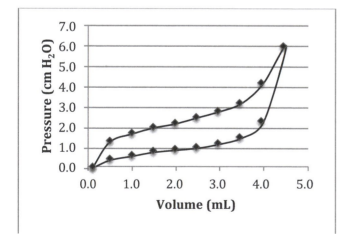

In a separate study the PV curves for the mechanical inflation of lungs for patients with no known lung disease, were compared with the lungs of patients that were diagnosed with emphysema and ILD, the results of which are shown below. In IDL, alveoli become fibrotic, which significantly affects lung gas volume. The observed effect of emphysema is thought to primarily result from changes in the elasticity of the lung tissue.

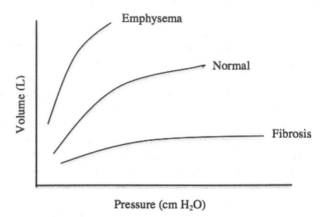

These plots can be mathematically fit using the following equation, where V is the volume at a given pressure P, V_{max} is the extrapolated volume at infinite pressure, A is a constant associated with the intercept on the volume axis, e is the base of the natural logarithm (2.178), and k is a constant associated with the amount of curvature of the plot. The compliance of the lung can be measured by the $\Delta V/\Delta P$ for the initial linear portion of the plot.

$$V = V_{max} - Ae^{-kP}$$

1. At what temperature were the PV experiments on the frog lung performed?

   A. 273 K
   B. 293 K
   C. 298 K
   D. 311 K

2. If just the lung is considered the system, which of the following terms best describes the PV experiments performed on the frog lung?

   A. isovolumetric
   B. isobaric
   C. isothermal
   D. adiabatic

3. Which of the following is true concerning the control experiments performed with the balloon?

   A. The amount of work done during inflation was greater than the amount of work done during deflation.
   B. The amount of work done during inflation was less than the amount of work done during deflation.
   C. The same amount of work was done during inflation as during deflation.
   D. No work was done during inflation or deflation.

4. Which of the following patients would do the most work to inhale an equivalent amount of air?

   A. A patient with emphysema.
   B. A patient with IDL.
   C. A patient with normal lung function.
   D. All patients do the same amount of work.

5. Which of the following is a true statement?

   A. The lungs of a patient with emphysema would be expected to have a higher degree of compliance and require more work per unit volume of air inhaled than normal.
   B. The lungs of a patient with emphysema would be expected to have a higher degree of compliance and require less work per unit volume of air inhaled than normal.
   C. The lungs of a patient with emphysema would be expected to have a lower degree of compliance and require more work per unit volume of air inhaled than normal.
   D. The lungs of a patient with emphysema would be expected to have a lower degree of compliance and require less work per unit volume of air inhaled than normal.

6. Which of the following best describes the entire experimental system used to measure the PV curves for the frog lung?

   A. It was an open system.
   B. It was an isolated system.
   C. It was a closed system.
   D. It was a potential system.

7. The volume coefficient of expansion for water is 2.07 x 10^{-4} K^{-1} at 25°C. If 900 mL of water are placed in a 1.0 L beaker at room temperature, what will the volume of the water contained in the beaker at its normal boiling point? Assume evaporation during the heating process is negligible.

   A. 902 mL
   B. 914 mL
   C. 938 mL
   D. 1000 mL

8. As air is brought into the body through the nasal cavity, heat is transferred from the sinus tissues to the air, in order to raise the temperature before the air enters the lungs. Which of the following best describes the process in which this heat is transferred?

   I. conduction
   II. convection
   III. radiation

   A. I only
   B. II only
   C. I and II only
   D. I, II and III

Use the following for questions 9 and 10.

Constant	Value
Specific Heat of ice	2.06 J/g K
Specific Heat of liquid water	4.18 J/g K
Specific Heat of steam	2.02 J/g K
Heat of fusion at 0°C	334 J/g
Heat of Vaporization at 100°C	2260 J/g

9. The compressor of a refrigerator used 178 W of power and ran for 30 minutes to convert 200. g of water at 25°C to an equivalent amount of ice at 0°C? What is the minimum amount of work the compressor would have to do to make the ice?

   A. 20.9 kJ
   B. 66.8 kJ
   C. 87.7 kJ
   D. 320 kJ

10. If 100 g of ice at 0°C are placed in an insulated cup containing 300 g of liquid water at 25°C, what will the temperature of the system be after reaching equilibrium, assuming that this is an isolated system.

    A. 273 K
    B. 281 K
    C. 292 K
    D. 298 K

SECTION 4
CONTENT REVIEW PROBLEMS

Use the following in questions 1 and 2:

A cube, 0.1 m on a side, is made up of six metal plates, insulated from each other (see figure). Plates A and D are opposite each other and maintained at 1000 V. Plates B and E are opposite each other and maintained at 0 V. Plates C and F are maintained at –1000 V. The elementary charge is 1.6×10^{-19} C.

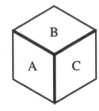

1. A charge of 10^{-14} C is pushed very slowly from the center of plate A straight across to the center of plate D. What is the work done by this force pushing the charge?

   A. -10^{-11} J
   B. 0 J
   C. 10^{-11} J
   D. 2×10^{-11} J

2. What is the change of potential energy of the system if an electron is transferred from plate A to plate C?

   A. -3.2×10^{-16} J
   B. -1.6×10^{-16} J
   C. $+1.6 \times 10^{-16}$ J
   D. $+3.2 \times 10^{-16}$ J

3. Two charges ($q_1 = 1.1 \times 10^{-8}$ C and $q_2 = 1.1 \times 10^{-9}$ C) are a distance 0.1 meters apart. How much energy is required to bring them to a distance 0.01 meters apart?

   A. 10^{-9} J
   B. 10^{-8} J
   C. 10^{-6} J
   D. 10^{-5} J

4. At the beginning of an experiment, two identical metal balls (radius 0.1 m) are neutral and considered to be at zero electrical potential. They are located far apart (5 m). Electrons are transferred by a mechanical technique from ball A to ball B, such that the system of balls and apparatus is isolated from the environment. After the transfer, ball A has acquired a potential of 10,000 volts and ball B a potential of –10,000 volts. Now, how much work is required to transfer 10^{-10} C from ball A to B?

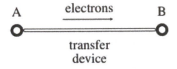

   A. -2×10^{-6} J
   B. -10^{-6} J
   C. 10^{-6} J
   D. 2×10^{-6} J

5. A charge $Q = 1.1 \times 10^{-5}$ C is fixed in space. Another charge $q = -10^{-6}$ C is 5 meters away. It is slowly moved 4 meters in a straight line directly toward the charge Q. How much work is required to move charge q?

   A. -0.08 J
   B. -0.016 J
   C. 0.016 J
   D. 0.08 J

6. A charge $Q = 1.1 \times 10^{-5}$ C is fixed at the origin. A second charge $q = 10^{-6}$ C is moved along a straight path from the point (0 m, 2 m) to the point (2 m, 0 m). How much work is performed in moving q along this path?

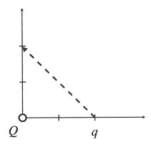

   A. 0 J
   B. 0.10 J
   C. 0.14 J
   D. 0.25 J

7. A dry cell (or battery) is in the shape of a cylinder of length l and diameter d. Its terminals have a small radius r, and the rating of the battery is voltage V. What is the energy required to bring one electron from the positive terminal to the negative terminal? (Charge on electron = q_e)

A. Vq_e
B. kq_e^2/r
C. $(kq_e^2/r^2)l$
D. $(Vq_e r)/l$

Use the following in questions 8 and 9:

Charges Q_1 and Q_2 (both 1.1×10^{-4} C) are located at $(-3$ m, 0 m) and at (3 m, 0 m) on the *xy*-plane. Point A is the point $(-1$ m, 0 m), point B is the point (1 m, 0 m), and point C is the point (0 m, 4 m).

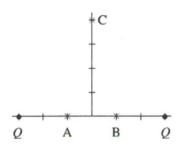

8. What is the potential difference between A and B?

A. 0 volts
B. 10^6 volts
C. 2×10^6 volts
D. 7.5×10^6 volts

9. What is the potential of C relative to a point an infinite distance away?

A. 2×10^5 volts
B. 4×10^5 volts
C. 5×10^5 volts
D. 7.5×10^5 volts

Use the following in questions 10 and 11:

A positive charge Q is held fixed at the origin. A positive charge q is on the positive *x*-axis and is let go. (Assume no friction.)

10. Which of the following describes the theoretical acceleration of q *after* it is let go?

A. Its acceleration decreases, eventually reaching zero.
B. Its acceleration decreases forever, but it never reaches zero.
C. Its acceleration decreases and then increases.
D. Its acceleration increases forever.

11. Which of the following describes the theoretical velocity of q *after* it is let go?
A. Its velocity increases and then decreases to zero.
B. Its velocity increases and then decreases, but it never reaches zero.
C. Its velocity increases forever but never becomes greater than a certain bound.
D. Its velocity increases forever without bound.

Use the following in questions 12–14:

When a proton encounters a large atomic nucleus, to a good approximation, we can assume the large nucleus is fixed in space. The main force between the nucleus and proton is electrostatic. Assume a nucleus of charge Q is fixed at the origin, and a proton (mass m, charge q) approaches it moving along the *x*-axis. Far away from the nucleus the proton has a velocity v, but as the proton approaches the nucleus, it slows and comes to a stop at a so-called *turning radius r*. (See figure.) Energy is conserved during this process.

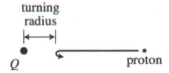

Note: The electric potential energy (or electrostatic energy) between two charged particles q_1 and q_2 a distance d apart is $E = kq_1q_2/d$.

12. Which of the following best describes the flow of energy?

A. potential to kinetic
B. kinetic to potential
C. kinetic to potential to heat
D. kinetic to potential and heat

13. Two protons are fired at the nucleus, the second with four times the velocity of the first. How would the electrostatic energy of the second proton at its turning radius compare with the electrostatic energy of the first proton at its turning radius?

   A. It would be greater by a factor of 16.
   B. It would be greater by a factor of 4.
   C. It would be greater by a factor of 2.
   D. It would be the same.

14. How would the turning radius be affected if the initial velocity *v* were increased by a factor of 4?
   A. It would decrease by a factor of 16.
   B. It would decrease by a factor of 4.
   C. It would decrease by a factor of 2.
   D. It would stay the same.

Use the following in questions 15 and 16:

A wire carries a current *I* which is traveling up the page. Point P lies off to the right.

15. What is the direction of the magnetic field at point P?

   A. Up the page.
   B. To the right.
   C. Out of the page.
   D. Into the page.

16. Which direction are electrons traveling in the wire?

   A. Up the page.
   B. Down the page.
   C. In a spiral.
   D. In a circle.

Use the following in questions 17 and 18:

In the figure the magnetic field is pointing down. A horizontal wire is shown.

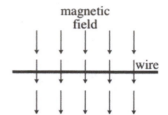

17. If an external force pulls the horizontal wire down the page, which of the following best indicates the direction of the force of the *magnetic field* on the electrons in the wire?

   A. Up.
   B. Into the page.
   C. Out of the page.
   D. There is no magnetic force.

18. If the horizontal wire is pulled out of the page toward you, which of the following best indicates the direction of the force of *magnetic field* on the electrons in the wire?

   A. Right.
   B. Into the page.
   C. Left.
   D. There is no magnetic force.

19. A proton is traveling to the right and encounters a region R which contains an electric field or a magnetic field.

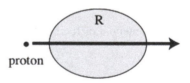

The proton is observed to speed up. Which is the best conclusion about the region R?

   A. There is a magnetic field pointing up the page.
   B. There is a magnetic field pointing down the page.
   C. There is an electric field pointing to the right.
   D. There is an electric field pointing to the left.

20. A proton is traveling to the right and encounters a region S which contains an electric field or a magnetic field.

The proton is observed to bend up the page. Refer to the following possibilities:

I. There is a magnetic field pointing into the page.
II. There is a magnetic field pointing out of the page.
III. There is an electric field pointing up the page.
IV. There is an electric field pointing down the page.
Which is the best conclusion about the region S?

A. I only.
B. II only.
C. I or III.
D. II or IV.

Use the following in questions 21 and 22:

A beam of electrons is traveling to the right. Point A is above the beam, as shown.

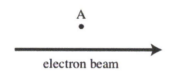

21. What is the direction of the electric field at point A?

A. Up the page.
B. Down the page.
C. Into the page.
D. Out of the page.

22. What is the direction of the magnetic field at point A?

A. Into the page.
B. Out of the page.
C. To the right.
D. To the left.

23. An electron beam is traveling to the right, and encounters a region R with a magnetic field pointing down, as shown. This region *also* has an electric field. We observe that the effects of the magnetic force and of the electric force cancel, so that the electron beam is straight.

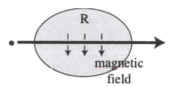

In which direction must the electric field point?

A. Up the page.
B. Down the page.
C. Into the page.
D. Out of the page.

Use the following in questions 24 and 25:

A current I is flowing through a wire loop as shown.

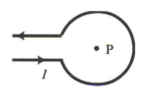

Point P is in the middle of the loop.

24. What is the direction of the magnetic field at point P?

A. Out of the page.
B. Into the page.
C. To the right.
D. To the left.

25. If a proton is at point P and moving upward (↑), what is the direction of the acceleration of the proton?

A. To the left.
B. To the right.
C. Up, that is, speeding up the proton.
D. Down, that is, slowing down the proton.

Passage 1

In a certain apparatus, a long wire along the z-axis carries a uniform charge on it. The resulting electric field outside the wire is directed away from the wire and has a magnitude given by

$$E = K/d$$

where

$$K = 30{,}000 \text{ Nm/C}$$

and d is the perpendicular distance from the wire to the point in question.

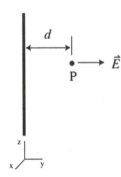

Charges near the wire experience forces due to the electric field. This is true of elementary particles, like electrons, as well as ions and molecules. Polar molecules have one end charged positively and the other end, negatively. The two sides of the molecule thus experience two forces.

If the electric field is great enough, the gas around the wire may undergo breakdown, that is, the molecules are ionized by the electric field.
For the following questions, use for the charge on an electron

$$q_{elec} = -1.6 \times 10^{-19} \text{ C}$$

26. What is the sign of the charge on the wire?
   A. Positive.
   B. Negative.
   C. Positive or negative.
   D. Positive and negative in equal amounts to make neutral.

27. What is the force on an electron located 0.01 meters from the wire?

   A. 1.9×10^{23} N toward the wire.
   B. 4.8×10^{-13} N toward the wire.
   C. 4.8×10^{-13} N away from the wire.
   D. 1.9×10^{23} N away from the wire.

28. Which of the following best depicts the electric field lines?

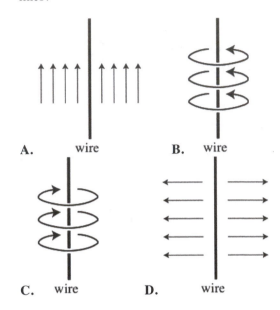

29. A fluoride ion (F^-) has a mass 19 times greater than a hydrogen ion (H^+). If a hydrogen ion and a fluoride ion are at the same location relative to the wire, how does the magnitude of the force on the fluoride ion compare to that of the force on the hydrogen ion?

   A. 19 times weaker.
   B. The same magnitude.
   C. 10 times stronger.
   D. 19 times stronger.

30. If a butanol molecule ($CH_3CH_2CH_2CH_2OH$) is near the wire, what is its most likely orientation?

   A. The methyl group will be near the wire.
   B. The methyl group will be away from the wire.
   C. The oxygen atom will be near the wire.
   D. The oxygen atom will be away from the wire.

Passage 2

If two parallel metal plates separated by a small gap are charged, one positively and one negatively, then there will be an electric field between the plates. If the electric field is larger than a certain threshold, then a spark may jump across the gap, partially discharging the plates. The threshold electric field depends on the type and pressure of the gas between the plates.

To see how a spark occurs, imagine a lone electron between the plates. It experiences a force and an acceleration, so it will move in the direction of the positive plate. Before it gets there, it is likely to collide with a gas particle. The average distance an electron travels before encountering a gas particle is the *mean free path*. The mean free path depends only on the number density of the gas, that is, the number of gas particles per unit volume. If the electron gains enough energy before colliding with the gas particle to ionize it, then after the collision there are more electrons to continue the process. The original electron loses much of its kinetic energy but is still available to accelerate and ionize other gas particles. (See figure.)

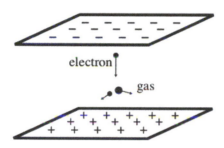

A lone electron thus undergoes acceleration and energy gain, followed by a collision, depositing energy into the gas particle and debris. Each collision releases several electrons, so the phenomenon grows exponentially. The process described is a run-away chain reaction. The result is a transfer of charge from one plate to the other. In addition, the discharge leaves many molecules in an excited state, which releases photons as they decay to the ground state.

For air at atmospheric pressure the threshold electric field is about

$$E_{th} = 3 \times 10^6 \text{ N/C}$$

You may also use the following:

$$k = 9 \times 10^9 \frac{\text{Nm}^2}{\text{C}^2}$$

$$Q_{elementary} = 1.6 \times 10^{-19} \text{ C}$$

r_0 = the average atomic radius = 6 x 10^{-11} meters
l_{mfp} = the mean free path = 8 x 10^{-9} meters

31. If an oxygen ion (O^{2-}) and an electron are both between the plates, which experiences the greater force?

   A. The oxygen ion by a factor of 8.
   B. The oxygen ion by a factor of 2.
   C. They experience the same magnitude of force.
   D. The electron experiences a much greater force because of its small mass.

32. How much force would a calcium atom experience if it were between the plates? (Assume the electric field is the threshold electric field for air.)

   A. 0 N
   B. 4.8 x 10^{-13} N
   C. 9.6 x 10^{-13} N
   D. 9.6 x 10^{-12} N

33. How would the threshold electric field change if the pressure of the gas were increased?

   A. The threshold would decrease because the mean free path would decrease.
   B. The threshold would decrease because the mean free path would increase.
   C. The threshold would increase because the mean free path would decrease.
   D. The threshold would increase because the mean free path would increase.

34. Sulfur hexafluoride is a dense gas which absorbs electrons. What would be the effect of replacing air with sulfur hexafluoride between the plates?

   A. The threshold would decrease because the density would be greater.
   B. The threshold would increase because the density would be greater.
   C. The increased density would increase the threshold, while the lone electrons would be absorbed, increasing the threshold even more.
   D. The lone electrons would be absorbed, increasing the threshold. (Density is not a factor.)

35. Which graph could be a typical graph of the electron described in paragraph 2 above?

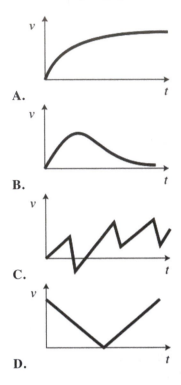

A.

B.

C.

D.

Use the following information in questions 36–40:

In the circuit shown, each light bulb has a resistance of 2 Ω, and the voltage source maintains a potential of 12 volts.

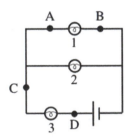

36. What is the current passing through the voltage source?

 A. 1 amp
 B. 2 amps
 C. 4 amps
 D. None of the above

37. Which dissipates more power, light bulb 1 or 3?

 A. Light bulb 1.
 B. They dissipate the same.
 C. Light bulb 3, by a factor 2.
 D. Light bulb 3, by more than a factor of 2.

38. What happens if points A and B are connected by a wire?

 A. Light 1 extinguishes.
 B. Light 1 extinguishes, and light 3 is brighter.
 C. Lights 1 and 2 extinguish, and light 3 is brighter.
 D. All lights extinguish, and the voltage source is shorted.

39. What happens to the voltage across light 3 if A and B are connected with a wire?

 A. It becomes zero.
 B. It stays the same.
 C. It increases but not to 12 volts.
 D. It becomes 12 volts.

40. What happens if points C and D are connected by a wire?

 A. Light 3 extinguishes.
 B. Light 3 extinguishes, and lights 1 and 2 burn dimmer.
 C. Light 3 extinguishes, and lights 1 and 2 burn brighter.
 D. The potential source is shorted.

Use the following in questions 41–42:

In the circuit shown, $R_1 = 100\ \Omega$, $R_2 = 200\ \Omega$, and $\Delta V = 6$ volts.

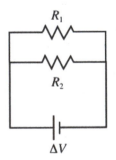

41. What is the total resistance for the circuit?

 A. 67 Ohms
 B. 100 Ohms
 C. 200 Ohms
 D. 300 Ohms

42. What is the voltage flowing through resistor 1?

 A. 2 volts
 B. 4 volts
 C. 6 volts
 D. None of the above

43. How much energy is dissipated by resistor 2 in 10 minutes?

    A. 108 J
    B. 720 J
    C. 7.2×10^3 J
    D. 7.2×10^4 J

Use the following in questions 44–46:

The heating element of a toaster is a long wire of some metal, often the alloy nichrome, which heats up when a potential difference is applied across it. In the U.S.A., plugging a toaster into the wall outlet is equivalent to applying a 120-V potential source across it. For these problems, consider a 300-W toaster connected to a wall outlet.

44. What is the resistance of such a toaster?

    A. 0.4 Ohms
    B. 2.5 Ohms
    C. 48 Ohms
    D. 3.6×10^4 Ohms

45. How could one increase the rate at which heat is produced?

    A. Use a longer wire.
    B. Use a thicker wire.
    C. Both A and B.
    D. None of the above.

46. In one experiment, we use a collection of toasters with various resistances. We record the power consumed by each. Which graph best represents the relationship between power consumption and resistance?

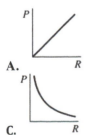 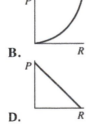

Use the following in questions 47–49:

A variable resistor is a resistor whose resistance can be adjusted by turning a knob. In a certain experiment a battery is connected to a variable resistor R. The potential difference across the resistor and the current through it are recorded for a number of settings of the resistor knob. Assume the battery can be modeled as an ideal potential source in series with an internal resistor.

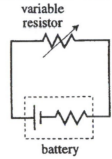

47. The emf of the potential source is 6.2 volts and the internal resistance is 0.1 Ω. If the variable resistor is set for 0.5 Ω, what is the current through it?

    A. 10.3 A
    B. 15.5 A
    C. 30.6 A
    D. 74.4 A

48. Consider the following possibilities:

    I. a small external resistance
    II. a large external resistance
    III. a small total current
    IV. a large total current

    When would it be a good approximation to ignore the internal resistance of the battery?

    A. II only
    B. II or III
    C. I only
    D. I or IV

49. From the resistances R and currents I mentioned in the experiment, we prepare a graph of $1/I$ versus R. Which of the following best represents that graph?

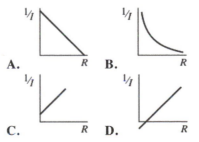

Passage 3

In a certain experiment, we place two metal plates of area A parallel to each other and separated by a distance d to form a capacitor. The copper disks are mounted on nonconducting stands in a dry room which does not allow the conduction of charge through the air. The two plates are connected with wires to the opposite ends of a DC cell. We can increase the capacitance of such a setup by inserting a nonconductor, called a dielectric in electrical engineering parlance, between the plates. In this case, the capacitance of the device is $C_{di} = \kappa C_{vac}$, where C_{vac} is the capacitance of the plates with a vacuum between them, κ is the dielectric constant of the nonconductor, and C_{di} is the new capacitance.

In Experiment 1 we place two copper circular disks of area A_1 a distance d_1 apart, thus creating a capacitor with capacitance C_1. We connect the two plates to opposite terminals of a battery which produces a potential ΔV_{bat}. This produces a positive charge Q_1 on one of the plates and an electric field E_1 between the plates.

In Experiment 2 we reproduce the setup in Experiment 1. This time, however, the two disks are connected to the opposite ends of a battery which produces four times the potential as that in Experiment 1 ($4\Delta V_{bat}$).

In Experiment 3 we reproduce the setup in Experiment 1. Then the wires are removed from the copper plates. We place cellulose nitrate (a dielectric with dielectric constant $k = 9$) between the plates.

50. What is the capacitance of the capacitor in Experiment 2?

    A. C_1
    B. $2C_1$
    C. $4C_1$
    D. $16C$

51. What charge is on the positive plate in Experiment 2?

    A. $Q_1/4$
    B. $Q_1/2$
    C. $2Q_1$
    D. $4Q_1$

52. What is the magnitude of the electric field between the plates in Experiment 2?

    A. $E_1/4$
    B. $E_1/2$
    C. $2E_1$
    D. $4E_1$

53. What charge is on the positive plate at the end of Experiment 3?

    A. $Q_1/9$
    B. Q_1
    C. $9Q_1$
    D. $81Q_1$

54. What is the magnitude of the potential difference between the plates at the end of Experiment 3?

    A. $\Delta V_1/9$
    B. $3\Delta V_1$
    C. $9\Delta V_1$
    D. $81\Delta V_1$

Passage 4

The Earth itself is a relatively good conductor. The atmosphere near the surface of the Earth, the troposphere and stratosphere, is composed mainly of neutral oxygen and nitrogen molecules, and it is a fairly good insulator.

About 30 km above the surface of the Earth, the atmosphere is composed mainly of ions. These ions are created by the bombardment of cosmic rays, and the low density of gas at that height inhibits their recombining to form neutral species. This portion of the atmosphere, called the ionosphere, is a good conductor. (See figure.)

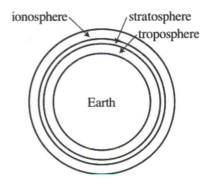

Thus, a very much simplified model of the Earth and its atmosphere consists of two conductors separated by an insulator. Furthermore, there is a net charge of -10^6 C on the surface of the Earth and a corresponding positive charge on the ionosphere. The potential between the Earth's surface and the ionosphere is about 9×10^5 volts. Thus the model roughly resembles a parallel-plate capacitor.

For these questions, you may consider the charge on the electron to be -1.6×10^{-19} C.

55. Considering the Earth and its atmosphere as a capacitor, what is its capacitance?

   A. 1.1 Farads
   B. 30 Farads
   C. 2.7×10^9 Farads
   D. 9×10^{11} Farads

56. What is a good approximation for the magnitude of the electric field in the Earth's atmosphere?

   A. 1.4×10^{-13} N/C
   B. 30 N/C
   C. 2.7×10^9 N/C
   D. 9×10^{10} N/C

57. What would be the change in potential energy of an electron which was transported from the Earth's surface to the ionosphere?

   A. -1.4×10^{-13} Joules
   B. -1.8×10^{-25} Joules
   C. 1.8×10^{-25} Joules
   D. 1.4×10^{-13} Joules

58. Which of the following best represents the electric field?

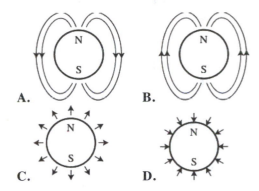

59. Assuming the electric potential at the Earth's surface is zero, which of the following *best* represents the electric potential as a function of height h above the Earth's surface?

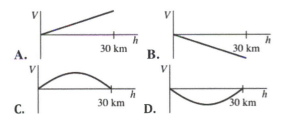

Passage 5

An electrostatic precipitator is a device used in industry to remove pollution from exhaust gas. It consists of a long thin wire surrounded by a conducting cylinder, such that a potential about 5×10^4 volts is maintained between the negative wire and the positive cylinder. (See figure.)

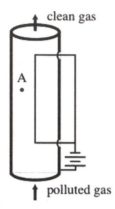

The resulting electric field inside the cylinder varies inversely with the distance from the center wire. Neutral particles of pollution are attracted to the center wire. The electric field near the wire is strong enough (greater than about 3×10^6 N/C) to ionize air, so the pollution particles are ionized negatively. They are attracted to the outer cylinder, where they collect and are eventually removed.

A typical energy requirement for such a device is about 300 Joules for each cubic meter of gas processed.

Note: The charge on an electron is -1.6×10^{-19} C. Point A is in the plane of the page.

60. If a sodium ion is at point A, in what direction would it experience a force?

    A. right
    B. left
    C. up
    D. down

61. If a $C_{10}H_{18}O_2$ molecule is at point A, in what direction would it experience a force?

    A. right
    B. left
    C. up
    D. down

62. If a fluorine atom were ionized to form fluoride (mass 3×10^{-26} kg) near the center wire, what is the best approximation for the maximum kinetic energy it could have by the time it reached the outer cylinder?

    A. 8×10^{-31} J
    B. 1.5×10^{-23} J
    C. 10^{-20} J
    D. 8×10^{-15} J

63. If the potential maintained across the wire/cylinder were increased, how would the capacitance of the device be affected?

    A. The capacitance would decrease.
    B. The capacitance would stay the same.
    C. The capacitance would increase.
    D. The capacitance could decrease or increase depending on the gas in the cylinder.

64. If the flow rate of gas through an electrostatic precipitator is 100 m³/s, what would be the electrical current through the device?

    A. 0 amps
    B. 10^{-2} amps
    C. 0.8 amps
    D. 3×10^4 amps

65. Which of the following best represents the electric field lines in the cylinder?

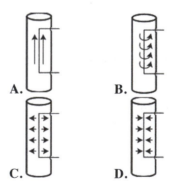

66. Which of the following is the closest analogy to the attraction of neutral particles of pollutants to the center wire?

    A. The aligning of a small magnet to Earth's magnetic field.
    B. The attraction between a chloride ion and a sodium ion in a salt crystal.
    C. The van der Waals attraction between two nitrogen molecules in air.
    D. A charged comb picking up pieces of paper.

Passage 6

When thunderclouds form, the base of the cloud is generally about 2 km above the surface of the Earth, while the top of the cloud may extend to about 8 km above the Earth. The charge structure is quite complicated. The top of the cloud has a strong positive charge; the middle of the cloud, a strong negative charge; and the bottom of the cloud, a weaker positive charge. Meanwhile the cloud induces a positive charge on the surface of the Earth. (See figure.) The resulting potential difference between the bottom of the cloud and the ground is around 10^8 volts.

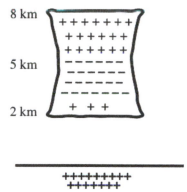

When lightning strikes, some of the negative charge of the cloud neutralizes the positive charge of the Earth. Approximately 4 Coulombs of negative charge pass from the ground to the cloud, forming a current of 20 kamps. This results in a huge release of energy in the form of dissociation, ionization, and excitation of molecules in air, the heating and expanding of gas, and electromagnetic radiation.

In places especially prone to lightning, it is helpful to install lightning rods. A lightning rod is a long piece of metal with one end embedded in the ground and the other end extending up higher than the surrounding buildings. The end in the air comes to a sharp point. The purpose of such a piece of metal is to conduct electrons from the Earth into the air and reduce the charge imbalance, thus reducing the probability of lightning. If lightning strikes anyway, it is more likely to strike the lightning rod than the buildings.

67. What is the approximate magnitude of the electric field in the air during a thunderstorm?

    A. 2×10^2 N/C
    B. 5×10^4 N/C
    C. 5×10^6 N/C
    D. 2×10^{11} N/C

68. What is approximate resistance for charge flow during a lightning strike?

    A. 5000 Ω
    B. 2×10^4 Ω
    C. 5×10^6 Ω
    D. 2×10^7 Ω

69. How much energy is released during a stroke of lightning?

    A. 8×10^4 Joules
    B. 4×10^8 Joules
    C. 2×10^{12} Joules
    D. There is not enough information to answer this question.

70. What is the approximate duration of a stroke of lightning?

    A. 2×10^{-4} seconds
    B. 5×10^{-3} seconds
    C. 2×10^{-2} seconds
    D. 0.5 seconds

71. Which of the following best represents the electric field near a lightning rod?

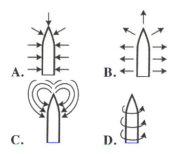

72. Which of the following is most likely to result in the light associated with lightning?

    A. dissociation of molecules
    B. excitation of molecules
    C. heating of air
    D. expansion of air

Passage 7

A number of aquatic species have evolved the capability to produce sizable electric fields. For some species this helps them to detect other organisms, either predator or prey. Other species, such as the electric eel, use this capability to stun or kill a predator or prey.

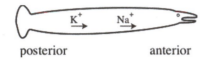

posterior   anterior

The organism generates the electric field in an "electric organ" which can take up most of the body cavity. The following description refers to a hypothetical electric organ, which includes many features by which these organs operate.

Electrocytes are flattened cells (like disks) which are stacked in a series, as shown in the figure below. During the equilibrium state, the cells actively exclude sodium ions (Na^+), creating a potential difference between the inside of the cell and the outside of the cell. The cell membrane is permeable to potassium ions (K^+), so the interior of the cell becomes enriched with K^+ ions, partially but not fully compensating for the potential difference due to the imbalance of Na^+ ions. The magnitude of the potential difference between the inside and outside is of the cell is about 0.1 V.

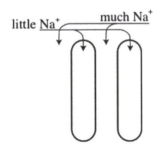

Equilibrium State

During the activated state, the posterior side of the cells becomes permeable to sodium ions, so they rush in through the posterior face due to the potential difference. Potassium ions rush in the same direction through the anterior face of the cell. The result is a potential difference across the whole organ, which acts, in effect, as a battery. (See the figure below.) The circuit is completed in the surrounding water, as shown in the second figure below.

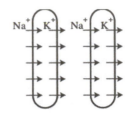

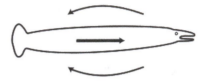

Activated State
(arrows show current flow)

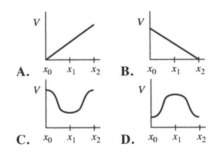

arrows show current flow

During the activated state, the current across the anterior and posterior faces of a cell in this hypothetical electric organ is 30 milliamps. The duration of a pulse is 2 milliseconds.

The charge on an electron is -1.6×10^{-19} C.

73. Consider x_0 and x_2 to be points in the extracellular medium and x_1 a point in the interior of the cell. During the equilibrium state, which graph best shows the electric potential as a function of x?

A. (graph) $x_0 \quad x_1 \quad x_2$ B. (graph) $x_0 \quad x_1 \quad x_2$

C. (graph) $x_0 \quad x_1 \quad x_2$ D. (graph) $x_0 \quad x_1 \quad x_2$

74. If the electric organ of a fish consists of 5000 electrocytes stacked in a series, what is the approximate total current through the fish during the activated state?

A. 30 milliamps
B. 75 amps
C. 150 amps
D. 300 amps

75. How much charge crosses the cell membrane during the activated state?

A. 1.6×10^{-19} C
B. 3×10^{-6} C
C. 6×10^{-5} C
D. 7×10^{-2} C

76. Which of the following best shows the electric field due to the fish during the activated state?

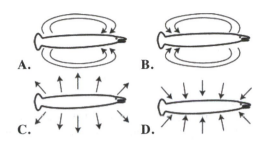

A.   B.

C.   D.

77. Which of the following best shows the magnetic field due to the fish during the activated state?

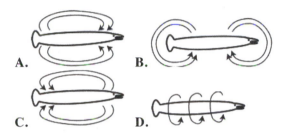

A.   B.

C.   D.

78. Which is a better conductor of electricity, fresh water or sea water?

A. Fresh water, because sea water is slightly more dense.
B. Sea water, because sea water is slightly more dense.
C. Fresh water, because ions impede current in sea water.
D. Sea water, because ions carry current in sea water.

Use the following information in questions 79 and 80:

Atomic masses of some isotopes

$_{0}^{1}\text{n}$	1.00866 amu
$_{1}^{1}\text{H}$	1.00783 amu
$_{1}^{2}\text{H}$	2.01410 amu
$_{2}^{4}\text{He}$	4.00260 amu
$_{3}^{7}\text{Li}$	7.01601 amu

79. In the Sun, four hydrogen nuclei react to form a helium nucleus, so that the net reaction looks like

$$4\,^{1}\text{H} \rightarrow\,^{4}\text{He} + 2\nu$$

where the neutrino is massless or nearly so. What is the mass deficit for this reaction?

A. 0.02872 amu
B. 0.03204 amu
C. 2.99477 amu
D. 5.01043 amu

80. Consider the interaction of one lithium atom (^{7}Li) and one hydrogen atom (^{1}H) to create two equal particles. What is the mass deficit for this reaction?

A. 0.01864 amu
B. 0.47129 amu
C. 1.02491 amu
D. 4.00260 amu

81. An isolated ^{8}Be atom will spontaneously decay into two alpha particles. What can be concluded about the mass of the ^{8}Be atom?

A. The mass is less than double the mass of the ^{4}He atom.
B. The mass is exactly double the mass of the ^{4}He atom.
C. The mass is greater than double the mass of the ^{4}He atom.
D. None of the above may be concluded.

82. Each second the Sun produces 3.9×10^{26} J. How much mass does it lose per second from nuclear processes alone? (Use $c = 3.0 \times 10^{8}$ m/s $h = 6.63 \times 10^{-34}$ J s.)

A. 7.8×10^{1} kg
B. 2.2×10^{9} kg
C. 4.3×10^{9} kg
D. 1.8×10^{68} kg

83. In a nuclear reaction the mass of the products is less than the mass of the reactants. This is not observed in a chemical reaction. Why not?

A. Mass is conserved in chemical reactions, which involve only the electromagnetic force.
B. The mass deficit in chemical reactions is too small to be observed by present techniques.
C. In chemical reactions, the mass deficit is balanced by a mass surplus.
D. In chemical reactions, the mass is held constant by the nucleus.

Passage 8

Certain toys found in cereal boxes display the phenomenon of phosphorescence. If a child exposes the toy to a bright light (for example, the Sun), then the toy will glow with a characteristic color when the child takes it into a dark closet.

The phenomenon of phosphorescence requires the interaction of light with three energy levels in an atom (or molecule). The figure below (not to scale) shows a hypothetical energy diagram in which the lowest state shown is the ground state ($E = 0$). When the toy is taken into the Sun, a photon causes a transition from the ground state to state 2. Almost immediately, the atom emits a photon, making a fast transition to state 1.

$$
\begin{array}{ll}
E_2 & 2 \\
E_1 & 1 \\
E = 0 & \text{ground} \\
& \text{state}
\end{array}
$$

The atom makes a transition to the ground state only slowly. Thus when the child takes the toy into a closet, he is able to observe the phosphorescent photons from this final transition. The transition from state 1 to the ground state is said to be *forbidden*, and it takes place by different (and thus slower) processes than the other transitions.

Let f_{abs} be the frequency of the absorbed photons, f_{fl} be the frequency of the photons emitted while the object is still in the sunlight, and f_{ph} be the frequency of the photons released in the closet. (Planck's constant is $h = 4.14 \times 10^{-15}$ eV s.)

84. How does f_{abs} compare to the f_{ph}?

    A. $f_{abs} < f_{ph}$
    B. $f_{abs} = f_{ph}$
    C. $f_{abs} > f_{ph}$
    D. It depends on the specific atoms used in the material.

85. How does f_{fl} compare to the f_{ph}?

    A. $f_{fl} < f_{ph}$
    B. $f_{fl} = f_{ph}$
    C. $f_{fl} > f_{ph}$
    D. It depends on the specific atoms used in the material.

86. Which of the following gives a correct expression for f_{ph}?

    A. $\dfrac{E_1}{h}$ **B.** $\dfrac{E_2}{h}$

    C. $\dfrac{(E_1 + E_2)}{h}$ **D.** $\dfrac{(E_2 - E_1)}{h}$

87. After the child brings the object into the closet, which atomic state is the most populated? That is, a number of atoms have electrons in the ground state, a number in state 1, and a number in state 2. Which number is greatest?

    A. The ground state is the most populated.
    B. State 1 is most populated.
    C. State 2 is most populated.
    D. Either the ground state or state 1 is the most populated.

88. Which is correct?

    A. The Sun emits photons of many frequencies, but only photons corresponding to the absorption frequency will be absorbed by the object.
    B. The Sun emits photons of many frequencies, but only photons corresponding to the absorption frequency make it through Earth's atmosphere.
    C. The Sun emits photons of one frequency, and the toy is constructed to absorb that frequency.
    D. The Sun emits photons of one frequency, and the toy converts the photons to the desired frequency.

Passage 9

Sample 1

We observe radioactivity from a sample of ^{209}Po (Sample 1), but the radioactivity is effectively blocked by a piece of thin (0.05 mm) gold foil. The radioactive efflux is made into a beam by placing the sample in a block of lead (Pb) with a hole which allows the particles to escape as shown in the figure below). In one experiment the beam is subjected to an electric field which points up. In another experiment the beam is subjected to a magnetic field which points down.

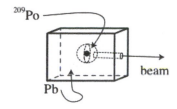

Sample 2

We obtain a pure sample of ^{66}Ga (Sample 2), which has a radioactivity level of 1000 mCi. We observe that the radioactivity is not blocked by a piece of thin metal foil, but it is blocked by several centimeters of aluminum. After 19 hours, the level of radioactivity is down to 250 mCi.

A beam is made of the radioactive efflux in the same way as mentioned for Sample 1. The beam is traveling to the east, and it enters a strong magnetic field pointing up. The beam veers to the south.

89. What is the product of the decay of ^{209}Po?

    A. ^{205}Pb
    B. ^{209}At
    C. ^{209}Bi
    D. ^{209}Po

90. When the beam from Sample 1 enters the electric field, what is the effect on the beam?

    A. The particles in the beam go faster.
    B. The particles in the beam slow down.
    C. The beam bends up.
    D. The beam bends down.

91. When the beam from Sample 1 enters the magnetic field, what is the effect on the beam?

    A. The beam bends up.
    B. The beam bends down.
    C. The beam bends to the left, as viewed from the top.
    D. The beam bends to the right, as viewed from the top.

92. What type of radioactivity is produced by ^{66}Ga?

    A. α
    B. β^+
    C. β^-
    D. γ

93. At what time after the beginning of Experiment 2 was the radioactivity level at 500 mCi?

    A. 9.5 hours
    B. 12.6 hours
    C. 15 hours
    D. None of the above is correct.

94. In Experiment 2, when will the level of radioactivity decrease to zero?

    A. 28 hours.
    B. 56 hours.
    C. 112 hours.
    D. It will last indefinitely.

Passage 10

The two dominant forces in the nucleus of an atom are the electromagnetic force, which is the repulsive force among protons, and the strong force, which is attractive among protons and neutrons. Many of the things we observe in nuclei can be explained by a balance of these two forces, combined with the Pauli principle for the particles in the nucleus. For instance, most stable nuclei have somewhat more neutrons than protons, although nonmassive stable nuclei have about the same number of neutrons as protons. Nuclear physicists say that these nuclei are in a *valley of stability*, so that

$$N \geq Z$$

where N is the number of neutrons and Z is the atomic number, and the symbol means that N is greater than or approximately equal to Z.

When the difference $N - Z$ is strongly positive, it is likely that a nucleus will decay by β^- decay, in which a neutron converts into a proton, an electron, and an antineutrino (which rarely interacts with matter).

When $N - Z$ is only slightly positive or even negative, then there are two likely modes of decay: β^+ decay and K-capture. In β^+ decay (also called positron decay), a proton is converted into a neutron, a positron, and a neutrino.

In K-capture, an electron from an orbital of the first shell (or K-shell, that is, the 1s orbital) combines with a nuclear proton to make a neutron and a neutrino. This often happens in nuclei in which positron decay is forbidden, for instance, because it is energetically unfavorable. K-capture is possible because there is some overlap of the first-shell orbital and the volume taken up by the nucleus, that is, the first-shell orbital has a nonzero amplitude at the center of the nucleus.

95. Which of the following represents the K-capture decay of ^{56}Ni?

A. $^{56}\text{Ni} \rightarrow \,^{56}\text{Co} + \text{e}^+ + \nu$

B. $^{56}\text{Ni} \rightarrow \,^{56}\text{Cu} + \text{e}^- + \bar{\nu}$

C. $^{56}\text{Ni} \rightarrow \,^{56}\text{Co} + \text{e}^- + \bar{\nu}$

D. $^{56}\text{Ni} + \text{e}^- \rightarrow \,^{56}\text{Co} \quad \nu$

96. What kind of nuclei would tend to undergo K-capture?

A. Nuclei with many more neutrons than protons.
B. Nuclei with more protons than neutrons.
C. Nuclei with a deficit of electrons.
D. Nuclei with protons in low energy orbitals.

97. Which of the following, if true, would explain why L-capture, the interaction of a nucleus with a second-shell electron, is extremely rare?

A. The second shell has greater energy than the first shell.
B. The second shell has a vanishing amplitude in the nucleus.
C. The second-shell electrons are easily removed from the atom.
D. The second-shell electrons cannot be converted to positrons.

98. When an atom undergoes K-capture, several photons are often observed in the vicinity of the event. Which is the best explanation for this?

A. The neutrino ionizes the surrounding atoms.
B. The neutron decays into particles which ionize surrounding atoms.
C. Electrons in outer shells make transitions to lower shells.
D. The positron interacts with an electron.

99. What happens to the difference $N - Z$ during normal beta decay?

A. decreases by 2
B. decreases by 1
C. increases by 1
D. increases by 2

100. What happens to $N - Z$ during alpha decay?

A. decreases by 4
B. decreases by 2
C. stays the same
D. increases by 4

Passage 11

One strategy in the fight against cancer involves the interaction of neutrons with a particular isotope of boron, called boron neutron capture therapy (BNCT). In BNCT, boron-10 is introduced into tumor cells, and the area is irradiated with slow neutrons. The interaction of a boron-10 nucleus and a neutron results in the production of an alpha particle with 2.3 MeV of kinetic energy.

A charged particle with large kinetic energy will lose that energy as it ionizes molecules that it passes by. In this case the alpha particles disrupt the DNA (among other molecules) of the tumor cells, effectively destroying cancerous tissue.

There are several problems with this method. It is important not to use a neutron flux so high that neutrons react substantially with oxygen and hydrogen in normal tissue, producing gamma rays. This sets an upper limit on the flux of neutrons and thus a lower limit on the necessary concentration of ^{10}B in tumor cells.

It has proven difficult to concentrate ^{10}B in tumor cells. One idea involves attaching boron to certain monoclonal antibodies which would recognize antigens on cancer cells. Another idea involves attaching boron to nucleosides, which tend to be taken up by dividing cells.

Another problem is finding a significant source of slow neutrons. Nuclear reactors are few, expensive, and relatively immobile. The isotope ^{252}Cf has been suggested as a source of neutrons. Although its main channel of decay is alpha, with a 2.6-year half-life, a significant fraction of it spontaneously fissions, yielding neutrons. Thus ^{252}Cf can be taken to the site where it is needed. The neutrons from the fission can be moderated and directed to the area to be irradiated.

101. In paragraph 1, when a slow neutron encounters a ^{10}B nucleus, what particle is created, in addition to the alpha particle?

    A. a proton
    B. a neutron
    C. ^{4}He
    D. ^{7}Li

102. Why do the neutrons used in irradiation not cause significant ionization and thus radiation damage of normal tissue?

    A. The neutrons do not contain any orbitals.
    B. The neutrons get captured before they have a chance to ionize anything.
    C. The neutrons have overall zero charge.
    D. The neutrons are not an elementary particle.

103. Paragraph 3 alludes to nuclear reactions which may be dangerous to normal tissue. Which of the following is a possibility, according to this paragraph?

    A. $^{16}O + {}^1n \rightarrow {}^{13}C + {}^4He$
    B. $^{16}O + {}^1n \rightarrow {}^{17}O + \gamma$
    C. $^{16}O + {}^1n \rightarrow {}^{17}F + \gamma$
    D. $^1H + {}^1n \rightarrow {}^2He + \gamma$

104. What is the immediate decay product for the alpha decay of ^{252}Cf?

    A. ^{252}Es
    B. ^{252}Bk
    C. ^{256}Fm
    D. ^{248}Cm

105. A sample of ^{252}Cf is shipped to a hospital, and 7.8 years later there are 0.01 moles of ^{252}Cf left. How much was shipped to the hospital in the first place?

    A. 0.01 moles
    B. 0.03 moles
    C. 0.04 moles
    D. 0.08 moles

106. Which reaction shows an example of the spontaneous fission mentioned in the last paragraph?

    A. $^{252}Cf \rightarrow {}^{250}Cf + {}^1n + {}^1n$
    B. $^{252}Cf \rightarrow {}^{149}Ce + {}^{100}Zr + {}^1n + {}^1n + {}^1n$
    C. $^{252}Cf + {}^1n \rightarrow {}^{150}Ce + {}^{100}Zr + {}^1n + {}^1n + {}^1n$
    D. $^{252}Cf + {}^1n \rightarrow {}^{250}Bk + {}^1H + {}^1n + {}^1n$

107. Why is it dangerous to have too large a neutron flux?

    A. The neutrons will ionize molecules in biological tissue.
    B. The neutrons will convert hydrogen and oxygen to other elements.
    C. The neutrons will react with hydrogen and oxygen to produce ionizing radiation.
    D. The neutrons will react with boron in normal cells, not just tumor cells.

Passage 12

The first method of imaging the interior of the human body came with the discovery of X-rays in 1895. A major advance in image resolution came with computerized axial tomography (CAT), a method of imaging which combines X-ray images from numerous axial viewpoints.

A new method is positron emission tomography (PET). PET allows us to obtain very precise tomographic information of a specialized nature. For instance, we can obtain information about cells which are metabolizing a large amount of glucose. In this method, an analog of glucose, 2-fluoro-2-deoxy-D-glucose, or FDG, is introduced into a person's bloodstream. The analog is incorporated into the cells along with normal glucose by the same carriers. Hexokinase converts FDG into FDG-6-phosphate, but its metabolism stops at that point, and the fluorine may be detected.

The key to this procedure is using the isotope ^{18}F in FDG, since ^{18}F is unstable to positron decay (half-life 110 minutes). In the production of this isotope, a cyclotron accelerates deuterons (^{2}H) toward a target of ^{20}Ne and H$_2$. A deuteron and a neon nucleus collide to form ^{18}F, which chemically reacts with the hydrogen gas to form hydrogen fluoride (H ^{18}F). This is used in the synthesis of FDG.

The cells which are metabolizing a large amount of glucose will have a high concentration of FDG tagged with ^{18}F. When a ^{18}F nucleus emits a positron, the positron travels several millimeters before slowing to a stop. It then reacts with an electron to form two photons, which are emitted 180° apart. These photons are detected by a ring of detectors circling the person's body. Thus the original site of the decay can be reconstructed.

Another use of PET involves the incorporation of the isotope ^{15}O (half-life 122 seconds) into water. This can be accomplished by bombarding a target of ^{14}N with protons from a cyclotron. The water (with ^{15}O) is introduced into the bloodstream. Detailed information can be obtained as to what capillaries are open or closed and therefore what areas of the brain are active.

108. Where does the kinetic energy of the positron go as it comes to a stop?

    A. sound
    B. ionization
    C. gravitational potential energy
    D. nuclear energy

109. In paragraph 3, when a deuteron collides with the ^{20}Ne, what particle is produced in addition to the ^{18}F nucleus?

    A. a gamma particle
    B. a proton
    C. a neutron
    D. an alpha particle

110. What does the ^{18}F nucleus become after positron decay?

    A. ^{17}O
    B. ^{18}O
    C. ^{18}Ne
    D. ^{19}Ne

111. What is a possible problem of using glucose tagged with ^{15}O?

    A. Glucose with ^{15}O would not be transported into the cells.
    B. Glucose with ^{15}O would be a poison to biological functioning.
    C. The half-life of ^{15}O might be too short to record its incorporation into cells.
    D. The isotope ^{15}O would not positron decay when incorporated into a carbon compound.

112. If a sample of ^{15}O is to have an activity of 10 mCi at a time 8 minutes after it is created and injected into the body, what must its activity be at the time it is synthesized?

    A. 60 mCi
    B. 80 mCi
    C. 120 mCi
    D. 160 mCi

113. In the last paragraph, a proton collides with a ^{14}N nucleus to create ^{15}O and what other particle?

    A. A gamma particle.
    B. A proton.
    C. A neutron.
    D. An alpha particle.

MATH REVIEW

SECTION 5
MATH ASSESSMENT

Unlike every other test we take in college, the MCAT won't let us have a calculator. As such, we have to have strong arithmetic skills, good estimation ability, and a very good number sense.

If you're already very comfortable with mathematical operations, then skip the following arithmetic assessment. Jump right to the Algebra 2 assessment and take that. If you're able to score very highly (95%+ correct) then you can skip the math review chapters that follow. You should skill go through the chapter on Interpreting Graphs and Experimental Design, as they have value for all test-takers. Similarly, a strong confidence and strong performance on the math assessments mean that you can likely skip the Math final at the end of the book as well.

On the other hand, if you struggle with doing math problems, or they're a major source of anxiety for you, then you should begin by carefully working your way through both assessment chapters that follow. Then go slowly and methodically through every problem in each Math Review chapter and every single question in the math final at the end.

This page intentionally left blank.

CHAPTER 16
ASSESSMENT: ARITHMETIC

A. INTRODUCTION

Many of us have been using a calculator so long that we've forgotten the fundamentals. Unfortunately, the MCAT is not going to cut us any slack here. The test will expect us to be able to do calculations involving basic functions and approximations with nothing more advanced than a pencil and paper.

B. ASSESSMENT EXAM

Section 1: Basic operations

1. $13 + 9 =$
2. $27 + 9.6 =$
3. $103 + 19 =$
4. $1152 + 879 =$
5. $989 + 11271 =$
6. $35 - 8 =$
7. $81 - 98 =$
8. $10.7 - 99 =$
9. $23 - 561 =$
10. $415 - 296 =$
11. $8 \times 7 =$
12. $12 \times 3 =$
13. $11 \times 1.1 =$
14. $3 \times 104 =$
15. $20 \times 213 =$
16. $64 / 4 =$
17. $36 / 1.2 =$
18. $3 \times 2 + 1 =$
19. $(4 + 2)(9 \times 1.8) =$
20. $4 / 2 + 1 \times 9 - 5 =$

Section 2: Fractions

21. $25 / 5 =$
22. $1/3 + 4/3 =$
23. $1/3 + 2/5 =$
24. $4/7 + 1/4 =$
25. $16/19 - 1/2 =$
26. $2/3 - 3/5 =$
27. $1/4 - 5/6 =$

28. $1/2 \times 1/3 =$
29. $4/9 \times 0.1 =$
30. $13/2 \times 2/13 =$
31. $1/2 \div 1/3 =$
32. $2/3 \div 3/2 =$
33. $12/5 \div 1/2 =$
34. $7/8 \div 5/4 =$
35. $3/4 \times 0.15 =$
36. $1/3 \div 1/5 \times 5/4 =$
37. $2/3 + 2/9 \times 1/3 =$
38. $1/4 \div 1/3 + 0.5 =$
39. $(4/5 + 0.2) \times 8/9 =$
40. $1/2 + 1/2 =$

Section 3: Percentages

41. 50% of $30 =$
42. 25% of $48 =$
43. 75% of $3/4 =$
44. 80% of 15% of $1,000 =$
45. 45% of $(9/10 \times 0.2) =$
46. 50% more than $50 =$
47. 10% more than $25 =$
48. 25% sale off an item that starts at $40 =$
49. A student scores 87% on a test of 200 questions. He got wrong $=$
50. A car starts at 50 mph, increases its speed by 10% and then decreases its speed by 10%. It ends at $=$
51. 15% less than $90 =$
52. 30% less than $0.0045 =$

53. 1.2% of 50 =

54. 2.5% of 10.1 =

55. A class of 40 students is 60% boys and among the boys 50% play soccer. The number of non-soccer playing boys is =

56. 10% of the sale price of a house is commission paid to the real estate agent. A house sells for $250,000. The real estate agent receives =

57. 36.6% of 1000 =

58. 50% more than 10% less than 50 =

59. 20% less than 25% more than 40 =

60. 100% of 100 =

Section 4: Roots, Scientific Notation

61. $4^2 =$

62. $11^2 =$

63. $105.23^0 =$

64. $0^{13} =$

65. $2^2 + 3^3 =$

66. $10^5 / 10^2 =$

67. $(5^2)^2 \times 5^{11} =$

68. $2^3 \times 4^3 =$

69. $1^5 + 2^4 + 3^3 =$

70. $\sqrt{169} =$

71. $\sqrt{4} + \sqrt{16} =$

72. $\sqrt{5} \times \sqrt{5} =$

73. $\sqrt{144} - \sqrt{25} =$

74. $\sqrt{32} =$

75. $\sqrt{50} =$

76. $\sqrt{(4/9)} =$

77. $3.2 \times 10^4 + 3.2 \times 10^4 =$

78. $2 \times 10^2 \times (4 \times 10^6)^2 =$

79. $1.5 \times 10^5 - 9.8 \times 10^4 =$

80. $\sqrt{(2.5 \times 10^9)} =$

Section 5: Estimation

81. $25.113 + 24.98 \approx$

82. $30.013 + 0.995 \approx$

83. $119.155 - 247.03 \approx$

84. $4.814 \times 9.21 \approx$

85. $1.0311 \times 483.3 \approx$

86. $1021.4 / 511.1 \approx$

87. $8.33332 / 29.4 \approx$

88. 31.14% of 99.8 $\approx$

89. 91.66% more than 1044 $\approx$

90. 12.555% less than 94.3 $\approx$

91. $4.1^2 \approx$

92. $5^{2.01} \approx$

93. $2^{3.8} \approx$

94. $\sqrt{98} \approx$

95. $\sqrt{160} \approx$

96. $\sqrt{38} + \sqrt{45} \approx$

97. $4.9(2.012^2 + \sqrt{24}) \approx$

98. $(51/99) + (31.22/63.998) \approx$

99. $6.022 \times 10^{23} + 9.88 \times 10^{22} \approx$

100. $\sqrt{(6 \times 10^{19})} + [9.1 \times 10^4]^2 \approx$

C. ANSWER KEY

Section 1: Basic operations

1. $13 + 9 = 22$
2. $27 + 9.6 = 36.6$
3. $103 + 19 = 122$
4. $1152 + 879 = 2031$
5. $989 + 11271 = 12260$
6. $35 - 8 = 27$
7. $81 - 98 = -17$
8. $10.7 - 99 = -88.3$
9. $23 - 561 = -538$
10. $415 - 296 = 119$
11. $8 \times 7 = 56$
12. $12 \times 3 = 36$
13. $11 \times 1.1 = 12.1$
14. $3 \times 104 = 312$
15. $20 \times 213 = 4260$
16. $64 / 4 = 16$
17. $36 / 1.2 = 30$
18. $3 \times 2 + 1 = 7$
19. $(4 + 2)(9 \times 1.8) = 97.2$
20. $4 / 2 + 1 \times 9 - 5 = 6$

Section 2: Fractions

21. $25 / 5 = 5$
22. $1/3 + 4/3 = 5/3$
23. $1/3 + 2/5 = 5/15 + 6/15 = 11/15$

24. $4/7 + 1/4 = 16/28 + 7/28 = 23/28$
25. $16/19 - 1/2 = 32/38 - 19/38 = 13/38$
26. $2/3 - 3/5 = 10/15 - 9/15 = 1/15$
27. $1/4 - 5/6 = 3/12 - 10/12 = -7/12$
28. $1/2 \times 1/3 = 1 \times 1 / 2 \times 3 = 1/6$
29. $4/9 \times 0.1 = 4/9 \times 1/10 = 4/90$
30. $13/2 \times 2/13 = 13 \times 2 / 2 \times 13 = 26/26 = 1$
31. $1/2 = 3/1 \div 1/2 \times 3/1 = 3/2$
32. $2/3 \div 3/2 = 2/3 \times 2/3 = 4/9$
33. $12/5 \div 1/2 = 12/5 \times 2/1 = 24/5$
34. $7/8 \div 5/4 = 7/8 \times 4/5 = 28/40 = 14/20 = 7/10$
35. $3/4 \times 0.15 = 3/4 \times 15/100 = 45/400 = 9/80$
36. $1/3 \div 1/5 \times 5/4 = 1/3 \times 5/1 \times 5/4 = 25/12$
37. $2/3 + 2/9 \times 1/3 = 2/3 + 2/27 = 20/27$
38. $1/4 \div 1/3 + 0.5 = 1/4 \times 3/1 + 1/2 = 5/4$
39. $(4/5 + 0.2) \times 8/9 = (4/5 + 1/5)(8/9) = 8/9$
40. $1/2 + 1/2 = 2/2 = 1$

Section 3: Percentages

41. 50% of 30 = 15
42. 25% of 48 = 12
43. 75% of $3/4 = 9/16$
44. 80% of 15% of $1,000 = 0.8(150) = 120$
45. 45% of $(9/10 \times 0.2) = 0.45(0.18) = 0.081$
46. 50% more than $50 = 1.5(50) = 75$
47. 10% more than $25 = 1.1(25) = 27.5$
48. 25% sale off an item that starts at $40 = 0.75(40) = 30$
49. A student scores 87% on a test of 200 questions. He got wrong = $0.13(200) = 26$
50. A car starts at 50 mph, increases its speed by 10% and then decreases its speed by 10%. It ends at = $0.9(1.1(50)) = 0.9(55) = 49.5$
51. 15% less than $90 = 0.85(90) = 76.5$
52. 30% less than $0.0045 = 0.7(0.0045) = 0.00315$
53. 1.2% of $50 = 0.012(50) = 0.6$
54. 2.5% of $10.1 = 0.025(10.1) = 0.2525$
55. A class of 40 students is 60% boys and among the boys 50% play soccer. The number of non-soccer playing boys is = $0.5(0.6(40)) = 12$
56. 10% of the sale price of a house is commission paid to the real estate agent. A house sells for $250,000. The real estate agent receives = $25,000
57. 36.6% of 1000 = 366
58. 50% more than 10% less than $50 = 1.5(0.9(50)) = 67.5$
59. 20% less than 25% more than $40 = 0.8(1.25(40)) = 40$
60. 100% of 100 = 100

Section 4: Roots, Scientific Notation

61. $4^2 = 16$
62. $11^2 = 121$
63. $105.23^0 = 1$
64. $0^{13} = 0$
65. $2^2 + 3^3 = 4+27 = 31$
66. $10^5 / 10^2 = 10^{(5-2)} = 10^3 = 1000$
67. $(5^2)^2 \times 5^{11} = 5^{2 \times 2} \times 5^{11} = 5^4 \times 5^{11} = 5^{(4+11)} = 5^{15}$
68. $2^3 \times 4^3 = (2 \times 4)^3 = 8^3 = 512$
69. $1^5 + 2^4 + 3^3 = 1 + 16 + 27 = 44$
70. $\sqrt{169} = 13$
71. $\sqrt{4} + \sqrt{16} = 2 + 4 = 6$
72. $\sqrt{5} \times \sqrt{5} = \sqrt{(5 \times 5)} = \sqrt{25} = 5$
73. $\sqrt{144} - \sqrt{25} = 12 - 5 = 7$
74. $\sqrt{32} = \sqrt{(16 \times 2)} = \sqrt{16} \times \sqrt{2} = 4\sqrt{2}$
75. $\sqrt{50} = \sqrt{(25 \times 2)} = \sqrt{25} \times \sqrt{2} = 5\sqrt{2}$
76. $\sqrt{(4/9)} = \sqrt{4} / \sqrt{9} = 2/3$
77. $3.2 \times 10^4 + 3.2 \times 10^4 = 6.4 \times 10^4$
78. $2 \times 10^2 \times (4 \times 10^6)^2 = 2 \times 10^2 \times 16 \times 10^{12} = 32 \times 10^{14} = 3.2 \times 10^{15}$
79. $1.5 \times 10^5 - 9.8 \times 10^4 = 15 \times 10^4 - 9.8 \times 10^4 = 5.2 \times 10^4$
80. $\sqrt{(2.5 \times 10^9)} = \sqrt{(25 \times 10^8)} = \sqrt{25} \times \sqrt{10^8} = 5 \times 10^4$

Section 5: Estimation

(for these questions, give yourself credit for a right answer if you were within 10-20% of the solution presented here)

81. $25.113 + 24.98 \approx 25 + 25 = 50$
82. $30.013 + 0.995 \approx 30 + 1 = 31$
83. $119.155 - 247.03 \approx 120 - 250 = -130$
84. $4.814 \times 9.21 \approx 5 \times 9 = 45$
85. $1.0311 \times 483.3 \approx 1 \times 484 = 484$
86. $1021.4 / 511.1 \approx 1000 / 500 = 2$
87. $8.33332 / 29.4 \approx 8 / 29$
88. 31.14% of $99.8 \approx 0.3(100) = 30$
89. 91.66% more than $1044 \approx 2(1000) = 2000$
90. 12.555% less than $94.3 \approx 0.88(100) = 88$
91. $4.1^2 \approx 16$
92. $5^{2.01} \approx 25$
93. $2^{3.8} \approx$ between 8 and 16, closer to 16
94. $\sqrt{98} \approx$ a little less than 10
95. $\sqrt{160} \approx$ between 12 and 13, closer to 13
96. 96. $\sqrt{38} + \sqrt{45} \approx 6.1 + 6.9 = 13$
97. 97. $4.9(2.012^2 + \sqrt{24}) \approx 5(4+5) = 45$
98. 98. $(51/99) + (31.22/63.998) \approx (50/100)+(32/64)=1$
99. 99. $6.022 \times 10^{23} + 9.88 \times 10^{22} \approx 6 \times 10^{23} + 1 \times 10^{23} = 7 \times 10^{23}$
100. $\sqrt{(6 \times 10^{19})} + [9.1 \times 10^4]^2 \approx \sqrt{(60 \times 10^{18})} + 81 \times 10^8 = 7.8 \times 10^9 + 8.1 \times 10^9 = 15.9 \times 10^9 = 1.59 \times 10^{10}$

D. ANALYSIS

Your performance on the assessment earlier should guide your work going forward.

Section 1: Basic Operations

Number Correct

20. Excellent! You have a strong foundation in basic operations and don't have anything to worry about on Test Day.
17-19. Good job, but be careful of careless errors. You may be tempted to dismiss a couple of mistakes, thinking "Oh I was just going too fast. That was sloppy and I would never do that on the real MCAT." But remember, practice makes permanent. If you practice moving too quickly and making sloppy mistakes, then you're more likely to perform that way on Test Day.
12-16. You hit some real issues here. This is a major concern, as the basics of arithmetic manipulation are the foundation of all the numbers you'll see on Test Day. You should work your way through the remaining math chapters, and complete all review problems and the final exam at the back of the book.
<12. You're going to need foundational work beyond the scope of this MCAT review book. You should pick up a review book for adult learners to help them regain the basic comfort with operations that is normally developed early on. Start now! If you neglect this foundational work, you will have a very tough time managing big parts of the science sections on the MCAT.

Section 2: Fractions

20. Excellent! You have a strong foundation in fractions and don't have anything to worry about on Test Day.
17-19. Good job, but be careful of careless errors. You may be tempted to dismiss a couple of mistakes, thinking "Oh I was just going too fast. That was sloppy and I would never do that on the real MCAT." But remember, practice makes permanent. If you practice moving too quickly and making sloppy mistakes, then you're more likely to perform that way on Test Day.
12-16. You hit some real issues here. This is a concern, as manipulating fractions is very common, especially in the chemical foundations section (think stoichiometry or the ideal gas law). You should work your way through the remaining math chapters, and complete all review problems and the final exam at the back of the book.
<12. You're going to need foundational work beyond the scope of this MCAT review book. You should pick up a review book for adult learners to help them regain the basic comfort with fractions that is normally developed early on. Start now! If you neglect this foundational work, you will have a very tough time managing big parts of the science sections on the MCAT.

Section 3: Percentages

20. Excellent! You have a strong foundation in percentages and don't have anything to worry about on Test Day.
17-19. Good job, but be careful of careless errors. You may be tempted to dismiss a couple of mistakes, thinking "Oh I was just going too fast. That was sloppy and I would never do that on the real MCAT." But remember, practice makes permanent. If you practice moving too quickly and making sloppy mistakes, then you're more likely to perform that way on Test Day.
12-16. You hit some real issues here. This is a concern, as manipulating percentages is very common, especially in the social sciences section (most research data is presented in percentages at some point). You should work your way through the remaining math chapters, and complete all review problems and the final exam at the back of the book.
<12. You're going to need foundational work beyond the scope of this MCAT review book. You should pick up a review book on percentages – something that will build up the foundations (think "Percentages for Dummies" or something similar). Start now! If you neglect this foundational work, you will have a very tough time managing big parts of the science sections on the MCAT.

Section 4: Roots, Scientific Notation

20. Excellent! You have a strong foundation in roots and exponents and don't have anything to worry about on Test Day.
17-19. Good job, but be careful of careless errors. You may be tempted to dismiss a couple of mistakes, thinking "Oh I was just going too fast. That was sloppy and I would never do that on the real MCAT." But remember, practice makes permanent. If you practice moving too quickly and making sloppy mistakes, then you're more likely to perform that way on Test Day.
12-16. You hit some real issues here. This is a concern, as manipulating roots, exponents, and *especially* scientific notation is very common throughout all three science sections. You should work your way through the remaining math chapters, and

complete all review problems and the final exam at the back of the book.

<12. You're going to need review work beyond the scope of this MCAT review book. You should pick up an additional math review book that covers these operations. Start now! If you neglect this foundational work, you will have a very tough time managing big parts of the science sections on the MCAT.

Section 5: Estimation

20. Excellent! You did a great job estimating and don't have anything to worry about on Test Day.

17-19. Good job, but be careful of careless errors. You may be tempted to dismiss a couple of mistakes, thinking "Oh I was just going too fast. That was sloppy and I would never do that on the real MCAT." But remember, practice makes permanent. If you practice moving too quickly and making sloppy mistakes, then you're more likely to perform that way on Test Day.

12-16. You hit some real issues here. This is a concern, as estimating your calculations is going to be the only way to get through the test in time. You should work your way through the remaining math chapters, and complete all review problems and the final exam at the back of the book.

<12. You'll need to get in *a lot* of practice with your estimating skills. Re-take this assessment a few times, work your way through the estimation part of the following chapters more than once, and do the same with the final exam. Try estimating as you go through everyday life. For example, when going grocery shopping, try keeping a running estimate of your bill in your head. When you check out, see how close your estimate was to the actual bill.

Overall Performance

90-100. Good job. Your arithmetic skills are solid. You can likely skip the arithmetic chapter, or perhaps just skip to the review problems at the end of that chapter.

75-89. You got a big majority of the questions correct, but still hit enough trouble that you'll want to invest in a thorough review. Work your way through all of the math chapters, carefully review all of the questions at the end of the chapters, and complete the final exam at the end of the book. Then come back and re-do this assessment.

50-74. You hit some real trouble on this assessment. You'll need to work your way through the math chapters very slowly and carefully. Read them over more than once, make study sheets, and complete the questions at the end of the chapter at least twice. Then take the final, review it, and re-take the final again a week later. Finally, come back and re-take this assessment to make sure you've built up your skills to the point you need for Test Day.

<50. You're going to need heavy-duty review to get yourself ready for the MCAT, including work beyond this prep book. Consider picking up additional math review books to build up your fundamentals.

CHAPTER 17
ASSESSMENT: ALGEBRA AND TRIGONOMETRY

A. INTRODUCTION

Many of us have been using a calculator so long that we've forgotten the fundamentals. Unfortunately, the MCAT is not going to cut us any slack here. The test will expect us to be able to do basic trig, logs, and algebra with nothing more advanced than a pencil and paper. Complete the following assessment exam if you are concerned about your math fundamentals

B. ASSESSMENT EXAM

Section 1: Probability and statistics

1. A drawer contains 4 black socks and 10 white socks. What are the odds of drawing out a white sock?
2. A drawer contains 4 black socks and 10 white socks. What are the odds of drawing out two white socks in a row?
3. A fair coin is tossed three times. What are the odds of getting three heads in a row?
4. A fair coin is tossed four times. What are the odds of getting at least one tails?
5. What are the odds of rolling two six-sided dice and getting at least one six?

Questions 6-13 use this data set:

$\{1, 2, 3, 3, 3, 4, 6, 7, 7, 7, 11, 45\}$

6. What is the mode(s) of the set?
7. What is the mean of the set?
8. What is the median of the set?
9. What is the range of the set?
10. If the 45 were replaced with a 4, what would happen to the standard deviation of the set?
11. If the 6 were replaced with a 72, what would happen to the standard deviation of the set?
12. What is the interquartile range of the set?
13. Which data point(s) is/are outlier(s)?

Questions 14-19 use this data set:

$\{5, 5.1, 5.2, 5.3, 5.4, 5.5, 5.6\}$

14. What is the mode(s) of the set?
15. What is the mean of the set?
16. What is the median of the set?
17. What is the range of the set?
18. What is the interquartile range of the set?
19. Which data point(s) is/are outlier(s)?

20. For a given couple's genetic makeup, there is a 1/2 chance that any son will be color blind and a 1/4 chance that any daughter will be colorblind. If the couple has two children, what are the odds that they will have a colorblind son and a color

blind daughter?

Section 2: Manipulating equations

21. Isolate d: $v_f^2 = v_i^2 + 2ad$
22. Isolate R: $PV = nRT$
23. Solve for x: $2x/3 + 5 = 5x$
24. Solve for x: $4x/5 = 2/3x$
25. Solve for x: $(5/x) + 10 = 14$
26. Solve for x+y: $5x - 10 = 5 - 5y$
27. Solve for x: $5 / x^2 = 1 / 5$
28. Solve for x: $(\sin 30°)/x = 5$
29. Solve for x:
    a. $x + y = 15$
    b. $3y/2 = 21$
30. Solve for x:
    a. $4x = 3y$
    b. $x = 15 - 3y$
31. Solve for x:
    a. $x(x + 2y) = 9 - y$
    b. $(2y/3) + 1 = 15/9$
32. Solve for v_f / v_i
    a. $v_f^2 = v_i^2 + 2ad$
    b. A car starts at 10 m/s and accelerates at 5 m/s² for 10m.
33. Find P_i / P_f
    a. $PV = nRT$
    b. A sample of gas has its volume cut in half and its temperature also cut in half.
34. Find V_i / V_f
    a. $PV = nRT$
    b. A sample of gas has its pressure tripled and its temperature doubled.
35. Find T_i / T_f
    a. $PV = nRT$
    b. A sample of gas has its pressure and volume both doubled.
36. Find F_i / F_f
    a. $F = GMm / r^2$
    b. Mass 1 is doubled and the distance between the masses is tripled.
37. Find F_i / F_f
    a. $F = GMm / r^2$
    b. Both masses are doubled and the distance between the masses is halved.
38. Find F_i / F_f

a. $F = kQq / r^2$
b. One charge is doubled, the other is halved, and the distance between the charges is doubled.

39. If a sample of gas has the pressure and temperature held constant, but the volume doubles, then what must be true:
   a. (Use $PV = nRT$)
40. Solve for x: $2 \log x = 10$

Section 3: Logarithms

Note: if no base is indicated, then it is the common log, $\log_{10}$

41. $\log_5 5 =$
42. $\log 1 =$
43. $\ln e =$
44. $2.3 \times \log_{10} e \approx$
45. $\log (3 \times 10^4) \approx$
46. $\log (X / Y) =$
47. $\log (1 / Q) =$
48. $\log 100 =$
49. $\log 0.001 =$
50. $\log 10 =$
51. $\log (5 \times 10^5) \approx$
52. $-\log (2.5 \times 10^{-15}) \approx$
53. $-\log (10^5) \approx$
54. $-\log (8 \times 10^{-2}) \approx$
55. $\log 1/100 =$
56. $\log X^Y =$
57. $\log 10^6 - \log 100,000 =$
58. $\log 50 + \log 2 =$
59. $\log 4,000 - \log 40 =$
60. $2 \times \log (\sqrt{10}) =$

Section 4: Trig

61. $\sin 0° =$
62. $\cos 30° =$
63. $\tan 45° =$
64. $\sin 60° =$
65. $\cos 90° =$
66. $\tan 180° =$
67. $\sin 30° =$
68. $\cos 45° =$
69. $\tan 60° =$
70. $\sin^{-1} 1/2 =$
71. $\cos^{-1} 1/2 =$
72. $\tan^{-1} 1 =$
73. $\sin^{-1} \sqrt{3} / 2 =$
74. $\cos^{-1} 0 =$
75. $\tan^{-1} \sqrt{3} =$
76. The hypotenuse of a 30-60-90 triangle is 4.2 meters long. The shorter leg is:
77. One leg of a 45-45-90 triangle is 20 meters long. The other leg is:
78. The longer leg of a 30-60-90 triangle is $\sqrt{6}$ meters long. The shorter leg is:

79. The hypotenuse of a 45-45-90 triangle is $6\sqrt{2}$ meters long. The sum of the lengths of the legs is:
80. $(\sin 30°)^2 + (\cos 30°)^2 =$

Section 5: Units

Note: for the following, use the following conversion factors:

1 yard = 3 feet = 36 inches
1 inch = 2.5 cm
1 Calorie = 1000 calories = 4184 J
1 pound (lb) = 4.45 N

81. 15.2 cm in mm =
82. 1,500 μJ in kJ =
83. 3.2 Gg in kg =
84. 0.0041 Ms in ms =
85. 2 m in inches =
86. 25 cm in inches =
87. A garden is designed to be 2 yards long and 6 yards wide. How many square feet is this:
88. An apartment is advertised as being 1881 square feet. This is how many square yards:
89. A meal is advertised as containing 100 Calories. How many joules is this:
90. To boil a certain cup of water will take 836800 J of energy. How many calories is this:
91. On earth, a person's weight is 100 pounds. On the moon, the person's weight in Newtons would be (approximate the gravitational force on the Moon as 1/5 that of Earth):
92. A bag of building materials weighs 8900 N. How many pounds is this:
93. An experiment is carried out at 298K. This is how many °C?
94. The boiling point of water in F, °C, and K is:
95. A car is able to drive 350 miles on a single tank of gas and the tank holds 15 gallons. How many miles per gallon does the car get:
96. A recipe calls for 10 g of flour and 20 g of sugar. A cook wishes to make 100 portions of this recipe. Flour is sold in 500g bags and sugar is sold in 250 g bags. The minimum number of bags of flour and sugar needed is:
97. 1 mile is 1.6 km and 1 gallon is 3.8 L. A car gets 40 miles per gallon. How many km per liter is this?
98. A butterfly flies at 24 inches a second. How many meters per minute is this?
99. The average adult human needs to consume 2000 Calories per day to maintain weight. How many joules per minute is this?
100. The freezing point of water in F, °C, and K is:

C. ANSWER KEY

Section 1: Probability and statistics

A drawer contains 4 black socks and 10 white socks. What are the odds of drawing out a white sock?

10 / 14

A drawer contains 4 black socks and 10 white socks. What are the odds of drawing out two white socks in a row?

$10/14 \times 9/13 = 90 / 182 = 45 / 91$

A fair coin is tossed three times. What are the odds of getting three heads in a row?

$1/2 \times 1/2 \times 1/2 = 1/8$

A fair coin is tossed four times. What are the odds of getting at least one tails?

No tails at all:

$1/2 \times 1/2 \times 1/2 \times 1/2 = 1/16$

At least one tails = $1 - 1/16 = 15/16$.

What are the odds of rolling two six-sided dice and getting at least one six?

$1/6 + 1/6 - 1/36 = 11/36$

Questions 6-13 use this data set:

{1, 2, 3, 3, 3, 4, 6, 7, 7, 7, 11, 45}

What is the mode(s) of the set?

3 and 7

What is the mean of the set?

8.25

What is the median of the set?

$(4+6)/2 = 5$

What is the range of the set?

$45 - 1 = 44$

If the 45 were replaced with a 4, what would happen to the standard deviation of the set?

Decreased standard deviation

If the 6 were replaced with a 72, what would happen to the standard deviation of the set?

An increased standard deviation

What is the interquartile range of the set?

75th percentile = 7

25th percentile = 3

IR = 7-3 = 4

Which data point(s) is/are outlier(s)?

The only outlier is the 45

Questions 14-19 use this data set:

{5, 5.1, 5.2, 5.3, 5.4, 5.5, 5.6}

What is the mode(s) of the set?

No mode

What is the mean of the set?

5.3

What is the median of the set?

5.3

What is the range of the set?

$5.6 - 5 = 0.6$

What is the interquartile range of the set?

IR = 5.5-5.1 = 0.4

Which data point(s) is/are outlier(s)?

No outliers

For a given couple's genetic makeup, there is a 1/2 chance that any son will be colorblind and a 1/4 chance that any daughter will be colorblind. If the couple has two children, what are the odds that they will have a colorblind son and a colorblind daughter?

Two ways for this outcome:

The first child is a son (1/2) who is colorblind (1/2) and the second child is a daughter (1/2) who is color blind (1/4) = $1/2 \times 1/2 \times 1/2 \times 1/4 = 1/32$

The first child is a daughter (1/2) who is colorblind (1/4) and the second child is a son (1/2) who is color blind (1/2) = $1/2 \times 1/4 \times 1/2 \times 1/2 = 1/32$

$1/32 + 1/32 = 1/16$

Section 2: Manipulating equations

Isolate d: $v_f^2 = v_i^2 + 2ad$

$d = (v_f^2 - v_i^2)/2a$

Isolate R: $PV = nRT$

$R = PV/nT$

Solve for x: $2x/3 + 5 = 5x$

$2x + 15 = 15x$

$15 = 13x$

$x = 15/13$

Solve for x: $4x/5 = 2/3x$

Cross multiply:

$12x^2 = 10$

$x^2 = 10/12 = 5/6$

$x = \sqrt{(5/6)}$

Solve for x: $(5/x) + 10 = 14$

$5/x = 4$

$4x = 5$

$x = 5/4$

Solve for x+y: $5x - 10 = 5 - 5y$

$5x + 5y - 10 = 5$

$5x + 5y = 15$

$x + y = 3$

Solve for x: $5 / x^2 = 1 / 5$

Cross multiply:

$x^2 = 25$

$x = 5$

Solve for x: $(\sin 30°)/x = 5$

$(1/2)/x = 5$

$1/2 = 5x$

$x = 1/10$

Solve for x:

$x + y = 15$

$3y/2 = 21$

$3y = 42$

$y = 14$

$x + 14 = 15$

$x = 1$

Solve for x:

$4x = 3y$

$x = 15 - 3y$

$4(15 - 3y) = 3y$

$60 - 12y = 3y$

$60 = 15y$

$y = 4$

$4x - 3(4)$

$x = 3$

Solve for x:

$x(x + 2y) = 9 - y$

$(2y/3) + 1 = 15/9$

$2y/3 = 15/9 - 1$

$2y/3 = 15/9 - 9/9$

$2y/3 = 6/9 = 2/3$

$2y = 2$

$y = 1$

$x(x + 2(1)) = 9 - 1$

$x(x+2) = 8$

$x^2 + 2x - 8 = 0$

$(x+4)(x-2) = 0$

$x = 2$ or -4

Solve for v_f / v_i

$v_f^2 = v_i^2 + 2ad$

A car starts at 10 m/s and accelerates at 5 m/s² for 10m.

$v_f^2 = (10)^2 + 2(5)(10) = 100 + 100$

$v_f = \sqrt{200}$

$v_f / v_i = \sqrt{200} / 10 = \sqrt{200} / \sqrt{100} = \sqrt{(200/100)} = \sqrt{2} \approx 1.4$

Find P_i / P_f

$PV = nRT$

A sample of gas has the volume cut in half and the temperature also cut in half.

$V_f = 0.5V_i$

$T_f = 0.5T_i$

$P_i / P_f = (nRT_i / V_i) / (nRT_f / V_f)$

$= (T_i / V_i) / (0.5T_i / 0.5V_i)$

$= (T_i / V_i) \times (0.5V_i / 0.5T_i)$

$= 0.5 / 0.5 = 1$

Find V_i / V_f

$PV = nRT$

A sample of gas has the pressure tripled and the temperature doubled.

$P_f = 3P_i$

$T_f = 2T_i$

$V_i / V_f = (nRT_i / P_i) / (nRT_f / P_f)$

$= (T_i / P_i) / (T_f / P_f)$

$= (T_i / P_i) / (2T_i / 3P_i)$

$= (T_i / P_i) \times (2P_i / 3T_i)$

$= 2/3$

Find T_i / T_f

$PV = nRT$

A sample of gas has the pressure and volume both doubled.

Doubling both P and V will quadruple the left side of the equation. To maintain the equation the right side must also quadruple. So T_f is four times T_i

$T_i / T_f = 1/4$

Find F_i / F_f

$F = GMm / r^2$

Mass 1 is doubled and the distance between the masses is tripled.

Doubling the mass would double the force. Tripling the radius will cut the force by 1/9. So the new force is 2/9 of the old force:

$F_i / F_f = 9/2$

Find F_i / F_f

$F = GMm / r^2$

Both masses are doubled and the distance between the masses is halved.

$M_f = 2M_i$

$m_f = 2m_i$

$r_f = 2r_i$

$F_i / F_f = (GM_im_i / r_i^2) / (GM_fm_f / r_f^2)$

$= (M_im_i / r_i^2) / (M_fm_f / r_f^2)$

$= (M_im_i / r_i^2) / (2M_i2m_i / [2r_i]^2)$

$= (M_im_i / r_i^2) \times (4r_i^2 / 2M_i2m_i)$

$= (1 / 1) \times (4 / 2 \times 2)$

$= 1$

Find F_i / F_f

$F = kQq / r^2$

One charge is doubled, the other is halved, and the distance between the charges is doubled.

Doubling one charge, Q, and halving the other charge, q, will cancel each other out. So the only change is doubling the distance, which will cut the force by a quarter:

$F_i / F_f = 4/1$

If a sample of gas has the pressure and temperature held constant, but the volume doubles, then what must be true:

(Use $PV = nRT$)

If volume doubles, the left side of the equation doubles. To maintain the equality, the right side must also double. This means n doubles.

Solve for x: $2 \log x = 10$

$\log x = 5$

$x = 10^5$

Section 3: Logarithms

Note: if no base is indicated, then it is the common log, $\log_{10}$

$\log_5 5 = 1$

$\log 1 = 0$

$\ln e = 1$

$2.3 \times \log_{10} e \approx 1$

$\log (3 \times 10^4) \approx \log 3 + \log 10^4 \approx 0.5 + 4 = 4.5$

$\log (X / Y) = \log X - \log Y$

$\log (1 / Q) = -\log Q$

$\log 100 = 2$

$\log 0.001 = -3$

$\log 10 = 1$

$\log (5 \times 10^5) \approx \log 5 + \log 10^5 = 0.7 + 5 = 5.7$

$-\log (2.5 \times 10^{-15}) \approx 15 - \log 2.5 = 14.7$

$-\log (10^5) = -5$

$-\log (8 \times 10^{-2}) \approx 2 - \log 8 \approx 1.2$

$\log 1/100 = \log 10^{-2} = -2$

$\log X^Y = Y \log X$

$\log 10^6 - \log 100,000 = 6 - 5 = 1$

$\log 50 + \log 2 = \log (50 \times 2) = 2$

$\log 4,000 - \log 40 = \log (4000 / 40) = 2$

$2 \times \log (\sqrt{10}) = \log (\sqrt{10})^2 = \log 10 = 1$

Section 4: Trig

$\sin 0° = 0$

$\cos 30° = \sqrt{3} / 2$

$\tan 45° = 1$

$\sin 60° = \sqrt{3} / 2$

$\cos 90° = 0$

$\tan 180° = 0$

$\sin 30° = 1/2$

$\cos 45° = \sqrt{2} / 2$

$\tan 60° = \sqrt{3}$

$\sin^{-1} 1/2 = 30°$

$\cos^{-1} 1/2 = 60°$

$\tan^{-1} 1 = 45°$

$\sin^{-1} \sqrt{3} / 2 = 60°$

$\cos^{-1} 0 = 90°$

$\tan^{-1} \sqrt{3} = 60°$

The hypotenuse of a 30-60-90 triangle is 4.2 meters long. The shorter leg is: 2.1 meters

One leg of a 45-45-90 triangle is 20 meters long. The other leg is: 20 meters

The longer leg of a 30-60-90 triangle is $\sqrt{6}$ meters long. The shorter leg is: $\sqrt{6} / \sqrt{3} = \sqrt{(6/3)} = \sqrt{2}$

The hypotenuse of a 45-45-90 triangle is $6\sqrt{2}$ meters long. The sum of the lengths of the legs is: $6+6 = 12$

$(\sin 30°)^2 + (\cos 30°)^2 = 1$

Section 5: Units

Note: for the following, use the following conversion factors:

> 1 yard = 3 feet = 36 inches
> 1 inch = 2.5 cm
> 1 Calorie = 1000 calories = 4184 J
> 1 pound (lb) = 4.45 N

15.2 cm in mm = 152

1,500 μJ in kJ = 1500×10^{-6} J x 1 kJ / 10^3 J = 1500 x 10-9 kJ = 1.5×10^{-6} kJ

3.2 Gg in kg − 3.2×10^3 kg

0.0041 Ms in ms = 4.1×10^{-3} Ms x 10^6s / 1 Ms x 10^3 ms / 1 s = 4.1×10^6 ms

2 m in inches = 200 cm x 1 in / 2.5cm = 80 in

25 cm in inches = 25cm x 1 in / 2.5cm = 10 in

A garden is designed to be 2 yards long and 6 yards wide. How many square feet is this:
> 6 feet x 18 feet = 108 ft²

An apartment is advertised as being 1881 square feet. This is how many square yards:
> 1881 ft² x 1 yd / 3 ft x 1 yd / 3 ft = 1881 ft² x 1 yd² / 9 ft² = 209 yd²

A meal is advertised as containing 100 Calories. How many joules is this:
> 100 Calories x 4184 J / 1 Cal = 418400 J = 4.184×10^5 J

To boil a certain cup of water will take 836800 J of energy. How many calories is this:
> 836800 J x 1 cal / 4.184 J = 200000 cal = 2 x 10^5 cal

On earth, a person's weight is 100 pounds. On the moon, the person's weight in Newtons would be (approximate the gravitational force on the Moon as 1/5 that of Earth):
> 100 pounds x 4.45N / 1 lb = 445 N
> 445 N_{EARTH} x 1/5 = 89 N_{MOON}

A bag of building materials weighs 8900 N. How many pounds is this:
> 8900 N x 1 lb / 4.45 N = 2000 lb

An experiment is carried out at 298K. This is how many °C?
> 25°C

The boiling point of water in F, °C, and K is:
> 212F, 100°C, 373K

A car is able to drive 350 miles on a single tank of gas and the tank holds 15 gallons. How many miles per gallon does the car get:
> 350 mi/tank x tank/15gal = 350/15 mi/gal = 70/3 = 23 1/3 mpg

A recipe calls for 10 g of flour and 20 g of sugar. A cook wishes to make 100 portions of this recipe. Flour is sold in 500g bags and sugar is sold in 250 g bags. The minimum number of bags of flour and sugar needed is:
> 10g flour x 100 portions = 1000 g flour
> 20g sugar x 100 portions = 2000g sugar
> 1000g flour / 500g = 2 bags
> 2000g sugar / 250g = 8 bags

1 mile is 1.6 km and 1 gallon is 3.8 L. A car gets 40 miles per gallon. How many km per liter is this?
> 40 mi/gal x 1.6km / 1mi x 1 gal/38L = 10x1.6/38 km/L = 16/38 = 8/19 km/L

A butterfly flies at 24 inches a second. How many meters per minute is this?
> 24 in /sec x 60sec/1min x 2.5cm/1in x 1m/100cm = 24x60x2.5 / 100 = 36 m/min

The average adult human needs to consume 2000 Calories per day to maintain weight. How many joules per minute is this?
> 2000 Cal/day x 4184 J / 1 Cal x 1 day / 24 hr x 1 hr / 60 min = 2000x4184 / 24 x 60 = 5811.1 J/min

The freezing point is: 32F, 0°C, 273K

D. ANALYSIS

Your performance on the assessment earlier should guide your work going forward.

Section 1: Probability and statistics

Number Correct

20. Excellent! You've got a strong foundation and don't have anything to worry about on Test Day.

17-19. Good job, but be careful of careless errors. You may be tempted to dismiss a couple of mistakes, thinking "Oh I was just going too fast. That was sloppy and I would never do that on the real MCAT." But remember, practice makes permanent. If you practice moving too quickly and making sloppy mistakes, then you're more likely to perform that way on Test Day.

12-16. You hit some real issues here. This is a major concern, as statistics and probability will show up frequently in both the biology (think Punnett squares) and psychology section. You should work your way through the remaining math chapters, and complete all review problems and the final exam at the back of the book.

>12. You're going to need foundational work beyond the scope of this MCAT review book. You should pick up a review book on basic probability and stats. Start now! If you neglect this foundational work, you will have a very tough time managing big parts of the science sections on the MCAT.

Section 2: Manipulating equations

20. Excellent! You don't have anything to worry about on Test Day.

17-19. Good job, but be careful of careless errors. You may be tempted to dismiss a couple of mistakes, thinking "Oh I was just going too fast. That was sloppy and I would never do that on the real MCAT." But remember, practice makes permanent. If you practice moving too quickly and making sloppy mistakes, then you're more likely to perform that way on Test Day.

12-16. You hit some real issues here. This is a concern, as manipulating equations is very common, especially in the chemical foundations section. You should work your way through the remaining math chapters, and complete all review problems and the final exam at the back of the book.

>12. You're going to need foundational work beyond the scope of this MCAT review book. You should pick up an algebra basics book right away. Start now! If you neglect this foundational work, you will have a very tough time managing big parts of the science sections on the MCAT.

Section 3: Logarithms

20. Excellent! You don't have anything to worry about on Test Day.

17-19. Good job, but be careful of careless errors. You may be tempted to dismiss a couple of mistakes, thinking "Oh I was just going too fast. That was sloppy and I would never do that on the real MCAT." But remember, practice makes permanent. If you practice moving too quickly and making sloppy mistakes, then you're more likely to perform that way on Test Day.

12-16. You hit some real issues here. This is a concern, since log scales show up very frequently in the Chemical Foundations section, and to a lesser extent in the Biological Foundations section. You should work your way through the remaining math chapters, and complete all review problems and the final exam at the back of the book.

>12. You're going to need foundational work beyond the scope of this MCAT review book. Pick up a review book on Algebra II basics right away. Start now! If you neglect this foundational work, you will have a very tough time managing big parts of the science sections on the MCAT.

Section 4: Trig

20. Excellent! You don't have anything to worry about on Test Day.

17-19. Good job, but be careful of careless errors. You may be tempted to dismiss a couple of mistakes, thinking "Oh I was just going too fast. That was sloppy and I would never do that on the real MCAT." But remember, practice makes permanent. If you practice moving too quickly and making sloppy mistakes, then you're more likely to perform that way on Test Day.

12-16. You hit some real issues here. This is a concern, as basic trig functions are going to show up almost any time you have to deal with vectors in the physical sciences section. You should work your way through the remaining math chapters, and complete all review problems and the final exam at the back of the book.

>12. You're going to need review work beyond the scope of this MCAT review book. You should pick up an additional math review book that covers these operations. Start now! If you neglect this foundational work, you will have a very tough time managing big parts of the science sections on the MCAT.

Section 5: Units

20. Excellent! You did a great job and don't have anything to worry about on Test Day.

17-19. Good job, but be careful of careless errors. You may be tempted to dismiss a couple of mistakes, thinking "Oh I was just going too fast. That was sloppy and I would never do that on the real MCAT." But remember, practice makes permanent. If you practice moving too quickly and making sloppy mistakes, then you're more likely to perform that way on Test Day.

12-16. You hit some real issues here. Units are one of the most important foundations of your math work, so this deserve *a lot* of extra attention. You should work your way through the remaining math chapters, and complete all review problems and the final exam at the back of the book.

>12. You'll need to get in a lot of practice with your units and unit conversion skills. Re-take this assessment a few times, work your way through the estimation part of the following chapters more than once, and do the same with the final exam.

Overall Performance

90-100. Good job. Your math skills are solid. You can likely skip the algebra and trig chapter, or perhaps just skip to the review problems at the end of that chapter.

75-89. You got a big majority of the questions correct, but still hit enough trouble that you'll want to invest in a thorough review. Work your way through all of the math chapters, carefully review all of the questions at the end of the chapters, and complete the final exam at the end of the book. Then come back and re-do this assessment.

50-74. You hit some real trouble on this assessment. You'll need to work your way through the math chapters very slowly and carefully. Read them over more than once, make study sheets, and complete the questions at the end of the chapter at least twice. Then take the final, review it, and re-take the final again a week later. Finally, come back and re-take this assessment to make sure you've built up your skills to the point you need for Test Day.

<50. You're going to need heavy-duty review to get yourself ready for the MCAT, including work beyond this prep book. Consider picking up additional math review books to build up your fundamentals.

SECTION 6
MATH REVIEW

The following chapters will walk you through the various aspects of math and data interpretation needed on the MCAT. The most important one is the last one on experimental design, as these concepts are important for all three science sections of the test. For the remaining chapters, use your performance on the assessment chapters to guide your work.

This page intentionally left blank.

CHAPTER 18
ARITHMETIC OPERATIONS

A. INTRODUCTION

The MCAT will expect you to be familiar with the foundational math operations covered in a typical pre-algebra level (ratios, percents, etc.) and then to apply those operations in a science context. If you're struggling with foundational pre-algebra math operations, you should pick up a math review book to cover those basics – something like an SAT or GRE review book would serve well here.

B. ESTIMATION

The MCAT will reward an ability to get close to the right answer much more than getting the exact right answer, simply because you'll get full credit in less time. When the answer choices are numbers they are almost always spread out quite a bit. This gives us plenty of wiggle room to estimate quite a bit.

When doing estimation, you should generally try to make your estimations cancel each other out. So for example, if you were trying to estimate:

403.7 x 3.9 =

Here, if you round the 403.7 down to 400, you should round the 3.9 up to 4. That way, the effect of those roundings will cancel each other out:

403.7 x 3.9 ≈ 400 x 4 ≈ 1600

5021 x 312 / 1599

Here, if we want to round 5021 and 312 down to 5000 and 300, we should also round 1599 down to 1500. This gives us:

5021 x 312 / 1599 ≈ 5000 x 300 / 1500 ≈ 1500000 / 1500 ≈ 1000

Notice if, instead, we rounded the 1599 up to 1600 we would get:

5000 x 300 / 1600 = 937.5

This is almost twice as far from the right answer as our first estimate:

5021 x 312 / 1599 = 979.7

Before doing any rounding, you should also check the answer choices to see how far apart they are.

C. PROBABILITY AND STATISTICS

The statistics you will see on the MCAT primarily revolve around two concepts: measures of central tendency and measures of variability. Measures of central tendency, such as mean, median, or mode, describe how a data set is clustered around its central data points. Measures of variability such as range and standard deviation tell us how tightly or loosely the data is clustered around those central points.

Mean

The mean is the arithmetic average of a set of data. You calculate the mean by adding up all of the numbers in the set and then dividing by the number of members in the set:

Mean = Sum of the values / Number of values

It is important to remember that the mean is not necessarily a number that's actually in the set. The mean can also be strongly influenced by a single very large or very small value. Consider the following examples:

Ages of people at John's retirement party: 53, 54, 56, 56, 61, 63, 65, 65

Mean = (53+54+56+56+61+63+65+65) / 8 = 473/8 = 59.125

Here, the average age is 56.9, which is not actually a number in the set. Now what if one of the attendees at the retirement part brought his granddaughter to the event?

Ages of people at John's retirement party: 1, 53, 54, 56, 56, 61, 63, 65, 65

Mean = (1+53+54+56+56+61+63+65+65) / 9 = 474/9 = 52.67

Here, a single data point – the one year old child – dragged the mean down to below every other person at the party.

So in the first example, the average age of about 59 was a good description of the people at the party – they were all folks who were right around 60 years old. In the second set, the mean isn't such a good description, because saying, "the average age at the party was in the low 50's" would not be an accurate description. The party consisted of people who were in their 50's to mid'60's. The tendency for the mean to be skewed by a small number of outlying data points often makes the median a better statistic to use.

Median

The median is the number that sits in the middle of a set of data when you arrange all of the numbers in a row. If there's an even number of data points, then the median is the arithmetic average of the two numbers that sit in the middle. Consider the examples from above:

Ages of people at John's retirement party: 53, 54, 56, 56, 61, 63, 65, 65

Here there are 8 data points. So you take the two numbers in the middle and average them:

Ages of people at John's retirement party: ~~53, 54, 56~~, 56, 61, ~~63, 65, 65~~

Median = (56+61) / 2 = 117 / 2 = 58.5

When we add the 1 year old child we had:

Ages of people at John's retirement party: 1, 53, 54, 56, 56, 61, 63, 65, 65

Now there are 9 data points, so only one number sits in the middle:

Ages of people at John's retirement party: ~~1, 53, 54, 56~~, 56, ~~61, 63, 65, 65~~

Median = 56

Notice that these two numbers are much closer together and more accurately reflect the age of the group even when the outlying data point of the 1 year old is considered.

Mode

The mode is the number that appears most frequently in a data set. There can be more than one mode, but if all numbers appear equally often, there is no mode. So for example:

Ages of people at John's retirement party: 1, 53, 54, 56, 56, 61, 63, 65, 65

Both 56 and 65 appear twice, so this is a set with two modes.

By contrast:

Ages of people at John's retirement party: 1, 53, 54, 56, 57, 61, 63, 65, 67

Now every single data point appears once, so there is no mode. One final example:

Ages of children on a little league team: 8, 9, 9, 9, 9, 9, 10, 10, 10, 10, 10, 11, 11, 11, 11, 11

In this set, the modes would be 9, 10, and 11. If the 8 were missing, there would be no mode.

The mode is a useful measure of the "average" of a set when the thing you're analyzing tends to happen very commonly at a certain point, and not very commonly at other times. For example, if you were analyzing the retirement age for police officers, the data set might look something like this:

Retirement age for police officers in a town: 55, 55, 55, 55, 55, 56, 56, 57, 70, 70

Mean: (55+55+55+55+55+56+56+57+70+70) / 10 = 584 / 10 = 58.4
Median: 55, 55, 55, 55, 55, 56, 56, 57, 70, 70 = (55+56) / 2 = 55.5
Mode: 55

Here, the mode is 55 and that seems to be the best description. If you were to ask, "What's the normal or average age for a police officer to retire?" this data set would seem to suggest most police retire at 55.

There are a couple of folks who stayed on for another year or two and then two outliers who retired much older. That drags the average up to 58.4, but that number is misleading since it gives them impression that police officers wait until their late 50's to retire. The median is a better description at 55.5 but again it conveys the idea that what's "normal" or "average" is to wait past 55, whereas the data set much more clearly demonstrates that the typical police officer retires at 55.

Range

The range of a set is a fairly limited tool. You simply take the largest data point and subtract from it the smallest data point. It can give you a sense of how wide the extremes in the set are, but tells you very little beyond that.

Ages of people at John's retirement party: 53, 54, 56, 56, 61, 63, 65, 65

For this set, the range would be: R = 65 − 53 = 12

Ages of people at John's retirement party: 1, 53, 54, 56, 56, 61, 63, 65, 65

For this set, the range would be: R = 65 − 1 = 64

So certainly this measurement tells us that the second set

Standard Deviation

Standard deviation is a measure of how spread out a data set is. The formula to calculate it is:

SD = $\sqrt{[(\Sigma\{x_i - x\}^2) / (n - 1)]}$

Fortunately, you don't have to memorize this equation. All you have to know is that a bigger standard deviation means a set of data is more spread out, and a smaller standard deviation means a data set that is more clustered around the middle.

One relationship you should know is how a standard deviation relates to the normal bell curve distribution:

Normal Curve

Standard Deviation

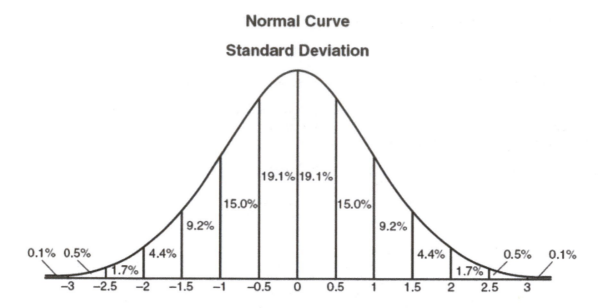

The normal distribution curve is an arrangement of data found in many different areas. If you were to plot out IQ scores, or MCAT scores, or the height of Americans, it would roughly form a normal distribution curve like this.

Here, "0" marks the mean of the data. Then each subsequent denotation is how many standard deviations away from the mean each part of the curve is. For the MCAT, you should know that 68.2% of the data points are going to lie within one standard deviation of the mean, that 95.4% are within two standard deviations, and 99.6% are within three standard deviations.

To put that in terms of the old MCAT scoring scale, in 2013 a score of about 25 was average on the 3 – 45 scale and the standard deviation was about 6 points. That meant that 2/3 of MCAT test takers scored in the range of 19 – 31 and over 95% of test-takers scores in the range of 13 – 37.

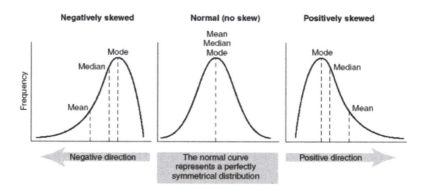

In addition to the normal distribution, the data set may also be skewed in one direction or another. If there are a lot of high-value outliers, the data set will be positively skewed. This pulls the mean up above the mode and median. An example might be income distribution in the US, with a smaller proportion of the population making much more money than is typical. Conversely, the data set might have more low-value outliers, giving a negatively skewed set. Those low-value data points will drag the mean down below the median and mode. An example might be the grades in a typical college biology 101 class: the bulk of students will get A's and B's, but a smaller fraction will bomb the class and those D's and F's will drag the average down.

Finally, a data set may represent two more common clusters of data. Such distribution is called bimodal:

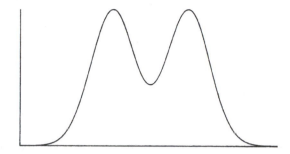

In this data set, there are two modes – two much more common outcomes, hence the name bimodal. An example might be how tall the average 90 year old is. The numbers will be quite different for men and women and so you will end up with two clusters – one for the average man and one for the average woman.

Percentile

A percentile is the percentage of data points falling below a given level. So, for example, imagine a class in which scores on a math test are as follows:

Math test scores: 43, 51, 69, 80, 81, 81, 81, 85, 85, 94

The person who scored a 43 on the test is at the 0th percentile. That is, 0% of the kids in the class scored below that person. The highest performing student – the one who got a score of 94 on the test, is at the 90th percentile. That is, 90 percent of the kids in the class scored below her. Notice that the range for percentiles is 0%ile to 99.9%ile. You cannot score 100th percentile because that mean scoring higher than everyone (even yourself!)

To bring that back to the normal distribution curve, we can say that a data point that is 1 standard deviation above the norm would be the 84th %ile. We can get that number by adding up all of the percentages in the chart that are less than 1 standard deviation above the mean (15+19.1+19.1+15+9.2+4.4+1.7+0.5+0.1)

Inter-Quartile Range

Another way to measure the distribution in a data set is through the inter-quartile range. To do this, a data set is first split into quartiles. Much like finding the median, finding quartiles first involves arranging the data set in order, and then splitting it into fourths. For example, let's say a class of MCAT students gets the following scores on a practice test:

490, 492, 494, 494, 500, 500, 501, 502, 502, 503, 509, 519

To split the group into quarters we get:

490, 492, 494 || 494, 500, 500 || 501, 502, 502 || 503, 509, 519

Those groups are then named the first quartile, second quartile, and so on.

To find the interquartile range, we use the equation: $IR = Q_3 - Q_1$

To get the value of Q_1, we take the highest value in in the first quartile and the lowest value in the second quartile and average them. We do the same with the highest value in the third and lowest value in the fourth quartile to find Q_3. For example:

$Q_1 = (494 + 494) / 2 = 494$
$Q_3 = (502 + 503) / 2 = 502.5$

$IR = 502.5 - 494 = 8.5$

The IR then also gives us a specific mathematical definition of an outlier data point. Any score that is 1.5 IR's below Q_1 or 1.5 IR's above Q_3 is considered an outlier.

Here, the IR was 8.5, so the outliers would be 12.75 points below Q_1 or above Q_3. That is, any score below 481.25 or any score above 515.25 would be considered an outlier data point. In our set above, the only outlier is the one student who got a 519.

Probability

When calculating probability, we must first start with the probability of an individual event, X:

P_X = number of favorable outcomes in which X occurs / total number of possible outcomes

For example, the odds of rolling a standard 6-sided die and getting an even number (2, 4, or 6) is:

P_{EVEN} = 3 / 6 = 1 / 2

If two events are independent, then the probability of one event does not affect the probability of the other. Rolling two dice would be an example of this. However, if two events are dependent, then you must change the odds of the second event based on the outcome of the first.

When calculating the odds of two events both happening, simply multiply the two probabilities together. This can be a bit confusing since we use the word "and" in English but use multiplication when doing the math.

For example:

1. What are the odds of rolling two dice and getting a 2 on one and a 2 on the other?

$P_{ROLL\ 2}$ = 1 / 6
$P_{ROLL\ 2}$ and $P_{ROLL\ 2}$ = 1/6 x 1/6 = 1/36

2. What the odds of flipping a coin three times and getting heads on all three flips?

P_{HEADS} and P_{HEADS} and P_{HEADS} = 1/2 x 1/2 x 1/2 = 1/8

When one event affects the other, you must account for that effect before multiplying the probabilities together:

1. A drawer has 10 white socks and 10 brown socks. What are the odds of drawing out a white sock and then another white sock?

$P_{FIRST\ WHITE\ SOCK}$ = 10 / 20
$P_{SECOND\ WHITE\ SOCK}$ = 9 / 19 (since we have already removed one white sock, there are only 9 white socks left and only 19 socks left in the drawer)

$P_{BOTH\ WHITE\ SOCKS}$ = (10 / 20) x (9 / 19) = 90 / 380 = 9/38

By contrast, when calculating the probability that one or the other of an event will occur, you must add the probabilities and then subtract the odds of them both happening. For example:

1. What are the odds of rolling at least one "2" on two six-sided dice?

P_{ROLL2} = 1/6
$P_{ROLL2\ TWICE}$ = 1/36
$P_{ROLL2\ ON\ EITHER}$ = 1/6 + 1/6 − 1/36 = 11/36

2. What are the odds of flipping heads on either of two fair coins?

$P_{\text{HEADS}} = 1/2$
$P_{\text{BOTH HEADS}} = 1/4$
$P_{\text{EITHER ONE IS HEADS}} = 1/2 + 1/2 - 1/4 = 3/4$

Finally, it is sometimes easier to calculate an event NOT happening and then using that to find the probability of an event happening. We must use:

$P_X + P_{\text{NOT X}} = 1$

For example:

1. The odds of rain are 20% each day for Monday, Tuesday, and Wednesday. What are the odds of rain on at least one day?

Here, the odds of no rain on a given day are 80% (remember X and Not X must add up to 1 or 100%). So the odds of no rain at all are:

$P_{\text{NO RAIN MONDAY}} \times P_{\text{NO RAIN TUESDAY}} \times P_{\text{NO RAIN WEDNESDAY}} = 0.8 \times 0.8 \times 0.8 = 0.512$

$P_{\text{NO RAIN AT ALL}} + P_{\text{RAIN AT LEAST ONCE}} = 1$

$P_{\text{RAIN AT LEAST ONCE}} = 1 - 0.512 = 0.488$

So there is a 48.8% chance of getting rain at least once.

2. What are the odds of flipping a coin five times and getting heads at least once?

Here, the odds of Not Heads is 1/2. To not get heads at least once means flipping the coin five times and getting tails every single time.

$P_{\text{NO HEADS, TAILS FIVE TIMES IN A ROW}} = 1/2 \times 1/2 \times 1/2 \times 1/2 \times 1/2 = 1/32$

$P_{\text{AT LEAST ONE HEAD}} + P_{\text{NO HEADS}} = 1$
$P_{\text{AT LEAST ONE HEAD}} = 1 - 1/32 = 31/32$

So, unsurprisingly, the odds of flipping a coin five times and getting heads one or more times is pretty high – 96.875%

D. ROOTS AND EXPONENTS

Manipulating roots and exponents is an essential part of doing MCAT math. Let's start with exponents.

There are a few key rules that we must memorize:

1. $N^0 = 1$

This is true for any number but 0. 0^0 is undefined and won't come up on the MCAT.

2. $N^X \times N^Y = N^{(X+Y)}$

A quick example can help show why this rule is true:

$5^2 \times 5^4 = (5 \times 5) \times (5 \times 5 \times 5 \times 5) = 5 \times 5 \times 5 \times 5 \times 5 \times 5 = 5^6 = 5^{(2+4)}$

3. $M^X \times N^X = (M \times N)^X$

Again, an example:

$2^3 \times 5^3 = 10^3 = 2 \times 2 \times 2 \times 5 \times 5 \times 5 = (5 \times 2) \times (5 \times 2) \times (5 \times 2) = (5 \times 2)^3 = 10^3$

4. $N^X / N^Y = N^{(X-Y)}$

For example: $5^5 / 5^2 = 5 \times 5 \times 5 \times 5 \times 5 / 5 \times 5 = 5 \times 5 \times 5 = 5^3 = 5^{(5-2)}$

5. $(N^X)^Y = N^{(X \times Y)}$

For example: $(5^2)^3 = 5^2 \times 5^2 \times 5^2 = 5^6 = 5^{(2 \times 3)}$

6. $(N/M)^X = N^X / M^X$

For example: $(2/3)^3 = (2^3) / (3^3) = 8 / 27$

7. $N^{(1/2)} = \sqrt{N}$

8. $N^{(-X)} = 1 / N^X$

In addition to knowing these eight rules, it can speed up your work tremendously and help you approximate to memorize the first twenty squares:

$1^2 = 1$	$5^2 = 25$	$9^2 = 81$	$13^2 = 169$	$17^2 = 289$
$2^2 = 4$	$6^2 = 36$	$10^2 = 100$	$14^2 = 196$	$18^2 = 324$
$3^2 = 9$	$7^2 = 49$	$11^2 = 121$	$15^2 = 225$	$19^2 = 361$
$4^2 = 16$	$8^2 = 64$	$12^2 = 144$	$16^2 = 256$	$20^2 = 400$

So if a question asks you to find the square root of 130, you likely won't need the exact number – you'll just need to know that it's between 11 and 12.

The two square root values that you must memorize are:
$\sqrt{2} \approx 1.4$
$\sqrt{3} \approx 1.7$

In terms of square root rules, simply apply the ones listed above for exponents. After all, a square root is just the exponent of 1/2 so all the rules listed above will apply to square roots as well.

E. SCIENTIFIC NOTATION

Scientific notation is a way to manage numbers that would otherwise be so big or so small that working with them would be extremely clumsy

$3,141,500 = 3.1415 \times 10^6$

Here, we've taken a number and re-expressed it in terms of scientific notation. The 3.1415 is the **coefficient** and the 10^6 is the **exponent**. The coefficient must be a number between -10 and 10 (exclusive) and the exponent can be any integer. It's possible to express numbers in "sort of" scientific notation just for ease of calculation – having a coefficient that's bigger than 10 or an exponent that's a decimal, for example. We'll see some examples like that shortly.

For numbers less than 1, use a negative exponent. For example:

$0.0001415 = 1.415 \times 10^{-4}$

You can also adjust how a number is expressed in scientific notation to help with certain calculations. If you want to make the exponent bigger, make the coefficient smaller, and vice versa.

For example:

$2,300 = 2.3 \times 10^3 = 0.23 \times 10^4 = 23 \times 10^2$

Remember that if the exponent is negative, a "smaller negative" is a bigger number! For example:

$0.00023 = 2.3 \times 10^{-4} = 0.23 \times 10^{-3} = 23 \times 10^{-5}$

Now let's look at how to carry out basic operations using scientific notation.

Addition and Subtraction with Scientific Notation

To add or subtract two numbers that are expressed in scientific notation, first adjust them so that they have the same exponent. Then add the coefficients but don't change the exponent. For example:

$0.000034 + 0.0000091 =$
$3.4 \times 10^{-5} + 9.1 \times 10^{-6} =$
$34 \times 10^{-6} + 9.1 \times 10^{-6} =$
$43.1 \times 10^{-6} =$
1.31×10^{-5}

$45{,}000{,}000 + 6{,}700{,}000 =$
$4.5 \times 10^{7} + 6.7 \times 10^{6} =$
$4.5 \times 10^{7} + 0.67 \times 10^{7} =$
5.17×10^{7}

Multiplication, Division, and Roots with Scientific Notation

To multiply or divide numbers in scientific notation, simply multiply or divide the coefficients as you would any other numbers, and then follow the exponent rules discussed above for the exponents. Often it is helpful to separate the coefficients and exponents to keep track of what you're doing. For example:

$(3 \times 10^{6}) \times (4 \times 10^{2}) = 3 \times 4 \times 10^{6} \times 10^{2} = 12 \times 10^{8} = 1.2 \times 10^{9}$

$(2 \times 10^{-3}) \times (7 \times 10^{-5}) = 2 \times 7 \times 10^{-3} \times 10^{-5} = 14 \times 10^{-8} = 1.4 \times 10^{-7}$

$(5 \times 10^{-8}) \times (5 \times 10^{6}) = 5 \times 5 \times 10^{-8} \times 10^{6} = 25 \times 10^{-2} = 2.5 \times 10^{-1} = 0.25$

$(6 \times 10^{8}) / (1.5 \times 10^{3}) = (6 / 1.5) \times (10^{8} / 10^{3}) = 4 \times 10^{5}$

$(3 \times 10^{4}) \times (6 \times 10^{-9}) / (9 \times 10^{-2}) = (3 \times 6 / 9) \times (10^{4} \times 10^{-9} / 10^{-2}) = 2 \times 10^{-3}$

When taking the root of a number in scientific notation, the most important thing to do is adjust the number so that the exponent can easily be dealt with. Remember that taking the square root means cutting the exponent in half, taking the cube root means taking $1/3$ of the exponent, and so on. For example:

$\sqrt{(6.4 \times 10^{9})} = \sqrt{(64 \times 10^{8})} = \sqrt{64} \times \sqrt{10^{8}} = 8 \times 10^{4}$

Significant Figures

The MCAT won't necessarily have questions that exactly test you on sig figs but you should generally be familiar with the rules:

1. Any number between the leftmost nonzero digit and the rightmost nonzero digit is significant.

So in the number 2300.02 all six of the digits are significant.

2. Zeroes are not significant if they are to the left of the leftmost nonzero digit.

So in the number 0045.2 the zeroes are not significant.
In the number 0.000403 the zeroes to the left of the four are not significant. The "4", "0", and "3" in a row are all significant.

3. Zeroes to the right of the rightmost nonzero digit are significant **only** if there is a decimal point.

So in the number 3020.00 all six digits are significant.

In the number 3020 the last zero on the right is **not** significant.
In the number 0.00012300 the 1, the 2, the 3, and the next two 0's are all significant.

4. When a number is being generated by a physical measurement in an experiment, the last digit is usually considered not significant since it's only an estimate.

CHAPTER 18 PROBLEMS

1. 35.112 / 7.2 is closest to:
   A. 3
   B. 5
   C. 210
   D. 35000

2. 2.011 x 105 / 43 is closest to:
   A. 0.5
   B. 5
   C. 6.5
   D. 12

3. (29.8 + 115)/(144.4) is closest to:

   A. 0
   B. 1
   C. 30.5
   D. 31

4. A gumball dispenser has 40 red gum balls and 60 blue gum balls. The odds of two blue gum balls in a row is closest to:
   A. 6%
   B. 24%
   C. 36%
   D. 100%

5. A couple's genetic makeup means any girl they have has a 10% chance of being albino and any boy they have has a 20% chance of being albino. If they have one child, the odds of it being albino are:
   A. 5%
   B. 10%
   C. 15%
   D. 30%

6. In a normal deck of 52 cards, there are 13 cards of each suit (clubs, spades, hearts, diamonds). What are the odds of drawing a club from the deck, replacing the card, and then drawing another club?
   A. 1/4
   B. 13/52 x 12/51
   C. 1/16
   D. 1/4 + 1/4

7. $\sqrt{180}$ =

   A. $6\sqrt{5}$
   B. 14
   C. $9\sqrt{2}$
   D. $18\sqrt{10}$

8. How many significant digits are in the numbers 250.00, 35, and 0.0020, respectively?

   A. 3, 2, 4
   B. 2, 2, 4
   C. 2, 2, 2
   D. 5, 2, 2

9. $\sqrt{(2.5 \times 10^{17})}$ =

   A. 1.4×10^{17}
   B. 6.25×10^{15}
   C. 2.5×10^{9}
   D. 5×10^{8}

10. $3 \times 10^{6} + 9 \times 10^{5}$ =

    A. 6×10^{5}
    B. 3.9×10^{6}
    C. 1.2×10^{6}
    D. 12×10^{11}

CHAPTER 19
ALGEBRA AND TRIGONOMETRY TOPICS

A. INTRODUCTION

You're going to see an awful lot of equations on the MCAT, and not just in the physics. The biology and biochemistry will give you experiments with all sorts of equations, and the general chemistry and organic chemistry have their equations as well. The MCAT typically won't ask you to solve equations in the way that a high school algebra class (or the GRE) would. But they will expect that you can do so, and they will then ask trickier, high-level relationship questions that presume that fundamental understanding. Run through the following chapter to brush up on your skills, and remind yourself of anything you might have forgotten.

B. MANIPULATING EQUATIONS

The MCAT will require you to be comfortable manipulating equations and variables roughly at the level of a high school Algebra I (or a little bit of Algebra II) course. To that end, we'll briefly review some foundational concepts here.

Direct and Inverse Relationships

Often the MCAT won't require you to solve for an exact number, if you can simply determine the relationship between the variables. They can either be direct or inverse. In a direct relationship, as one variable increases, the other increases as well. With inverse relationships, as one variable increases, the other goes down.

The equation for a direct relationship is:

$A / B = k$

where k is some constant. Alternatively, it could be presented as:

$A_1 / B_1 = A_2 / B_2$

A classic example of this kind of direct relationship is Charles's law, which states that temperature and volume of a gas are directly related:

$V_1 / T_1 = V_2 / T_2$

Inverse relationships are typically presented as:

$R \times Q = k$

$R_1 Q_1 = R_2 Q_2$

Again, a classic example of this is Boyle's law, which states that pressure and volume of a gas are inversely related:

$P_1 V_1 = P_2 V_2$

Graphically, these relationships typically look like this:

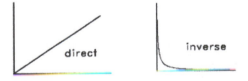

Systems of Equations

"Systems of equations" simply refers to situations in which you have two unknown variables and two different equations. To manipulate systems of equations on the MCAT, you will want to use substitution or combination. Let's consider the following two equations:

$2x + 9y = 31$

$3y - x = 7$

To solve, we can use either substitution or combination. Let's start with substitution. First, take one of the equations and isolate a variable. Let's take the second equation and isolate x:

$3y - x = 7$
$3y = 7 + x$
$3y - 7 = x$

Now we can substitute this value, $(3y - 7)$ into the first equation:

$2(3y - 7) + 9y = 31$
$6y - 14 + 9y = 31$
$15y - 14 = 31$
$15y = 45$
$y = 3$

Now that we know that y is three, we can plug that value back into one of the original equations:

$3(3) - x = 7$
$9 - x = 7$
$x = 2$

And so we have solved that x = 2 and y = 3.

To do combination, you will simply add the two equations together. For example, if you had the equations:

$3 \times 2 = 6$

$3 + 1 = 4$

You could add the left side of both equations and the right side of both equations and you'd still have a valid equation:

$(3 \times 2) + (3 + 1) = 6 + 4$
$6 + 4 = 10$

And notice we still have a true equation at the end. For this process to be helpful with algebra, we will need one of the equations to cancel out one of the variables. In our first equation we had "2x" and in the second we had "-x". So make the x cancel out, multiply the second equation by 2:

$3y - x = 7$
$2(3y - x) = 2(7)$
$6y - 2x = 14$

We can now add the two equations together:

$$2x + 9y = 31$$
$$+ \ 6y - 2x = 14$$
$$2x + 9y + 6y - 2x = 31 + 14$$
$$9y + 6y + 2x - 2x = 45$$
$$15y = 45$$
$$y = 3$$

And since we've done everything correctly, we arrive at the same answer as before – that y is three.

C. TRIGONOMETRY

As with so many other concepts on the MCAT, understanding trig starts with memorizing the basic concepts. Let's start with the definitions you'll be expected to know:

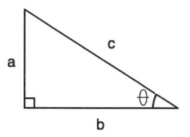

Sine:
sin θ = opposite / hypotenuse = a / c

Cosine:
cos θ = adjacent / hypotenuse = b / c

Tangent:
tan θ = opposite / adjacent = a / b

Inverse sine:
$\sin^{-1}$ (a/c) = arcsin (a/c) = θ

Inverse cosine:
$\cos^{-1}$ (b/c) = arccos (b/c) = θ

Inverse tangent:
$\tan^{-1}$ (a/b) = arctan (a/b) = θ

Rather than trying to calculate trig values, you should simply memorize the common values likely to show up on the MCAT. If you learn the following values, you'll be set for 99% of what you're likely to see on the MCAT:

sin 0° = $\sqrt{0}$ / 2 = 0
sin 30° = $\sqrt{1}$ / 2 = 1/2 = 0.5
sin 45° = $\sqrt{2}$ / 2 ≈ 0.7
sin 60° = $\sqrt{3}$ / 2 ≈ 0.87
sin 90° = $\sqrt{4}$ / 2 = 2/2 = 1
sin 180° = 0

Notice the pattern here – the denominator in each case is 2 and for the numerator you simply count up from 0 to 4 and take the square root.

cos 180° = 1
cos 90° = $\sqrt{0}$ / 2 = 0
cos 60° = $\sqrt{1}$ / 2 = 1/2 = 0.5

$\cos 45° = \sqrt{2} / 2 \approx 0.7$
$\cos 30° = \sqrt{3} / 2 \approx 0.87$
$\cos 0° = \sqrt{4} / 2 = 2/2 = 1$

Notice the pattern here – the denominator in each case is 2 and for the numerator you simply count up from 0 to 4 and take the square root.

$\tan 0° = 0$
$\tan 30° = \sqrt{3} / 3$
$\tan 45° = 1$
$\tan 60° = \sqrt{3}$
$\tan 90° = $ undefined
$\tan 180° = 0$

Unfortunately, there's not such an easy pattern for tangent!

Finally, the MCAT will expect you to have memorized the ratios between the sides for the 30-60-90 and the 45-45-90 right triangles. Here they are:

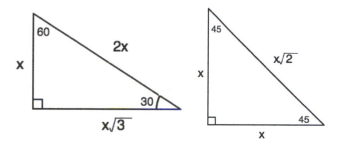

D. LOGARITHMS

The MCAT includes a number of equations based on logarithms that you will be expected to use. For example:

$pH = - \log [H+]$
$\Delta G = - RT \ln K_{eq}$

A logarithm is simply the inverse of an exponent. That is:

$10^A = B$
$\log_{10}B = A$

Since you will mostly be dealing with powers of ten, you should be very familiar with $\log_{10}$, and if no number is listed, simply assume that it is log base 10. You should also know the following:

$\log 0.01 = -2$
$\log 0.1 = -1$
$\log 1 = 0$
$\log 3 \approx 0.5$
$\log 10 = 1$
$\log 100 = 2$

You won't be expected to calculate the exact value of log 2 through log 9, and usually on the MCAT you can simply estimate all of them as ≈ 0.5 (that is, just some value between 0 and 1).

The log rules you will need to know are:

1. $\log_X 1 = 0$
2. $\log_X X = 1$
3. $\log (N \times M) = \log N + \log M$
4. $\log (N / M) = \log N - \log M$
5. $\log (N^M) = M \times \log N$
6. $- \log N = \log (1 / N)$

The only other log besides $\log_{10}$ you are likely to encounter on the MCAT is $\log_e$, or the natural log, ln. Euler's number, e, is about 2.7. You may find that you need to convert between $\log_{10}$ and ln, so use the following conversion:

$$2.3 \times \log_{10} N = \ln N$$

Log Scales: pH and Decibels

By far the two most common cases in which you will use log scales in when working with acid-base problems or with decibels. Remember that every "step" on a log scale means 10x more of whatever's being measured. So moving from pH 4 down to pH 3 means a solution that is ten times more acidic.

When solving for pH, use the following shortcut:

$$pH = - \log [H+] = - \log [A \times 10^{-B}] = B - \log A$$

And remember we said that "log A" can simply be rounded off to 0.5 so long as A is a number between 1 and 10. For example, what is the pH of a solution whose $[H+] = 4 \times 10^{-8}$?

$$pH = - \log [H+] = - \log [4 \times 10^{-8}] = 8 - \log 4 \approx 7.5$$

The situation is slightly trickier with decibels (dB) since the decibel equation involves a ratio and puts a x10 into the equation itself:

$$dB = 10 \log (I / I_o)$$

For example, a 63 decibel sound is how much louder than a 23 decibel sound?

First, we see that this is a change of 40 decibels:

$$40 = 10 \log (I / I_o)$$
$$4 = \log (I / I_o)$$

The discussion of what I_o is and why the equation is set up as a ratio is beyond the scope of our discussion about log scales. For now, suffice to say that we see going from a 23 decibel sound to a 63 decibel sound involves 4 steps on a log scale – meaning the 63 decibel sound is 10^4 times louder. So the answer is, "The 63 decibel sound is ten thousand times louder (more intense) than the 23 decibel sound."

CHAPTER 19 PROBLEMS

1. Solve for x: 3x / (x+2) = 5

A. 5
B. -5
C. -10
D. -2

2. Solve for x:
2y – x = 5
2x + 3y = 18

A. 3
B. 4
C. 4.5
D. 14

3. Isolate log A: pH = pKa + log (A/HA)

A. log A = pH/pKa + log HA
B. log A = pH – pKa + log HA
C. log A = pH + pKa / log HA
D. log A = log HA (pH – pKa)

4. sin 30° =

A. 0
B. 1/2
C. $\sqrt{2}$ / 2
D. 1

5. cos 180° =

A. 0
B. - 1/2
C. $\sqrt{2}$ / 2
D. - 1

6. tan 0° =

A. 0
B. 1/2
C. $\sqrt{2}$ / 2
D. 1

7. $\log_4 4$ =

A. 0
B. 1
C. 4
D. 512

8. log 25 + log 4

A. 0
B. 2
C. 29
D. 10^{29}

9. log (1/1000) =

A. 0.001
B. 3
C. -3
D. -1000

10. $2 \log_5 \sqrt{5}$

A. 1
B. 2
C. 5
D. 25

CHAPTER 20
INTERPRETING GRAPHS

A. INTRODUCTION

One of the most important skills you will need on Test Day is interpreting graphs and figures. The majority of the science passages you'll see on the MCAT will have some sort of table, graph, or figure with them. When you see any figures, you should always take a careful look at them as soon as you start your work on the passage. Focus on:

1. Title, Units, Axes, Labels

By far the most important thing to do when you see a figure is get yourself oriented to what it's even showing you. If it's a graph, what are the axes labeled? What are the units?

2. Trends

Are the numbers going up? Down? Random? What's the slope of the line if it's a graph?

3. Extremes, Outliers, Intercepts

If it's a graph, where does it intersect the x or y axis? Do the trend lines intersect at any point? Are there extremes? Big jumps in trends? Who's the biggest and smallest category?

4. What does the text say?

Finally, to pull it all together, you should see what the text has to say about the figure. Does it tell you something about the data in the figure? Does the data in the figure tell you something about the graph?

B. THE CARTESIAN PLANE

The basic coordinate system you will see on the MCAT will be the standard Cartesian plane, with a vertical y-axis and a horizontal x-axis. Units on the axes will typically be at standard intervals – each square will be 1 unit (for the sake of convenience, they may draw the graph with 1 square representing 5 units, 10 units, etc.)

To express information on a Cartesian plane, we use an ordered pair of coordinates, first listing the x coordinate and then the y coordinate. For example, in the graph below, the points (2, 3), (-5, 1), and (4, -2) have been plotted.

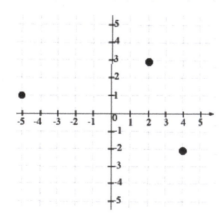

C. LINEAR GRAPHS

When representing data in a Cartesian plane, one of the most common forms you will see on the MCAT is a simple linear plot, with the classic formula structure y = mx+b. The m variable represents the slope:

m = slope = $\Delta y / \Delta x$

When analyzing a graph, remember that the units on the axes are important – the slope represents the units on the y-axis divided by the units on the x-axis. For example:

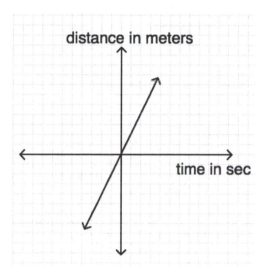

Here, we see a line that goes up by two units for every 1 unit along the x-axis. Thus its slope is 2 and the equation described by the line is d = 2t. The units for the slope would be m/s and so we can infer that the slope represents to velocity.

In the y=mx+b formula, the "b" variable represents the y-intercept, the point at which the line crosses the y-axis. For example, in the following graph, the y-intercept is 2:

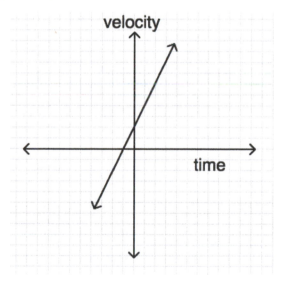

The slope is 2 and the y-intercept is 2, giving an equation y = 2x + 2. Since it is a graph of velocity vs. time the equation would be v = 2t+2 and the slope would represent (m/s)/s or m/s^2 which we can infer is acceleration.

Let's look at a couple of examples that would be linear based on some classic formulas you'd see on Test Day. The idea gas law is PV = nRT. If we graph this with PV on the y-axis and T on the x-axis we would get:

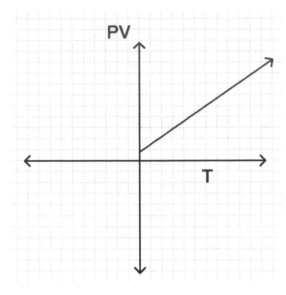

Here the line does not cross the y-axis into negative x values since temperature cannot be negative on the Kelvin scale. The slope of the line is "nR" and we remember that R is a constant and n is the number of moles of gas. So as temperature increases, the value of P x V increases linearly. The slope doesn't change at all because neither n nor R is changing.

In the kinematic equation $v_f = v_i + at$ we can see that v_f is the y-axis, t is the x-axis, a is the slope, and v_i is the y-intercept. Such a graph would look like the velocity vs. time graph depicted above.

D. CONIC SECTIONS

The MCAT will also present you with many relationships that are not just straight lines. Most commonly, you'll see parabolic relationships, exponential relationships, and logarithmic ones. Here's a quick look at what they look like.

Here's a graph of the exponential relationship $y = 10^x$

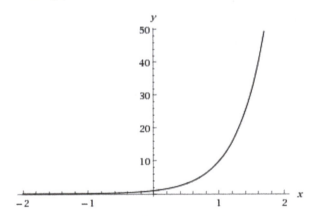

You see this kind of exponential curve in the Arrhenius equation: $k = Ae^{-E_a/RT}$ if you were to plot the rate constant k vs. the exponent E_a/RT.

In a parabola, the dependent variable changes as the square (or cube, etc.) of the independent variable. The classic example is $y = x^2$ and the graph looks like this:

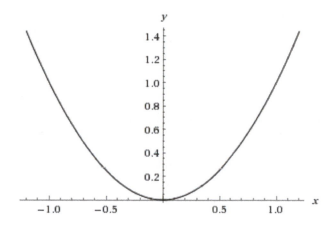

This parabolic relationship would be seen in the kinetic energy equation, for example, $KE = (1/2)mv^2$ if you were to plot KE versus velocity.

Finally, in a logarithmic relationship of $y = \log x$, y increases quickly at first but then slows down dramatically:

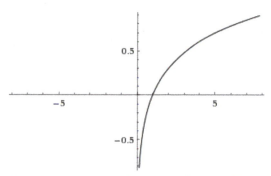

The classic example of this would the pH or decibel scales, $pH = -\log [H^+]$ and $dB = 10 \log I$.

E. SEMILOG AND LOG-LOG SCALES.

The MCAT will also give you graphs in which the x and y axes are not labeled in a linear fashion, which each box on the graph representing 1 unit, but rather the distance between the boxes representing a fixed ratio – that is, each line on the graph is ten times more than the one before it.

In a semilog graph, the y-axis is graphed in this ratio fashion while the x-axis is still labeled a unit at a time. Data is graphed this way when the value on the y-axis increases very quickly, and graphing it in a regular linear plot would be unwieldy. For example, imagine a graph of the mass of bacteria growing in a colony (measure in μg) plotted vs. time. The graph would increase very slowly at first, but would grow very rapidly as the colony keeps doubling over and over. On a simple linear plot the graph would shoot off the top of the chart pretty quickly, but in a semilog plot it might look like this:

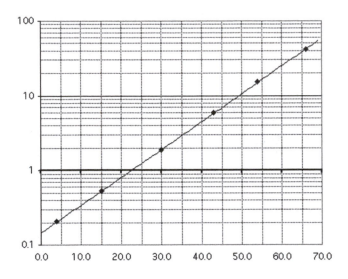

You may also see a log-log plot on the MCAT, although this is much less likely. In a log-log plot, both the x and y axes are listed as a constant ratio between segments, rather than a constant interval:

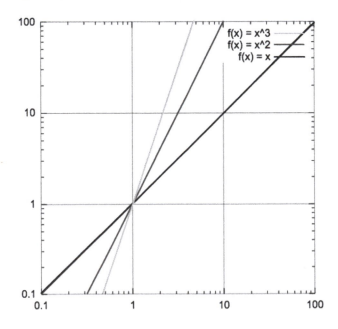

F. Other Charts and Graphs

Pie Charts

Pie charts are used to represent parts of a whole – the entire circle must represent 100% or the total number of data points. Pie charts are popular when showing demographic or epidemiological data. Their value lies in providing a quick, visually intuitive way to represent how much a total is made up of various groups (how big a "piece of the pie" each group takes). To be useful, however, the number of categories expressed in the pie must be relatively small. Compare the two pie charts below. In the first, the data is clear and easy to understand, but in the second the large number of categories makes the chart much less helpful.

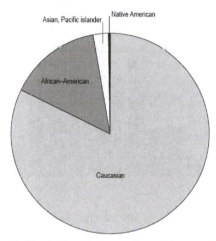

Figure 1F Racial breakdown of population of Indiana

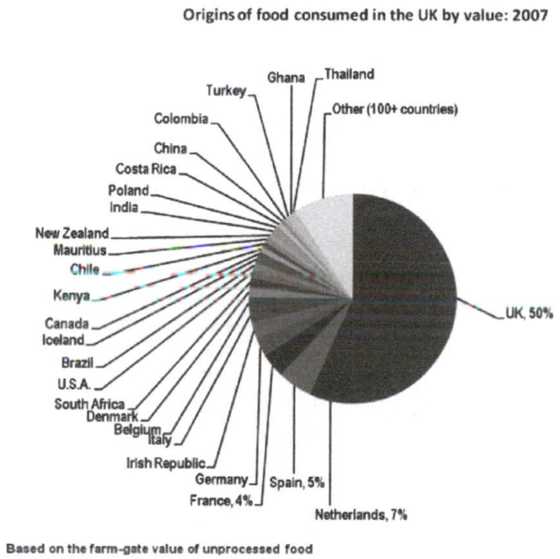

Origins of food consumed in the UK by value: 2007

Based on the farm-gate value of unprocessed food

Figure 2F Country of Origin for Food consumed in the UK

Bar Graphs

Bar graphs present data sorted by category. They allow for quick comparison across groups. One type of bar graph is a histogram, in which the categories are various numerical values or ranges. For example, the chart below is a histogram of MCAT Verbal Reasoning Scores from the 2013 test administrations.

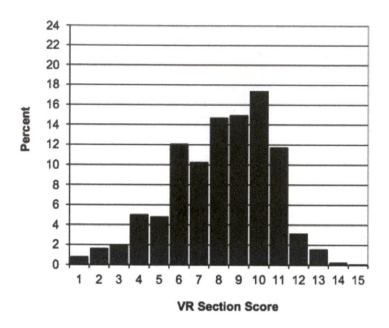

Box-and-Whisker Plot

In a box-and-whisker plot data is graphed to show several things at once. The bottom edge of the box is the 25th %ile, the top edge of the box is the 75th %ile, the line in the middle of the box is the median, and the whiskers extend out to the minimum and maximum values in the data set.

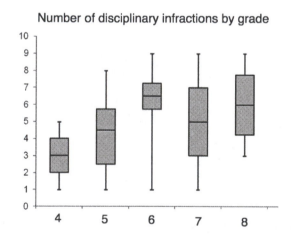

Other Representations of Data

Data may, of course, also be represented in any number of other ways. Symbols may be used to represent numbers in any way that makes it more visually compelling and easy to understand at a glance. For example, showing data spread out geographically can also provide quick, useful information.

CHAPTER 20 PROBLEMS

Questions 1-2 use the following graph:

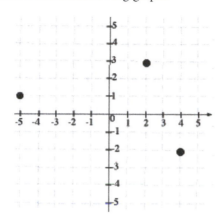

1. What is the slope of a line connecting the points $(2, 3)$ and $(4, -2)$?
   A. -2.5
   B. -0.4
   C. 0.4
   D. 2.5

2. What is the slope of a line connecting the points $(-5, 1)$ and $(2, 3)$?
   A. -7/2
   B. -2/7
   C. 2/7
   D. 7/2

Questions 3-5 use the following graph:

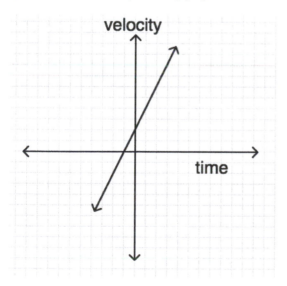

3. If each vertical unit on the graph represents 5 m/s and each horizontal unit represents 1 s then this object has a vi of:
   A. 2 m/s
   B. 5 m/s
   C. 10 m/s
   D. 10 m/s^2

4. If each vertical unit on the graph represents 5 m/s and each horizontal unit represents 1 s then this object has an acceleration of:
   A. 1 m/s^2
   B. 5 m/s^2
   C. 10 m/s^2
   D. 25 m/s^2

5. If each vertical unit on the graph represents 5 m/s and each horizontal unit represents 1 s then from t=0 to t=3 the total distance covered by this object is:
   A. 15 m
   B. 39 m
   C. 45 m
   D. 75 m

Questions 6-8 use the following graphs:

Graph I:

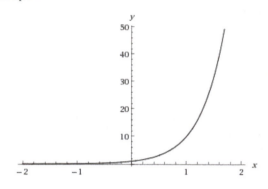

Graph II:

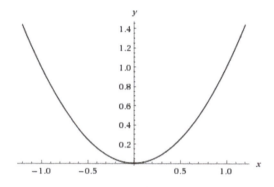

Graph III:

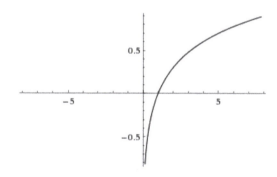

8. Which of the graphs above would best represent the binding curve for hemoglobin and oxygen *in vivo*?
   A. I
   B. II
   C. III
   D. None

Questions 9-10 use the following graph:

Number of disciplinary infractions by grade

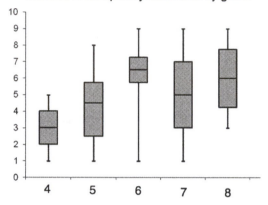

9. The data set for which grade shows the largest range?
   A. 4
   B. 5
   C. 6
   D. 7

10. The data set for which grade shows a 25th and 75th percentile that are the closest together?
   A. 4
   B. 5
   C. 6
   D. 7

6. Which of the graphs above represents an exponential relationship?
   A. I
   B. II
   C. III
   D. None

7. Which of the graphs above would best represent the relationship $d = v_f^2/2a$ if d were graphed on the y axis and v_f on the x axis?
   A. I
   B. II
   C. III
   D. None

CHAPTER 21
UNITS

A. INTRODUCTION

The MCAT will expect you to be familiar with a wide array of metric units. The good news is that most of these will be very familiar from your previous class work. The unit conversions discussion at the end is especially important, as converting between units is a skill tests on all of the science sections. Be sure to get in plenty of practice, and always be mindful of the units as you do your problem solving.

B. UNITS TO KNOW

The SI system has both base and derived units. You should be familiar with all of the base units and the derived units listed here.

SI Base Units

Unit	Symbol	Quantity measured
meter	m	length
kilogram	kg	mass
second	s	time
ampere	A	current
kelvin	K	temperature
mole	mol	amount of substance
candela	cd	luminosity

SI Derived Units

Unit	Symbol	Derivation	Quantity measured
hertz	Hz	s^{-1}	frequency
newton	N	$kg \cdot m \cdot s^{-2}$	force
pascal	Pa	$kg \cdot m^{-1} \cdot s^{-2}$	pressure
joule	J	$kg \cdot m^2 \cdot s^{-2}$	energy
watt	W	$kg \cdot m^2 \cdot s^{-3}$	power
coulomb	C	$s \cdot A$	charge
volt	V	$kg \cdot m^2 \cdot s^{-3} \cdot A^{-1}$	potential, emf
farad	F	$kg^{-1} \cdot m^{-2} \cdot s^4 \cdot A^2$	capacitance
ohm	Ω	$kg \cdot m^2 \cdot s^{-3} \cdot A^{-2}$	resistance
tesla	T	$kg \cdot s^{-2} \cdot A^{-1}$	magnetic field strength
degree Celsius	°C	K	temperature

C. CONVERSIONS

Converting between metric units starts with knowing the prefixes used in the metric system. They are:

Exponent	Prefix	Abbreviation
10^{12}	tera	T
10^9	giga	G
10^6	mega	M
10^3	kilo	k
10^2	hecta	h
10^1	deka	da
10^{-1}	deci	d
10^{-2}	centi	c
10^{-3}	milli	m
10^{-6}	micro	μ
10^{-9}	nano	n
10^{-12}	pico	p

When converting from one metric unit to the next, start by expressing the number in base units and then convert to the new prefix. Here are some examples:

1200 kJ is how many mJ?

$1200 \text{ kJ} = 1200 \times 10^3 \text{ J}$

$1200 \times 10^3 \text{J} \times (1 \text{ mJ} / 10^{-3} \text{ J}) = 1200 \times 10^6 \text{ mJ} = 1.2 \times 10^9 \text{ mJ}$

62 Gm is how many km?

$62 \text{ Gm} = 62 \times 10^9 \text{ m}$

$62 \times 10^9 \text{ m} \times (1 \text{ km} / 10^3 \text{m}) = 62 \times 10^6 \text{ km} = 6.2 \times 10^7 \text{ km}$

405 mΩ is how many MΩ?

$405 \text{ m}\Omega = 405 \times 10^{-3} \text{ }\Omega$

$405 \times 10^{-3} \text{ }\Omega \times (1 \text{ M}\Omega / 10^6 \text{ }\Omega) = 405 \times 10^{-9} \text{ M}\Omega = 4.06 \times 10^{-7} \text{ M}\Omega$

D. CONVERTING BETWEEN ENGLISH AND METRIC

The MCAT won't expect you to memorize English units, but it may provide you with the conversion factor and then ask you to convert between them. The only conversion factor you should memorize is between temperature scales – Fahrenheit to Celsius to Kelvin.

You should, however, be familiar with the general scale of these conversions so you know if your answers make sense as you solve questions:

Base Unit	Equivalent Unit	Metric Unit
1 mile	5280 feet, 1760 yards	1.6 km
1 foot	12 inches	30.48 cm
1 inch	1/12 foot	2.54 cm
1 Calorie	1000 calories	4184 J
1 pound	16 ounces (oz)	4.45 N
1 gallon	4 quarts, 16 cups, 128 fluid oz	3.79 L

Temperature conversions

Converting between Celsius and Kelvin is easy enough – simply take the Kelvins and subtract 273 to get the Celsius value. Converting between Celsius and Fahrenheit is a little more complex, using the formula below:

$F = (9/5)C + 32$
$C = K - 273.15$

Temperature	Fahrenheit	Celsius	Kelvin
Water freezing	32 F	0°C	273 K
Standard Conditions	77 F	25°C	298 K
Water boiling	212 F	100°C	373 K

E. DIMENSIONAL ANALYSIS

One of the most important skills you can bring with you into the room on Test Day is a mastery of the relationships between SI units, and an ability to manipulate the units given in a problem or passage. Many times, even if you forget the equation, or can't figure out what's going on in the passage, if you "make the units work" you can get the right answer.

For example, if you were given a problem which said that a machine which does 150 watts of work operates for 10 seconds at a potential of 5 volts, and then asks you how many coulombs of charge were moved, you may not be sure what equation, if any, applies to this situation. However, if you remember the unit conversions:

Volt = Joule / Coulomb

Watt = Joule / s

You can use those unit conversions to find the answer:

$V = J/C$
$W = J/s$
$J = VC = Ws$

$VC = Ws$
$(5V)(C) = (150W)(10s)$
$C = 300$ coulombs

Next, a common issue in dimensional analysis is converting between units when one of the units is squared or cubed. When doing so, be sure to apply the conversion as many times as needed to get the desired units at the end. Here are a couple of examples:

10 m^2 is how many cm^2?

10 m^2 x (100 cm / 1 m) x (100 cm / 1 m) =

10 m^2 x (10000 cm^2 / 1 m^2) =

100000 cm^2

1,500 mL is how many m^3?

1,500 mL x (1 cm^3 / 1 mL) = $1,500 \text{ cm}^3$

$1,500 \text{ cm}^3$ x (1 m / 100 cm) x (1 m / 100 cm) x (1 m / 100 cm) =

$1,500 \text{ cm}^3$ x (1 m^3 / 10^6 cm^3) = $1,500$ x 10^{-6} m^3 = 1.5 x 10^{-3} m^3

Finally, dimensional analysis can lead you to the right answer even in cases where the discussion in the passage doesn't relate to typical SI or English units, and for which there is no equation. Simply set up the conversion with the units in the answer choices in mind, and then apply whatever conversions you're given to make the remaining units cancel out. Here are a couple of examples with nonsense units:

A woman has 6 zops. Every 2 zops are worth 3 square zaps and a single zap is only worth 1/5 of a zip. How many square zips does she have?

The conversions they gave us: 2 zop / 3 zap^2 and 5 zaps / 1 zip

To convert zops to zip^2:

6 zop x (3 zap^2 / 2 zops) x (1 zip / 5 zap) x (1 zip / 5 zap) =

6 zop x (3 zap^2 / 2 zops) x (1 zip^2 / 25 zap^2) =

6x3/2x25 zip^2 = 18 / 50 = 36/100 = 0.36 zip^2

A man has a freeble that holds 12 plunks. The going rate is five dollars a plunk. The man has 6 dups that he can sell and he knows he can get $20 per dup. If he sells all of his dups how many times can he fill he freeble with plunks?

The conversions they gave us: 1 freeble / 12 plunk, 1 plunk / $5, 1 dup / $20, and that the man has 6 dups

To find how many freebles he can get:

1 freeble / 12 plunk x (1 plunk / $5) x ($20 / 1 dup) x 6 dup = 2 freebles

CHAPTER 21 PROBLEMS

1. Which of the following is equal to a joule?
   A. $kg \cdot m^2 \cdot s^{-1}$
   B. $kg \cdot m \cdot s^{-2}$
   C. $N \cdot m^{-1}$
   D. $W \cdot s$

2. The SI unit for charge is divided by the SI unit for current. This gives:
   A. time.
   B. volt.
   C. electron-volt.
   D. force.

3. 3.21 g is how many kg?
   A. 0.00321
   B. 0.0321
   C. 3.21
   D. 3210

4. 642 GJ is how many nJ?
   A. 6.42×10^{-18}
   B. 6.42×10^{11}
   C. 6.42×10^{18}
   D. 6.42×10^{20}

5. A Fahrenheit scale reads -40°F. This is how many °C?
   A. -72 °C
   B. -40 °C
   C. -22.2 °C
   D. -8 °C

6. Standard thermodynamic conditions are P = 1 atm and T = 298 K. This is what temperature in Celsius?
   A. 0 °C
   B. 25 °C
   C. 77 °C
   D. 298 °C

For questions 7-8 use the following conversions:
1 inch = 2.5 cm
1 cal = 4.184J

7. A meal is advertised as containing 963 kcal. How many joules is this?
   A. 4.03×10^{-6} J
   B. 3,891 J
   C. 963,000 J
   D. 4,029,192 J

8. A particular fabric is sold at $1 for every ten square inches. Which of the following is closest to the cost of two thousand square centimeters, at this rate?
   A. $0.30
   B. $3
   C. $30
   D. $300

9. A person runs at 1.5 m/s and her strides are 0.75 m long. The track she is walking around is 150 meters long. How many strides will it take her to complete a loop around the track?
   A. 100 strides
   B. 112.5 strides
   C. 150 strides
   D. 225 strides

10. A person runs at 1.5 m/s and her strides are 0.75 m long. The track she is walking around is 150 meters long. How long will it take her to complete a loop around the track?
    A. 100 s
    B. 112.5 s
    C. 150 s
    D. 225 s

Chapter 22
Experimental Design

A. INTRODUCTION

Constructing an experiment isn't just a matter of getting the Mythbusters crew together and playing with some toys in the workshop. Good scientific research involves very careful application of the scientific method and research procedures. At the beginning of the book we started by introducing a basic framework for the scientific method, but we will expand on it here.

The process is carried out as follows:

1. **Generate a question** about the world based on some confusing phenomenon, previous scientific work, or speculation.

Often science research starts because something's confusing – we don't understand why something works out the way it does. An anomaly in research data, and area not covered by our current theories, etc.

For example, a social science researcher might wonder, "Why do girls perform worse on standardized tests of math, even though they often get better grades and more schooling?"

2. Do **background research**

You don't just jump right from a question to a test. You first have to investigate the issue to see what others have already discovered.

In our example, the researcher might uncover the notion of Stereotype Threat when it comes to performance on standardized tests. She might see that certain minority groups will perform worse on a test due to anxiety about conforming to a negative stereotype, and decide to investigate whether that also happens to girls on math tests.

3. Construct a **hypothesis** in the form of an if/then statement.

The hypothesis is the researcher's best guess about what the answer to the question is. In our example it might be, "If girls experience stereotype threat with respect to math performance, they will perform worse on a math test than they otherwise would."

4. Construct and **conduct experiments** to test the hypothesis and **interpret the data**.

This is the step that most people think of when they imagine scientists at work – the process of carrying out research protocols and doing statistical analysis of the data. While this certainly can make up the bulk of the time, money, and effort, we mustn't forget about all of the work that came before. Often scientists will say that what makes a great scientist is someone how knows how to "ask the right questions", rather than simply carry out good protocols. In our example, the scientists might give a series of math tests to subjects with differing instructions at the beginning to see if stereotype threat has an effect.

5. **Publish and verify** the results.

To enter the realm of "scientific knowledge" the information needs to be disseminated, typically in a peer-reviewed journal. Others who work in the field can then review the work and carry things forward, by designing their own research around whatever new questions are raised by the study.

B. CONSTRUCTING SCIENCE RESEARCH

When designing one's experiments, there are several factors to consider when developing the research question. One set of criteria that has been suggested is the PICOT criteria:

Population: what specific patient population will be investigated?

Intervention: what is the intervention that will be carried out on these patients?

Comparison group: who will your intervention group be compared against?

Outcome: what is the outcome that will be measured?

Time: what is the appropriate timeline to follow up with subjects?

In addition to these criteria for evaluating your research question, the practicality and value of the researcher itself can be evaluated with the FINER criteria:

Feasible: is the research in question feasible given time and budget constraints?

Interesting: would the results be interesting to the researcher and the scientific community?

Novel: is this research investing something new?

Ethical: would this procedure be acceptable to the institutional review board and does it meet the ethical standard of the professional community and the community at large?

Relevant: is this work relevant to current state of scientific knowledge and to future research?

Controls

When constructing an experiment, it is essential to have a control group. We've all been told that over and over in our science classes, but it's important to remember why. The simple act of carrying out an experiment may itself change the results – such that we end up seeing results that are not due to whatever new thing we're testing, but simply by virtue of doing the study itself. We should also remember that the materials we use in the lab are not flawless. A control is one way to make sure we didn't get a "bad batch" of something that we ordered from the supply company.

Let's consider a hypothetical study on the doubling time of cells in culture. A scientist begins by growing the cells in a standard nutrient broth and finding that it takes them 21.2 minutes to double. He checks this against the previous literature and sees that the typical doubling time for these types of cells is anywhere from 18 to 22 minutes. So this control shows him that his cells are a normal batch and there's nothing wrong with his nutrient broth, his test tubes, etc. This is an example of a **negative control**. These cells were not altered in any way, and the dependent variable – doubling time – was unchanged, as expected.

Next, he wishes to test the effect of drug X, a new drug that should hypothetically interfere with a certain metabolic pathway. It is well known that drug Q, another drug on the market does interfere with that pathway. So in his second test, the scientist administers drug Q and notices that the doubling time increased to 36 minutes. This is a **positive control** – something was done in the experiment where it is known that the dependent variable will change. Here, the scientist has established that his cells respond in the expected way to having the metabolic pathway disrupted by drug Q.

Finally, he can test drug X. If he administers it and sees the doubling time increase above 21.2 minutes, he knows that the drug has had an effect. If the results are similar to those for drug Q, the hypothesis that it interferes with the same pathway is slightly strengthened.

In medical studies with human patients, the typical positive control is the current standard of care. The typical negative control would be a placebo pill.

Causation

It's usually almost impossible to prove causation in studies, especially social science studies, with human subjects. There are simply too many variables to control all of them. With social science researcher, we simply seek to establish a strong correlation – a relationship between the independent and dependent variables.

In basic science research, where the experimenters can tightly control all relevant variables, it is often much easier to establish causality. To do so, experimenters demonstrate that a change in the independent variable leads to a change in the dependent variable. By showing that the change in the independent variable always leads to the same result in the dependent variable –

and then also showing that the result doesn't occur in the absence of the change to the independent variable – basic science researchers can establish causality.

Error, Precision, and Accuracy

Error can creep into an experiment from a number of sources. First, the experimenters or subjects may allow their biases, either consciously or unconsciously to affect the results. This is discussed more below with double-blind trials. Next, an experimenter may overtly express bias by choosing to either ignore data that don't fit the hypothesis, or choosing not to publish results that don't fit the researcher's own biases.

An example of this is detection bias, in which a researcher is more likely to detect something that fits with his or her previous notions. For example, a physician may be aware that there is a higher incidence of HIV infection in a certain sub-group of hit patients. When he sees a new patient who is a member of that sub-group, he may be more likely to screen for HIV, thus skewing the epidemiological data.

The **Hawthorne effect**, or **observation bias**, creeps in when the subjects alter their behavior simply because they know they're being observed. For example, in a study of new diet plans, people participating in the study may alter other lifestyle habits – exercise, sleep patterns, etc. – simply because they know they're being assessed for the effectiveness of a diet.

Next, error can be the systematic result of instruments that give faulty readings or measurements that are being made incorrectly. The goal in collecting data should be to be both accurate and precise.

Accuracy or validity is how close the data collected is to the true value. If a given instrument or measure is able to generate a series of results that are clustered around the true value, then the results are said to be accurate.

Precision or reliability refers to the ability of a measure to give consistent results in a narrow range of possible results. If the measure or instrument gives the same results under the same conditions every time, it is a very precise measure.

It is possible for results to be accurate, but not precise, and vice versa:

Accurate, precise: the results are close to the true value and tightly clumped around the true value.
Accurate, imprecise: the results are close to the true value but are clumped very loosely (would have a large standard deviation)
Inaccurate, precise: the measurements are very tightly clustered, but not around the true value (usually the result of a mis-calibrated instrument)
Inaccurate, imprecise: the results are clumped very loosely around the wrong answer.

C. RESEARCH ETHICS AND HUMAN SUBJECTS

In the Psychological Foundations sections, you're likely to encounter experiments involving human subjects. There are very strict rules about the ethics of experiments involving human subjects. The core ethical concept to be aware of is **informed consent**, in which the subject is adequately informed about the nature of the process, and then is mentally and legally competent to give consent to it.

This core concept of informed consent falls under the general umbrella of respect for autonomy. Broadly speaking, there are four ethical categories that medical intervention (whether experimental or not) must meet: beneficence, acting the good of the person receiving the treatment; nonmaleficence, doing no harm (or least not doing more harm than good); social justice, treating similar patients similarly and working to ensure equal distribution of healthcare resources; and finally respect for autonomy, allowing patients to make decisions based on informed consent.

These broad ethical categories also include other general requirements in medical intervention:

• Honesty
• Confidentiality
• Special protection for vulnerable populations (children, prisoners, the disabled)
• Differences in care may not be based on factors such as race, religion, gender, or sexual orientation
• Assessments must be carried out in the least invasive and potentially harmful manner

Human Subjects

When carrying out the classic experimental approach, researchers will vary the independent variable and measure the dependent variable, as they would in any experiment. Alternatively, researchers can conduct observational experiments.

Because people are not petri dishes, it would be impossible (and unethical) to attempt to control them with the level of precision used in a test tube. As such, the data more often leads to correlations rather than causal conclusions.

Researchers gather data and then use regression analysis to determine the relationships between the variables. Researchers will investigate data that is binary (yes v. no), continuous (performance on an IQ test), or categorical (race, gender). Regression analysis is discussed further below.

More commonly in the social sciences, researchers carry out observational studies. This is often because carrying out an experimental study would be impossible or unethical (e.g. it would be impossible to change someone's race or religion, and it would unethical to even try). Observational studies vary on how they observe the subjects: forward in time, backward in time, or at one point in time.

Studies that look forward in time are cohort studies. They divide groups into cohorts based on some factor (male v. female, high educational attainment v. low) and follow the cohorts over many years, checking in with them periodically to assess outcomes. Studies that look backwards in time are case-control studies. Here, people are identified who have already developed the outcome of interest and then researchers look back to see if a person had a given risk factors. Those "cases" are then compared against "controls" who don't have the disease. For example, researchers might examine 50 children who were born with low birth weight and 50 who weren't, and then look back at the prenatal care the mother received.

Finally, studies that examine people at a given point in time are cross-sectional studies. Those simply gather data on a large cross-section of a group at a particular time, and ask a question at that point in time. For example, a cross-sectional study might look at 5 year olds who are in pre-school programs and those who aren't, and compare their developmental progress at that point.

Because observational studies only lend themselves to correlations, the data must be very strong to suggest that there is an underlying causal connection. The relationship must be linked in time (with the cause always preceding the effect). It must be a strong, consistent, and proportional relationship (meaning if there's more of the cause, there's more of the effect). The connection must be consistent with past research, plausible, and alternatives must have been ruled out. If all of these criteria have been met, researchers may be able to deduce a causal relationship from correlation data.

Should we Treat?

When research has been completed and the data compiled, it then leads to the question as to whether the studied intervention should actually be carried out in patients. First, the data must have the statistical power to indicate that the studied intervention actually had an effect. But much more important, researchers will need to determine whether the treatment is clinically relevant. After all, a new surgical procedure may has a statistically significant change – say a 3.5 day average recovery time instead of a 3.75 day average recovery time – but such a change may be irrelevant to overall patient health.

When considering whether or not a new treatment modality should be implemented, clinicians must consider factors such as:

• Cost – if a new treatment costs ten times more, but is only marginally more effective, then it may be unethical to use a treatment that will put the patient in great financial distress for only marginal gains.
• Side effects – a treatment may be more effective but have side effects that are so deleterious that they create a net decrease in patient well-being.
• Accessibility – if a patient would, for example, be required to fly across the country to access the treatment, removing them from the social supports of family and friends, it may not be the best choice.
• Pain, inconvenience, intrusiveness – the overall process of receiving the treatment should not create a "treatment is worse than the disease" situation for the patient; even an improvement in outcomes may not be worth it for the patient if the treatment is lengthy, painful, and intrusive.

D. PRACTICAL CONCERNS: THE MATH AND THE MONEY

Finally, we should consider some practical concerns about experimental design. Researchers don't have an infinite amount of time, money, or manpower. They must also be wary of unintended biases and be sure that what they're studying is actually proving what they're setting out to prove.

Statistical Measures in Experiments

In addition to the basic numerical statistics discussed in an earlier chapter, the MCAT will expect you to be familiar with the various statistical tests used by researchers to demonstrate that their findings are real. You won't have to actually calculate the various factors discussed below, but you'll need to be familiar with them. These are all part of the practical considerations in the construction and evaluation of experiments. After all, an experiment whose results cannot be analyzed statistically is often near-useless to researchers.

Independent, Dependent, and Confounding Variables

Variables are the things measured by researchers in the course of their experiments. Independent variables are the ones the researchers directly manipulate, and dependent variables are the ones they measure. Typically such data is represented graphically with the independent variable graphed along the x-axis and the dependent variable graphed along the y-axis.

Independent variables might include time, temperature, age, socioeconomic status, or organism size. Dependent variables are whatever effect the researchers are looking for. In the social sciences that might be something like IQ, income, symptoms, etc.

A confounding variable is one that the researchers did not account for in their experiment and which alters their results. An example might be a study that analyzes the effects of stereotype bias on math performance by race, but that fails to account for socioeconomic class. Any results obtained would be suspect, since participants may have scored more poorly simply because they were from a lower socioeconomic class, not due to their race.

In the hard sciences, an experiment designed to test two chemistry mechanisms might have a confounding variable of pH if one of the chemicals produces a side product that is an acid and the researchers failed to properly buffer their solutions to prevent changes in pH. In the social sciences, an experiment that showed a correlation between household income and children's college completion could not make the causal assertion that "having higher income causes you to be more likely to complete college." A confounding factor might be that having parents who went to college makes it more likely that the children will complete college. Or having parents with a certain personality style both makes them more likely to have a higher income **and** have children who complete college.

Sampling and Bias

Sample size (usually denoted with N) is simply the number of data points developed in an experiment. In the social sciences and biology, this usually means the number of people or number of organisms in the experiment. The larger the sample size, the higher the statistical power of the experiment. While more is always better, it is usually impossible to test every possible case or every possible person, so a smaller sample of the whole must be taken.

The group of every possible person or organism is the population, out of which the sample is selected. The population could be very broad – every single human would have many billions in the population – or it could be much narrower. The population of 25 year old females living in France with North African ancestry who have completed college and self-identify as queer would be a much smaller population.

Typically, experimenters try to take a random sample of the population under study, simply because studying every single individual would be impossible. If researchers wished to assess the levels of DDT present in hawks, they could not capture and assess every hawk. Instead, they would have to capture a random group of hawks and test them, and then extrapolate to the whole population.

When researchers attempt to generate a random sample but instead get a biased, or non-random sample, an error can be introduced into the results. One example of such an unintended biased sample was in the polling results for the 2008 US presidential elections. Polling companies called people before the election to ask them who they intended to vote for. But such companies were depending on traditional land lines rather than cell phones. As it turned out, those voters who only used cell phones tended to skew both younger and more Democratic in their voting patterns. As a result, the election resulted in a much bigger win for the Democratic candidate than had been predicted.

Some other common types of bias include: geographic bias (surveying people in only one area), self-selection bias (only surveying those who choose to participate), pre-screening bias (only including those participants who saw the initial screening questions), and healthy population bias (using only people who are more likely than average to be healthy in the study).

The t-test

The t-test is a very common statistical measure used when analyzing experimental data. It's a way to see if the mean of two data sets are actually different, or if the difference is simply due to chance. For example, researchers might measure the mean doubling time of a certain bacterial population as 25.2 minutes, then administer a drug and find the new mean doubling time to be 21.5 minutes. Are these two numbers actually different, or is the difference merely due to chance?

This is where a t-test would be used. For the MCAT, you won't have to actually know how to calculate a t-test. Instead, you will have to be familiar with the importance of p-values. After performing a t-test and comparing it to a table of p-values, experimenters can determine if the difference they've observed is significant or not. Typically, a p-value must be below 0.05 for any observed difference to be statistically significant. This means that there is only a 5% chance that the observation was due to chance alone, and there is a 95% chance that the observed difference is real.

In our previous example, let's imagine the experimenters found that the p-value for the two means (25.2 minutes and then 21.5 minutes) was 0.15. This would mean that there is an 85% chance that those two numbers really are different, and a 15% chance that the difference observed is just due to random chance. You might think that's pretty good – "Hey, 85% chance of a real difference sounds good to me!" but researchers are a careful, conservative bunch. They only assert that their observations are statistically significant if they're *at least* 95% sure that it's real.

The Null Hypothesis

The tests discussed above are all done in relation to the null hypothesis. The null hypothesis says that whatever we're testing is irrelevant, not true, or there is no difference between the populations. We more often think not of proving our hypothesis, but rather of rejecting the null hypothesis.

For example, let's say we're testing a hypothesis that says that increasing the temperature of a cell broth will lower the doubling time of that population of cells. The null hypothesis would be, "Raising the temperature of a cell broth will have no effect on doubling time." We then set out disprove the null hypothesis. If we can conclusively disprove it, then our original hypothesis is much more likely to be true.

When comparing our results to the null hypothesis, it is possible to get it right or make an error:

1. Type I error = the null hypothesis is true, but we reject it

This is a **false positive**. We think our hypothesis is true, but in reality the null hypothesis is true.

In health care, a false positive can be relatively harmless, or *very* dangerous. For example, you might think you have a fever because you feel flushed, and so you take an aspirin. If you're otherwise healthy, a single aspirin poses no real risk. If it turns out you didn't actually have a fever, then your self-assessment was a false positive, albeit a harmless one. By contrast, a false positive that said a patient has cancer (when in fact she doesn't) could be *very* harmful if it lead to a lengthy and unnecessary round of damaging chemotherapy.

2. Type II error = the null hypothesis is false, but we accept it

This is called a **false negative**. Our hypothesis was true, but we reject it and accept the null hypothesis.

In health care, this would be "missing the diagnosis" – the patient *had* the condition, but we told him that he didn't. Just as with a false positive, a false negative can have consequences that are very mild (if the condition is benign or would clear up on its own) or are fatal.

3. Null hypothesis is true, and we accept the null hypothesis.

This would be an example of confidence. We had a hypothesis, but it was wrong, and we demonstrated that it was wrong. If our results have statistical significance, and the stronger our results are, the more **confidence** our study has.

4. The null hypothesis is false, and we reject the null hypothesis.

Here our hypothesis was true and we figured out that it was true (and that the null hypothesis was wrong). If we have good results, and a strong, well-constructed study, we would say our results have power. The better our results, and the more likely that we're right, the more **power** our study has.

Positive and Negative Correlation

When comparing independent and dependent variable, researchers look to see how closely correlated they are. This relationship is expressed as a correlation coefficient (usually denoted R) that ranges from -1 to +1. A correlation value of -1 would indicate perfect negative correlation. A value of +1 indicates perfect positive correlation, and 0 indicates no correlation at all.

A data set with no correlation, when graphed, will not demonstrate any particular relationship:

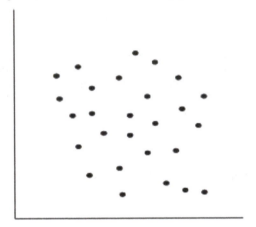

Figure 1 No correlation

Compare that to a data set with a negative correlation. In the figure below, the correlation is a very strong relationship, because the data points all lie very close to the line:

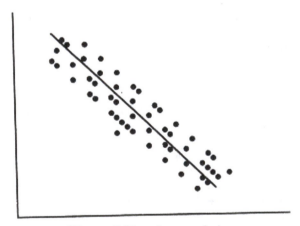

Figure 2 Negative correlation

And finally, here's an example of a positive correlation (in the graph below, R is approximately +0.6):

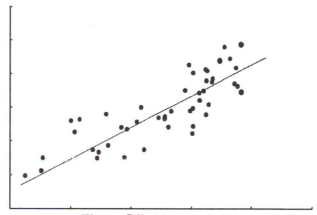

Figure 3 Positive correlation

We remember, though, that correlation does not prove causation. Two things may be correlated – even *perfectly* correlated, even though one does not directly cause the other.

Validity and Reliability

For an experiment or test to have value, it must be both valid and reliable.

Validity is a measure of how well a given experiment is actually measuring what it sets out to measure. If a study has internal validity then it means that the study has internally been well constructed, using things like large random samples, safeguards against confounding variables, reasonable and reliable processes and instruments, etc. If a study is internally valid, we can then assess whether it has external validity – can the results of the experiment be generalized to other settings. After all, if a study only shows that X is related to Y *for this experimental group*, then it's not very valuable for drawing conclusions about the larger population. To have external validity, an experiment must tightly control any situational variables in the execution of the study. Finally, construct validity refers to how well a given assessment (a survey, a test, etc.) actually measures what it claims to measure – has it been properly constructed to measure the relevant thing.

Reliability refers to how consistent and repeatable an experiment or assessment is. Test-test reliability refers to the fact that a good test should give stable results over time. For example, if you took the MCAT once a year every year without doing any prep or practice (although why on Earth would you want to do something like that?!), you would get basically the same results every time because the MCAT has good test-test reliability. One other form of reliability is inter-rater reliability. That means that if an assessment is carried out by different researchers, they should generate similar results. For example, the SAT includes an essay that a person grades on a scale of 1-6. The SAT essay has good inter-rater reliability because the same essay will be given the same (or nearly the same) score regardless of which person scores it.

Biases and the Double-Blind Randomized Controlled Trial

When conducting research, especially with human subjects, it is extraordinarily easy to skew the results due to unintended biases on the part of the researchers or the subjects. If the subjects know that they're getting a new experimental drug, they may over-state the results due to the placebo effect. If the researchers know which subjects are getting the new treatment and which are getting the placebo, they may unconsciously skew the results through their tone or body language when communicating with patients.

To avoid these problems, researchers use randomized controlled trials, and whenever possible they use a double-blind protocol. In a randomized controlled trial, the subjects are randomly assigned to the experimental group and to the control group. This prevents any bias in who gets assigned to which group. The control group will receive either no treatment, a placebo, or the current standard treatment.

In a blind trial, the patients do not know whether they are receiving the placebo or the experimental treatment. This helps prevent any biased reactions from the subjects. Some people, for example, may feel (perhaps unconsciously) that if they are getting a fancy new experimental treatment, they "should" get better, and so will report a larger improvement in their symptoms than they otherwise would. While a blind trial is helpful, it can still introduce biases through unintended communication from the researchers.

To prevent this, researchers use a double-blind trial in which neither the subjects, nor the researchers, know who is receiving the treatment and who is receiving the control. All of the data identifying which is the control and which is the experimental group are held by a person who is not directly interacting with the patients, and it is only after the data have been collected and analyzed that researchers "remove the blinds" to see what the results show.

FINAL EXAM
PHYSICS CONTENT REVIEW

Note: unless friction, air resistance, or viscosity is explicitly mentioned, neglect them. Estimate g = 10 m/s².

1. A driver drives 1 km northwest and then 1 km northeast. What is the magnitude of his displacement?

A) 1 km
B) 1.4 km
C) 2 km
D) 4 km

2. A driver drives 1 km northwest and then 1 km northeast. What is the positive difference between his distance and displacement?

A) 0.6 km
B) 1 km
C) 2 km
D) 2.4 km

3. Two children push a box northward. The bigger child pushes with a 200 N force and the younger child pushes with a 100 N force. Their father pushes southward with a 300 N force. Which of the following must be true?

A) The box is moving northward at a constant speed.
B) If the box is moving, it cannot be moving northward or southward.
C) The box is stationary.
D) The box is not accelerating.

4. A person cycling at 2 m/s accelerates at 1 m/s² over a distance of 10.5 m. His final velocity is:

A) 3 m/s
B) 5 m/s
C) 10.5 m/s
D) 12.5 m/s

5. A car traveling at 50 m/s comes to rest. The car's brakes are capable of creating a deceleration of 12.5 m/s². Over what distance does the car come to rest?

A) 4 m
B) 10 m
C) 100 m
D) 2500 m

6. The chain that a tugboat uses to pull a ship is designed to pull a ship at a constant 10 m/s with a maximum force of 150 kN. When the tugboat first begins pulling a boat that is the maximum weight, how does the tension in the chain compare to 150 kN?

A) Significantly less than 150 kN
B) Slightly less than 150 kN
C) Exactly equal to 150 kN
D) Slightly more than 150 kN.

7. A 3 kg spherical object is dropped from the top of 150 m tall building. A second object with a mass of 35 kg and shaped in a cube is thrown downward from the same building at the same time, with an initial velocity of 5 m/s. Which object experiences a greater change in velocity during the first 1.4 seconds of the fall?

A) The 3 kg sphere
B) The 35 kg cube
C) Neither
D) The 3 kg sphere, so long as air resistance is neglected.

8. Galileo is standing on top of the Learning Tower of Pisa and he drops two spheres from it at the same time: 1 kg metal sphere and a 0.1 kg wooden sphere. The gravitational force on the objects:

A) is the same since all objects fall at the same speed.
B) is greater for the metal sphere.
C) is greater for the wooden sphere.
D) is the same so long as the objects are dropped from the same height.

9. A ball is thrown straight upwards. At what point in the ball's path is there the largest angle between its momentum and acceleration vectors?

A) During the entire trip up
B) During the entire trip down
C) Just after being released
D) Just before hitting the ground

10. An inclined plane with an angle of 45° to the horizontal has a 50 kg box resting on it. What is the approximate magnitude of the friction force needed to keep the box stationary?

A) 50 N
B) 250 N
C) 350 N
D) 500 N

11. What is the SI unit for momentum?

A) kg
B) N
C) kg•m / s^2
D) kg•m/s

12. For an box placed on an inclined plane, if the angle of the incline is lowered from a 45° to a 30° angle with respect to the horizontal, then the friction force:

A) will decrease.
B) will increase.
C) will remain the same.
D) will increase or decrease depending on the mass of the object and μ.

13. An object is thrown horizontally at 12 m/s from a window 200 m above the ground. After 0.5 s the object's speed is closest to:

A) 5 m/s
B) 12 m/s
C) 13 m/s
D) 17 m/s

14. A person pushes a desk across a tile floor at a constant speed of 0.5 m/s. Another person pushes the same desk, but at a constant speed of 0.75 m/s. The desk has a mass of 100 kg and the coefficient of friction is μ = 0.2. Which of the following is true?

A) The man pushing the desk at 0.75 m/s has to overcome a greater friction force.
B) The man pushing the desk at 0.5 m/s has to overcome a greater friction force.
C) The desk is experiencing a greater magnitude of forces (but not a greater net force) when being pushed at 0.75 m/s.
D) The same kinetic friction force is present in both cases.

15. A forklift holds a 100 kg weight 10 m in the air and then slowly lifts it to 25 m in the air. How much work is done holding the weight in the air and hoisting it up further, respectively?

A) 0 J and 15 kJ
B) 10,000 J and 25,000 J
C) 0 J and 25 kJ
D) 15 kJ and 25 kJ

16. A sled dog is pulling a sled along icy level ground. The tether between the dog and the front of the sled makes an angle of 30° to the horizontal. The sled and rider have a mass of 243 kg and the tension in the tether is 3000 N. If the dog pulls the sled for 50 m at a constant speed, approximately how much work has the dog done?

A) 2,4300 J
B) 30,000 J
C) 130,000 J
D) 150,000 J

17. A 200 kg object starting from rest is accelerated to 20 m/s in 4 seconds. The power required to do this is equal to:

A) 10 W
B) 10 kW
C) 40 W
D) 40 kW

18. A student drops a 2 kg bowling ball out of a window 10 m off the ground. When the ball is 1.4 m from the surface of the ground, what is the total mechanical energy of the falling ball?

A) 20 J
B) 28 J
C) 200 J
D) 280 J

19. A chamber filled with Neon is increased in pressure from 2.3 atm to 4.3 atm in an isovolumetric process. During the process, the work done on the gas is:

A) dependent on the temperature.
B) 202, 650 J
C) unknown unless intermolecular forces are compensated for.
D) 0 J.

20. In the three-rope pulley system below the mass m = 15 kg. What is the tension in each of the three ropes?

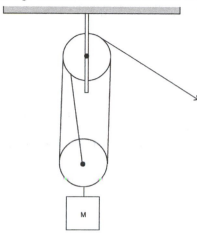

A) 45 N
B) 50 N
C) 150 N
D) 450 N

21. In the two-rope pulley system below the mass is 10 kg. How much work is done lifting the mass 1 m?

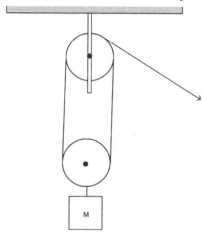

A) 10 J
B) 33 J
C) 100 J
D) 300 J

22. In the four-rope pulley system below, the mass is 20 kg and is being lowered with an acceleration of 2 m/s^2. What is the tension in each of the four segments of rope?

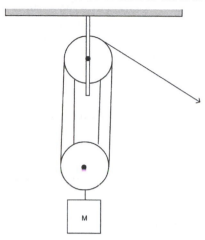

A) 20 N
B) 40 N
C) 160 N
D) 200 N

23. Each of the following is a non-conservative force EXCEPT:

A) electrostatic force.
B) friction.
C) air resistance.
D) viscosity.

24. A satellite moves in geosynchronous orbit around the Earth. Which of the following is true regarding this motion?

A) The velocity of the satellite does work.
B) The velocity does no work but the gravitational force does work.
C) The potential energy of the satellite increases as it moves around the Earth.
D) $W_{net} = 0$

25. The cartilage between vertebrae can be modeled as a spring system. If the cartilage is first compressed 2 mm and then compressed 4 mm, the potential energy stored in the cartilage has:

A) been cut in half.
B) remained the same.
C) doubled.
D) quadrupled.

26. Assume a system with perfect conservation of mechanical energy. A metal sphere with a mass of 50 g is dropped from a 1 m height. It hits a small platform attached to a spring, compresses the spring, and then is bounced back upwards by the spring. The same experiment is then repeated with a 5 g plastic sphere. Which of the following is true of this experiment:

A) Both the metal and plastic spheres will compress the spring the same amount.
B) The metal and plastic sphere experience equal acceleration and equal gravitational force.
C) Both the metal and plastic spheres will bounce up to the same height.
D) V_{final} as measured just before impact with the spring is greater for the metal sphere.

27. Mechanical advantage is measured as:

A) a ratio of work.
B) a ratio of power.
C) a ratio of force.
D) a ratio of potential energy.

28. Efficiency is a ratio that compares:

A) input force to output force.
B) input work to output work.
C) temperature as measured relative to absolute zero.
D) performance relative to the performance of a Carnot engine.

29. An object starts at 0°C and warms to 20°C. Its temperature has increased by how many degrees Fahrenheit?

A) 0
B) 20
C) 36
D) 68

30. A small footbridge is built of steel and is 5 m long. The trail's typical winter temperature is -10 °C and typical summer temperature is 80°C. The footbridge expands how far during a season change from winter to summer? ($\alpha = 1 \times 10^{-5} K^{-1}$)

A) 0.40 cm
B) 0.45 cm
C) 45 cm
D) 4.5 m

31. Heat transferred from the Sun to the Earth moves via:

A) radiation.
B) conduction.
C) pressure waves.
D) convection.

32. A person is making spaghetti and stirring the pot of boiling water with a metal spoon. The person burns their hand on the spoon. This heat was transferred via:

A) radiation.
B) conduction.
C) pressure waves.
D) convection.

33. A researcher wishes to melt a 500 g sample of a substance, starting from a temperature of 25 °C. The melting point of the substance is 1050 °C, its specific heat is 125 J/kg•K and its latent heat of fusion is 6.4 x 10^4 J/kg. Which of the following is closest to the amount of heat that must be added?

A) 3 kJ
B) 30 kJ
C) 60 kJ
D) 90 kJ

34. A cat lies in a sunny patch on the floor to warm up. Assume the cat's specific heat is the same as water and that the cat lies in the sun for an hour. If the sun is creating a net transfer of heat into the cat of 4.44 x 10^{-2} W, the cat has a mass of 4 kg and the cat starts at 38 °C, approximately how warm will the cat be by the end of the hour?

A) 36 °C
B) 38 °C
C) 40 °C
D) 238 °C

35. In an adiabatic compression:

I. the temperature of the gas goes up.
II. the net work is 0.
III. work is done on the gas.

A) I only
B) II only
C) I and II only
D) I and III only

36. Each of the following are state functions EXCEPT:

A) Gibbs free energy
B) Density
C) Heat
D) Entropy

37. In a heating system in a house, water is heated to 150 °C in a pressurized boiler in the basement and this super-heated water is forced through metal pipes to units in each room, warming them and then cycling the cooler water back to the boiler. The heat transfer in this system can be described as:

A) convection then conduction.
B) conduction.
C) convection.
D) radiation then convection.

38. Heat is added to a liquid. Which of the following must be true of this heat transfer?

A) The temperature increases.
B) The temperature decreases.
C) The temperature remains the same.
D) Cannot be determined without more information

39. A student has a mixture of ink and water and he agitates the beaker to thoroughly mix the two substances. He then does the same with a beaker full of oil and water. He then lets both uniform mixtures stand overnight. The next morning, the oil has completely separated to the top of the beaker but the ink and water mixture remains unchanged. Overnight, which of the following occurred:

A) the entropy of the ink and water mixture increased.
B) the entropy of the ink and water mixture decreased.
C) the entropy of the oil and water mixture decreased.
D) the entropy of the oil and water mixture increased.

40. Two samples of liquid with equal mass and boiling points both start at room temperature and are heated at the same rate. Sample A begins boiling before Sample B. This could be due to:

A) Sample B has a higher heat of fusion.
B) Sample A having a lower specific heat.
C) Sample B having a higher latent heat of vaporization.
D) Sample A having a lower boiling point.

41. A calorie is:

A) equal to 1/4.184 J.
B) the same thing as a Calorie.
C) the amount of energy needed to raise one gram of water by one Kelvin.
D) the only form of energy that can result in a phase change.

42. In the diagram below, the work done by the gas is closest to:

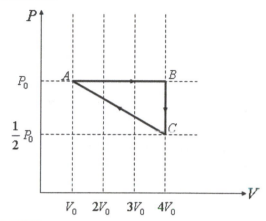

A) $P_0 V_0$
B) $1/2(P_0 V_0)$
C) $3/4(P_0 V_0)$
D) $3/2(P_0 V_0)$

43. The human body is a very highly organized system. Given that the entropy of the universe is always increasing, the human body:

A) illustrates the effect of extra-scientific principles on human life.
B) is able to exist because metabolism increases the entropy of the universe.
C) relies on the decrease in entropy created when a lipid bilayer spontaneously forms in aqueous environment.
D) engages in anabolic behavior that violates thermodynamic principles.

44. A leak develops in a bomb calorimeter. The device has now gone from:

A) an isolated system to an open system.
B) a closed system to an open system.
C) a closed system to an isolated system.
D) a perfectly functioning calorimeter to one in which heat gained from the environment will distort test results.

45. It is possible to add heat to a system but have the temperature remain the same if:

I. the system is going through a phase change.
II. the system does work.
III. the system is composed only of solids.

A) I only
B) II only
C) II and III only
D) I and II only

46. In an isothermal process, 450 J of work are added to a system. Heat flow must consist of:

A) 450 J of heat into the system.
B) 0 heat flow.
C) 450 J out of the system.
D) 900 J out of the system.

47. A child swims to the bottom of a swimming pool holding two toys. One is a plastic dog with a density of 1.2 g/cm^3 and the other is a model truck of density 2.4 g/cm^3. The gauge pressure on the plastic toy is 1.3 atm. What is the gauge pressure on the truck?

A) 0.65 atm
B) 1.3 atm
C) 2.6 atm
D) cannot be determined without knowing the volume of the truck.

48. What is the tension on the rope in the diagram below, assuming the ρ water = 1 g/cm^3, the ρ of the object is 2 g/cm^3 and its volume is 10 cm^3?

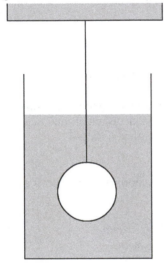

A) 0.01 N
B) 0.1 N
C) 0.2 N
D) 20 N

49. A child swims to the bottom of a swimming pool holding two toys. One is a plastic dog with a density of 0.2 g/cm^3 and the other is a model truck of density 0.4 g/cm^3. The child releases both toys. Which of the following is true regarding their acceleration?

A) The dog accelerates more quickly.
B) The truck accelerates more quickly.
C) They accelerate at equal rates.
D) Acceleration depends on depth.

50. In a given piston, the pressure is doubled. If the surface area of the piston remains constant, then the force in the piston:

A) is halved.
B) remains the same.
C) is doubled.
D) is quadrupled.

51. If the cross-section area of a pipe constricts so that it is one-quarter its original area, then the velocity of the fluid flowing through the narrow end:

A) is one-quarter the velocity at the wide end.
B) must be the same velocity throughout.
C) is determined by the pressure in the pipe.
D) is four times the velocity at the wide end.

52. A hydraulic lift is constructed with piston 1 having a radius of 0.1 m and piston 2 having a radius of 2 m. If a 10 N force is applied to piston 1, then the force at piston 2 will be:

A) 5 x 10^{-2} N
B) 10 N
C) 200 N
D) 4000 N

53. The speed of the blood through the arterioles is much higher than the speed of the blood flow through the venules. Assuming laminar flow and no fluid loss or gain, which of the following most likely explains this observation?

A) Veins have valves but arteries do not.
B) Arteries are generally located higher in the body than veins.
C) The total cross-sectional area of the arterioles is much lower than the venules.
D) The arterioles experience greater force from the heart.

54. A person inflates the front and rear tires of their car. The front tires are inflated until they give a gauge pressure reading of 2.2 atm. The rear tires are inflated until the total pressure inside them is 3.5 atm. Of the following answer choices which one gives the ratio of the gauge pressure in the front to rear tires?

A) 22:35
B) 22:25
C) 35:22
D) 202,650:615,319

55. An ice cube floats in water with 10% of its volume above the surface of the water. The system is then transported to the moon where the gravitational force is 1/6 that of Earth. The ice cube then floats with:

A) 16.7% of its volume above the surface.
B) 16.7% of its volume below the surface.
C) 0.67% of its volume above the surface.
D) 90% of its volume below the surface.

56. In the diagram below, the magnitude of the force attracting the negative charge towards the positive charge is:

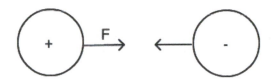

A) 1/2 F
B) F
C) 2F
D) F²

57. What happens to the magnitude of the force acting on the negatively charged object if the distance between the two objects is decreased to half its original distance?

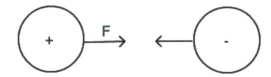

A) 1/2 F
B) F
C) 2F
D) 4F

58. An electron is moving from left to right at speed v. There is a magnetic field pointed from right to left. The electron will accelerate:

A) in the same direction, faster.
B) in the opposite direction, decelerating.
C) out of the plane of the page.
D) not at all.

59. An electron is moving from left to right at speed v. There is a magnetic field pointed downwards in the plane of the page. The electron will accelerate:

A) in the same direction, faster.
B) in the opposite direction, decelerating.
C) out of the plane of the page.
D) not at all.

60. An electron is moving from left to right at speed v. There is an electric field pointed from right to left. The electron will accelerate:

A) in the same direction, faster.
B) in the opposite direction, decelerating.
C) out of the plane of the page.
D) not at all.

61. Each of the following is an expression for potential EXCEPT:

A) N/m
B) V
C) J/C
D) N•m/C

62. If the spheres are moved twice as far apart, the force between them will be:

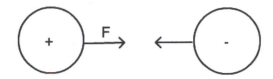

A) 1/4 F
B) 1/2 F
C) F
D) F²

63. In an electrical field generated by a point charge +Q, the potential is zero at:

A) distance = 0.
B) any distance equal to the radius of the charge.
C) at any point on an equipotential line running antiparallel to the field line vector.
D) infinite distance away.

64. A 12-volt car battery is used to do 120 J worth of work on a charge. The charge is:

A) 10 C
B) 12 C
C) 120 C
D) 1440 C

65. During a single flash of a strobe light, 1.2 C of charge passes through the circuit in 0.02 s. This is:

A) 0.0125 A
B) 0.024 A
C) 60 A
D) 120 A

66. A resistor has its resistivity doubled and its length halved. The new resistance is:

A) halved.
B) the same.
C) doubled.
D) increased by a factor of 3/2.

67. When a galvanic cell is constructed, its emf is 2.2 V. When hooked up to a circuit with a 4 ohm resistor, it is found to provide a current of 0.5 A. The battery's internal resistance is:

A) 0.2 ohm
B) 0.4 ohm
C) 1.1 ohm
D) 2.2 ohm

68. Voltage can be altered using a transformer, but a transformer neither adds nor subtracts energy. If a step-down transformer is used to convert 20 kV to 120 V, then the ratio $I_F : I_I$ must be:

A) 1:1
B) 1:6
C) 6:1
D) 500:3

69. What is the total resistance in the circuit below?

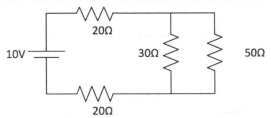

A) 20 Ω
B) 58.75 Ω
C) 70 Ω
D) 120 Ω

70. In the circuit below, what is the ratio of the current flowing through the first 20 Ω resistor and the second one?

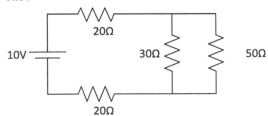

A) 1:1
B) 1:2
C) 2:1
D) 5:1

71. In the circuit below, what is the ratio of the voltage drop across the 30 Ω resistor to the voltage drop across the 50 Ω resistor.

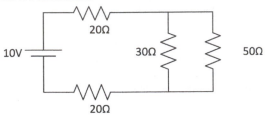

A) 3:5
B) 5:3
C) 1:1
D) 25:9

72. Which of the following will double the capacitance of a capacitor?

I. Doubling the surface area
II. Inserting a dielectric with a dielectric constant of 2
III. Doubling the distance between the plates

A) I only
B) I and II only
C) I and III only
D) I, II, and III

73. An ideal voltmeter should have:

A) infinite resistance.
B) zero resistance.
C) all of the current in the circuit passing through it.
D) a total current of $\sqrt{2} \cdot I_{TOT}$ passing through it

74. A man playing a didgeridoo is able to create a resonant hum in the instrument by vibrating his lips on one end at 80 Hz. If he then picks up an identically constructed didgeridoo and vibrates his lips at 82 Hz, he will:

A) not get a resonant tone.
B) hear the same note.
C) hear a lower-pitched note.
D) hear a louder note.

75. A pregnant woman is having an ultrasound of her fetus performed. The machine is able to generate an image based on:

A) the attenuation of the reflected sound wave.
B) the time it takes for the sound to be reflected.
C) the wavelength of the reflected wave.
D) the degree of refraction of the incident wave.

76. Two planes are flying towards each other. Each plane is flying at half the speed of sound, which is 340 m/s. A radar beam from one plane, emitted at 15 kHz, would be detected by the other plane at:

A) 7.5 kHz
B) 15 kHz
C) 30 kHz
D) 45 kHz

77. Two boys are standing on a maglev train that is moving due south at 150 m/s. One boy throws a ball due north to the other boy, who is standing 5 m away in the same train car. The ball makes a tone at 800 Hz as it flies. The boy catching the ball will perceive a tone that is:

A) significantly lower than 800 Hz
B) equal to 800 Hz
C) slightly higher than 800 Hz
D) significantly higher than 800 Hz.

78. A wave with a period of 0.01 s travels at 10 m/s. Its wavelength is:

A) 0.1 m
B) 0.01 m
C) 0.002 m
D) 0.001 m

79. An organ pipe is closed at one end and open at the other. It is 2 m long. What is the wavelength of the fundamental harmonic produced by the instrument? (v_{sound} = 340 m/s)

A) 1/2 m
B) 1 m
C) 2 m
D) 8 m

80. A sound goes from 22 dB to 52 dB. The intensity of the sound has increased by a factor of:

A) 2.4
B) 30
C) log 52
D) 1000

81. A closed tube instrument produces a tone at its third harmonic. The tone has a frequency of 170 Hz. What is the length of the instrument? (v_{sound} = 340 m/s)

A) 0.5 m
B) 1.0 m
C) 1.5 m
D) 3.0 m

82. A man escapes from the sinking Titanic. While swimming underwater, he hears the large boom of the rear section of the ship breaking off from the front section of the ship. He is startled and pokes his head above the water when he then hears the sound again. This perception is likely due to:

A) auditory hallucination from the trauma of the event.
B) sound travelling faster in liquids than in gases.
C) the temperature differential between the water and the air.
D) Doppler effect at the air-water interface.

83. Which of the following represents a frequency of light in the visible range?

A) 8×10^4 Hz
B) 2×10^6 Hz
C) 4.5×10^{14} Hz
D) 1.4×10^{28} Hz

84. While shaving, a man's face is 1.5 m in front of a plane mirror. The distance between his face and the reflection appears to be:

A) 0 m.
B) 1.5 m.
C) 3.0 m.
D) infinite.

85. The radius of curvature of a 1.5 m x 3.0 m rectangular plane mirror is:

A) 0.75 m
B) 4.5 m
C) 9.0 m
D) infinite.

86. An object is placed at the focal point of a converging lens. The image is:

A) infinitely far away.
B) real, inverted, and placed at the focal point on the opposite side of the lens.
C) upright, virtual, and behind the object.
D) real, upright, and between the object and the lens.

87. A beam of light is refracted from air into water. Which of the following remains the same?

I. Frequency
II. Wavelength
III. Color

A) I only
B) II only
C) I and III only
D) I, II, and III

88. Light moves through three media. First air, then medium 1 with an n = 1.5 and then into medium 2 with an n = 3.0. The angle of incidence is 45°. Which of the following is closest to the angle of refraction in medium 2?

A) 65°
B) 45°
C) 40°
D) 15°

89. An image is placed in front of a concave mirror at a distance less than the focal length. The image produced is:

A) real and upright.
B) real and inverted.
C) virtual and upright.
D) virtual and inverted.

90. A two lens system is constructed such that the magnification of the first lens is 2.5 and the magnification of the second lens is -2.5. The total magnification produced by the system is:

A) -6.25
B) -5
C) 0
D) 1

91. Which of the following can produce a virtual image:

A) a plane mirror.
B) a convex lens.
C) a convex mirror.
D) all of the above.

92. A beam of light with frequency 2.7×10^{11} Hz is incident on a piece of metal (assume a negligible work function). What is the approximate speed of the ejected electrons? (h = 6.6×10^{-34} J•s and mass of electron = 9×10^{-31} kg)

A) 20,000 m/s
B) 200,000 m/s
C) 400,000 m/s
D) 4×10^{31} m/s

93. Which of the following correctly characterizes the Bohr model of the atom?

I. Energy levels that are discrete.
II. Electrons may move from n = 2 to n = 4 only by emitting a photon whose energy matches the energy difference between the two levels.
III. The electron only moves from one energy level to another by absorbing or emitting a photon.

A) I only
B) I and III only
C) II and III only
D) I, II, and III

94. A hydrogen atom's electron falls from a higher energy level to a lower one, emitting 1.6×10^{-18} J. What is the approximate wavelength of this photon? (h = 6.6×10^{-34} J•s)

A) 2.5×10^{15} m
B) 1.6×10^{33} m
C) 1.2×10^{-7} m
D) 3.3×10^{7} m

95. A researcher shines a beam of IR light on a metal and then shines a beam of UV light on the metal. The UV light generates a current in a circuit, but IR light does not. This is because:

A) UV light has a longer wavelength than IR light.
B) UV light impacts the metal with greater kinetic energy than the IR light.
C) The collisions between the IR light and the electrons of the metal are nonelastic.
D) UV light has an energy level higher than the work function but IR light does not.

96. Zinc, with an atomic mass of 67, emits a negatively charged particle and becomes ^{67}Ga. This process is:

A) β decay.
B) α decay.
C) electron capture.
D) gamma decay.

97. A given isotope decays every 6 hours. After one day, how much of the sample remains?

A) 4/6
B) 1/8
C) 1/16
D) 1/32

98. An oxygen nucleus is fissioned such that it breaks up into α particles. How many alpha particles could be created?

A) 2
B) 3
C) 4
D) 8

99. A nucleus undergoes one α decay, two β decays, and three γ decays. The difference between the atomic mass of the starting nucleus and the daughter nucleus is:

A) 2
B) 4
C) 6
D) 9

100. Which of the following is a SI base unit?

A) Ohm
B) Coulomb
C) Gram
D) Kelvin

Final Exam
Math Skills Review

Note: throughout this exam, where calculating an exact answer would be cumbersome, use approximation. Logarithm functions are all base 10 or natural log.

1. $13 + 9 =$

2. $3.4 + 87 =$

3. $120 / 20 =$

4. $125 / 0.1 =$

5. $8 \times 7 =$

6. $2 \times 18 =$

7. $5 \times 150 =$

8. $0.1 \times 38 =$

9. $3.6 \times 10.1 =$

10. $0.02 \times 0.05 =$

11. $2 \times \sqrt{2} =$

12. $\sqrt{5} \times \sqrt{5} =$

13. $3^3 + 2^4 =$

14. $6^2 \times \sqrt{6} =$

15. $10^5 / 10^2 =$

16. $5^5 \times 25^2 =$

17. $\sqrt{140} =$

18. $2^3 + 2^5 =$

19. $(\sqrt{10000}) / 100 =$

20. $(2^2 + 3^3) / (2 + 3)^2 =$

21. $23 \times 10^{14} \times 2 \times 10^{-6} =$

22. $5 \times 10^5 + 2 \times 10^6 =$

23. $(6 \times 10^{12}) / (3 \times 10^{10}) =$

24. $\sqrt{(1.6 \times 10^{17})} =$

25. $(7 \times 10^3)^2 / (\sqrt{(4.9 \times 10^{-17})}) =$

26. $\log 1 =$

27. $\log 30 =$

28. $\log 300 - \log 200 =$

29. $\log 20 + \log 5 =$

30. $\log (1/1000) =$

31. $\log (3 \times 10^6) =$

32. $\log (8 \times 10^{-7}) =$

33. $-\log (3 \times 10^{-10}) =$

34. Simplify $([x^2 + 3x^2] / 4x^3)$

35. $\sin 0° =$

36. $\sin 45° =$

37. $\sin 90° =$

38. $\cos 30° =$

39. $\cos 60° =$

40. $\cos 180° =$

41. $\tan 0° =$

42. $\tan 30° =$

43. $\tan 45° =$

44. $\tan 180° =$

45. $\sin^{-1} 1/2 =$

46. $\sin^{-1} 1 =$

47. $\sin^{-1} \sqrt{2}/2 =$

48. $\cos^{-1} 0 =$

49. $\cos^{-1} \sqrt{3}/2 =$

50. $\cos^{-1} 1/2 =$

51. $\tan^{-1} 1 =$

52. $\tan^{-1} \sqrt{3} =$

53. $\tan^{-1} \sqrt{3}/3 =$

54. kilo- means:

55. giga- means:

56. micro- means:

57. pico- means:

58. 1 Calorie is how many joules?

59. 1 inch is approximately how many centimeters?

60. $1\ N \times 1\ m \times 1\ C^{-1} =$

61. $1\ kg \times 1\ m^2 \times 1\ s^{-2} =$

62. $1\ kg \times 1\ m \times 1\ s^{-1} =$

63. Solve for x: $2x + 2y = 10;\ 3x + y = 15$

64. Given $E = hf$ and $E = 1/2 \times mv^2$ solve for mass in terms of Planck's constant

65. Given $P_1V_1 = nRT$ and $P_1V_1 = P_2V_2$ solve for V_2 in terms of n and V_1.

66. In the equation $A_1B_1 = A_2B_2$ the variable have what relationship?

67. In the equation $X_1/Y_1 = X_2/Y_2$ the variables have what relationship?

68. All else held constant, in the equation $PV = nRT$, if T goes up what happens to P? to n?

69. All else held constant, in the equation $PV = nRT$ if V goes down what happens to P? to T? to n?

70. $3.612 \times 10.025 / 4.9987 =$

71. $101,325 \times 3.14159 / 99,011.2 =$

72. $500^{0.2}$ is approximately =

73. What is the maximum value of $3\sin\theta +1$?

74. What is the minimum value of $2 - 2\cos\theta$?

75. In the equation $R = k[X]^2$ the value of [X] is given in molarity and the value of k is given in $L \times mol^{-1} \times sec^{-1}$. What are the units of the rate?

76. Cats need a base energy intake of 2×10^4 J / day plus an additional 2×10^3 J per kg of body weight. Dogs need a base energy intake of 8×10^3 J/day plus an additional 4×10^3 J per kg of body weight. At what weight would a dog and a cat have the same caloric needs per day?

77. In a study of the relative effectiveness of a new drug, which of the following would qualify as a positive control group?

A) A group receiving a placebo
B) A group receiving double the dose of the experimental drug
C) A group not enrolled in the study
D) A group receiving the treatment that is currently the standard drug

78. In a study of the relative effectiveness of a new drug, which of the following would qualify as a negative control group?

A) A group receiving a placebo
B) A group receiving double the dose of the experimental drug
C) A group not enrolled in the study
D) A group receiving the treatment that is currently the standard drug

For questions 79-81, refer to the following diagram:

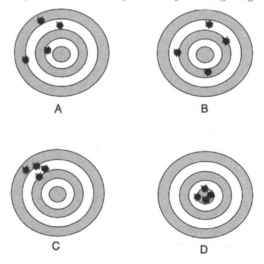

79. Which represents a precise but inaccurate array?

80. Which represents an accurate but imprecise array?

81. Which is neither accurate nor precise?

82. Is validity more concerned with accuracy or precision?

83. Is reliability more concerned with accuracy or precision?

84. An observational study of health in people that follows a group with diabetes and group without over a period of time would be a(n):

A) case-control study.
B) cohort study.
C) cross-sectional study.
D) double-blind study.

85. An observational study of health in people that analyzes a large group of people at a single point in time would be a(n):

A) case-control study.
B) cohort study.
C) cross-sectional study.
D) double-blind study.

86. A study in which the researchers administering a drug do not know whether it is the experimental drug or a control nor do the patients would be a(n):

A) case-control study.
B) cohort study.
C) cross-sectional study.
D) double-blind study.

For questions 87 – 90 use the following data set:

$\{23, 19, 6, 35, 23, 21\}$

87. Find the mean.
88. Find the mode.
89. Find the median.
90. If the 23 were replaced with a 95, the standard deviation of the set would:

91. In the normal distribution curve, approximately how much of the data set lies within one standard deviation of the mean?

92. In a negatively skewed data set, the mean is:

A) less than the median.
B) more than the median.
C) equal to the median.
D) not able to be calculated.

93. When assessing the level of cannabis consumption in a population, usage was especially high among the 10 – 19 age group and the 60 – 69 age group. This represents a distribution that is:

A) negatively skewed.
B) positively skewed.
C) normal.
D) bimodal.

94. A data set may include an outlier for any of the following reasons EXCEPT:

A) a data that is highly skewed with a long tail.
B) a measurement error.
C) the normal distribution curve.
D) a true anomaly.

95. The probability that a child will be born male is 1/2. The probability that the child will have blue eyes in 1/5. The probability that a child will be shorter than both parents is 1/10. What is the probability that a child will be male, not have blue eyes, and be shorter than his parents?

96. The probability of a child have blue eyes is 1/5, brown eyes 1/2, and green eyes 1/4. What is the probability that a child will have blue or green eyes?

97. A test for a certain disease has a 90% chance of detecting the disease if a person has the disease. A new test is developed that has a 95% chance of detecting the disease if the person has the disease. This new test:

A) will produce fewer false positives.
B) will produce fewer false negatives.
C) should be more successful.
D) should be used by any ethical physician.

98. A test for a certain disease has a 2% chance of detecting the disease if a person does not have the disease. A new test is developed that has a 0.2% chance of detecting the disease if the person does not have the disease. This new test:

A) will produce fewer false positives.
B) will produce fewer false negatives.
C) should be more successful.
D) should be used by any ethical physician.

99. An experiment in which the hypothesis being tested is not true and the experimenters gather a wealth of scientific data to show that the hypothesis is, in fact, not true have generated a study with high:

A) power.
B) p-value.
C) chance of type II error.
D) confidence.

100. An experiment in which the hypothesis being tested is true and the experimenters gather a wealth of scientific data to show that the hypothesis is, in fact, true have generated a study with high:

A) power.
B) p-value.
C) chance of type II error.
D) confidence.

CHAPTER 1 SOLUTIONS

1. A. We start with the information 1.1×10^{-12} g. Unit analysis takes us to the answer:

$$1.1 \times 10^{-12} g \left(\frac{1 \text{ microbe}}{6 \times 10^{-16} g} \right) = \frac{1.1}{6} \quad 10^{-12 \quad 16} \text{ microbes}$$

$$\approx 0.2 \times 10^4 \text{ microbes}$$

$$\approx 2000 \text{ microbes}$$

Here we estimate (1.1)/6 to be about 0.2, which is close enough to give us an answer. Remember, all you need is an answer. You do not need to calculate a second digit.

2. B. The question again is, "How much?" We have information in mL, and we want it in mg. Thus we write

$$422.4 \text{mL} \left(\frac{8.4 \mu g}{1 \text{mL}} \right) \left(\frac{1 \text{mg}}{10^3 \mu g} \right) \approx \frac{400 \cdot 8}{1000} \text{mg}$$

$$\approx \frac{3000}{1000} \text{mg}$$

$$= 3 \text{ mg}$$

Here we estimated 4 times 8 = 30. This is close enough to yield the answer B.

3. C. Here we start with 1 molecule H_2O. Then we can convert to mol and g:

$$1 \text{ molec} \left(\frac{1 \text{ mol}}{6.02 \times 10^{23} \text{ molec}} \right) \left(\frac{18 \text{ g}}{1 \text{ mol}} \right) \approx \frac{18}{6} \quad ^{-23}$$

$$\approx 3 \times 10^{-23} g$$

4. C. We can guess that the amount of time required is proportional to the temperature change desired, so let's start with that. Next, we want to cancel the units °C, so we add a factor of 4.2×10^3 J/kg°C, giving

$$5°C \frac{4.2 \times 10^3 J}{kg°C}$$

We want to cancel kg, so we can just place a factor of 10 kg in the numerator, giving

$$5°C \frac{4.2 \times 10^3 J}{kg°C} \frac{10 kg}{1}$$

To cancel J, we can use the J from the power the resistor dissipates 2 W = 2 J/s. Thus

$$5°C \frac{4.2 \times 10^3 J}{kg°C} \frac{10 kg}{1} \frac{s}{2J}$$

At this point we rejoice, because we have seconds in the numerator. Now we cut everything down to one digit and quickly multiply. This gives

$$\Delta t = \frac{5 \cdot 4 \cdot 10^3 \cdot 10}{2} s = \frac{20}{2} = 10^4 s \quad 10^5 s$$

This is close to choice C.

Does this method always work? Clearly you cannot answer every conceivable question by looking at units. But it is surprising how many questions can be answered this way, specifically any question in which all the formulas involved are simple proportionalities without unitless proportionality constants.

5. B. We know this involves the ideal gas equation, but how do we start a unit analysis? Since we know we want to end up with K in the numerator, we can just place it there at the outset:

$$\frac{K \text{ mol}}{0.0821 \text{ L atm}}$$

Now we cancel L and atm, giving

$$\frac{K \text{ mol}}{0.0821 \text{ L atm}} \frac{2 \text{ L}}{1} \frac{10 \text{ atm}}{1}$$

We can cancel mol if we think of a connection between mol and the 16 g Ar, so that we write

$$\frac{K \text{ mol}}{0.0821 \text{ L atm}} \frac{2 \text{ L}}{1} \frac{10 \text{ atm}}{1} \frac{40 \text{ g}}{\text{mol}} \frac{1}{16 \text{ g Ar}}$$

$$\approx \frac{2 \cdot 10 \cdot 40}{0.08 \cdot 16} K$$

$$\approx \frac{100 \cdot 2 \cdot 10 \cdot 40}{8 \cdot 16} K$$

$$\approx \frac{10,000}{16} K$$

$$\approx 700 K$$

In the second step above, we multiplied numerator and denominator by 100. In the third step we calculated 2 · 40/8 = 10. Most calculations go pretty quickly if you look for these shortcuts. Our answer is close enough for us to realize the correct answer is B.

6. B. If the diameter of a circle increases by a factor of 4, the radius increases by a factor of 4 also. (If you do not believe this, try it with a few numbers.) The circumference increases by a factor of 4 as well.

7. C. Clearly the area increases, but since the radius is squared in the formula, the area increases by a factor of 4^2 = 16. The π in the formula does not make any difference.

8. D. This time there is an r^3 in the formula, so the volume increases by a factor of 4^3 = 64.

9. B. If the volume of a sphere decreases by a factor of 27, then its radius must decrease by a factor of 3, since $3^3 = 27$. If the radius decreases by a factor of 3, then the diameter decreases by a factor of 3 as well. Again, you should try this method with some numbers if it does not make sense to you.

10. C. If the radius increases by 30%, that is the same as increasing by a factor of 1.3, since $(1 + 30/100) = 1.3$. If the radius increases by a factor of 1.3, then the area increases by a factor of $1.3^2 = 1.69$. An increase by such a factor is an increase by 69%, so the answer is C. Keep in mind that you need to know how to manipulate numbers like this quickly.

11. B. Since l is in the numerator, T increases if l does. If l increases by a factor of 4, then T increases by a factor of

$$\sqrt{4} = 2$$

12. B. A problem like this is easier if we solve for l, giving

$$l = g(2\pi T)^2$$

$$l = 4\pi^2 g T^2$$

A decrease by 20% in the period is equivalent to multiplying the period by $(1 - 20/100) = 0.8$. If the period is multiplied by 0.8, then the length is multiplied by $0.8^2 = 0.64$. We can rewrite $0.64 = (1 - 36/100)$. Thus the length decreases by 36%.

13. B. Since g is in the denominator, a decrease in g results in an increase in T. If g decreases by a factor of 6, then T increases by a factor of

$$\sqrt{6} = 2.4$$

Of course, you do not have to work out the square root. A glance at the answers indicates that B is correct.

14. B. Since m is in the numerator, an increase in m will increase T. This results in a decrease in frequency f. Since m changes by a factor of 4, the period changes by a factor of

$$\sqrt{4} = 2$$

The frequency changes by a factor of 2, so the answer is B. This approach is the most straightforward way to do the problem. Any time spent calculating the value of k is wasted time.

15. A. First, if the period is larger for mass P, then mass P must be larger. Next, for there to be a change of 36 in the period, there must be a change of 1296 inside the square root. Thus the answer is A.

16. C. Since we have $(1 + 50/100) = 1.5$, the period is multiplied by 1.5. Thus the frequency is multiplied by $(1.5)^{-1} = 0.67$. We rewrite $0.67 = (1 - 33/100)$, so the frequency decreases by 33%.

17. D. If s increases by a factor of 9, then V increases by a factor of 81. Do not let the 1/3 in the formula throw you off. If it did, try the problem with numbers to see why the 1/3 does not matter.

18. B. This is a simple proportionality.

19. C. In this case, both s and h increase by a factor of 3. The increase in s causes V to increase by a factor of 9, and another factor of 3 comes from the h.

Passage 1

20. C. The separation of the plates is unchanged, so the electric field increases by a factor of 9.

21. B. According to the first equation, the electric field and the plate separation are inversely related, so an increase in d results in a decrease in E, so that B is the answer. If this is unclear, solve for E in the first equation.

22. B. For this question we need to remember that a helium nucleus has two protons (its atomic number on the periodic table), so the bare helium nucleus has twice the charge of a proton. Thus the force on it is twice as great.

23. B. If the separation of the plates increases by a factor of 2, then the electric field decreases by a factor of 2. And the force on the proton decreases by a factor of 2.

24. A. The voltage V and electric field E are proportional, so A is correct. For C to be correct, the equation would need to be $V = Ed + V_0$.

Passage 2

25. D. Since r is in the denominator, if r decreases, then the force increases. If r changes by a factor of 2, then the force changes by a factor of $2^2 = 4$.

26. B. The distance r is multiplied by 1.25. Thus F is multiplied by $1.25^{-2} = (5/4)^{-2} = (4/5)^2 = 0.8^2 = 0.64 = (1 - 36/100)$. The force decreases by 36%.

27. C. Concerning choice A, a factor of 4 in both q_1 and q_2 will result in a factor of 16 in F, so this choice is incorrect. If F is to stay the same, and q_2 increases, then the distance r must increase, so choice B is incorrect. A factor of 4 in q_2 is equivalent to a factor of 2 in r, since $2^2 = 4$. Another way to see this is to solve for r, which you should do if this discussion was unclear.

28. D. If the charge on one ball increases by a factor of 4 (from 2 C to 8 C), then the force must increase by a factor of 4.

29. C. We can eliminate A and B immediately, since F decreases as r increases. We can eliminate D, since F does not have a linear relationship with r (that would look like $F = kr + c$). As r approaches 0, the force becomes infinite, so C is a good choice. Also, as r becomes large, F approaches 0 but never reaches it.

30. B. If both balls acquire a charge q, then the force between them is given by

$$F = \frac{kq^2}{r^2}$$

which is equivalent to $F = ar^2$, a quadratic equation. Thus the answer is B.

CHAPTER 2 SOLUTIONS

1. C. The mass of the mobile unit does not change just because we transport it to a different place.

2. A. We add the fly's velocity to the car's velocity in order to obtain its total velocity relative to the ground. We move the fly velocity vector so that its tail coincides with the tip of the car velocity vector. The resulting total is just west of north (see diagram). In the choices, only choice A shows the correct total vector. The choice does not show the fly vector already moved. You must do that.

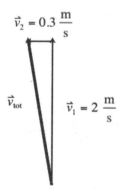

$$\vec{v}_2 = 0.3\ \frac{m}{s}$$

$$\vec{v}_{tot}$$

$$\vec{v}_1 = 2\ \frac{m}{s}$$

3. B. From the diagram of the previous solution, we can see that the answer must be slightly larger than 2 m/s and certainly not as large as 2.3 m/s, so B is correct. To do the numbers, we use the Pythagorean theorem:

$$(v_{tot})^2 = \left(2\ \frac{m}{s}\right)^2 + \left(0.3\ \frac{m}{s}\right)^2$$

$$= 4.09\ \frac{m^2}{s^2}$$

$$v_{tot} = 2.02\ \frac{m}{s}$$

4. A. First we move the horizontal vector, so its tail is on the tip of the top vector. Then we move the bottom vector, so its tail is on the tip of the horizontal vector. The resulting sum is the arrow from the first tail to the last tip (see diagram).

$$\vec{v}_{tot}$$

5. C. Again we sequentially place the tail of one vector on the tip of the previous one. The resulting sum is zero (see diagram). We could see this in the diagram anyway, since the arrows seem to cancel out each other.

$$\vec{v}_{tot} = \vec{0}$$

6. A. They exert the largest net force when they pull the same direction (see figure), giving the total 7000 N. They exert the smallest net force when they are directly opposed to each other, giving 1000 N. Therefore it is not possible for the net force to be 500 N. If this is unclear, try drawing a few vector diagrams to get a total of 500 N.

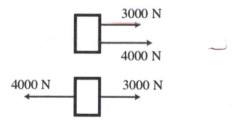

3000 N

4000 N

4000 N   3000 N

7. B. If they pull at right angles, then we need to apply the Pythagorean theorem (see figure):

$$(F_{tot})^2 = (3000\ N)^2 + (4000\ N)^2$$

$$F_{tot} = 5000\ N$$

3000 N

4000 N $\vec{F}_{tot}$

8. A. Since she starts from rest, her initial velocity is zero.

9. A. Again, she ends at rest.

10. B. The net displacement is $\Delta s = 27$ km $= 27{,}000$ m. The total time is $\Delta t = 75$ min $= 4500$ s. Thus the average velocity is $v_{avg} = \Delta s/\Delta t = 6$ m/s.

11. D. During these 9 s, she was accelerating uniformly, so we can write the equation:

$$v_2 - v_1 = a\Delta t$$

$$v_2 = v_1 + a\Delta t$$

$$= 0 \text{ m/s} + (2.5 \text{ m/s}^2)(9\text{s})$$

$$= 22.5 \text{ m/s}$$

12. B. Since the car is accelerating uniformly, we can write $a = \Delta v/\Delta t = (30 \text{ m/s} - 5 \text{ m/s})/10 \text{ s} = 2.5 \text{ m/s}^2$.

13. C. Since the car is accelerating uniformly, we can write $v_{avg} = 1/2 \, (v_1 + v_2) = 17.5$ m/s.

14. C. We can write the equation

$$\Delta x = 1/2 \, (v_1 + v_2)\Delta t$$

$$= 1/2 \, (5 \text{ m/s} + 30 \text{ m/s})(10\text{s})$$

$$= 175 \text{ m}$$

15. B. We want a formula which relates distance, velocity, and time, so we write

$$v = \frac{\Delta x}{\Delta t}$$

Now Δx is the same, while we want v to increase by a factor of 3. To do this we need Δt to decrease by a factor of 3. You could probably do this without writing down the formula. Other problems will not be so simple.

16. A. We want to know change of velocity Δv, while we know acceleration $a = 0.3$ m/s^2, the time interval $\Delta t = 3$ s, and the initial velocity $v_1 = 1.5$ m/s. We need the definition of acceleration:

$$a = \Delta v/\Delta t$$

$$\Delta v = a\Delta t$$

$$= (0.3 \text{ m/s}^2)(3 \text{ s})$$

$$= 0.9 \text{ m/s}^2$$

So we did not need the value of v_1 at all. The key to many problems is making an inventory of what we know and what we want.

17. B. We know $\Delta y = -10$ m, $a = -10$ m/s^2 (approximately), $v_1 = 0$ m/s (because it is dropped). We want Δt. Thus we have

$$\Delta x = v_1 \Delta t + \frac{1}{2}\Delta a \; t^2$$

$$-10\text{m} = \frac{1}{2}\left(-10 \frac{\text{m}}{\text{s}^2}\right)\Delta t^2$$

$$\Delta t = \sqrt{2}\,\text{s} = 1.4\text{s}$$

18. B. If we want v_2, we use the equation:

$$v_2^2 = v_1^2 + 2a\,\Delta x$$

$$v_2^2 = \left(0\frac{\text{m}}{\text{s}}\right)^2 + 2\left(-10\frac{\text{m}}{\text{s}^2}\right)(-10\text{m})$$

$$v_2 = 10\sqrt{2}\,\frac{\text{m}}{\text{s}}$$

$$= 14\frac{\text{m}}{\text{s}}$$

19. B. We know $v_1 = 20$ m/s, $a = 1.2$ m/s^2, and $\Delta t = 5$ s. Thus $\Delta x = v_1\Delta t + 1/2 \, a(\Delta t)^2 = 115$ m.

20. C. We know $a = -0.1$ m/s^2, $v_2 = 0$ m/s (because it comes to a stop), and $\Delta t = 5$ s. We use the following equation:

$$v_2 - v_1 = a\Delta t$$

$$v_1 = v_2 - a\Delta t$$

$$v_1 = (0 \text{ m/s}) - (-0.1 \text{ m/s}^2)(5\text{s})$$

$$= 0.5 \text{ m/s}$$

21. B. We know $v_1 = 0.2$ m/s and $a = -0.05$ m/s^2. If we want to know how long it takes to stop, we add the datum $v_2 = 0$ m/s. Thus we have

$$v_2 - v_1 = a\,\Delta t$$

$$0\frac{\text{m}}{\text{s}} - 0.2\frac{\text{m}}{\text{s}} = -0.05\frac{\text{m}}{\text{s}^2}\;t$$

$$\Delta t = \frac{-0.2\frac{\text{m}}{\text{s}}}{-0.05\frac{\text{m}}{\text{s}^2}}$$

$$= 4 \text{ s}$$

22. A. We still use $v_1 = 0.2$ m/s and $a = -0.05$ m/s^2, but now we have $\Delta t = 6$ s. The net displacement is obtained from

$$\Delta s = v_1\Delta t + 1/2 \, a\Delta t^2$$

$$= (0.2 \text{ m/s})(6 \text{ s}) + 1/2 \ (-0.05 \text{ m/s}^2)(6 \text{ s})^2$$

$$= 0.3 \text{ m}$$

It is important to pay attention to signs in this problem, translating "up" into positive and "decelerating" into negative. Also note that the ball travels further than 0.3 m, going 0.4 m up the slope before heading back. The net displacement is the difference between final position and initial position.

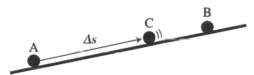

23. C. Here we have $v_1 = -5$ m/s, $\Delta t = 10$ s, and $v_2 = 10$ m/s. We can obtain acceleration from its definition: $a = (v_2 - v_1)/\Delta t = 1.5 \text{ m/s}^2$.

24. A. We obtain the net displacement from $\Delta x = 1/2(v_1 + v_2) \Delta t = 25$ m.

25. C. We want an equation which relates v, Δx, and Δt. This is $v = \Delta x/\Delta t$. If v increases by a factor of 3, then Δt must decrease by a factor of 3, so the answer is C.

26. A. Here we know that $v_1 = 25$ m/s, $x_1 = 3000$ km, $a = 0.02$ m/s^2, and $\Delta t = 500$ s. We want x_2. We know that $\Delta x = x_2 - x_1$, so we can calculate

$$\Delta x = v \Delta t + \frac{1}{2}\Delta a \ t^2$$

$$=(25\frac{\text{m}}{\text{s}})(500\text{s}) + \frac{1}{2}\left(0.02\frac{\text{m}}{\text{s}^2}\right)(500\text{s})^2$$

$$= 15000\text{m}$$

$$= 15\text{km}$$

Thus $x_2 = 3015$ km. Remember to be careful with the units.

27. B. We calculate $\Delta x = 1/2 \ (v_1 + v_2)\Delta t = 4.4$ m.

28. B. We want an equation involving velocity and time and possibly acceleration. Let's look at the equation

$$a = \frac{\Delta v}{\Delta t}$$

Here a is constant and Δt increases by a factor of 3. Thus Δv increases by a factor of 3 as well, giving B as an answer. Another way to see this is to rewrite the equation:

$$\Delta v = a\Delta t$$

so an increase in Δt yields an increase in v.

29. C. The figure in the problem shows a car which starts from rest, speeds up to a cruising speed which it maintains, then slows to a stop. Let's keep this in mind.

The figure above shows v versus t, and we want to pick the best graph for x versus t. From point A to point B, there is no area under the graph, so the displacement is zero, and all the choices show this. From B to C, there is an increasing amount of area under the curve, eliminating choices B and D which show a jump in x versus t. From C to D, there is area under the curve, so Δx is positive for every interval Δt. This means x is increasing, which is shown only in choice C. After E, the velocity goes to zero, and Δx goes to zero. This means that no more increments get added to x. *But this does not mean that x returns to the x-axis (as in choice A).*

30. B. Between A and B, the instantaneous slope is zero (see figure). Between points B and C, the instantaneous slope jumps to a constant value, eliminating A and C as choices. Between C and D, the instantaneous slope is zero, so the acceleration jumps back down to zero, so B is correct. Between points D and E, the acceleration is negative.

Passage 1

31. A. The initial velocity is just that at the beginning of the experiment.

32. B. The average velocity is $v_{\text{avg}} = \Delta x/\Delta t$. The net displacement is $\Delta x = 1.35$ m $-$ 1.35 m $= 0$ m.

33. D. This question consists entirely of words, but let us write an equation anyway. Uniform acceleration means a is constant, and $a = \Delta v/\Delta t$. Thus Δv and Δt are in a constant ratio. If one of the choices expresses this fact, then that would be the solution. (If not, we will have to think some more, perhaps find another equation.) D is the correct answer.

34. D. We apply the definition of acceleration:

$$a = \frac{v_2 - v_1}{\Delta t}$$

$$= \frac{0.6\,\frac{m}{s} - \left(-0.6\,\frac{m}{s}\right)}{1s}$$

$$= 1.2\,\frac{m}{s^2}$$

35. A. Since acceleration is positive, the vector points in the forward direction (according to the sign convention of the passage).

36. B. For any 0.5-s interval in the chart, the acceleration ($\Delta v/\Delta t$) is a constant 1.2 m/s², even for the intervals near t = 1.5 s, where the velocity is zero. Thus B is the best answer.

CHAPTER 3 SOLUTIONS

1. D. From the first law of motion, a force balance on an object implies it has constant velocity. From this we conclude that the force of gravity and the drag force due to the air are *exactly balanced*.

2. D. Since there is only one force, there must be a net force on the object; there is no way for forces to be balanced. From the first law of motion, we conclude that the object is not undergoing uniform motion, so it is speeding up, slowing down, or changing direction. But none of the choices can be definitely concluded.

3. C. Since the car is not undergoing uniform motion (it is slowing), it has a net force on it. In fact, the net force points in the opposite direction the car is going.

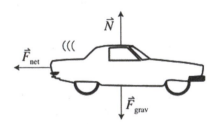

4. C. Since the object is moving with uniform motion, the forces on the object must be balanced. Since there are exactly two forces, the only way for them to be balanced is that they be of equal magnitude in opposite directions, which is choice C. If you chose B, think of the example of the paratrooper falling in question 1, in which the downward force of gravity is balanced by the upward force of the air drag.

5. B. In case 1, we move the tail of F_B to the tip of F_A (see figure). The sum, F_{net}, is drawn from the first tail to the last tip, giving a magnitude of 700 N. So choice B is correct. The same method for case 2 yields a magnitude 100 N. For case 3, we need to apply the Pythagorean theorem to obtain a magnitude 500 N.

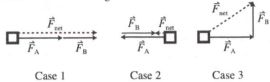

Case 1   Case 2   Case 3

6. A. (This was a review problem.) We calculate a = (3.5 m/s – 1.5 m/s)/3 s = 0.67 m/s².

7. A. We calculate $F_{net} = ma$ = (60 kg) (0.67 m/s²) = 40 N.

8. C. We calculate a = (20 m/s – 0 m/s)/(12 s) = 1.67 m/s².

9. A. We calculate (from Chapter 2) Δx = 1/2 (0 m/s + 20 m/s) (12 s) = 120 m.

10. C. The magnitude of the net force is given by $F_{net} = ma$ = 167 N.

11. C. The vertical forces, which are balanced, are gravity (down) and the normal force of the ground (up). The one horizontal force accelerates the tiger, and it is due to the ground pushing forward. This may seem strange, but it is a result of the third law of motion. The tiger pushes the ground backward. There is then an equal force of the ground on the tiger pushing forward, even though there is no "active" agent creating the force. But it has to be the ground pushing the tiger forward, since that is the only thing touching him. Certainly he does not push himself forward (what would that even mean?).

12. B. We want an equation which connects force, acceleration, and mass. This is $F = ma$. Since we are looking for the change in acceleration, we can write this equation $a = F/m$. If the mass decreases by a factor of 2, then the acceleration increases by a factor of 2.

13. C. As in question 12, we write $a = F/m$. If F increases by a factor of 3 and m increases by a factor of 3, then a remains the same.

14. A. We draw a diagram (see figure). We cannot calculate the acceleration using the methods of the previous chapter, but we can find a net force. In one dimension, we can call east positive, so F_{net} = 0.0015 N – 0.0010 N = 0.0005 N. Thus we can find acceleration a = F_{net}/m = 0.0005 N/0.0005 kg = 1 m/s².

0.0010 N   0.0015 N

15. B. We draw a diagram (see figure). We can obtain the net force by applying the Pythagorean theorem. The net force is 13000 N. From this we obtain the magnitude of the acceleration $a = F_{net}/m = 26$ m/s^2.

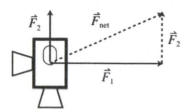

16. C. We draw a diagram (see figure). We include the vertical forces of gravity and the normal force, which add to zero (that is, balance each other). There is nothing touching the truck except the ground (the girl has already let go), but there must be another force because the truck is changing velocity. This force is the drag force, pointing backward. (There is no forward force.) We want to know the magnitude of the drag force, since this is also the net force. We obtain the acceleration $a = (0$ m/s $- 15$ m/s$)/5$ s $= -3$ m/s^2. Thus, in magnitude, the net force is $F_{net} = ma = 12$ N.

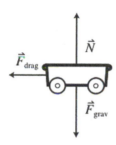

17. B. We draw a diagram showing the forces on the mass (see figure). There is the force of gravity and the tension in the string, which pulls up. The net force (with down as positive) is $F_{net} = (0.8$ kg$)$ $(10$ m/s$^2) - 6$ N $= 2$ N. The sign indicates the net force is down. Now we can calculate the acceleration $a = F_{net}/m = 2$ N$/0.8$ kg $= 2.5$ m/s^2.

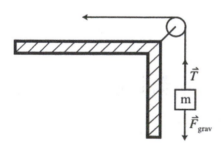

18. B. We draw a diagram showing the forces on the woman. Since she is traveling at constant velocity, the net force on her is zero, and the forces are balanced. Thus the force of the floor against the woman's feet has the same magnitude as the force of gravity on her. This is just the first law of motion. If you chose C, then you need to study the first law of motion again.

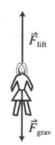

19. B. We can calculate an estimate of acceleration $a = \Delta v/\Delta t = (1$ m/s$)/(7$ s$) = 1/7$ m/s^2. Thus the total mass is given by $m = F_{net}/a = 900/(1/7)$ kg $= 6300$ kg. The mass of the rocket case is then $(6300 - 3300)$ kg $= 3000$ kg. This is close to B.

20. C. We need an equation which connects time and mass (which differs from A to B). We also have information about F, v_1, and d. We can use $F = ma$ and $d = v_1\Delta t + 1/2\, a(\Delta t)^2$. Combining these, we obtain

$$d = v_1 + \frac{1}{2} a\, t^2$$

$$= \frac{1}{2}\left(\frac{F}{m}\right)\Delta t^2$$

$$\Delta t = \sqrt{\frac{2dm}{F}}$$

So if m increases by a factor of 4, then time increases by a factor of

$$\sqrt{4} = 2$$

21. A. First we draw a diagram (see figure). The vertical forces balance. The net horizontal force is $F_{net} = 105$ N $- 30$ N $- 70$ N $= 5$ N. The net force is forward, so the car is speeding up.

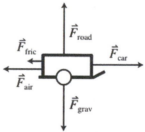

22. C. The force which accelerates the car must be a force of some agent acting on the car, so that fact narrows the choices to C and D. The acceleration is horizontal, so the net force must be horizontal, therefore C is correct. The car exerts a force on the road, so that (third law) the road exerts a force on the car.

Passage 1

23. D. Choices A and B are irrelevant, and comparisons, such as those in choice C, are meaningless if the units do

not match. The correct choice is D. From the table we can see that equal jumps of time (for example, 0.2 s to 0.4 s) result in equal jumps of velocity (0.1 m/s to 0.2 m/s). This is consistent with the statement that $\Delta v/\Delta t$ is a constant, or that acceleration is constant.

24. B. It seems as if acceleration would be a useful quantity to calculate, so let's choose the interval from $t = 0.0$ to 0.2 s, obtaining $a = \Delta v/\Delta t = (0.1$ m/s $- 0.0$ m/s) / $(0.2$ s $- 0.0$ s) $= 0.5$ m/s^2. Now we can look at the interval from $t = 0.0$ s to 0.9 s. We want to find Δx, and we have $\Delta t = 0.9$ s, $v_1 = 0.0$ m/s, and $a = 0.5$ m/s^2. From this we calculate $\Delta x = 1/2\ a(\Delta t)^2 \approx 0.20$ m.

25. B. Gravity certainly acts on m. The only thing touching mass m is the string, so B is correct. (See figure.)

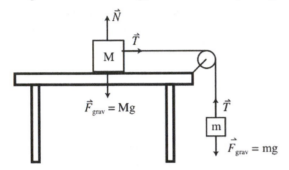

26. B. The things touching mass M are the table and the string. It is true that the tension in the string is, in some sense, caused by mass m, but M does not know or care what the other end of the string is connected to. It only cares that there is a force due to a string which is directed to the right.

27. C. By definition, we have $v_{avg} = \Delta x/\Delta t = (0.09$ m $- 0.0$ m)/$(0.06$ s $- 0.0$ s) $= 0.15$ m/s.

28. C. Only the table and the string are touching mass M, but the string has no tension in it, so the answer is C.

CHAPTER 4 SOLUTIONS

1. B. The fact that the stars revolve about their combined center of mass is irrelevant for calculating the force of gravity between them. That depends only on their masses and the distance between their centers. Since we have $F_{grav} = Gm_1m_2/d^2$, if one of the masses decreases by a factor of 2, then F_{grav} decreases by a factor of 2.

2. A. The factor of d^2 in the denominator indicates that if d increases by a factor of 2, then F_{grav} decreases by a factor of $2^2 = 4$.

3. B. If m_1 decreases by a factor of 2, and m_2 increases by a factor of 5, then F_{grav} changes by a factor of 5/2.

4. B. I hope this one did not fool you. The mass of an object does not change just because you transport it somewhere.

5. A. Objects in free fall on the Moon have a constant acceleration due to gravity 1.6 m/s^2 for the same reason that free-fall objects have $a = 9.8$ m/s^2 here on Earth. This comes from setting $F_{net} = ma$ equal to $F_{grav} = mg$, so that $a = g$. In this case, we have

$$a = -1.6 \text{ m/s}^2$$

$$v_1 = 0 \text{ m/s}$$

$$\Delta y = -2 \text{ m}$$

$$\Delta t = ?$$

$$\Delta y = v_1\Delta t + 1/2\ a\Delta t^2$$

$$-2 \text{ m} = 1/2\ (-1.6 \text{ m/s}^2)\Delta t^2$$

$$\Delta t^2 = 2.5 \text{ s}^2$$

We only need to work as far as Δt^2 in order to eliminate choices B, C, and D.

6. C. The weight of the block on the Moon is an exact analogy to its weight on Earth: $F_{grav} = mg_{Moon} = 20$ N.

7. D. On Earth (or on any planetary body), we get the acceleration due to gravity on the surface by assuming that gravity is the only force acting on an object. So we set $F_{net} = ma$ equal to $F_{grav} = Gm_{planet}m/r^2$, where r is the radius of the planet:

$$ma = \frac{Gm_{planet}m}{r^2}$$

$$a = \frac{Gm_{planet}}{r^2}$$

See Example 2 in Section A. Now if the radius of the planet were multiplied by 0.5, then the acceleration due to gravity would be *divided* by $(0.5)^2$, giving us 40 m/s^2. (We expect an increase, since the acceleration increases if radius decreases.) But the mass of Mars is 0.1 of Earth's mass, so a factor of 0.1 in the numerator brings the acceleration down to 4 m/s^2.

8. A. This time the relevant equation is

$$F_{grav} = \frac{Gm_{sun}m_{planet}}{d^2}$$

where d is the distance from the Sun to that planet. The mass of Mars is 0.1 times that of Earth, so that is a factor of 0.1. Another factor comes from the distance from the Sun to Mars, which is 1.5 times greater, so we *divide* by $(1.5)^2$, yielding about 0.04.

9. D. The equation we need for this problem and the next is

$$F_{grav} = \frac{Gm_{Earth}m_{moon}}{d^2}$$

where d is the distance between the Earth and the Moon. If d decreases by a factor of 3, then F_{grav} increases by a factor of $3^2 = 9$.

10. A. The Earth's gravitational pull on the Moon is the same as the Moon's on the Earth. That's the third law of motion. (Why does the Moon in its orbit move so much more than the Earth, then?)

11. C. In problem 7, we worked out the surface acceleration due to gravity of a planet. Since we are looking for radius, we can solve for it, so we have

$$r = \sqrt{\frac{Gm_{planet}}{a}}$$

If the new planet has the same mass as Earth, but a larger acceleration due to gravity, then the radius must be smaller. And if a changes by a factor of 3, then r changes by a factor of $\sqrt{3}$, so the answer is B. (We don't need to know $\sqrt{3}$ to figure out which choice is right.)

12. B. We want to relate acceleration and time, so we want an equation that involves these quantities. (We have seen enough of these problems to realize $v_1 = 0$.) We can use

$$h = v_1\Delta t + 1/2\ g\Delta t^2$$
$$h = 1/2\ g\Delta t^2$$
$$\Delta t = \sqrt{\frac{2h}{g}}$$

If g increases by a factor of 3, then Δt decreases by a factor of $\sqrt{3}$.

13. A. Since weight is the force of gravity on an object, and there are no massive planetary bodies around, the weight is zero.

14. B. The acceleration is $a = (0\ m/s - 0.5\ m/s)/(4\ s) = -0.125\ m/s^2$. (This was a review question.)

15. B. Once we have the acceleration, we can calculate a mass $m = F/a = (0.08\ N)/(0.125\ m/s^2) = 0.64\ kg$.

16. A. Certainly there is the force of gravity, down. There is nothing else touching the can opener, so gravity is the

only force. Since there is no horizontal force, there is constant horizontal motion. But horizontal motion *does not* imply a horizontal force (see the first law of motion).

17. B. Since we have a force diagram, we next need to inventory the information relevant to the vertical motion. We have $a_y = -10\ m/s^2$ and $\Delta t = 2\ s$. Because the opener is traveling *horizontally* when it leaves Barbara's hand, we have $v_{1y} = 0\ m/s$. Since we want to know Δy, we use the equation $\Delta y = v_{1y}\Delta t + 1/2\ a_y(\Delta t)^2 = 20\ m$.

18. A. Since we are looking for Δx, we now inventory the horizontal information. We have $a_x = 0\ m/s^2$ and $v_{1x} = 1.5\ m/s$. Thus we have $\Delta x = v_{1x}\Delta t + 1/2 a_x(\Delta t)^2 = 3\ m$.

19. C. The problem asks for v_{2y}, so we write $v_{2y} = v_{1y} + a_y\Delta t = -20\ m/s$. Since only positive choices are listed, we choose the magnitude 20 m/s.

20. B. We can calculate $v_{2x} = v_{1x} + a_x\Delta t = 1.5\ m/s$. Of course, we don't really have to do a calculation, since we know that the horizontal velocity is constant as long as there are no horizontal forces on the opener.

21. B. As the ball just leaves the table, it is going 1.5 m/s horizontally, so $v_{1x} = 1.5\ m/s$.

22. A. Since the initial velocity is horizontal, we have $v_{1y} = 0\ m/s$.

23. A. We draw a diagram including all the forces (see figure). Since nothing is touching the ball, gravity is the only force. Thus $F_{grav} = mg = (0.2\ kg)\ (10\ m/s^2) = 2\ N$.

24. C. Since the ball simply drops the height of the table, we have $\Delta y = 1.25\ m$.

25. B. For horizontal information, we have $a_x = 0\ m/s^2$ and $v_{1x} = 1.5\ m/s$, which is not enough to obtain Δt. For vertical information, we have

$$\Delta y = -1.25\ m$$

$$a_y = -10\ m/s^2$$

$$v_{1y} = 0\ m/s$$

We can calculate

$$\Delta y = v_{1y}\Delta t + 1/2\ a_y\Delta t^2$$

$$\Delta t^2 = 2\Delta y/a_y$$

$$\Delta t^2 = 0.25 \ \text{s}^2$$

We do not really need to take the square root to figure out the answer. If choice A is right, then $(\Delta t)^2 = (0.26 \ \text{s})^2 \approx 0.12 \ \text{s}^2$ (wrong). If choice B is right, then $(\Delta t)^2 = (0.5 \ \text{s})^2 = 0.25 \ \text{s}^2$. (Do not feel the need to work every arithmetic problem to its end.)

26. A. There is no horizontal force on the ball.

27. A. We want Δx. Since we now have Δt, we have enough information to calculate

$$\Delta x = v_{1x}\Delta t + 1/2 \ a_x\Delta t^2$$

$$\Delta x = 0.76 \ \text{m}$$

Passage 1

28. D. For the student running along the roof, he starts from rest ($v_1 = 0$ m/s) and ends up running $v_2 = 5$ m/s. We have $\Delta x = 5$ m, and we want Δt. We use $\Delta x = 1/2 \ (v_1 + v_2)\Delta t$ to obtain $\Delta t = 2$ s.

29. B. The acceleration on the roof is one problem; the falling is another. For Δt, we need the vertical information:

$$\Delta y = -7.2 \ \text{m}$$

$$a_y = -10 \ \text{m/s}^2$$

$$v_{1y} = 0 \ \text{m/s}$$

$$\Delta t = ?$$

We use the equation

$$\Delta y = v_{1y}\Delta t + 1/2 \ a_y\Delta t^2$$

to obtain $(\Delta t)^2 = 1.44 \ \text{s}^2$. We can eliminate choice A, and choice C is too large, so B is right.

30. B. We know gravity pulls down and the roof pushes up, and these forces add to zero. In addition, there must be a force accelerating the student forward (to the right). Surprisingly, it is the roof which exerts the force forward. His feet push backwards on the roof, and the roof (by the third law of motion) pushes forward on him.

31. A. We know gravity pulls down. Since nothing else touches the student, there is no other force.

32. D. Since the student's fall takes $\Delta t = 1.2$ s, the horizontal displacement is $\Delta x = v_{1x}\Delta t + 1/2 \ a_x(\Delta t)^2 = 6$ m.

33. B. All during the fall the student has the same horizontal velocity 5 m/s.

CHAPTER 5 SOLUTIONS

1. C. The force diagram should include gravity, pointing down. Nothing else is touching the orange, except the problem mentions that wind exerts a horizontal force, so we add that. The force diagram is shown.

2. C. The only vertical force is due to gravity, so $F_y = F_{grav} = mg = 30$ N.

3. C. At the top of the orange's path we have $v_{2y} = 0$ m/s. Since this is vertical information, let's see what other vertical information we have. We have $a_y = -10$ m/s^2 and $v_{1y} = 5$ m/s. We want Δt, so we write $v_{2y} = v_{1y} + a_y\Delta t$ and obtain $\Delta t = 0.5$ s.

4. B. We want a_x. The horizontal information we have is $v_{1x} = 0$ and $F_x = 6$ N. We don't have enough information for the equations of Chapter 2, but we can use $a_x = F_x/m = (6 \ \text{N})/(3 \ \text{kg}) = 2 \ \text{m/s}^2$.

5. B. Since we know a_x, v_{1x}, and Δt, we can find $v_{2x} = v_{1x} + a_x\Delta t = 0 + (2 \ \text{m/s}^2)(0.5 \ \text{s}) = 1 \ \text{m/s}$.

6. B. First we draw a force diagram. This problem has those key words "at constant velocity", which means there is a force balance on the shoe. The horizontal forces are equal in magnitude so that their vector sum is zero, so B is correct. If you chose C, then go back and read the section on the first law of motion.

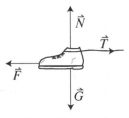

7. C. First we draw a force diagram (see figure). In addition to gravity, we have two forces, normal and tension, due to two things touching the crate. There is no friction. The gravitational force vector can be separated into two components (see figure).

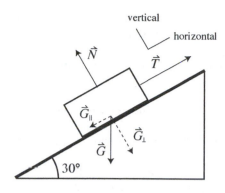

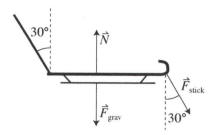

From trigonometry we know

$$\frac{G_\perp}{G} = \cos 30°$$

$$G_\perp = G \cos 30°$$

This gives us choice C.

8. B. We get this from the same diagrams shown in the solution for 7.

9. C. If we take the sum of all the perpendicular forces (in the text we called them "vertical"), we obtain $N - G_\perp = (F_{net})_y$. The negative sign denotes the "downward" direction of $G_\perp$. But the crate is moving at a constant velocity, which tells us that the acceleration is zero, and the net force is zero. Thus $N - G_\perp = 0$, giving choice C.

10. A. As we noted, the net force is zero because of the information we have on the acceleration.

11. B. This time we take the sum of parallel forces ("horizontal"), and we obtain $T - G_\| = (F_{net})_x = 0$. Again, we know the horizontal component of the net force is zero because the crate is moving at constant velocity. Thus the answer is B.

12. B. There are two things touching the sled: the ground and the stick. So, in addition to gravity pointing down, we draw the normal force pointing up and the force due to the stick pointing down/right. There is no friction (which would act to the left). So B is the correct answer (see figure).

13. A. We use the following diagram to obtain the vertical component of the stick's force.

Using trigonometry, we obtain

$$\frac{F_x}{F_{stick}} = \sin 30°$$

$$F_x = F_{stick} \sin 30°$$

$$= (20\text{N})\left(\frac{1}{2}\right)$$

$$= 10\text{N}$$

14. B. Using the same diagram as in solution 13, we obtain $F_y/F_{stick} = \cos 30°$, and $F_y = 17$ N.

15. D. In order to obtain the normal force, we need to consider all the vertical forces. We can obtain the vertical component of the net force by looking at the force diagram, so we write

$$(F_{net})_y = N - mg - F_y$$

Here we have used $F_{grav} = mg$ and have chosen "up" to be positive. But we know that the sled is not moving up or down, so the vertical acceleration a_y is zero. And from second law of motion, we know that $(F_{net})_y = ma_y = 0$. The above equation becomes

$$0 = N - mg - F_y$$

$$N = mg + F_y$$

$$= (5 \text{ kg})(10 \text{ m/s}^2) + 17 \text{ N}$$

$$= 67 \text{ N}$$

16. B. In the last problem, we talked about the vertical component of the net force being zero. We can tell from the force diagram that there is a net force, however, and this net force is the horizontal component F_x.

17. C.

The acceleration of the sled is given by $a_x = (F_{net})_x/m = 2.0$ m/s^2

18. D. The books are following a straight path. By turning the wheel, the driver pulls her car door into the path of the books, giving the impression that the books have a force on them.

19. B. The direction of the velocity vector is always changing but not its magnitude. At the moment shown in the diagram, the velocity vector is pointing in the direction of the stopper's motion, that is, B.

20. A. The tangential acceleration is zero, since the speed is constant. However, because the stopper is moving in a circle, the velocity vector is changing direction, and the acceleration vector points toward the center of the circle.

21. A. Since the acceleration vector $\vec{a}$ points toward the center, we can conclude that the net force $\vec{F}_{net} = m\vec{a}$ points toward the center as well.

22. B. The centripetal force is provided by the string, which is a force of tension.

23. B. If the string were to break, then there would no longer be a force to affect the velocity vector. The velocity vector would be constant (first law of motion), so B is correct.

24. A. Because the car moves in a circle, we know there is a centripetal acceleration and a centripetal force. This narrows the choices to A and C. There is no reason to assume there is a force acting forward on the car, especially since the tangential acceleration is zero (because of the car's constant speed). Hence A is correct. If you chose C, perhaps you were thinking that motion in the forward direction implies there must be a force in the forward direction. Not so.

25. C. The acceleration is given by $a_{cent} = v^2/r = (3$ m/s$)^2/(4$ m$) = 2.25$ m/s^2.

26. C. Once we know the acceleration of the car, we necessarily know the net force on the car: $F_{net} = ma = (1200$ kg$)(2.25$ m/s$^2) = 2700$ N.

27. C. To see that the centripetal force is due to friction, consider what would happen if there were no friction between the tires and the road. The car would simply slide straight forward into the other lane.

28. A. Gravity and the normal force add to zero. We know there is a net force toward the center of the wheel, because the beetle is moving in a circle, so this narrows our choices to A and C. Choice C includes a force in the forward direction, but since the wheel is rotating at

constant speed, there is no tangential acceleration and no reason to assume there is a tangential force.

29. C. The acceleration can be calculated $a = v^2/r = (2$ m/s$)^2/(0.5$ m$) = 8$ m/s^2.

30. B. Once there is no longer a centripetal force, there is no longer a centripetal acceleration. According to the first law of motion, the velocity vector would be constant.

31. A. We consider the fixed point to be the origin, and we add the angles ϕ_A and ϕ_B to the diagram of the meter stick (see figure).

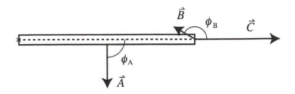

For force A, the value of ϕ is 90°. Thus torque is

$\tau = rF\sin\phi$
$= (0.5$ m$)(10$ N$)\sin90°$
$= 5$ Nm.

The torque is clockwise, so the sign is negative.

32. B. For force B, the value of ϕ is 150°, but when we calculate torques we can always use the smaller angle 30° (see figure). The torque is

$$\tau = rF\sin\phi$$
$$= (1.0 \text{ m})(5 \text{ N})\sin30°$$
$$= 2.5 \text{ Nm}.$$

The torque is counterclockwise, so the sign is positive.

33. B. For force C, the angle ϕ is 0°, so $\sin\phi = 0$, and the torque is zero. We can see this from the diagram, in which force C does not tend to produce any rotation about the fixed point.

34. A. We draw a diagram (see figure) showing the forces on the meter stick.

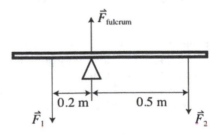

The net torque on the meter stick about the fulcrum must be zero. Since the torque due to the force of the fulcrum is zero, we have

$$\tau_{net} = 0$$
$$-F_1r_1 + F_2r_2 = 0$$
$$-(6 \text{ kg})(10 \text{ m/s}^2)(0.2 \text{ m}) + m_2(10 \text{ m/s}^2)(0.5 \text{ m}) = 0$$
$$m_2 = 2.4 \text{ kg}$$

35. C. We draw a diagram (see figure) showing all the forces on the rope. Since the weight of the book acts at point B, the torque is zero (because $r = 0$ m).

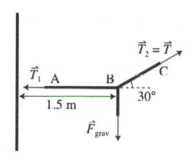

36. A. The force is perpendicular to the line connecting B and A, so $\phi = 90°$. We have

$$\tau = -(1.5 \text{ m})(4 \text{ kg} \cdot 10 \text{ m/s}^2)1$$
$$= -60 \text{ Nm}.$$

37. C. The tension due to the person pulling the rope acts at the point B, so the torque due to this tension is zero (since $r = 0$ m).

38. D. The easiest way to do this problem is to take torques about point A and to apply torque balance. The torque due to the horizontal rope is zero, and we have

$$\tau_{net} = 0$$
$$= -(1.5 \text{ m})(40 \text{ N}) + \tau_2,$$
$$\tau_2 = 60 \text{ Nm}.$$

This makes sense, because the torque due to the weight of the book about A should be balanced by the torque of the tension T about A.

A more difficult way to do the problem is to calculate T using force balance $(F_{net})_y = 0$ and obtaining $T = 80$ N. Then apply the definition of torque.

39. A. We draw a diagram (see figure) showing all the forces on the seesaw itself.

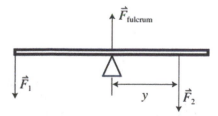

Since there is a torque balance about the fulcrum, we may write

$$F_1(2 \text{ m}) - F_2(y) = 0,$$
$$(30 \text{ kg} \cdot 10 \text{ m/s}^2)(2 \text{ m}) - (40 \text{ kg} \cdot 10 \text{ m/s}^2)(y) = 0,$$
$$y = 1.5 \text{ m}.$$

Now $y = 1.5$ m represents the distance from the fulcrum to Scott's seat. Thus he sits 0.5 m from the end.

40. A. We draw a diagram showing all the forces on the meter stick (see figure).

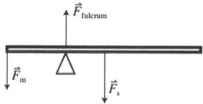

If we take torques about the fulcrum, then the fulcrum force will not have a torque. Torque balance becomes

$$(m \cdot 10 \text{ m/s}^2)(0.3 \text{ m}) - (0.6 \text{ kg} \cdot 10 \text{ m/s}^2)(0.2 \text{ m}) = 0$$
$$m = 0.4 \text{ kg}$$

41. D. We draw a diagram showing all the forces which contribute to torques about the axis of pulley B (see figure).

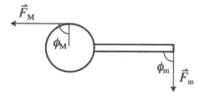

The torque due to the weight of mass m is

$$\tau = (L)(mg)1$$

42. C. We can take torques about the axis of pulley B. In both cases we have $\sin\phi = 1$, and torque balance yields

$$(d/2)(Mg)1 - (L)(mg)1 = 0$$
$$M = 2mL/d$$

43. C. We draw a diagram showing all the forces on the forearm (see figure).

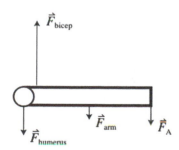

The torque due to the weight of mass A is

$$\tau_A = (0.4 \text{ m})(1.5 \text{ kg} \cdot 10 \text{ m/s}^2)1$$
$$= 6 \text{ Nm}.$$

44. B. The torque due to the weight of the arm is

$$\tau_{\text{arm}} = (0.2 \text{ m})(2 \text{ kg} \cdot 10 \text{ m/s}^2)1$$
$$= 4 \text{ Nm}.$$

45. C. Torque balance about the elbow yields the following equation:

$$-(0.4 \text{ kg})(1.5 \text{ kg} \cdot 10 \text{ m/s}^2) -$$
$$(0.2 \text{ m})(2 \text{ kg} \cdot 10 \text{ m/s}^2) +$$
$$(0.02 \text{ m})F_{\text{biceps}} = 0$$

$$F_{\text{biceps}} = 500 \text{ N}.$$

CHAPTER 6 SOLUTIONS

1. B. We draw a diagram with all the forces. The two things touching the block are the ground, which contributes the normal force and friction, and the rope, which contributes tension. We also include gravity. We can read the horizontal component of the tension from the diagram.

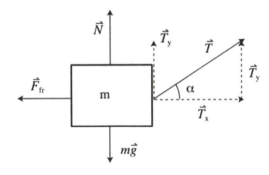

2. D. Since the normal force is vertical, we add all the vertical forces to obtain $(F_{\text{net}})_y$, so that

$$(F_{\text{net}})_y = N + T_y - mg$$

But $(F_{\text{net}})_y$ is ma_y, and the vertical acceleration is zero because the block is not changing its velocity up and down. Thus $(F_{\text{net}})_y = 0$, and

$$0 = N + T_y - mg$$

$$N = mg - T_y$$

$$= mg - T\sin\alpha$$

3. C. Our first thought for this question is the definition, $F_{\text{fr}} = \mu_k N$, but none of the answers corresponds to this, since N is not mg. Choices C and D mention the tension T, so let's look at the force diagram again. The problem states that the block's velocity is constant, implying $a_x = 0$. Thus we must have $(F_{\text{net}})_x = 0$.

We can also get an expression for $(F_{\text{net}})_x$ from the diagram:

$$(F_{\text{net}})_y = T_x - F_{\text{fr}}$$

$$0 = T_x - F_{\text{fr}}$$

$$F_{\text{fr}} = T_x = T\cos\alpha$$

4. B. Since the surfaces are not slipping, the friction is static friction.

5. C. We draw a diagram showing all the forces.

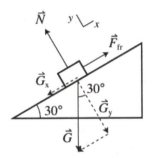

Since only the steel is touching the copper block, the only forces besides gravity are the normal force and friction. We choose axes which are tilted compared to the level ground, and divide the gravitational force into two components. In order to find the normal force, we look at the "vertical" forces, so we write

$$(F_{\text{net}})_y = N - G_y$$

But $(F_{\text{net}})_y$ is zero, since a_y is zero. So we have

$$0 = N - G_y$$

$$N = G_y$$

$$= mg\cos 30°$$

$$= (2 \text{ kg})(10 \text{ m/s}^2)(0.87)$$

$$= 17 \text{ N}$$

We do not really need to do the last few calculations. Since we know cos30° is somewhat less than 1, we know that the normal force is somewhat less than $mg = 20$ N.

6. A. Since the block is not moving, it is not accelerating, and $F_{net} = 0$.

7. B. Since there is force balance on the block, we must have $(F_{net})_x = 0$. But from the diagram we know that $(F_{net})_x = F_{fr} - G_x$, so that we have

$$0 = (F_{net})_x$$
$$= F_{fr} - G_x$$
$$F_{fr} = G_x$$
$$= mg\sin 30°$$
$$= (2\text{ kg})(10\text{ m/s}^2)(1/2)$$
$$= 10\text{ N}$$

8. A. By definition, we have $\mu = F_{fr}/N = (10\text{ N})/(17\text{ N}) = 0.58$.

Passage 1

9. A. We draw a force diagram including the force of gravity.

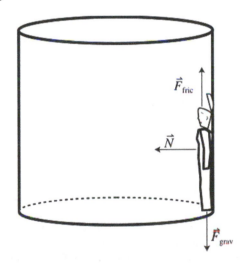

The only thing touching the rider once the floor drops is the side of the drum, which exerts a normal force that ends up being toward the axis of rotation. It also exerts a frictional force, which is up (balancing gravity). For uniform circular motion, we know the net force must be toward the center of rotation, so we can see that this force diagram is complete.

10. A. From the diagram we can see that the normal force provides the centripetal force.

11. A. Because the motion is uniform circular rotation, the acceleration vector points toward the center of rotation.

12. C. The rider traverses the circumference of the circle $(2\pi R)$ during each period of time T. Thus his speed is $2\pi R/T$.

13. A.

The upward force must balance the gravitational force, so the magnitude of the upward force must be Mg as well.

14. D. The force of friction (which is the upward force in the previous question) must be less than the maximum possible static friction $(F_s)_{max} = \mu_s N$:

$$Mg < \mu_s N$$

But N is the centripetal force, so we substitute $N = Mv^2/R$ to obtain

$$Mg < \mu_s \left(M \frac{v^2}{R} \right)$$

Dividing both sides by M and multiplying by R/v^2 gives

$$\frac{gR}{v^2} < \mu_s$$

Translating this into words gives choice D.

Passage 2

15. B. According to the passage, equation (1) is valid as long as the Reynolds number is greater than about 100, so, using equation (2), we have

$$Re > 100$$
$$\frac{\rho vl}{\eta} > 100$$
$$\frac{\left(1.29\, \frac{\text{kg}}{\text{m}^2} \right) v(2\text{m})}{1.8 \times 10^{-5}\, \frac{\text{kg}}{\text{m}^3}} > 100$$
$$v > \frac{100\left(1.8 \times 10^{-5} \right)}{(1.29)(2)}\, \frac{\text{m}}{\text{s}}$$
$$v > 10^{-3}\, \frac{\text{m}}{\text{s}}$$

16. B. The diagram shows the car, modeled by a block shape.

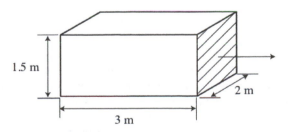

The arrow shows the direction the car would go, so the shaded face is the cross section we are interested in. The

423

area is $A = (1.5 \text{ m}) (2 \text{ m}) = 3 \text{ m}^2$. The length of the car does not matter.

17. A. We apply equation (1) to obtain

$$F_{drag} = C\rho A v^2$$

$$= (0.2)\left(1.29 \frac{\text{kg}}{\text{m}^3}\right)\left(3\text{m}^2\right)\left(30 \frac{\text{m}}{\text{s}}\right)^2$$

$$= 700\text{N}$$

18. D. For turbulence we need the Reynolds number to be greater than about 2×10^5, so we have

$$R_e > 2 \times 10^5$$

$$\frac{\rho v l}{\eta} > 2 \times 10^5$$

$$\frac{\left(1.29 \frac{\text{kg}}{\text{m}^2}\right)v(2\text{m})}{1.8 \times 10^{-5} \frac{\text{kg}}{\text{m}^3}} > 2 \times 10^5$$

$$v > 1.4 \frac{\text{m}}{\text{s}}$$

This is just an estimate, so choice D is about right.

19. B. We apply equation (1) again, so we have $F_{drag} = (0.2) (10^3 \text{ kg/m}^3) (0.01 \text{ m}^2) (2 \text{ m/s})^2 = 8 \text{ N}$.

20. B. We draw a force diagram for the drop at terminal velocity.

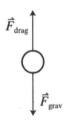

The two forces are equal in magnitude, so we can write

$$Mg = C\rho A v^2$$

$$v = \sqrt{\frac{Mg}{C\rho A}}$$

Let's compare this terminal velocity for the two situations, on Earth and on Venus. The question states that M, the mass of the drop is the same, g is the same, A is the same, and C is a constant. The density of the respective atmospheres is different, however. Looking at the choices, we exclude I. The density of the atmosphere depends on temperature and pressure, so choice B is correct.

CHAPTER 7 SOLUTIONS

1. C.
The force diagram is shown. The direction of travel is shown by a dashed vector, to distinguish it from forces. We have $W_{rope} = (30 \text{ N}) (10 \text{ m}) \cos 30° = 260 \text{ J}$.

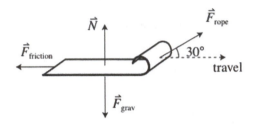

2. A.
The normal force and the direction of travel are perpendicular, so $\cos\phi = 0$.

3. B.
The gravitational force and the direction of travel are perpendicular, so $\cos\phi = 0$.

4. A.
The words "constant velocity" tell us that the net force is zero. Thus the total work is zero.

5. B.
The friction does negative work on the sled. The only other work is from the rope (question 1), that is, 260 N. Since the total work is 0 J, the friction must do –260 J.

6. B.
The box is not sitting on a surface, so there is no normal force. The man is certainly pushing up. Is he pushing forward? There is no reason to think so, since the box is moving at constant speed in a straight line.

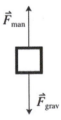

7. A.
The force of the man is perpendicular to the direction of the box's motion, so $\cos\phi = 0$. What is going on here? The reason our intuition is poor is that the man does a fair amount of microscopic work inside his striated muscles in order to maintain a force. Such muscles are extremely inefficient. That energy ends up as heat, which radiates from his body.

8. A.
We have $p = mv = (4 \text{ kg}) (3 \text{ m/s}) = 12 \text{ kg m/s}$.

9. C.
We have $E_K = 1/2 \, mv^2 = 1/2 \, (4 \text{ kg}) (3 \text{ m/s})^2 = 18 \text{ J}$.

10. C.
A force diagram is shown, although we do not need it in this case. We deduce there must be a frictional force since the net force is zero. The horse is pulling in the same direction as the direction of travel so $\cos\phi = 1$. Also Δx is $v\Delta t$.

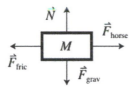

11. B.
The gravitational force is perpendicular to the direction of travel, so $\cos\phi = 0$.

12. D.
We have v_1, F and Δt, which do not combine in any way to make energy. If we had the mass of the cart we could obtain the acceleration from F, then the final velocity, and then the energy. If we had the distance traversed, we could use $W_{tot} = F\Delta x$. But we do not have those things.

13. B.
Gravity and the normal force are balanced vertical forces. Since the car is slowing down, which is accelerating backwards, there must be a net force backwards, and this is provided by friction (or braking). The force diagram is shown below.

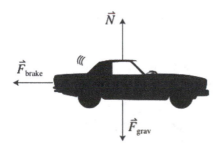

14. A.
Change in energy is always final minus initial. Thus we have $E_{K2} - E_{K1} = 0 \text{ J} - 1/2 \, (1000 \text{ kg})(20 \text{ m/s})^2 = -2 \times 10^5$ J.

15. A.
The only force doing work is the road, so the work done by the road is the total work. But this is the same as the change in kinetic energy.

16. D.

In this case the direction of travel is in the opposite direction of the road's force, so $\cos\phi = -1$. Thus $W = F\Delta x$ $\cos\phi$ yields 8000 N.

17. C.
This is one of the cases in which the simple statement of the conservation of energy holds. The only force acting on the cat is gravity. (See figure.)

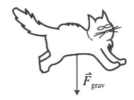

We set

$E_{K1} + E_{P1} = E_{K2} + E_{P2}$,
$0 + mgH = E_{K2} + 0$,
$E_{K2} = (4 \text{ kg})(10 \text{ m/s}^2)(3 \text{ m})$
$= 120 \text{ J}$.

18. C.
Use $E_K = 1/2 \, mv^2$, but just estimate the square root.

19. C.
As in problem 17, we obtain $E_{K2} = mgH$. If H were doubled, then E_{K2} would double.

20. A.
Setting now E_{K2} to $1/2 \, mv_2^2$, we obtain $1/2 \, mv_2^2 = mgH$. Notice that m cancels, and this yields

$$v_2 = \sqrt{2gH}$$

This looks more complicated than the variable relationships we have seen, but it is not. If H increases by a factor of 2, then v_2 increases by a factor of $\sqrt{2}$ which is 1.41.

21. A.
Momentum is always conserved as long as there is no unbalanced external force. The external forces here are gravity and the normal force, which are balanced. The internal forces are the forces that the carts exert on each other. Choices B and D are equivalent, so neither can be the answer. In fact, the collision is not elastic. It is not completely inelastic because the carts do not stick together.

22. A.
Using conservation of momentum gives

$p_1 = p_2$,
$m_A v_{1A} + m_B v_{1B} = m_A v_{2A} + m_B v_{2B}$,
$(1 \text{ kg})(0.5 \text{ m/s}) = (2 \text{ kg})v_{2B}$,
$v_{2B} = 0.25 \text{ m/s}$.

23. C.

The initial kinetic energy is $E_{K1} = 1/2\, m_A v_{1A}^2 = 0.125$ J.
The final kinetic energy is $E_{K2} = 1/2\, m_B v_{2B}^2 = 0.0625$ J.
The ratio is 0.5.

24. B.
The efficiency is defined in this problem as ratio of energy expended due to air resistance to energy consumed. The energy expended due to air resistance is $W_{air} = F_{air} D \cos\phi$, where $\cos\phi$ is 1 because the road is level. The total energy consumed is simply $n\Delta H_{rxn}$.

25. D.
The problem makes no mention of how efficiency depends on speed. On the other hand, the energy expended to overcome air resistance will increase as the square of the velocity. In many situations the efficiency is defined as the ratio of useful work to input energy, the rest of the energy wasted as heat. This problem is different in that the efficiency is defined as the ratio of energy consumed by a given drag to input energy.

26. C.
The answer is not A or B, because the car has as much kinetic energy before as after, since it goes at one speed, and as much potential energy before as after, since it travels on level ground. The energy starts as chemical energy, so D is incorrect.

27. D.
The amount of energy expended is $\Delta E = P\Delta t$, by definition. This is equal to the increase of the potential energy of the box. The energy does not go anywhere else: not into heat because the transfer is 100% efficient and not into kinetic energy because the box moves slowly and at constant speed. Setting $P\Delta t$ equal to mgH yields $H = 40$ m. Note the $30°$ angle had nothing to do with the answer.

28. A.
See the answer to problem 27.

29. A.
In this case the power is 120 Watts. This gives an energy expenditure of $(120\text{ W})(60\text{ s}) = 7200$ J. The energy which becomes potential energy is 720 J because of the 10% efficiency. If this is set equal to mgH, then $H = 1.8$ m.

30. A.
If the current and the potential difference were both doubled, then the power would increase by a factor of 4. If the energy expended is the same in $\Delta E = P\Delta t$, then Δt decreases by a factor of 4.

31. D.
The first method of doing pulley problems involves drawing a force diagram for the bottom pulley, as shown. This gives the force equation $T + T - mg = 0$, so that $T = 1/2\, mg$.

The second method involves imagining that the end of the rope is pulled 1 meter. That means that 1 meter of rope goes over the upper pulley, and 0.5 meters of rope are taken from either side of the lower pulley. The angle α has no part in this problem. The work done by the pulling is the work done pulling the mass, so $T (1\text{ m}) = mg (0.5\text{ m})$ and $T = 1/2\, mg$.

32. A.
The force diagrams are shown. Clearly the second tension is double the first tension.

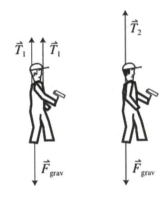

33. C.
Many students are tempted to choose 300 N, thinking that the two weights add. The force diagram below shows that the tension in either string is 150 N. The right string exerts 150 N on the force meter, the left string exerts 150 N on the force meter, and the force meter records 150 N.

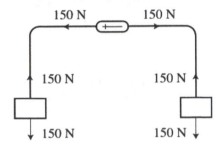

34. B.
The first method is the easier method for this pulley problem. The force diagram for the lower pulley is shown. Thus $T + T + T - mg = 0$, so that $T = 1/3\, mg$.

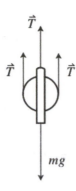

CHAPTER 8 SOLUTIONS

1. C.
A diagram of a human head is shown.

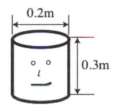

The area over which the force is acting down is the top of the head $\pi r^2 = \pi (0.1\ m)^2$. We multiply this by atmospheric pressure, which we approximate as 10^5 N/m². This is a force in Newtons. If m is the number of kilograms we are seeking, then this force is mg. Thus $m = [\pi (0.1)^2\ 10^5/10]$ kg $= 310$ kg.

2. C.
We draw a force diagram as shown.

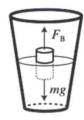

The second step is to write a force equation. Because the cork is not accelerating, we can write $F_B - mg = 0$. Let m and V be the mass and volume of the cork. We replace m with ρV. We replace F_B with $\rho_{water}\ V_{disp}\ g$, but V_{disp} is $3V/4$, according to the problem. We cancel g and V to obtain $\rho / \rho_{water} = 3/4$.

3. B.
The force diagram is same as that for the previous problem. The force equation is again $F_B - mg = 0$. In this problem V_{disp} is $0.9V$. Solving, we obtain $\rho / \rho_{water} = 0.9$.

4. D.
The force diagram is the same as that in the previous problems. In this problem, we want an equation which includes the volumes in and out of the fluid. Again we have $F_B = mg$, but we call the displaced volume V_{in}, and the total volume of iron we call $V_{in} + V_{out}$, so we have

$$F_B = mg$$

$$\rho_{Hg} V_{in} g - \rho_{Fe}(V_{in} + V_{out})g$$

$$(\rho_{Hg} - \rho_{Fe})V_{in} = \rho_{Fe}V_{out}$$

$$V_{out}/V_{in} = (\rho_{Hg} - \rho_{Fe})/\rho_{Fe} = \rho_{Hg}/\rho_{Fe} - 1$$

5. C.
The buoyancy force is $F_B = \rho_{air} V_{disp}\ g$, but V_{disp} is the volume of the man m/ρ_{man}. Thus $F_B = (\rho_{air} / \rho_{man})\ mg = 1.2$ x 10^{-3} (686 N) = 0.8 N.

6. D.
This is a simple application of the ideal gas law $PV = nRT$. (Did you recognize R in the answer choices?) The quantity n/V, which is P/RT, is the number of moles per volume, that is, number of moles per liter, if P is in atm, R is in L atm/ K mol. If we multiply by the atomic mass 4 grams/mole, we obtain density. There is a factor of 1000 to convert liters to cm³. Note that temperature T must be measured in Kelvins, and 27° C is 300 K.

7. D.
First, we draw a force diagram, as shown.

We assume the balloon is not accelerating, so we write

$$F_B - m_{He}g - Mg = 0.$$

We replace F_B and m_{He} and cancel the factor g, so we have

$$\rho_{air}Vg - \rho_{He}Vg - Mg = 0,$$
$$(\rho_{air} - \rho_{He})V - M = 0,$$
$$V = M/(\rho_{air} - \rho_{He})$$

8. D.

We apply the formula

$$P = P_{atm} + \rho g h$$
$$= (1.0 \times 10^5 + 10^3 \cdot 10 \cdot 5) \, \text{Pa}$$
$$= 1.5 \times 10^5 \, \text{Pa}.$$

9. A.
The gauge pressure is defined as

$$P - P_{atm} = \rho g h = 5 \times 10^4 \, \text{Pa}.$$

10. A.
The gauge pressure is:
$$\rho g h = 10^3 \, \text{kg/m}^3 \times 10 \, \text{m/s}^2 \times 1\text{m} = 10^4 \, \text{Pa}$$

11. A.
The questions here are a bit confusing, so let us think about what the muscles which expand the lungs do. During normal breathing conditions, the pressure inside your lungs is similar to the pressure outside, so these forces balance. To breathe in, you exert a small force to expand the push out the chest (and pull down the diaphragm). A force diagram for the chest is shown, where P_{in} is the pressure of gas inside the lung, and P_{out} is the pressure of fluid outside your lung.

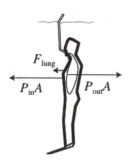

Underwater, however, the force P_{out} is greater than P_{in} by an additional $\rho g h$. Thus for question 10, we would say that the pressure the lungs are expanding against is the difference $P_{out} - P_{in}$. The best answer is

A. If you chose C, you were thinking along the right track, but it is not the total outside pressure that makes breathing difficult; it is the net pressure, that is, the difference in pressure.

The force F_{lung} must balance the two pressure forces, so the force is most nearly the product of the gauge pressure and the area of the chest. The best answer is A.

12. D.
The pressure at the top of the column on the right side is simply the atmospheric pressure P_{atm}. Pascal's law states that the pressure at point Q is the same (see figure).

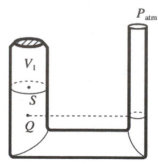

If we apply hydrostatic equilibrium to the points Q and S (at the top of the column at the left), we obtain

$$P_Q = P_S + \rho_{Hg} g (h_1 - h_2),$$
$$P_S = P_{atm} - \rho_{Hg} g (h_1 - h_2).$$

13. A.
This is a simple application of Pascal's law.

14. A.
Since the pressures are the same $P_1 = P_2$, we can substitute an expression for force $P = F/A$. Thus $F_1/A_1 = F_2/A_2$, and $F_1 = (A_1/A_2)F_2$.

15. B.
The long way to do this is to realize that a change of volume on one side of the press is the same as a change of volume on the other side of the press. If the piston on the right moves Δx_1 and the load moves Δx_2, then

$$\Delta V = A_1 \Delta x_1 = A_2 \Delta x_2.$$

But

$$W_1 = F_1 \Delta x_1 = P A_1 \Delta x_1 = P \Delta V,$$

and

$$W_2 = F_2 \Delta x_2 = P A_2 \Delta x_2 = P \Delta V.$$

The short way to see this is to realize that the flow of energy is from the piston doing the work on the fluid to the fluid doing work on the load, increasing its potential energy. We assume no energy is lost to friction, so we must have $W_1 = W_2$.

16. B.
This is an application of hydrostatic equilibrium. The pressure at the top of the column is zero, and the pressure at the bottom of both flasks is $\rho_{Hg} g h$.

17. A.
Hydrostatic equilibrium allows us to write

$$P_{res} = P_{atm} + \rho_{fluid} g (h_2 - h_1),$$

which becomes

$P_{res} - P_{atm} = \rho_{fluid}g(h_2 - h_1).$

The left side is constant. On the right side, if ρ_{fluid} increases, then $h_2 - h_1$ decreases.

18. B.

Compare this problem with the needle in Example 2 of Section E. The circumference about the needle turned out to be twice the length of the needle. Here we have bent the needle into a rectangle, so the length L that goes into $F_{max} = \gamma L$ will be $L = 2(l + w + l + w)$. This is not like a rectangular bug foot (see Example 1 of Section E) in the water. The circumference for the thread has to go all around the outside as well as all around the inside.

19. A.

The relevant length for the wire circle is $I_{wire} = 2(2\pi r)$, just like Example 2 in Section E. The coin's relevant length is $2\pi r$, just like Example 1.

20. B.

Since water is incompressible, the flow rate must be constant along the flow.

21. A.

If the flow rate is 0.06 m³/s, and the area of the pipe at B is $\pi(0.03 \text{ m})^2$, then the flow velocity is $v = f/A = 21$ m/s.

22. D.

Certainly one expression for the velocity at point B is $f/\pi r_B^2$, but that is not any of the choices. But the velocity at point B is related to the velocity at point A as well. Since we know $f_A = f_B$, we can write $v_A\pi r_A^2 = v_B\pi r_B^2$. From this we get choice D.

23. A.

The area of contact is the area of the side of the piston, that is, $2\pi rl$. The distance between the sliding surfaces is Δr, so the viscosity equation gives choice A.

24. B.

Work is force times distance times $\cos\phi$. We can draw a force diagram. There are four forces we are concerned with, since we are ignoring gravity. The problem mentions the viscous force. There are pressure forces for the two faces of the piston. In addition, the shaft is attached to the piston, and it is by moving the shaft that the piston does useful work. We are interested in the work done by the atmospheric pressure. The force is $P_{atm}A = P_{atm}\pi r^2$. The distance the piston moves is $v\Delta t$, so that B is the correct answer.

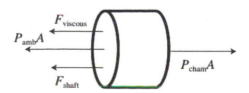

25. C.

The quantity f gives the revolutions per second. Each revolution represents a distance $2\pi R$, that is, the circumference. Thus the velocity is $2\pi Rf$.

26. A.

Torque is force times radius times $\sin\phi$. The torque of the rod must balance the retarding torque due to the viscous force. The viscous force is $F_{vis} = \eta Av/d$, and the relevant radius is R. Because the force is perpendicular to the radius vector, we have $\sin\phi = 1$. Thus the retarding torque is $\tau = R\eta Av/d$, and this is also the torque of the rod.

27. B.

Increasing the flow rate increases the likelihood of turbulence, so A is incorrect. Making the joints smooth does not seem to do anything at first glance, but perhaps this would remove obstacles that would create turbulence, so B is a possibility. Reynolds number says nothing about temperature, so C is also incorrect. Increasing the radius of the pipe increases the likelihood of turbulence, so D is incorrect, and the answer must be B.

28. B.

We can consider a streamline which goes from the reservoir (pressure P_{res}, $v = 0$) to the nozzle (pressure P_{atm}, velocity desired). Since gravity plays no role, the ρgh terms drop out. Bernoulli's equation gives

$$P_{res} + \frac{1}{2}(0)^2 = P_{atm} + \frac{1}{2}v^2$$

$$v = \sqrt{\frac{2(P_{res} - P_{atm})}{\rho}}$$

29. A.

We can consider a streamline which goes from the reservoir to the top of fountain (pressure P_{atm} and $v = 0$), so that Bernoulli's equation gives

$$P_{res} + \frac{1}{2}\rho(0)^2 + \rho g(0) = P_{atm} + \frac{1}{2}(0)^2 + \rho gh$$

$$h = \frac{P_{res} - P_{atm}}{\rho g}$$

30. B.

The viscosity depends only on the substance and not on the situation, so A is incorrect. The water does develop turbulence, and this would disqualify the flow from Bernoulli's principle, so B is a possibility. C is irrelevant, as well as D, so B is correct. The energy of the flow goes into turbulence and eventually into heat.

31. C.

This is similar to an example worked in the text. The fact that the hose goes over the top of the tank does not change the application of Bernoulli's principle. A streamline can be said to go from the top of the tank (pressure P_{atm}, $v = 0$)

through the hose to the other end (pressure P_{atm}, velocity desired). Bernoulli's equation becomes

$$P_{atm} + \frac{1}{2}\rho(0)^2 + \rho g h_3 = P_{atm} + \frac{1}{2}\rho v^2 + \rho g(0)$$

$$h = \sqrt{2\rho h_3}$$

32. B.
This is a question about hydrostatic equilibrium, so $P_{bottom} = P_{atm} + \rho g(h_3 - h_1)$.

33. B.
Looking at the answers, we see that the question writer intends for us to apply Bernoulli's equation. A streamline goes from the reservoir (pressure P_{res}, velocity 0) to the pipe 2 with no gravity gradient, so Bernoulli's equation becomes $P_{res} + 0 = P_{atm} + 1/2\ \rho v_2^2$, so B is correct.

34. B.
Relating the velocity v_1 to velocity v_2 is a matter of continuity. The flow f has to be the same all along the flow, so $A_1 v_1 = A_2 v_2$. Thus B is correct.

35. C.
Again we can apply Bernoulli's principle. The answer choices do not refer to v_2, so let us take for the two points, a point in the reservoir and a point in the constricted pipe, and see where that leads. If nowhere, then we can try again:

$$P_{res} + 1/2\ \rho(0)^2 = P_1 + 1/2\ \rho v_1^2$$
$$P_1 = P_{res} - 1/2\ \rho v_1^2$$

CHAPTER 9 SOLUTIONS

1. D.
If we draw a force diagram for the mass (shown below), then we see that the gravitational force and the spring force add to zero, so they must be equal in magnitude (second law of motion). The magnitude of the force is $F_{grav} = (0.8\ \text{kg})(10\ \text{m/s}^2) = 8.0\ \text{N}$. We use the spring equation to calculate $x = F_{spring}/k = (8.0\ \text{N})/(2.5\ \text{N/m}) = 3.2$ m. Since the spring is being stretched, we add that to the resting length 0.15 m, for a total 3.35 m.

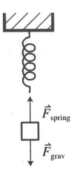

2. A.
Before we started pulling, the forces due to spring and gravity were balanced. Then we increased the spring force. The *increase* in spring force is given by $\Delta F_{spring} = k\Delta x = (2.5\ \text{N/m})(0.10\ \text{m}) = 0.25\ \text{N}$. Another way to get the same result is to realize the new extension x is 3.2 m + 0.1 m, so the force exerted by the spring is $F_{spring} = (2.5\ \text{N/m})(3.3\ \text{m}) = 8.25\ \text{N}$ up. The force of gravity is 8.0 N down, for a net force 0.25 N up. (See figure.)

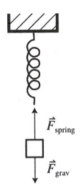

3. D.
We can draw a force diagram for the mass (shown below). (There are two forces not shown: the force of gravity and the normal force of the table, which sum to zero.) The spring provides the centripetal force, so we can write $F_{spring} = mv^2/R$. Solving for v gives $v = 2$ m/s. One revolution is the equivalent of the circumference $C = 2\pi R \approx 12$ m. Thus the time it takes is $C/v \approx (12\ \text{m})/(2\ \text{m/s}) = 6$ s, which is closest to D.

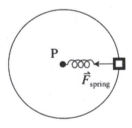

4. B.
The extension x is given by $x = F_{spring}/k = (10\ \text{N})/(50\ \text{N/m}) = 0.2$ m. Since the radius of the circle of revolution is 2 m and since the spring is pulling, the resting length of the spring must be 1.8 m.

5. A.

We simply use $E_K = 1/2\ kx^2 = (0.5)$ (50 N/m) (0.2 m)^2 = 1 J. Of course, on the real MCAT, the answer to a problem would not depend on the answer to a previous problem.

6. A.
The figure below shows a force diagram for the bob. The net force must be either up or down or zero. The velocity vector is changing direction, so the acceleration cannot be zero, and in fact, there must be a centripetal component to the acceleration. These two facts together imply the acceleration is up.

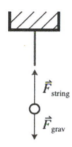

7. A.
Thus also the net force is up. Questions 6 and 7 are the same because of the second law of motion.

8. C.
If you try to work out the forces involved, things get tangled pretty quickly. This is a conservation of energy problem, and energy is converted from potential to kinetic, so we write

$E_{K1} + E_{P1} = E_{K2} + E_{P2}$

$0 + 1/2\ kx^2 = 1/2\ mv^2 + 0$

$1/2\ kx^2 = 1/2\ mv^2$

The displacement of the spring is increased by a factor of 4 in our experiment, so the initial stored energy is increased by a factor of 16. The velocity must increase by a factor of 4, and $v_2 = 4v_1$.

9. B.
Again, this is a conservation of energy problem. This time the displacement is the same in both experiments, so the stored energy is the same at the beginning of the experiment, and the kinetic energy is the same at the end of the experiment. The larger mass does not affect the final kinetic energy but its velocity would be less.

10. C.
The energy begins as gravitational potential energy. Just before the ball hits the spring, it has its maximum kinetic energy. The energy is then converted to spring potential energy.

11. C.
The change in gravitational energy is $-mgL$. The change in spring potential energy is $1/2\ kx^2$. These should add to

zero, since energy is conserved (there is no change from begin point to end point in kinetic energy):

$$-mgL + \frac{1}{2}kx^2 = 0$$

$$x = \sqrt{\frac{2mgL}{k}}$$

12. C.
The period is the time for one oscillation. If 20 oscillations take 60.0 s, then one oscillation takes 3 s.

13. A.
The frequency is the number of oscillations per unit time, so $f = 1/T$.

14. A.
Clearly the choices intend for us to use frequency information (not $F_{spring} = kx$). The equation is

$$f = \frac{1}{2\pi}\sqrt{\frac{k}{m}}$$

$$2\pi f = \sqrt{\frac{k}{m}}$$

$$(2\pi f)^2 = \frac{k}{m}$$

$$k = m(2\pi f)^2$$

$$k = (0.1)\left(2\pi \frac{20}{60}\right)^2$$

15. A.
The amplitude is the size of the displacement *from the equilibrium position*. The mass travels 0.15 m to the left of equilibrium and 0.15 m to the right of equilibrium in one oscillation. So the amplitude is 0.15 m.

16. B.
The relationship between frequency and spring constant is given by

$$f = \frac{1}{2\pi}\sqrt{\frac{k}{m}}$$

If k increases then f increases. If k increases by a factor of 2, then f increases by a factor of $\sqrt{2}$, that is, 1.41. Increasing by a factor of 1.41 is the same as increasing by 41%.

17. D.
There is no relationship between amplitude and spring constant. Any amplitude may be chosen for the oscillation.

18. B.

In an oscillating system, the energy is going back and forth between two or more forms (so A is incorrect). It cannot dissipate as heat, so D is incorrect. Gravitational potential energy plays no role in the problem, so C is also incorrect. Indeed, spring potential and kinetic are the two forms of energy.

19. A.
Remember that whenever there is a collision involving sticking or crunching or what-have-you, momentum is likely to be the only conserved quantity. During the brief moment of the collision, the spring does not do anything, so the potential energy does not come into play. And the kinetic energy before the collision turns into heat (mostly). Momentum is conserved because there are no external forces during the collision: gravity is balanced with the normal force, and the spring is not compressed and hence exerts as yet no force.

20. B.
Momentum is not conserved, the external force being the spring which acts on mass B. Although kinetic energy is clearly not conserved, the sum of kinetic and potential is.

21. B.
We need to use conservation of momentum (the clue is that the collision involves sticking), so that if the initial velocity is v_0, then we write

$P_{before} = P_{afeter}$

$m_A v_0 + m_B(0) = (m_A + m_B)(0.2 \text{ m/s})$

$v_0 = \dfrac{(0.1+0.4) \text{ kg}}{0.1 \text{ kg}}\left(0.2\dfrac{\text{m}}{\text{s}}\right)$

$v_0 = 1.0$ m/s

22. A.
If we try to think of forces, we will get confused, because the spring force keeps changing. Again this is an energy problem, in which the kinetic energy (after the collision) gets completely converted to potential energy:

$1/2\ (m_A + m_B)v^2 = 1/2\ kx^2$

$1/2\ (0.5 \text{ kg})(0.2 \text{ m/s})^2 = 1/2\ (50 \text{ N/m})x^2$

$x = 0.02$ m

23. A.
The acceleration is the greatest when the net force is the greatest, that is, when the spring is compressed or extended. The net force is to the right when the spring is extended. Some readers confuse acceleration with velocity (or speed) and think that the block must be moving when the acceleration is great. This is not so.

24. D.

During the collision, most of the initial kinetic energy gets dissipated as heat. The choices involving chemical energy would also be possibilities (since the tearing and grasping of Velcro is chemical), but any answer must also involve heat, so D is the best answer.

25. B.
These are the two conditions for resonance to occur. A strong coupling will generally not allow energy to build up.

26. C.
The wavelength is the distance from peak to peak.

27. A.
The period is 2 s, so the frequency is $f = 1/T = 0.5$ Hz.

28. A.
The velocity is given by $v = \lambda f = (4 \text{ m}) (0.5 \text{ Hz}) = 2$ m/s.

29. A.
The amplitude is from equilibrium point to peak.

Passage 1

30. C.
Our first thought is to use the information about linear density, but there is no way to find the tension in the string. What other formula do we have for wave velocity? Well, $v = \lambda f$, and we know $f = 660$ Hz. We can get the wavelength just by knowing that the note 660 Hz refers to the fundamental. The fundamental has a wavelength $\lambda = 2 (0.65 \text{ m}) = 1.3$ m.

31. A.
For the D string we can use $\lambda = 1.3$ m, so that $f = v/\lambda = 294$ Hz. We do not have to do the calculation. If we look at the choices, we see only one choice less than 382.

32. C.
The fourth harmonic (see the figure in problem 40) has a wavelength $\lambda = 1/2\ (0.65 \text{ m}) = 0.325$ m, yielding $f = v/\lambda = 1175$ Hz.

33. C.
The first node occurs one fourth of the way from the neck end. Since the neck is a node as well, there must be a node at the midpoint and three fourths of the way down. This corresponds to a wavelength 0.325 m, as in problem 3 (above).

34. A.

The sixth harmonic has five nodes (not including the ends). This is shown in the figure. The wavelength is $\lambda = 1/3\ (0.65 \text{ m}) = 0.22$ m.

35. D.

Increasing the frequency by 3% is the same as increasing it by a factor of 1.03, which means increasing the wave velocity (recall $v = \lambda f$, and λ does not change) by a factor of 1.03. Now $T = v^2\mu$, and μ does not change, which means T is increased by a factor of $(1.03)^2 \approx 1.06$, which is an increase of 6%.

CHAPTER 10 SOLUTIONS

1. C.

We simply apply the formula $\beta = 10 \log_{10} [(10^{-6}$ W/m^2)/(10^{-12} W/m^2)] $= 10 \log_{10}[10^6] = 10 (6) = 60$ decibels.

2. A.

In Section B we discussed how intensity varies as the inverse square of the distance from the point source of sound. If distance increases by a factor of 3, then intensity decreases by a factor of $3^2 = 9$.

3. A.

The 40 W goes out in all directions. If you stand 6 m away from the sound, then you can imagine a ball around the speaker of radius 6 m. The total surface area of that ball is $4\pi r^2$. (If you have forgotten this formula, then take a minute to memorize it.) Since intensity is power per area, we can write

$$I = \frac{P}{A}$$

$$= \frac{40\,\text{W}}{4\pi(6\,\text{m})^2}$$

$$\approx \frac{40}{4 \cdot 3 \cdot 36}\frac{\text{W}}{\text{m}^2}$$

$$\approx \frac{10}{100}\frac{\text{W}}{\text{m}^2}$$

$$\approx 0.1\frac{\text{W}}{\text{m}^2}$$

We estimated $\pi \approx 3$ and $3 \times 36 \approx 100$. Look for these shortcuts.

4. B.

The intensity I is *proportional* to the power, so an increase by a factor of 10 in power leads to an increase by a factor of 10 in intensity. But β is related to the *logarithm* of intensity. An increase by a factor of 10 leads to an addition of 10 to β. You can also work this out by using the formula, and plugging any number you want in for area (like 1 m^2). But it is better to think it through as we have done here.

5. C.

Since the problem said the sound was barely perceptible, that means that the intensity at Betsy's ear was $I_0 = 10^{-12}$ W/m^2. Since the mosquito was 1 m away, we can imagine a ball 1 m in radius around the mosquito (see figure).

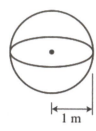

If 10^{-12} W emerges from each area 1 m^2, then for this ball, with area 4π (1 m)^2, the power must be

$$P = 10^{-12} \frac{W}{m^2} \left[4\pi(1 \text{ m})^2 \right]$$
$$= 1.3 \times 10^{-11} \text{ W}$$

This is the power produced by one mosquito. To obtain the energy produced in 100 s, we write

$$\Delta E = P\Delta t$$
$$= (1.3 \times 10^{-11} \text{ J/s})(100 \text{ s})$$
$$= 1.3 \times 10^{-9} \text{ W}$$

6. D.
In the last problem we determined that the power produced by one mosquito was 1.3×10^{-11} W. To power a 10-W bulb, we would need (10 W)/(1.3×10^{-11} W) $\approx$ $10/10^{-11} = 10^{12}$.

7. B.
If a mosquito were 10 m away (instead of 1 m), then the intensity of the sound would be $10^2 = 100$ times less. Thus there would have to be 100 mosquitoes in order to be barely perceptible.

8. B.
Moving from 30 to 3 m away decreases the distance by a factor of 10, and this increases the intensity by a factor of 100 (two factors of 10), and this adds 10 to β twice, so β = (20 + 10 + 10) decibels. You can work this problem by explicitly using the formula, but that is more difficult.

9. D.
If we consider the displacement of air particles, then the closed end is a node and the open end is an antinode. The fundamental wave form is shown in the figure. The 1.5 m shows merely a quarter of a full wave, so the wavelength is 6 m.

10. A.
Thus the frequency is $f = v/\lambda$ = (343 m/s)/(6 m) = 60 Hz.

11. B.
The second harmonic has one more node than the fundamental, and it is shown in the figure. What is shown is only three quarters of a wavelength. We can write $(3/4)\lambda = 1.5$ m to obtain $\lambda = 2$ m.

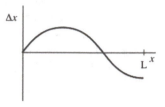

12. A.
The fifth harmonic has four more nodes than the fundamental. This is shown in the figure. There are 2 1/4 = 9/4 wave forms present, so we may write $(9/4)\lambda = 1.5$ m to obtain $\lambda = 2/3$ m.

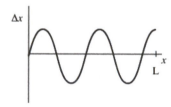

13. A.
The wavelength λ is still 6 m for the fundamental, since the length of the tube does not change, and we apply $f = v/\lambda$.

14. D.
If we consider the displacement of air particles, then both ends are antinodes, and we need at least one node in the pipe, even for the fundamental. This is shown in the figure. This is half a wave, so the wavelength is 0.2 m, since the pipe length is 0.1 m.

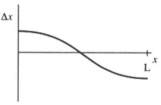

15. C.
Thus the frequency of the fundamental is $f = v/\lambda$ = (343 m/s)/(0.2 m) = 1700 Hz.

16. B.
The fourth harmonic has three more nodes than the fundamental, for a total of four nodes. The ends are still antinodes. This is shown in the figure. There are two wavelengths packed in the 0.1 m, so $\lambda = 0.05$ m.

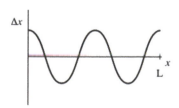

17. B.
Sound speed and frequency are related by $f = v/\lambda$, where λ is constant since it is simply twice the length of the organ pipe. If sound speed is 2% slower, then v decreases by a factor of 0.98, and f decreases by a factor of 0.98. Thus f decreases by 2%.

18. A.
The beat frequency in this case is $f_{beat} = 29.1$ Hz – 27.5 Hz $= 1.6$ Hz. Thus the period is $T = 1/f = 0.6$ s.

19. D.
The problem states that the beat frequency is twice a second, or 2 Hz. This means that the E string frequency differs from true 660 Hz by 2 Hz. Thus it could be 658 Hz or 662 Hz.

20. D.
Choices A, B, and C look really tempting, since sound needs to come into it somehow. We know, however, that the energy starts in the strings and ends up as sound. Choice D describes sound in another way. After all, sound is a wave, which is a "sloshing back and forth" of kinetic and potential energy. Thus, D is the answer, the first medium being the guitar string and the second medium being air.

21. C.
Choice A is tempting since the mini-passage is about beats, but we hear beats only at the end of the procedure. For choice B, interference is the addition of two waves in the same medium, which is what happens when waves from both strings combine, but that is not the excitation of the C_4 string. Choice C is when energy gets transferred from one oscillator to another of similar frequency by a weak coupling, so C is the answer. Choice D, dispersion, is the spreading of waves due to the dependence of wave speed on frequency (which we have not discussed).

22. A.
The beat frequency between the notes is $f_{beat} = f_2 - f_1 = $ (784.87 – 783.99) Hz = 0.88 Hz.

23. B.
The figure shows the fundamental and the third harmonic for the C_4 string. The fundamental frequency is given by $f_1 = v/(2L)$. The frequency of the third harmonic is given by $f_3 = v/(2/3\ L) = 3\ f_1$. Thus to get the frequency of the fundamental, we need to divide 784.87 Hz by 3.

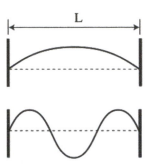

24. D.
The emitter is moving, and we choose the minus sign in the denominator because we want the answer to be greater than 420 Hz. Thus we have

$$f_{det} = \frac{350}{350 - 50}(420\ \text{Hz})$$
$$= \frac{7}{6}(420\ \text{Hz})$$
$$= 490\ \text{Hz}$$

25. C.
This time the detector is moving, and we choose the positive sign in the numerator to obtain an answer greater than 420 Hz (again they are approaching). Thus

$$f_{det} = \frac{350 + 50}{350}(420\ \text{Hz})$$
$$= \frac{8}{7}(420\ \text{Hz})$$
$$= 480\ \text{Hz}$$

26. B.
Again the emitter is moving, but this time we choose the positive sign:

$$f_{det} = \frac{350}{350 + 50}(420\ \text{Hz})$$
$$= \frac{7}{8}(420\ \text{Hz})$$
$$= 367.5\ \text{Hz}$$

27. D.
If the car were to hear the frequency, the frequency it would hear is given by

$$f_{det} = \frac{350 + 50}{350}(42\ \text{Hz})$$
$$= \frac{400}{350}(42\ \text{kHz})$$

Now if it were to re-emit this frequency, the frequency detected by the police detector would be

$$f_{det} = \frac{350}{350-50} f_{car}$$

$$= \frac{350}{300} \frac{400}{350} (42 \text{ kHz})$$

$$= \frac{4}{3} 42 \text{ kHz}$$

$$= 56 \text{ kHz}$$

This is the equivalent of sending a signal and having it reflect from a moving target. There are two Doppler shifts.

Passage 1

28. B.
According to paragraph 1, the wavelength must be shorter than the target insect. Thus the frequency must be greater than $f = v/l_{insect} = 34300$ Hz $= 34.3$ kHz.

29. B.
The sound pulse must travel from the bat to the insect, be reflected, and travel back again, for a total of 6 m. The time required is $\Delta t = \Delta x/v = 0.017$ s.

30. B.
Since the insect and the bat are moving in the same direction at the same speed, there is no Doppler shift, and the detected frequency is simply 30 kHz. If you want to make sure, you can work this problem like problem 27 above.

31. C.
Higher harmonic content refers to higher frequencies being present in addition to the fundamental. These higher harmonic frequencies thus have shorter wavelength. This would not really aid in distance measurement, so choice A is incorrect. Stunning the insect? Choice B is also incorrect. There is a sentence in paragraph 1 which indicates that C is plausible, since shorter wavelengths are more likely to be reflected if the wavelength of the fundamental is too large. If the harmonics are Doppler shifted, then so is the fundamental, so choice D is incorrect.

32. D.
If the tree could detect a frequency, it would detect

$$f_{tree} = \frac{343}{343-15} 50 \text{ kHz}$$

If it re-emitted this frequency, then the bat would detect a frequency given by

$$f_{det} = \frac{343+15}{343} f_{tree}$$

$$= \frac{358}{343} \frac{343}{328} (50 \text{ kHz})$$

$$= 55 \text{ kHz}$$

There are two Doppler shifts.

You do not need to do the calculation to obtain the answer. Given the fact that the bat and the tree approach each other, the frequency must be increased, so D is the only possible answer.

33. B.
The bat does not hear frequencies which are too far from those it sends out. Choice D is definitely not right, but it is interesting to think why. Why is such an adaptation completely useless?

CHAPTER 11 SOLUTIONS

1. C.

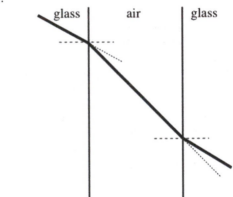

As the light beam goes from the glass to the air, it bends away from the normal (so the refracted beam makes a larger angle with the normal than the incident beam), and this eliminates A and B. As it passes into the glass it bends toward the normal.

2. C.

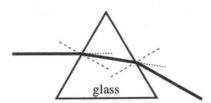

The dashed line shows the normal, and at the first interface the light bends toward the normal, which is down. At the second interface (normal is dashed line), the light bends away from the normal, which is down.

3. C.

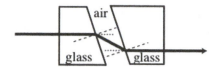

As the light beam passes into the glass, the incident angle is 0°, so the transmitted ray is still horizontal. Passing into the air, the light bends down, away from the normal. At the interface with glass, the beam bends toward the normal, back to horizontal. Thus the answer is C. To see that the beam is indeed exactly horizontal, you need to work out Snell's law.

4. B.

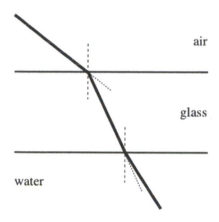

At the first interface, from air to glass, the beam bends toward the normal (A and D are incorrect), and at the second interface, the beam bends away from the normal (C is incorrect).

5. A.

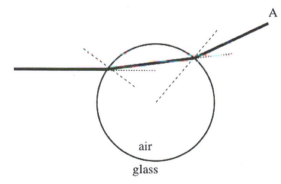

At the interface to air, the beam bends away from the normal, which is a radius, shown dashed. At the interface to glass, the beam bends toward the normal, which is again up.

6. C.
Snell's law becomes

$N_r \sin\theta_r = n_i \sin\theta_i$

$1.00\sin\theta_r = (4/3)\sin 30°$

$\sin\theta_r = (4/3)(1/2)$

$\sin\theta_r = 2/3$

$\theta_r = \sin^{-1} 2/3$

7. A.
The reflected angle has the same magnitude as the incident angle.

8. C.
For the critical angle, we must have the refracted angle be 90°:

$n_i \sin\theta_{crit} = n_r \sin 90°$

$(4/3)\sin\theta_{crit} = 1$

$\sin\theta_{crit} = 3/4$

$\theta_{crit} = \sin^{-1} 3/4$

9. D.
The equation for critical angle becomes (setting $\theta_r = 90°$)

$n_i \sin\theta_{crit} = n_r \sin 90°$

$1.00\sin\theta_{crit} = 1.414(1)$

$\sin\theta_{crit} = 1.414$

Since sine cannot be greater than 1, there is no critical angle. There is a critical angle, and total internal reflection, only for light beams traveling from a slow medium encountering a fast one.

10. B.
The frequency of light is the same, although the wave speed, and thus wavelength, changes.

11. D.
In this case the incident angle is 60°, since the problem states that the angle with the horizontal is 30°. Thus,

$\theta_i = 60°$

$n_r \sin\theta_r = n_i \sin\theta_i$

$\sqrt{3}\sin\theta_r = (1.00)\sin 60°$

$\sqrt{3}\sin\theta_r = \frac{\sqrt{3}}{2}$

$\sin\theta_r = \frac{1}{2}$

$\theta_r = 30°$

If the refracted angle is 30°, then the ray makes an angle with the surface which is 60°.

12. A.
The frequency of the beam does not change as it goes from air to a salt crystal, but the wave speed does, so we have $\lambda = v_{light}/f$. Thus $\lambda = c/nf$. Since n increases by a

437

factor of 1.7, the wavelength must decrease by a factor of 1.7, so the answer is A.

13. B.

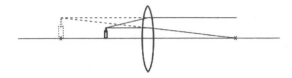

The figure shows the ray diagram. From this we can see the answer is B. If you want to use equations, you can write

$$\frac{1}{f} = \frac{1}{d_i} + \frac{1}{d_o}$$

$$\frac{1}{4m} = \frac{1}{d_i} + \frac{1}{2m}$$

$$\frac{1}{d_i} = \left(\frac{1}{4} - \frac{1}{2}\right) m^{-1}$$

$$= -\frac{1}{4} m^{-1}$$

$$d_i = -4 \text{ m}$$

where the negative sign indicates the image is on the same side as the object.

14. B.
From the diagram we observe the image is upright and virtual, since the rays must be extended to intersect.

15. D.
The magnification can be read from the diagram, or we can write

$$m = -\frac{d_i}{d_o}$$

$$= -\frac{-4 \text{ m}}{2 \text{ m}}$$

$$= 2$$

16. C.

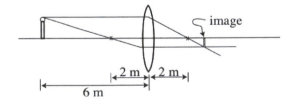

The figure shows the ray diagram, from which we see the image is inverted and real.

17. C.

Since the index of refraction depends on the frequency, and the focal length depends on the refraction of the beam in the lens, dispersion causes the focal length to depend on frequency.

18. B.

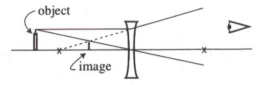

The figure shows the ray diagram. From it we can read the position of the image close enough to realize that B is the answer. The equation is

$$\frac{1}{f} = \frac{1}{d_i} + \frac{1}{d_o}$$

$$\frac{1}{-3m} = \frac{1}{d_i} + \frac{1}{4m}$$

$$d_i = -\frac{12}{7} \text{ m}$$

19. B.
The magnification is given by

$$m = -\frac{d_i}{d_o}$$

$$= -\frac{-\frac{12}{7} \text{ m}}{4 \text{ m}}$$

$$= \frac{3}{7}$$

The candle image has a height

$$d_i = \frac{3}{7}(21 \text{ cm})$$

$$= 9 \text{ cm}$$

20. C.
We can get the focal length from the following equation:

$$\frac{1}{f} = \frac{1}{d_i} + \frac{1}{d_o}$$

$$\frac{1}{f} = \frac{1}{4m} + \frac{1}{2m}$$

$$f = \frac{4}{3} \text{ m}$$

21. B.
The magnification is given by

$$m = -\frac{d_i}{d_o}$$

$$= -\frac{2\text{ m}}{4\text{ m}}$$

$$= -\frac{1}{2}$$

where the negative sign indicates the image is inverted.

22. D.

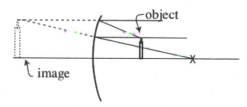

The figure shows the ray diagram for the candle 6 m from the mirror. From the diagram we can see that the image is about 12 m behind the mirror. The equation becomes

$$\frac{1}{f} = \frac{1}{d_i} + \frac{1}{d_o}$$

$$\frac{1}{12\text{m}} = \frac{1}{d_i} + \frac{1}{6\text{m}}$$

$$d_i = -12\text{ m}$$

where the negative sign indicates the image is behind the mirror.

23. C.
We can read this from the diagram, or we can calculate m $= -d_i/d_o = -(-12\text{ m})/(6\text{ m}) = 2$.

24. C.

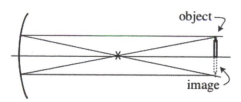

From the diagram we see the image is in the same position as the object but inverted. If we wanted to do the calculation, we would write

$$\frac{1}{f} = \frac{1}{d_i} + \frac{1}{d_o}$$

$$\frac{1}{12\text{m}} = \frac{1}{d_i} + \frac{1}{24\text{m}}$$

$$d_i = 24\text{ m}$$

25. C.
From the diagram we see the image is inverted and real.

26. C.
If the object is an infinite distance away, then the focus is on the focal plane, 12 m in front of the mirror. To see this in the equation, we write

$$\frac{1}{f} = \frac{1}{d_i} + \frac{1}{d_o}$$

$$\frac{1}{12\text{m}} = \frac{1}{d_i} + \frac{1}{\infty}$$

$$d_i = 12\text{ m}$$

27. C.

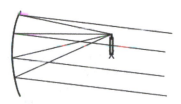

Conversely to the previous problem, light rays that start at the focus end up parallel.

28. A.

29. A.

30. B.

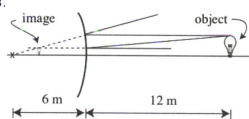

These answers can be read from the ray diagram (see figure).

31. B.

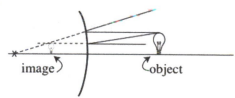

The figure shows the ray diagram.

32. B.
We calculate the focal length as follows:

$$\frac{1}{f} = \frac{1}{d_i} + \frac{1}{d_o}$$

$$\frac{1}{f} = \frac{1}{-4\text{ m}} + \frac{1}{2\text{ m}}$$

$$\frac{1}{f} = \frac{1}{4}\text{m}^{-1}$$

$$f = 4\text{ m}$$

where the positive sign indicates the mirror is converging.

33. C.
The magnification is given by $m = -d_i/d_o = -(-4\text{ m})/(2\text{ m}) = 2$.

Passage 1

34. B.
The light emerging from the first (left) polarizer has half the intensity of the original source, since the horizontal component has been taken out of it. All of the resulting light passes through the second (right) polarizer, since it is already vertically polarized. Thus the final beam has half the intensity of the original.

35. D.
The light emerging from the first polarizer has half the intensity of the original source, and it is vertically polarized. The second polarizer cuts out the vertical component and passes the horizontal component, so the resulting intensity is zero.

36. C.
Again, the light emerging from the first polarizer is vertically polarized and has intensity $1/2\ I_0$. After it goes through the optically active substance, it may have *any* orientation, since that information is not given in the problem. If the beam ends up horizontally polarized, then the resulting intensity is $1/2\ I_0$. If it ends up vertically polarized, then the intensity is zero. If the more probable situation arises that the beam is somewhere between these two extremes, still polarized but at some oblique angle, then the resultant intensity is between 0 and $1/2\ I_0$.

37. C.
Since the light is absorbed, the energy turns to heat.

38. D.
The passage states (paragraph 1) that radiation is emitted perpendicular to the wire. For the antenna in question 5, most of the radiation is emitted east, west, up, down, and so on, but none is emitted north and south.

CHAPTER 12 SOLUTIONS

1. A.
For a repulsive force to exist, the balls must have like charge.

2. D.
At first it seems as if III can be definitely concluded. Then we remember that a charged object can attract a neutral object if it induces a charge, so D is the correct answer.

3. A.
By Coulomb's law, as the distance increases by a factor of 4, the force decreases by a factor of 4^2.

4. D.
Both charges increase by a factor of 2. Both contribute an increase of a factor of 2 to the force.

5. B.
By Coulomb's law, the force exerted by one charge on the other has the same magnitude as the force the other exerts on the first. This is an example of Newton's third law.

6. B.
This can be obtained by process of elimination. In choice A, the positive charges are concentrated in an area. Their mutual repulsion would cause them to move apart, so choice A is out. In choices C and D, the charges in the middle would be repelled by the charged ball and move to the left. So choices C and D are out.

7. B.
The positive charges will repel each other and, being free to move, will move as far apart as possible. Thus they will end up distributed as in choice B.

8. D.
The positive charges will repel each other, but not being free to move, they will remain where they are placed. The correct answer is D.

9. D.
First let's draw a diagram with all the forces. If Q and $-Q$ are 2×10^{-6} m apart, then q is 10^{-6} m from Q.

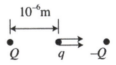

The force to the right due to charge Q is $F_{elec} = kQq/d^2 = 10^{-5}$ N, where we have used $d = 10^{-6}$ m. The force due to the charge $-Q$ is also to the right and has the same magnitude. The forces add to yield 2×10^{-5} N.

10. C.
First let's draw a diagram with all the forces.

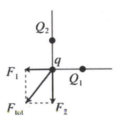

The magnitude of the force in the $-x$-direction is given by Coulomb's law, so that $F_1 = 3 \times 10^{-5}$ N. Likewise $F_2 = 4 \times$

10^{-5} N. We obtain the total force by the Pythagorean theorem, $F_{tot} = 5 \times 10^{-5}$ N.

11. A.
First let's draw a diagram with all the forces on charge q.

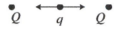

The forces add to zero.

12. A.
The sodium ion Na^+ is positively charged and attracts the oxygen atom. Oxygen is slightly negative because it is more electronegative than the hydrogen atoms to which it is attached.

13. C.
First, we draw a diagram.

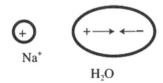

The water molecule can be modeled as having a positive end and a negative end, so that is how we will draw it. The sodium ion exerts a force on each end, as shown. The repulsive force is greater than the attractive force because the positive end is nearer the sodium ion, and Coulomb's law states that the force varies as the inverse square of the distance.

14. A.
First we draw a diagram, showing the electric field from the various charges. (The vector E_1, is due to charge Q_1 at $x = -10^{-3}$ m.)

Note that because point P is closer to the negative charge, the vector to the left is longer. The sum will be to the left, so the answer is A.

If we want to calculate the numbers, we calculate the magnitude

$$E_2 = \frac{kQ_2}{d_2^{\,2}}$$

$$= \left(9 \times 10^9 \, \frac{Nm^2}{C^2}\right) \frac{\left(1.1 \times 10^{-9} \, C\right)}{\left(10^{-3} \, m\right)^2}$$

$$= 10^7 \, \frac{N}{C}$$

Likewise we calculate the magnitude

$$E_1 = \frac{kQ_1}{d_1^{\,2}}$$

$$= \left(9 \times 10^9 \, \frac{Nm^2}{C^2}\right) \frac{\left(1.1 \times 10^{-9} \, C\right)}{\left(2 \times 10^{-3} \, m\right)^2}$$

$$= 2.5 \times 10^6 \, \frac{N}{C}$$

Subtracting these yields the result A.

15. D.
First we draw a diagram, showing the electric field from the various charges.

Both electric field vectors point toward the negative charge, and both vectors have a magnitude

$$E_1 = \left(9 \times 10^9 \, \frac{Nm^2}{C^2}\right) \frac{\left(1.1 \times 10^{-11} \, C\right)}{\left(5 \times 10^{-3} \, m\right)^2}$$

$$= 4 \times 10^3 \, \frac{N}{C}$$

Since there are two vectors of equal magnitude, the result is D.

16. A.
First we draw a diagram, showing the electric field from the various charges.

Note that the electric fields are of the same magnitude and point in the opposite direction, so the total electric field at that point is zero.

17. A.
First we draw electric field vectors into the diagram.

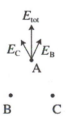

The horizontal components add to zero, and the vertical components are both up, away from the charges. Thus the answer is A.

18. B.
First we draw electric field vectors into the diagram.

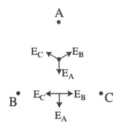

The electric fields due to charges B and C add to zero, so the total electric field at point D is down.

19. A.
The electric fields due to the various charges add to zero.

20. B.
First we draw a diagram, showing the electric field from the various charges.

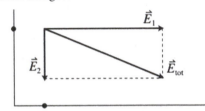

We read the direction from the diagram.

21. D.
Since $F = qE$, and the charge q for an electron is negative, F is the in opposite direction from E.

22. A.
The positively charged top plate will create a downward electric field, and a negatively charged bottom plate will create a downward field as well. Choice B will create an upward field, and choices C and D will not create electric fields at all.

23. B.
The force diagram for the ball is shown.

Force balance yields $F_{elec} - mg = 0$. What do we use for F_{elec}? We do not have data for Coulomb's law, but we do have an electric field. Thus we write $QE - mg = 0$, where Q is the charge on the ball. We obtain $Q = -2.25 \times 10^{-6}$ C for the ball, where we have used $E = 400$ N/C, and we have taken up to be positive. In order to check the sign on the charge, we realize that the electric force must be up. If the electric field is down, then a positive charge would experience a downward force. So the charge must be negative, so the electric force will balance gravity.

24. A.
We apply the formula $F = q_{proton}E = (1.6 \times 10^{-19}$ C) (4 x 10^4 N/C) = 6.4×10^{-15} N.

25. C.
The relevant equation is $F = QE$. Since E is constant, and Q is twice as large for the alpha particle (helium has two protons and two neutrons), the force is twice as large.

26. D.
We need to relate acceleration to data in the problem. Let's start with $F = ma$, or

$a = F/m$

where F is the force on the proton (or electron), and m is the mass of the proton (or electron). The force is given by $F = qE$, in both cases, so

$a = qE/m$

The electron has a charge of opposite sign, E is constant, and m is 2000 times smaller. Therefore, the acceleration of the electron is of opposite direction and 2000 times greater.

27. C.
The positive end of the water molecule would experience a force in the same direction as the electric field, that is, up. The negative end of the molecule would experience a force in the opposite direction of the electric field, that is, down. The energy would be minimized, therefore, if the hydrogen end pointed up and the oxygen end down, so C is the answer.

28. A.
Note that this is not the orientation derived in problem 27. Let's draw a diagram showing the forces, and drawing the water molecule as a dipole. The forces cancel. (This is not like those problems in which one arrow is longer than the other, because the electric field here is uniform.)

29. C.
From the above diagram, we see that the molecule tends to be compressed.

Passage 1
30. A.
The frequency of the radiation is the same as the frequency of the alternating current, 10^7 Hz. The

wavelength of the radiation is $\lambda = c/f = (3 \times 10^8 \text{ m/s})/(10^7 \text{ Hz}) = 30$ m. For a quarter-wave antenna (see paragraph 3), the length would be 7.5 m.

31. D.
According to the passage, the electric field "points along the same axis as the current" that produces it. Since the antenna is vertical, the current it carries is vertical, so the electric field is vertical as well.

32. B.
The magnetic field is perpendicular to the direction of propagation (north/south) and to the electric field (up/down). So the magnetic field must point east/west.

33. B.
The electric field points up and down, so the force on the electrons in the antenna is up and down as well. The electrons should be free to move in this direction if an alternating current is to be set up. Thus the antenna should be vertical.

34. B.
When you think of an electric field, you should immediately think of force on a charge. Choice B is correct in that the force creates the current. (Choice C is incorrect because the electrons are not bound to individual atoms.)

35. A.
The energy starts as electrical.

CHAPTER 13 SOLUTIONS

1. C.
The electric current is the amount of charge going by a point in the circuit per unit time. In a flow of water, the analogous parameter is the amount (volume) of water going past a point per unit of time, the volume flow rate. Note that the current is the same for resistors in series, and the volume flow rate is constant along a flow (if there is no branching), which is not true of flow velocity.

2. D.
Height gives a measure of the energy per mass required to place water at that point, just as electric potential is a measure of the energy per charge required to place a charge at that point.

3. C.
A battery pumps charge from one electric potential to another.

4. C.

A pool is a large supply of water from which you can take or to which you can add water without disturbing it. A ground is a large supply of charge.

5. A.
We can label the circuit diagram with currents and voltages. Clearly, the current which flows through resistor 2 is the current which flows through the entire circuit. To obtain this current, we can combine resistors. Since they are in series, we simply add in order to obtain the equivalent circuit shown below.

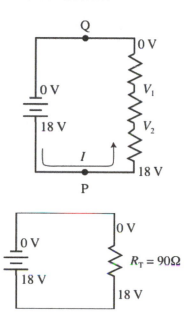

The current, from Ohm's law, is $I = (18 \text{ V})/(90 \ \Omega) = 0.2$ A. If you chose C, then you probably tried to apply Ohm's law by substituting in 18 V for the potential drop across the resistor. But the potential drop is not nearly so large, as is shown in the first diagram of this solution. We need to consider the entire circuit to obtain the current in any one place. This is like water in a pipe, in that the current at one point is affected by conditions (such as a partial blockage) both upstream and downstream.

6. B.
See the above explanation.

7. C.

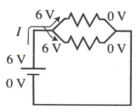

In the circuit diagram we label voltages and currents. The current splits into two unequal pieces. The current through resister 1 is given by Ohm's law: $I_1 = 6 \text{ V}/1 \ \Omega = 6$ A. The current through resister 2 is $I_2 = 6 \text{ V}/2 \ \Omega = 3$ A. Of course, this is not surprising, since we would expect that the lesser resistance would have the greater current if the voltage drops are equal.

8. B.
See above explanation.

9. D.
We label the voltages and currents in the circuit diagram, beginning with 0 volts at the short end of cell 1. Because of the jump of $V_1 = 6$ V, we label the wire on the other side 6 volts. The short end of the cell 2 is 6 V, so a jump of 9 V means the wire on the other side is 15 V. Thus the potential drop across the resistor is 15 V. Ohm's law gives us $I = 15 \text{ V}/60 \ \Omega = 0.25$ A.

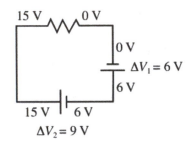

10. B.

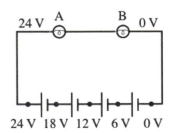

Since the bulbs are in series, the current through them is the same.

11. C.
We label voltages and currents in the circuit diagram. We can read off that the potential difference between C and D is 18 V.

12. D.
In this case, Ohm's law is $\Delta V_i = IR_i$, since I is constant. The light bulb with the higher resistance has a proportionally higher potential drop.

13. C.

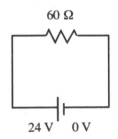

To obtain the total current, we draw an equivalent circuit, combining the voltage sources and the two resistor light bulbs (see figure). Ohm's law yields 0.4 A.

14. C.
For this question, we can simply apply Ohm's law to obtain $\Delta V_1 = I_1 R_1 = (2 \text{ A}) (4 \ \Omega) = 8$ V.

15. B.
Since resistors 1 and 2 are in series, the current going through them must be the same.

16. B.

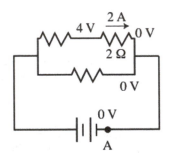

Since the current through resistor 2 is 2 amps, the voltage drop across it is $I_2 R_2 = 4$ V. If we label point A to be 0 V, then a jump of 4 V will bring us to point B.

17. B.

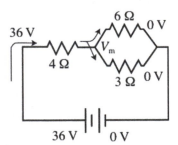

We can label the circuit diagram with voltages and currents, but this does not give us the answer immediately because we do not know the potential drop across resistor 1. (If you chose D, you should pay attention to this point.) First let's combine resistors 2 and 3, as shown in the equivalent circuit below. The resulting resistance is given by

$$\frac{1}{R_T} = \frac{1}{6\Omega} + \frac{1}{3\Omega}$$
$$\frac{1}{R_T} = \left(\frac{1}{6} + \frac{1}{3}\right)\frac{1}{\Omega}$$
$$\frac{1}{R_T} = \frac{1}{2\Omega}$$
$$R_T = 2\Omega$$

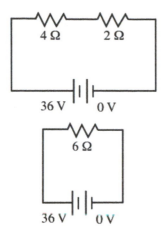

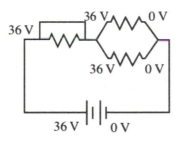

(If you chose C, you forgot to take the final reciprocal.) We combine the resistors in series to obtain the equivalent circuit shown. The total current is 6 amps, which is also the current through resistor 1.

18. B.
Since resistors 2 and 3 are in parallel, the voltage drop across both of them are the same.

19. A.

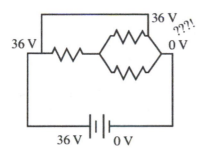

The resulting new circuit is shown in the diagram. The potential drop across resistor 2 is the full 36 V. Thus the voltage increases when A and B are connected.

20. D.

The resulting new circuit is shown in the diagram. But what is this? Definitely a problem. We have shorted the circuit. Do not try this at home.

21. A.

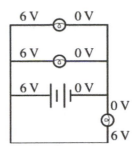

On the circuit diagram, we label the potentials. The current splits into three pieces. By Ohm's law we can calculate the current through light bulb 2, $I_2 = (6 \text{ V})/(20 \text{ }\Omega) = 0.3$ A. From this we can get power, $P_2 = I_2 \Delta V_2 = 1.8$ Watts = 1.8 J/s. In 10 seconds, 18 Joules are dissipated.

22. C.

23. C.

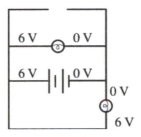

If the connection through light bulb 1 were interrupted, then we obtain the circuit shown. The electric potential across light bulb 2 is the same 6 V that it was before, so it burns in the same way.

Question 23 is essentially the same question. The 6-V potential across light bulb 3 does not change if current through light bulb 2 is interrupted.

24. D.

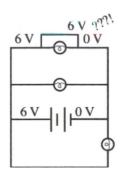

The short is made clear in the resulting circuit diagram. If you tried this in real life the battery would get very hot while a large current surged through the wire connection.

25. A.

445

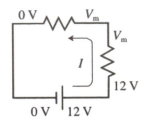

We draw potentials and currents on the circuit diagram, but we know neither the potential drop nor the current for resistor 1. We can obtain this current, however, by combining resistors. Since the resistors are in series, we obtain $I = 12 \text{ V}/6\ \Omega = 2$ A. Thus the current through resistor 1 is 2 A, and the potential difference across it is $I R_1 = 4$ V. Thus the power dissipated is $P_2 = I_2 \Delta V_2 = 8$ Watts.

26. D.

From the circuit diagram (Problem 25) we can see that the sum of the potential drops across the resistors must be 12 V. We could obtain another relationship, since the current through both resistors is the same. Thus

$$I_1 = I_2$$
$$\frac{\Delta V_1}{R_1} = \frac{\Delta V_2}{R_2}$$
$$\Delta V_1 = \frac{1}{2}\Delta V_2$$

but this does not correspond to any of the choices.

27. A.

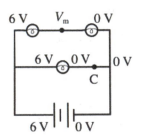

We draw in potentials and currents in the circuit diagram. Introducing a resistor at point C would split the potential drop across light bulb 3, decreasing the power $P_3 = (\Delta V_3)^2/R_3$, so choice D is out. Decreasing the emf of the battery would decrease the power of resistor 3, so C is out. If we hold the potential drop across light bulb 3 constant, then a decrease in the resistance will increase the power since, again, $P_3 = (\Delta V_3)^2/R_3$. So A is correct.

28. C.

The power dissipated (that is, the energy per unit time) is constant. If the question had asked, "What is the energy dissipated look like as a function of time?", then D would have been the answer. B might have been the answer if the source were alternating current.

29. B.

Since current can no longer go through the wire with light bulb 1, light bulb 2 extinguishes. Choices A and C are

eliminated. Does light bulb 3 burn brighter? The potential drop across light bulb 3 is not a function of what happens in the upper wire. The potential across it remains 6 V. Its current does not change, and the power it dissipates does not change.

30. D.

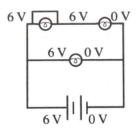

We draw a new circuit with A and B connected. In this new circuit, light bulb 2 has the full 6 volts across it, so it burns brighter.

Passage 1

31. C.

There is an electric field E_1 between the plates, and the force on a charged particle is given by $F_{elec} = QE_1$. Since a helium nucleus has twice the charge of a proton, the force on it is double.

32. A.

In Experiment 2 the increase in distance results in a decrease in capacitance by a factor of 3 (see equation). Since ΔV is the same in Experiment 2, the charge ($Q = C\Delta V$) decreases by a factor of 3.

33. A.

The electric field is simply given by $E = \Delta V/d$, so an increase in d by a factor of 3 results in a decrease in the electric field by a factor of 3.

34. B.

Once the wires are removed from the plates, no more charge may be transferred, so the charge must stay the same. This is a situation in which the question becomes easy if we visualize the charges and think about the experiment. The question is difficult or intractable if we rely on rote memorization of equations.

35. C.

The capacitance is decreased by a factor of 2 since the distance is increased by a factor of 2. The charge is still Q_1 since there is no way for it to change. Thus the potential between the plates *must* change. The only equation we have relating voltage and charge is $\Delta V = Q/C$, so ΔV increases by a factor of 2.

CHAPTER 14 SOLUTIONS

1. D.
The force on the proton is given by $F = qE$. This gives us the acceleration from $a = F/m$, and since we are given the initial velocity $v_1 = 0$ m/s, the final velocity is given by $v_2 = v_1 + a\Delta t = (qE/m) \Delta t = (1.6 \times 10^{-19}$ C$)(1.6 \times 10^2$ N/C$)(10^{-4}$ s$)/(1.7 \times 10^{-27}$ kg$) = 1.5 \times 10^6$ m/s. (Notice how easy it is to do the arithmetic if the variables are manipulated first and the numbers substituted afterwards.)

2. C.
The force on a particle is simply $F = qE_0$. The charge on the deuteron (one proton and one neutron) is the opposite of the charge on the electron. Thus the forces on the two are the same in magnitude.

3. A.
The symbol $^{20}F^-$ represents an ion with a nucleus of 9 protons (hence F) and 11 neutrons (hence mass number 20) and 10 electrons outside the nucleus (hence the overall charge). For this problem, the overall charge is all that is needed. Since $F = qE_0$, the magnitudes of the forces are the same.

4. A.
The magnitude of the acceleration is given by $a = F/m = qE_0/m$. The electric field is constant, of course. The charges of the proton and the electron are equal in magnitude and are opposite in sign. The proton is 2000 times more massive, so its acceleration is 2000 times smaller.

5. C.
We have $a = qE_0/m$ from Problem 4. Now ^{1}H has one half the charge of ^{4}He (decreasing the acceleration by a factor of 2) and one fourth the mass (increasing the acceleration by a factor of 4). The result is an increase by a factor of 2, as expressed in answer C.

6. B.
The nuclei have the same charge (both have one proton). The forces on both are the same.

7. D.
If we write the atomic numbers explicitly, we obtain

$$^{235}_{92}U \rightarrow {}^{141}_{56}Ba + {}^{92}_{36}Kr + ?$$

The subscripts already add to 92, so adding a proton ($^1_1$H) on the right would ruin the sum. On the other hand, the superscripts add to 235 on the left and to 233 on the right. If we add two neutrons to the right ($^1_0$n + $^1_0$n), then the sum becomes correct.

8. B.

The reactants are $^3_2$He + $^3_2$He. Thus the superscripts must add to 6, so C is not the answer. The subscripts must add to 4, so A and D are eliminated.

9. C.
The left side of the reaction is represented by

$$^{15}_7N + {}^1_1H \rightarrow ?$$

so the superscripts add to 16 and the subscripts add to 8. This eliminates A and B (recall that γ represents no protons and no neutrons). The problem with choice D is that $^2_3$Li cannot exist, since the mass number (total number of protons and neutrons) must be greater than the atomic number (number of protons).

10. C.
The energy of the transition is the same as the energy of the photon $E_{ph} = hf = h(c/\lambda) = 1.3 \times 10^{-18}$ J. Therefore the new energy level differs from the ground state (0 J) by 1.3 $\times 10^{-18}$ J. Is it positive or negative? Since the ground state represents the lowest energy, the excited state must be $+1.3 \times 10^{-18}$ J.

11. D.
There are three possible transitions, as shown in the figure below. Thus D is the answer. In order to get the frequencies listed, we calculate $f_1 = (1$ eV $- 0$ eV$)/(4.14 \times 10^{-15}$ eV s$) = 2.4 \times 10^{14}$ Hz, and cetera.

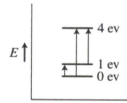

12. D.
The six possible transitions are shown in the figure below.

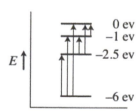

13. B.
The lower limit for visible light is 4.0×10^{14} Hz, which corresponds to $E_{photon} = hf = (4.14 \times 10^{-15}$ eV s$)$ $(4.0 \times 10^{14}$ Hz$) = 1.7$ eV, and the upper limit corresponds to $E_{photon} = (4.14 \times 10^{-15}$ eV s$)$ $(7.5 \times 10^{14}$ Hz$) = 3.1$ eV. The only transition to fall in these limits is from -2.5 eV to 0 eV.

14. C.
The young scientist calculates a photon energy $E_{photon} = hf = (4.14 \times 10^{-15}$ eV s$)$ $(4.8 \times 10^{14}$ Hz$) = 2.0$ eV. Since this is a transition from the ground state, it must be a transition from -5 eV (the ground state) to -3 eV (an excited state).

15. B.
The energy of transition is the same as the energy of the photon $E_{ph} = hf = (4.14 \times 10^{-15}\ \text{eV s})(2.01 \times 10^{14}\ \text{Hz}) = 0.83\ \text{eV}$. Thus the excited state is 0.83 eV above the ground state at -5.37 eV. So the energy level is at -4.54 eV.

16. B.
The wavelength is given by $\lambda = c/f$.

17. C.
The frequency given in the choices corresponds to $E_{\text{transition}}/h$. If a photon has any energy greater than this, then 5.37 eV of the energy will liberate the electron from the atom, and the rest of the energy will go into the kinetic energy of the electron.

18. B.
We write the nuclear reaction

$$^{55}_{28}\text{Ni} \rightarrow ?+\ ^{0}_{+1}\text{e} + \nu$$

The subscript of the daughter nucleus must be 27, and the superscript must be 55. Thus the daughter is $^{55}_{27}\text{Co}$.

19. D.
We write the nuclear reaction

$$? \rightarrow\ ^{222}_{88}\text{Ra} +\ ^{4}_{2}\text{He}$$

The subscript of the parent nucleus is 90, and the superscript is 226. Thus the parent is $^{226}_{90}\text{Th}$.

20. C.
We write the nuclear reaction

$$^{238}_{92}\text{U} \rightarrow\ ^{4}_{2}\text{He} +\ ^{0}_{-1}\text{e} +\ ^{0}_{-1}\text{e} +\ ^{4}_{2}\text{He} + ?$$

Thus the daughter is $^{230}_{90}\text{Th}$.

21. C.
If we add in the subscripts and add notation to the beta particles, we obtain

    A. $^{1}_{1}\text{H} +\ ^{1}_{1}\text{H} \rightarrow\ ^{2}_{1}\text{H} + \gamma$

    B. $^{1}_{1}\text{H} +\ ^{1}_{1}\text{H} \rightarrow\ ^{2}_{2}\text{He} + \gamma$

    C. $^{1}_{1}\text{H} +\ ^{1}_{1}\text{H} \rightarrow\ ^{2}_{1}\text{H} +\ ^{0}_{+1}\text{e}^{+} + \nu$

    D. $^{1}_{1}\text{H} +\ ^{1}_{1}\text{H} \rightarrow\ ^{2}_{1}\text{H} +\ ^{0}_{-1}\text{e}^{-} + \bar{\nu}$

Choice B does not have heavy hydrogen as a product, and choices A and D do not satisfy the criteria that the sub- and super-scripts have the same sum on both sides.

22. A.
Recall that the symbol for the neutron is n or $^{1}_{0}\text{n}$. The only reaction which satisfies the criteria is A.

23. C.
Eight thousand years is five half-lives. If we multiply 1 gram by 1/2 five times, we obtain $(1/2)^5$ g = 1/32 g = 3.1 x 10^{-2} grams.

24. C.
A decrease in radioactivity from 300 to 20 mCi is a decrease of about a factor of 16, that is, four factors of 2. Four half-lives corresponds to 57.2 days, which is close to C. The formal way to do this problem is to write

$$200\left(\frac{1}{2}\right)^{n} = 30$$

$$200\left(\frac{1}{2^{n}}\right) = 30$$

$$2^{n} = \frac{200}{30}$$

$$2^{n} = 15$$

$$n \approx 4$$

25. C.
A glance at the answers indicates we need get only an estimate. We want to know how much uranium we need to obtain 10^{12} J. The amount of mass that needs to be converted each second is given by

$$E = mc^2$$

$$10^{12}\ \text{J} = m\left(3 \times 10^{8}\ \frac{\text{m}}{\text{s}}\right)^2$$

$$10^{12}\ \text{J} = m\left(10^{17}\ \frac{\text{m}^2}{\text{s}^2}\right)$$

$$m = 10^{-5}\ \text{kg}$$

$$m = 10^{-2}\ \text{g}$$

Passage 1

26. B.
We see from the energy level diagram that the smallest energy from ground state to excited state is from $n = 1$ to $n = 2$. The difference in energy is

$$E_{\text{photon}} = (-3.4 - -13.6)\ \text{eV}$$

27. D.
By definition, ionization energy is the amount of energy required to remove an electron from an atom (or molecule) in its ground state. The energy level diagram shows this to be 13.6 eV.

28. A.
The photon energy corresponds to the difference between the two energy states. Certainly B and C are incorrect. It is not the case that we must merely have enough energy to reach the next rung of the ladder. We have to hit it exactly. Compare this with problem 17, where we wanted

to ionize the atom. In that case we can hit the atom with a photon of greater energy because the excess goes into kinetic energy. We have no way of soaking up the extra energy in this case.

29. C.
Both momentum and energy are conserved because there are no external forces in this scenario. Energy is converted from one form to another: from the energy of an excited state to photon energy and (much less) kinetic energy of the recoiling atom.

30. D.
We want the longest wavelength, which means the smallest frequency (since $f = c/\lambda$), which means the smallest energy (since $E = hf$). If we look at the energy level diagram for the differences between levels, we see there is a transition corresponding to a largest energy, but the energy difference can get as small as you like (at the upper end of the diagram).

CHAPTER 15 SOLUTIONS

1. B
The passage states that the experiments were conducted at 20°C. To convert the temperature to the Kelvin scale, add 273.

$$20 + 273 = 293 \text{ K}.$$

2. C
In this system heat is readily exchanged with the surroundings, which maintains the temperature at 20°C. An adiabatic system does not exchange heat with the surrounding and changes temperature. The pressure and volume of the gas in the lung change.

3. C
The passage states that "As a control, a balloon was used to repeat the experiment and no hysteresis was observed." Since the inflation and deflation PV curves are the same, the same amount of work was done.

4. B
IDL is the result of fibrosis, which makes the lung less elastic, requiring more work to inflate the lung. This is readily seen in the second figure in the passage, which compares a normal lung to the lung of a patient having emphysema and IDL. Note that the volume is on the y-axis in this plot. To inhale the same amount of air as a normal lung the pressure for the IDL lung would have to be much greater and much more work (area under the PV curve, when volume is on the x-axis) would have to be done. Alternatively, more than one breath would be required, also requiring more work.

5. B
As stated in the passage, "The compliance of the lung can be measured by the $\Delta V/\Delta P$ for the initial linear portion of the plot." A steep slope corresponds to a more compliant (easily expanded) lung. The slope of the emphysema patient was clearly more compliant than the normal patient's lung. The work corresponds to the area under the PV curve when volume is plotted on the x-axis. It takes less work to expand a more compliant lung. The problem with emphysema is that the air passages have been compromised due to obstruction, making it more difficult to get air in and out of the lung prior to reaching the equilibrium lung volume for a given pressure.

6. A
Once the valve that connected the system to the air was closed, the experimental system consisted of the lung tissue and the air contained within the lung, plastic tubes, syringes and manometers. Heat was readily exchanged with the surroundings, but not matter. Therefore, by definition this is a closed system. While the volume of air in one portion of the system, the lung, does change, the total amount of air within the entire system does not change, because "Air was injected into the lung using S2".

7. B
The change in volume per change in temperature is equal to the coefficient of expansion α times the original volume. The change in volume will be

$$\Delta V = \alpha \, V \, \Delta T = (2.07 \times 10^{-4} \text{ K}^{-1})(900 \text{ mL})(75 \text{ K}) = 14 \text{ mL}$$

Therefore, the total volume when the water reaches 100 °C will be $900 + 14 = 914$ mL.

8. C
In order for heat to be transferred from the sinus tissue to the air, the heat must be transferred by conduction, but additionally, some of the heat is transferred within the air by convection as it passes through the nasal cavity.

9. C
The amount of heat that must be removed from the water to convert it into ice, will be the sum of the heat that must be removed to cool the liquid water from 25°C to 0°C [4.18 J/g°C x 200 g x 25°C = 20900 J], and the amount of heat that must be removed to cause the freezing of the water [334 J/g x 200 g = 66800 J], which is 87.7 kJ.

10. A
To completely melt the ice, the liquid water would have to supply 334 J/g x 100 g = 33400 J of heat. If the water is cooled from 25°C to 0°C, the amount of heat available is 4.18 J/g°C x 300 g x 25°C = 3150 J, which is not enough to completely melt the ice. The system will come to equilibrium in which there is a mixture of liquid water and a small amount of ice, both of which are at 0°, which is 273 K.

CHAPTER 18 SOLUTIONS

1. B.
Estimate as 35/7 = 5

2. B.
Estimate as 2 x 100 / 40 = 200/40 = 5

3. B.
Estimate as (30+115) / 145 = 1

4. C.
First blue gum ball = 60/100
Second blue gum ball = 59/99 (estimate as 60/100)

60/100 x 60/100 = 6/10 x 6/10 = 36/100 = 36%

5. C.
(50% $_{\text{CHANCE OF BOY}}$ x 10% $_{\text{ALBINO}}$)+ (50% $_{\text{CHANCE OF GIRL}}$ x 20% $_{\text{ALBINO}}$) = 15%

6. C.
Odds of drawing a club = 13/52 = 1/4

Replacing the card returns the deck to its original state, so the odds of the second club are also 1/4.

Odds of two clubs = 1/4 x 1/4 = 1/16

7. A.
Factor out:

$\sqrt{180} = \sqrt{(36 \times 5)} = \sqrt{36} \times \sqrt{5} = 6\sqrt{5}$

8. D.
The decimal makes the two zeros at the end of the 250 significant, so there are 5 sig figs in the first number. That makes the right answer D.

9. D.
Convert so the exponent is an even number, to make it easier to cut in half:

$\sqrt{(2.5 \times 10^{17})} = \sqrt{(25 \times 10^{16})} = \sqrt{25} \times \sqrt{10^{16}} = 5 \times 10^8$

10. B.

Convert so they both have the same exponent and then add the coefficients:

$3 \times 10^6 + 0.9 \times 10^6 = 3.9 \times 10^6$

CHAPTER 19 SOLUTIONS

1. B.
$3x / (x+2) = 5$
$3x = 5(x+2)$
$3x = 5x + 10$
$-2x = 10$
$x = -5$

2. A.

$2y - x = 5$
$2(2y - x = 5)$
$4y - 2x = 10$

$[4y - 2x = 10]$
$\underline{+[2x + 3y = 18]}$
$7y = 28$
$y = 4$

$2(4) - x = 5$
$8 - x = 5$
$x = 3$

3. B.

$pH = pKa + \log(A/HA)$
$pH - pKa = \log(A/HA)$
$pH - pKa = \log A - \log HA$
$pH - pKa + \log HA = \log A$

4. B.

Sine of 30° is 1/2.

5. D.

Cosine of 0° is 1 and cosine of 180° is -1.

6. A.

Tangent of 0° is 0.

7. B.

$\text{Log}_X X$ is always equal to 1.

8. B

$\log A + \log B = \log (A \times B)$
$\log 25 + \log 4 = \log (25 \times 4) = \log 100 = \log 10^2 = 2$

9. C

$-\log A = \log (1/A)$

log (1/1000) = - log 1000 = - log 10^3 = -3

10. A

$2 \log_5 \sqrt{5} = \log_5 (\sqrt{5})^2 = \log_5 5 = 1$

CHAPTER 20 SOLUTIONS

1. A.
Slope = $\Delta y / \Delta x$ = 3 – (-2) / 2-4 = 5 / -2 = -2.5

2. C.
Slope = $\Delta y / \Delta x$ = 1 – 3 / -5 – 2 = -2 / -7 = 2/7

3. C.
The initial velocity will be where t=0 which is the y-intercept on this graph. The y-intercept is two boxes up on the graph and the question tells us that each one is 5 m/s. So the v_i is 10 m/s.

4. C.
Acceleration is m/s / s or m/s^2. On this graph, acceleration is represented by the slope of the line. The line slopes up 2 units for every 1 unit over. That's 10 m/s up and 1 sec over, for an acceleration of a = 10 m/s / 1 s = 10 m/s^2

5. C.
Distance is measured in meters. The vertical axis is m/s and the horizontal is in sec. To find meters, we multiply them together – that is, we must find the area under the curve to get the total meters travelled. The shape under the curve consists of a rectangle with dimensions 10x3 (for an area of 30) and a triangle with dimensions 15x6 (for an area of 45). Thus the total area under the curve is 75. (Remember the y-axis is 5 m/s per line)

6. A.
Graph I represents the curve of the line y = 10^x, which is an exponential relationship.

7. B.
Graph II represents the curve of the line y = x^2 which is the kind of parabola that would be described by the equation in the question.

8. D.
Hemoglobin binding to oxygen is a sigmoidal curve, and none of the graphs presented are sigmoidal.

9. C.
In a box-and-whisker plot, the outer edges of the whiskers indicate the range of the data. Here, the grade 6 had the widest whiskers, indicating the largest range in number of disciplinary infractions.

10. C.
In a box-and-whisker plot, the top and bottom edges of the box indicate the 75th and 25th percentiles. Thus the smallest box would indicate the 75th and 25th percentiles that are the closest together. Here, the smallest box is for grade 6.

CHAPTER 21 SOLUTIONS

1. D.
A watt is a joule per second, so a joule is a watt times a second.

2. A.
Current, amps, can be expressed as charge per time, coulombs / seconds.

Amp = Coul / sec

Rearranging this equation we get:

sec = Coul / Amp

Thus charge divided by current gives time.

3. A.
3.21g x (1 kg / 10^3 g) = 3.21 x 10^{-3} kg = 0.00321 kg

4. C.
642 GJ x (10^9 J / 1 GJ) x (10^9 nJ / 1 J) = 642 x 10^{18} nJ = 6.42 x 10^{20} nJ

5. B.
F = (9/5)(°C) + 32
-40 = (9/5)(°C) + 32
-72 = (9/5)(°C)
(-72)(5/9) = °C
-40 = °C

6. B.
K = °C + 273
298 = °C + 273
25 = °C

7. D.
963 kcal x (1000 cal / 1 kcal) x (4.184 J / 1 cal) = 4,029,192 J

Note that you can estimate this as 1000 x 4000 to see that the answer will be around 4 million, which is enough to get the question right.

8. C.

451

$1 / 10$ in^2 x (1 in / 2.5 cm) x (1 in / 2.5 cm) x 2000 cm^2 =
$32

9. C.
150m x (1 stride / 0.75 m) = 200 strides

10. A.

150m x (1 s / 1.5 m) = 100 s

Section 1 Content Review Problems

Passage 1

1. B.
In order to determine n, we need two experiments where everything stays the same except for the area, so that we can investigate the results of a change in area. As for choice A, the object changes and the area does not, so that is out. In choice B, area changes from 1.5 to 3.0 cm², and nothing else changes, so B is correct. Choice C is incorrect because the velocity is the only thing that changes. In choice D, both A and v change, so we would not be able to tell how much change in F is due to A and how much is due to v.

2. D.
In the previous solution, we realized that experiments 4 and 6 have the property that all the input variables stay the same except for velocity v, which increases by a factor of 4. The force increases by a factor of 16, which means that p must be 2. That is, if p is 2, then an increase by a factor of 4 in v results in an increase by a factor of 4^2 in the force.

3. B.
In choice A, experiments 1 and 2 both use a cork ball. For choice C, many input variables are altered between experiments 1 and 6, so it is impossible to isolate the effect of object density. As for choice D, experiments 4 and 6 both use a steel ball. Choice B involves two experiments in which only the density of the object changes.

4. A.
As for choice A, experiments 1 and 2 could be used to determine p, since the velocity changes and nothing else does. Once p is determined, k can be determined by substituting in values from either experiment 1 or 2. Thus experiments 1 and 2 are sufficient. We can exclude choices B and C (not minimum sets). As for choice D, there is not enough information to obtain p or k.

Passage 2

5. B.
If v increases by a factor of 2, then the required energy increases by a factor of $2^2 = 4$.

6. C.
If Julie increases her speed by 20%, then she multiplies her speed by 1.2. Thus the required energy is multiplied by $(1.2)^2 = 1.44$, which is an increase of 44%.

7. B.
Comparing Scott's car to Laura's, all the linear dimensions are increased by a factor of 2 (see figure). The cross-sectional area A is width times height ($A = hw$), so if both h and w increase by a factor of 2, then A increases by a factor of 4. Thus the required energy increases by a factor of 4. The increase in length does not matter.

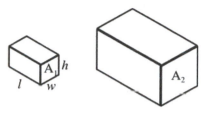

8. C.
Julie increases her speed by a factor of $55/50 = 1.1$, so the energy increases by a factor of $1.1^2 = 1.21$. This is an increase of 21%.

9. C.

Simplifying the equation in the passage, we can set the relationship between A and D as: $A_1D_1 = A_2D_2$. Plugging in 1 for A_1 and D_1, and 0.8 for A_2 (a 20% reduction in area), we can see the D_2 is 1.25, or a 25% increase.

10. B.
The following figure is x versus t. We can obtain v versus t by looking at the instantaneous slope at various times. This gives the points shown in the second figure.

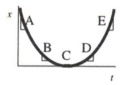

To obtain the acceleration, we need to take the instantaneous slope at various points in the second figure, but clearly the slope is always positive (and probably constant).

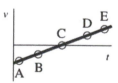

11. A.
The net displacement is $\Delta x = x_2 - x_1$, the difference between final and initial position. But in this case x_1 and x_2 are the same, so the net displacement is zero.

12. C.
In words, we can say that the velocity starts large and decreases to a stop. Then it increases again. Just this description alone might lead us to recognize C as the answer.

The figure shows how successive areas under the curve v versus t result in successive increases in the curve x versus t. Note that the fact that v is always positive translates into the fact that x is always increasing.

We can also work this problem by taking the choices and working backward, taking instantaneous slopes, in order to find which would produce the given v versus t.

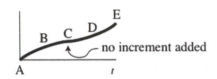

13. B.
Taking instantaneous slopes of v versus t gives an acceleration which is constant and negative until the cusp. Then it is constant and positive. This is shown in choice B.

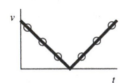

14. B.
The net change in velocity $\Delta v = v_2 - v_1$ is simply zero, since the velocity starts and ends with the same value.

15. A.
The car is backing up at the beginning of the problem, so the velocity is negative. The only choice to show this is A. The flat portion in the center of choice A is when the car is stopped. The later flat portion shows the constant velocity while going forward.

16. C.
The car accelerates exactly twice: while it slows to a stop going backward (positive acceleration) and while it speeds from a stop going forward (positive acceleration). When the car is cruising at constant velocity, the acceleration is zero, so C is the correct choice. By the way, choice B shows a sketch of x versus t.

Passage 3

17. B.
We apply the formula $\Delta x = v_1 \Delta t + 1/2\, a(\Delta t)^2 = (0\text{ m/s})(4\text{ s}) + 1/2\,(10\text{ m/s}^2)(4\text{ s})^2 = 80\text{ m}$.

18. B.
The equation which involves change in velocity Δv and time is the definition of acceleration:

$$g = \Delta v / \Delta t$$

$$\Delta v = g \Delta t$$

$$\Delta v = g(t_2 - t_1)$$

19. C.
Since velocity starts at zero, we can eliminate D. The instantaneous slope for the graph of v versus t must be a constant $g = 9.8\text{ m/s}^2$. The graph to which this applies is C.

20. B.
Let's be clear about this by writing an equation. The equation involving Δv is the definition of acceleration (see solution to problem 2 above). Thus $\Delta v = g \Delta t$. The acceleration g is constant, and Δt is the same for the two situations (both have $\Delta t = 1$ s). Thus Δv is the same. The velocity increases at a constant rate throughout the fall.

21. A.
We can calculate the height at the four clock readings:

$$\Delta x\,(t = 1\text{s}) = v_1 \Delta t + 1/2\, a \Delta t^2$$

$$= (0\text{ m/s})(1\text{ s}) + 1/2\,(10\text{ m/s}^2)(1\text{ s})^2$$

$$= 5\text{ m}$$

$$\Delta x\,(t = 2\text{ s}) = 20\text{ m}$$

$$\Delta x\,(t = 3\text{ s}) = 45\text{ m}$$

$$\Delta x\,(t = 4\text{ s}) = 80\text{ m}$$

Thus from 1 to 2 s, the object falls 15 m, while from 3 to 4 s, the object falls 35 m. This confirms our intuition that the distance fallen is greater for the later time interval. Notice the difference between this problem and the previous one.

22. D.
We use the equation involving Δx, Δt, and the acceleration (since we know its value):

$$\Delta x = v_1 \Delta t + 1/2\, g \Delta t^2$$

We have $v_1 = 0$ m/s, so we write

$$\Delta x = 1/2\, g \Delta t^2$$

If the time interval Δt increases by a factor of 3, what happens to Δx? Apparently it increases by a factor of 9.

23. C.

Choice A is nonsense. Choice B is a true statement, but it cannot be an adequate explanation for the fact, since the lead and styrofoam balls fall at the same rate, and the force of gravity is presumably different on those two balls as well. Choice C is a good candidate, since the passage mentions air resistance as a caveat. Choice D is irrelevant.

24. B.

The gravitational force acts on the stove, pulling it toward the Earth. The answer is B.

25. D.

The paired force is the gravitational force of the stove on the Earth, that is, arrow D.

26. A.

Forces A and B represent the normal force and gravitational force on the stove. If these were not balanced, the stove would not undergo uniform motion (first law), so A is correct. Choice B is not a true statement. Choice C is not even a correct statement of the second law of motion, which states that the acceleration is proportional to *net* force. Choice D concerns two forces which act on different objects.

27. D.

Forces A and C are paired. Force A is the upward contact force of ground on the table, and force C is the downward contact force of the table on the ground.

28. C.

There is certainly gravity, and there is an upward force from the road to balance it. There must be another force, because the car has an acceleration vector pointing backwards, hence the frictional force. The correct choice is C. There is no force pushing the car forward. It continues going forward for a while because that is what cars do, by the first law of motion. The force diagram is shown in the solution for problem 3.

29. B.

Gravity acts, of course. What else is touching the arrow? Nothing, so B is correct. (See figure.)

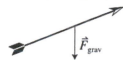

30. B.

The Sun's gravity acts on Mars. What else touches the planet? Nothing, so B is correct. The Sun's gravity changes the course of Mars, which would be a straight line away from the solar system, into the circular orbit. (See figure.)

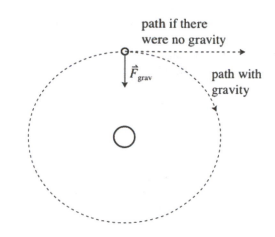

Passage 4

31. A.

We have encountered two ways of calculating acceleration: We can get the acceleration over an interval by calculating $a = \Delta v/\Delta t$. Or we can obtain acceleration from $a = F_{net}/M$. Since we do not want acceleration over an interval (like 0 to 90 s) but at an instant ($t = 0$ s), we will use the second approach, if possible. We draw a force diagram (see figure). The net force is given by $F_{net} = F_{thrust} - Mg = 2.86 \times 10^7$ N $- (2.0 \times 10^6$ kg$) (10$ m/s$^2) = 8.6 \times 10^6$ N. Thus we obtain acceleration $a = F_{net}/M = 4.3$ m/s^2.

32. A.

The passage states that 3400 kg of fuel are burned each second, and that this rate is fairly constant. The remaining mass after 300 s is 2.0×10^6 kg $- (300$ s$) (3400$ kg/s$) = 1.0 \times 10^6$ kg.

33. C.

Choice A is not even a true statement. Choice B is a true statement, but v increasing with time indicates only that the ship is speeding up, hence having positive acceleration. The ratio of Δv to Δt is the acceleration, so if this ratio is increasing, the acceleration is increasing. Choice C is correct. The ratio Δx to Δv does not have any obvious meaning.

34. C.

According to the passage, the mass of the ship decreases as it burns its fuel. In addition, there is reason to assume the force is constant, since the rate of fuel burning is approximately constant. The connection of force, mass, and acceleration is $a = F_{net}/M$, so if M decreases, then a increases. Thus C is correct.

35. B.
In order for the shuttle to accelerate, there must be a force on it by some agent. The third-law-pair force must be a force of the shuttle on that agent. This narrows the choices to A and C. Since there is little air in space, A is ruled out. The shuttle pushes off from the exhaust, and that is what creates the force which accelerates it forward, according to the third law of motion. (See figure.)

36. A.
Since gravitational force is given by $F_{grav} = mg$, and since Barbara's coins have four times the mass of Alice's coins, the force on them is four times as large.

37. B.
The acceleration of Alice's coins is a constant 9.8 m/s² down, as is the acceleration of Barbara's.

38. B.
The vertical acceleration a_y is the same for both coins, and the initial vertical velocity v_{1y} is the same for both coins. The vertical displacement for the fall is certainly the same, so in the equation $\Delta y = v_{1y}\Delta t + 1/2\, a_y (\Delta t)^2$, all the parameters are the same. This question combines the two ideas in this chapter, namely, for *freely falling bodies* near the surface of the Earth the vertical acceleration is 9.8 m/s² down, and for *all bodies* vertical motion is independent of horizontal motion.

39. A.
Both coins have the same vertical velocity. In addition, Barbara's coins retain their horizontal velocity.

40. C.
First, let's draw a diagram showing all the forces on the wagon body.

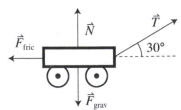

The handle and the ground are touching the wagon, so we include the tension force of the handle T and the upward force of the ground N. The problem mentions friction, so

we include that as well. There are four forces on the wagon. We can redraw the force of the handle as the sum of two components, as shown in the second figure.

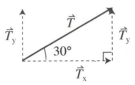

We calculate T_x as follows:

$$T_x/T = \cos 30°$$

$$T_x = T\cos 30°$$

41. B.
We calculate T_y as follows:

$$T_y/T = \sin 30°$$

$$T_y = T\sin 30°$$

42. A.
The gravitational force is vertical, so its horizontal component is zero.

43. D.
The vertical component of the gravitational force is the magnitude of the force, which is $F_{grav} = mg$.

44. A.
We don't have enough information to add up the force vectors, but we don't need to. The problem states the wagon is nonaccelerating (velocity is a constant 2 m/s), so $a = 0$ m/s² and $F_{net} = 0$ N.

45. C.
Gravity is acting on the bale, of course. The rope exerts a tension force. The force diagram is shown. Note that the bale is *not* in free fall.

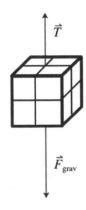

46. B.
If "up" is positive, then the net force is given by $F_{net} = 4000$ N $-$ (500 kg) (10 m/s²) $= -1000$ N. We have used a negative sign for gravity since it points down.

47. B.

We can calculate the acceleration $a = F_{net}/m = 1000$ N/500 kg = 2 m/s^2.

48. C.

On Earth, the hammer lands first because of air resistance, but if there is no air, then they have the same acceleration (about 1.6 m/s^2). Concerning choice D, of course they do not fly off, but they move along with the Moon in the same way that the grapefruit moves along with the ship. See the example in the text. This is the same way that a passenger moves along with a swiftly moving train.

49. B.

There is the force of gravity, down, and the normal force, up. The only thing touching the ball is the floor, which can cause only a normal force and possibly a frictional force. Since the problem states there is no friction, choice B is correct. Concerning choice C, there is nothing pushing the ball to the right, since it simply retains its initial motion. Choice D adds in a leftward force, presumably of friction, which the problem says is not there.

50. D.

If, as the problem states, the ball is going to the right at 0.3 m/s at time $t = 0$ s, then without any horizontal forces, it will continue to go 0.3 m/s forever. The problem is idealized, but without any information about a horizontal force, there is no way to calculate a horizontal acceleration or a horizontal change in velocity.

Passage 5

51. A.

We estimate density as follows:

$$\rho = \frac{m}{v}$$

$$= \frac{m}{\frac{4}{3}\pi r^3}$$

$$= \frac{2.0\times10^{30}\,\text{kg}}{4\left(1.4\times10^4\,\text{m}\right)^3}$$

Here we have estimated $\pi = 3$. Next we estimate $1.4^3 = 1.4 \cdot 1.4 \cdot 1.4 = 2 \cdot 1.4 = 3$, so we have

$$\rho = \frac{10^{30}}{2\cdot3\cdot10^{12}}\frac{\text{kg}}{\text{m}^3}$$

$$= \frac{10}{6}\cdot10^{29-12}\frac{\text{kg}}{\text{m}^3}$$

$$= 1.6\times10^{17}\frac{\text{kg}}{\text{m}^3}$$

The arithmetic is spelled out so that you can see how you can do a lot of fast estimating and still get a reasonable answer. Even on questions which involve much less arithmetic, you should always be looking for shortcuts.

52. C.

The acceleration due to gravity is given by

$$a_g = \frac{GM}{r^2}$$

where M is the mass of the body, and r is the radius. The passage states that M for a neutron star is the same as M for the Sun, but r is 50,000 times smaller. That means a_g is greater by a factor of $(50,000)^2$.

53. A.

The force due to gravity is

$$F_{grav} = \frac{GMm}{d^2}$$

where G is the gravitational constant. Considering the two situations in the problem, we know the mass of the neutron star is the same as the mass of the Sun. The mass of the two planets is the same. The distance d is the same for the two situations. The force of gravity does not depend on the size of the bodies but on the distance from center to center.

54. B.

Choice A is not relevant to the things which happen 2000 km away from the neutron star. Concerning choices C and D, the surface gravity of the neutron star is also irrelevant. Choice B correctly states that the force of gravity between near things is greater than between far things. This difference is enough to pull a body apart.

55. B.

We draw a diagram, including the three forces on the crate. We choose "horizontal" and "vertical" to be parallel and perpendicular to the surface, respectively, and we divide gravity into components (see figure).

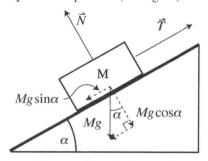

Since the normal force is "vertical", let us consider the vertical component of $F_{net} = a$. From the diagram we obtain

$$(F_{net})_y = N - Mg \cos\alpha$$

But we know that $a_y = 0$, because the crate is not moving up or down. This implies $(F_{net})_y = 0$, and we have

$$0 = N - Mg \cos\alpha$$

$$N = Mg \cos\alpha$$

56. D.
If we consider the "horizontal" component of $F_{net} = Ma$, then we can obtain from the diagram

$$(F_{net})_x = T - Mg \sin\alpha$$

where we have taken the positive direction to be up the incline. The acceleration is

$$a_x = \frac{\left(F_{net}\right)_x}{M}$$

$$= \frac{T}{M} - g \sin\alpha$$

57. A.
The force inward is due to friction between the runner's shoes and the track. It may seem surprising that there is not a force forward, since the runner is actively running. There is a horizontal acceleration, and thus net force, only at the beginning of the race when the runner is accelerating. When she is going at a constant speed, she expends effort pushing down with the foot in contact with the track and moving it back fast enough.

58. C.
The net force is given by $F_{net} = ma$, and the only acceleration is centripetal, so we have $a = a_{cent} = v^2/r$.

59. B.
The frequency is the number of revolutions per unit of time. Each revolution represents a trip of length $2\pi R$. So the velocity is the total distance per time, that is, $v = 2\pi Rf$. If f is doubled, then v is doubled.

60. C.
On the other hand the centripetal acceleration is $a_{cent} = v^2/r$, so a_{cent} is increased by a factor of 4.

61. B.
The person experiences a centripetal acceleration because he is moving in a circle, and he experiences a tangential acceleration because he is speeding up.

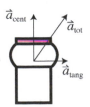

The tangential acceleration is in the same direction he is going. It would point the opposite way if he were slowing down. Adding the two vectors together gives the result B (see figure).

62. A.
In one second the centrifuge sample undergoes 50 revolutions, and each revolution is the circumference $2\pi r = 2\pi (0.1$ m). Thus in one second the sample travels 50 $(0.2\pi$ m), giving a velocity 10π m/s.

63. B.
If there is no gravity, then there is no net force, and Jupiter follows a straight line at constant speed, maintaining the same velocity vector as it had when the gravity was cut off.

Passage 6

64. B.
Each day the man travels a distance given by the circumference of the Earth $C = 2\pi R_{Earth}$.

65. C.
In order to calculate the centripetal force $F_{cent} = ma_{cent}$, we need the mass of the man and the centripetal acceleration. We can find the centripetal acceleration $a_{cent} = v^2/R_{Earth}$ if we know his velocity and the radius of the Earth. It seems that D is the correct answer. The problem with choice D is that we can calculate the velocity once we know the period and radius (as in the previous problem).

66. D.
Since the man is traveling in a circle at constant speed, his acceleration vector points toward the center of rotation, and so does the net force vector. For this to be so, the magnitude of the gravitational force must be greater than the magnitude of the force of the ground.

67. A.
The gravitational force for the two men is the same. Since the scale reading on a rotating Earth is less than the gravitational force, the correct answer is A.

68. C.
According to Newton's law of gravitation, if the distance in the denominator is less, then the gravitational force is greater.

69. A.
The radius vector is shown in the diagram.

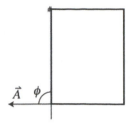

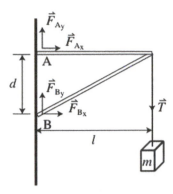

We calculate torque

$\tau = rF\sin\phi$
$= (0.4 \text{ m})(20 \text{ N})1$
$= 8 \text{ Nm}$.

The torque is clockwise, so its sign is negative.

70. C.
There are two ways to calculate the torque of force B about the pivot (see diagram).

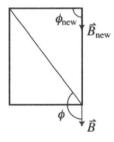

The more difficult way leaves B in the lower right corner. In the easier way we can move B. Since B points down, we can slide it directly up (maintaining its direction) to the upper right corner. Now we have $r = 0.3$ m and $\sin\phi = 1$, so that $\tau = (0.3)(10 \text{ N}) = 3$ Nm. The sign is negative because the torque is clockwise.

71. B.
The torque is zero since $\sin\phi$ is zero. Another way to see this is to note that force C would slide right through the pivot, so its torque must be zero. (See figure.)

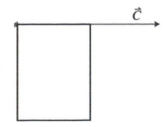

72. C.
We draw a diagram showing all the forces on the two rods (see figure).

We do not know if the forces are to the left or right, but the equation will tell us later on if our choices were right. If we take torques about A, then torques due to F_{Ax}, F_{Ay}, and F_{By} are zero. Torque balance becomes

$dF_{Bx}\sin90° - lT\sin90° = 0$,
$dF_{Bx} - lT = 0$,
$dF_{Bx} - lmg = 0$,
$F_{Bx} = lmg/d$.

The positive sign tells us that our choice was correct, that is, that F_{Bx} points to the right.

73. A.
If we take torques about B, then torques due to F_{Ay}, F_{Bx}, and F_{By} are zero. We can calculate the torque due to the tension in the wire easily by sliding the force down the string to the point shown in the figure.

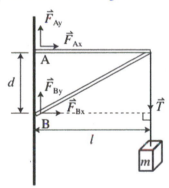

The torque is $-lT$, so that the torque balance is

$-dF_{Ax}\sin90° - lT\sin90° = 0$,
$-dF_{Ax} - lmg = 0$,
$F_{Ax} = -lmg/d$.

The negative sign tells us that the direction of F_{Ax} is to the left.

74. D.
The sum of the vertical forces must be zero, so we have

$F_{Ax} + F_{Bx} - mg = 0$,
$F_{Ax} + F_{Bx} = mg$.

And this makes sense, because the wall is providing the upward force which adds to the one downward force of gravity of the brick.

75. D.
We draw a diagram showing all the forces on the rod (see figure).

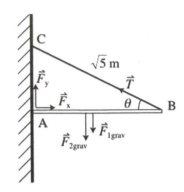

We can use the Pythagorean theorem to obtain the length of the wire. The torque due to the tension in the wire about point A is given by

$$\tau = (2\text{ m})T\sin\theta =$$

$$(2\text{ m})T\frac{1}{\sqrt{5}}$$

Thus the ratio τ/T is given by dividing both sides by T, so we have

$$\frac{\tau}{T} = \frac{2\text{ m}}{\sqrt{5}}$$

76. C.
We do not know F_x and F_y, so we can obtain an equation without them if we take torques about point A. Torque balance becomes

$$(2\text{m})T\sin\theta - (1\text{m})F_{1\text{grav}}\sin90° - (1\text{m})F_{2\text{grav}}\sin90° = 0$$

$$(2\text{ m})T\frac{1}{\sqrt{5}} - (1\text{ m})\left(1\text{ kg}\cdot10\frac{\text{m}}{\text{s}^2}\right)1 -$$

$$(1\text{ m})\left(2\text{ kg}\cdot10\frac{\text{m}}{\text{s}^2}\right)1 = 0$$

$$(2\text{ m})T\frac{1}{\sqrt{5}} = 30\text{ kg}\frac{\text{m}^2}{\text{s}^2}$$

$$T = 15\sqrt{5}\text{ N}$$

77. C.
If we take torques about point B, then F_x and T do not appear in the equation, so torque balance becomes

$$-(2\text{m})F_y\sin90° + (1\text{m})F_{1\text{grav}}\sin90° + (1\text{m})F_{2\text{grav}}\sin90° = 0$$

$$-(2\text{m})F_y\sin90° + (1\text{m})(1\text{ kg}\cdot10\text{ m/s}^2)\sin90° + (1\text{m})(2\text{ kg}\cdot10\text{ m/s}^2)\sin90° = 0$$

$$F_y = 15\text{ N}.$$

78. D.
This time we eliminate F_y and T from the torque balance by taking torques about point C. The torque due to F_x is (1 m) F_x, since $\phi = 90°$. We can get the torques due to $F_{1\text{grav}}$ and $F_{2\text{grav}}$ by sliding the forces upwards, that it, opposite the direction the vectors point (see figure).

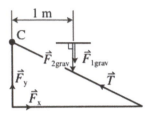

Then we can write the torques at sight, and torque balance becomes

$$(1\text{m})F_x\sin90° - (1\text{m})F_{1\text{grav}}\sin90° - (1\text{m})F_{2\text{grav}}\sin90° = 0$$

$$(1\text{m})F_x - 20\text{ Nm} - 10\text{ Nm} = 0$$

$$F_x = 30\text{ N}.$$

79. B.
We draw a diagram with all the forces on the leg (see figure).

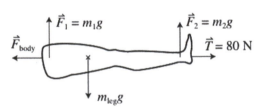

If we take torques about point B, we eliminate F_{body}, T, and m_2g from the torque balance, leaving just m_1 and the mass of the leg, so we write

$$(0.6\text{ m})(10\text{ kg}\cdot10\text{ m/s}^2) - (0.9\text{ m})(m_1\cdot10\text{ m/s}^2) = 0$$
$$m_1 = 6.67\text{ kg}$$

80. B.
To obtain an equation with just m_1 and m_2, we can take torques about the center of mass of the leg, so torque balance becomes

$$-(0.3\text{ m})(m_1\cdot10\text{ m/s}^2) + (0.6\text{ m})(m_2\cdot10\text{ m/s}^2) = 0$$

Dividing by 10 m/s^2 and solving yields

$$-0.3\text{ m} + 0.6\,m_2 = 0$$

$$m_2/m_1 = 1/2$$

We could obtain the same result by figuring out $m_2 = 3.33$ kg with the same method used in the previous problem.

81. C.

The tension exerted by the body must be equal in magnitude to the one other horizontal force, the tension due to the weight of the 8-kg mass. We write

$-F_{body} + T = 0,$
$F_{body} = T$
$= (8 \text{ kg})(10 \text{ m/s}^2)$
$= 80 \text{ N}.$

82. B.

First we draw a diagram with all the forces.

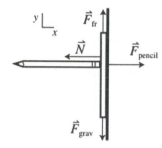

The wall and the pencil touch the card. The problem states that the pencil exerts a horizontal force (see diagram), and the wall exerts a normal force and a frictional force. The normal force is perpendicular to the surface and the frictional force parallel to it, even if the surface is vertical. The gravitational force is simply $F_{grav} = mg = (0.004 \text{ kg}) (10 \text{ m/s}^2) = 0.04 \text{ N}.$

83. D.

Since we are assuming the card is not moving, the acceleration a_x is zero, and we have $(F_{net})_x = 0$. But $(F_{net})_x = F_{pencil} - N$, so the normal force is equal in magnitude to F_{pencil}, which is given in the problem.

84. B.

Force balance allows us to conclude that the frictional force is equal to the gravitational force (as in question 10).

85. A.

The friction in this problem is static friction. We know this friction must be less than the quantity $\mu_s N$ in order for the friction to be sufficient to keep the surfaces from slipping. Since we have $\mu_s N = (0.2) (0.4 \text{ N}) = 0.08 \text{ N}$, and F_{fr} is less than this, there is no slipping.

86. D.

First we draw a diagram including all the forces.

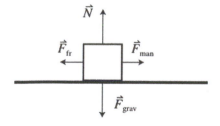

The man is pushing to the right, and the ground exerts a normal force and a frictional force. Since the washer is not moving, its acceleration is zero, and we have force balance. From the diagram we can see that the normal force and the gravitational force add to zero, so their magnitudes must be equal. Thus we have $N = F_{grav} = 1000$ N.

87. B.

Force balance tells us that the man's force and the frictional force are equal in magnitude, so $F_{fr} = 700$ N. Did you calculate $F_{fr} = \mu_s N = 800$ N? Remember, this is the calculation for the *maximum* static friction. The actual static friction force can have any magnitude from zero up to this maximum.

88. C.

The man would have to exert a force in excess of the maximum possible friction, that is,

$$(F_{stat})_{max} = \mu_s N$$
$$= (0.8)(1000 \text{ N})$$
$$= 800 \text{ N}.$$

89. B.

We have gravity, pointing down. The road exerts a force normal to its surface. Also, there is a force of friction. Since the car is going uphill with its brakes applied and tires skidding, the kinetic friction force is parallel to the surface and downhill. The force diagram is shown.

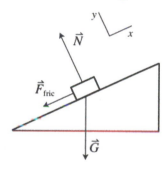

90. C.

The components of gravity are shown in the diagram below.

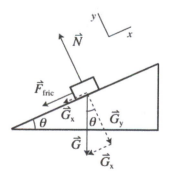

We calculate G_x as follows:

$$G_x/G = \sin\theta$$
$$G_x = G\sin\theta$$
$$G_x = mg\sin\theta$$

91. B.
We can obtain the net vertical force from the diagram, so we have

$$(F_{net})_y = N - G_y$$

But the car is not moving up or down, so $a_y = 0$ and $(F_{net})_y = 0$, so we have

$$0 = N - G_y,$$
$$N = G_y$$
$$= G\cos\theta$$
$$= mg\sin\theta.$$

92. C.
We cannot obtain the force of friction from the force diagram because we do not have a force balance and do not have any information about the acceleration. But we can calculate $F_k = \mu_k N$.

93. C.
The net force is the same as the sum of all the horizontal components of the forces, so

$$(F_{net})_x = F_{fr} + G_x$$

$$= \mu_k N + mg\sin\theta$$

where we have taken "downhill" to be positive.

94. A.
Because the car is turning at constant speed, we know the net force points toward the center of the turn. There is no force in the direction the car is going because the car is neither speeding up nor slowing down. The force diagram is shown, in which we view the car from the rear and the turn is to the left.

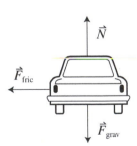

95. C.
Friction supplies the centripetal force. (The turn would be impossible if the surface were frictionless.) Since the tires are not slipping on the road, the appropriate friction is static.

96. C.

The acceleration is centripetal acceleration given by $a_{cent} = v^2/r = (8 \text{ m/s})^2/10 \text{ m} = 6.4 \text{ m/s}^2$.

97. D.
From the force diagram we can see that the normal force and gravity balance, so that $N = 10,000$ N.

98. A.
If we know the acceleration, we can calculate the net force $F_{net} = ma = 6400$ N.

99. A.
Remember that the expression $\mu_s N$ gives the maximum force of static friction. If any more friction is required by a situation, then surfaces begin to slip. In this case, this would mean the car goes into a skid. But $\mu_s N = (0.9)(10,000 \text{ N}) = 9000$ N, which is large enough. Thus the car will not go into a skid.

Passage 7

100. A.

If there is no air, then the only force is the force of gravity:

$$(F_{net})_y = F_{grav}$$

But the force of gravity is mg, and the acceleration is given by

$$ma_y = mg$$

$$a_y = g$$

So, if we call "up" positive, then $a_y = -10 \text{ m/s}^2$, and $v_{1y} = 3$ m/s. Also, to obtain the height, we write

$$v_{2y}^2 = v_{1y}^2 + 2a_y\Delta y$$

$$0 = \left(3\frac{m}{s}\right)^2 + 2\left(10\frac{m}{s^2}\right)y$$

$$\Delta y = 0.45 \text{ m}$$

101. B.
We calculate the drag $F_{drag} = (0.2)(1.3 \text{ kg/m}^3)(\pi(0.03 \text{ m})^2)(3 \text{ m/s})^2 = 7 \times 10^{-3}$ N.

102. C.

According to the passage, the air resistance must be small compared to the other forces in the situation, but this is just the force of gravity.

103. A.

As the ball travels away from the center of the Earth, the force of gravity decreases slightly, since

$$F_{grav} = Gm_1m_2/r^2$$

104. A.

If air resistance is included, there is an initial force down while the ball is going up, so the maximum height is less. The ball loses energy to air resistance, so its speed just before hitting the ground will be less than in the idealized problem.

105. C.

Even if the density of air changed appreciably (it does not), it would not help cats survive a greater fall. This holds for choice B as well. Regarding choice C, if cats stretch their legs, then this increases their cross-sectional area, which would decrease their terminal velocity, so is a viable possibility for an answer. Regarding D, the statement is true, but the fact would not help a cat to have a lesser terminal velocity from a greater fall.

SECTION 2 CONTENT REVIEW PROBLEMS

1. B.
Using $E_K = 1/2\ mv^2$ gives us $v = 8$ m/s.

2. C.
Whenever we see force and distance, we think of energy and the equation $W = F\Delta x\cos\phi$. In this case, $\cos\phi = 1$, so that $F = 130$ N. The force is the force that the track, through friction, exerts on his feet.

3. A.
After the cannonball leaves the cannon, there is nothing touching it besides air, and we are ignoring air resistance.

4. C.
We use $E_{K1} = 1/2\ mv^2$.

5. A.
We use $E_{P2} = mgh$.

6. C.
The only force acting on the cannonball is gravity, so the simple statement of the conservation of energy holds in this case, and we write

$$E_{K1} + E_{P1} = E_{K2} + E_{P2}$$
$$1/2\ mv_1^2 + 0 = 1/2\ mv_2^2 + mgh_2$$
$$v_2^2 = v_1^2 - 2gh_2$$
$$= \left(100\frac{m}{s}\right)^2 - \left(2\cdot 10\frac{m}{s}\cdot 180\ m\right)$$
$$= 6400\ m^2/s^2$$
$$v_2 = 80\ m/s$$

7. C.
Since the kinetic energy is decreasing, I is false. Since the potential energy is increasing, II is false. The sum is conserved, because gravity is the only force acting on the ball, so the simple statement of the conservation of energy holds.

8. C.
The momentum is large and directed up at the beginning, but it goes to zero by the end. The unbalanced force is gravity.

9. B.
Gravity is the only force on the ball in flight, and it does work on the ball, so A is false. The energy starts as kinetic and ends as potential, so B is true. C is false. The force of the hand ceases to play a role after the ball leaves the touch of the hand, so D is false.

10. A.

Here we have enough information to apply the definition, $E_K = 1/2\ mv^2 = 1/2\ (2.005\ kg)\ (1.5\ m/s)^2 = 2.25$ Joules. It is safe to round 2.005 to 2.

11. C.
In this question we are talking about part 1 of the event: a collision involving hot wood and partially combusted organic compounds, that is, energy lost as heat. This resembles a car collision, so conservation of momentum is the relevant concept. We write

$$p_1 = p_2,$$
$$m_{bullet}v_{bullet} + m_{block}v_{block} = (m_{block} + m_{bullet})v_{after},$$
$$(0.005\ kg)v_{bullet} = (2.005\ kg)\left(1.5\frac{m}{s}\right)$$
$$v_{bullet} \approx \frac{2}{0.005}1.5\frac{m}{s} = 600\frac{m}{s}$$

12. B.
In this question we are talking of part 2 of the event. The forces on the block (with bullet) are gravity and the tension of the strings. But the tension is always perpendicular to the direction of travel, so the tension forces do no work, and the simple statement of the conservation of energy applies:

$$E_{K1} + E_{P1} = E_{K2} + E_{P2},$$
$$1/2\ mv_{after}^2 + 0 = 0 + mgh,$$
$$h = \frac{\dfrac{1}{2}v_{after}^2}{g} = \frac{\left(1.5\dfrac{m}{s}\right)^2}{2\left(10\dfrac{m}{s^2}\right)}$$
$$= 0.11\ m = 11\ cm.$$

13. C.
Certainly the energy starts as kinetic, so the answer is A or C. But during part 1, there is no change in the potential energy of anything, so A is incorrect. Most of the kinetic energy of the bullet goes into heat, some goes into kinetic energy of the block, and a little stays as kinetic energy of the bullet.

14. A.
The block is moving at first, and by the time it stops, its height is greater. So the energy goes from kinetic to potential.

15. A.
Since the speed is constant, the kinetic energy is constant and therefore conserved. The potential energy is not constant but increases. Option III sounds attractive, but the cart as a system is not isolated, since the winch does work on it, and so its energy is not conserved. The proper statement for the conservation of energy in this problem is this: The potential energy increase of the cart is given by the work done by the winch. Remember to follow the energy flow.

16. B.
This is the correct, although contrived, answer. It is correct because the forces are, in fact, balanced and the momentum stays constant throughout the problem. It is contrived because this information does not allow you to calculate anything of use.

17. A.
The net force on the cart is zero, so $W_{tot} = F_{net}\Delta x \cos\phi$ is zero. Remember that the total work is a measure of the energy that goes into the *kinetic energy* of the cart. In this problem, winch energy goes into potential energy of the cart. A is true. B and C are false because kinetic energy, being constant, plays no role. Both the winch and gravity do work, so D is false.

18. B.
The acceleration down the incline is $a = g \sin\theta$. Thus mass is irrelevant and both will have the same v_f.

19. B.
We could do these problems by drawing forces, taking components, obtaining accelerations, and finally velocities. Conservation of energy gives us the answer much more quickly. The only two forces on the rocks are gravity and the normal force, so the simple statement of the conservation of energy applies. We write

$E_{K1} + E_{P1} = E_{K2} + E_{P2}$,
$mgh_1 = 1/2\, mv_2^2$,
$v_2^2 = 2gh_1$,

Notice that the angle α or β never appears at all, and the mass of the rock m or M cancels in the second step above. The only thing that matters, counterintuitively, is the height from which the rocks fall.

20. B.
This problem is more difficult. The reason that two rocks, one more massive than the other, take the same time to fall is that at each point along the path their accelerations are the same, their velocities are the same, and they take the same time to fall. The same is true in this problem. Once we determine that the acceleration of rock M is the same as rock m then they must take the same time to slide down. We can see that their accelerations are the same in the force diagrams below.

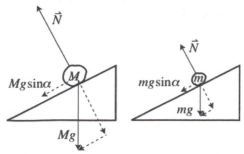

The horizontal components $F_{net} = ma$ for the respective diagrams is

$$Mg\sin\alpha = Ma_x, \qquad mg\sin\alpha = ma_x,$$
$$g\sin\alpha = a_x, \qquad g\sin\alpha = a_x,$$

In the above cases the accelerations are the same because the factor m cancels. This situation is the same as the case with falling masses (Section 4.C).

21. C.
The analysis in the previous problem should convince you that if the angle is greater, then the acceleration is greater, and the time of fall is less. Even if we do not think through the analysis, we can consider the extremes of a very small α, which would make the rock take a long time to slide, versus a large β (steep slope), which would be almost free fall. Thus the time is shorter.

22. C.
The energy required to get from A to B is given by the work done against air resistance. The work done by the air is $W_{air} = F_{air}\Delta x$, where Δx is the distance between the cities, which is a constant. Thus we have $W_{air} = C\rho Av^2\Delta x$, and if v is doubled, then W_{air} is increased by a factor of 4.

23. C.
An increase from 50 to 55 mph is 10%, that is, a factor of 1.1. Since W_{air} varies as v^2, W_{air} must increase by a factor of $1.1^2 = 1.21$, which is an increase by 21%.

24. D.
Power is given by $P = F_{air}v = C\rho Av^3$, so an increase by a factor of 2 in velocity yields an increase by a factor of $2^3 = 8$ in power.

Passage 1

25. B.
It is true that there are more particles on the left side of the reaction, but that would tend to make the pressure go down, not up, so A is false. The pressure goes up because the temperature goes up, so B seems a good choice. Spontaneous reactions can have either an increase or a decrease in pressure, so C is incorrect. D is incorrect for the same reason.

26. C.
The amount of work done is $W = F\Delta x \cos\phi = (P_{burn}A)(l)(1) = P_{burn}Al$. The quantity ΔH_{rxn} is given in Joules per mole of reactants going across the reaction equation, that is, per mole of O_2. Thus the amount of energy used is $n\Delta H_{rxn}$.

27. B.
The first answer we think of is number ratio, since the coefficients in a reaction refer to the number of atoms/molecules/formula units or whatever. But that is not a choice. Mass ratio is wrong, so A is excluded. For ideal gases, volume ratio is proportional to number ratio, and since the reactants are gases, B is a good choice. C is

nonsense. D is irrelevant since the reactants are at the same temperature.

28. D.
One of the reactants would be in excess. The heat of reaction is unchanged, so A is false. The combustion would still ignite, so B is out. The answer is C or D. If any of the intermediates in the reaction were stable compounds, then some of those compounds could end up in the waste gas. But the reaction of hydrogen with water is clean, and the waste gas would contain only leftover hydrogen or oxygen.

29. A.
If the reaction were performed isothermally, then the number of gas particles would be less after the reaction than before the reaction. Since pressure at a given volume and temperature is proportional to the number of gas particles by the ideal gas law, the pressure would decrease.

30. A.
When the gases are introduced in the chamber, the ideal gas law is $P_{atm}AL = n_{tot}RT_{amb}$, where n_{tot} is the number of total moles of both gases. Only one third of those molecules are oxygen, so A is correct.

31. A.
We have assumed that the piston movement is small and the pressure stays about the same. If the piston movement were larger, the increase in volume would decrease the pressure. The gas in the chamber is doing work against the piston, so the internal energy of the gas must decrease. The temperature must decrease as well.

Passage 2

32. D.
If the collision is isolated, then there are no external forces and momentum is conserved, so I is true. The word "elastic" implies that kinetic energy is conserved, so II is true. The total energy is always conserved in an isolated collision, so III is true. Thus the answer is D.

33. C.
The equation looks complicated, but it does not look as forbidding if we break it down. Consider the left-hand side. There is an energy and a distance, which reminds us of force, from the equation $W = F\Delta x \cos\phi$. The quantity energy divided by distance has the units of force.

34. D.
On the right-hand side of the equation, everything is constant except N, Z, and z. In this question we are comparing ^3H and ^3He, so the only difference is z. That is, ^3H has $z = 1$ and ^3He has $z = 2$. Since z is doubled, ^3He must lose 4 times as much energy per unit distance.

35. B.

The only difference in the two nuclei is the mass, which plays no role in equation (1).

36. C.
Since both gases are at STP, the ideal gas equation guarantees that the two gases have the same number of moles per unit volume, hence N is the same. Neon has 10 electrons per gas particle, and helium has 2 per particle. So neon has a Z which is 5 times larger and removes 5 times as much energy per unit distance.

Passage 3

37. C.
The slowing of the car implies the momentum is decreasing, but an unbalanced external force does not necessarily nullify the conservation of energy, just the conservation of momentum, so A is false. The conservation of energy takes entropy into account if heat is included in the accounting of the energy of the system, so B is false. If heat is transferred to the air, that is, out of the system, then energy is not conserved for that system, and C is true. Option D makes little sense.

38. D.
The energy of motion is turned into heat, so the equation is

$$1/2 \, M_{car}v^2 = C_V m_{brake}\Delta T,$$

$$\Delta T = \frac{M_{car}v^2}{2C_V m_{brake}}$$

39. C.
The initial kinetic energy of the car is $1/2 \, M_{car}v^2$, of which $1/2 \, aM_{car}v^2$ actually gets transferred to the flywheel. Thus we write

$$1/2 \, aM_{car}v^2 = 1/2 \, (MR^2)\omega^2,$$

$$\omega = \sqrt{\frac{aMcar}{M}} \, \frac{v}{R}$$

40. B.
We have learned that the force on a mass Δm moving in a circle of radius R is $\Delta m v^2/R$. We also know that the velocity $v = 2\pi R/T$, where T is the period, that is, $T = 1/f$. Putting all this together with $\omega = 2\pi f$ given in the passage yields $F = \Delta m \omega^2 R$.

41. A.
The car initially has kinetic energy $1/2 \, M_{car}v^2$. Of this, only energy $1/2 \, aM_{car}v^2$ is placed into the flywheel. And of this, only energy $1/2 \, abM_{car}v^2$ is transferred back into kinetic energy, which is $1/2 \, M_{car}v_2^2$. Thus

$$\frac{1}{2}M_{\text{car}}v_2{}^2 = \frac{1}{2}M_{\text{car}}abv^2$$

$$v_2 = \sqrt{ab}\;v$$

42. B.
The change in potential energy is $\Delta E_P = mg\Delta h$. We multiply this by 0.40 before setting it equal to $1/2\;mv^2$ Thus, using $\Delta h = 50$ meters,

$$\frac{1}{2}mv_2{}^2 = 0.4mg\Delta h$$

$$v = \sqrt{0.8g\Delta h}$$

$$= 20\,\frac{\text{m}}{\text{s}}$$

Passage 4

43. C.
When the car goes from point C to point D, the only forces acting on it are gravity and the normal force. The normal force does no work, so we can use the simple statement of the conservation of energy. The initial kinetic energy is very small, so

$$E_{P2} + E_{K2} = E_{P1} + E_{K1},$$
$$E_{K2} = MgH_1.$$

44. C.
In order to obtain the velocity, we use the above equation and set kinetic energy to $1/2\;Mv^2$.

45. C.
The situation is the same for the car going from point C to F as it is in going from C to E. The only forces ever operating are gravity and the normal force, so the simple statement of energy conservation works:

$$E_{K1} + E_{P1} = E_{K2} + E_{P2},$$

$$0 + MgH_1 = 1/2\;Mv^2 + MgH_2,$$

$$v = \sqrt{2g(H_2 - H_1)}$$

46. A.
The normal force never does work. This is because its direction is normal to not only the surface but to the motion of the object as well.

47. D.
Gravity, certainly, is acting down. The only thing touching the car is the tracks, which provide a normal force, down. Thus gravity and the normal force together provide the centripetal force. So if we are counting forces,

there are two. If you chose C, you need to review the section about the first law of motion.

48. D.
This is analogous to the books in the car in Section 5.D, which get "pulled" toward the door when the car turns. No such thing happens, of course. The books are going in a straight path and the car's door turns into their path. In this case, the blood would be going along a straight path, but the body is pulled by a centripetal force (from gravity and the normal force) away from the blood.

49. C.
A glance at the answers shows expression which look like centripetal force and gravity. The force diagram is shown.

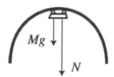

Gravity and the normal force add to make the net force, which is centripetal and leads to the acceleration of the car. On the one hand we can write $F_{\text{net}} = N + Mg$. On the other we write $F_{\text{net}} = M\alpha_{\text{cent}}$. Thus

$$N + Mg = M\,\frac{v_F{}^2}{R}$$

$$N = M\,\frac{v_F{}^2}{R} - Mg$$

This is close. Now we need to remember that the radius of the circle R is half the diameter, which is H_2, so the answer is C.

50. C.
The friction on the tracks plays no role in our current analysis and plays only a small role in reality. Since A is not a likely answer, let's look at the others. The bumpers are used to stop the car at the end of the ride, and they rely on friction. If the coefficient of friction is reduced, this could be disastrous. The cars are stopped by rubbing past the bumpers, so the friction is kinetic. By reducing the mass, the park operators reduce the amount of force necessary to negatively accelerate the cars to a stop.

51. A.
The energy in the motor certainly starts out as electrical. If the bumpers dissipate the energy, then the energy ends up as heat. In the ride itself, energy is sloshed back and forth from kinetic to potential.

Passage 5

52. C.
The definition of kinetic energy involves mass and velocity, and we know neither, so A and B are not right.

Choice C mentions force, and there is a connection between force and energy, the equation $W = F\Delta x\cos\phi$. Does this equation apply in this case? The change in kinetic energy is given by the total work done on an object, that is $F_{net}\Delta x\cos\phi$, so the equation does apply. The quantity Δx is the length of the barrel, and we have $\cos\phi = 1$.

53. C.
Pressure and temperature go together in the ideal gas equation, and though we may have the volume of the "reaction flask", we do not have the number of moles, so A is not the answer. It seems difficult to connect velocity with pressure, so let us look for a better answer than B. Pressure and force together remind us of the definition of pressure $P = F/A$. Since we have the cross-sectional area of the cannon, this is a connection between force and pressure. C is the answer.

54. A.
The rate of reaction does depend on surface area, concentration, and temperature, but grain size affects only the surface area. So A is the answer. Only a catalyst could reduce the activation energy.

55. B.
Since the reaction is irreversible, the entropy change is positive, so A is false. The reaction is spontaneous, so the free energy change must be negative.

56. B.
The energy starts as chemical energy and turns to heat after burning. The whole point of a cannon is to convert energy to kinetic energy of the ball. Note that the conversion of heat to kinetic energy is inefficient. Among the choices given, however, B is the best answer.

57. D.
This is like a problem we have done before. Because of the following calculation:

$$E_{K1} + E_{P1} = E_{K2} + E_{P2} ,$$
$$1/2\ mv^2 = mgh,$$
$$h = v^2/2g$$

we see that we do not need anything besides the ball velocity upon leaving the cannon.

SECTION 3 CONTENT REVIEW PROBLEMS

1. A.
First we draw a diagram. In addition to gravity, there are two forces on the necklace due to the two things touching it: the water (buoyant force) and the string (tension). The reading on the force meter is the magnitude of the tension.

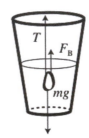

We write the force equation

$$T + F_B - mg = 0,$$
$$T = mg - F_B$$
$$= mg - \rho_{H2O}Vg$$
$$= (m - \rho_{H2O}V)g$$
$$= (50.0 - 4.82)\text{kg}/1000 \cdot 9.8\text{m/s}^2$$
$$= 0.44 \text{ N}.$$

We would have gotten the right answer by estimating g to be 10 m/s^2.

2. D.
This problem is similar to other problems we have done. In order to achieve force balance, the sink must exert a force $mg - \rho_{water}V_{disp}g$. The problem gives all the information except V_{disp}. The capacity of the cup is not the same as the volume the cup displaces when it is under water.

3. C.
Even if the pump draws a perfect vacuum, the column will not rise above 10 m. Consider the situation shown, which turns out to be impossible.

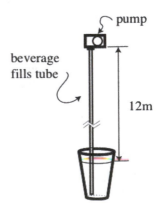

The pressure at the top of the column is P_{top}, and we write

$P_{atm} = P_{top} + \rho_{beverage}gh,$
$P_{top} = 10^5$ Pa $- (10^3$ kg/m$^3)(10$ m/s$^2)(12$ m$)$
$= -2 \times 10^4$ Pa.

This is impossible. Even the best pump can draw at best zero pressure, never a negative pressure. The water column would fall, so that the top of the column would have zero pressure and the evacuated space above it would also have zero pressure.

4. B.
We can obtain the height of the water column by setting P_{top} to 0. Thus, $P_{atm} = P_{top} + \rho gh$ becomes $h = P_{atm}/\rho g$. Using a different straw clearly has no effect, but decreasing ρ will increase h.

5. C.
We have to careful of units in this problem. Pressure is the connection between gas data and information about force. We do not need $PV = nRT$, because we already know $P = 2$ atm. In order to calculate force, however, we need Pascals, so P is approximately 2×10^5 Pa. Using $F = PA$, where $A = 0.01$ m^2 (the area of one face), we obtain that F is approximately 2000 N.

6. A.
We draw a diagram as shown below.

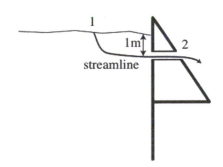

streamline

This reminds us of a Bernoulli question (especially with the explicit "ignore viscosity"), and we can draw a streamline as shown. The pressures at points 1 and 2 are both P_{atm}. The velocity at point 1 is essentially 0. If the top of the ocean is the standard height, then the height of point 2 is -1 m. Bernoulli's equation becomes

$P_1 + 1/2\, \rho v_1^2 + \rho gh_1 = P_2 + 1/2\, \rho v_2^2 + \rho gh_2,$
$P_{atm} + 0 + 0 = P_{atm} + 1/2\, \rho v_2^2 + \rho gh_2,$
$v_2 = \sqrt{-2gh_2}$

$= \sqrt{-2\left(10\dfrac{m}{s^2}\right)(-1\ m)} \approx 4.5\dfrac{m}{s}$

7. A.
If we know the flow velocity, we can obtain the flow rate from $f = Av = (.01$ m$)^2 (4.5$ m/s$)$.

8. A.
Since the problem asks for force, we draw a force diagram.

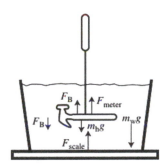

The pressure of the water can be obtained by hydrostatic equilibrium: $P_{water} = P_{atm} + \rho gh$, where h is 1 m.

Thus, since the finger is not accelerating, we write

$P_{water}A - P_{atm}A - F_{boy} = 0,$
$F_{boy} = (P_{water} - P_{atm})A$
$= \rho ghA$
$= (10^3$ kg/m$^3)(10$ m/s$^2)(1$ m$)(0.001$ m$)^2$
$= 1$ N.

9. A.
This is similar to problem 36. There we learned that a force meter provides a force, and the reading tells us what the force is. A force diagram is shown.

Since the hammer is not accelerating, the force equation is $F_{meter} + F_B - m_h g = 0$. We know $m_h g = (0.79$ kg$)\,(10$ m/s$^2)$ $= 7.9$ N. The displaced volume is simply the volume of the hammer, that is, $m/\rho_{steel} = 100$ cm^3, so that $F_B = \rho_{water} V_{disp}\, g = 1$ N (by the time the units are straightened). Thus F_{meter} is $(7.9 - 1)$ N $= 6.9$ N.

10. C.
The force diagram for the water is shown in the same diagram. We have not discussed the force that the hammer exerts on the fluid, but by Newton's third law of motion, its magnitude must be the same 1 N we calculated in the previous problem. Recall that a scale provides a force, and the reading tells the magnitude of the force provided. Since the water is not accelerating, the force equation is $F_{scale} - F_B - m_w\, g = 0$. Thus $F_{scale} = 50$ N $+ 1$ N $= 51$ N.

Passage 1
11. A.
Well, points P_1 and P_2 are in the water, and P_2 is above P_1, so the pressure at P_1 should be greater by ρgh. It is confusing, though, since the pressure at P_1 must be P_{atm}. The air just above P_2 must have pressure P_{atm}. Usually the

pressure on one side of a boundary between two substances is the same as the pressure on the other side, but this is not true if the boundary is curved, as when a meniscus forms.

12. C.
Certainly there are pressure forces, but these balance (both are $F = P_{atm}\pi r^2$). The surface tension pulls the column up, balancing the force of gravity.

13. C.
The pressure at the top of the column is given by $F = PA = P_{atm}\pi r^2$. We use the air pressure since it is the air that exerts the downward force on the column.

14. C.
The force due to gravity is $F_{grav} = mg = \rho V g = \rho \pi r^2 h g$.

15. C.
The length of the line of contact is the circumference of the straw, so $L = 2\pi r$.

16. B.
The force diagram for the column of water is shown.

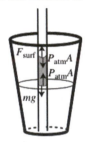

Since nothing is accelerating, the force equation becomes the following:

$$P_{atm}A + F_{surf} - P_{atm}A - mg = 0,$$
$$F_{surf} = mg,$$
$$2\pi r\gamma = \pi r^2 h\rho g,$$
$$h = 2\gamma/r\rho g.$$

From this we see that height h increases proportionally as r decreases.

Passage 2

17. B.
In this model a maximum height is obtained by setting the pressure at the top of the column to zero. Thus, $P_{bottom} = P_{top} + \rho gh$ becomes $P_{atm} = 0 + \rho gh$. Thus $h = P_{atm}/\rho g = 10^5$ Pa / $(10^3$ kg/m$^3)$ $(10$ m/s$^2)$ = 10 m.

18. D.
According to this equation, the height h depends only on the atmospheric pressure, the density of the fluid, and the acceleration due to gravity.

19. C.

The passage mentions that the surface tension and the gravitational force must add to zero. Thus, $2\pi r\gamma - \rho\pi r^2 hg = 0$ (as in the previous passage). This becomes

$$h = 2\gamma/r\rho g =$$
$$\frac{2\left(0.072\,\dfrac{N}{m}\right)}{\left(2\times10^{-7}\,m\right)\left(10^3\,\dfrac{kg}{m^3}\right)\left(10\,\dfrac{m}{s^3}\right)} =$$

72 meters.

20. A.
In this model the height is inversely proportional to the radius.

Passage 3

21. D.
The main difference between the inner and outer chambers is the presence of enzymes in the outer chamber. Enzymes are catalysts which reduce the activation energy. Choice A may play a role, but a smaller one.

22. D.
We apply the formula $f = Av = \pi (0.01$ cm$)^2$ $(1200$ cm/s$) = 0.4$ cm^3/s, where we have done the necessary unit conversions.

23. C.
Any object, whether it be a cannon ball or a drop of beetle spray, accelerates down at 10 m/s^2 if gravity is the only force acting on it at the surface of Earth. The initial velocity is 12 m/s up, and the final velocity is 0 m/s. We can obtain the distance traveled by

$$v_2^2 = v_1^2 + 2ah$$
$$h = -\frac{v_1^2}{2a}$$
$$= -\frac{\left(12\,\dfrac{m}{s}\right)^2}{2\left(-10\,\dfrac{m}{s^2}\right)}\quad 7.2\ m$$

An alternate solution involves using energy conservation: $E_{P1} + E_{K1} = E_{P2} + E_{K2}$. A third solution could involve Bernoulli's equation, using the points just outside the abdomen and the top of flight for the spray.

24. B.
A catalyst affects activation energy but has no effect on the heat of reaction.

25. A.

Choice A reminds us of Bernoulli's principle, which might give an estimate of the pressure inside the outer chamber, even if some energy is dissipated as heat. Indeed there is no reason to assume the flow is not turbulent and not viscous. But if Bernoulli's principle applies, then A is a good estimate. Choices B, C and D definitely remind us of an ideal gas, but the passage clearly stated that the spray is a liquid, so these choices are definitely incorrect.

26. A.
The connection between force and pressure is $F = PA$, so the answer is A or B. The pressure inside the chamber is pushing in the opposite direction as the atmospheric pressure outside the chamber, so A is correct.

27. B.
The table in the passage allows us to calculate the heat released per mole of quinone produced. We need to know the concentration of quinone to know how much heat per quantity of solution is produced. Thus A is incorrect: not enough information. Once we know the heat available per quantity of solution, then we can use the heat capacity to get the temperature change. B is correct. As for choice C, the heat of reaction is necessary but it is derivable from information in the passage. As for choice D, the volume of the chamber is unnecessary information, since the question is about intensive properties of the solution and not about extensive properties. That is, the question is not about how much stuff there is, but about quantities that do not depend on volume (such as temperature).

Passage 4

28. B.
Option A seems good, except it is the purpose of the *filter screen* to filter out byproducts, so this is not a likely possibility. The rupture film would certainly keep in the reactants, increasing the concentration and speeding the reaction. B is a likely possibility. The rupture film does keep the reactants dry, but that is important during the days and years before the accident, not the 1–5 ms during the reaction, so C is incorrect. There is no catalyst involved, so D is incorrect.

29. A.
In the absence of other information about entropy, it is reasonable to assume that the reaction which produces the most gas has the largest entropy increase. At a given temperature gases tend to have much more entropy than liquids and solids.

30. B.
Using $PV = nRT$, we note that $1000 / (0.0821) (300)$ is the number of moles of gas we desire. Multiplying by 6/9 (because of the reaction coefficients) yields the number of moles of sodium azide required. Multiplying by the molar mass (65 grams/mol) yields the number of grams required.

31. D.
Having the bag deflate will not affect the temperature appreciably, so A is incorrect. There are a number of ways to ensure that a bag will not burst (safety valve, and so on) that are better than having it deflate, so B is incorrect. The energy of collision or, rather, the work that must be done on the driver to stop him is a constant (equal to the negative of his kinetic energy before the collision), so C is incorrect. The language of choice D reminds us of $W_{tot} - F\Delta x$. And, indeed, the presence of an airbag increases the distance over which the decelerating force acts: not all at once at the steering wheel, but "gradually" over 0.3 meters. This decreases the force and reduces grievous bodily harm.

32. C.
It is not clear how a larger area of the bag could affect the flow rate. A larger area of the nozzle could increase the flow rate, but the question is asking about the airbag, so A and B are incorrect. Option C reminds us of the formula $P = F/A$. If A is increased, and F is the same, then pressure is reduced, hence the cushioning effect. Thus C is correct. D makes a correct statement, but does not lend advantage to the driver, so it is incorrect.

33. D.
Option A, chemical to heat, misses the point. If this were a reaction that generated a lot of heat that then dissipated, then A would be a possibility. The point of energy release in an airbag is that the airbag is actually inflated. So A is incorrect, as well as B. Option C seems like a possibility, since the bag seems to gain kinetic energy, which might later be turned to heat. Option D is a better description; however, since the true energy flow involves pushing back the atmosphere and not in moving the bag (which has little mass).

34. A.
All the options are reasonable byproducts except A, which involves Na or O in bizarre valence states.

Passage 5

35. B.
In the figure shown,

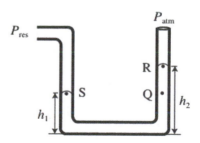

the pressure at point Q is the same as the pressure at point S, the reservoir pressure (Pascal's law). Hydrostatic equilibrium dictates that $P_Q = P_{atm} + \rho g(h_2 - h_1)$.

36. D.
The pressure all along the flow is the same, except for the tiny region where Barometer 2 disturbs the flow. Thus the pressure measured by Barometer 1 is the same as the upstream pressure. If we take the streamline shown in the figure, then upstream we have pressure P_1 and desired velocity v, and at the point in front of the barometer we have pressure P_2 and $v = 0$. Bernoulli's equation becomes

$$P_1 + \frac{1}{2}\rho v^2 = P_2 + \frac{1}{2}\rho(0)^2$$

$$v = \sqrt{\frac{2(P_2 - P_1)}{\rho}}$$

37. C.
Since the flow must go through a smaller area, the velocity must increase to maintain the same flow rate $f = Av$.

38. A.
Bernoulli's equation (neglecting the gravity terms) is

$$P_3 + \frac{1}{2}\rho v_3^2 = P_4 + \frac{1}{2}\rho v_4^2$$

If v_4 is greater than v_3, then P_4 is less than P_3. But do not rely on the equation; remember that for flow along a streamline, the pressure increases when the velocity decreases.

39. B.
If the fluid is incompressible, then $f = A_3 v_3 = A_4 v_{4new}$, regardless of viscosity. Thus v_{4new} is the same as v_4.

40. A.
Bernoulli's equation can no longer be used to obtain pressure, but perhaps we can figure out the answer by figuring out where the equation breaks down. The equation is a statement of energy conservation. If viscosity is added, then viscosity converts some energy into heat. Thus, we have

$$P_3 + \frac{1}{2}\rho v_3^2 = P_4 + \frac{1}{2}\rho v_4^2 + \frac{\text{heat energy}}{\text{volume}}$$

Comparing this with the equation in problem 4 above, we see that in this equation P_4 must be smaller (the $1/2\,\rho v_4^2$ term is the same; see previous problem). The key to this problem is remembering that Bernoulli's equation is about energy. Viscosity robs the flow energy, creating heat, thus reducing pressure from the prediction given by the Bernoulli equation.

41. D.
This is a question about geometry only. If the diameter of a circle increases by a factor of 4, how does the area change? We know $A = \pi r^2$. If the diameter increases by a factor of 4, the radius increases by a factor of 4, and the area increases by a factor of 16. If this seems counterintuitive, see Section 1.D.

42. A.
The passage stated that $\mu = \rho A$. Thus if the diameter is decreased by a factor of 2, then the radius is decreased by a factor of 2, the area is decreased by a factor of 4, and the linear density is decreased by a factor of 4.

43. C.
We want to increase the wave velocity by a factor of 1.3. Since $v^2 = T/\mu$, we want to increase T by $(1.3)^2 = 1.69$, that is, we want to increase T by 69%.

44. B.
Since we want to keep v the same and T the same, we therefore (since $v^2 = T/\mu$) want to keep μ the same. Thus we have

$\mu = \text{const}$,
$\rho A = \text{const}$,
$\rho \pi r^2 = \text{const}$.

The density ρ is to decrease by a factor of 4, so the radius increases by a factor of 2, and the diameter increases by a factor of 2. Thus it is 0.8 mm.

45. A.
The two waves, if superposed, would add to zero at every point.

46. D.
The question does not say whether the wave arrives in phase or out of phase or in between. The duck's oscillation could be as little as 1 m (out of phase) or as much as 7 m (in phase).

47. A.
Since the midpoint is the same distance from both speakers, and the speakers produce waves that are in phase, the waves must arrive at the midpoint in phase. If this explanation is unclear, visualize the following. Two crests are emitted by the speakers at the same time. They travel at the same velocity toward the center, and they arrive at the same time. Accordingly, the center is an antinode.

48. C.
The distance from the microphone to speaker 1 is 1.3 m, and its distance to speaker 2 is 0.7 m. We are interested in the *difference* in phase, which is the difference in distance, relative to wavelength. We calculate

$$\frac{d_2 - d_1}{\lambda} = \frac{1.3m - 0.7m}{0.8m} = 0.75$$

If this were a whole number, then we would have an antinode. If it were a half-odd integer (0.5, 1.5, 2.5, etc.), then we would have a node.

49. B.
As in the previous problem, we calculate

$$\frac{d_2 - d_1}{\lambda} = \frac{1.6m - 0.4m}{0.8m} = 1.5$$

We have a node.

50. C.
If the waves are out of phase, the combination has its minimum amplitude of (0.5 – 0.3) Pa = 0.2 Pa. If the waves are in phase, the combination has its maximum amplitude 0.8 Pa.

51. C.
The fundamental is shown in the first figure below, while the first harmonic is shown in the next figure. We can read from the figures that $\lambda_1 = 4$ m, and $\lambda_2 = 2$ m.

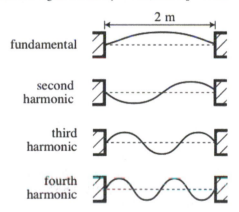

52. A.
Since the frequency is inversely related to the wavelength (from $v = \lambda f$), the ratio f_1/f_2 is 1/2. We could also write

$$\frac{f_1}{f_2} = \frac{\frac{v}{\lambda_1}}{\frac{v}{\lambda_2}} = \frac{v}{\lambda_1} \cdot \frac{\lambda_2}{v} = \frac{\lambda_2}{\lambda_1} \quad 0.5$$

53. C.
The third harmonic is shown in the figure above. One the one hand, we can read the wavelength from the figure. If this is not clear, we can also write that there are 3/2 wavelengths contained in the 2 m, so that we write

$3\lambda/2 = L$

$\lambda = 2L/3$

$\lambda = 4m/3$

54. B
The fourth harmonic is shown. We can see there are two wavelengths in the 2 m, so that we write

$2\lambda = L$

$\lambda = L/2$

$\lambda = 1$ m

55. B.
The fundamental does not have a node at the midpoint, but the second harmonic does, so this is the lowest frequency that can make a sound. Its frequency is given by

$f = v/\lambda$

$= (3 \times 10^4 \text{ m/s})/2m$

$= 1.5 \times 10^4$ Hz

56. C.
The third harmonic is the first mode with a node at the "third" point, so the frequency is given by

$f = v/\lambda$

$= (3 \times 10^4 \text{ m/s})/1.333m$

$= 2.25 \times 10^4$ Hz

Passage 6

57. B.
Choice A is true but does not do a good job of explaining anything. Choice B refers to the transition from deep to shallow water, which happens over length scales very long compared to the 10-m ocean waves. The pool waves hit the sharp boundary of the side of the pool and are reflected. Choices C and D are true but irrelevant.

58. D.
As waves, the energy is initially both kinetic and potential, which the MCAT refers to as mechanical. Choices A and B do not express what happens when a wave breaks, and the mechanical energy goes into another form. There are no chemical changes, so C is incorrect. Choice D is reasonable. The source of friction is the sandy beach.

59. A.
According to the second paragraph, a wave has its best chance of being transmitted if it has short wavelength.

60. D.

Choice A is incorrect, since we certainly do not want to convert light energy to anything else. Choice B is incorrect, since the situation more closely resembles paragraphs 1 and 2, the coating providing a gradual transition. Visible light waves have a small wavelength, so a thin coating would suffice. This would decrease the reflectivity.

61. C.
Choice A is incorrect, since the point is that the snow is *not* reflecting sound, resulting in your not hearing it. Choice B would be a good explanation, if the coat of snow were thick compared with the wavelength of sound (paragraph 2). This is not the case. It must be the case that the snow absorbs the sound energy, turning it to heat.

62. B
Choice A is incorrect, because the transition from air to wood is abrupt. Choice B seems likely. There is nothing to indicate C is correct. Choice D is definitely incorrect, since the frequency of a wave stays constant as it travels from place to place. There is nothing in the passage indicating a change of frequency.

Passage 7

63. D.
We apply $v = \lambda f$, using the speed of sound in air.

64. D.
According to the first paragraph, the wavelength must be smaller than the observed object. A wavelength of 10^{-3} m corresponds to a frequency of about 1.5×10^6 Hz in biological tissue, where we use $v = 1500$ m/s.

65. A.
The lowest frequency is 20 Hz, so $T = 1/f = 1/(20 \text{ Hz}) = 0.05$ s.

66. D.
The two real choices are B and D. Since there is tearing and rupturing involved, there must be chemical bonds broken, so D is it.

67. D.
Frequency is not directly connected to intensity. Amplitude and intensity are connected, but amplitude is not mentioned among the choices.

68. D.
Choices A and B are irrelevant. Concerning choice C, the problem is not energy reflecting off the organ but being absorbed by it. This is an example of resonance, and there must be a weak coupling between two oscillators: the sound is one and the oscillating organ is the other.

69. D.
The equation here is given by

$$f = \frac{1}{2\pi}\sqrt{\frac{k}{m}}$$

$$k = m(2\pi f)^2$$

$$= (0.5\text{kg})\left(2\pi \frac{1}{0.2}\right)^2$$

$$\approx \left(\frac{1}{2}\right)\left(2 \cdot 3 \cdot \frac{10}{2}\right)^2 \frac{\text{N}}{\text{m}}$$

$$\approx 450 \frac{\text{N}}{\text{m}}$$

Passage 8

70. A.
Use $\lambda = v/f$.

71. B.
We use $f_{\text{beat}} = f_1 - f_2 = 80 \text{ kHz} - 70 \text{ kHz} = 10 \text{ kHz}$.

72. D.
In the upper figure we see the beat, so T refers to the beat period, which is $1/f_{\text{beat}}$. The reason that the power never reaches zero is that the outgoing wave has a larger amplitude than the incoming wave.

73. A.
Maxima correspond to times when the two waves are in phase.

74. D.
Because the detected frequency is lower, the vehicle is receding, but there is no way to know from the passage whether it is doing so directly away or at an angle. The Doppler effect happens in three dimensions, and we have discussed only the one dimension parallel to the motion (which is the important one).

Passage 9

75. C.
You may have been tempted to choose D, but the question asks for the wavelength of the wave *in the pipe*, not the wavelength of the wave in the air, so we cannot use 343 m/s. The passage describes the vibration as having antinodes at the midpoint and ends and a node at the one-quarter point. This is shown in the figure. One wavelength corresponds to the length of the pipe.

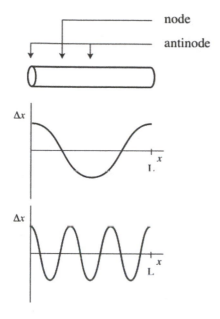

node
antinode

Δx

I.

Δx

L.

76. A.
We use $f = v/\lambda$.

77. C.
The waves in the pipe are analogous to waves on a string, and the hammer blow is a transverse blow. Sound waves in air must be longitudinal.

78. B.
We need to introduce at least one more node. If we introduce another node between the end and the place where the string attaches, that forces us to include three more nodes. The second fundamental is shown in the figure above. Three waves fit in 0.8 m, so the wavelength is 0.27 m.

Passage 10

79. B.
This is the definition of interference. Diffraction is the spreading of waves. Beats is a particular phenomenon which occurs when waves of similar frequency interfere. Difference tones have to do with the way the ear processes sound.

80. C.
The passage says that a note of average frequency turns on and off. Thus the perceived frequency is (30.87 Hz + 32.70 Hz)/2 = 31.79 Hz.

81. B.
This question asks for the beat frequency (times per second), so f_{beat} = 32.70 Hz − 30.87 Hz = 1.83 Hz.

82. C.
Choices A, B, and C all share the property that the difference is the desired frequency 110 Hz, but choice D is excluded. Choices A and B include frequencies lower

than 110 Hz, which cannot possibly be harmonics, so A and B are incorrect.

83. B.
The pressure in the room does not change markedly from the equilibrium pressure. Sound is tiny variations of pressure. If the vertical axis were marked $\Delta P = P - P_{eq}$, then an answer like A would be appropriate.

84. C.
According to paragraph 3, sound of two frequencies f_1 and f_2 enter the ear. Choice A is definitely wrong, especially with a wavelength drawn onto the graph. For that the horizontal axis must be a space coordinate like x. Choice B might show a portion of the power spectrum after some processing, but the frequency $f_1 - f_2$ does not enter the ear. The ear constructs the difference tone later. Choice C is correct. Choice D might have been correct if time were the horizontal coordinate.

Passage 11

85. B.
Since Alice is an equal distance from the speakers, and the speakers are emitting sound waves in phase, wave crests arrive at her location in phase. Thus she is at an antinode. Bob has moved to a position of relative silence, which must be a node.

86. C.
The waves arrive out of phase where Bob is sitting, because the wave from the left speaker takes a bit longer to arrive. When a crest from the right speaker is arriving, the corresponding crest from the left is still in transit. By the time it arrives, a trough is arriving from the right speaker.

87. D.
The sum of the two distances is not significant and cannot be derived from the information.

88. D.
The key here is that, for Bob, the waves arrive out of phase. When crest is coming from the left speaker, trough comes from the right. The difference is half a wavelength.

89. C.
Alice is positioned equidistant from the speakers, so for her the waves will still be in phase, so A and D are incorrect. Bob's location at a node depends on the wavelength of the sound, which we change when we change the frequency.

90. C.
Experiment 2 is the prescription for creating beats.

91. C.
We use the equation

$$\frac{1}{f_{tot}} = \frac{1}{f_1} + \frac{1}{f_2}$$

$$\frac{1}{f_{tot}} = \frac{1}{2\text{ m}} + \frac{1}{4\text{ m}}$$

$$\frac{1}{f_{tot}} = \frac{3}{4}\text{ m}^{-1}$$

$$f_{tot} = \frac{4}{3}\text{ m}$$

92. B.
The first lens has a power $P_1 = 1/f = 1/2$ D. We want a combination with total power $P_{tot} = 1/f_{tot} = 1/3$ D. Thus $P_2 = P_{tot} - P_1 = -1/6$ D.

93. B.
The focal length is 1/3 m, so the lens is a converging lens.

94. D.
The power of the combination is the sum of the powers.

Passage 12

95. C.
This is an application of the equation $f = c/\lambda = (3 \times 10^8$ m/s)$/(520 \times 10^{-9}$ m$) = 5.8 \times 10^{14}$ Hz.

96. C.

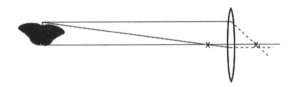

The figure shows the ray diagram for this problem. The diagram is not too much help in this problem, so we calculate

$$m = -\frac{d_i}{d_o}$$

$$= -\frac{0.025\text{ m}}{0.25\text{ m}}$$

$$= -0.1$$

Since the magnification is –0.1, the size of the image is $(0.1)(0.01\text{ m}) = 10^{-3}$ m and inverted.

97. A.
The subtended angle can be calculated from information in the third paragraph, that is, the ratio of the spatial separation of the top and bottom of the moth to the distance from the moth to the eye. Thus the angle is 0.01 m/0.25 m = 0.04 radians, which is about 2.3°.

98. D.

The desired power of the combination of corrective lens plus eye lens is 1/0.025 m = 40 D. Since $P_{combo} = P_{eye} + P_{correct}$, we must have $P_{correct} = 5$ D.

99. A.

The figure shows the red light focused on the retina. This lens refracts the blue light more than red light and hence focuses blue rays in front of the red focus. The figure exaggerates the case.

100. D.
According to the passage, if the camera is diffraction limited, then the resolution depends on the size of the lens (that is, light gathering hole) and the wavelength of the light used. Choices A, B, and C address neither of these issues. Increasing the size of the entire camera would increase the size of the lens, which would increase the resolution, by decreasing the resolution angle.

101. B.
Trying to determine if two dots are separate or blurred is analogous to trying to distinguish two headlights, so the information is in paragraph 3. The resolution of the eye is the ratio of dot separation to standing distance, so we write

$$2 \times 10^{-4} = 0.002\text{m}/D$$

$$D = 10\text{ m}.$$

You must stand 10 m away.

102. A.
The best resolution we can hope for is diffraction limited, for which $\theta_{diff} = \lambda/d = (520 \times 10^{-9}$ m$)/(2.4\text{ m}) = 2 \times 10^{-7}$ rad. We have used green light as being representative of visible light.

103. C.
UV light has a shorter wavelength than visible light, so the diffraction angle $\theta_{diff} = \lambda/d$ would decrease, giving a better resolution, assuming the apparatus is diffraction limited.

104. D.
Concerning choice A, a larger pupil does allow in more light, but this does not explain a decrease in resolution. For choice B, the opposite is true: a larger pupil allows more directional information to enter the eye, which should improve resolution if there were not another factor present. For choice C, both cats and humans contend with

chromatic aberration (see question 5). The large lens introduces spherical aberration, so D is correct.

SECTION 4 CONTENT REVIEW PROBLEMS

1. B
The clue here is the combination of energy and charge, so the equation to use is $W = q\Delta V$. Although the problem specifies that the path is straight across, the energy is path independent, so we do not need that information. Thus

$$W = q(V_D - V_A) = (10^{-14}\ \text{C})(1000\ \text{V} - 1000\ \text{V}) = 0\ \text{J}.$$

2. D
Again we use

$$W = q\Delta V = q(V_C - V_A)$$

$$= (-1.6 \times 10^{-19}\ \text{C})(-1000\ \text{J/C} - 1000\ \text{J/C})$$

$$= 3.2 \times 10^{-16}\ \text{J}$$

Let's check the sign. Moving a positive particle from 1000 V to –1000 V is downhill, so moving an electron is uphill, that is, an increase in energy.

3. D.
Whenever we see a problem about work or energy with charges, we know to write $W = Q\Delta V$. Let's consider the charge q_1 to be fixed and move charge q_2 from initial distance r_i to final distance r_f (see figure).

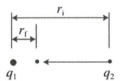

Then, we have

$$W = q_2\left(V_f - V_i\right)$$

$$= q_2\left(\frac{kq_1}{r_f} - \frac{kq_1}{r_i}\right)$$

$$= 1.1 \times 10^{-9}\ \text{C}\left(\frac{\left(9 \times 10^9\ \frac{\text{Nm}^2}{\text{C}^2}\right)\left(1.1 \times 10^{-8}\ \text{C}\right)}{0.01\ \text{m}} - \frac{\left(9 \times 10^9\ \frac{\text{Nm}^2}{\text{C}^2}\right)\left(1.1 \times 10^{-8}\ \text{C}\right)}{0.1\ \text{m}}\right)$$

$$= 10^{-5}\ \text{J}$$

Note that we get the same answer if we consider q_2 fixed and move q_1.

4. A.
Whenever we see a problem about work or energy with charges, we know to write $W = Q\Delta V$. The charge we want

to transfer is $Q = 10^{-10}$ C. Thus we have $W = (10^{-10}$ C$)$ ($-10,000$ V $- 10,000$ V$) = -2 \times 10^{-6}$ J.

A positive charge going from 10,000 V to $-10,000$ V is going downhill, so the negative sign is correct.

5. A.
Whenever we see a problem about work or energy with charges, we know to write $W = Q\Delta V$. If we try to apply $W = F\Delta x\cos\phi$, we are dead in the water, because, as the charge moves, F changes. In this case the charge q starts at point A, where the potential due to Q is $V_A = kQ/r_1 = 2 \times 10^4$ V, where we use $r_1 = 5$ m. It moves to point B, which is $r_2 = 1$ m away from Q, so $V_B = kQ/r_2 = 10^5$ V. The work required is

$$W = q\Delta V$$

$$= (-10^{-6} \text{ C})(-10^5 \text{ J/C} - 2 \times 10^4 \text{ J/C})$$

$$= -0.08 \text{ J}$$

Does the sign make sense? Since we are moving a negative charge nearer a positive one, we expect that the energy required be negative.

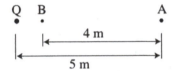

6. A.
Whenever we see a problem about work or energy with charges, we know to write $W = Q\Delta V$. If we try to apply $W = F\Delta x\cos\phi$, we are lost. The potential at the starting point A is $V_A = kQ/r_1$, where r_1 is 2 m. The potential at the ending point B is $V_B = kQ/r_2$, where r_2 is 2 m. Thus the potential at the two points is the same, and no energy is required. This is the equivalent of moving a rock from one point 50 m above sea level to another point 50 m above sea level. You may move the rock uphill and downhill, but the total work required is zero, because you pull as much energy out of the rock as you put into it.

7. A.
Whenever we see a problem about work or energy with charges, we know to write $W = Q\Delta V$. In this case, Q is the charge of the electron, and ΔV is the voltage rating of the dry cell.

8. A.
If we work out the electric potential at points A and B, we obtain

$$V_A = \frac{kQ}{r_1} + \frac{kQ}{r_2}$$

where $r_1 = 2$ m and $r_2 = 4$ m. But the calculation for V_B involves the same numbers, except that $r_1 = 2$ m and $r_2 = 4$ m. So $V_B = V_A$, and the potential difference is zero volts.

9. B.
The electric potential at point C is given by

$$V_A = \frac{kQ}{r_3} + \frac{kQ}{r_4}$$

$$= 2\left(\frac{\left(9 \times 10^9 \ \frac{\text{Nm}^2}{\text{C}^2}\right)\left(1.1 \times 10^{-4} \ \text{C}\right)}{5 \text{ m}}\right)$$

$$= 4 \times 10^5 \text{ volts}$$

since $r_3 = r_4 = 5$ m. (Use the Pythagorean theorem.)

10. B.
Its acceleration is given by force divided by mass, and the force is an inverse-square law with respect to distance. The force decreases as q moves away from Q, for the force decreases forever, never reaching zero.

11. C.
Since the acceleration is always positive (that is, away from charge Q), the velocity will increase forever. (There is no friction force in the problem to slow it down.) This narrows the answer to C or D. To distinguish between these possibilities we need an energy argument. The energy of the system starts as electrical potential energy, and is given by $E_{elec} = kQq/r$, where r is their initial distance. (Recall that the electrical potential energy is the energy required to bring a system together from charges starting at infinity.) After the charge Q has moved very far away, the energy of the system is all kinetic: $1/2 \, mv^2$. But since E_K can never be greater than kQq/r, there is a limit on the size of v. (See the figure for a sketch of v versus t.)

12. B.
The energy starts as kinetic and ends as electrical potential. In order for there to be heat, there must be a large number of particles in random motion. Heat is not an appropriate concept with just two particles.

13. A.
The energy is conserved, so there is no energy entering or exiting. Furthermore, there is no heat generation or such nonsense, so the initial kinetic energy ($1/2 \, mv^2$) is entirely converted to electrical potential energy. Thus if v is increased by a factor of 4, then the initial kinetic energy is

increased by a factor of 16, as is the final electrostatic energy.

14. A.

We derived the expression for the electric potential energy in Example 4 of Section F. (Note: The denominator is r, not r^2. This is not Coulomb's law, which is about force. This is an equation about energy.) If we set the expression for the initial kinetic energy equal to the final electrostatic energy, we obtain

$$\frac{1}{2}mv^2 = \frac{kQq}{r}$$

$$r = \frac{2kQq}{mv^2}$$

Clearly v and r are inversely related, so if v increases by a factor of 4, then r decreases by a factor of 16.

15. D.

Using the right hand, point the thumb up, so that the fingers curl counterclockwise when viewed from the top. At point P the magnetic field is into the page.

16. B.

If the current is up, then the electrons (being negative) must be flowing down.

17. D.

The external force pulls the wire, so the electrons move in the same direction as the magnetic field. Thus there is no magnetic force on the electrons.

18. C.

Using the left hand, point the fingers down the page and the thumb toward you. The palm faces left, the direction of the magnetic force.

19. C.

Since the proton is speeding up, there is work being done on it, so it cannot be a magnetic force speeding it up. The acceleration of the proton is to the right, so the force is to the right. The electric field must be to the right as well.

20. C.

There is a force on the proton up the page. If it is an electric force, then the electric field points up the page. If it is a magnetic force, then the force would be provided by a magnetic field pointing into the page.

21. B.

If a proton is placed at point A, it experiences no magnetic force (it is not moving). But it will feel the attraction toward the electrons, down the page. This indicates that the direction of the electric field is down (toward the electrons). It does not matter that the electrons are moving.

22. A.

The tricky part here is realizing that if the electron beam moves to the right, then the current points to the left. Using the right hand with the thumb pointing left (or the left hand with the thumb pointing right, either one), the fingers curl in the direction into the page at point A.

23. D.

We use the left hand (because electrons are negative) to figure out the direction of the magnetic force. The fingers point down and the thumb to the right. The palm faces out of the page, so that is the direction of the magnetic force. We are told that the electric force opposes it, so it must be into the page. If the electric field points out of the page, then its force on an electron is into the page (because the electron is negative).

24. A.

No matter what point along the wire loop we choose, if we apply the right hand rule, we obtain a magnetic field pointing out of the page.

25. B.

Using the right hand, point the fingers out of the page and the thumb up. The palm faces to the right, so the answer is B. Choices C and D are definitely out anyway, because a magnetic force cannot speed up or slow down a particle (that is, it does no work).

Passage 1

26. A.

Since the electric field is directed away from the wire, this indicates that the charge on the wire is positive.

27. B.

At a distance 0.01 m from the wire, the electric field is $E = (3 \times 10^4 \text{ Nm/C})/(0.01 \text{ m}) = 3 \times 10^6$ N/C. To obtain force, we calculate $F = q_{elec} E = 4.8 \times 10^{-13}$ N. Since the electric field is directed away from the wire, the force on the electron is toward the wire.

28. D.

The electric field lines point in the same direction that the field points, that is, away from the wire.

29. B.

The force of a charged particle in an electric field is simply $F = QE$. The charge on the fluoride ion is due to an extra electron, so it is -1.6×10^{-19} C. The charge on the hydrogen ion is 1.6×10^{-19} C. Thus the force on the fluoride is the same in magnitude and opposite in direction.

30. C.

In a butanol molecule, the oxygen atom is the most electronegative atom, so it is negatively charged relative to the rest of the molecule. Since the electric field points away from the wire, the negative oxygen experiences a force toward the wire.

Passage 2

31. B.
The force on a charged particle in an electric field is $F = QE$, so the oxygen ion (O^{2-}) experiences twice the force.

32. A.
A calcium atom has no charge, so the force on it would be zero.

33. C.
Increasing the pressure would put the gas particles closer to each other, so an electron could not travel as far before colliding with a particle. Thus the mean free path would decrease. If the electron is not able to travel as far, then the energy it gains is less. (The kinetic energy it gains is about $F_{elec}\, l_{mfp}$, from the standard formula for work.) Thus the electron is not likely to create a spark. A greater electric field is required, so the threshold is higher.

34. D.
The mass density does not have anything to do with this phenomenon, so choices A, B, and C are out. It is true that an electron absorber will inhibit the phenomenon like killing a baby in its crib.

35. C.
This graph shows the constant acceleration (due to the constant force) of the electron in the parts of the graph which have a small positive slope. The rapid decreases in velocity are the times of collision where the electron loses energy.

36. C.

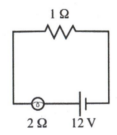

In order to obtain the total current, we need the total resistance of the circuit. Lights 1 and 2 are in parallel, so we can combine their resistances to obtain 1 Ω. The resulting equivalent circuit is shown above. The last two resistors can be combined to obtain 3 Ω as shown below. The total current is 4 amps.

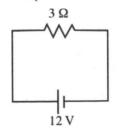

37. D.

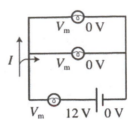

It is difficult to know how the potential across light 1 compares with the potential across light 3. On the other hand, the whole current through the potential source goes through light 3 and splits in half before going through lights 1 and 2. (Later it recombines and returns.) Since the power dissipated is $P_{res} = I^2 R$ and resistance is the same for lights 1 and 3, the fact that light 3 has twice the current means it dissipates 4 times the power.

38. C.

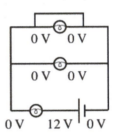

The resulting circuit diagram is shown. The new wire ensures that the potential on both sides of lights 1 and 2 is zero. So these lights extinguish. On the other hand, light 3 gets the full 12 volts, so it burns brighter.

39. D.
See the diagram above.

40. C.

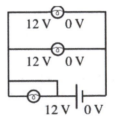

The new circuit diagram is shown. The new wire ensures that the potential on both sides of light 3 is zero, so it goes out. Lights 1 and 2 are brighter.

41. A.
We apply the equation for resistors in parallel:

$$\frac{1}{R_T} = \frac{1}{R_1} + \frac{1}{R_2}$$

$$= \left(\frac{1}{100} + \frac{1}{200}\right)\frac{1}{\Omega} = 0.015\frac{1}{\Omega}$$

$$R_T = 67\Omega$$

42. D.
Voltage does not flow. The question makes as much sense as asking what height is flowing in a river.

43. A.
The potential drop across resistor 2 is 6 volts, so the current through it is $I_2 = 0.03$ A, and the power dissipated by it is $P_2 = 0.18$ Watts. In 600 s, it dissipates $E = P_2\Delta t = 108$ Joules.

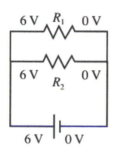

44. C.

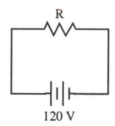

The circuit diagram is simply that shown above. Since the power is given by $P = I\Delta V$, we obtain the current from $I = 300$ W/120 V = 2.5 A. The resistance is 120 V/2.5 A = 48 Ω.

45. B.
Combining the power equation with Ohm's law yields $P = (\Delta V)^2/R$, where $\Delta V = 120$ V is a constant. To increase power, we want to decrease the resistance. A longer wire will increase resistance, while a thicker wire will decrease it, since $R = \rho l/A$.

46. C.
In the previous problem we mentioned $P = (\Delta V)^2/R$, where $\Delta V = 120$ V is a constant. If we graph P versus R, we obtain something like C.

47. A.

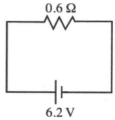

Ignoring the unfamiliar symbol and the dashed lines around the battery, we see that this is just a circuit with two resistors in series. We can combine the resistors into one with resistance $R_T = R + R_{int}$ (see figure). Ohm's law yields the result, which we can estimate by $I = 6$ V/0.6 Ω = 10 A.

48. B.
Since R_{int} is added to the external resistance of the circuit, we can ignore it if the external resistance is large (see the above solution). If the external resistance is large, then the current is small, so either II or III would allow us to ignore the internal resistance.

49. C.
The formal solution to the problem involves writing down Ohm's law for this circuit and then solving for $1/I$:

$$V_{emf} = I(R + R_{int})$$

$$\frac{1}{I}V_{emf} = (R + R_{int})$$

$$\frac{1}{I} = \frac{1}{V_{emf}}R + \frac{R_{int}}{V_{emf}}$$

$1/I$ is not proportional to R, but this equation has the familiar $y = mx + b$ form, with positive slope and positive y-intercept. Let's say you did not think of that. We know that as resistance R increases, the current I decreases, which means $1/I$ must increase, so that eliminates A and B. In choice D, there is a resistance where $1/I$ is zero, and the current is infinite. But you cannot obtain that from this circuit, so choice D is out.

Passage 3

50. A.
We have changed the potential across the plates, but we have not changed the capacitor itself. Thus its capacitance does not change. (Capacitance depends only on the capacitor itself, not on the applied potential.)

51. D.
The capacitance does not change, so the charge must increase by a factor of 4, since we have $Q = C\Delta V$.

52. D.
The electric field is $E = \Delta V/d$, so the electric field increases by a factor of 4.

53. B.

After the wires are removed, no charge can be transferred from one plate to the other. The dielectric is a nonconductor.

54. A.
The charge Q is constant, but the capacitance increases by a factor of 9. Thus the potential $\Delta V = Q/C$ decreases by a factor of 9.

Passage 4

55. A.
Capacitance is defined as charge per potential. Both are given in the passage.

56. B.
The formula $\Delta V = E\Delta x$ works here, where Δx is the separation between the Earth's surface and the ionosphere. The Earth and the ionosphere are like a parallel-plate capacitor which has been bent into a sphere.

57. A.
The work required is given by $W = q\Delta V = (-1.6 \times 10^{-19} \text{ C})(9 \times 10^5 \text{ J/C}) = -1.4 \times 10^{-13} \text{ J}$. But we are unsure about the sign. The Earth has a negative charge, so taking an electron away from it is easy: a downhill ride, so to speak. Thus the change in potential energy is negative.

58. D.
The electric field points away from a positive charge and toward a negative one. Thus it points toward the Earth and away from the ionosphere. The other two pictures are reminiscent of the Earth's magnetic field.

59. A.
Since the passage said that the potential difference between the ionosphere and the Earth's surface is 9×10^5 volts, we can exclude C and D. For a proton, going from the surface to the ionosphere is uphill, that is, going to greater potential energy away from the Earth's negative charge. Therefore A is the correct answer.

Passage 5
60. A.
A sodium ion (Na^+) is positively charged, and the negatively charged central wire will attract it.

61. A.
It does not matter what kind of molecule this is. The only thing that matters is its neutral charge. The passage states that it will be attracted to the wire.

62. D.
Since this question is about energy and charges, our guess is that we will use $W = q\Delta V$ somewhere. A fluoride ion near the negative wire has high potential energy, so it gains kinetic energy as it moves away from the wire. The change in potential energy is $q\Delta V = (-1.6 \times 10^{-19} \text{ C})(5 \times$

$10^4 \text{ J/C}) = -8 \times 10^{-15} \text{ J}$. (Recall: a fluoride ion has one extra electron, so its charge is the same as an electron.) The increase in kinetic energy is thus 8×10^{-15} J, since energy is being conserved. Now some energy may be lost to heat, and so on, so this is actually the maximum energy available.

63. B.
The main formula we have for capacitance is $C = Q/\Delta V$, which may tempt you to think that an increase in potential would lead to a decrease in capacitance, but this is not so. The capacitance of a device is fixed by the construction of that device, and the amount of stored charge goes up proportionally as the potential. An increase in potential would result in an increase in the charge on the wire Q_{wire}, but the capacitance remains the same.

64. C.
The only thing we can do with the new piece of information is to combine it with the information in the third paragraph, to obtain the power usage of $P = (300 \text{ J/m}^3)(100 \text{ m}^3\text{/s}) = 3 \times 10^4$ Watts. The question asks for current, and the only connection we know of between power and current is potential difference. Aha! $I = P/\Delta V = (3 \times 10^4 \text{ J/s})/(5 \times 10^4 \text{ J/C}) = 0.8 \text{ C/s}$.

65. D.
The electric field lines point away from the positive charge and toward the negative charge.

66. D.
The attraction of neutral particles to a charged wire is like a charged comb attracting neutral pieces of paper. Choice A does not refer to charges at all. Choice B involves two charged particles, and choice C involves two neutral species. Choice D refers to a charged and a neutral species, just like the wire and the pollutants. A charge is induced on the pollutants, and the resulting net force is attractive (see chapter text).

Passage 6

67. B.
We have several formulas involving electric field: $E = kQ/r^2$ for a point charge, $E = \Delta V/\Delta x$, and $F = qE$. We are not given the charge of the cloud in the passage (and even if we were, it would be difficult to get E from it), nor are we given a force on a charge. But we are told the potential ΔV between the cloud and the Earth and the distance Δx between them. Thus $E = (10^8 \text{ J/C})/(2 \times 10^3 \text{ m}) = 5 \times 10^4$ N/C. (To get the units, recall J = Nm.)

68. A.
The main formula with resistance in it is Ohm's law. Do we have enough information? Yes, the current is given in the second paragraph $I = 20$ kamps. We can write $R = \Delta V/I = (10^8 \text{ V})/(2 \times 10^4 \text{ A}) = 5 \times 10^3 \text{ }\Omega$.

69. B.

Let's go through the passage scanning for information that could go together to get an energy estimate. The first piece of information is 2 km, but that is not helpful. (If a single object moved 2 km under the influence of a constant force, we could obtain its energy $W = F\Delta x \cos\phi$, but there is no information about force.) Next we are given the potential between cloud and ground, and we could get an energy if we knew an amount of charge that was transferred. But we are given that in the next paragraph. Thus $W = q\Delta V = (4\ \text{C})(10^8\ \text{J/C}) = 4 \times 10^8\ \text{J}$. (This represents the work done on the charge by the electric field.)

70. A.

This is easy if we remember that current is the rate at which charge moves, $I = Q/\Delta t$. Thus $\Delta t = Q/I = (4\ \text{C})/(2 \times 10^4\ \text{C/s}) = 2 \times 10^{-4}\ \text{s}$.

71. B.

Since the electric field points away from a positive charge, it will point away from the positive lightning rod, especially away from the very positively charged tip.

72. B.

Visible light results from the electrical transition of electrons in atoms and molecules. Dissociation of molecules may produce some light, but excitation of molecules is a better answer. (Ionization and recombination would have been another good answer, if it had been a choice.) Heating and expansion of air is lower on the energy scale, producing merely thunder.

Passage 7

73. C.

According to the third paragraph, the positive sodium ions are transported to the outside of the cell. The outside of the cell acquires a positive charge and a higher potential. So C is the correct choice. The diffusion of potassium ions lessens the effect, but the qualitative picture is the same.

74. A.

The cells are stacked in series. Thus the current through all the cells is the same, and the total current is simply 30 milliamps. Remember, the currents add up if the components of the current are in parallel. The voltages add up in series.

75. C.

We know the current during the activated state is 30 mA. Current is the rate at which charge is transferred, so if the time for the activated state is 2 ms, then the charge transferred is $I\Delta t = (30 \times 10^{-3}\ \text{C/s})(2 \times 10^{-3}\ \text{s}) = 6 \times 10^{-5}$ C.

76. B.

The electric field points away from positive charges and toward negative charges. So where are the charges during the activated state? A glance at Figures 1 and 3 shows that the fish pushes positive charges from its tail to its head, so a positive charge collects at the head of the fish, and a negative charge at its tail. Thus the answer is B.

77. D.

To obtain the magnetic field, we need to consider the current. The main current during the activated state is along the fish from tail to head. The right-hand rule applied to this implies a magnetic field circling the body in the direction shown in choice D. The secondary currents outside the fish in the fourth figure reinforce this magnetic field. On problems like this one, if you are in doubt, choose one typical point and apply the right-hand rule. For instance, choose the point under the fishes belly. If the magnetic field there is to the right, choose A; up, B; left, C; or into the page, D.

78. D.

Sea water has the charge carriers which make it more conductive.

79. A.

We calculate

$$m_{\text{def}} = 4\,(1.00783\ \text{amu}) - 4.00260\ \text{amu}$$

80. A.

The reaction we seek is

$$^{7}_{3}\text{Li} + ^{1}_{1}\text{H} \rightarrow\ ^{4}_{2}\text{He}\ \ ^{4}_{2}\text{He}$$

We calculate

$$m_{\text{def}} = (7.01601 + 1.00783 - 2\,(4.00260))\ \text{amu}$$

81. C.

The original ^{8}Be must have more mass than the final products in order for the reaction to occur. The mass deficit is converted into the kinetic energy of the resulting products.

82. C.

This is a simple application of $E = mc^2$.

83. B.

Choices C and D are nonsensical. Choice A is possible, but in fact the principle of mass-energy conservation is completely general. The energy of a reaction must be in the form of mass before the reaction occurs. It is, however, quite small for chemical reactions, about a million (10^6) times smaller than for nuclear reactions.

Passage 8
84. C.

The energy level diagram makes clear that the largest transition is the transition of absorption, from the ground state to the highest energy level. Thus those photons have the most energy and the highest frequency.

85. D.
On the other hand, nothing in the passage indicates that the energy difference between levels 1 and 2 should be less than (or greater than) the energy difference between level 1 and the ground state.

86. A.
The question refers to the transition from state 1 (E_1) to the ground state ($E = 0$), so the frequency is $f = (E_1 - 0)/h$.

87. D.
Clearly state 2 is not very populated, since transitions out of state 2 to state 1 (or to the ground state) occur very quickly. Otherwise, the passage is silent on this issue, so D is the answer.

88. A.
The Sun emits photons of all sorts of frequencies; that is what makes the colors of the rainbow. And many photons make it through the atmosphere.

Passage 9

89. A.
The text mentioned that alpha radiation is not very penetrating, able to be blocked even by several centimeters of air. Beta and gamma radiation are more penetrating. Because this radiation is blocked by a single sheet of gold, it must be alpha radiation, so the product must be ^{205}Pb.

90. C.
The only information we need here is that the alpha particles are positive. In an electric field which points up, they will experience a force up.

91. C.
We need only know that the alpha particles are positive. Applying the right hand rule for magnetic force indicates a force to the left as viewed from the top.

92. B.
Since the radiation is blocked by several centimeters of aluminum, it is not gamma radiation. But it is not alpha radiation, since a sheet of metal foil fails to block it. Is it normal beta radiation or positron radiation? The information from the magnetic field indicates the particles are positive. Thus the decay is positron decay.

93. A.
After 19 hours, the radioactivity of the sample decreases by a factor of 4, that is, two half-lives. Its half-life is 9.5 hours, which is what the question asks for.

94. D.
Each 9.5 hours sees a decrease by a factor of 2 in radioactivity. Therefore, the sample will never have zero radioactivity. (However, there must be a last atom to decay, so the answer "indefinitely" is better than "forever".)

Passage 10

95. D.
Choice A represents the positron decay, which is forbidden for subtle quantum reasons. Choice B represents normal beta decay, which does not happen for this nucleus. Choice C does not have balanced subscripts. Choice D fits the description in the question.

96. B.
According to the passage, K-capture happens under the same conditions which promote positron decay, that is, proton-rich nuclei. That is to say, nuclei with more protons than neutrons have a negative $N - Z$.

97. B.
According to the passage, the possibility of electron capture is nonzero only if there is some overlap of the electron wave function and the nucleus, so if the orbital has vanishing amplitude near the nucleus, the probability of capture is small.

98. C.
Choice A is incorrect because the neutrino hardly interacts with matter (see paragraph 2). The whole point of K-capture is to turn one of the many protons into a neutron, so the neutron is not likely to change back, and choice B is incorrect. Since K-capture pulls an electron from the innermost shell, that orbital is empty and can be filled by another electron from outer shells. This is accomplished by emitting photons, so choice C is a possibility. There is no positron created, so choice D is incorrect.

99. A.
During normal beta decay, a neutron goes away (N decreases by 1) and a proton appears in its place (Z increases by 1). The net effect is $N - Z$ decreases by 2.

100. C.
During alpha decay, both N and Z decrease by 2, so $N - Z$ stays the same.

Passage 11

101. D.
We write the reaction

$$^{10}_{5}B + ^{1}_{0}n \rightarrow ^{4}_{2}He + \ ?$$

The only choice for the missing particle that satisfies the criteria that the superscripts and subscripts add up is

$$^{7}_{3}Li$$

102. C.
Choice A is nonsensical. Choice B misses the point, since the question asks *why* these neutrons do not tend to ionize the tissue. The passage indicates (paragraph 2) that a charged particle with large energy is ideal for ionizing tissue, so a neutron with no charge and little energy will do little harm. Choice C is a likely possibility. Choice D is excluded since neutrons are an elementary particle.

103. B.
Choices C and D do not have the superscripts and subscripts balanced. Choice A does not satisfy the description in the passage, in that there is no gamma ray in the products.

104. D.
The reaction is

$$^{252}_{98}Cf \rightarrow {}^{4}_{2}He + {}^{248}_{96}Cm$$

105. D.
The 7.8 years represents 3 half-lives, so the original sample decreased by a factor of 2 three times. The original sample must have been 0.08 moles.

106. B.
Choice A is spontaneous neutron drip, not fission. Choice B is correct. Choice C is nearly correct, except the reaction is not spontaneous. For a reaction to be spontaneous there can be only the one reactant. Choice D is excluded for the same reason.

107. C.
This is a paraphrase of the second sentence of paragraph 3.

Passage 12

108. B.
Most of the energy goes into the ionization of molecules. The energy comes from nuclear energy.

109. D.
We write the reaction

$$^{2}_{1}H + {}^{20}_{10}Ne \rightarrow {}^{18}_{9}F \quad \text{?}$$

The particle which balances the superscripts and subscripts is $^{4}_{2}He$, which is an alpha particle.

110. B.
We write the reaction

$$^{18}_{9}F \rightarrow {}^{0}_{+1}e + \text{?}$$

The nucleus which balances the superscripts and subscripts is

$$^{18}_{8}O$$

111. C.
Glucose marked with ^{15}O would react chemically (almost exactly) the same as glucose with ^{16}O, so choices A and B are incorrect. The chemical environment of the nucleus hardly affects its decay, which is entirely due to nuclear physics, so D is out. In fact, a half-life of 128 seconds is very short. Just for your information, the other problem is that the glucose gets completely metabolized before there is a chance to detect its presence. The FDG tends to build up in the cell since it cannot be metabolized as easily.

112. D.
The 8 minutes is about 4 half-lives, so the activity must have decreased by a factor of 2 four times. Its initial activity was 160 mCi.

113. A.
We write the reaction

$$^{1}_{1}H + {}^{14}_{7}N \rightarrow {}^{15}_{8}O + \text{?}$$

This equation seems to be already balanced. The only particle which can be placed in the products without disturbing the balance is a gamma particle.

FINAL EXAM: PHYSICS CONTENT REVIEW SOLUTIONS

1. B.
   The magnitude of the displacement is the hypotenuse of the right triangle, so $1^2 + 1^2 = c^2$, $c = \sqrt{2} = 1.4$ km.

2. A
   The distance that was traveled was 2.0 km and the displacement is 1.4 km. The difference is 0.6 km.

3. D
   The net force is the sum of all the forces acting on the box. In this case the net force is zero, which means that the box is not accelerating. We can't tell based on the information provided, if the box is stationary or moving with a constant velocity.

4. B
   The kinematic equation for this problem is $V_f^2 = V_i^2 + 2ad$, where $V_i = 2$ m/s, $a = 1$ m/s^2 and $d = 10.5$ m. $V_f^2 = 2^2 + 2(1)(10.5) = 25$ and $V_f = \sqrt{25} = 5$ m/s

5. C
   The kinematic equation for this problem is $V_f^2 = V_i^2 + 2ad$, where $V_i = 50$ m/s, $V_f = 0$ m/s, and $a = -12.5$ m/s. $0^2 = 50^2 + 2(-12.5)d$. $d = (-2500)/(-25) = 100$ m.

6. D
   In order to start moving there must be a net force that will cause an acceleration. Since the tension in the chain and frictional forces must result in a net zero force when the velocity is a constant, the force must have been slightly greater than 150 kN to cause the initial acceleration.

7. C
   Assuming that wind resistance is negligible for both objects, the acceleration is due to gravity, which will be the same for both objects, regardless of mass or shape.

8. B
   The gravitational force is the weight of the object, $F_g = mg$. The object with more mass, weighs more.

9. A
   Momentum is a vector and is mass times velocity. While the ball is going up, the velocity and momentum vectors are up, but the acceleration due to gravity is down, such that there is a 180° angle between the momentum and acceleration vectors.

10. C
    The weight of the box is $(50$ kg$)(9.8$ m/s$^2) = 490$ N. The component of the weight that is parallel with the incline is $\sin 45°(490$ N$) \sim 350$ N. To remain stationary the frictional force must be equal in magnitude to the parallel component of the weight.

11. D
    The SI system is a set of physical measurements with base units of meters, kilograms, seconds, amperes, degrees Kelvin, candelas, and moles. Momentum is mass (kg) times velocity (m/s), hence the corresponding SI unit of momentum.

12. B
    The frictional force will equal the component of the weight of the box that is parallel with the incline. The smaller the angle, the larger the parallel component.

13. C
    The speed will be slightly faster than the horizontal speed, due to the additional vertical component resulting from gravitational acceleration, which can be calculated using $g = (V_f - V_i)/t$, $V_f = (10$ m/s$)(0.5$ s$) = 5$ m/s. Using the Pythagorean theorem $(12$ m/s$)^2 + (5$ m/s$)^2 = c^2$, $c = \sqrt{169} = 13$ m/s.

14. D
    Both men are pushing the desk at a constant speed, therefore there is no acceleration and the net force is zero. Therefore, since in both cases the weight of the desk is the same, the applied force is equal to the kinetic frictional force, $F_f = mF_N$.

15. A
    Work is force times displacement. There is no work done just holding the weight, since there is no displacement. The force is the weight of the object, 100 kg x 9.8 m/s$^2 \sim 1000$ N and the work is 1000 N x $(25$ m $- 10$ m$) = 15000$ Nm $= 15$ kJ.

16. C
    If the dog is pulling with a constant speed, then the horizontal component of the tension times the displacement will be the work done by the dog, therefore, $\cos 30°(3000$ N$)$ x 50 m $= 129,000$ J.

17. B
    Power is the work per unit time. In this case, the work is equal to the change in kinetic energy. Since the object starts at rest, $\Delta KE = KE_f = 1/2$ $mV^2 = (0.5)(200$ kg$)(20$ m/s$)^2 = 40,000$ J, and $P = W/t = (40000$ J$)/(4$ s$) = 10,000$ J/s $= 10$ kW.

18. C
    The total mechanical energy (KE + PE) of the ball (assuming no rotation) will equal the kinetic energy just before hitting the ground, which is also equal to the gravitational potential energy prior to dropping the ball. Therefore, PE $= mgh = (2$ kg$)(9.8$ m/s$^2)(10$ m$) = 200$ J

19. D
    To do work, there must be a change in the volume of the gas.

20. B
    The weight of the mass is approximately 15 kg x 9.8 m/s$^2 \sim 150$ N. Since there are three supporting ropes, the tension is $(150$ N$)/3 = 50$ N.

21. C

The work will be the weight of the object times the displacement, or W = (10 kg)(9.8 m/s²)(1 m) = 100 J. This will also be the gravitational potential energy that was gained and the work done pulling the rope, W = (50 N)(2 m) = 100 J.

22. B

The net force must equal the sum of the vertical forces, $F_{net} = F_{down} + F_{up}$, therefore, (20 kg)(-2 m/s²) = (20 kg)(-10 m/s²) + F_{up}, so F_{up} = 160 N. Since there are four ropes, the tension will be one quarter of the total upward force, or 40 N.

23. A

This question is essentially asking "Which of the following is a conservative force?" When a conservative force does work, the amount of work is independent of the path taken.

24. D

To do work there must be a parallel component between the force and the displacement. In this case the force vector, gravity, is perpendicular to the infintesimally small displacement (δd, not Δd) vector. Furthermore, since the satellite returns to the same spot after each cycle, the net displacement for each cycle is zero.

25. D

The equation for spring potential energy is PE = 1/2 k(Δx)². Therefore, doubling the displacement Δx, quadruples the potential energy stored in the spring.

26. C

Assuming both objects are dropped from the same height, in both cases, the gravitational potential energy, will be converted into kinetic energy during the fall, which will then will be converted into spring potential energy, which will then be converted back into the upward kinetic energy, which will then return the object back to the same height, having the same gravitational potential energy as when it started. The object with more mass will have a greater initial gravitational potential energy, which will also affect the relative amount of kinetic energy (not velocity, g is constant) and spring potential energy at each stage, but if the energy is conserved, it must return to the same height as it started.

27. C

Mechanical advantage is defined as the ratio of the output force to the input force for a simple machine.

28. B

Inefficient machines have energy (work) losses due to things like friction.

29. C

As the poem goes:

Zero degrees Celsius is freezing.
Ten degrees is not.
Twenty degrees is warm.

Thirty degrees is hot.

Therefore, 20 °C is warm, or about 68 °F, but the question asks how much the temperature "increased." So, 0 °C is 32 °F, and the difference is 68 °F - 32 °F = 36 °F.

30. B

The ratio of the change in length ΔL to the change in temperature ΔT is equal to the coefficient of expansion α times the original length L, therefore, ΔL = αLΔT = (1 x 10⁻⁵ K⁻¹)(5 m)(90 °C) = 0.0045 m or 0.45 cm.

31. A

The vast majority of the heat transferred through the vacuum of space is transferred by way of electromagnetic radiation.

32. B

The heat was transferred by the molecular collisions between the hot fluid, water, to the metal and ultimately to the skin, by way of conduction.

33. D

The total amount of heat required will be the sum of the heat need to warm the solid substance from 25 °C to its melting point, 1050 °C, and the heat needed to melt the solid.

$$Q_1 = mC\Delta T$$
$$= (0.500 \text{ kg})(125 \text{ J/kg•K})(1025 \text{ K})$$
$$= 64000 \text{ J}$$
$$Q_2 = H_f m$$
$$= (6.4 \times 10^4 \text{ J/kg})(0.500 \text{ kg})$$
$$= 32000 \text{ J}$$
$$Q_t = Q_1 + Q_2 = 96,000 \text{ J or 96 kJ}$$

34. B

A watt is a joule per second, therefore multiplying the power and time in seconds, gives Q = (4.44 x 10⁻² W)(3.6 x 10³ s) = 160 J. The specific heat of water is 4.18 J/g K, so the temperature change will be

ΔT = (160 J)/(4.18 J/g K)(4000 g) = 0.0096 °C

Therefore, the temperature of the cat after one hour will be 38 °C + 0.0096 °C ~ 38°C.

35. D

There is a temperature change in an adiabatic process and during compression there are many more collision between gas molecules, causing an increase in the average kinetic energy, so Roman numeral I is true. If the system is the gas within the container, then work must be done on the system to cause the volume to change, therefore Roman numeral II is false and Roman numeral III is true.

36. C

A state function does not depend upon the path taken to achieve that situation, whereas, a path function does. Many thermodynamic properties, such as Gibbs free energy and entropy are state functions, and volume and density are state functions, but heat and work are not. This may seem counter-intuitive, but consider an example: if a block of wood is pushed across a table in a straight line, it will produce less heat due to friction than if it was pushed in a zig-zag path.

37. A

The heat transfer within the fluid (water) is convection, whereas the heat transfer from the fluid to the solid pipes is by conduction.

38. D

If the liquid is at a temperature somewhere in the liquid phase range, then the added heat would cause the temperature to rise, however, if the added heat is causing a phase change the temperature would remain the same.

39. D

The key to this question is the process that occurs overnight and the ink and water system had already reached equilibrium shortly after mixing. Spontaneous processes increase entropy, unless work is done on the system. The work (mixing) that was done on the oil and water system, was prior to the overnight period, therefore, since the separation of the oil and water overnight was a spontaneous process, it increased entropy.

40. B

The heat of fusion involves the phase change between solid and liquid, which is not necessary, and the heat of vaporization determine how much heat is required to completely convert the liquid to the gas phase, not when it will start boiling. The question clearly states that the two liquids have the same boiling points. If the specific heat (J/g•K) of sample B is larger than sample A, it will take more heat to raise the temperature of liquid B to the boiling point.

41. C

Choice C is the definition of a calorie.

42. C

The work done during one cycle of the process involving the gas is the area of the triangle, $W = 1/2 \Delta P \Delta V = 1/2 (P_0 - 1/2P_0)(4V_0 - V_0) = 1/2 (1/2P_0)(3V_0) = 3/4P_0V_0$.

43. B

Metabolism does work on the various systems comprising the body, thereby, overall increasing the entropy of the universe.

44. A

A bomb calorimeter is designed to be a system in which heat and matter are not exchanged with the surroundings, which is an isolated system. When the hole develops, matter and heat can be exchanged with the surroundings, which is the definition of an open system.

45. D

If a phase change occurs the temperature of the system does not change and if the volume of the system can change, the heat will be doing work and the temperature can also remain the same. If

the system is composed of only solids, the added heat will be distributed between the solids by conduction and the average kinetic energy (temperature) of the solids will increase.

46. C

If the overall process does not cause a temperature change (isothermal), then the work done on the system must also be coupled with a process that removes the same amount of energy from the system.

47. B

The pressure is the force per unit area exerted by the water surrounding the toys. Since both toys are at the same depth, they experience the same pressure.

48. B

The net force is zero, which is the sum of the weight of the object, the buoyant force of the water and the tension in the rope, $0 = F_g + F_B + F_T$.

F_g = 2 g/cm³ x 10 cm³ x 10^{-3} kg/g x -10 m/s² = -0.2 N (down)
F_B = 1 g/cm³ x 10 cm³ x 10^{-3} kg/g x 10 m/s² = 0.1 N (up)
$0 = -0.2 N + 0.1 N + F_T$
$F_T = 0.1 N$

49. A

The object with the lower density will experience a greater buoyant force and therefore accelerate upward faster.

50. C

Pressure is force per unit area (P = F/A) and there is a direct relationship between pressure and force.

51. D

Based on the continuity equation, the area A times the velocity V must be constant C within the pipe, C = VA. Therefore, since A an V are inversely related, if the area is decreased by one quarter, the velocity must be four times faster.

52. D

The pressure (P = F/A) that the fluid exerts throughout the fluid is the same, therefore we can say that $F_1/A_1 = F_2/A_2$. Since the surface area of the piston is πr^2, we can rewrite this equation as $F_1/r_1^2 = F_2/r_2^2$ and substitute the appropriate values.

$(10 N)/(0.1 m)^2 = F_2/(2 m)^2$
$F_2 = (10)(2)^2/(0.1)^2$
$F_2 = (40)(10^2) = 4000 N$

53. C

The speed of blood is inversely related to the total cross-sectional area of all of a particular type of blood vessel within the body.

54. B

The gauge pressure is the total pressure minus atmospheric pressure (1 atm). Subtracting atmospheric pressure from the total pressure for

SOLUTIONS

the rear tires gives a gauge pressure of 2.5 atm and a ratio of 2.2:2.5.

55. D

The weight of the ice cube (force of gravity) down is equal to the buoyant force up. The magnitude of the buoyant force is equivalent to the weight of the liquid water that is displaced. Gravity does not change the density of ice or the density of liquid water. Since weight is mass times the acceleration of gravity, on the moon the acceleration of gravity (9.8/6) will affect the weight of the ice and the buoyant force by the same amount, and there will still be 10% of the ice floating above and below the surface of the water.

56. B

According to Newton's third law, forces act in pairs, equal and opposite.

57. D

According to Coulomb's law there is an inverse square relationship between the force and the distance between the objects, $F = kQ_1Q_2/r^2$. Decreasing the distance between the objects by half will increase the force by a factor of four.

58. D

In order for there to be a force acting on the moving charged particle there needs to be a component of the velocity that is perpendicular to the magnetic field.

59. C

According to the right hand rule, this situation would result in a force acting on a positively charged particle that would be pointed into the page. However, since this is a negatively charged particle, the force is directed out of the page.

60. A

Electric field lines indicate the direction of force that would act on a positive test charge. In this case, a positive test charge would be accelerated in the opposite direction of its velocity, but a negatively charged particle will be accelerated in the same direction as its velocity.

61. A

One definition of a volt, choice B, is the electric potential energy per unit of charge, or Coulombs, flowing through a circuit. The unit for energy is the Joule, which is equivalent to the unit for work, N•m, therefore choice C and D are equivalent to each other and to the volt.

62. A

According to Coulomb's law there is an inverse square relationship between the force and the distance between two charged objects, therefor $F = 1/2^2 = 1/4$.

63. D

According to Coulomb's law there is an inverse square relationship between two charged objects, therefor $F = 1/\infty^2 = 0$.

64. A

A volt is the electrical potential energy per unit charge, V = PE/q, therefore,
$$12 V = (120 J)/q$$
$$q = 120/12 = 10 C$$

65. C

An ampere is the amount of charge, in Coulombs, that passes through a circuit per second, A = Q/t, therefore
$$A = (1.2 C)/(0.02 s) = 60 A$$

66. B

Resistance R, is directly related to both the length L and the resistivity ρ, but inversely related to the cross sectional area A,
$$R = \rho L/A$$

67. B

The voltage drop across the resistor is V = IR = $(0.5 A)(4 \Omega) = 2 V$, therefore the difference between the emf of the cell and the voltage drop of the resistor must be due to the internal resistance of the cell.

68. D

The ratio of the currents is the same as the ratio of the voltages, since there is a direct relationship between current and voltage according to Ohm's law.

69. B

For the two resistors in parallel, the equivalent resistance is
$$1/R_e = 1/30 + 1/50$$
$$1/R_e = 5/150 + 3/150$$
$$1/R_e = 8/150$$
$$R_e = 18.75 \Omega$$
This equivalent resistor would be in series with the two 20 Ω resistors.
$$R_e = 20 + 20 + 18.75 = 58.75 \Omega$$

70. A

The 20 Ω resistors are in series with one another, so the same amount of current must flow through both resistors.

71. C

Parallel resistors experience the same voltage drop, but can have different currents. For resistors in series, the current is the same, but voltages can be different.

72. B

The equation for capacitance C is
$$C = \varepsilon A/d$$
where ε is the permittivity of the dielectric, A is the surface area of plate overlap, and d is the distance between the plates. Capacitance is directly related to both ε and A, but inversely related to d.

73. A

If the volt meter did not have a very large resistance, then it would provide a parallel path through which charge would flow. As a result the equivalent circuit would have less resistance and a lower voltage for the same amount of

current. If the resistance of the voltmeter is near infinity, then the equivalent resistance R_e of the circuit will be essentially the same as the resistance of the circuit R_c without the voltmeter.
$$1/R_e = 1/R_c + 1/\infty$$

74. A

Resonance occurs when the wavelength of a vibration corresponds with the dimensions of a particular cavity within an instrument. The walls of the cavity cause reflections, which result in constructive interference of the waves. If the second instrument is identical to the first, then changing the frequency of the vibration changes the wavelength and will not produce constructive interference, with no resonance amplification occurring.

75. B

When a wave interacts with a new material, some of the wave is reflected. By knowing the speed of the wave and the time necessary to detect the reflected wave, the position of the interface between the materials can be calculated.

76. B

Radar waves travel at the speed of light – a speed so much faster than the speeds of the planes that the Doppler shift will be minimal.

77. C

Since both boys are on the train traveling at the same speed, their relative speed is 0 m/s. Since the ball producing the sound is traveling towards the boy that is perceiving the tone, the Doppler effect will cause the frequency and pitch of the sound increase slightly.

78. A

The speed of the wave is equal to the wavelength λ times the frequency f of the wave, $v = \lambda f$. Since the period T is the inverse of the frequency, combining the relationships gives
$$\lambda = vT = (10 \text{ m/s})(0.01 \text{ s}) = 0.1 \text{ m}$$

79. D

For a closed tube resonator of a particular length L, the harmonics occur with wavelengths λ, where $\lambda = (4/n)L$ where n = 1, 3, 5... and so on. For the fundamental the wavelength will be four times the length of the tube.

80. D

The change in the loudness of the sound was 30 decibels (dB), or 3 B, where Bells are defined as the $\log_{10}$ of the intensity ratio of the sounds.
$$B = \log I/I_o$$
$$3 = \log I/I_o$$
$$I/I_o = 10^3$$

81. C

For a closed tube resonator of a particular length L, the harmonics occur with wavelengths λ where L = (n/4) λ, and n = 1, 3, 5, ... and so on. Since $\lambda = v/f$, we get the equation

$$L = (n/4)(v/f)$$
$$L = (3/4)(340 \text{ m/s})/(170 \text{ s}^{-1})$$
$$L = 1.5 \text{ m}$$

82. B

The speed of sound in air is 334 m/s, whereas the speed of sound in water is 1482 m/s.

83. C

Visible light occurs in the 400-800 nm range of the electromagnetic spectrum. Wavelength λ times frequency f equals the speed of light c.
$$f = c/\lambda$$
$$f = (3.0 \times 10^8 \text{ m/s})/(400 \text{ nm} \times 10^{-9} \text{ m/nm}) = 7.5 \times 10^{14} \text{ s}^{-1}$$
$$f = (3.0 \times 10^8 \text{ m/s})/(800 \text{ nm} \times 10^{-9} \text{ m/nm}) = 3.75 \times 10^{14} \text{ s}^{-1}$$

84. C

For a plane mirror, the distance between the object and the mirror is the same as the distance the image is behind the mirror, because the focal length f is infinity. Using the mirror equation
$$1/f = 1/d_o + 1/d_i$$
$$0 = 1/(1.5 \text{ m}) + 1/d_i$$
$$1/d_i = -2/3$$
$$d_i = -3/2 = -1.5 \text{ m}$$
Hence the distance between the man's face and the image is 3.0 m.

85. D

A plane mirror has a focal point with an infinite distance. It produces a virtual image behind the mirror, whose distance from the mirror is the same as the distance from the object to the mirror.

86. A

When the object is beyond the focal point, the image is inverted and real. As the object is moved towards the lens and closer to the focal point the image moves away from the lens, and once the object reaches the focal point the image is infinitely far in front of and behind the mirror, because it is changing from real to virtual. A truly confusing situation for your brain.

87. C

When light is refracted its speed and wavelength change, but frequency does not. The color of the light is dependent on the refractive index of the aqueous humor, so the color you perceive does not change.

88. D

While we could do a calculation using Snell's law, $n_1\sin\theta_1 = n_2\sin\theta_2$, twice, it is not necessary, since at each interface the light will bend towards the normal, because the index of reaction increases. We can immediately eliminate choices A and B. Choice C is only slightly smaller than the angle of incidence and we would expect a significantly smaller angle of refraction.

89. C

The ray diagram for this situation is

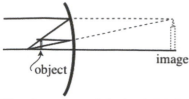

If an image is upright (upright), it must be virtual.

90. A

The image of the first lens will be the object for the second lens. The equation for magnification is $M = h_i/h_o$. For the first lens, where the magnification is +2.5, the h_i will be 2.5 times bigger than the h_o. For the second lens, now h_o = 2.5, and if the magnification is -2.5, then -2.5 = $h_i/(2.5)$, so h_i = (2.5)(-2.5) = -6.25 bigger than the original object.

91. D

A virtual image results when light rays do not converge and the image appears to be upright, whereas a real image results when light rays converge and produce an inverted image. Both a plane mirror and a concave mirror always produce virtual images. A convex lens can produce a virtual image when the object is located between the surface of the lens and the focal point.

92. A

The energy of the photon, $E = hf$, will equal the kinetic energy, $KE = 1/2\ mv^2$ of the electron, therefore $v = \sqrt{(2hf/m)}$.

$v = [2(6.6 \times 10^{-34}\ \text{J}\bullet\text{s})(\ 2.7 \times 10^{11}\ \text{s}^{-1})/(\ 9 \times 10^{-31}$ kg)$]^{1/2}$
$= [4.0 \times 10^{8}]^{1/2} = 2.0 \times 10^{4}$ m/s

93. B

The Bohr model of electron structure does rely on discrete energy levels, therefore Roman numeral I is true. Roman numeral II is false since quantized amounts of energy must be absorbed to increase the principle quantum number, and emitted to decrease the principle quantum number, making Roman numeral III true.

94. C

Since $c = \lambda f$ and $E = hf$, the $E = hc/\lambda$, therefore λ = (6.6 x 10^{-34} J$\bullet$s)(3.0 x 10^{8} m/s)/(1.6 x 10^{-18} J) = 12.4 x 10^{-8} m or 1.24 x 10^{-7} m.

95. D

For electromagnetic radiation, wavelength and energy are inversely related with high energies corresponding to short wavelengths. The IR radiation is not energetic enough to eject the electron from the metal and cause ionization, i.e. the photoelectric effect.

96. A

The product nuclear particle is a beta-negative particle, $_{-1}^{0}\beta$. In electron capture, the electron is coming from an inner core shell of electrons and combines with a neutron to produce a proton in the nucleus, hence the atomic number also goes up.

97. C

After one day the isotope will have experienced (24 h)/(6 h) = 4 half-lives. Each half-life reduces the amount by half, therefore $0.5^4 = 0.0625$ = 1/16.

98. C

The most abundant isotope of oxygen has eight protons and eight neutrons. An alpha particle has two protons and two neutrons, $_{8}^{16}O \rightarrow 4\ _{2}^{4}\alpha$

99. B

Of the three nuclear particles in this question, only the alpha particle (helium nucleus) has a mass number, $_{2}^{4}\alpha$.

100. D

The SI system is a set of physical measurements with base units of meters (m), kilograms (kg), seconds (s), amperes (A), degrees Kelvin (K), candelas (cd), and moles (mol). The Ohm (Ω) is derived unit of electrical resistance (kg m^{2}s^{-3}A^{-2}). A coulomb (C) is a derived unit of charge (A$\bullet$s). The base unit of mass is the kilogram (kg), not the gram (g).

FINAL EXAM: MATH SKILLS ANSWER KEY

1. 21
2. 90.4
3. 6
4. 1250
5. 56
6. 36
7. 750
8. 3.8
9. 36.36
10. .001
11. 2.8
12. 5
13. $3^3 + 2^4 = 27 + 16 = 43$
14. $6^2 \times \sqrt{6} = 6^2 \times 6^{0.5} = 6^{2.5} \approx 36 \times 2.5 = 90$
15. $10^5 / 10^2 = 10^3 = 1000$
16. $5^5 \times 25^2 = 5^5 \times (5^2)^2 = 5^5 \times 5^4 = 5^9 = 3125$
17. $\sqrt{140} \approx 12$
18. $2^3 + 2^5 = 8 + 32 = 40$
19. $(\sqrt{10000}) / 100 = 100 / 100 = 1$
20. $(2^2 + 3^3) / (2 + 3)^2 = (4 + 27) / (5)^2 = 31 / 25 \approx 30/25 = 1.2$
21. $23 \times 10^{14} \times 2 \times 10^{-6} = 23 \times 2 \times 10^{14} \times 10^{-6} = 46 \times 10^8 = 4.6 \times 10^9$
22. $5 \times 10^5 + 2 \times 10^6 = 0.5 \times 10^6 + 2 \times 10^6 = 2.5 \times 10^6$
23. $(6 \times 10^{12}) / (3 \times 10^{10}) = 6/3 \times 10^{12}/10^{10} = 2 \times 10^2$
24. $\sqrt{(1.6 \times 10^{17})} = \sqrt{(16 \times 10^{16})} = \sqrt{16} \times \sqrt{10^{16}} = 4 \times 10^8$
25. $(7 \times 10^3)^2 / (\sqrt{(4.9 \times 10^{-17})} = [7^2 \times (10^3)^2] / [\sqrt{(49 \times 10^{-18})}] = [49 \times 10^6] / [7 \times 10^{-9}] = 7 \times 10^{15}$
26. $\log 1 = 0$
27. $\log 30 = \log (3 \times 10) = \log 3 + \log 10 \approx 0.5 + 1 = 1.5$
28. $\log 300 - \log 200 = \log (300/200) = \log 1.5 \approx$ some decimal between 0 and 0.5
29. $\log 20 + \log 5 = \log (20 \times 5) = \log 100 = 2$
30. $\log (1/1000) = \log 10^{-3} = -3$
31. $\log (3 \times 10^6) = \log 3 + \log 10^6 \approx 0.5 + 6 = 6.5$
32. $\log (8 \times 10^{-7}) = \log 8 + \log 10^{-7} \approx 0.9 + (-7) = -6.9$ (any answer between -6.1 and -6.9 would suffice)
33. $-\log (3 \times 10^{-10}) = - (\log 3 + \log 10^{-10}) \approx - (0.5 + (-10)) = 10 - 0.5 = 9.5$
34. Simplify $[x^2 + 3x^2] / 4x^3 = 4x^2 / 4x^3 = x^2/x^3 = x^{-1}$
35. $\sin 0° = 0$
36. $\sin 45° = \sqrt{2} / 2$
37. $\sin 90° = 1$
38. $\cos 30° = \sqrt{3} / 2$
39. $\cos 60° = 1/2$
40. $\cos 180° = -1$
41. $\tan 0° = 0$
42. $\tan 30° = \sqrt{3} / 3$
43. $\tan 45° = 1$
44. $\tan 180° = 0$
45. $\sin^{-1} 1/2 = 30°$
46. $\sin^{-1} 1 = 90°$
47. $\sin^{-1} \sqrt{2}/2 = 45°$
48. $\cos^{-1} 0 = 90°$
49. $\cos^{-1} \sqrt{3}/2 = 30°$
50. $\cos^{-1} 1/2 = 60°$

51. $\tan^{-1} 1 = 45°$
52. $\tan^{-1} \sqrt{3} = 60°$
53. $\tan^{-1} \sqrt{3}/3 = 30°$
54. kilo- means: 10^3
55. giga- means: 10^9
56. micro- means: 10^{-6}
57. pico- means: 10^{-12}
58. 1 Calorie is how many joules? 4184 (note 1 calorie is 4.184)
59. 1 inch is approximately how many centimeters? 2.5
60. $1 N \times 1 m \times 1 C^{-1} = V$
61. $1 kg \times 1 m^2 \times 1 s^{-2} = J$
62. $1 kg \times 1 m \times 1 s^{-1} =$ trick question! Measure of momentum, but not a derived unit.
63. Solve for x: $2x + 2y = 10$; $3x + y = 15$
$2x + 2y = 10$
$x + y = 5$
$y = 5 - x$
then substitute:
$3x + (5 - x) = 15$
$2x + 5 = 15$
$2x = 10$
$x = 5$
64. Given $E = hf$ and $E = 1/2 \times mv^2$ solve for mass in terms of Planck's constant
Set equal to each other: $E = hf = 1/2 mv^2$
$hf/v^2 = 1/2 m$
$2hf / v^2 = m$
65. Given $P_1V_1 = nRT$ and $P_1V_1 = P_2V_2$ solve for V_2 in terms of n.
P_1V_1 is equal to both P_2V_2 and equal to nRT, so set them equal to each other:
$P_1V_1 = P_2V_2 = nRT$
Then isolate V_2:
$V_2 = nRT/P_2$
66. In the equation $A_1B_1 = A_2B_2$ the variable have what relationship? Inverse
67. In the equation $X_1/Y_1 = X_2/Y_2$ the variables have what relationship? Direct
68. All else held constant, in the equation PV = nRT, if T goes up what happens to P? to n?
If T goes up, P goes up
If T goes up, n goes down
69. All else held constant, in the equation PV = nRT if V goes down what happens to P? to T? to n?
If V goes down, P goes up.
If V goes down, n goes down.
70. $3.612 \times 10.025 / 4.9987 \approx 3.6 \times 10 / 5 = 36 / 5 = (35 + 1) / 5 = 35/5 + 1/5 = 7.2$
71. $101,325 \times 3.14159 / 99,011.2 \approx 10^4 \times 3 / 10^2 = 3 \times 10^2 = 300$
72. $500^{0.2}$ is approximately $= 500^{1/5} =$ between 3 and 4
73. What is the maximum value of $3\sin \theta + 1$? max value of $\sin \theta$ is 1.
$3(1) + 1 = 4$

74. What is the minimum value of $2 - 2\cos\theta$? To minimize the expression, maximize $\cos\theta$:
$2 - 2(1) = 0$

75. In the equation $R = k[X]^2$ the value of $[X]$ is given in molarity and the value of k is given in $L \times mol^{-1} \times sec^{-1}$. What are the units of the rate? M/s

76. Cats need a base energy intake of 2×10^4 J / day plus an additional 2×10^3 J per kg of body weight. Dogs need a base energy intake of 8×10^3 J/day plus an additional 4×10^3 J per kg of body weight. At what weight would a dog and a cat have the same caloric needs per day?
Let x be the mass where they need the same energy every day. Set up the following equations:
Cats: Energy = 20,000 + 2000x
Dogs: Energy = 8000 + 4000x
Set them equal:
20,000 + 2000x = 8000 + 4000x
12000 = 2000x
6 = x
Dogs and cats have the same energy needs if they are both 6 kg.

77. D
78. A
79. C
80. B
81. A
82. Accuracy
83. Precision
84. B
85. C
86. D
87. 21.2
88. 23
89. 22
90. If the 23 were replaced with a 95, the standard deviation of the set would: increase
91. In the normal distribution curve, approximately how much of the data set lies within one standard deviation of the mean? 68%

92. A
93. D
94. C

95. The probability that a child will be born male is 1/2. The probability that the child will have blue eyes in 1/5. The probability that a child will be shorter than both parents is 1/10. What is the probability that a child will be male, not have blue eyes, and be shorter than his parents?
Male: 1/2
Not blue: 4/5
Shorter: 1/10
1/2 x 4/5 x 1/10 = 4/100 = 4%

96. The probability of a child have blue eyes is 1/5, brown eyes 1/2, and green eyes 1/4. What is the probability that a child will have blue or green eyes?

Blue: 1/5
Green: 1/4
1/5 + 1/4 = 0.2 + 0.25 = 0.45 = 45%

97. B
98. A
99. D
100. A